Investigative Interviewing

The Conversation Management Approach

Investigative Interviewing

The Conversation
Management Approach

Second Edition

Eric Shepherd and Andy Griffiths

OXFORD
UNIVERSITY PRESS

OXFORD

UNIVERSITY PRESS

Great Clarendon Street, Oxford, OX2 6DP,
United Kingdom

Oxford University Press is a department of the University of Oxford.
It furthers the University's objective of excellence in research, scholarship,
and education by publishing worldwide. Oxford is a registered trade mark of
Oxford University Press in the UK and in certain other countries

First Edition published in 2007

Second Edition published in 2013

Impression: 3

Published in the United States of America by Oxford University Press
198 Madison Avenue, New York, NY 10016, United States of America

British Library Cataloguing in Publication Data

Data available

Library of Congress Control Number: 2013940573

ISBN 978–0–19–968189–1

Printed in Great Britain by
Ashford Colour Press Ltd, Gosport, Hampshire

Dedications

From Eric
Rosaleen, a stór mo chroí, agus Luke, mo mhac ghile.... gan iad, gan a.

From Andy
To my wife Jacqui, and children Megan and Iwan for their continued support
in every endeavour. My love and thanks in equal measure.

Acknowledgements

As with the first edition the scope and the detail of this book would not have been possible without the help of hundreds of colleagues, both within and outside the police service.

Space does not allow us to list all those to whom we are grateful for their advice, reflections, conversation and assistance. We are particularly indebted to Alison Knight. Mark Robinson, John Kelly, Sarah Gregg, Rich Barnston, Steve Peck, Steve Retford, Steve Davies, Jenny Ingram, Barney Jones, Alan Grainger, Sally Nicholls, Mel Paley, Padge Pagett, Paul Haywood, Jez Prior, Gail Brehany, Kevin Smith, Steve Tilney, Ian Hynes and Dave Walsh.

Two people deserve special mention. Lindsay Hudson for the many hours spent together with the first author creating the interview activity maps, and Panagiotis Maounis who kindly created excellent visual materials.

The original project was born of an idea by Andrea Oliver, then at OUP. Many thanks to dear Andrea. However we owe the greatest thanks to Lucy Alexander, and Sally Pelling-Deeves who kept us both on the straight and narrow and ensured that this second edition saw the light of day.

Contents

Contents

How to use this book

What is common to all

If you are reading this page you are likely to be involved in some way in the practice of investigation, either operationally—as a practitioner, supervisor, or manager—or designing, delivering, or managing the training of individuals occupying these roles.

Mention investigation and most people immediately say that this is the task of the police service or other agencies. However, ask people to identify other contexts in which professionals investigate, and they are able to list many—in both public and private sectors. This underlines the fact that investigation occurs across a very wide spectrum.

Whatever the context in which you operate your task is to protect individuals, groups, institutions, the community, or society as a whole. You do this by responding to, and then solving or resolving, a problematic occurrence or set of circumstances that has affected, is affecting, or has the potential to affect them. Whether you are operating in the public or the private sector of the economy, professional performance involves three interdependent areas of skill.

- Case management skills.
- Handling people skills.
- Finding out facts skills.

The common denominator in every investigation—irrespective of context—is a problem-solving cycle, enquiry, and the universal effort of translating information to evidence. Every investigation involves information processing, reflection, and reasoning in order to define and continuously re-define the situation, to make decisions (judgements and choices under conditions of risk and uncertainty), to plan, prioritize, and assign actions, and to act (which may be not doing something).

Common activities in any investigations are:

- the identification and location of sources of information;
- the gathering of information—most particularly through interviewing, ie *purposive conversations* conducted to achieve investigative aims through coverage of specific objectives—and the recording of the gathering process and its outcome;
- the collation and analysis of gathered information;
- the evaluation of information in terms of its validity relative to the reliability of its origin—leading to some information being accorded the status of evidence, of a perceived degree of strength and sufficiency.

Common to all and irrespective of context is the influence exerted by mindset upon the investigative endeavour, particularly prior to, during, and following any purposive conversations. Of course different contexts of enquiry demand particular subject-matter expertise:

- *knowledge* and *awareness* of the domain relevant to the problematic occurrence or set of circumstances;
- requisite *understanding*—knowing how domain knowledge and awareness must, should, or could be applied;
- *skills*—applying domain knowledge, awareness, and understanding in a performance that fulfils investigative aims and objectives, and when subjected to scrutiny, is deemed

competent, proper, morally acceptable, defensible, and compliant with the letter and spirit of relevant law, regulations, ordinances, and guidelines for professional best practice.

Practical *experience*—a history of exposure to, observation of, actual participation in, and recognition and reward (particularly praise, kudos, advancement, and a reputation)—is particularly important. It is also precarious since it can operate for good or bad. Experience is the medium within which we all develop, and demonstrate, our investigative mindset: a fixed mental attitude or disposition that predetermines how we interpret, and respond to, a situation in a habitual manner.[1]

These commonalities transcend geographical borders. They exist despite:

- differences in government, civil administration, or legal system;
- differences in—or absence of—rules, guidelines, and codes of practice;
- differences in—or absence of—infrastructures to ensure regulation, compliance, and observance of the law, rules, guidelines, and codes of practice.

Common to all are already existing or emergent demands for transparency and accountability in the performance of case management, handling people, and finding out facts. These demands stem from public awareness, ever increasing in this digital age, of the necessity to protect ourselves—as individuals, institutions, and as a society—from investigative practitioners who believe the ends justify the means and act expediently. Recording technology renders open to scrutiny the investigator's behaviour and treatment of the interviewee and of information. History has shown that it leads to the reduction and disappearance of unethical conversation, of the misuse of power, of lying and trickery, and of misconduct and oppression: all traditional behaviours aimed at inducing the interviewee to say things that he or she otherwise would not, or not to say things the he or she otherwise would.

This book presents an approach to investigative interviewing that is founded upon conversation management—managing the conversation with the interviewee ethically:

- to facilitate the maximum disclosure of information initially and thereafter across the course of the interview;
- to enable the comprehensive capture, rapid analysis and timely response to the fine-grain detail of the interviewee's disclosures.

It is an approach that is applicable in any investigative setting.

The material in this book

The material in this book is not a substitute for professional training and experience gained doing the 'job'. It extends both of these essential aspects of practitioner development. Whatever point you are at in your career, in whatever context of investigation you are operating, and whatever investigative interviewing role you are fulfilling, the material in this book will provide the context and additional content to whatever you have learned thus far, are learning at this moment, or will learn in the future:

- whether in the safe learning environment of the training establishment;
- or the precarious learning environment of real life interviewing.

---

[1] Dweck, C.S. (2006) *Mindset: How you can Fulfil your Full Potential*. New York: Random House.

Many readers of this book will be working in the criminal justice context in which the conduct of investigation and interviews is subject to statute law, legal rulings in appellate courts, and the provisions of official regulations and guidelines. Being both English and having worked in the criminal investigative context for some 30 years apiece, we firmly believe that readers in other jurisdictions throughout the world will have no problem casting what we say into their working context, finding relevance and value in the material we present in this book. On grounds of common sense and to assist our readers working in the crime context of England, Wales, and Northern Ireland, we cite legal references, regulations, and guidelines for this jurisdiction.

Complexity and flexibility

Nearly 70 years ago Myers, one of the founding fathers of modern interviewing, observed that little was known psychologically about what goes on in an interview. He felt that the relationship between the interviewer and the interviewee was very subtle, very fluid, and defied attempts at any simple statement of procedures. Some 40 years later Oppenheim, an outstanding academic, interviewing practitioner, colleague, and friend of the first author echoed Myers when he said that interviewing, if thought about seriously, is a task of daunting complexity.

An interview is a *purposive conversation*: a verbal exchange to achieve your investigative aim and objectives. In common with every conversation, interviewing involves relationship: two people relating as human beings. The *influence* that you exert—the impact that you make and your management of interview as an event, its course and conduct (yours, the interviewee's, and that of any third party)—is critical. Your influence significantly determines what the interviewee relates to you from the outset and throughout the conversation. It is the basis of your ability to *persuade* the interviewee (or any other person present) to consider his or her conduct or what he or she has said. Without appropriate influence you will not be able to *negotiate* different terms of engagement when faced with the challenge posed by inappropriate behaviour, resistant behaviours, or the demand to converse with the individual in special circumstances.

The skills of interviewing

Ethical, effective interviewing requires you to take into account the nature of, and the conditions affecting, the psychological processes—thoughts, feelings, attitudes, and behaviour—involved: the interviewee's, your own, and those of any third party participant. Since the human mind and body are inextricably related, you also have to be mindful of physical and physiological factors. Awareness of this complexity brings with it the demand for flexibility.

The twin demand to grasp the complexity of factors involved and, aware of these, to behave flexibly marks out interviewing as a *higher order interpersonal skill*. Such skill is essential but counts for nothing if you cannot secure maximum grasp of the fine-grain detail, registering and retaining what is there—and crucially what is not there—in the material before your ears and eyes.

The higher order interpersonal skill of interviewing therefore relies upon having *higher order information processing*—study—*skills*: effective reading, methodical observation, intent and active listening, and a better than average ability to hold detail in working memory. You have to become passionate about detail and a master of detail, dominating detail in order to identify areas for action and probing; evaluating; action planning; communicating to others what you know, what you don't know, and what must, should, and could be known, and what needs to be done to achieve these objectives.

Confronting and coping with complexity

The content of each chapter in this book provides the foundation for that to come in subsequent chapters and strikes links with material in preceding chapters. This will enable you to cope with the 'daunting complexity' that Oppenheim spoke about. Growing awareness and underpinning knowledge will give you the confidence to take into account the psychological, physical, and physiological factors when managing your conversations with the entire range of individual: witnesses (including victims), suspects, and third parties.

Your journey from conversational basics to asking the right question provides you with a body of knowledge that will enable you to develop your interpersonal skills to manage conversation and to trigger fuller if not maximum disclosure. This book provides examples of these skills in action. You will see people's voices represented in italics.

Of course the voice of the interviewer in these examples is illustrative not definitive. The italics are an invitation to use your own voice and your own words. Don't be self-conscious. Rather like learning another language from a book, find a quiet spot, and practise saying the illustrative words aloud. Then follow this by saying things aloud using your own words to capture the spirit of the message and the meaning of the illustrative voice.

Productive pausing

Typically books on interviewing do not represent the vital behaviour of pausing. In this text pausing is represented by the symbol ^. Two of these symbols—^ ^—represent a one or two second interval, rather as if you said to yourself silently 'pause, pause…pause, pause'. The more symbols used the longer the pausing. In order to gain a sense of the significance of the pause, read the narrative voice aloud, pausing for the requisite period shown by the symbol.

You will probably think that the pausing is too long, perhaps uncomfortably long! This is the key point. Persevere. Move outside your 'comfort zone': use longer pauses. Skilled investigative interviewing is actually slowed down talk. Pausing is essential. It gives you time to think, to observe, and to create the 'space' for the interviewee who may well 'come in' to take the talking turn. Then transfer this deliberate pausing into your everyday interviewing. You will be, as Joan Morris, a colleague of the first author, said, 'Making the pause work for you.'

Dealing with detail

Core themes of this text are vigilance to detail and that quality evidence takes time. Much space is devoted to developing your information processing skills, and to applying with increasing expertise a range of information processing tools. The Reference Section at the end of the book gives fuller explanations of a number of these tools.

The alternative to being serious about detail—skimming over detail and operating on a selectively constructed, gist understanding of matters—is a rush to get it wrong and the rapid route to destroying any prospect of a quality investigation.

The skill of flexibility

As you progress through the book the demand to think, act, and respond flexibly to circumstances and the content of disclosure emerges as one of the hallmarks of skilful conversation management from your earliest planning onwards. Flexibility is integral to skilled active listening and to expertise in asking the right question at the right time in the right way.

Taking a risk

Although potentially scary and always carrying a measure of risk, being flexible is a skill that has to be developed like any other. An interviewer who is fearful to be flexible, or who has not developed the capacity to act flexibly, is in effect operating in 'auto pilot'. This certainly reduces the risk but at extraordinary cost: the creation of avoidable barriers, alienating the interviewee, and impoverished disclosure by the interviewee in terms of quality and quantity of detail.

Navigating flexibly

In the chapters that consider interviews of particular types of interviewee there are maps that show the activities involved at each stage of managing an interview from initial planning through to evaluation and beyond. These maps underline yet again the 'daunting complexity' of what is involved when managing conversation within the framework of the deceptively simple sequence of steps.

A map of any kind is a two-dimensional representation of a terrain which is multi-dimensional. The map is not the territory. The interview activity maps are no exception. They can never be a rigid route—an action sequence—that must be followed slavishly in your investigative journey with each and every interviewee. The maps are a flexible guide. Should you meet an unforeseen obstacle, or indeed an unexpected but welcome opportunity, take pride and gain pleasure in being a flexible navigator.

Differences in perspective

Occasions will arise when the perspective we give in this book differs on a particular issue from that presented in an official source (eg policy or guideline) or the view of an authority figure (eg trainer, supervisor, manager, lecturer, speaker, or writer). When this happens it is only underlining how right Myers and Oppenheim were. Because interviewing *is* complex there will always be different ways of looking at a 'problem'. Being categorical helps but always at some cost.

We have always viewed difference in perspective as a positive rather than a negative. It is a reminder of the need to reflect upon the difference, to exercise common sense relative to the circumstances, and to note your reasons for doing something this way rather than another. Such reflection and recording are essential to the development of expertise and essential evidence if and when called upon later to explain the decisions and actions taken prior to, during, and after interviewing to achieve your investigative aim and objectives.

Fundamentals

The Conversation Management Approach to Investigative Interviewing

1.1 Chapter overview

This chapter reviews the nature of investigation, highlighting how moral, legal, and regulatory requirements now define acceptable conduct of investigative practitioners, particularly in interviews. In particular, technology—the recording of interviews—will increasingly render the interviewing process transparent and make interviewers accountable for their behaviour.

We consider the origins and the key elements of the conversation management approach to investigative interviewing: an approach born of technology rendering unethical, oppressive interrogation unacceptable, and which focuses on creating a relationship with the interviewee—whether a suspect or a witness—that facilitates:

- maximum spontaneous disclosure;
- maximum capture of fine-grain detail;
- rapid, timely identification of issues and anomalies requiring probing—questioning to obtain expansion and explanation.

We describe the fundamental GEMAC framework of conversation management. We conclude with an overview of the PEACE model of investigative interviewing and the ABE model for interviewing vulnerable witnesses. Born of the conversation management approach, both have great merit and are incorporated into this text.

1.1.1 Chapter objectives

This chapter will enable you to:

- appreciate key aspects of investigation, two opposing mindsets adopted by practitioners, and ACCESS—a model of investigative decision-making and action;
- know the origins of the conversation management approach to investigative interviewing;
- understand the key elements of this approach contained within the GEMAC framework;
- appreciate two developments of this approach—the PEACE model and the ABE model for interviewing vulnerable witnesses.

1.2 Investigation

The word 'investigation' comes from the Latin *vestigium* meaning 'trace' or 'footprint': investigation is the search for the trace or footprint and, if done professionally, demands commitment to enquire in detail, to observe carefully, and to examine systematically (Figure 1.1).

What is common to every context of investigation is the commitment of human resource—practitioner, supervisory, and managerial—and increasingly the application of technology, in the acquisition, management, and use of information to protect the well-being of individuals, groups, institutions, the community, or society as a whole by solving or resolving a problematic occurrence or set of circumstances. Common to all such occurrences and circumstances is a *case*—an instance of harm that has happened, is happening, or has the potential to happen.

Investigations can be reactive or proactive.

- **Reactive investigation** is a response to an instance of harm. It is usually overt, although circumstances may require the use of covert methods.
- **Proactive investigation** seeks to prevent the occurrence of harm.

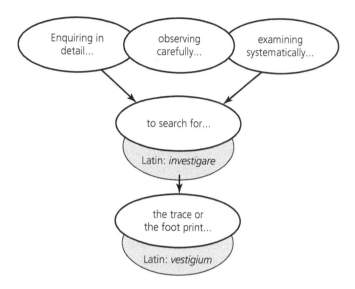

Figure 1.1 The nature of investigation

1.2.1   The journey from information to evidence

Investigation involves probing from the known to the unknown in order to establish the offence or the intention to offend, the circumstances of its actual or potential occurrence, and the most likely offender. This gives rise to detail that differs in status: information, fact, and evidence.

Information

This is detail that has not undergone the test of *validity*, ie checking whether it is accurate or real. In addition, you need to consider the *reliability*—the trustworthiness—*of the source* of the information: to what extent can this be trusted to provide accurate or real information. Often it will not be possible—or appropriate—to assess trustworthiness in the very early stages of an investigation. However, as the amount of information grows, and facts and evidence emerge, the issue of reliability becomes increasingly important.

Fact

In most cases this is information which has been successfully validated, ie its accuracy or reality has been established. The highest level of accuracy is *physical* confirmation that something is the case, ie it really was raining at 1.20 am in that part of the country; the wound was four centimetres deep and to the right groin.

Information passing this test is *hard fact*.

In contrast, the greater part of the information that you obtain and deal with is *soft 'fact'*: utterances and assertions within accounts given by witnesses (a term which includes victims, eyewitnesses, and every other type of witness, including police officers and civilian staff) and suspects. Very rarely there is physical confirmation of detail contained within a reported utterance or assertion, eg a CCTV with parallel sound recording of an incident in the entrance to a night-club.

A less stringent form of validation is *corroboration*, ie one or more people giving accounts containing detail that converges—providing a measure of mutual or collective confirmation. Some accounts can never be corroborated, eg where only the suspect and the alleged victim were present; where the victim is the only witness and has survived but is unable to give an account; where there are no witnesses and two suspects are giving opposing versions of 'what happened' or other matters.

Another less stringent form of validation is *consistency*. Assertions by one individual fit in with those made by another: rather than saying the same thing (confirmation), the assertions are akin to pieces of a jigsaw that fit together.

Soft facts are precarious. In everyday life people make use of stereotyped beliefs as mental shorthand to make sense of the world, eg it is widely believed that the more people who say something the more true it is. A moment's thought reveals that this is a wholly dangerous belief: if two or more people say the same thing—or what is sensed to be the same thing—it would be foolish to treat this as a hard fact.

Investigators have to guard against such stereotyped thinking.[1] What appears to be convergence or consistency could arise from two or more people talking to each other or others before—or even after—initial attendance by the police at an incident. What appear to the police as accounts which corroborate or fit together may be in reality a *post hoc* (after the event) illusion. An apparently coherent account from two or more sources may well have arisen from a process of influencing, shaping, and contamination of their accounts. People—including police officers—are particularly disposed to produce and to contribute to a consensus as to 'what happened' or a critical description.

Investigators are also at risk of treating the complainant's version as hard fact. They may go further, asserting (wholly inappropriately and improperly) to the suspect that what the complainant says is the 'truth', automatically defining as untrue anything said by the suspect that differs.

On occasions investigators do not attempt to validate information. They—or whoever directs them—decide that:

- validation would be pointless because the information has limited or no potential to inform the investigation;
- the information may have the potential to inform the investigation, but lack of time, human resource, or budget demands validation of other information that offers a potentially better return, ie a greater likelihood of emerging as persuasive evidence.

Very rarely do investigators consider seriously or at all the issue of the *reliability*—the trustworthiness—of witnesses. What they assert is all too often uncritically accepted as true.

Evidence

This is information and/or fact that indicates—either unequivocally or arguably beyond all reasonable doubt—that a suspected individual committed the offence.

The investigation may fail to uncover evidence directly pointing to the individual having committed the offence. However, on occasions information and facts taken in the round constitute *circumstantial evidence* that points to the individual's culpability.

The process of reduction

The journey from information to evidence during the investigation process is inevitably subject to attrition, ie gradual reduction (Figure 1.2).

What investigators gather will always be less than the total material generated by the offence. This reduction will stem in part from physical factors, eg availability of material,

---

[1] Wagenaar, W., van Koppen, P., and Crombag, H. (1993) *Anchored Narratives: the Psychology of Criminal Evidence*. Brighton: Harvester Wheatsheaf; Wagenaar, W. and Crombag. H. (2005) *The Popular Policeman and Other Cases*. Amsterdam: Amsterdam University Press.

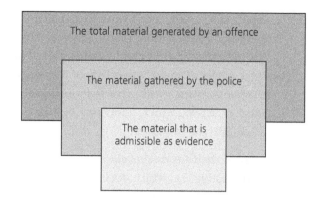

Figure 1.2 Attrition of material during the investigation process (ACPO/Centrex)[2]

and from organizational constraints beyond the control of investigators, eg lack of personnel, lack of financial resource to fund a particular line of investigation. However, much of this reduction stems from practitioners operating with a mindset that:

- adversely affects the quality of information gathering and information management;
- accounts in great measure for critical further reduction: the amount of material eventually admissible as evidence.

The dysfunctional mindset: defensive avoidance

There are many pressures in the workplace: volume of work, shortage of staff, limited time and resources, and restricted budgets. These are liable to lead investigators to adopt a mindset that is inconsistent with quality performance: *defensive avoidance*.[3] More cases can be worked more quickly and with less 'grief' by not enquiring in detail, by not observing closely, and by not examining systematically—in sum, defensively avoiding detail.

Defensive avoidance is a decision to minimize the mental demands and to evade the complexity and implications of detail. It is characterized by taking the 'short cut' as much as possible.

- **'Begging the question'**. The investigator assumes something to be the case—established or proven—or to have been done.
- **Freezing**. The investigator succumbs to *premature closure* (stops considering other alternative explanations) and fails to revise the current *case theory*—the mental model concerning the commission of an offence: what is likely to have happened, the likely motive, and the likely offender (usually in global terms). The investigator believes ('knows') the suspect is guilty, and uncritically accepts the available evidence—despite its status or quality.
- **Seizing**. The investigator is drawn to material that:
  — grabs attention because it stands out as vivid, memorable, dramatic, or emotionally charged;
  — demands little or no mental effort because it 'fits';
  — is readily noted.
- **Relevance filtering, rapid editing, and rapid action**. The investigator 'knows' what he or she needs to know, thus defining anything else as irrelevant, ie not worth knowing. This enables expeditious turn around of work through:

---

[2] ACPO/Centrex (2005) *Practice Advice on Core Investigative Doctrine*. Cambourne: ACPO/Centrex.
[3] Mortimer, A. and Shepherd, E. (1999) 'Frames of Mind: Schemata Guiding Cognition and Conduct in the Interviewing of Suspected Offenders' in A. Memon and R. Bull (eds), *Handbook of the Psychology of Interviewing*. Chichester: Wiley.

— rapid skim reading, eg of witness statements within the crime file, scanning for 'key facts' that fit the current case theory and existing case knowledge;

— the reduction of 'key facts' to 'bullet points' that are easily grasped and handled;

— the conduct of 'quick' interviews of witnesses and the creation of 'quick' statements that are consistent with what the investigator already knows or believes;

— the conduct of a 'quick' interview with the suspect, effectively seeking responses that agree with the 'key facts'.

The common theme is *confirmation bias*, ie the search for information that confirms prior belief and ignoring that which does not, motivated by several different characteristics.[4] The reward for working with detail in this manner—avoiding detail that does not fit—is *rapid closure*.

- The problem is clear and uncomplicated.
- There is a definite answer to the problem.
- The problem is quickly resolved—with the prospect of a quick result.

Defensive avoidance is expedient and expeditious. It produces a quick result. Often circumstances later reveal that it was an investigative failure—a 'rush to get it wrong'—with catastrophic implications, particularly in terms of miscarriages of justice.[5]

- A high proportion of investigatively significant detail within information and evidence is never registered.
- Although the investigator is likely to detect a 'thin' story or contradiction—the most obvious anomaly or oddity—there is little or no chance of detecting the many other forms of anomaly that require an investigative response: missing detail, gaps, jumps, 'non-barking dogs' (detail that could be reasonably expected to be mentioned but is not), 'sidestepping' (avoiding saying something), 'pat' (learned) detail, non-specificity (vagueness and ambiguity), inconsistency, and narrative contrast (variation of amount of detail across the account and in responses).

Most of these anomalies have to do with what is not there, what is not being disclosed. Relevance filtering and rapid editing denies the investigator awareness of these significant anomalies that require probing.

Defensive avoidance, characterized by relevance filtering, rapid editing, and rapid action, generates poor evidence. Historically this has led to very large numbers of cases being withdrawn at court for lack of real evidence. Where trials have proceeded, they have failed for want of quality evidence.

The alternative mindset: vigilance to detail

The alternative mindset to defensive avoidance is *vigilance*:[6] the decision to be attentive, observant, and circumspect in respect of detail. Common sense argues that the life-blood of effective investigation is a comprehensive grasp of the fine-grain detail (FGD). An investigator who is not committed to all the detail—warts and all—is a contradiction in terms. Vigilance to detail is mentally and physically demanding. The pressure can be markedly

---

[4] Ask, K. (2006) 'Criminal Investigation: Motivation, Cognition and Emotion in the Processing of Criminal Evidence' University of Gothenburg, Sweden: Unpublished PhD thesis <https://gupea.ub.gu.se/bitstream/2077/676/1/gupea_2077_676_1.pdf>.

[5] Rossmo, D.K. (2009) *Criminal Investigative Failures*. Boca Raton, FL: CRC Press.

[6] Janis, I. and Mann, L. (1979) *Decision Making: A Psychological Analysis of Conflict, Choice, and Commitment*. New York: Macmillan.

eased by operating with a model of investigation that assists thinking and action in the gathering and processing of detail.

1.2.2 The ACCESS model of investigation

ACCESS is a mnemonic of the six stages of problem-solving involved in any investigation (Figure 1.3).

Assess, action plan, and prepare

Assess

You have to assess the case before you. This demands that you dominate the detail of the information and evidence in terms of *knowledge detail* and *event detail*.[7]

- **Event detail**. In a reactive investigation this is particularly detail of actual events, episodes (periods of time), and continuous states (circumstances, conditions, positions, states of affairs, phases) occurring within the *material time frame*—the span of time leading up to, during, and following upon the incident. In a proactive investigation this is detail of events, episodes, and continuous states that have occurred up to the present moment and with a potential to happen.
- **Knowledge detail**. This is background information without which you would find it difficult, if not impossible to make sense of any narrative. This will of course be case specific, but includes identities (the people directly and indirectly involved or mentioned or referred to, their descriptive and biographical detail), relationships, associations, groups, institutions, organizations, locations, objects, vehicles, data, processes, procedures, routines, rituals, plans, and intentions.

Furthermore you have to assess the validity of the information and evidence you have, and assess the reliability of its source.

Assessment enables you to know what you know, and crucially to identify what you do not know and what you need to know. This is fundamental to subsequent action planning and preparation.

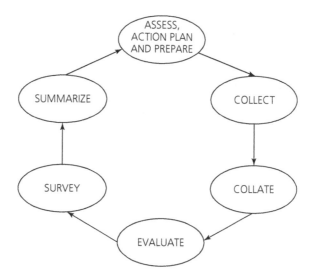

Figure 1.3 ACCESS: a systematic cycle of investigation

---

[7] Shepherd, E. (2008) *SE3R: A Resource Book*. Fourth edition. East Hendred: Forensic Solutions.

Action plan

You must specify:

- *what* you need to know in terms of information and evidence to be collected;
- *why* you need to know it;
- the *how*—the investigative actions to collect the knowledge (what needs to be done, by whom);
- the *priority placed on action*: must do, should do, could do;
- *by when* the action needs to be completed.

In the case of intended interviewing, you must draw up:

- an *interview plan* specifying investigative aims and objectives;
- an *interview strategy* where it is a complex, serious case forecast to require multiple interviews of one or more individuals.

Prepare

This involves getting ready in all senses of the word to collect the specified information and evidence.

Collect

You and, where applicable, your colleagues engage in investigation, interviewing, or both to get the specified information and evidence.

Collate

Collation is the systematic recording and organization of emergent information and evidence collected in investigative actions and interviews.

Evaluate

Evaluation involves reflection: reviewing the detailed product of investigative actions and interviewing.

- Using the action plan, interview plan, and interview strategy to conduct a *gap analysis*—to identify any mismatch between the intended and the actual outcome.
- Determining the value added—additional and unanticipated information and evidence.
- Making judgements concerning information and evidence that has been collected depending upon its nature:
  - *validity* (accuracy; reality) of assertions;
  - *reliability* (trustworthiness) of the source of the information/evidence and the manner in which it was obtained;
  - *continuity* (the chain of custody of physical evidence);
  - *integrity* (procedures taken to protect physical evidence from contamination, damage or tampering).

Survey

Here reflection is taken up a level. You adopt a methodical, comprehensive 'helicopter' view of your investigative effort and the outcomes of this.

Summarize

This is a written record and/or verbal briefing that spells out succinctly the case as it currently stands, its management, and progress to date. This sets the scene for you to enter the investigative cycle yet again: **Assess, action plan, and prepare**—and so on.

1.2.3 Moral, legal, and regulatory requirements

A defining property of a free, civilized society is the expectation of every citizen that those tasked with investigation in any context will conduct themselves properly in their enquiries.

- **Acting *ethically***. Respecting the dignity and rights of any citizen—whether or not known or believed to be a suspect—to be treated with respect, to be listened to, not to be exploited, and to exercise freedom of choice.
- **Acting with *integrity***. Able to be trusted to do the right thing in their treatment of information and individuals—to tell the truth, to act honestly and with fairness, and not to manipulate—even when there is no chance of getting caught for acting otherwise.

Society is no longer willing to pay the cost of miscarriages of justice—ruined lives, compensation, and erosion of faith in the law and those tasked with protecting the law—arising from improper conduct by investigators and their managers acting above the law. Legislation that requires transparency and accountability is the only protection for citizens from unethical, corrupt, dishonest, and self-serving behaviour by investigators.

Investigators and investigation managers therefore have to act *lawfully* as well as ethically and with integrity:

- in the search for detail enabling reconstruction of an actual or intended illegal act or omission, and of the mental state accompanying it;
- when disclosing information and evidence—whether used or not in the prosecution of the individual.

Central and local government institutions, as well as others in the public sector, and organizations, institutions, and companies in the private sector:

- require the maintenance of a continuous record—an audit trail—of the investigation, particularly advice, discussion, decisions, plans, and actions;
- already, or will increasingly, require the electronic recording of interviews.

Electronic recording renders the interviewing process transparent: what happened, how, and to what effect. It enables assessment of the reliability of the interviewee as a source of valid information,[8] particularly when it reveals what would otherwise not come to light.

- **Inappropriate interviewer behaviour.** Evidence that the content of the interviewee's account was influenced, shaped, or misrepresented by the conduct of the interviewer.
- **Factors that rendered the individual vulnerable to inappropriate interviewer behaviour.** For example, evidence of the interviewee's emotional state, level of fatigue, developmental disadvantage (due to being young or old, or having a learning disability),

---

[8] Gudjonsson, G.H. (2006) 'The Psychological Vulnerabilities of Witnesses and the Risk of False Accusations and False Confessions' in A. Heaton-Armstrong, E. Shepherd, G. Gudjonsson, and D. Wolchover (eds), *Witness Testimony: Psychological, Investigative and Evidential Perspectives*. Oxford: Oxford University Press; Gudjonsson, G.H. (2003) *The Psychology of Interrogations and Confessions: A Handbook*. Chichester: Wiley.

or psychological make-up (including the disposition to acquiesce, be compliant, or be suggestible).

The legal or regulatory requirement to record interviews has steadily spread across the world, though it has yet to be introduced universally within North America. Recording will reveal, and render unacceptable, the widespread practices advocated in the *interrogation* of suspects—individuals deemed by investigators to be probably guilty on the basis of:

- information, evidence, or investigator belief in the individual's guilt;
- responses or behaviours observed during—but not always—a prior *investigative interview* which the investigator interprets as deceptive and indicative of guilt.[9]

The aim of the interrogation is not investigation. It is to persuade the suspect to tell the truth. Although there is acknowledgement that this might be a truthful assertion of innocence, in practical terms it is difficult for an innocent suspect to achieve.

- The investigator already believes that the suspect is more likely to be guilty than innocent.
- The encounter consists of a *monologue* during which:
  — the investigator does not focus on 'if' the suspect committed the offence but 'why':
    o producing evidence (which can be untrue) pointing to the suspect's guilt;
    o offering the suspect persuasive arguments—reasons and excuses—that serve to psychologically (not legally) justify or minimize the moral seriousness of offending;
  — if the suspect rejects the investigator's arguments, objects, and continues to assert innocence, the investigator:
    o dominates the talking turn;
    o ignores the suspect's objections and assertions;
    o seeks to render the suspect silent and then compliant: giving the investigator the required 'truth', an admission of guilt, and then signing a confession statement.

It remains to be seen if interrogation—in North America and in other countries where practitioners have long used and argued the merits of these oppressive, non-investigative practices to secure the 'truth'—will survive the transparency of recording, even more so as the efficacy of these techniques is being called increasingly into question through empirical reseach.[10]

It is now some 30 years since the first legal requirement[11] in the Western world to record all suspect interviews. It revealed unacceptable behaviours that led to successful appeals against conviction, and hastened the demise of the interviewing/interrogation distinction. Since then, video-recording has also been introduced, not only for suspects but for key and vulnerable witnesses. With rapid advances in technology, the ever-reducing cost of recording equipment, and the ubiquitous mobile phone, we believe that it is only a matter of time before all interviews will be electronically recorded.

In the meantime, it is the case that in investigations in contexts other than crime, investigators are increasingly subject to scrutiny and are increasingly accountable for

---

[9] Hess, J.E. (2010) *Interviewing and Interrogation for Law Enforcement*. Second edition. New Providence, NJ: Matthew Bender and Co; Inbau, F.E., Reid, J.E., Buckley, J.P., and Jayne, B.C. (2013) *Criminal Interrogations and Confessions*. Fifth edition. Burlington, MA: Jones and Bartlett Learning; Inbau, F.E., Reid, J.E., Buckley, J.P., and Jayne, B.C. (2005) *Essentials of the Reid Technique: Criminal Interrogations and Confessions*. Sudbury, MA: Jones and Bartlett; Zulawski, D.E. and Wicklander, D.E. (2002) *Practical Aspects of Interview and Interrogation*. Second edition. Boca Raton, FL: CRC Press.

[10] Meissner, C.A., Redlich A.D., Bhatt, S., and Brandon, S. (2012) *Interview and Interrogation Methods and their Effect on True and False Confessions*. Campbell Systematic Reviews 2012:13.

[11] Police and Criminal Evidence Act 1984, applying to England, Wales and Northern Ireland: commonly referred to by its acronym—PACE.

their decisions and their conduct, particularly towards those whom they question. They have to demonstrate compliance with government, institutional, and professional regulation. Those commissioning their services are particularly averse to investigation that gives rise to complaint to an ombudsman or tribunal, or to civil litigation. Written statements are no longer taken at face value. The process that gave rise to the statement is now questioned, as well as the content of the document drafted by the interviewer for the individual to sign. For this reason, across the spectrum of investigative context, electronic recording of interviews—once a revolutionary and resisted idea—has become commonplace because it protects the investigator and the interviewee.

The transparency brought about by technology was the spur to the creation of the conversation management approach to investigative interviewing.

1.3 The conversation management approach to investigative interviewing

1.3.1 Origins

In 1983 the first author had been working with the police service for some time as a consultant psychologist. He was very aware of the investigative culture of expediency and expeditiousness that resulted in dysfunctional and unethical conduct of investigations and questioning of witnesses and suspects. When working both operationally and within the training establishment he had met the pervasiveness of defensive avoidance: how officers minimized mental demands and evaded complexity, engaged in 'short cut' thinking—begging the question, freezing, seizing, relevance filtering, rapidly editing, and acting.

Confirmation bias and rapid closure were the defining characteristics in almost every investigation and questioning exchange. Interviewing was a low-status activity: compressing what the individual said into a written statement, drafted by the officer for signature by the individual. The first author was only too aware that more than half of the forensically significant detail went unregistered or was not noted down by the officer, and thus never got into the statement. Interviewing of witnesses was very much an exercise in confirmation rather than investigation: the officer already 'knew' the 'facts', particularly if he or she had interviewed a previous witness or knew the outcome of interviews by other officers.

Interrogation—questioning of suspects—was deemed to be a high-status activity: a craft learned by observing others, and then doing it, in unmonitored interview rooms, in cells, and in locations to which the suspect was taken from the police station. Yet again, confirmation bias and rapid closure reigned. Furthermore, the service was a 'confession' culture. The two-fold aim of interrogation was not investigative—it was to secure an admission of guilt from an individual 'known' or believed to be guilty, and to then secure a written confession signed by the suspect.

Having had experience in a former career as an interrogator and trainer of personnel to resist interrogation, the first author was able to observe and to draw objective conclusions about the tactics used by officers: to sap the suspect's will, to render the suspect silent and compliant, to give up resisting, to give in, and to give the suspect's tormentor—often tormentors—what was demanded. Their conduct was oppressive. Although many appeal rulings had found this to be the case,[12] oppressive conduct was still the order of the day: suspects had to be induced to say things that they otherwise would not, or not to say things that they otherwise would. He found this wanting in terms of ethics, effectiveness, and the

---

[12] For example, *R v Priestley* (1965) 50 Cr App R 183; *R v Prager* (1972) 56 Cr App R 151.

harm that it did—and would increasingly do—to the individuals on the receiving end, the reputation of the service, and to public perceptions of the service and the public's faith in the criminal justice system to 'do it right, and to get it right'.

The Police and Criminal Evidence Bill before Parliament—subsequently enacted in 1984 as the Police and Criminal Evidence Act (PACE)—contained a provision for mandatory electronic recording in designated police stations of interviews with suspects. The first author reasoned that, although it might take a decade to install equipment in every designated police station and for recording to become universal, technology would gradually reveal to the courts and render unacceptable the conduct of officers interrogating suspects. He saw the law and technology providing the opportunity to develop an entirely new *ethical* approach to questioning suspects—investigative interviewing—aimed at achieving investigative aims and objectives, not at securing a confession.

He reasoned that being ethical was not enough. Investigative interviewing had to be effective—judged in terms of the extent to which the interviewer was able to manage the conversation with the suspect in order to:

- facilitate maximum spontaneous disclosure initially and in response to subsequent questioning;
- capture as comprehensively as possible the fine-grain detail (FGD), systematically analyse this, and respond appropriately and in a timely manner.

As a practising psychotherapist and psychologist, the first author knew that clinical professionals are investigators who have the same task of conversing to facilitate maximum disclosure that will enable the clinician to achieve his or her investigative aims and objectives. Any interview they conduct is similarly a 'difficult conversation'.[13] For a wide range of reasons the situation has the potential to become 'tricky', even if it did not start off as such or has not already become problematic.

- The professional, the interviewee, and any third party present may feel uncomfortable, anxious, angry, or frustrated.
- There is a potential for conflict because those involved have different goals, needs, wants, beliefs, and opinions.
- Interviewees and third parties are liable to engage in inappropriate behaviour.
- Interviewees frequently resist because:
  — they are facing circumstances that are psychologically challenging and stressful;
  — they feel vulnerable;
  — their self-esteem is implicated;
  — there are important issues at stake;
  — the outcomes are uncertain;
  — they feel strongly about what is being discussed and about the person who is asking them to disclose.

These practitioners consciously manage conversation to create a *positive relationship* with individuals of all kinds who vary greatly in their *willingness* to engage and to disclose, and in their *ability to tell*. They have to transform this positive relationship into a *working relationship*[14] in which both involved have a shared understanding of the aims, the goals, and their respective tasks, and where participants develop a positive bond. To achieve this and

---

13 Stone, D. Patton, B., and Heen, S. (1999) *Difficult Conversations*. London: Penguin.

14 Gelso, C. and Carter, J. (1985) 'The Relationship in Counselling and Psychotherapy: Components, Consequences, and Theoretical Antecedents' *Counselling Psychologist, 13*, 155–243.

the aims and objectives of the investigation, a clinician must have a commitment to ethical conduct and respect for human rights, and possess the essential underpinning knowledge, understanding, and skills.

Commitment to ethical conduct

Morality has to do with a particular outlook on the world, a set of values about the way the world ought to be in respect of *rationality*—appropriate forms of logical relationship—and *sociality*—appropriate forms of social relationship. Many people are not conscious of having a particular moral perspective or set of values. Despite this, an examination of history and across cultures suggests that two central moral concepts are *respect for the person* and the *obligation to tell the truth*.

The two concepts are interdependent. Observing both protects *integrity* (from the Latin *integer*, meaning the whole): the entirety, the whole society, of which the person is taken to be representative. It is therefore no accident that the cornerstone of law is respect for the person, and the application of law rests upon telling the truth. The observance of both distinguishes a free from a totalitarian society. In a free society, investigative professionals—irrespective of the context in which they work—behave lawfully or in accordance with a code of conduct. In a totalitarian society they behave expediently.

The everyday process of living poses people as individuals with the task of translating their implicit, cloudy moral perspective into action. This is the essence of *ethics*—deliberate thought into action deemed to be 'right'—moral, justifiable, and defensible. The central concept of ethics is *obligation*—what *ought* to be thought and done. Ethical action presupposes freedom of choice to act one way rather than another. Which of the possible courses of action to take depends upon the individual's interpretation of conduct which is ethical. The evidence for this choice is how he or she converses with the person opposite.

Any investigator has a responsibility to respect the rights of the interviewee (or indeed any third party present).

- A right to his or her own opinions, views, and ideas—that may differ from the investigator.
- A right to a fair hearing.
- A right to refuse to participate.
- A right to choose what to disclose, when, and in what detail.
- A right to refuse a request for information.
- A right to object to or to counter information or evidence, arguments, or proposals.
- A right to have feelings and to express these if he or she chooses.
- A right to be 'human'—to get it wrong.
- A right to be himself or herself—the same or different from the other person or other people.

The investigator has a task to do, as well as being a fellow human being, and therefore has commensurate rights.

- He or she has a right—derived from his or her professional role and requirement to progress the investigation—to manage the course of the conversation and to influence the content of the exchange by making *assertions*—making statements, observations, and comments, giving explanations, posing questions, and giving feedback.
- He or she has the same human rights as the interviewee—most particularly to a fair hearing.

He or she has to be prepared to:

- assert in the sense of being *assertive*—engaging in verbal and non-verbal behaviours—to elicit information or to invite the interviewee (or third party) to behave in another way;
- not assert at a particular time.

An ethical investigator never engages in *aggressive* behaviour:

- ignoring the other person's human rights;
- dismissing the needs, wants, opinions, feelings, and beliefs.

Essential underpinning knowledge, understanding, and skills

Clinical professionals typically have a body of underpinning knowledge, understanding, and skills that enables them to manage the conversation with the individual to achieve their investigative aim and objectives.

- They know the *psychological basics*: how memory works, about communication, and the dynamics of conversation.
- They know the importance of *assessment, action planning,* and *preparation* prior to the encounter.
- They know how to *influence* ethically:
  — the individual's perceptions of the professional;
  — the emergence of a positive relationship;
  — the course of the encounter as a series of stages—paying attention to explanation before it begins, at its outset, and throughout;
  — the individual to disclose spontaneously—asking the right question in the right manner, observing and monitoring the individual's behaviour continuously, listening intently (to the FGD) and actively (to detect clues to emotion and attitude).
- They know what is involved when seeking to *persuade* the individual ethically—not resorting to dishonesty or trickery—when inviting him or her:
  — not to engage in inappropriate behaviour or resistance;
  — to reflect on information and evidence;
  — to reflect on his or her disclosures and those of others;
  — to consider alternative ways of perceiving and acting.
- They know what is involved when on those few occasions they seek to *negotiate* ethically with the individual to secure his or her involvement or co-operation.
- They know the importance of *evaluation* following the encounter.

The first author was working as a consultant with Merseyside Police, one of the forces in England chosen to pilot tape-recorded interviewing of suspects. Given the revelatory nature of recordings in the pilot study, it was apparent to all that the days of traditional interrogation tactics to secure admissions and obtain confessions were numbered. Furthermore, since Merseyside was to be the first service in the country to have technology in every designated police station, there was a pressing need for a new approach to questioning suspects.

The first author developed a conversation management approach to interviewing founded upon a commitment to ethical conduct and essential underpinning knowledge, understanding, and skills. The approach he devised was equally applicable to witnesses and suspects. He reasoned that suspects, like victims, are special forms of witness. Suspects give witness—testimony—concerning their personal knowledge or awareness of, presence at, or involvement in an event or set of circumstances.

Whether conversing with a suspect or witness, the interviewer:

- has to take into account the same psychological, conversational, and disclosure considerations;
- prior to meeting the interviewee, has to assess, to action plan, and prepare;
- at the outset of the exchange—on first meeting—has to establish and thereafter sustain a positive relationship;
- across the course of the exchange up to the point of departure has consciously:
  — to influence the individual;
  — to influence the course of the conversation;
  — to facilitate maximum disclosure;
  — to make sense of the individual's behaviour and disclosed detail;
  — to judge when to engage in ethical persuasion or ethical negotiation.

  In effect, the interviewer manages the conversation—viewed as a process and as verbal and non-verbal content—through four distinct stages summarized by the acronym GEMAC: **G**reeting, **E**xplanation, **M**utual **A**ctivity (monitoring/assertion), **C**losing.
- after the exchange, has to evaluate the interview and its outcome in the context of the investigation as a whole.

The first author was invited to assist in the establishment of the Merseyside Interview Development Unit, and appointed co-director with a very experienced detective, Frank Kite, who had overseen the tape-recording pilot scheme. The first author trained Frank and his team of trainers in the conversation management approach to interviewing, which he and they were then to deliver to practitioners.

In the following sections we summarize the basic elements of the conversation management approach to investigative interviewing. From the outset, the first author developed and continued to develop investigative and interviewing tools to assist the interviewer to capture, manage, make sense of, and to make use of information prior to, during, and following the interview.

1.3.2 The psychological, conversational, and disclosure basics

Any practitioner seeking to conduct an investigative interview must know the facts concerning remembering and forgetting offence-related experience:

- the interviewee's memory task;
- attention, perception, and memory;
- the three stages of remembering;
- factors affecting acquisition of detail;
- factors affecting retention of detail in long-term memory;
- retrieval of detail from long-term memory;
- memory for facial detail.

These issues are covered in Chapter 2 (Remembering and Forgetting Offence-Related Experience).

The practitioner must have a secure understanding of:

- channels of communication used in conversation;
- how conversation works;
- how people seek to manage a conversation they have initiated;
- two dimensions of managing conversation: control and concern.

These issues are covered in Chapter 3 (Conversation: From Everyday Talk to Ways of Relating and Changing Minds).

Knowledge of the processes involved in telling and listening, and key features and forms of disclosure, is essential. An interviewer needs to know about:

- how people disclose their experience;
- anomaly;
- deceptive disclosure;
- making sense of disclosed detail.

These issues are covered in Chapter 4 (Telling and Listening: Disclosing and Making Sense of Disclosed Detail).

1.3.3 Prior to meeting: assessment, action planning, and preparation

Ability to engage in conversation management from first meeting through to departure rests upon fulfilling these tasks: the first step in the ACCESS model of investigation.

Planning and preparation are necessary to maximize the investigative and evidential value of the interview by dominating information concerning:

- the interviewee: personal attributes, background, well-being, actual or potential vulnerabilities;
- the offence;
- the context in which the offence or offending took place.

Awareness of these factors enables a decision to be made as to:

- the right person—the most suitable practitioner—to conduct the interview;
- the right place in which to conduct the interview;
- the right time at which to interview.

The interviewer, together with colleagues where applicable, has to manage the information available using a range of tools. This assists the process of interview planning. Where applicable, this plan will be within the framework of the overall interview strategy.

The difference between an interview strategy and an interview plan

In investigations into serious offences, an interview strategy places the forthcoming interview, or all interviewing, in the context of the overall investigation. The investigators working collaboratively, or, in serious and complex cases, the assigned interview adviser together with an external adviser, formulate the interview strategy.

An interview plan is a tactical document. It specifies:

- the aim of the interview;
- the objectives: the key topics—matters or issues—that need to be covered;
- how these will be achieved in practical terms.

Other areas of planning and preparation

Where the interviewer must:

- decide what will be disclosed before the interview when briefing any third party due to be present;
- if there is a second investigator, brief on the tasks he or she will fulfil in the interview;
- where applicable, brief the interpreter;

- make administrative arrangements;
- attend to personal preparation.

Planning and preparation are covered in Chapters 6 (Managing Information), which introduces useful tools described in greater detail in the Reference Section. Planning and preparation are also covered in Chapter 8 (Right Person, Right, Place to Interview, Right Time to Interview, and Right Duration of Interviewing) and in chapters that describe the application of the conversation management approach to interviewing witnesses (Chapters 13 to 15) and suspects (Chapters 16 to 19), and when interviewing in special circumstances (Chapter 20).

1.3.4 The exchange: influencing ethically

Mindful responsive relationship-building behaviours: RESPONSE

Everything an interviewer says or does, and the way he or she says and does it, constitutes the interviewer's *response* to the interviewee as a person. This evidences the extent to which the interviewer is committed to be mindful that the interviewee like the interviewer:

- is a human being;
- has a self concept;
- has a sense of self-esteem;
- has the same rights, needs, concerns, and sensitivities as the interviewer or any other human being.

RESPONSE is an acronym, a sequence of letters that summarize and act as a mnemonic—memory jogger—of the key responsive behaviours that signal:

- the interviewer is mindful of the interviewee as a person;
- wishes to foster and sustain a positive, constructive relationship between the two of them (Box 1.1);

R	Respect
E	Empathy
S	Supportiveness
P	Positiveness
O	Openness
N	Non-judgemental attitude
S	Straightforward talk
E	Equals talking 'across' to each other

Box 1.1 RESPONSE: mindful behaviours for relationship-building

If the interviewer manifests RESPONSE behaviours across the course of the entire interview, he or she will exert significant positive influence:

- upon the relationship between himself or herself and the interviewee;
- over the course of the encounter;
- on the extent to which the interviewee will be disposed to work with the interviewer, the degree of detail disclosed by the interviewee.

If the interviewee is vulnerable in any way, the interviewer will need to pay even more attention to some behaviours—mindful of the particular vulnerability. In Chapter 5 (RESPONSE: Mindful Behaviours for Relationship Building) we cover these matters in greater detail.

Creating a positive impact

A range of behaviours can positively or negatively impact, affecting the interviewer's potential to influence the course of the interview and the relationship with the interviewee:

- dress and appearance;
- posture;
- eye-contact;
- how the interviewer smiles;
- how the interviewer shakes hands;
- gestures that draw the interviewee's attention;
- the interviewer's vocal behaviour;
- the interviewer's use of language.

It follows, therefore, that at the point of very first contact, the interviewer must make a *positive impact* upon the interviewee. This is achieved by *congruent communication*. By this we mean that the interviewer's:

- non-vocal, non-verbal behaviour: dress and appearance, posture, eye-contact, facial expressions, body movements, gestures;
- vocal verbal and non-vocal behaviour: the way he or she expresses himself or herself and the way in which the interviewer speaks and uses his or her voice;
- listening behaviour

must all 'say' the same thing.

We cover the issue of conversational impact in Chapter 3 (Conversation: From Everyday Talk to Ways of Relating and Changing Minds).

Greeting the interviewee (the G of GEMAC)

The 'first four minutes'

When the interviewer first greets the interviewee, the act of greeting is the first stage of a process that psychologists call *set induction*.

- The term *set* seems unusual, but it has to do with the core tasks of preparation, as in 'setting up', or 'setting the table', 'Are you all set?', 'Is the alarm set?'
- *Induction* has to do with the *strategy* followed and the *tactics* applied to create the right mindset within the interviewee: disposing him or her:
  — to engage in a working relationship;
  — to disclose spontaneously detail that enables the achievement of the interview aim and objectives.

Greeting and what follows immediately thereafter is a social act, and so psychologists refer to it as *social set induction*. In the world of psychotherapy and counselling, practitioners know the significance of social set induction and refer to it as the 'first four minutes'.[15] In the context of a police investigation, in the case of a suspect with whom the interviewer has had no prior contact, these early minutes will occur in the custody area. In the case of a witness, the location will vary:

---

[15] Zunin, L. and Zunin, N. (1992) *Contact: The First Four Minutes*. New York: Ballantine.

- if deemed not to require special care interviewing, this is likely to be at his or her home or other location;
- if deemed to require special care interviewing, this will normally be in a location with dedicated recording and monitoring facilities.

In other investigative contexts, investigators have the same task: managing the 'first four minutes' to best effect.

The way the interviewer greets the interviewee sends signals to the interviewee about the relationship that the interviewer wishes to establish between the two of them. These signals are transmitted crucially by:

- the form of address that the interviewer uses towards the interviewee;
- shaking hands.

Reciprocity

If we receive something from another person we feel obliged to reciprocate by giving something back. This applies in all human social exchanges.[16] It is the basis of all conversation, communication of relationship, and the act of relating to one another as human beings. If we perceive someone is feeling a particular emotion towards us, we convey back to them our awareness of this, they feel more able to continue talking. For example, if someone says *Good morning* and smiles as you enter a location, you reciprocate by saying something similar and smiling back, and say whatever you are minded to say.

Reciprocity is a major facilitator of conversation. For example, *I'm Andy Griffiths, and you are?* said while extending a hand towards the interviewee will be met with a name, and almost always a hand.

Reciprocity can easily be woven into attention to creature comforts, with the interviewer making a low-key self-disclosure. The term creature comforts refers to those matters which will make the interviewee feel comfortable. With very few exceptions, a small gesture will generate enormous goodwill from the interviewee.

INTERVIEWER: *It's chilly in here. I'm going to get something to drink before we get started. Would you like a drink?*

INTERVIEWEE: *Er...yeah...tea..., thanks.*

INTERVIEWER: *How do you like it?*

INTERVIEWEE: *Strong please...with milk...and a couple of sugars.*

INTERVIEWER: *Right. Let's sort that right away.*

Skilled use of such simple self-disclosure by the interviewer is very influential. The interviewer in effect trusts the interviewee not to exploit the interviewer's approachable behaviour and the thoughts that he or she shares with the interviewee. Similarly, the interviewee recognizes that the interviewer will not exploit the interviewee's corresponding approachable behaviour and disclosure of his or her thoughts.

In addition to creating the conditions for mutual trust, such low-key self-disclosure is the basis for fostering a positive psychological bond. This bond does not necessarily have to be one of liking. Mutual acceptance and respect are the substance of early bonding. Liking, if it happens at all, may take time, but it can also be immediate. Common sense argues that reciprocity, once demonstrated, should be continuous.

---

[16] Cialdini, R. (2011) *Influence: Science and Practice.* Boston: Allyn and Bacon.

Explanation (the E of GEMAC)

Explanation—giving information in such a way as to maximize comprehension—is termed by psychologists as *cognitive set induction.*

Explanation has increasingly been recognized to be a core professional skill. Despite this, explaining is an activity that is very often poorly performed.[17] It follows that the interviewer's capacity to influence the course of, the interviewee's contribution to, and conduct within the interview will rely in great measure on how empathically and effectively the interviewer puts the interviewee 'in the picture'. This is particularly important in investigative interviewing, since interviewees—whether witnesses, victims, or suspects—are:

- characteristically anxious: about what is going to happen, what will be expected, how they will perform relative to expectations;
- liable to be pre-occupied mentally, engaged in a 'guessing game'—trying to work out what is going to be covered, how, and in what detail.

Explanation begins within or soon after the 'first four minutes': when the interviewer effects introductions, explains his or her role, and outlines briefly what matters are all about, and what is to happen. Explanation is picked up again at the outset of the interview and thereafter occurs across the entire course of the interview to maximize the interviewee's comprehension throughout.

Preliminary orientation

Before commencing the interview 'formally', the interviewer needs to give a preliminary orientation—a brief explanation—to the interview which covers:

- the elements of the 'formal' opening stage of the interview—including introductions;
- indicating, or showing, recording equipment that will be used—explaining why it is being used and subsequent access to a copy of the recording.

Formal introductions within the interview location

In the interview location, the interviewer must effect formal introductions for the record (electronic and otherwise). Each person must introduce himself or herself—first the interviewer and then the interviewee. Where there are third parties present, the interviewer must invite each one to introduce himself or herself and explain his or her role to avoid any confusion, concerns, and apprehensions within the interviewee.

Formal explanation

This must include four elements.

Reason for the interview

This is the 'why'. Whether the interviewee is a witness or suspect he or she must know the rationale for the conversation.

Route Map

Letting the interviewee know the main topics that the interviewer wants to cover—equating to a map of the route that the interviewer would like the interview to take—makes

---

[17] Hargie, O. and Dickson, D. (2004) *Skilled Interpersonal Communication: Research, Theory and Practice.* Fourth edition. Hove, East Sussex: Routledge.

sense. It creates shared understanding: *rapport*. This reduces anxiety and removes apprehensions, assisting further the emergence of a positive working relationship.

In laying out these main topics as a *Route Map*, the interviewer creates an explicit understanding. When the interviewer raises the topic following the Explanation stage, or later in the interview, most interviewees understand that it is over to them to start talking about that topic.

An explicit Route Map provides the interviewer with enormous potential:

- to influence the course of the interview;
- to manage appropriately instances when the interviewee 'drifts off course' or starts disclosing on a matter that has greater priority or earlier than the interviewer wishes to address it;
- to manage behaviour by the interviewee or a third party that risks diverting the interviewer from achieving his or her interview objectives.

Routines

This is the 'housekeeping' aspect of the interview: the 'what' in terms of:

- what the interviewer will be doing across the course of the interview, eg referring to notes, taking notes, producing and showing material (ie information and evidence);
- where applicable, what the second investigator will be doing, ie taking notes.

Expectations

This is a crucial element in the cognitive set induction of the interviewee. Here the interviewer spells out the 'contract' between the interviewee and the interviewer: what each can expect of the other. The Expectations are the 'ground rules'. These rules differ from one investigative context to another. However, the following 'ground rules' apply in every context.

- **To be observed by the interviewee:**
  - To disclose in detail.
  - Not to rush.
  - To think before, and after, saying something.
  - To say if he or she does not understand or needs to ask something.
  - To say if he or she finds it difficult to give an answer.
  - To say if he or she needs something.
  - To ask questions at any time.
- **To be observed by the interviewer:**
  - Not to interrupt.
  - Where necessary, to ask the interviewee to slow down, to stop from time to time, or to go over something again.

The interviewer must check back with the interviewee to confirm comprehension of each 'rule'. Where necessary, the interviewer will have to explain again, and keep on explaining, until the interviewee indicates that he or she has grasped the 'rule'. At the point the interviewee confirms comprehension, he or she effectively signs up to the 'contract' to behave in this manner.

These matters are covered in more detail in Chapter 9 (Right Start, Right Question, and Right Manner of Questioning).

Mutual activity (the MA of GEMAC)

Monitoring

The interviewer must:

- observe continuously, listen intently and actively to the interviewee's verbal and non-verbal disclosures;
- comprehensively capture—holding in working memory, recording in a note or other written or visual form—the FGD of disclosed detail;
- analyse disclosed detail in order to detect anomaly and other issues that require probing, explanation, or expansion within the interview or investigation following the interview.

These matters are covered in Chapter 6 (Managing Information) and Chapter 7 (Active Listening, Observing, and Assessing), and useful tools are described in the Reference Section.

Assertion

By assertion we mean the interviewer:

- using the right question and the right manner of questioning to maximize spontaneous initial disclosure, to respond to this, and to trigger and to respond to subsequent disclosure—both verbal and non-verbal;
- assisting the interviewee's remembrance of offence-related detail.

These matters are covered in Chapter 9 (Right Start, Right Question, and Right Manner of Questioning) and Chapter 10 (Assisting Remembrance of Offence-Related Detail).
Assertion also involves the interviewer:

- engaging in *ethical persuasion* in response to:
  — anomalous disclosures by the interviewee;
  — resistance—verbal, emotional, and even physical behaviour by the interviewee—that blocks the interviewer's efforts to engage in appropriate conversation;
- engaging in *principled negotiation*, when necessary, in special circumstance interviews.

These matters are covered in Chapter 11 (Responding to Inappropriate or Disruptive Behaviour and to Resistance), Chapter 13 (Interviewing the Witness: Key Considerations), and Chapter 20 (Interviewing in Special Circumstances).

Closing (the C of GEMAC)

Professional closing of the interview is the final aspect of set induction. The interviewer reinforces the positive working relationship and 'sets the scene' by:

- expressing appreciation of the interviewee's co-operation and contribution;
- evidencing the interviewer's grasp of the interviewee's disclosures and the interviewer's openness to feedback by providing a concise summary of key ideas/detail from across the interview and inviting confirmation, correction, and expansion;
- providing a 'forward focus': telling the interviewee what is going to happen next;
- inviting questions;
- shaking hands;
- departing on a positive note.

1.3.5 After the exchange: evaluation

This is the next stage in the ACCESS investigation model. The evaluation should be conducted by the investigator, the second investigator (where applicable), and—where applicable and appropriate—by a peer or interview adviser.

The focus is on developing the investigation: contributing to the surveying and summarizing of matters antecedent to engaging in the next assessment, action-planning and preparation for further interviewing, further investigation, or both. Logic argues that evaluation must occur immediately post-interview and certainly before any subsequent interview. There may be some occasions—for example when there are critical issues and implications requiring immediate response to what the interviewee says or does within the interview—when evaluation is conducted within the interview.

Evaluation involves reflection upon:

- **the product**: information and evidence that emerged in the interview;
- **the process**: the relationship between the interviewee and the interviewer, significant behaviour change, points of misunderstanding;
- **the conduct of the interview**: observance of legal and regulatory requirements, procedures, guidelines, and recommended good practice.

Evaluation to achieve investigative objectives, and also to develop professional practice, is covered in Chapter 12 (Evaluation: The Last Piece of the Jigsaw), where reference is made to tools developed by both authors and which are described in more detail in the Reference Section.

1.4 PEACE

1.4.1 Origins

It took almost a decade from the time the Police and Criminal Evidence Act 1984 (PACE) mandated the electronic recording of interviews of suspects before the traditional notion of interrogation was dispensed with in England, Wales, and Northern Ireland. Following a series of high-profile cases in which the Court of Appeal overturned convictions based on false confessions obtained by interrogation, the Home Office in London decided that the police service should have a single national model of investigative interviewing that:

- was not focused on obtaining confessions from suspects;
- increased the investigative potential of witness interviewing.

1.4.2 The basic PEACE model

The first author was a member of the Home Office Working Party appointed to advise and to assist a national project team tasked with developing the national model. Early on, it was decided that the model would be framed on the conversation management approach to investigative interviewing, incorporating materials donated by the first author and the Merseyside Police.

The project team devised an acronym—PEACE—which is a nice play on the abbreviation PACE, cleverly summarizing and assisting remembrance of the five stages of managing the interview process (Box 1.2).

P	Planning and preparation
E	Engage and explain
A	Account
C	Closure
E	Evaluate

Box 1.2 PEACE: the national model of investigative interviewing in England, Wales, and Northern Ireland

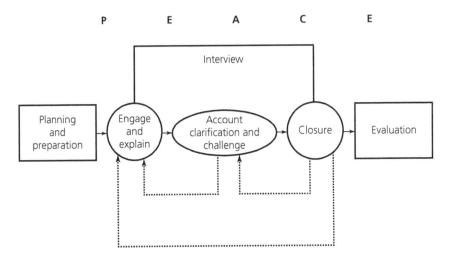

Figure 1.4 The current PEACE model

Responsibility for the further development passed to the National Crime Faculty (NCF). The model quickly evolved to specify two further activities—Clarification and Challenge—in addition to Account within the A stage (Figure 1.4).

Clarification

The view of the NCF was that in any interview there are two distinct perspectives on matters: the interviewee's and the interviewer's. Although the interviewee may disclose material spontaneously in his or her account, and answer probing questions about this:

- these disclosures may not, and very often will not, mention matters that the interviewer wants to know about;
- there will usually be issues about which the interviewee will have no knowledge but the interviewer will want to ask questions about.

Across the years different terminology has been used to differentiate these two perspectives. Originally they were called the *interviewee's agenda* and the *police agenda*. Because the word 'agenda' has a negative connotation, the alternative terms *interviewee areas* and *interviewer areas* were introduced. Latterly another term was introduced as an alternative to interviewer areas: *investigatively important information* (which we refer to as I[3]).

Challenge

The original PEACE model gave no advice on what to do if the interviewee:

- gave an account that was anomalous;

- gave anomalous responses to questions concerning the account or matters introduced by the interviewer.

Challenging is now considered to be the final stage in the interviewing process in which anomaly—particularly inconsistency and contradiction—is brought to the interviewee's attention and an explanation requested.

We have reservations about the use of the word challenge, believing that it is an unfortunate word, conveying a tenor of combativeness and of throwing down the gauntlet. We acknowledge and respect that the police service in England, Wales, and Northern Ireland will continue with this choice of word notwithstanding its negative connotation.

The process is in effect a review, the elements of which in an interview of a suspect are captured by the mnemonic FAIR:

- **Final Anomaly Investigation**
- **Reasons to suspect.**

We cover the FAIR review in Chapter 16 (Interviewing the Suspect: Key Considerations).

Following discussions between the first author and a colleague Ian Hynes, Ian has defined the activities with the A stage of PEACE as:

- Account
- Clarify
- Compare and contrast.[18]

We consider that 'compare and contrast' is an accurate and constructive description of what an interviewer may have to do in an interview of a witness or a suspect. The first author has incorporated this description into PEACE training that he delivers to practitioners in public and private sector institutions.

1.4.3 The free recall interview

The *free recall interview* is a simple development of the PEACE model that can be followed in interviews of eyewitnesses.

- 'Setting the scene', ie context reinstatement.
- Free recall.
- Encouraging repeated attempts to recall.
- Identifying topics/episodes for expansion and explanation—using conventional probing questions.

In Chapter 10 we explain how to assist an interviewee's remembrance of offence-related detail.

1.4.4 Development of PEACE

It is now 20 years since the introduction of PEACE. The model remains the foundation of the interview strategy advocated by the senior leadership of the police service in England, Wales, and Northern Ireland. Over that period, a national steering group has worked to ensure the model remains fit for purpose and responsive to change.

---

[18] Personal communication: Eric Shepherd and Ian Hynes.

Principles of investigative interviewing

i.   The aim of investigative interviewing is to obtain accurate and reliable accounts from victims, witnesses, or suspects about matters under police investigation.

ii. Investigators must act fairly when questioning victims, witnesses, or suspects. Vulnerable people must be treated with particular consideration at all times.

iii. Investigative interviewing should be approached with an investigative mindset. Accounts obtained from the person who is being interviewed should always be tested against what the interviewer already knows or what can reasonably be established.

iv. When conducting an interview, investigators are free to ask a wide range of questions in order to obtain material which may assist an investigation.

v.   Investigators should recognize the positive impact of an early admission in the context of the criminal justice system.

vi. Investigators are not bound to accept the first answer given. Questioning is not unfair merely because it is persistent.

vii. Even when the right of silence is exercised by a suspect, investigators have a responsibility to put questions to them.

Figure 1.5 Principles of Investigative Interviewing (NPIA, 2009)

- Legal developments such as a change to the law relating to the right to silence,[19] and the introduction of 'bad character'[20] have been incorporated into training.
- A tiered approach to competency has been introduced so that investigators are trained for the level of criminality their work encompasses.
- Developments in technology have been made to improve the quality of recordings.

The overall approach is detailed in a published strategy[21] that has updated the principles of interviewing issued when PEACE was originally implemented (Figure 1.5).

1.5   *Achieving Best Evidence*: the Phased Interview

The Youth Justice and Criminal Evidence Act 1999 (YJCEA) (as amended by the Coroners and Justice Act 2009) introduced the category of vulnerable witnesses, being:

- children vulnerable by reason of their age—under 18;
- individuals who have a mental disorder;[22]
- individuals significantly impaired in relation to intelligence and social functioning—who have a learning disability.

These individuals are eligible for special measures, which include interviewing, the conduct of which must be mindful of their vulnerability. Official guidance for interviewing of these

---

[19] Criminal Justice and Public Order Act 1994.

[20] Criminal Justice Act 2003.

[21] National Police Improvement Agency (2009) National Interview Strategy <http://www.acpo.police.uk/documents/crime/2009/200901CRINSI01.pdf>.

[22] As defined by the Mental Health Act 1983, as amended by the Mental Health Act 2007.

individuals is contained in *Achieving Best Evidence* (ABE),[23] which specifies that following essential planning and preparation, there should be a *phased approach* to interviewing.

- Rapport;
- Free narrative account;
- Questioning;
- Closing the interview.

This is followed by evaluation.

It will be immediately clear that the phased interview is a conversation management approach, underlined by the fact that ABE requires the interviewer:

- to establish rapport and a positive working relationship with the individual;
- to be extremely flexible: adjusting conversation and questioning to the particular limitations of the individual.

ABE also specifies special interviewing techniques, including the Cognitive Interview/ Enhanced Cognitive Interview (CI/ECI) developed by Geiselman and Fisher[24] to enhance witness memory performance by using various techniques. We discuss cognitive interviewing in Chapter 10 (Assisting Remembrance of Offence-Related Detail).

1.6 Advantages and disadvantages of linear goal models

The original conversation management framework—GEMAC—does not spell out specific goals: it specifies the interdependent activities—monitoring and assertion (that constitute Mutual Activity—MA) in which the interviewer has to engage skilfully. In contrast, PEACE, its free recall development, and the ABE Phased Interview are linear goal models. They specify what needs to be achieved between the point of opening and closing in terms of goals. This has clear advantages when explaining to learners what needs to be achieved. However, it risks creating a mindset that *all* the goals have to be achieved within a single interview. It is very much the case that busy investigators—faced with a significant case load, under time pressure, and the requirement to get things 'turned round'—will tend to view the interview as a time-constrained one-shot, one-stop event with little or no prospect of further interviewing at this time or even in the future.

The downside of this is that the imperative to get all the goals achieved in a single encounter risks driving the process faster than is sensible. A rapidly delivered 'thin' account is typically accepted as the 'norm': 'what all interviewees give'. Rather than giving feedback and asking the interviewee to have another go—this time with more detail—all too many investigators immediately shift to Clarify, selecting topics to be probed. All too often probing is inadequate and unsystematic. There is too little questioning to obtain expansion and explanation. The interviewer moves too quickly to the next topic, and the next, and the next. In the PEACE context, Clarification can very often become a rapid exercise in confirming prior knowledge—information and evidence in the 'file'—rather than facilitating fuller disclosure. All too often the interviewer embarks immediately into Challenging. The interviewer counters the interviewee's responses and confronts the interviewee with the mismatch between what the interviewee has said and what the interviewer 'knows'. This done, the interview is brought to a conclusion.

---

[23] Ministry of Justice (2011) *Achieving Best Evidence in Criminal Proceedings: Guidance on Interviewing Victims and Witnesses, and Guidance on Using Special Measures*. London: HMSO.

[24] Fisher, R.P. and Geiselman, R.E. (1992) *Memory-enhancing Techniques for Investigative Interviewing: The Cognitive Interview*. Springfield, Ill: Charles C. Thomas.

Common sense argues that circumstances dictate that not all the goals specified in the model can or should be addressed in a single interview. A professional interviewer judges when it is the right time for a break. Taking a break is sensible for example when:

- the interviewee has given a very full first account that may have taken some time;
- probing on a topic, or only a few topics, has given rise to a large amount of detail that is actually or potentially significant;
- the interviewee is showing signs of exhaustion, struggling to cope, stress, or distress;
- the interviewer recognizes that there is a lot to take in or there are issues that need to be thought about before interviewing progresses further.

There are numerous factors relating to the offence that might influence the decision to achieve just one goal—a very detailed account—or extensive probing on a topic or number of topics. Factors that are likely to lead the interviewer to take a break before beginning another interview include:

- the nature of the offence;
- the complexity of the offence;
- the age of the offence—the time elapsed between the offence and the interview;
- the period of time across which offending took place and the frequency of offending;
- the number of offences to be accounted for;
- the time frame over which offending took place;
- situational factors;
- the interviewee's psychological make-up;
- the interviewee's psychological (mental and emotional) and physical state;
- the interviewee's reaction to being interviewed and responses when asked to disclose detail or to answer probing questions—all may very well dictate that more than one interview is necessary;
- the need to defuse the situation—where the interviewee's response is extremely aggressive, disruptive;
- the interviewee needs to compose himself or herself, for example, being unable to stop crying or being uncontrollably angry;
- the interviewee's behaviour is wholly disruptive;
- the investigator's need to get his or her head around the disclosed detail;
- the investigator's need to compare and contrast the interviewee's disclosures with the FGD of prior information and evidence;
- the disclosures that have questioned the validity or reliability of information and evidence known prior to the interview;
- the need to validate detail that the interviewee has disclosed in the interview;
- the need to conduct further investigations;
- if the nature of the exchange indicates a 'clash of personalities'—the absence of a positive relationship between the interviewer and interviewee, or, although it may be positive, little of investigative substance is being achieved.

These issues underline our observations in *How to use this book*: the conversation management approach requires you to confront complexity and to be flexible.

1.7   PEACE and ABE within this text

Chapters 13 to 19 cover the application of the conversation management approach to investigative interviewing of witnesses and suspects. Throughout we have presented this within the frameworks of PEACE (applied to witnesses and suspects) and ABE (applied to vulnerable witnesses).

Arguments advocating more appropriate terminology (FAIR review; compare and contrast), the emergence of the free-recall interview, and the ABE phased interview all underline the fact that PEACE is more of a framework than a 'one size fits all' model.

In this text we have left intact the terminology of PEACE as a model. In the interview maps showing the activities at each stage with different categories of witness and suspect we have preserved the terminology of PEACE, as well as including our own modifications.

1.8 Chapter summary

In 1990 the first author gave a presentation on conversation management entitled 'Ethical Interviewing'.[25] He argued that established ways of thinking and acting when it comes to interviewing had to yield to those aspects of the service that were stirring most deeply within individuals who wanted to do the job professionally. Among these officers was a growing awareness of the rightness and wrongness of certain attitudes and actions, and the gnawing internal and external reverberations that result if the service failed to act according to this awareness. Ethical interviewing could only exist if the ethos were right. He indicated his liking for the Greek distinction concerning time: *chronos*—measured time, time past, and time to come; and *kairos*—the right time. He argued that for the good of the police service and society, it was *kairos*—the right time to abandon interrogation and to engage in investigative interviewing using the conversation management approach.

This chapter has provided you with an overview of the origins of this approach, of the required ethical commitment, and of the underpinning knowledge, awareness, and skills, of the psychological and practical elements of the GEMAC framework. You now know the elements and the defining features of conversation management models that have evolved over the past 20 years: PEACE, the free recall interview, and the ABE Phased Interview.

---

[25] Paper presented at the *Policy for Interview Training Seminar*, Council of the Association of Chief Police Officers of England, Wales and Northern Ireland, 19–21 September 1990 at the Metropolitan Police Training School, London.

Remembering and Forgetting Offence-Related Experience

2.1 Chapter overview

This chapter examines the mental processes involved when people remember and forget an event, and focuses on those factors with a potential to affect whether a witness or suspect remembers or forgets offence-related experience. An understanding of these processes is fundamental to effective investigative interviewing.

2.1.1 Chapter objectives

This chapter will enable you to:

- understand the interviewee's memory task;
- appreciate the interdependence of attention, perception, and memory;
- understand the three stages of remembering an event;
- have a sound grasp of the range of factors that affect acquisition of event detail, and subsequent storage and retrieval of event detail;
- understand how facial detail is acquired, stored, and retrieved.

2.2 The memory demands of interviewing and being interviewed

When we interview witnesses and suspects, we are seeking detailed disclosure of their remembrance—the contents of their memory—of their experience of a particular event or episode occurring prior to the interview, and of a person or persons involved.

There is much more to memory than retrieval or recall. An interview—like every conversation—makes very large mental demands. Both participants have to make sense of a stream of information issuing from the other person. Each has to concentrate, to consciously pay attention, and to hold on to—and make sense of—what the other person is saying or doing, and what has gone before—what was said and done earlier.

For the interviewee, this mentally demanding conversation will be anything but a casual or informal chat. He or she may be a reluctant, unwilling, or unhappy participant. This is a conversation with a person with power and the authority—rather like a parent—to determine what gets talked about, when, for how long, and in what degree of detail. A conversation with implied expectations and obligations: to co-operate and to disclose detail in response to the authority person's requests and questions about 'something' of actual or potential significance, and with likely implications for the individual and those mentioned or involved.

Conducting an interview is particularly mentally demanding. How you manage the course of the interview, the extent to which you create a working relationship, you facilitate maximum disclosure, and you achieve your interview aim and objectives—all rely on your memory and on your ability to concentrate and to process information. These are the cognitive tools required to implement your interview plan, to monitor the interviewee's verbal and non-verbal communication, to pose questions, to capture, analyse, and respond at the appropriate time to the fine-grain detail of the interviewee's disclosures and to changes in his or her behaviour. Where others are present in the conversation, the mental demands upon you are even greater!

2.3 Attention, perception, and memory

Our ability to make sense of circumstances and situations that confront us and to make decisions—judgements and choices—about appropriate actions relies on three interdependent aspects of our mental functioning (Figure 2.1).[1]

- **Attention**. The mental capacity to concentrate, observe, and to listen that we devote to processing available information.
- **Perception**. The interpretation or construction we place on circumstances to which we are exposed.
- **Memory**. The mental processes that we use to acquire, store, retain, and later retrieve information.

2.3.1 Attention

How we attend necessarily affects how we respond to—and perform in—a set of given circumstances, an event, an everyday conversation, or an interview. We have only a finite amount of mental resource available for the task of attention. We are able to attend *selectively*, choosing what information has our attention. We can also *divide* our attention—varying the amount, or level, of our attention that we devote to two or more tasks. Our ability to attend selectively and to distribute our attention points to the role of perception in guiding our attention.

Of great significance is our *attention span*: the amount of time that we can concentrate without being distracted. Attention can be *focused* or *sustained*. Focused attention is a short-term response to something that attracts our awareness, eg the ring of a telephone, or an unexpected occurrence. After a few seconds we return to what we were originally doing or think about something else. Sustained attention is a longer-term response which enables us to achieve something over a period of time. Being able to sustain attention without being distracted is crucial in the context of an investigative interview.

Ability to sustain attention varies with age: young children find it difficult, performance improves with developing maturity, and tends to decline in older years. The digital age has adversely affected attention spans in the community. With each successive generation, the effect is greater due to the pervasiveness of television as a medium and ever-increasing use of modern technology: mobile phones, electronic devices, and the extensive use of the Internet.

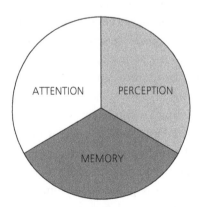

Figure 2.1 Attention, perception, and memory

---

[1] Styles, E.A. (2005) *Attention, Perception and Memory: An Integrated Introduction.* Hove: Psychology Press.

Most teenagers and adults are able to sustain attention on one thing for about 20 minutes. They then need to refocus, enabling them to do the same thing for another 20 minutes. After 40 minutes, attention rapidly declines: a break is necessary. This is why you should never interview an adult for more than 40 minutes. The interviewee and you, and any third party present, have reached the limits of your ability to concentrate, take in, and deal with what has happened and been exchanged in the interview. In the case of children, young people, and the elderly, you should match the duration of the interview to allow for their age.

Within the course of the interview, attention ebbs and flows. In Chapter 1 we high-lighted the significance of the 'first four minutes'.[2] The first four or so minutes constitute a period of adjustment, mental settling down, in which the individual is particularly alert to communication—particularly non-verbal—and conduct that send messages about the rela-tionship that exists, or you wish to create, between you. He or she will gradually focus, increasing attention on the verbal content of your messages. For this reason you should keep the pace down, pausing as you make introductions, and add each successive element of your Explanation: the Reason for the interview, the Route Map, and the Routines.

You should aim to deliver the 'contract'—Expectations—no earlier than five minutes into the interview. At this point the individual is entering a period of optimal focus which typic-ally lasts for some 10–20 minutes. The individual is highly receptive to what you are saying and in a state of readiness to give a first account, hopefully in accordance with the contract, and thereafter to respond to your questions. You will be optimally focused to capture, ana-lyse, and respond in a timely manner to whatever the individual discloses. By continuously working to place the individual in the talking turn is the way to ensure he or she sustains attention.

Factors affecting attention

A very large number of factors have the potential to affect an individual's attention and resultant response and performance, eg in a conversation.

Relevance, significance, interest, and motivation

If, for whatever reason, the individual does not sense something as relevant, significant, or interesting—or lacks motivation—he or she is unlikely to devote much, if any, attention to processing available information.

Physical factors

Current physical state and health affect concentration. Fatigue, lack of stamina, pain, phys-ical discomfort, and other symptoms divert attention and make it difficult to keep track. Similarly, any visual and auditory impairment will adversely affect performance.

Lack of—or disrupted—sleep affects all aspects of thinking on the following day. The individual struggles to pay attention, to concentrate, to remember, to pull things together, and to hold information in memory.

Time of day

We are diurnal animals. Our biological rhythms are such that our ability to attend, to con-centrate, and to follow declines with the onset of darkness and with our need to sleep dur-ing the night.

---

[2] Zunin, L. and Zunin, N. (1992) *Contact: The First Four Minutes*. New York: Ballantine.

Distractors

Location and ambient conditions, eg temperature, background noise, interruptions, can significantly disrupt attention.

Distractibility

If the individual's thoughts are elsewhere, if he or she is dwelling on something else, this will impair concentration. He or she will not attend or be unable to grasp fully, or to any meaningful extent, what is happening or what is being said.

The need to drink, eat, urinate, or excrete significantly affect ability to pay attention and to concentrate—increasingly so as the need becomes more pressing. This is especially the case if the individual has ingested alcohol or opiates. These drugs—and many which are prescribed or bought over-the-counter (OTC)—have a dramatic diuretic effect. The individual becomes dehydrated and needs to drink liquid, experiencing this subjectively as thirst and rendering the individual distractible.

Alcohol and opiates also affect blood sugar level. The individual becomes temporarily hypoglycaemic and commonly experiences dysphoria: feeling unwell, emotionally and mentally 'down', and indifferent. These symptoms affect ability to concentrate until such time as food—containing sugar or carbohydrate—is taken and digested. An individual with diabetes who has become hypoglycaemic will be similarly unable to process information effectively until blood sugar level has been restored.

If an individual is significantly addicted to nicotine, he or she needs to smoke before engaging in any activity that requires sustained attention and concentration. The individual will become increasingly distractible as the interval increases since he or she last smoked. Similarly, if an individual is taking a prescribed medication one or more times a day for a psychological condition (see later), this may cause increasing distractibility in the period leading up to taking the drug. He or she may continue to be distractible for a period thereafter.

Some individuals who are so heavily addicted to recreational drugs may need medication to render them calm enough to cope with the mental demands of an interview.

Emotion

Intense feelings (eg frustration, embarrassment, guilt, remorse, anger, fear, sadness, happiness, disgust, surprise, acute anxiety, or acute depression) typically triggered by a specific event or circumstances can significantly influence attention and ability to concentrate.

Mood

More general, pervasive, and prolonged feelings (eg enduring anxiety, depression, or a combination of these) are characteristically not caused by a specific event or circumstances. Their effects are typically cognitive, occasioning the individual to think at length, to brood, or to ruminate—activities that inhibit attention, concentration, ability to keep track and to grasp matters.

As described previously, an individual may experience temporary mood change—dysphoria—as a result of a drop in blood sugar level which affects ability to process information.

Stress

There are many aspects to stress, all of which have a potential to affect attention. Stress is the physiological and emotional response to a stressor—any demand to adapt to current circumstances. The body releases hormones that increase physical strength, energy, and readiness—enabling the individual to engage or to exit (the 'flight or fight' response).

Again underlining that perception affects attention, people experience stress when they feel that they cannot control what is happening. This subjective stress in response to a stressor can occur in parallel with physiological and emotional stress. It can significantly affect attention and ability to concentrate, to follow, and to comprehend. Again striking the interdependent relationship between experience, perception, and attention, some stressors cumulatively debilitate mentally and physically, erode overall mental functioning, and adversely affect capacity to attend and to concentrate. These include 'life stress' events (eg bereavement, divorce, moving home, redundancy) and 'micro-stressors'—enduring stress-inducing circumstances (eg continuing unemployment, constant arguments, straightened finances).

Psychological 'make-up'

A wide range of factors within an individual's psychological 'make-up' can—either alone or in combination—variously impact upon an individual's attention, concentration, and ability to 'keep up', to remain on track, and grasp matters. These include:

- Stage of development and level of mental functioning (particularly young and very young children; individuals with learning difficulties; the elderly).
- The individual experiencing psychological problems or having a psychological condition.
- Disposition: the individual may have a personality that renders him or her a poor attender. For example, extreme extroverts characteristically struggle to maintain attention and to stay on target. They are easily diverted. They prefer to be doing something other than paying attention—talking!

Psychological conditions

Many psychological conditions are characterized by problems with attention and concentration. Medication alleviates problems experienced by those who are being treated for an *affective disorder*—anxiety, depression, mania, and hypomania—or *Attention Deficit and Hyperactivity Disorder* (ADHD). Such individuals will become increasingly distractible as they approach the time for their next medication.

Drugs

Nicotine exercises a powerful stimulant and sedative effect. If an individual smokes one or more cigarettes per hour averaged across the day, he or she has a significant dependency. An individual dependent on nicotine will experience the need to smoke in order to concentrate and to relax. As pointed out previously, he or she will be distractible if he or she has not been able to smoke prior to the interview.

Recreational drugs such as alcohol and opiates significantly impair mental functioning. An individual under the influence of such drugs—and for some time afterwards while suffering the after-effects of the drug—will be unable to concentrate, follow, understand, or remember with any reliability.

As pointed out previously, drugs, especially alcohol and opiates, have a diuretic effect and affect blood sugar level, rendering the individual distractible.

Language barriers

Language and how it is delivered can create significant barriers to attention, ability to follow and to grasp, as well as affecting the individual's perception of what is going on.

Difficult words, jargon, utterance length, and speed of delivery compound any difficulties arising from physical factors, distractibility, emotion, mood, stress, developmental and intellectual disadvantage, psychological problems, being under the influence of a drug, not having English as a first language, or any combination of these. The individual will struggle, missing detail and missing the point, and may cease paying attention.

2.3.2 Perception

Perception and memory are inextricably entwined. Our personal *frame of reference* (FOR)—the product of our accumulated experience—is multi-faceted, combining our ideas about the world, expectations, aspirations, desires, values, attitudes, preconceptions, and prejudices. We describe in the next section how this knowledge provides us with mental shorthand—enabling us to cope with complexity—and a mind-set that disposes us to respond in a characteristic way.

We are so used to accessing, applying, and acting upon our FOR that much of the time we are relatively unconscious of its role in our lives.

- It determines the relevance and the significance of, and our interest in, the information—and the source of the information—to which we are exposed.
- It motivates us to pay attention.
- It guides our attention, influencing us to select particular detail from all information that is potentially available.
- It influences what sense we make of this selected detail.
- It removes uncertainty and ambiguity, keeping our anxiety level down and keeping us 'ahead of the game' in terms of actions and reactions: our own and those of other people.
- It can work against us, leading us to behave dysfunctionally by going into 'auto pilot'—we've seen it (all) before—and 'shoe-horning'—applying an established way of perceiving and acting to cope with an entirely novel experience, rationalizing that 'it worked for that...so I'll do it for this'.

Other factors mentioned earlier that affect the way we perceive are subjective stress and cumulative exposure to stressors. In addition, developmental and intellectual disadvantage, as well as psychological problems, restrict an individual's ability to make sense of matters and in turn adversely affect attention, concentration, and ability to follow what is going on.

2.3.3 Memory

Memory does not function like a single unitary organ such as the heart or liver. It is much more complex, comprising a series of interconnected systems serving different purposes and behaving in different ways. For ease of explanation, psychologists usually explain memory in terms of information flowing through three sub-systems: *immediate* memory, *working* memory, and *long-term* memory (Figure 2.2).[3]

These sub-systems interact with each other. As information passes through, it is held in a distinctive manner for varying duration. Information which enters, and is later recalled, is influenced by what we were—and are now—attending to and the sense we made—and are now making—of it.

---

[3] Baddeley, A., Eysenck, M., and Anderson, M. (2009) *Memory.* Hove: Psychology Press.

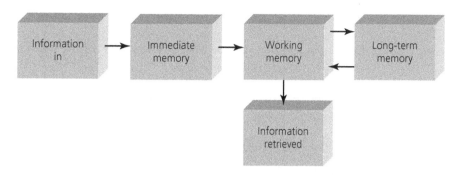

Figure 2.2 The flow of information through the memory system

Immediate memory

Sometimes called *sensory* memory or *buffer store*, immediate memory is the point at which information in the environment impinges on our senses, and in varying degree enters our awareness. At this point the information is fleeting, short lived and unstable. A good example of immediate memory is when someone gives you their telephone number straight off without pausing. You are not likely to remember all the digits and will find yourself asking the person to repeat the number for you.

Working memory

Working memory is where we are able to hold consciously in mind—and work with—several pieces of information at the same time, relating these to each other. Information enters working memory from immediate memory and from long-term memory—our accumulated store of experience (see later in this chapter). We rely on our working memory in order to understand what is being said to us, or what we are looking at, in the light of what has gone before and what we expect to come. Similarly, when we wish to say something, it is a working memory task: thought comes to mind, as do the words, and then we literally speak our mind.

It follows that any conversation—particularly one with some personal importance—makes multiple demands on an individual's working memory:

- to *talk*;
- to *listen* in readiness to talk;
- to *follow* what is being said now and was said before this point in the conversation, and earlier, by the other person or others present;
- to *grasp the significance* of what is now being said and was said before this point and earlier—of questions posed, of responses, or of disclosures—by the individual, the other person, or others present;
- to *remember* what was said before this, and earlier, by the individual, the other person or others present.

People vary greatly in terms of the capacity and efficiency of their working memory. Those who are disadvantaged developmentally, psychologically, or experiencing the effects of a changed state of consciousness (for whatever cause) will be at a disadvantage in terms of their working memory performance.

Long-term memory

This comprises our experience accumulated across our lifetime organized into bodies of knowledge: semantic memory and episodic memory.

Semantic memory

This is our personal store of 'general knowledge' of the world based upon our experience that we have mentally organized as:

- *factual knowledge*, eg our language; subject matter knowledge
- packages of *'typical' knowledge*.

'Typical' knowledge exists in two forms.

- **Stereotypes**. These comprise our categorical notions about types of people, types of situation, types of circumstance, and characteristic behaviour in given situations and circumstances. This is the stuff of pre-conception, prejudice, exclusion, exclusiveness, and a closed mind. They lie at the heart of relevance filtering, excessive editing, and confirmation bias described in Chapter 1.
- **Scripts**. These comprise our notions of typical ways of acting, and responding, in a given type of situation and given set of circumstances. This is the stuff of the routines, the rituals, and agendas that we and other people typically follow in everyday life, eg going for a meal, filling the car with petrol.

Our stereotype and script knowledge combined with our hopes, aspirations, what we want to happen and to achieve provide us with our FOR.

Episodic memory

We store information concerning events, 'one-off' happenings we experience, as episodes. This episodic memory comprises stored knowledge with multiple facets: a sequence of actions occurring at a particular point in time, in a specific situation, within a set of particular circumstances, involving maybe ourselves but frequently another person or people with particular features or behaving in a particular way. We bring to bear our FOR and our semantic memory with its stereotype and script contents to enable us to make sense of these multiple facets of the 'one-off' situation before us.

Given that people differ greatly in their life experience, each person will have a distinctive semantic memory and different FOR. Each individual's episodic memory for an event will necessarily be *idiosyncratic*: a unique mix of detail.

This has important implications for us as interviewers. We should expect individual differences in the detail disclosed, in terms of amount, focus, content, breadth, depth, and quality, as well as interpretation, explanation, and justification.

Single occurrences—repeated occurrences

Often a witness or suspect will be disclosing detail about an episode that was indeed a 'one-off' happening: a single occurrence. However, we have to make allowances for an interviewee who is being invited to disclose detail about an instance of a repeated occurrence, eg a victim of abuse that has occurred frequently over a period of time, perhaps even years. Any one instance will of course be a 'one-off' episode that occurred at a particular time and under particular circumstances. However, because the abuse occurred repeatedly, it has become a script within semantic memory—typical ways in which the offender acted, and the victim responded. This means that the victim may have difficulty differentiating a particular instance in time. Because of this the individual may struggle to describe the actual sequence of offending behaviour, instead reporting a stereotyped sequence: a script memory.

Similarly, an individual who has committed multiple, serial, or repeated offences may well have the problem of differentiating between separate instances of offending across a period of time. They may well remember anchoring detail, such as the place, the circumstances, and even the victim, but may have problems describing the actions and sequence of actions.

Chapter 10 describes a technique that enables you to help an individual to dis-embed a particular instance from a series of repeated occurrences, and thus decrease the potential for reporting a script memory.

2.4 Remembering offence-related experience

For offence-related detail to become part of an individual's stock of experience and to be remembered—and shared with another or others subsequently—this detail has to go through three stages: *acquisition*, *storage*, and *retrieval*.[4] Failure to pass through any one of these stages will result in an inability to remember the event.

2.4.1 Acquisition

Acquisition involves the registration, or encoding, of particular detail as a *memory trace* in our memory system. At the stage of acquisition, the information is in the form of electrical activity within, and throughout, the individual's brain.

Core (central) detail and peripheral detail

Detail that strikes us as salient, and we attend to, is likely to become *core* or *central* to our subsequent remembrance of matters. Core detail will very often be the main action detail, is often remembered with great clarity if it sticks out, and in a subsequent account may be 'priority' detail remembered initially with some conviction and perhaps great accuracy.

In contrast, we give minimal attention and thought to other detail. This *peripheral* detail is less likely to be registered securely and is liable to be less accurately recalled.

People differ greatly. We cannot make assumptions about the core/peripheral distinction. What emerges as core detail to one person will not be core detail to another. Similarly, what might be peripheral detail to one might be central to another. This does not alter the fact that we register action and activity detail more readily than descriptive detail.

The constructive process of making sense

At the point an event is initially registered the individual is making sense of it—putting a *construction* on it—based upon his or her stock of knowledge in long-term memory. At this stage memory is *constructive*.

Factors affecting acquisition of offence-related detail

Two types of factor have a potential to affect attention and perception, and therefore the acquisition (encoding), of offence-related detail: *event factors* and *personal factors*.[5]

---

[4] Parkin, A. (1999) *Memory: A Guide for Professionals.* Chichester: Wiley.

[5] Loftus, E.F., Wolchover, D., and Page, D. (2006) 'General Review of the Psychology of Witness Testimony' in A. Heaton-Armstrong, E. Shepherd, G. Gudjonsson, and D. Wolchover (eds), *Witness Testimony: Psychological, Investigative and Evidential Perspectives.* Oxford: Oxford University Press.

Event factors

Duration of exposure

The longer the individual was exposed to the event, object, or person the greater the potential for detail to be registered.

Frequency of exposure

If an individual observes an event, object, or person more than once during a period of time, or on a number of occasions, this increases the potential to register more, and better quality, detail.

Physical factors

The degree of visibility, level of illumination, and distance between the individual and the observed event, object, or person will necessarily influence the amount and quality of detail detected.

Salience

We are disposed to register some detail because it is salient: attracting our attention and therefore becoming potentially memorable. Some detail may strike us as interesting, novel, unusual, or otherwise out of the ordinary. Similarly, people have a tendency to attend to, and remember, detail which is striking in sensory terms, eg it is colourful, bright, or noisy. Again, people differ: you cannot assume that all people will have perceived particular detail as salient.

Type of detail

Some kinds of detail pose a particular perceptual challenge, eg height, build, gait, duration, details of a conversation, distance, speed, the colour—or particular point in the sequence—of a traffic light. It appears that different memory processes are involved in the perception of facial detail. Memory for facial detail is covered later in this chapter.

Gravity of the event

Violence attracts attention. People are more likely to remember the details of a violent offence than one involving no violence. The gravity of the offence strongly influences registration of key detail and subsequent performance in identification procedures. Such performance cannot be guaranteed, eg those whose attention was elsewhere—who 'couldn't bear to look' or the timid—are likely to have registered very little.

Weapon focus

The production or use of a weapon narrows attention to this object. This *weapon focus* affects perception of other detail, rendering this peripheral and less likely to be registered.

Personal factors

The nature of attention, factors described earlier that affect attention, and aspects of the individual's FOR necessarily affect the acquisition of offence-related detail. Some have the potential to exercise particular influence.

Division of attention

As pointed out earlier, an individual has only a finite amount of mental resource available for the task of attention. Focusing on—and devoting conscious attention to—particular details necessarily implies the rest of the available detail is hardly registered, if at all. There is an inverse relationship between memory for peripheral detail and accuracy of identification of the offender: the more peripheral detail attended to, the less accurate the identification.

Differences in what is attended to

We are much more likely to register personally relevant information. However, it is not possible to predict what will strike a particular individual as personally relevant and therefore what he or she will attend to. Whereas one individual who is assaulted might pay attention to the attacker's face, the focus of attention of another individual in the same situation might be entirely different. Even though looking at the attacker's face, the individual's attention—thoughts—could be directed to means of escape and not to registering the details of the face.

It follows that where more than one individual is involved, either as a suspect or witness, there will be differences in what they attended to, what they registered, and their perceptions.

Expectations

An individual's expectations—a key aspect of his or her FOR—significantly affect attention and perception. These expectations may stem from:

- stereotypical knowledge concerning people (bias; prejudice; categorical thinking—'looks like a criminal'), about typical situations, and scripts which we saw earlier are typical actions and responses within typical situations;
- prior knowledge of the particular person or people involved and the circumstances.

Although there is conflicting evidence, we need to be alert to potential differences that predispose people to notice and to make sense of detail, eg age, gender, and culture.

Mood, emotion, and stress

We saw earlier that mood, emotion, and stress affect how we attend to, and perceive, everyday life events. It follows that an individual's *internal state*—how he or she subjectively feels and his or her associated thoughts—has the potential to affect the acquisition of offence-related detail. If the experience is extremely stressful or emotionally arousing, particularly if it induces fear in response to a threat to life, or physical or sexual integrity, this internal state can result in:

- 'weapon focus' described earlier, ie narrowing the focus of attention to the weapon held by the person posing the threat;
- *dissociative* symptoms:
  - a reduction in the quantity—but not quality—of detail registered: this later emerges as recall that lacks coherence, may be jumbled, but is accurate;
  - distortion in sensation, eg sounds appearing louder or failing to hear sound; things appearing very large or very small; duration being telescoped—'no time at all' or very protracted;
  - in extreme cases, a temporary disconnection with what is 'going on': numbing or the experience of 'not happening to me' experience; an 'out of body' experience.

Limitations in psychological 'make-up'

It is important to point out that an individual with a limitation in his or her psychological make-up can still provide accurate—truthful—information, but may not be able to provide substantial quantities of information.[6] In Chapter 11 we describe techniques that you can use to assist the individual's remembrance of offence-related detail. We indicate which techniques are unsuitable for very young children or the significantly learning disabled.

Physical limitations

Any limitation in terms of visual and auditory acuity, whether due to age, disability, illness, or infirmity, or the individual not wearing the appropriate aid at the time of the event, will necessarily affect the quality of detail registered.

Ingested substances

A wide range of substances (eg alcohol, cannabis, tranquillizers, opiates, ecstasy) can significantly affect attention and perception, and therefore the acquisition of detail.[7] For example, the individual may register the act of hitting someone, but not register where the hitting took place, who was struck, and how. Acquired detail may be distorted or misattributed, eg the individual may remember something being said, but be mistaken as to who said what to whom, and what was said in reply. The extent of the effect depends on dose, ie the amount ingested and the period over which it was ingested. The impairment caused can range from negligible to severe.

Impairment follows a very characteristic pattern usefully described as 'transition': as the amount of drug in the individual's body increases, so the acquisition of information becomes progressively, and increasingly, disrupted and eventually halted with the onset of unconsciousness. This process of transition from sobriety to intoxication is often characterized by intermittent periods of non-awareness before total loss of consciousness. During these periods the individual has no conscious remembrance of what happened, the course of events, others involved, and other detail. It is possible for an individual who is unconscious through high alcohol intake to be the victim of a sexual assault, not waking up because the assault occurred during deep sleep (termed stage 3 or 4 'non-dreaming' sleep).[8]

There comes a point at which consciousness is lost completely, but this may be punctuated by 'islands' or fragments: points at which the individual regains fleeting conscious awareness sufficient to register some information. Victims of rape under the influence of alcohol, drugs, or a combination of these often report such 'islands'.

A dramatic move from sobriety to total 'blackout', ie a complete loss of consciousness, can occur if an individual has ingested an extremely large amount of alcohol, recreational drug, or a combination of these in a very short space of time, eg in a four-hour period consuming five glasses of spirits or 20 glasses of beer. Alcoholic blackout is common in individuals with a history of heavy drinking, especially with previous blackouts. The common factor is a very high blood alcohol level at the time of the offence. Individuals who have blacked out may still report 'islands' of fleeting consciousness.

---

[6] Murphy, G.H. and Clare, I.C.H. (2006) 'The Effect of Learning Disabilities on Witness Testimony' in A. Heaton-Armstrong, E. Shepherd, G. Gudjonsson, and D. Wolchover (eds), *Witness Testimony: Psychological, Investigative and Evidential Perspectives*. Oxford: Oxford University Press.

[7] Curran, H.V. (2006) 'Effects of Drugs on Witness Memory' in A. Heaton-Armstrong, E. Shepherd, G. Gudjonsson, and D. Wolchover (eds), *Witness Testimony: Psychological, Investigative and Evidential Perspectives*. Oxford: Oxford University Press.

[8] Fenwick, P. (1999) 'Witness Testimony in Sleep and Dream-related Contexts' in A. Heaton-Armstrong, E. Shepherd, and D. Wolchover (eds), *Analysing Witness Testimony: A Guide for Legal Practitioners and Other Professionals*. Oxford: Oxford University Press.

Traumatic injury

If the individual receives a traumatic head injury rendering him or her unconscious—in coma—for a significant period of time, ie several hours or even longer, the individual will experience *anterograde amnesia*—the period up to a point of receiving the injury will be a blank. Even if detail had been attended to prior to the injury, consolidation in memory was disrupted by the head injury. A simple yardstick is that any long period of coma renders the individual unreliable to give an account for what happened in the blank period.

Where the individual gradually loses consciousness, eg as blood pressure drops as a result of being stabbed or being shot, attention narrows and the ability to register detail declines. Memory for what happened during this process will be questionable and the reliability of the witness cast into doubt.

2.4.2 Storage

Memory traces of core and, to a lesser extent, peripheral detail concerning a set of circumstances—for example a sequence of events at a location involving people engaging in actions including conversation—are stored as episodic memory. Initially electrical activity—comprising the memory traces—is distributed over the brain and in key areas of the brain. This increases biochemical activity. Change occurs at the synapses (gaps) at the end of nerves. Memory for the event is biochemically structured throughout the individual's brain.

Factors affecting retention of detail in long-term memory

Forgetting

Detail in store is subject to decay, following a characteristic 'forgetting curve': a rapid, initial decrease followed by a gradual falling off over a period of days. The curve is less steep if the detail is autobiographical—has to do with the individual himself or herself—or is impactful and meaningful. Indeed, all the evidence points to the fact that individuals are remarkably able to retain personally relevant detail, ie intimately involving them or those who are significant to them.[9]

Arguably much more significant than forgetting are the ways in which stored memory is liable either to resist sensible reflection or, much more likely, to change.

Freezing

We met the notion of freezing in Chapter 1 when describing the process of having a fixed perception on matters. In terms of memory, an individual may describe 'what happened' soon after the experience in very confident, unequivocal, even insistent terms. There is a risk that, whether accurate or not, such positive, emphatic assertions are subject to freezing: becoming fixed in the individual's memory and enduring in all later accounts.

Post-event information

Individuals are vulnerable to new information presented to them after the event about the circumstances, actions, or an individual or individuals. This *post-event information* (PEI) can fundamentally affect the individual's original remembrance. PEI can occur in many forms, eg:

- details, recollection, and views expressed by others, eg who also observed, who were involved, or who are investigating;

---

[9] Schacter, D.L. (2007) *How the Mind Forgets and Remembers: The Seven Sins of Memory.* London: Souvenir Press.

- material within the media, eg television reconstructions and replayed recordings; newspaper reports, including photographs and E-fit reconstructions.

PEI may facilitate, or trigger, accurate remembrance of forgotten detail, and accurate modification and extension of what the individual remembers. However, against this must be weighed the *contamination* effect of PEI.[10]

Overwriting

PEI—particularly if the source expresses it confidently—can distort or 'over-write' detail that the individual accurately registered and held in store.

Compromise memory

If later information conflicts with the detail stored in memory, people are prone to form a *compromise memory*. They revise what might be an accurate remembrance to align with the content of the PEI.

People at particular risk of incorporating PEI

An individual with a vulnerable psychological 'make-up'—who is compliant ('goes along with it' in order not to be the 'odd one out'), is suggestible (distrusting his or her memory such that he or she accepts what is said by another person), or both—is likely to incorporate detail from PEI which he or she did not experience or could not have experienced.

The vulnerability of particular detail to PEI

PEI is generally more liable to modify memory for peripheral detail. The potential of misleading or contradictory PEI to contaminate stored memory is least immediately after the experienced event, and increases across time.

Difficulty proving the effect of PEI

Whether PEI genuinely facilitated an individual's accurate recall or actually implanted an inaccurate memory is extremely difficult to prove. Very often only objective evidence, eg CCTV, can disprove implanted inaccuracy.

Change in the character of the stored detail

Retained detail is liable to decay and to undergo change. The quantity tends to shrink and the quality—accuracy—tends to decline as:

- the remembered detail becomes less precise and more vague through the processes of compression and generalization;
- some detail evolves acquiring a different quality, greater significance, and salience: other less 'meaningful' detail becomes less memorable and is forgotten.

Change in episodic memory is particularly likely to occur in the third stage of remembrance, *retrieval*.

2.4.3 Retrieval

Retention does not necessarily imply that something can, or will, be retrieved. We are not machines that can electronically record visual and auditory information in the way that

---

[10] Davies, G. (1999) 'Contamination in Witness Memory' in A. Heaton-Armstrong, E. Shepherd, and D. Wolchover (eds), *Analysing Witness Testimony: A Guide for Legal Practitioners and Other Professionals*. Oxford: Oxford University Press.

technology can, eg a video or audio recorder. Our selective attention and preferential, partial perception ensure that we will only ever catch and comprehend a proportion of the available information. We are biased towards registering action and activity, and thus find it easier to retrieve event detail than descriptive detail. We glue bits of information together as a coherent description or story of 'what happened': a narrative. When we consciously attempt to retrieve or to recall an event:

- we are searching our memory store;
- we are gathering and marshalling fragments;
- we are bringing these fragments into working memory to be literally worked upon.

2.5 Retrieval of detail from long-term memory

At the point an event is initially registered, the individual is making sense of it—putting a *construction* on it—based upon his or her stock of knowledge in long-term memory. At this stage memory is *constructive*. Thereafter, every time the individual retrieves detail concerning this event, whether willingly or not, this is a process of *reconstruction*, not replication.

Reconstruction involves accessing fragments of information from long-term memory and placing these in working memory. As with the point of initial registration, the reconstruction will predominately concern action and activity. Descriptive detail is relatively lacking. People tend to report action and activity happening much more recently than it did.

Each time the individual engages in retrieval, he or she does not access and place in working memory exactly the same episodic information, in exactly the same degree of detail, in the same order of telling. Each reconstruction will necessarily differ from its predecessor. The prospects of core detail being retrieved more consistently are necessarily greater than for peripheral detail. Although the variability in core detail would be expected to be less—particularly when the narrative has been reconstructed repeatedly—there will still be variation. Variation in peripheral detail on successive attempts at retrieval is entirely natural.

All investigators and criminal justice professionals need to understand the implications of reconstruction.

- Absence of replication does not mean that the individual is giving an inaccurate or untruthful account.
- Excessive degree of replication is a cause for concern. It could be a 'pat'—rehearsed—account, described in Chapter 1.

2.5.1 Private reflection

Much retrieval occurs through the process of private reflection. Typically the individual's initial attempt at reconstruction is likely to reveal that he or she has:

- some problems in remembering the precise sequence of events;
- difficulty in terms of missing detail.

As the individual dwells longer on the event, and with each subsequent attempt to retrieve episodic detail from long-term memory, an increasingly coherent narrative emerges.

Such reflection upon reconstructed material is a natural, unavoidable, but risky business.

- In their long-term memory, people have script knowledge concerning events they have never personally faced before, eg a mugging. These scripts are *second-hand experience*, mostly derived from the media. These scripts tend to have fewer steps than occur in a real life event. Hence an individual who has been mugged—and had never been mugged before—is likely to access the second-hand 'mugging' script to 'work out' (deduce or guess) the missing or unclear bits in his or her remembrance of the event. The risks are that:

— the deduction or guess may be entirely wrong;

— script detail might overwrite and distort accurate remembrance;

— the incorrect deduction or guess becomes part of the stored memory.

- Repeated reconstruction has the effect of *rehearsal*, establishing in the individual's mind what is in effect a learned representation. The risk is that any inaccuracy becomes a learned 'fact'.

2.5.2 Conversational retrieval

Retrieval commonly occurs in conversation at any time after the incident. As pointed out earlier, the risk is of PEI, particularly from a confident source, contaminating the individual's memory or inducing the construction of compromise memory.

2.5.3 Guided retrieval

An investigative interview is an exercise in guided retrieval. This presents a challenge to the interviewer. Characteristically, people do not like to be asked questions. It puts them 'on the spot'. A witness or suspect is in this situation for the entire duration of the interview. The interview is not, and never could be, a normal conversation. To a greater or lesser extent it is a learning relationship. The investigating officer uses instruction and questioning to guide the individual's process of retrieval.

The status of the questioner

Interviewers are 'powerful people'. We shall consider such people in greater detail in Chapter 4 (Telling and Listening: Disclosing and Making Sense of Disclosed Detail). Suffice to say at this moment that:

- interviewees perceive interviewers to already have knowledge of matters, and know the answers;
- interviewers are able to influence strongly what gets talked about, when, and for how long.

The retrieval environment

Much but not all research has shown that the *external physical environment*, or physical context, in which the details of an event were acquired (encoded) is a powerful trigger to retrieval. A crime reconstruction either physically on the ground or through the medium of television presents external cues that may potentially jog people's memory: taking people back to the one or more key locations, enabling them to observe typically an enactment of the movements of a role player dressed to match a key individual.

In many instances, taking the individual physically back to the scene is not possible or appropriate.

- It may be impractical because of time and resource constraints, the location has changed, the ambient conditions, eg weather, cannot be replicated.
- It could be ethically unacceptable because of the risk of trauma to the interviewee arising from visiting the location, observing an enactment, or being invited to re-live what happened in this particular location.

An individual can enhance his or her remembrance of an experienced event by mentally reinstating the context of the event.[11] The individual concentrates hard, thinking back to the time of the event, where necessary assisted by a 'time anchor', eg a birthday, to locate this in time. He or she creates an image in his or her mind of:

- the physical location and where the individual was located;
- what was going through his or her mind at the time;
- how he or she was feeling;
- his or her thoughts at the time;
- his or her physical state at the time.

Mental context reinstatement is a highly effective but there are risks.

- The process can be stressful and induce distress.
- The induced stress and distress may hinder retrieval, make it difficult for the individual to disclose, or both.

Context reinstatement must therefore be managed sensibly, sensitively, and skilfully and its effects closely monitored.

Questioning

Research has consistently confirmed key facts.

- Spontaneous narrative—free recall—is best for retrieval and reporting of detail that is accurate but at the price of completeness.
- Probing is necessary to achieve completeness but at the risk of inaccuracy.

Probing questions can be inappropriately posed in two ways.

- **Using suggestive rather than neutral wording**, eg *groped* instead of *touched*, *smashed into* (suggesting speed) instead of *collided*.
- **Using a suggestive type of question**:
  - leading, eg *Wasn't he attacking him on the ground?*
  - option, eg *Did he punch or jab him in the eye?*
  - inappropriate confirmatory, eg *Did he kick him?*

The implications of suggestive wording are extremely serious.

- Some interviewees come to believe that they 'knew it all along'.
- Some interviewees construct a compromise memory: revising their accurate remembrance to align with the suggested content of the questioning.
- Suggestible interviewees who have no remembrance or who distrust their memory:
  - reason that the interviewer's words, the offered options, and the direction of the question represent the true nature of circumstances;
  - 'go along' with and endorse this misleading representation.

If the interviewer engages improperly in contaminating, suggestive questioning *before* the invitation to give a free recall, the risk is that misleading and inaccurate suggested material becomes part of the individual's narrative. If the inappropriate questioning occurs after free recall, the individual's responses will lead to inaccurate expansion or amendment of the narrative, or both.

---

[11] Fisher, R.P. and Geiselman, R.E. (1992) *Memory-enhancing Techniques for Investigative Interviewing: The Cognitive Interview*. Springfield, Ill: Charles C. Thomas.

Chapter 1 observed that where witness interviews are not recorded, fellow investigators and the criminal justice system can never know whether inappropriate questioning produced the statement. The problem is compounded by the continued inappropriate practice of ensuring 'seamlessness' in the accounts of two or more witnesses. Suggestive wording and suggesting questions ensure that the content of the retrieved account of this and any subsequent witness converges with and does not contradict the account of the preceding witness.

2.5.4 Confident retrieval

The public at large, and in particular those involved in the criminal justice system, have stereotyped perceptions of confidence concerning retrieved detail. They tend to interpret confident retrieval—sureness of its accuracy—as indicative of actual accuracy. The research evidence is clear that there is no correlation—no association—between asserted confidence of recall and the accuracy of recalled material. A person can be supremely confident and yet totally incorrect in his or her remembrance. An individual who is unconfident about his or her recall can be wholly correct. Age has a compounding effect. Although adults are more likely than their young counterparts to make mistakes in memory, they are more likely to insist that they are right and be believed.

Despite increasing awareness of this lack of correlation, many police officers and many other criminal justice professionals—including the judiciary—remain steadfastly credulous concerning the positive link between confidence and accuracy of remembrance. If the person giving the account comes across as confident, has a positive demeanour, this enhances his or her credibility, lending even greater credence to what he or she is confidently recalling. The enduring power of this stereotype is the reason why public and private sector investigators and expert witnesses attend training on how to give evidence confidently. It is also why the Court of Appeal has directed that witnesses should not undergo such preparation.[12]

2.5.5 Asserted amnesia

The individual may assert *amnesia*, total inability to recall the event which involved him or her either as a witness or suspect. Amnesia *can* occur. However, most crime-related amnesia is feigned.[13]

Organic amnesia

A medical condition, eg brain trauma or epilepsy, can produce a *total blackout*. Information about the event, although registered before the blackout, is never stored, hence there is nothing to retrieve. As pointed out earlier, ingested substances can also cause blackout.

- It involves an extremely large amount of alcohol, recreational drug, or a combination of these taken in a very short space of time.
- It is common in individuals with a history of heavy drinking, especially with previous blackouts.

---

[12] *R v Momodou and Limani* [2005] EWCA Crim 177.

[13] Christianson, S.A., Merckelbach, H., and Kopelman, M. (2006) 'Crime-related Amnesia' in A. Heaton-Armstrong, E. Shepherd, G. Gudjonsson, and D. Wolchover (eds), *Witness Testimony: Psychological, Investigative and Evidential Perspectives*. Oxford: Oxford University Press.

Dissociative amnesia

Extreme emotion can, as explained earlier, have a dissociative effect adversely affecting the quality and the coherence of registered and stored detail. In contrast, the individual asserting dissociative amnesia is saying that there is *nothing* in store because he or she was excessively aroused or agitated at the time of the event. This form of amnesia is rare and most clinicians view it with healthy scepticism.

Genuine and feigned amnesia

Most asserted amnesia is feigned. Feigned amnesia—also called *instrumental amnesia*—is a variation of passive deception. The individual is asserting inability to remember as a tactic. The individual reasons that amnesia for the *critical period* during which the offence occurred:

- prevents the police from questioning about the offence;
- enables denial of responsibility for personal conduct or performing a particular act.

Asserted amnesia is particularly likely where the offence appears premeditated or goal-driven, eg to achieve arousal or gratification, or to obtain an advantage. It is very common in cases of murder, sexual offending, domestic violence, causing death by dangerous driving, and even fraud. Some 20–30 per cent of people who commit violent crimes claim amnesia for the critical period.

Potential indicators of genuine amnesia

There are a number of potential indicators of genuine amnesia.

- The individual made no effort to resist arrest or may have given himself or herself up.
- The memory impairment is very often consistent with organic amnesia.
- Akin to many rape victims, the individual reports 'islands', ie fragments of fleetingly regained awareness.
- The individual has a long alcohol history, with instances of previous alcoholic blackout.
- The individual had a very high blood alcohol level when arrested at the scene or soon afterwards.

Potential indicators of feigned amnesia

Experts find it difficult to distinguish between organic, dissociative, and feigned amnesia. There are likely to be opposing opinions given at court. Nonetheless, there are some useful potential indicators of feigned amnesia that every investigator should know about.

- The individual has clear remembrance of circumstances and events occurring immediately prior to the *critical period* during which the offending occurred.
- Memory loss for the critical period is total.
- There is unreal specificity about the period of total memory loss, eg *I don't remember anything from the time I left the house until I opened the door and saw the police officers.*
- Remembrance is relatively clear for circumstances and events occurring after the specified end of the amnesic period.
- The individual asserts emphatically that any attempt at retrieval, however partial, is a waste of time.
- The individual reports pervasive memory 'symptoms', ie having a 'really bad memory' and experiencing severe problems with remembering in everyday life before and/or since the offence took place.

- The individual 'evidences' his or her pervasive memory 'symptoms' by scoring bizarrely on memory assessment tasks, with scores lower than those achieved by severely brain-damaged individuals.

Claims of alcoholic blackout are very common amongst those feigning amnesia. The greater the seriousness of the offence, the more likely such a blackout will be asserted. There are a number of potential indicators that this is a bogus claim.

- There is no reporting of 'transition' from sobriety to intoxication. We saw previously that typically, as people become more and more intoxicated, they experience progressively poorer recall and then intermittent periods of non-awareness before losing consciousness.
- There is no reporting of 'islands'—fragments of fleetingly regained awareness—after blacking out.
- There is no corroborative evidence that the individual was drinking excessively, particularly within the hours prior to the critical period.
- Critically, there was an absence of excessively high blood alcohol level at time of arrest.

2.5.6 Recovered memory

The term *recovered memory* refers to remembering an actual event after a period of time during which the experience was forgotten. It is entirely different to remembrance of an event that the individual recalls having consciously sought to 'put out of mind'. Those who report recovered memory do not remember adopting this strategy.

Psychologists in the main accept that where the memory of an event is recovered spontaneously, there are few grounds to doubt the validity of what is reported. This said, there is always the possibility that the recovered memory is false, ie what the individual now asserts as having happened did not happen.[14]

Recovered memory of an event should be viewed with scepticism if it emerged in circumstances that increase the likelihood of a false remembrance.

- Counselling or therapy which involves:
  — close, sustained reflective scrutiny and discussion in which the individual initially denied such experience;
  — pressure and suggestive practices, eg hypnosis, regression, guided fantasy, to remember events for which the individual initially asserted no memory.
- Conversations with a family member, friend, or a religious person which encouraged retrieval of forgotten experience.

Confident remembrance

Earlier in this chapter it was pointed out that confident assertion is no indicator of the validity (accuracy) of what is asserted. It is necessary to ask the individual who reports recovered memory key questions.

- Whether he or she has considered the possibility that the recovered memory might be inaccurate.
- How he or she has come to the conclusion that the recovered memory is accurate.

---

[14] Brewin, C. (2006) 'Recovered Memory and False Memory' in A. Heaton-Armstrong, E. Shepherd, G. Gudjonsson, and D. Wolchover (eds), *Witness Testimony: Psychological, Investigative and Evidential Perspectives*. Oxford: Oxford University Press.

Concerns raised by confident assertion of recovered memory are tempered if the individual:

- describes initial uncertainty about the remembered event;
- has attempted to validate the remembrance, ie taking the effort to check circumstances that obtained at the time.

Vividness, degree of detail, and intensity of emotion

People who have undergone a traumatic experience, eg involvement in an accident or a serious assault, often have 'flash backs': involuntary, intrusive, vivid, often sensory experience of the event, and often accompanied by acute emotion. However, the evidence shows that in some cases these 'flash backs' relate to events that never happened. It follows that in the case of recovered memory, although the individual reports persuasively an experience that is vivid, includes sensory information, and the feeling of strong emotion, this kind of detail is no guarantee that the event actually happened.

Prosecution and defence will call experts who will examine and offer opinions concerning:

- the individual's assertions concerning recovered memory;
- the context in which this remembrance emerged.

As there is no professional consensus either in favour of or against the validity of recovered memory, ultimately it will be for the court to decide as to the individual's reliability and the credibility of what he or she asserts.

2.6 Memory of facial detail

The indications are that the experience of observed facial detail is processed differently to other offence-related information. Nonetheless, the same factors which affect acquisition, storage, and retrieval of other information apply to memory of facial detail.[15]

2.6.1 Acquisition

Critical questioning about the observed face

At the time the individual observes and acquires detail about the observed face, he or she is unconsciously engaged in a process of decision-making.

- Is this face familiar to me? Have I come across this face—this person—before?
- How is this face familiar to me? How and where do I know this face—this person—from?
- What is this person's name whose face seems familiar?

Order of facial information processing

People tend to observe facial information in a predictable sequence.

- **Initial attention to hair.** The colour, style, and the effect of the observed person's hair on the outline of his or her face.
- **Secondary attention to eyes.** In particular colour.
- **Very little attention to other features.** Information concerning mouth, lips, chin is scarcely registered if at all.

---

[15] Ainsworth, P.B. (1998) *Psychology, Law and Eyewitness Testimony.* Chichester: Wiley.

Unusual or distinctive features

Distinctive or unusual features strike people as salient, but they tend to pay hardly any attention to other detail. However, as with event detail, people differ greatly on the matter of the salience of features. It cannot be assumed that people will report the same feature or features as striking.

Very attractive faces are much more likely to be registered as such. 'Average', 'normal', or 'usual' faces do not stand out. People struggle and fail to describe such faces.

Cross-cultural differences

People find it difficult to register detail of an individual who is not from their racial group. The explanation for this lies in the individual's FOR. For example, white people follow the 'first hair, then eyes, maybe other features' sequence of facial information processing described earlier. This sequence is potentially of little value if they are observing a black person. The hair and eye detail of black people tends to be relatively uniform, hence the white observer is unable to differentiate black faces on these two criteria. Oriental faces pose similar problems.

Gravity of the offence

We saw that the gravity of the offence is liable to focus attention. This may enhance registration of facial detail.

2.6.2 Storage of facial detail

The longer a facial image is in store the more likely it is to undergo change. This has major implications for identification procedures. Those conducted soon after the offence will be more investigatively useful than those conducted some time after.

2.6.3 Retrieval

Retrieving facial detail from store raises two problems: the limitations of language and proneness to error.

Limitations of language

It is surprising, and sobering, that although the research has shown that we are biologically programmed to look at faces and spend an extraordinary amount of time gazing at other people's faces, most people have a very limited vocabulary to describe faces. Most descriptions are in general terms. Precision is much more likely to come from an individual who has a personal interest in, or a wider general knowledge of, describing features.

For example, a witness may well have a visual image of an observed person having a V-shaped growth of hair towards the centre of the forehead. This is called a 'widow's peak' but knowledge of this term is not widespread. Luckily most people will resort to a form of non-verbal communication that overcomes lack of language. They use their fingers, or hands, to draw out in space—on their own head or someone else's—the shape of the feature they cannot put words to. These finger or hand movements are called *illustrators* because they fulfil this task: making up for our lack of words or augmenting our stumbling attempts to describe. Try describing someone you know or can see as you look up from this book. You will quickly appreciate the labelling problem and how quickly you need to resort to illustrators to supplement your words or to substitute for words altogether.

It is important to appreciate the implication of people's limited ability or inability to give a verbal description. The individual has nonetheless the image in his or her head. Common sense argues, therefore, that an individual's difficulty in describing an offender's face verbally should not preclude the individual from participation in an identification procedure.

Proneness to error

People are highly prone to error when retrieving facial detail. Two key factors have the potential to affect adversely what a person retrieves.

- **Misleading information about faces.** Exposure to images, eg in the media or shown by the police, constitute PEI that can distort or overwrite the individual's memory for the face in question.
- **Mislabelling.** The individual recognizes the face as familiar, but recalls incorrectly where the face was seen and registered. The result is the face is mislabelled as the perpetrator. Mislabelling can often occur following the publicizing of a description in the media, eg on the BBC *Crimewatch* television programme, or in a newspaper.

Verbal descriptions of faces are notoriously fallible. Research has shown that a verbal description is subject to freezing and can interfere with later recognition of the perpetrator in an identification procedure. However, if the description is vague or inaccurate there is less likelihood of freezing.

2.7 Chapter summary

Remembrance of offence-related detail—the circumstances, locations, events, participants, and the entire range of potentially material fact—lies at the heart of the accounts given by witnesses and suspects. Effective interviewing of a witness or suspect relies upon a sound understanding of how attention, perception, and memory interrelate. If you remain constantly aware of the how information passes through the memory system, and of the many factors that affect registration, storage, and retrieval, your interviewing will not pose a threat to the integrity of the interviewee's disclosures.

3

Conversation: From Everyday Talk to Ways of Relating and Changing Minds

3.1 Chapter overview

This chapter reviews conversation, the medium through which people relate to each other and relate their experiences to each other. Ability to manage conversation skilfully rests upon a secure understanding of the dynamics of conversation, how the manner in which an individual converses can create very different kinds of relationship, and how a range of behaviours can impact upon the other person, creating crucial perceptions concerning sincerity and professionalism. We conclude with an examination of ethical persuasion and ethical negotiation, forms of conversation that are founded upon respect for the person, the obligation to tell the truth, and mutual respect for rights and responsibilities.

3.1.1 Chapter objectives

This chapter will enable you to:

- understand the multiple channels of communication used in conversation;
- understand how conversation works;
- understand how people seek to manage a conversation that they have initiated and may do so thoughtfully or thoughtlessly;
- recognize the four quadrants of conversational behaviour reflecting an individual's choices in terms of *control* of the exchange and the focus of *concern*: self-centred or taking account of the other person's perspective;
- understand which quadrant is consistent with socially skilled interviewing to achieve investigative goals;
- be aware of the interdependence of influence, persuasion, and negotiation;
- engage in behaviours that will create a positive impact upon people, enabling you to engage in ethical persuasion, and, where applicable, ethical negotiation.

3.2 Words and deeds: channels of communication used in conversation

When people converse they are exchanging ideas with another person on one or more topics. The word conversation comes from an old French word *converser* meaning 'to keep company with another using words and deeds'. This definition captures the fact that when conversing people use their whole body to relate in both senses of the word:

- to pass on information concerning their experience, and to acknowledge information concerning the other person's experience;
- to signal what kind of relationship exists—or they wish to exist—between the two of them.

Words and deeds comprise two channels of communication: *verbal* and *non-verbal*. Box 3.1 provides an illustrative—not exhaustive—summary of these channels and shows the four uses to which they can be put. Some 70 per cent of communication is non-verbal. A common label given to non-verbal communication is 'body language'. This is unfortunate because much significant non-verbal behaviour is *vocal*, ie created by the voice not by movements of the body. Take, for example, 'tone of voice'. This is particularly significant vocal non-verbal behaviour used in conversation. The term refers to two different uses, which we have called for convenience *tone of voice*[1] and *tone of voice*[2].

CHANNEL (vocal = using voice; non-vocal = not using voice)		USE			
		Expressing thoughts and ideas	**Expressing attitude, emotion, and stress**	**Fostering conversation**	**Signalling relationship**
Verbal (words or equivalent)	*Vocal* (spoken language)	Narrative Description Request Question Response Argument, etc	Focused language use, eg *We shouldn't be talking about this; I'm absolutely furious; Bloody hell!*	Supportive phrases, eg *I see.*	• Form of address • Relationship description, eg *I feel that I can trust you.*
	Non-vocal (sign language)				
Non-verbal	*Vocal* (called *paralanguage*)	• Stress (key idea) • Intonation	• Tone of voice[1] (speech quality; way of vocalizing) — Rhythm — Speed, eg gabbling — Volume, eg raising or dropping of voice — Pitch, eg high, low, shrill • Dysfluency, eg stammering • Sighing	• 'Following' noises, eg *mmm; uh-huh* • Laughter	• Tone of voice[2] (manner of speaking), eg warm; reassuring; submissive (inferior); dominant (superior); condescending; sarcastic; belittling; hectoring; harsh
	Non-vocal	• Illustrators (describing a shape, trajectory, route travelled, location, layout, relative positions, an image— 'mental picture'— or rhythm/tempo with hand or finger) • Pointing • Gestures (replacing or reinforcing words) • Enactment (acting out actions; 'what happened')	• Reflex reaction, eg blushing, crying, change in breathing • Eye contact, eg direct (anger), intermittent (anxiety), gazing down (sadness) • Facial expression, eg concern; distress; hostility • Adaptors, eg fidgeting, grooming, fiddling with hair, fingers, etc, 'lint' picking • Hands, eg trembling • Trunk, eg shaking • Lower limb • 'Leakage', eg feet tapping; knee tremor • Posture, eg relaxed; tense	• Facial expression, eg smile (showing respect and open attitude); empathy signals (showing concern, etc) • Eye contact, eg sustained gaze = interest • 'Guggling' (nodding at a stressed key idea within an utterance) • Appropriate silence = *I'll just listen. Carry on.* • Open handed gesture = over to you; keep going • Posture, eg open • Proximity, eg forward lean	• Touch, eg shaking hands; signalling empathy • Facial expression, eg disdain • Proximity (intimate space: 0–18 inches; personal space: 3–4 feet; public space: over 4 feet) • Orientation, eg face-to-face (potentially confrontational); ten-to-two (collaborative); turned away (not relating)

Box 3.1 Channels of communication used in conversation

- **Tone of voice**[1]. Changes in the *physical quality* of a speaker's voice send potentially significant messages about his or her feelings, eg level of stress, emotional state, attitude to the topic being talked about, or the conversation itself.
- **Tone of voice**[2]. The *manner* in which a person speaks sends potentially significant relationship messages, eg whether he or she feels positively or negatively towards the other person; whether he or she feels superior or inferior.

3.2.1 Expressing thoughts and ideas

For those who are able to speak, the verbal channel of words is the primary medium for vocally expressing thoughts and ideas to the other person. People use non-verbal behaviour:

- to reinforce their words vocally, eg stressing the key ideas in what they are saying;
- to substitute for words altogether, eg by using an illustrator—moving a finger or hand in space—to trace out shapes or to indicate direction of movement; by making a gesture wagging a finger to say 'no' or raising a thumb to indicate approval. Of course, these same non-verbal behaviours can parallel words sending these messages.

3.2.2 Expressing attitude, emotion, and stress

Attitude, emotion, and stress evoked by the other person, the conversation, a particular topic can be expressed verbally, eg by a comment, an outburst, or a resort to profanity. However, the primary function of non-verbal behaviour is to communicate feelings, both vocally and non-vocally, eg growing and intense arousal, negativity, discomfort, or distress.

Tone of voice plays a significant part in conversation. Physical movements, eg facial expression, gestures, hand and leg activity, are readily detected. People interpret these vocal and non-vocal non-verbal behaviours as 'vibes'. These messages are very potent. If they are not in keeping with what the person is saying, in effect he or she is sending a 'mixed message'. People are disposed to believe the non-verbal rather than the verbal. Because of this, people who wish to create a positive impression in a conversation will seek to consciously control their non-verbal behaviour: to hide their feelings. Vocal non-verbal behaviour does not present too much of a problem, eg consciously not raising one's voice. It takes more conscious effort to control facial movements and upper body movements, eg deliberately not frowning or not tapping fingers impatiently. Controlling leg and foot movement is particularly demanding, eg you have to devote attention to your what your body is doing at the very moment that you are talking or listening, and to consciously ensure that you do not tap your foot or jig your leg up and down.

3.2.3 Fostering conversation

Most poor conversationalists do not realize how much behaviour—particularly non-verbal—fosters conversation by making people more responsive and receptive. SOFTENS (Box 3.2) is a useful acronym that serves as a mnemonic summarizing key conversation fostering behaviours. These behaviours evidence that you really are paying attention to, and empathizing with, the other person. In particular, nodding ('guggling') at the key ideas within the individual's utterances signals that you are following and registering what he or she is saying. For your part, saying supportive words and making supportive

S	Signs of sincerity	• A smile shows that you are receptive and open. • An appropriate facial expression shows that you understand the other's situation, eg looking concerned.
O	Open posture	• Keeping your hands away from your mouth and your arms uncrossed. • If seated, sitting comfortably (*not* slouching) rather than 'to attention'. — Works best if you are at the appropriate distance from each other: — sharing each other's *personal space* (3–4 feet between you) if standing • if sitting, 3–4 feet between the middle of your shins and the middle of the other person's shins. [*Note:* You should not be in each other's *intimate space* or be too far away in *social space*.] • You should be appropriately orientated, particularly if sitting, ie chairs placed at 'ten-to-two on the clock face' angle (a little more than 90 degrees) rather than face-to-face which some might feel was being 'pushy' or confrontational.
F	Forward lean	• Leaning slightly forward signals you are interested, listening, and want the person to keep talking. • Leaning slightly further forward at critical points signals empathy, eg when the other person discloses feelings.
T	Touch	• Shaking hands on meeting and departing. • Symbolic touching, ie raising your hand and touching the individual's shoulder in the visible profile that you have of the individual in your field of vision. [*Note: Not* physical touch: this could be taken as inappropriate, unwanted touching, and lead to a complaint or allegation.]
E	Eye contact	• Look straight at the other person. • Maintain maximum eye contact: but don't stare! Sends the message that: • *I am listening.* • *I am paying attention.* • *I am interested.* • The other person should carry on talking.
N	Nods	'Guggling' at the key ideas that the individual stresses in his or her utterances sends the message that: • you are following what is being said; • you understand what is being said/the individual's position.
S	Supportive sounds and silence	Helping the individual to talk—and keep talking—by: • saying supportive words, eg *I realise it's difficult;* ^^ ^^ • making supportive noises, eg *Uh-huh;* ^^ ^^ • just listening rather than talking—creating a long pause, ie silence.

Box 3.2 SOFTENS: key conversation fostering behaviours

noises (in effect 'guggling' vocally) send the same message. Not saying anything—simply pausing instead—creates the opportunity for the individual to talk—if he or she has not done so already—or to continue talking if he or she has stopped talking momentarily. In effect you are consciously managing the talking turn, something that we focus on later in this chapter.

In this text we use the symbol ^^ throughout to signify a one to two second pause; thus ^^ ^^ represents a three to four second pause. The ^^ symbol highlights the significance of, and makes it easier for you to create in your mind, a pause before, between, and after illustrative utterances and guidance, eg on questioning and listening in this text.

3.2.4   **Signalling relationship**

From very early childhood onwards, people learn that there are two types of relationship based on perceptions of power—dominance, submissiveness, equality—to determine who talks, who listens, who decides what gets talked about, when, in what detail, and for how long.[1]

- **'Up–down' relationships.** One person occupies a higher status than the other. He or she exercises more power over what gets said, when, and how. Typical 'up–down' relationships are: parent–child; teacher–pupil, doctor–patient; manager–managed. The problem about these relationships is that awareness of difference in status can, and often does, prevent people being open in what they say.

- **'Across' relationships.** The participants signal to each other that status does not enter into it: they are on an equal footing. 'Across' relationships are much more productive than 'up–down' because both parties want to be responsive and receptive. A person of notionally higher status can consciously behave in a way that signals that this is an 'across' relationship. In effect he or she is signalling that 'I may have the superior power and knowledge but I want this to be a collaborative, talking "across" relationship'.

People signal the relationship that they believe exists—or wish to exist—and relative status in the relationship in a number of ways

Form of self-address

When first meeting, or speaking to, someone, there are five possible forms of self-address when introducing yourself. Each form gives the other person an immediate clue as to the relationship that you wish to exist between the two of you.

- **Frozen.** *I'm Shepherd.* This signals that my view is that we are distant from each other. At one time this was quite common but is relatively rare now. It sends a definite 'I'm "up", you're "down"' message.

- **Formal.** *I'm Mr Shepherd.* This is quite common: title ('handle') plus second name. It is becoming less and less common, increasingly giving way to Consultative. It does put a distance between you and the other person, but it signals a respectful 'across' relationship.

- **Consultative.** *I'm Eric Shepherd.* This is very widespread. You are signalling that you will not object if the individual calls you by your first name, but you may choose not to use his or her first name. It is consistent with an 'across' relationship.

- **Informal.** *I'm Eric.* This signals that you do not mind being called by your first name. It is consistent with an 'across' relationship. It is a matter for you whether you want the witness or suspect to call you by your first name. It is the case that if you call the interviewee by his or her first name but don't allow him or her to address you by your first name, you are in fact sending a subtle message: 'I'm "up"—the parent figure—so don't call me by my first name; you're "down"—the child figure—so I'll call you by your first name'.

- **Intimate.** *I'm Sheppsey.* These are nicknames or very personal forms of address. Only appropriate for conversations with special people, eg one's intimate group of friends. Of

---

[1] Watzlawick, P., Beavin, J., and Jackson, D. (1967) *Pragmatics of Human Communication.* New York: Norton.

course you should never use this form to refer to yourself in a working context when you are relating to a witness or suspect.

The relationship loop

This is a very subtle first step towards creating a working relationship in a face-to-face encounter.

- Extend your hand as you introduce yourself, using the consultative form of self-address, eg *I'm Eric Shepherd, the Duty CID officer.*
- Start shaking the interviewee's hand as you check his or her name, eg *And you are...?*
- Listen to the reply and, still shaking the person's hand ask, *And how would you like me to call you?*
- Echo immediately what he or she says. For example, if he says *Liam*, simply say his name, echo how you would like to be called, finishing your handshake as you say this, eg *Liam ^^ OK Liam, please call me Eric. ^^^^*
  - **If the individual selects a more formal form of address than the one you used to refer to yourself**: You should accept this, recognizing that the individual has indicated a desire for a more distant relationship between the two of you.
  - **If he or she selects an intimate form of address, eg** *Call me Scouse*: You should respect this. It would make no sense, and prejudice the relationship, if you were to say that you were uncomfortable with the form chosen by the person.

If you are conversing on the telephone, or via video-line, adjust what you say to allow for the absence of hand-shaking.

The rules about form of address

There are two cardinal rules concerning form of address.

- **Shift from formal or consultative to informal is permissible**. If prior to, or during the course of, the interview you would like to move to use of first names you can do so, but you need to request permission to call the other person by his or her first name, eg *I'm happy for you to call me Ian. Can I call you* (person's first name)? If the person says no, don't be offended or take it to heart, simply stick with the individual's preferred form of address.
- **Shift from informal to formal is not permissible**. You should never make this shift, eg having called the person *Liam* you cannot switch to addressing him *Mr Hudson*. If you make such a change to formal the other person:
  - would be right to conclude that the relationship between you had changed;
  - could be forgiven for thinking that you are insincere, ie that you really didn't mean what you were saying when you were on first name terms.

Manner of speaking

It is not what a person says explicitly but very much the way that he or she says it—his or her *manner of speaking* (tone of voice[2])—that indicates powerfully how he or she views the relationship: the 'distance' or 'difference' between the two of you, his or her view of you as a person. Even very young children and those with significant learning difficulties can pick up these vital clues in a person's manner of speaking. This has crucial implications for interviewers.

3.3 How conversation works

3.3.1 The process of conversing

The cornerstone of conversation is co-operation. Without co-operation there is no conversation. Conversation is a highly ritualized, rule-bound activity. Very few people learn formally about how conversation actually works, and only then in adult life. We 'pick up' the rituals and the rules for conversation from our earliest interactions with our mothers and our observation of, and participation in conversations, particularly within the family, with friends, and with 'powerful people' such as teachers.[2] (You will recall from Chapter 2 that interviewers are 'powerful people'. We shall return to this matter on many more occasions.)

The rules

The rules of conversation are implicit in many senses: being basic, unspoken, and integral to a process of sharing time and yourself with another human being. There are four rules.

1. **Conversation requires co-operation. If the other person will not engage there is no conversation.** When you forgo the opportunity to engage for whatever reason, this will potentially confuse or offend the other person who only knows that the opportunity was there but you didn't take it.
2. **Signal your co-operation by being responsive to the other person.** Your response to the other person demonstrates a desire to see his or her point of view, to give of yourself, to share time and your thoughts.
3. **Once started you are obliged to continue.** This distinguishes conversation from a passing word or recognition or acknowledgement, eg saying *Morning Alison!* as you pass compared to *Morning Alison. How are you?*
4. **Discontinuing and departing must not confuse or offend.** Conversation is investment in mutual relationship. Rather like failing to take the opportunity to engage in conversation, disengagement is a decision not to spend more of one's time or of oneself. At its most basic level it is a form of rejection. When this is done abruptly 'without a word'—no explanation, justification, or excuse—the confusion and offence can be considerable.

Turn taking

At the heart of conversation lies *reciprocity*: the mutual activity of *turn taking*, participants switching between occupancy of the *talking turn* and the *listening turn*.[3] Conversation starts when one person initiates the exchange. Using the words of the theatrical world, he or she takes and has 'the floor'—occupying the talking turn. While this is happening, the other participant occupies the listening turn.

At some point there will be an exchange of the talking and listening turn. The one who had the talking turn relinquishes 'the floor' to take the listening turn, allowing the other person to take the talking turn. The process of turn taking is highly ritualized.

Voluntary exchange of turn

The speaker passes the talking turn by:

• gazing at the listener;

---

[2] Wardaugh, R. (1985) *How Conversation Works*. Oxford: Blackwell.
[3] Graddol, D., Cheshire, J., and Swann, J. (1994) *Describing Language*. Buckingham: Open University Press.

- making a comment, inviting comment, making a request, or asking a question;
- continuing to gaze at the listener.

The pressure is then on the listener to take the 'floor'. The origins and nature of this pressure go right back to our baby days and are described later.

Earlier in this chapter we explained how the third of the final SOFTENS behaviours—just listening rather than talking, creating a long pause, ie silence—gives the other person the opportunity to talk (the talking turn) or to continue talking after a momentary pause (to retain the talking turn).

Foregoing or refusing the talking turn

Although the speaker passes the talking turn, the listener may forego, or refuse, the 'floor', in effect passing the talking turn straight back by:

- gazing at the speaker;
- saying nothing.

The pressure is then on the listener to take the 'floor'. The origins and nature of this pressure are again described later.

Involuntary exchange of turn

The listener makes a demand for the 'floor':

- non-verbally, eg making a gesture or moving his or her chair;
- verbally, eg *I need to come in there*.

Origins of turn taking

The origins of turn taking lie in early mother and baby interaction.[4] The mother looks at the baby initially, she then fleetingly gazes away, then gazes back at the child and says something, eg *What a lovely little boy!* Having stopped talking, the mother has created a period of silence during which she continues to gaze at the baby. The baby eventually makes a noise. It does not matter what this is. During this time the baby may retain eye contact, or gaze away before restoring eye contact, with its mother. As soon as the baby falls silent the mother gazes away fleetingly, then gazes back at the child and says something else, setting in train another exchange of talking and listening turn.

In effect the mother instils in the baby awareness of a reciprocal 'on'–'off' activity. The baby learns that:

- the mother makes a noise;
- the mother creates silence while continuing to look at the child;
- the child makes a noise while the mother continues to look;
- the child stops making a noise;
- the mother makes a noise, and so on.

The pressure to take the talking turn

The power of this reciprocal 'on'–'off' activity with our mother is considerable. It creates an expectation to respond when someone is speaking to us, stops talking, and maintains eye contact with us. If we do not say something, we experience growing psychological pressure

---

[4] McTear, M. (1985) *Children's Conversation*. Oxford: Blackwell.

to fulfil the expectation: to say something, anything, rather than nothing. We later learn as we acquire language that if the other person concluded his or her talking turn with a request or a question, it is a matter of obligation for us to take the talking turn to give an answer. Because we are obliged to respond, if we do not, the internal pressure and our discomfort at not answering become even greater.

The speed of the change in turn

The speed of the change in talking turn is remarkably quick. When adults and older children are conversing, it can be thousandths of a second between one person ceasing to talk and the other starting to talk.[5] This rapidity tends to create conversations which can seem rather superficial, frustrating, and even depressing. Because the exchange happens so quickly, there is characteristically only pause for breath. There is never, literally, pause for thought.

Some people need time to think—eg those who are developmentally disadvantaged through tenderness of years, advanced years, or learning disability. Taking the example of younger children, they definitely need more time to think, and if you take time to listen you can almost hear the 'cogs' turning. Their pause for thought is very long compared to the barely existent pause in adult conversation.

When young children of similar age are conversing, the interval between one child relinquishing the talking turn and another assuming the talking turn is characteristically long. They cope with these long pauses. An eavesdropping adult might come, incorrectly, to the conclusion that what is going on is children talking 'at' each other rather than 'to' each other.

When they do take the talking turn you can continue to hear the 'cogs'. They typically stop and start, repeat phrases and words, trying to fashion in language primitively formulated thoughts. We just have to be patient, listen, and leave them with the talking turn. However, all too many adults do not do this. This accounts for some rather sad and frustrating behaviour in conversations between adults and children.

- The unaware adult speaker relinquishes the talking turn.
- The child says nothing—while the 'cogs' turn.
- The adult feels the conversational pressure of the silence, and feels that he or she should say something, having construed the child's silence as indicating one or more of the following:
  — the child has not been paying attention;
  — the child has not understood;
  — the child is unwilling to say anything.
- The adult sees this as an opportunity to 'crack on' because:
  — time is short;
  — the adult is busy;
  — the adult already knows the answer; or
  — any combination of these.
- The adult 'fills the pause', takes back the talking turn, and starts to talk.

This sequence creates the *open–closed confirmatory 'yes'/'no' sequence* of questioning that adults use excessively when talking to children, eg *What did you do today? Did you...?* The adult does no more than ask the child to confirm what is in the adult's head. Children learn this sequence from their parents. As growing children, teenagers, and as adults they apply it widely in their everyday conversations. Investigators use it excessively when interviewing

---

[5] Romaine, S. (1984) *The Language of Children and Adolescents: The Acquisition of Communicative Competence.* Oxford: Blackwell.

suspects and also when interviewing the generality of witnesses, as recording would prove if it took place!

The result is that many investigators, although they would be distressed to be made aware of this, talk 'at' rather than 'with' interviewees—especially children, elderly people, and those with learning disability or a communication disorder, eg cerebral palsy. They are unaware that their behaviour saddens or alienates these interviewees.[6] Yet investigators typically get fed up, or experience even stronger emotions, when they are on the receiving end of someone, eg a supervisor or a manager, who will not allow them to get a 'word in edgeways'.

Talking time

Whenever a participant occupies the talking turn this contributes to the total amount of his or her talking time across the course of the conversation.

3.3.2 Topic selection and progression

Participants introduce topics either by making a comment, inviting a view, or asking a question. After an exchange of information on a particular topic, one of the participants moves the conversation forward by raising another topic.

3.4 How people seek to manage a conversation they have initiated

3.4.1 Conversational goals

People engage in conversation to achieve particular goals. The most minimal exchange is a simple greeting to acknowledge the other person as you cross paths. Your goal is *interpersonal*: to communicate personal recognition (literally *re-knowing*). In many conversations our goals are *practical*, eg we engage the other person in conversation to obtain information.

Conversation is inherently anxiety-inducing. We cannot really anticipate what the other person will say in response to what we say. To make the course of the conversation, and content of the person's responses, more predictable we have to exercise some degree of control over both. There is no escape: we have to manage the conversation as a staged event, and the exchange of information to achieve our practical goals. There is a potential problem. The other person will be drawing significant conclusions from our behaviour, potentially affecting their view of us and their participation in the exchange.

3.4.2 The universal script

Other than the passing greeting, when people initiate conversation they follow a universal script.[7] As pointed out in Chapter 2, a script is a stereotyped sequence of actions.

- **Opening**. One person initiates the conversation.
- **Exchanging**. The participants take turns in the mutual activity of talking and listening, sharing the talking time between them as:
  — they introduce topics;

---

[6] Marchant, R. and Gordon, R. (2001) *Two-Way Street: Communicating with Disabled Children and Young People.* Leicester: NSPCC.

[7] Hargie, O. and Dickson, D. (2004) *Skilled Interpersonal Communication: Research, Theory and Practice.* London: Routledge.

— they respond to questions about topics;
— they make or invite comment.

- **Closing**. One of the participants signals that the conversation is at an end.

Opening the conversation

'Firsts' and 'lasts' have a particular psychological importance to us. How something begins and ends impacts upon us: conversations are no exception.

Greeting

A minimal act of common courtesy is plain good manners: showing respect for the other person. SOFTENS behaviours (see Box 3.2), particularly eye contact and smiling, communicate responsiveness.

In 'service' settings people very often act impersonally. They act thoughtlessly, failing to make any form of greeting—verbal or non-verbal—mindlessly moving straight to the focusing topic.

Focusing topic

This topic—raised either in the form of a statement, comment, or observation, question, or request—draws the other person's attention to what the individual has in mind.

Exchanging

Having received the other person's response to the focusing topic, the person manages the exchange to achieve his or her goals. Again, this can reflect whether the individual is acting thoughtfully or thoughtlessly—how mindful he or she is of the other person.

Thoughtful behaviours

- Ensuring the other person has equal—or more access—to the talking time.
- Allowing the other person's latitude to contribute freely.
  - **Raising topics in a way that facilitates disclosure**. Making a statement, comment, or observation, or posing an *open* question, ie one that does not constrain (*Could you tell/explain/describe...? How...? What* (requesting a narrative)...? *In what way...? Why...?*).
  - **Pausing**. This gives the other person time to think and to marshal thoughts before taking the talking turn.
- Using the supportive behaviours summarized in SOFTENS.
- Listening closely to the person's responses.

Thoughtless behaviours

- Talking most of the time.
- Following an *agenda*—introducing and progressing topics of relevance to achieving personal goals.
- Limiting the other person's latitude to contribute freely.
  - **Making pre-emptive assertions**. The person pronounces a state of affairs as a 'fact' in the form of a statement, comment, or observation to be accepted unquestioningly by the other person.

— **Asking constraining questions**. These suggest the answer, ie confirmatory 'yes'/'no' questions (*Is that OK?*), leading questions (*You did say that didn't you?*), or option questions (*Was that the last time or the time before?*).

— **Not giving the other person time to think ('filling the pause')**. The speaker asks a question—signalling a switch in the talking turn—but before the other person can say anything, the individual pre-emptively 'fills the pause' by taking the talking turn. This may be either to answer his or her own question, or to ask another question or a series of questions.

• Disrupting the person when he or she has the talking turn.

— **Overtalking**. The person may feel impelled to start talking even though the other person is still talking. In addition to being disruptive, it is rude and counter-productive, underlining the wisdom of the saying that 'you are not learning anything when you are talking'.

— **Interrupting**. The individual's overtalking may induce the other person to give up the talking turn. Interrupting disrupts the other person's mental and spoken flow, and he or she may find it difficult—and may not feel inclined—to pick up the thread and continue on this matter.

— **Rapid topic changing**. Also called 'topic hopping', the individual switches the topic suddenly without warning and with no apparent logic to another topic, challenging the other person's ability to keep up logically and conversationally.

• Disruptively listening.

— **Being inattentive**. The individual may not listen at all—in effect being a 'non-attender'—evidenced by a lack of supportive non-verbal, non-vocal behaviour. The individual may randomly listen—consciously or unconsciously 'tuning "in"' and 'tuning "out"' to the content of what the other person is saying. Clues that the person is 'tuned "out"' include the same absence of supportive non-verbal behaviour or a minimal vocal response, eg a hollow noise indicative of not really listening or not really being interested.

— **Assuming**. The individual hears what he or she wants to hear and believes that he or she already knows the answer before it is given. Frequently assumers trigger the answer they want to hear by asking *constraining* questions (confirmatory 'yes'/'no', leading, option). They may even go further, interrupting to complete what the other person is saying (*I know what you're going to say*).

— **Word picking**. An extreme version of an assumer, the word picker puts his or her own biased interpretation upon a word or phrase used by the other person, and makes this a topic for corrosive conversation.

Closing

People tend not to put too much thought, time, or effort into ending conversations in order to depart or to switch their attention to a non-conversational task. Often closing is impromptu, ie spontaneous, done without any planning or indeed any conscious attention to the other person's perceptions.

Typically people warn the other person of their imminent departure non-verbally.

• Putting or patting hands on the arms of the chair—as if about to rise.
• Patting thighs or the table.
• Rising or moving forward in the chair.
• Looking towards and aligning towards the exit.
• Breaking eye contact.
• Looking at one's watch or looking towards a clock within shared vision.

- Making an action indicative of departure or wish to perform another activity, eg reaching for keys, bag, or a book.

The manner in which the person closes the conversation verbally greatly determines how these non-verbal actions are perceived. Careless verbal closing can give offence, something likely to make the memory of the conversation even more negative.

Thoughtful verbal closing

- Recognizing the other person's position/circumstances, eg *I know that you're busy.*
- Acknowledgement of the other person's contribution, eg *That was really helpful. I've learned a lot.*
- Expression of gratitude, eg *I appreciate you giving me your time.*
- Continuity of contact ('future perspective'), eg *See you again next week.*
- Well-wishing comment, eg *Take care.*

Thoughtless verbal closing

Very often this is a combination of:

- peremptory gratitude, eg *Thanks*; and
- minimal parting utterance before physically departing or looking away, eg *Bye.*

The individual's abrupt verbal closing has the effect of sending one or more powerful relationship messages to the other person.

- The individual does not find, or no longer finds, the exchange beneficial or desirable.
- The individual is frustrated with the other person, his or her conduct, and contribution to the conversation, the content of the conversation, or any combination of these.
- The individual has 'better things to do' than to talk further with the other person or on these matters.

3.5 Control and concern: the two dimensions of managing conversation

3.5.1 Control of the exchange

Psychologists have long recognized that in every conversation people make a decision as to the extent to which they will seek to control the exchange in terms of:

- access to the talking turn and therefore the talking time;
- topic selection and progression.

Our behaviour reflects our decision along a dimension of *control* extending from *total control* of the conversation (dominance) through appropriate assertion to *total lack of control* (submissiveness).

3.5.2 Concern

Irrespective of the degree of control, our behaviour reflects our decision along a dimension of *concern*. At one end is *concern for yourself*—excluding from consideration the other person and his or her perspective. The other person perceives you as being self-centred, pursuing your 'agenda' by behaving mindlessly or thoughtlessly. At the other end of this dimension is *concern for the other person*: consciously behaving in a manner that takes into account the other person and his or her perspective.

3.5.3 Putting the dimensions together

Combining the two dimensions creates four quadrants (Box 3.3): each a pattern of conversational behaviour that evidences the control you exert and the focus of your concern, yourself or the other person.[8]

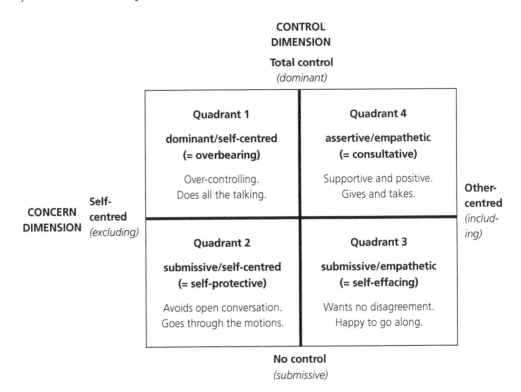

Box 3.3 Combining control and concern: the four quadrants of conversational behaviour

People who exhibit Quadrant 1 or Quadrant 2 behaviours are oppressive. They make the other person feel used, uncomfortable, and unwilling to talk too much. Socially skilled individuals exhibit Quadrant 3 and 4 behaviours. They make the other person feel valued, motivating him or her to talk. If you have practical goals—as you have in an investigative interview—Quadrant 4 behaviours (assertive/empathetic) offer the best prospect of getting the person to collaborate with you to achieve your goals.

3.6 Influence, persuasion, and negotiation

Influence—behaving in a manner that impacts positively on the other person—is a key determinant of whether he or she will relate to you as a person and engage actively and collaboratively in conversation. Interviewers have no choice: they have to exert influence from first meeting right up to the moment of departure. This applies whether the other person is the interviewee or a third party.

---

[8] Lefton, R., Buzzotta, V., Sherberg, M., and Karraker, D. (1977) *Effective Motivation through Performance Appraisal.* Cambridge, Mass.: Ballinger.

At some point, whether within the interview location or elsewhere, you will need to engage in *persuasion*: inviting the interviewee or a third party to:

- reflect upon what he or she has said or not said, or upon the way he or she is behaving;
- recognize the implications of what has been said or the behaviour;
- consider changing what has been said, or to disclose detail, or to behave differently.

In most circumstances, persuasion is as far as you can go because there are constraints imposed upon you, eg the law, regulations, procedures, official guidelines. However, there will be occasions, particularly when interviewing in special circumstances, in which there is a fundamental conflict of interests—actual or potential, eg:

- when there is a legal obligation upon the interviewee to disclose;
- when you are seeking intelligence or information on other offences;
- when you cannot disclose information or evidence to trigger disclosure.

In these situations, moving the conversation forward to achieve your aims and objectives is a matter of *negotiation*.

3.6.1   The relationship between influence, persuasion, and negotiation

Influence, persuasion, and negotiation are interrelated. Figure 3.1 shows that influence—the range of behaviours that impact upon the individual—is the common denominator.

- Persuasion requires behaviours that impact upon the individual. In addition, it requires behaviours to remove obstacles by winning the interviewee over, and aligning him or her to your perspective.
- Negotiation also requires behaviours that impact upon the individual. In addition, it requires behaviours to reconcile opposing interests—yours and the interviewee's—sufficiently to move the interviewee to do something even if he or she disagrees with it, or is unhappy to do it.

In sum, influence determines initial and subsequent perceptions of relationship. Persuasion takes influence further. It combines perceptions of relationship with compelling, reason-based argument. It is the intellectual 'face' of influence. The interviewer uses reasoning to convince the individual of the merits of acting differently—in a way that will enable achievement of the interviewer's goals or point of view. Negotiation also takes influence further to move the individual to do something that he or she would much rather not do.

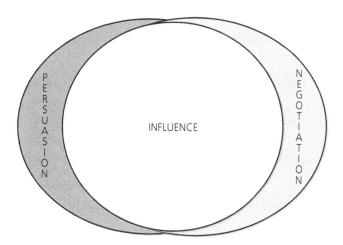

Figure 3.1 The relationship between influence, persuasion, and negotiation

It is about seeing the other person's point of view and making concessions in order to make it worth the individual's while to accept the least upsetting and unpalatable way of the two of you working together.

3.6.2 Respect for the person and the obligation to tell the truth

Interviewers are powerful people. Persuasion and negotiation are precarious exercises in power. Society expects interviewers at all times, irrespective of the circumstances, to observe two fundamental moral concepts: *respect for the person* and the *obligation to tell the truth*. It is no accident that these concepts are the cornerstone of law,[9] and their observance distinguishes a free from a totalitarian society.

If interviewers observe these moral concepts, then we can rely upon them at the very moment they are seeking to influence, to persuade, and to negotiate to protect the integrity of the individual and our society of which he or she is a representative. On the other hand, the individual, truth, law, and society as a whole are all at risk if an interviewer abuses power to achieve expedient ends: engaging in unethical persuasion and negotiation by:

- distorting reality by telling lies;
- engaging in trickery;
- coercing the individual to say and do things that he or she otherwise would not, or not to say or do things that he or she otherwise would.

3.6.3 Mutual respect for rights and responsibilities

In Chapter 1 we indicated that an interviewer has a responsibility to respect the fundamental rights of the interviewee (or indeed any third party present).

- The right to his or her own opinions, views, and ideas—that may differ from the interviewer.
- The right to a fair hearing.
- The right to refuse to participate.
- The right to choose what to disclose, when, and in what detail.
- The right to refuse a request for information.
- The right to object to or to counter information or evidence, arguments, or proposals.
- The right to have feelings and to express these if he or she chooses.
- The right to be 'human'—to get it wrong.
- The right to be himself or herself—the same or different from the interviewer.

It follows that in performing your role as interviewer to achieve ethically your investigative aim and objectives, you have rights commensurate with having a job to do and with also being human.

- You have the right—derived from your professional role and requirement to progress the investigation—to manage the course of the conversation and to influence the content of the exchange by making *assertions*—making statements, observations, and comments, giving explanations, posing questions, and giving feedback.
- You have the same human rights as the interviewee—most particularly to a fair hearing.

Your behaviour when you are seeking to persuade, or negotiate with, the individual is evidence of your continued attention to mutual rights and responsibilities. The individual has

---

[9] Kant, I. (1964) *Fundamental Principles of the Metaphysics of Morals.* Translated by H. Paton. New York: Harper and Row.

a right to expect this of you. You may hope but you cannot presume that the individual will respect your rights: as the professional, as a fellow human being, or both. This is why the conversation management approach to interviewing emphasizes the necessity of establishing a positive relationship—consciously engaging in reciprocity, manifesting RESPONSE behaviours, and fostering and sustaining rapport—shared understanding—through continuous explanation. The very beginning of relationship—and how it evolves thereafter—and your potential to manage the conversation and the course of events rely upon your ability to influence the individual through the totality of your conduct towards the individual.

3.6.4 Influence

Favourable and unfavourable impression

First impressions count. Your subsequent behaviour will either validate or invalidate these impressions. People form immediate and vivid impressions of each other within the first five seconds. It takes the next five minutes to add 50 per cent more impression—positive or negative—to that made in the first five seconds.

Influence is about impression management—seeking to generate and then to reinforce within the mind of the interviewee positive—favourable—perceptions of you as a person and as a professional: definitely not perceptions that are negative—unfavourable (Box 3.4).

Favourable	Unfavourable
Confident	Uncertain
Friendly	Aloof
Caring	Condescending
Professional	Bored
Helpful	Disinterested
Genuine	Ungenerous
Sincere	Superficial

Box 3.4 Favourable and unfavourable impressions

In Chapter 1 we explained how positive impact is achieved by *congruent communication*. By this we mean that:

- your non-vocal, non-verbal behaviour: dress and appearance, posture, eye contact, facial expressions, body movements, gestures;
- your vocal verbal and non-vocal behaviour: the way you express yourself and the way in which you speak and use your voice;
- your listening behaviour

must all 'say' the same thing.

If you are interviewing on the telephone it follows that your vocal behaviour and your listening behaviour have to be congruent.

Dress and appearance

You must dress, groom, and appear appropriate to the environment you are in, as well as to yourself.

The significance of dress and appearance

Even before you open your mouth your dress and appearance communicate your attitude and your concerns: how you feel about yourself and the extent to which you care about the impression you make. Your dress and appearance are the crucial immediate ingredients to establishing *initial credibility* as a professional in the eyes of the interviewee or a third party.

Be appropriate

There is not so much a right or wrong way to dress, or groom, as an appropriate way. It should be appropriate in the eyes of the perceiver. You have to exercise empathy yet again: get round to his or her side of the circle of perception and ask yourself what would be his or her expectations—the dress and appearance of a professional investigator wishing to conduct an interview in these circumstances. A good exercise is to ask five people that you trust to give you their expectations.

Dress at the conscious level

We are creatures of habit. We tend to wear the same types of clothing and groom in the same old way. Take a careful and conscious look at your habitual dress and appearance.

Ask yourself the hard question: To what extent is the way that I currently dress and groom consistent with people's expectations? If there is a gap, you need to close this by abandoning your habitual ways and consciously dress and groom to impress positively.

Posture

While there is no absolute right or wrong way to stand or to sit. How you 'hold' yourself physically is commonly construed as a reflection of how you hold yourself mentally, and the regard that you have for yourself and the encounter. Slumped posture is perceived negatively: as the outward manifestation of indifference, helplessness, sunken spirits, lack of energy or commitment. In contrast, overly erect posture is negatively construed as signalling 'up–down' relationship, emotional distance, or tension. Similarly, sitting rigidly on the edge of your chair can interpreted as being mentally 'on edge', keyed up, and under pressure.

Generally, people will respond to the observed behaviour in accordance with the message they think it sends. They react negatively to negative posture. Your posture should therefore signal that you are in a state of readiness but appropriately relaxed, fully engaged, and involved.

- When standing, take the 'ready position', with your weight slightly forward enabling you—undetectably—to flex up and down on the balls of your feet. This signals energy and confidence, and prevents you from rocking back and forth or side to side, which observers find disconcerting.
- When sitting, place your body well into the chair and lean slightly forwards. This places you in the right position to engage in SOFTENS behaviours when these are required. If you are male, or a female wearing trousers, you will find sitting with your legs slightly apart both comfortable and construed as you being 'open'. If you are female wearing a skirt or dress, an appropriate and comfortable position is to cross your legs at the ankles.

When seated don't remain in the same position for a protracted period: move your body forward and back from time to time. If you are male, or a female wearing trousers, you can cross and uncross your legs. If you are female and wearing a skirt or dress you can alternate inclining your legs or move them forwards or backwards.

Eye contact

Eye communication is the most important interpersonal skill for any interviewer.

Focus of gaze

You need to look at the person's eyes, occasionally switching your gaze to his or her forehead before returning to look at his or her eyes again.

Sustained eye contact

In face-to-face communication the basic rule is that the person in the talking turn should gaze at the listener, maintaining sustained eye contact. The normal duration for this is between 5 to 15 seconds. In the majority of exchanges listeners are comfortable with being gazed at by the speaker for some 5 to 15 seconds. The person in the listening turn is likewise expected to gaze at the speaker, 'guggling' at the key ideas in what is being said. This evidences that he or she is paying attention, concentrating, following, and registering the detail.

You need to develop the skill of sustaining eye contact when in the talking turn. It sends the message that you are confident in what you are saying. Similarly you have to maintain eye contact when the interviewee or third party is talking. You have to stay 'on target', gazing at the individual whether you are in the talking or listening turn. This said, you have to avoid giving the impression that you are staring at the individual. It is also the case that some interviewers feel uncomfortable maintaining sustained gaze—either when speaking or listening.

Two simple techniques can 'soften' your sustained gaze—such that it is not perceived as staring—and also help you to relax your eyes—since sustained eye contact is tiring.

- While continuing to focus on the speaker's eyes, systematically lengthen and shorten the focal length of your gaze, ie look at a point in space—for instance the wall—just behind his or her head but in line with his or her eyes, then look at a point just short of his or her eyes. This relieves eye-strain by relaxing the cilial muscles that adjust the corneas (lenses) of your eyes. It also has the effect of 'softening' your gaze and reducing the risk of creating the impression that you are staring at or—even worse—'staring down' the individual.
- Switch your focus from the speaker's eyes to his or her forehead. This is particularly helpful if the individual is being difficult or resistant.

Breaking eye contact

When we are speaking we are allowed to break eye contact with our listener intermittently, but only fleetingly, in order to access our thoughts. Breaking eye contact in any other way is a problem. This occurs in two ways.

Eye dart

When people feel under pressure when they are speaking, they have a tendency to glance at anything other than the listener. Their eyes dart around, signalling nervousness, like a frightened rabbit. Once they start looking at anything other than the listener, this actually increases the likelihood of continuing to look in any direction other than the listener. Listeners find this disconcerting and, crucially, the speaker loses credibility.

You must therefore consciously resist darting your eyes when you feel under pressure. Re-double your effort at maintaining eye contact.

Slow blink

This is when an individual keeps his or her eyelids closed for up to two or three seconds while speaking. It is a means of relieving inner pressure by:

- substituting a lecture to a 'blank screen' for real conversation;
- not having to see the listener's reactions to what the speaker is saying.

Slow blinking sends very powerful, negative messages, eg *I don't want to be here, I'd rather not be talking to you*. When you feel under pressure you have to resist closing your eyes and resorting to slow blinking. Consciously put your effort into keeping your eyes open and targeted on the interviewee or third party.

Facial movement

Smiling

People who smile are considered more sincere, sociable, and competent. You should smile at the individual on first, and any subsequent, meeting, and across the course of the encounter at appropriate times.

Pause briefly before smiling

Don't smile immediately. A rapidly appearing smile risks you being perceived as not being authentic and untrustworthy. Allow a short interval—around half a second—before starting to shape your smile.

Minimal, fuller, and Duchenne smiles

If your smile on first encounter involves *minimal movement* (corners of the mouth upturned but no teeth showing) and is fleeting, you are liable to be perceived as insincere and 'going through the motions' (a feature of Quadrant 2 behaviour).

Across the course of the encounter and in the interview proper, guard against minimal smiles. Called 'ghost' smiles, they frequently occur when people feel angry or resent having their views dismissed or rejected. They also occur when people are feeling anxious or threatened. 'Ghost' smiles always evoke negative perceptions: the person construes you as unsure, being rattled, or lacking ability to assert yourself.

In contrast, a fuller smile (corners of the mouth upturned but with some area of teeth revealed) tends to last longer and is perceived as genuine. However, the most positively impactful smile is a Duchenne smile. This involves greater amplitude in the movement of the mouth, and simultaneous raising of the cheekbones that causes movement in the muscles around your eyes—creating wrinkles ('crow's feet', also called 'E' lines). Duchenne smiles last longer—about a second—and are universally perceived as genuine and welcoming.

Duchenne smiling has a warming power that can melt the hardest resolve. So always put conscious effort and muscle into your smiling!

Eyebrows

Raising your eyebrows slightly can be an appropriate signal of concern (see SOFTENS). Resist significantly raising your brows, since this signals amazement, shock, or being 'thrown' by what the individual is saying.

Frowning and scowling

You should consciously avoid frowning and definitely never scowl. Frowning is perceived as you being judgemental: inconsistent with other RESPONSE behaviours that you are manifesting, and therefore risking you being viewed as insincere. People also frown when they are 'losing it' in terms of being perplexed and struggling to grasp what is being disclosed or the issue.

Frowning and scowling give the individual the impression that you are reacting emotionally (suppressing your anger) or are unable to cope with the individual's behaviour (particularly if he or she is 'pushing back'—resisting, objecting to, or rejecting your assertions) or what is being disclosed.

Jaw movement

A relaxed jaw signals just that: you are calm, not perturbed or emotionally unsettled by what is being disclosed or by the individual's behaviour. People associate thrusting the chin forward with aggression, annoyance, and being combative.

Handshake

In Western culture, it is a natural mark of respect when you first meet someone to offer your hand—a sign of openness and approachability—in order to shake hands—signalling warmth and solidarity. Repeating this ritual when you depart reinforces these perceptions.

We recommend that you offer your hand before you say anything to the other person—irrespective of his or her age or gender—and follow this through with a handshake. People who are younger than you and those whose circumstances and lifestyle are very different from yours do not expect an interviewer to show respect in the form of an extended hand and a subsequent handshake. This simple, unexpected act is a cause of genuine surprise and sets the individual up to engage in a positive relationship.

The individual may fumble his or her part of the handshake. However, for your part you have created a very positive impact as a person and a professional, wanting to relate to the individual.

You need to focus consciously on six aspects of shaking hands to create a positive impact.

- **Offer your hand positively**. Extend your hand towards the individual in a smooth trajectory. Don't move it up and down. As the other person moves his or her hand towards you guide the 'horn' of your hand (the 'V' shaped webbed part between your thumb and index finger) towards the 'horn' of the individual's hand.
- **Completeness**. Gently but firmly push the 'horn' of your hand against the 'horn' of the other person's hand. The two 'horns' must connect. If this does not happen the result will not be a real handshake.
- **Firmness**. Squeeze the individual's hand firmly—don't crush it. The fleshy area of the hand down from the base of the little finger to the wrist is called the 'ball'. When you squeeze, wrap the tips of your fingers round this 'ball' and gently and firmly pull up with your fingers. If you do not squeeze the individual's hand—particularly if you have not connected the 'horns' of each other's hands—the result will be a limp—'wet fish'—handshake.
- **Duration**. Shake hands for a few seconds. A brief handshake is construed negatively as merely 'going through the motions'. If it is a short-lived 'wet fish' handshake, the perception will be even more negative.
- **Energy**. Move the person's hand up and down with appropriate energy. Don't vigorously pump, as this overwhelms. Lack of energy, however, is another defining feature of a limp handshake.
- **Eye contact**. Maintain eye contact with the person throughout. If you do not, you will be perceived as insincere—'going through the motions'—with your real attention elsewhere, or both.

Shaking hands brings a bonus. You can use this contact to detect whether the person's palm is:

- clammy or moist—a potential indicator that the he or she is psychologically/physiologically aroused or anxious;
- dry—indicative of calmness.

Some investigators have problems shaking hands with an individual who appears not very warm or friendly, or seems tired. These are the people with whom you really need to shake hands. It is also the case that some investigators, particularly in the crime context, are reluctant to shake hands with suspects—particularly those whose lifestyle is far from that of the investigator or who are deemed to have perpetrated an outrageous or heinous offence.

Our view is that if you find it difficult to shake hands with a 'lesser' person, you should ask yourself hard questions as to why. Until you overcome your own psychological barriers it makes no sense to attempt to shake hands with people with whom you would rather not associate. The result will be a 'wet fish' handshake. This risks you being perceived negatively by the other person: as going through the motions, having negative perceptions of the individual as a person.

There are cultural differences. If you are male you should never shake the hand of a Muslim female.

Hand and arm movements

Particular hand movements are perceived negatively and must be consciously avoided:

- covering your mouth when talking (interpreted as 'not sure' or 'reluctant to say this');
- very obvious adaptors/excessive level of adaptors, eg grooming, moving pens and paper around (interpreted as 'nervous');
- hand-wringing;
- finger-pointing/jabbing;
- tapping fingers;
- fist-thumping;
- arms crossed high (interpreted as 'unapproachable');
- arms crossed low (interpreted as 'for protection').

Body movement

Some body movements quickly draw the other person's attention and evoke negative perceptions:

- fidgeting;
- 'jigging': bursts of, or even continuous, rapid up and down movement of legs or thighs;
- tapping feet.

Proximity

We tend to choose a particular distance from the other person depending upon how we feel towards that person at a given time, the context of the conversation, and our interpersonal goals (what we want to get out the conversation and the relationship). There are four distances: *intimate* (skin contact out to about 18 inches); *personal* (ranging from about 18 ins/about 50 cm to about 4 ft/about 1.25 m); *social* (about 4 ft/about 1.25 m to about 12 feet/about 4 m); and public (extending from about 12 ft/about 4 m outwards).

Personal distance is the zone which predominantly applies when interacting with an interviewee or third party. Its closer phase is the distance at which most couples stand from each other in public. There is still a risk of the other person, particularly one of the opposite sex, sensing this is 'too close for comfort'. As a professional, stand just that bit further away—three to four feet. This is optimum distance for you to engage in SOFTENS behaviours (see Box 3.2). It places you just beyond the person's reach—you are literally at 'arm's length' from each other and will not be perceived as 'crowding' the person or being invasive. There is another benefit. Should the individual become physically aggressive you are beyond striking distance.

Physical barriers, proximity, and orientation in the interview room

A table or desk between you and the interviewee is a physical barrier which generates within the interviewee a sense of psychological distance.

- It reduces the impact you have on the individual, making it harder to foster a psychological bond.
- You cannot engage in the complete range of psychologically positive SOFTENS behaviours.
- Individuals are relatively unaware of, and find it difficult to control, their lower trunk, leg, and foot movements. A table or desk will obscure the lower half of the individual's body, denying you the ability to monitor and to detect potentially significant movement. (See BASELINES in Chapter 7 (Active Listening, Observing, and Assessing), and in the Reference Section).

Wherever possible, place the interviewee where you have a full view of his or her body. Face-to-face orientation is perceived negatively, being construed as confrontational. In contrast, an oblique orientation generates positive perceptions: conversational, consultative, or confiding. Figure 3.2 shows how to place your chairs obliquely—in a 'ten-to-two'—orientation. If you cannot move the table or desk out of the way, sit at the desk and place the individual away from the desk, in the open space, still achieving a 'ten–to-two' orientation (Figure 3.3). As shown in the figures, always place any third party to the far side of the interviewee. Never allow the third party to sit between you and the interviewee.

When sitting, you need three to four feet distance between your shins and those of the interviewee. If you sit any closer your feet and legs will be within each other's intimate space.

- When setting up the interview location, set the chairs up at an appropriate distance, obliquely orientated to each other ('ten-to-two').

INTERVIEWER   INTERVIEWEE

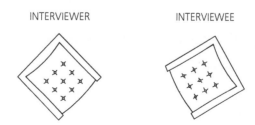

Figure 3.2 'Ten-to-two' seating positions: no table

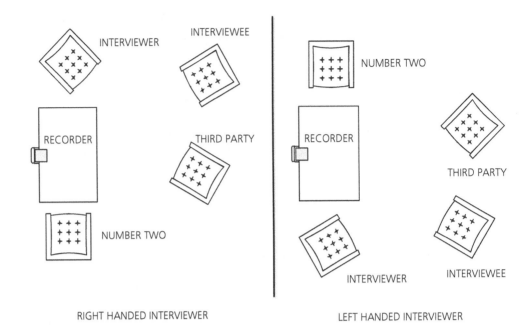

RIGHT HANDED INTERVIEWER · LEFT HANDED INTERVIEWER

Figure 3.3 'Ten-to-two' seating positions: with table

- Sitting in your chair, extend your legs, towards the other chair, stretching your toes to their fullest extent.
- Place a coin or a pen on the floor at the tip of your shoe.
- Move to the other person's chair.
- Extend your legs and feet as far forward as you can, then push the chair forwards or backwards until your extended toes touch the coin or the pen. If you know the individual to be taller than you, make allowance for this.

When the interviewee eventually sits in the chair, both of you will be at an optimum distance from each other. Because the seating is at 'ten-to-two', when he or she breaks eye contact and gazes away, you will have a side-on, profile view. This makes it very easy to monitor even more BASELINES behaviours, such as blink rate, blood vessels, and breathing.

Use of language

As a professional, you cannot expect people to change the way that they understand you. A little mis-communication—partial misunderstanding—is normal and predictable in every conversation. The only valid test that you are communicating clearly is the result: the interviewee's reaction and the content of his or her response to what you have said or asked.

Clear communication begins with you, not the other person. You have to be conscious of the way that you use language when you converse with an interviewee.

Monitor and mirror the individual's language

You need to listen intently to the individual's use of language—particularly in terms of:

- vocabulary (everyday words vs more 'educated', bookish words);
- word length (short—one or two syllables—vs a high proportion of long—three or more syllables);
- utterance length (short utterances vs longer utterances, particularly using words that extend these, eg *which, who, whether*).

If you detect that the individual uses mostly short, everyday words, in short utterances, you need to mirror this pattern by observing the mnemonic KISS—Keep It Simple and Short. Simple words, no jargon, and short utterances will ensure that you communicate clearly and will be understood.

'Red flag' words and phrases

Some words and phrases can alienate, confuse, or provoke a negative response, even anger and hostility. These are called 'red flag' words and phrases.

'Red flag' words

There are many of these. Two to avoid are *We* and *It*.

'We' (referring to the other person)

Using the word 'we' (a plural) to refer to the other person (very much a singular) is alienating. It signals an 'up'–'down' relationship: a superior talking in a condescending, rebuking, or menacing way, or in a manner to a subordinate—rather like a teacher addressing a small child who does not grasp that he or she has done something wrong, or needs to be warned.

> *We need to think very carefully about this ^^ (=* **You** *don't understand the significance and I'm warning you)*

'It'

'It' is an extremely ambiguous word. You cannot assume the other person knows what you are referring to when you use 'it'. You have to define clearly and concretely what you mean by 'it'.

> *I know it was normal. By that I mean everybody . . . ^^*

'Red flag' phrases

Common examples of 'red flag' phrases that should be avoided include:

> *I can't pretend that there will not be a delay . . .*
> *With respect . . .*
> *I hear what you say . . .*
> *If you must . . .*
> *I don't quite know how to say this . . .*
> *I disagree . . .*
> *I assume . . .*

Vocal behaviour

Your voice is the primary vehicle conveying your message. The sound of your voice conveys your level of alertness and energy, and the way you feel about yourself and what you are doing. Your vocal behaviour will contribute greatly to perceptions of you as 'confident' or 'not sure' and the extent to which you come across as credible—on top of things and engaged (Box 3.5).

To improve your vocal behaviour make a copy of Box 3.5 and then listen to recordings of your interviews, using the detail of the box as a checklist. Consciously work to develop those aspects of your voice that you have ticked in the 'Not sure' column.

Behaviour	'Confident'	'Not sure…'
Rhythm	Smooth flow with pauses	Erratic, chopped up
Speed (pace)	Measured	Fast with occasional pauses for breath; extremely slow
Volume	Appropriate	Too quiet, almost whispering; too loud
Pitch	Steady, dipping down at the end of utterances	Wavering; rising up at the end of expressed ideas and posed questions
Articulation	Clear and rounded	Mumbling; clipped
Breathing	Deep and even	Shallow; irregular
'Um…' 'Er…'	Minimal	Frequent

Box 3.5 Vocal behaviours: 'confident' and 'not sure'

Verbal echoing and behaviour mirroring

Verbal echoing is saying what the other person has just said. It is a very effective indicator that you are paying attention and are registering what he or she has said. Behaviour mirroring occurs automatically in everyday conversational life: people unconsciously replicate each other's gestures, mannerisms, and postures. Echoing and mirroring are potent tools for influencing another person subconsciously—communicating a sense of rapport and forming a bond.

The skill is to mirror behaviours that can positively impact on your management of the conversation. If the interviewee leans forward, eg to share something that he or she holds as significant or confidential, you should mirror by leaning forward.

There are a couple of warnings.

- Mirroring too quickly after the other person—and excessively engaging in rapid mirroring—may be detected and risks you being perceived as insincere, or even odd. Pause for two to four seconds before you mirror.
- Common sense argues that you should not echo utterances or mirror behaviours that are alienating, improper, dysfunctional, or unhelpful.

3.6.5 Persuasion

When you seek to persuade an individual, you are attempting to convince him or her that it is reasonable to take an appropriate action, or remove the obstacle that prevents the individual from acting appropriately. Persuasion is about removing obstacles by winning the other person over, and aligning the individual to your perspective. Fundamental to persuasion are:

- honesty in presenting information or facts (evidence);
- freedom of choice—to accept or to reject what is being presented or represented;
- respect for the individual's decision.[10]

We have pointed out earlier that psychologically manipulating the individual—offering invalid, insincere, manipulative reasons, excuses, or arguments, lying (creating a false

---

[10] Perloff, R.M. (2010) *The Dynamics of Persuasion: Communication and Attitudes in the 21st Century*. Fourth edition. New York: Routledge.

representation of reality), or using subterfuge and trickery—is exploiting the individual's vulnerability and ignorance. It is unethical.

If the interviewer does not respect the individual's right to dissent and to have his or her decision respected and accepted, and pressures the individual by conversing unethically—denies the individual's right to the talking turn and to be listened to without being over-talked and interrupted—this is not winning over by reason. This is oppression: conduct aimed at rendering the individual compliant—such that he or she will say things that he or she otherwise would not, or not say things that he or she otherwise would.

Ethical, skilled persuasion is characterized by the following.

- Having a clear idea of:
  — your argument(s);
  — the evidence to back up your argument(s);
  — the benefit(s) to the individual should he or she take an appropriate action.
- Moral commitment:
  — to tell the truth;
  — to respect the individual as a person;
  — to respect the individual's freedom to dissent and to choose.
- Keeping calm.
- Engaging in Quadrant 4 behaviours:
  — engaging continuously in RESPONSE behaviours;
  — being appropriately assertive.
- Listening intently to what is said and listening actively to how it is said.
- Engaging in SOFTENS behaviours.
- Ensuring the individual fully understands by:
  — being explicit at all times;
  — presenting your position in a straightforward, matter-of-fact manner.
- Cope with rejection of your argument—using positive rather than negative language, eg instead of saying *You're wrong about that* say:

  I accept that ^^ ^^ however let's look more at what's at issue ^^ ^^ *or*
  I accept that ^^ ^^ however I want you to know (consider) ^^ ^^

- If necessary, re-stating your position (the argument, the evidence, the benefits).
- Having re-stated your position, if the individual is still not convinced, accepting that:
  — he or she probably never will be convinced;
  — further presentation of your position will evoke a negative response and erode the relationship that you have established with the individual.

When persuasion works, it tends to work relatively quickly.

3.6.6 Negotiation

In most circumstances persuasion is not only enough, it is as far as you can go given the constraints imposed upon you by the law, regulations, procedures, and guidelines. However, there will be instances when you are faced with the task of negotiation—particularly in special circumstance interviewing, eg when there is a legal obligation upon the interviewee to disclose, when you are seeking to obtain information on other offences or intelligence, or in counter-terrorism where you cannot disclose evidence.

In these circumstances there is an actual or potential conflict of interest. Your task is to reconcile interests—yours and the individual's—sufficiently so that the individual will do something even if he or she disagrees with it. This is done by giving the individual enough concessions to make co-operation worthwhile.

Whereas persuasion is about *telling*, negotiation is about *selling* or, put another way, trading. Persuaders give reasons, negotiators give concessions. Negotiation must, however, be *principled*. Principled negotiation means each seeing things from each other's perspective. This is the basis for progressing from acknowledgement to adjustment of your respective positions—concessions—to arrival at a mutually satisfactory agreement: a 'win'–'win' as opposed to a 'win'–'lose' outcome.

Ethical, skilled negotiation is characterized by many persuasion behaviours and a few others.

- Preparing thoroughly.
- Always identity your BATNA (best alternative to a negotiated agreement)—the outcome acceptable to you in the event of not reaching agreement.
- Moral commitment:
  — to tell the truth;
  — to respect the individual as a person;
  — to respect the individual's freedom to dissent and to choose.
- Being explicit at all times.
- Keeping calm.
- Displaying patience.
- Not being rattled by time pressure.
- Engaging in Quadrant 4 behaviours:
  — engaging continuously in RESPONSE behaviours;
  — being appropriately assertive.
- Listening intently and actively.
- Engaging in SOFTENS behaviours.
- Systematically questioning and probing (see Chapter 9):
  — to understand barriers to resolution—particularly the individual's inhibitions, fears, aspirations, and his or her perceptions of constraints, available choices, and latitude to act in a given way;
  — to gauge the individual's motives, priorities, needs, interests, issues;
  — to clarify generalizations;
  — to test assumptions.
- Identifying:
  — the key issues;
  — areas of common ground.
- Probing for areas of movement—offering brief, tentative proposals.
- Resisting—or keeping to a minimum—the making of instant counter-proposals to those made by the individual.
- Rarely saying *No*.
- Regularly summarizing areas of agreement.
- Taking a break if the individual consistently rejects your proposal:
  — summarize your proposal;
  — state you will stop the interview for [duration] to allow the individual to reflect.
- Distinguishing between 'needs'—important matters, issues, or points that you cannot compromise upon—and 'interests'—where you can concede ground.
- Knowing when to compromise (agree to concede what is demanded) where necessary—but minor ones at first.
- Remembering the power of reciprocity: if you give something, the other person feels obliged to give something in return.
- Allowing the individual to save face—if necessary by making small concessions.
- Reinforcing agreement psychologically and the relationship subliminally by smiling sincerely or making an appreciative gesture.

3.7   Chapter summary

Skill in conversation management to achieve investigative goals fundamentally rests upon an intimate understanding of how conversation works. It is essential to know how we use conversation as a medium to relate: to express our thoughts, ideas, attitudes, emotions, stress and distress, and to signal relationship, whether perceived or wished for. Also, we need to be aware of how our conversational behaviour evidences our decisions in terms of controlling the exchange and whether we are concerned for the other person's perspective on what is happening. How you converse builds upon, and enhances, the impact of the first impression that you make on first meeting the other person. This greatly influences the other person and the relationship that will exist between you, and will have implications for your ability to persuade the individual, or to negotiate with him or her.

4

Telling and Listening: Disclosing and Making Sense of Disclosed Detail

4.1 Chapter overview

This chapter examines the decision-making of interviewees—the truthful, the deceptive, and those who confabulate—when asked to tell an interviewer about offence-related detail. It describes the choice an interviewer has to make when listening to the interviewee's disclosures—to pay maximum attention or to relevance filter—scanning for facts deemed to have a bearing. Knowledge of the implications of each option is vital, since the wrong choice is liable to prejudice the relationship and the investigation.

4.1.1 Chapter objectives

This chapter will enable you to:

- understand why individuals with nothing to hide follow a 'less is best' strategy for disclosing detail when interviewed;
- have a sound grasp of the different forms of anomaly that occur in people's disclosure of offence-related detail;
- understand the three ways in which individuals lie when disclosing detail and the hurdles a liar has to jump for lying to be effective;
- recognize the four forms of confabulation;
- understand the high price paid for relevance filtering when listening to an interviewee's disclosures.

4.2 Telling: how people disclose their experience

4.2.1 Pitching it appropriately

Whenever we disclose our experience to another person we devote some thought, to a greater or lesser extent, to the other person's likely interest or reaction. This thought guides our decision-making as to how we will pitch—express—our disclosure: what we will say and how we will say it. This disposition to bear in mind the other person's view goes right back to our infant days. At some point every baby makes a major psychological leap when, assisted by games such as 'peek-a-boo', it comes to realize that 'there is something going on' inside the object it is looking at. The baby works out 'what is going on' from the responses that it observes to its behaviour. It develops an awareness of *social desirability*, which behaviours evoke a favourable response and which trigger disapproval. So the baby consciously 'pitches' its behaviour to trigger an approving response.

For the rest of our lives our attention to social desirability becomes a major determinant of whatever we disclose in a conversation. Most people want the listener at the end of the encounter to emerge with a positive view of them. Very few would want a listener to feel negatively disposed towards them. People can cope with indifference, but some more so than others.

For some people, attention to social desirability is not a concern: they are indifferent to what the other person thinks of them.

- The individual may feel too busy to care.
- If emotionally burned out, the individual may not care what the other person thinks.
- Psychopaths (sociopaths) are unable to empathize and are incapable of genuinely taking into account what is 'going on inside' the other person.

4.2.2 Factors affecting how we pitch our disclosure

The difficulty of the conversation

Some conversations are particularly difficult for us and will affect how we pitch what we disclose. In Chapter 1 it was pointed out that a 'difficult conversation'[1] is one in which:

- we feel vulnerable;
- our self-esteem is implicated;
- issues important to us are at stake;
- we fear the consequences whether the issues are raised or not;
- the outcomes for us are uncertain;
- we feel, positively or negatively, about:
  — what is being discussed;
  — the person we are conversing with.

Difficult conversations occur in everyday life; people who view each other as equals or in a superior–subordinate relationship engage in disclosure that is personally exposing for either participant or both.

Many difficult conversations occur within the setting of an interview. Most people do not like being interviewed at the best of times. From Chapter 1 onwards we have recognized that it is a conversation, but it is certainly not a 'normal' conversation. It is not an exchange between equals. The person asking the questions is in charge. He or she determines the course and the content of the exchange. This role necessarily puts him or her in the 'up' position, and defines the respondent as 'down'. The respondent in this position follows the norm, first learned in question–answer exchanges with parents, and then in the classroom. When asked a question, an answer—disclosure of what is in the respondent's mind—is expected.[2]

If it is not the best of times when the question–answer exchange happens, when the implications of whatever is disclosed are extremely significant for the respondent, this conversation will be really difficult. This is the position in which the witness and the suspect find themselves.

The listener's 'reward' power

'Reward' power refers to an individual's capacity to respond to what we do in the form of approval (reward) or disapproval (punishment). This power to reward that which is perceived as appropriate, right, acceptable, or pleasing, or to punish that which is considered inappropriate, wrong, unacceptable, and displeasing is extremely potent. This leads us to think very carefully before we say anything: most especially in difficult conversations.[3]

The listener's feedback

As explained earlier, we have a lifetime's experience of monitoring a listener's response for feedback as to whether we are pitching—or have pitched—our disclosure appropriately, ie acceptably. The response can be verbal, non-verbal, or a combination of the two. In Chapter 3 the point was made that people are particularly alert to non-verbal communication,

---

[1] Stone, D., Patton, B., and Heen, S. (1999) *Difficult Conversations*. London: Penguin.

[2] Dillon, J. (1990) *The Practice of Questioning*. London: Routledge.

[3] Hargie, O. and Dickson, D. (2004) *Skilled Interpersonal Communication: Research, Theory and Practice*. London: Routledge.

the primary medium for sending messages about feelings. It follows that we are particularly sensitive to non-verbal clues that we are getting the pitch of our disclosure right or wrong. Those who are vulnerable in any way are likely to be especially anxious on this account, and to be distressed if they sense the messages say that they do not have the listener's approval.

4.2.3 'Powerful people'

Some listeners have greater power than others to reward or punish for the pitch of our disclosure. Their views of us or the decisions they make have a greater effect upon us than others'. Our conversations with them are going to be difficult because of their significance. We are extremely sensitive to their feedback.

The earliest 'powerful people' in our lives were our parents, soon followed by teachers and other non-family or relatively unfamiliar people, eg doctors. The common factor is that they engage us in 'finding out' conversation in which they question us in order to make important decisions about us and what happens to us. If an individual finds himself or herself cast in the role of witness or suspect, he or she will be having potentially difficult conversations with particularly 'powerful people'—police officers—as they seek to obtain disclosure of the individual's remembrance of case-relevant detail.

Characteristic features of 'powerful people'

Cumulatively, our experience of conversing with 'powerful people' provides us with a mental stereotype of how they behave. People anticipate such people will exhibit thoughtless Quadrant 1 conversational behaviours described in Chapter 3:

- Talking most of the time.
- Following their own agenda.
- Limiting the other person's latitude to contribute freely: making pre-emptive assertions, asking constraining questions, and 'filling pauses'—not giving the other person time to think.
- Disrupting the other person when he or she is talking by overtalking, interrupting, and rapidly changing the topic.
- Disruptively listening: not paying attention, assuming—and even telling the person—they already know the answer, and word-picking.

The right pitch for disclosing to 'powerful people'

Because we experience 'powerful people' as typically overbearing, dominant, and essentially self-centred individuals who ask questions and make us feel uncomfortable and used, at a very early age we engage in 'inner editing' and follow the 'less is best' strategy.

Inner editing

When we engage in *inner editing* we think about what we could mention and from this select that which we feel it appropriate to mention. Because people differ, there are many factors that could influence their editing decisions. Box 4.1 gives an illustrative, not exhaustive, list of potential influences. Some individuals may find it difficult to engage in inner editing because they are extremely stressed or are suffering from a clinical condition where one of their symptoms is *over-inclusive thinking*, inability to stop thinking about many things all at once.

Capacity to engage in confident conversation
- Level of self-esteem.
- Level of social skill.
- Ability to assert.

Sources of 'inner pressure'
- Situational stressors: significant life events (eg separation; bereavement; loss of job); micro-stressors (eg stressful domestic life; continuous arguments; poverty).
- Gender, eg 'gender gap'; notions of proper/improper conduct and communication for a male/female.
- Age, eg 'generation gap'; notions of age appropriate/inappropriate conduct and communication.
- Ethnicity/culture, eg proper/improper or proscribed conduct and communication.
- Motivational factors, eg interest, shame, embarrassment, guilt, resentment.
- Emotions: apprehension, fear, dread, anxiety, depression.
- Physical factors, eg exhaustion, debilitation, lack of sleep, lowered blood sugar.
- Substance dependency, eg heavy smoker needing to smoke.

Individual differences in psychological make-up
- Attention, working memory, and comprehension problems associated with:
  — developmental immaturity (young; old);
  — learning disability;
  — illiteracy;
  — long-term substance abuse, eg alcohol, cannabis;
  — medication, eg increasing distractibility as drug wears off;
  — psychological disorder, eg anxiety condition (neurosis), reactive depression; unipolar depression; bipolar depression (depression and mania); psychosis.
- Disposition, ie tendency to:
  — acquiesce (unreflectively agree);
  — comply ('go along' in order to be approved);
  — be suggestible (resolve memory distrust by accepting offered information);

Box 4.1 Potential influences upon inner editing

The 'less is best' strategy

In conversation with a 'powerful person' we put our inner editing into effect by making further decisions concerning amount of detail and the timing of disclosure. Typically, we engage in the 'less is best' strategy: not telling the 'powerful person' too much spontaneously. We reason that there is little likelihood of being perceived negatively because 'powerful people':

- already know the answer;
- are used to not being told a lot spontaneously;
- quickly take control of the talking turn;
- select the topics to be talked about, when, and in what detail;
- pose questions that narrow our response options in order to obtain endorsement of what they know or believe to be correct:
  — closed confirmatory 'yes'–'no' questions, eg *Did you…?*
  — leading questions which suggest the desired answer, eg *Didn't you…?*
  — option questions giving a choice of alternatives they deem the only alternatives.

Implementing the 'less is best' strategy when conversing with a 'powerful person' has the potential to benefit both parties.

- The 'powerful person' is happy because he or she gets the answers he or she wants.
- The 'powerful person' rewards us verbally and non-verbally for our appropriate, right, acceptable, or pleasing disclosures.
- By taking charge, the 'powerful person' reduces the likely duration of the conversation.

- Keeping spontaneous disclosure to a minimum benefits us because we render a difficult conversation less difficult.

Not everyone is disposed to engage in the 'less is best' strategy.

- Some people characteristically talk a lot. They tend to be labelled 'windbags'.
- Some find it difficult not to give, or feel impelled to give, very large amounts of detail. Their conversation is circumstantial and filled with trivia. They witter on.
- For some people, *pressure of speech*—talking rapidly and at length—is a feature of a psychological disorder, eg mania, hypomania, schizophrenia.
- Some people when intoxicated cannot stop talking.

In the vast majority of cases you can anticipate that when you interview a witness or suspect that he or she will engage in inner editing. For the remainder of this chapter the focus will therefore be upon disclosure by these key individuals and making sense of their disclosure.

4.3 Anomaly: the outcome of inner editing and following the 'less is best' strategy

When a witness or suspect engages in inner editing and follows the 'less is best' strategy, this will lead to potential anomaly in what he or she tells you. Box 4.2 shows the very wide range of anomaly that occurs in people's disclosures.

An individual may not intend to give you an inaccurate or unhelpful account or description. However, inner editing and the 'less is best strategy' have the potential to prevent you achieving your investigative objectives.

- Although wanting to be entirely genuine, the individual may deny you critical detail.
- The edited, anomalous disclosures of genuine individuals are difficult to distinguish from the edited, anomalous disclosures of those who seek to deceive.

4.4 Deceptive disclosure

4.4.1 Deception

This is the strategic intention of an individual to lie, creating in the mind of another person a false perception of reality.[4]

- **Lying is strategic.** By deceiving, the individual seeks a gain or an advantage which extends beyond the confines of the conversation.
- **Lying is intentional.** Lying is deliberate behaviour. It is not an accident.
- **A false perception.** The individual wants the other person to believe something to be the case which the deceiver knows to be untrue, inaccurate, and misleading.

4.4.2 Lying behaviour

'Lie signs': a health warning

Among the highest selling 'pop' psychology texts are those describing particular behaviours as 'lie signs'—indicators of deception. Many institutions and individuals have invested

---

[4] Ekman, P. (2001) *Telling Lies: Clues to Deceit in the Marketplace, Politics, and Marriage.* New York: Norton.

'Thin' story

The narrative lacks detail throughout. It has the character of an 'agenda', comprising a limited number of steps, with no detail given about any of the steps, or what happened between one step and the next.

Missing detail

The disclosure lacks detail on this matter.

Gaps

Between two points in the narrative it lacks one or more steps.

Jumps

- A significant gap in time, eg *I saw him at the bar around eleven last night. This morning around ten or so I heard that he'd been found dead.*
- A sudden shift in location, eg *We were fighting like cats and dogs in the kitchen. I made it up to her in the bedroom.*

Absence of reasonably expected detail: 'non-barking dog'

The individual gives no detail about an event or an issue that people in general could be reasonably expected to mention.

[Note: The term 'non-barking dog' was coined by the first author having read the story in Conan Doyle's *Memoirs of Sherlock Holmes* in which stable dogs—who characteristically bark at strangers—did not bark when a racehorse was stolen from its stable.]

Vagueness

The disclosure is general or unspecific, eg *We have problems. I had to give her a slapping.* 'Problems' and 'slapping' have multiple meanings.

Ambiguity

The detail has two meanings.

'Sidestepping'

- Use of the passive that avoids naming the doer of an action, eg *I was forced to agree; a plan was being put together.*
- Using 'not really' to avoid giving detail, eg *I couldn't really describe him.*
- Answering a question with a question, eg *Now would a respectable man like me ruin my reputation by doing such a thing?*

'Pat'

The individual's account is odd because the sequencing of detail is highly unusual.
- Events are described in chronological order with little or no narrative reversal. (Narrative reversal occurs when the order of telling is not the order in which events happened, eg *I called my Mum after I put the kids down.* It is very natural. It is highly unusual to tell a complete narrative without narrative reversal occurring.)
- Too many descriptive words precede the item described, eg *it was a small, torn, white, plastic Tesco's bag.* Usually people put no more than two descriptive words before the item, eg *a small Tesco's bag.* Often people use just one, eg *a Tesco's bag.* They describe in reverse, typically tacking on descriptive words, eg *a Tesco's bag…small…white. It was torn.*

When asked to repeat the account:
- these features occur again
- the person uses the same or very similar words and phrasing.

Inconsistency

Something said later does not 'fit' with something:
- said earlier by the individual; or
- said elsewhere by the individual or another person.

Contradiction

The individual gives more than one version.

Narrative contrast

The amount of detail for circumstances preceding and following an offence or significant event differs from the amount of detail given when describing the event. It occurs in two forms.
- There is a greater level of detail concerning circumstances preceding and following the event relative to level of detail about the event.
- There is a greater level of detail concerning the event relative to circumstances preceding and following the event.

Box 4.2 Common anomalies found in accounts and descriptions

in training in the use of techniques and technology claimed to detect 'lie signs' in a person's behaviour.

- **Non-verbal behaviour** eg change in voice, eye movements, direction of gaze, and facial movements.
- **Verbal—spoken and written—behaviour**, eg use of language; using emphatic phrases (*to be honest...*; *frankly...*; *to tell the truth...*; *on my Mother's life*); using phrases inviting support (*you know...*; *innit...*); using the passive form of verbs (*I was forced to join in*).
- **Vocal behaviour.**

There is lack of objective, empirical research evidence for 'lie signs' in the scientific literature.[5] It is therefore necessary to apply a health warning in respect of manifest behaviours purported to be 'lie signs'.

- There is no such thing as categorical lying behaviour, ie non-verbal or verbal behaviour that *always* occurs when an individual is lying.
- Non-verbal behaviours deemed to be 'lie signs' are the observable manifestation of physiological and psychological arousal. Arousal can indeed be experienced by people who are telling lies, and they manifest change in their non-verbal behaviour. However, people who are not lying but are aroused because they are experiencing stress, strong emotion, or embarrassment also exhibit the same observable behaviour.
- People who are entirely innocent use in their everyday lives the forms of verbal behaviour deemed to be 'lie signs'.

Because of these very obvious shortcomings, our criminal justice system does not accept any form of non-verbal or verbal behaviour, whether observed by a practitioner or identified by technology, as evidence or even indicative of deception. The courts require investigative interviewers to find evidence of deception within the *content* of what an individual discloses.

4.4.3 Ways of lying when disclosing

Truth and lies

Lying is rather like filling a basket with scraps of paper bearing information. Typically, the liar will put into the basket some, perhaps even many, scraps bearing truthful detail. The liar also places in the basket scraps bearing two types of deceptive information: untrue details represented as the truth, and non-specific detail. The third way in which a liar deceives is evasion: not putting particular information in the basket at all. These three forms of lying that occur in the content of accounts and responses constitute a *passive-active* dimension.

Passive lying

The individual avoids disclosing detail by simply not mentioning something. Evasion—giving less than the 'whole picture'—is the most common form of lying in everyday life and in the crime context. It offers great benefits to the liar.

- It takes little or no mental effort.
- The less the individual says, the less likely it will be that he or she will be 'caught out'.

---

[5] Vrij, A. (2008) *Detecting Lies and Deceit.* Chichester: Wiley.

- Not saying something induces no inner (psychological) pressure or much less than when 'making something up'.
- Because there is little or no inner pressure, the risk of manifesting non-verbal behaviour indicative of stress is relatively low.

There are potential clues to the individual evading and thus only giving 'half the picture'.

- **Anomalous lack of detail.** 'Thin' account; significant missing detail; significant gaps; significant jumps; 'non-barking dogs'; 'sidestepping'.
- **Answering a question with a question.**
  — To block a line of questioning, eg Interviewer: *Could you tell me why you kept the Rolex having found it on the floor in Tesco's?* Interviewee: *Why would a man of my standing steal a watch?*
  — To narrow the focus of questioning, eg Interviewer: *So what did he look like?* Interviewee: *What you mean?* Interviewer: *A description.* Interviewee: *What of?* Interviewer: *What he was wearing.*
- **Attempting to change the topic.** Interviewee: *Rather than asking me about* [Topic A] *you should be asking me about* [Topic B]; Interviewee: *I tell you what I can say and that is* [discloses on a completely different issue].
- **Referring to someone else to answer**, eg Interviewee: *Look I'm not your man for that kind of detail. You need to speak to* [name of person].
- **Measured, evasive responses ('reeling out bus tickets')**, eg Interviewer: *Could you describe the bag?* Interviewee: *It was black.* Interviewer: *And...* Interviewee: *Leather.* Interviewer: *Anything else?* Interviewee: *Medium-sized.* And so on...
- **'Blanking' an echo probe**, eg Interviewee: *He got up and hit me.* Interviewer: *Hit you?* Interviewee: *Yeah.* (Interviewee remains silent, gazing at interviewer, indicating that he or she has relinquished the talking turn.)

In Chapter 1 it was pointed out that those who have the mindset of defensive avoidance and engage in the traditional approach to statement taking are concerned with relevance filtering, editing, and compressing what the individual says. Because interviewers focus on what the individual says, they never register what he or she did not say—potential clues to deception.

'Half-way house'

Being non-specific—vague or ambiguous—is a very common way of lying because it has several benefits.

- It takes some but not a lot of mental effort.
- Listeners make assumptions about non-specific detail. They jump to an unfounded conclusion that they know what the individual means by his or her vague or ambiguous word or phrase.
- Like evasion, it induces little or no inner pressure: the risk of exhibiting non-verbal behaviour indicative of stress is similarly low.

When the interviewee says something non-specifically and this is detected (something that may well not happen), it saves time and effort for the interviewer:

- to jump to the conclusion—assume—that he or she knows what the interviewee means, especially if this confirms what the interviewer knows or believes;
- to not bother probing—requesting an expansion or explanation—now or later.

Very little of the totality of vagueness and ambiguity in accounts and responses is ever noted or probed.

Active lying

Active lying—presenting real lies, ie untruths as the truth—constitutes the smallest part of lying. There are sound reasons for this.

- It takes mental effort to construct a real lie.
- For many, but by no means all, people constructing and telling real lies induces inner pressure, potentially observable as a change in non-verbal behaviour.

A number of anomalies are likely to occur when an individual is actively lying.

- **'Thin' account.**
- **Narrative contrast.**
- **'Pat' account.** Potentially indicated by lack of narrative reversal and too many descriptors preceding the item described.
- **Inconsistency.**
- **Contradiction.**
- **'Matter of fact' manner.** The absence of any strength of feeling, eg outrage, indignation, or distress at what was happening, when disclosing on subject matter that could be expected to occasion a strong reaction. (Note: 'Matter of fact' manner is qualitatively different behaviour to that of a person who has been emotionally traumatized and numbed by his or her experience.)
- **Few or imprecise illustrators.** As explained in Chapter 3, we use movements with our hands or fingers to describe visually:
  — an image of what we experienced, eg a shape, trajectory, route travelled, location, layout, relative positions;
  — rhythm/tempo.

Illustrators have the effect of validating what is being described verbally, ie they provide a realistic, relatively precise non-verbal representation. If the individual is asked to illustrate with his or her finger or hand particular detail, eg relative positions or a route taken, and simply lifts and makes gross generalized movements, this is a warning bell. It is likely that this individual has no idea of what he is attempting to illustrate with his or her hands.

4.4.4 Hurdles to effective lying

To be effective in the task of creating a false perception of reality, a liar has to negotiate four hurdles.

First hurdle

This is a motivational hurdle. The would-be deceiver has to anticipate being questioned at some point and feel moved to make the mental effort to prepare in advance.

Most would-be liars clear this hurdle.

Second hurdle

The individual has to create a *story line*. This is a sequence of events rather like a script in a play. Typically, a liar's story line will comprise only a limited number of events. This reduces that mental demand involved in constructing and memorizing the story line. However, the nature of the offence will often dictate the complexity of the individual's story line. Hence a fraudster, paedophile, or a perpetrator of serious, serial offences is likely to construct a detailed story line.

Another strategy used by would-be liars is to transpose the detail of a corresponding period from another day and represent this as what happened on the day the offending took place. Because the transposed detail did take place, this makes it easier to give a relatively detailed account. However, the would-be liar still has to construct a script to accommodate the 'joins', ie the transition between the events that took place on the day of the offending and the start and end points of the transposed account of what happened on another day. These are the weakest points in the deceptive narrative, potentially detectable as narrative contrast.

Whatever their strategy, most would-be liars clear this second hurdle.

Third hurdle

Having given his or her story line, the individual has to cope with being probed about this. Interviewers typically ask for expansion or explanation of the account or topics selected by the interviewer. This forces the individual to improvise: rapidly constructing 'on the hoof' untruths in working memory and representing these as true detail.

Extempore lying is very difficult. The mental (cognitive) demand to generate spontaneous detail that flows, and appears coherent and plausible, is extremely great. A significant proportion of would-be liars struggle to negotiate this hurdle.

Fourth hurdle

The individual knows that he or she must not give contradictory or inconsistent responses. He or she has to remember all that he or she has said, extending from the detail of his or her first account right through to the latest 'on the hoof' construction in working memory. This is extremely difficult. Most people do not have the working memory capacity to devote to the dual tasks of:

- improvising new untruths;
- retaining what they just said before this latest creation, what they said before that, and before that, right back to the beginning of the exchange.

The mental demands are extreme at this stage. Many would-be liars fall at this hurdle, but many more do not because interviewers help them to succeed in their lies.

4.4.5 How interviewers help a liar to succeed

An interviewer can help a liar to succeed in his or her lies.

- The interviewer must make clear the 'contract' to disclose in detail: *tell me everything you can; there can't be too much detail; take your time, there's no rush; taking your time will help you to remember the detail we need*. This contract:
  — makes it clear that the 'less is best' rule does not apply in this conversation;
  — liberates a truthful witness or suspect to disclose in detail;
  — puts the would-be liar under tremendous pressure to go beyond his or her story line (script). Failure to spell out the contract relieves the stress on the would-be liar.
- The interviewer only registers some of the detail within the scraps of information placed in the basket.
- To continue with analogy of the basket, the interviewer fails to remember all of the scraps of paper that the liar placed in the basket—especially those the individual produced rapidly when probed for additional detail.

- The interviewer fails to make appropriate sense of, and fails to probe exhaustively, two key aspects of the liar's disclosures.
  - **What the liar says.** The anomalous detail within the scraps of information placed in the basket indicative of non-specificity (half-way house) or untruths represented as the truth (active lying).
  - **What the liar does *not* say.** Detail that is anomalous because it has not been stated at all (evasion).
- If the interviewer dominates the talking turn and the talking time, there is no pressure at all on the interviewee, who merely sits and listens to the interviewer.
- As observed earlier, the interviewer responds inappropriately to missing detail and vagueness by relying on assumptions, prior knowledge, and preconception:
  - to fill missing detail;
  - to interpret what the individual meant by a particular non-specific usage.
- The interviewer responds inappropriately to 'sidestepping' by changing the topic rather than instructing the individual to take his or her time because there is no rush.

4.4.6 Confabulation

The term *confabulation* comes in the Latin word *fabula* meaning 'tale'. A person confabulates when he or she discloses something that is not true but does not fit completely within the definition of a lie. Confabulation may be:

- imagined detail;
- an assertion which is not true made to create a favourable impression and to gain respect.

'Filling in gaps' in experience

The interviewee may be unable to recall 'what happened' or to describe something. For some reason he or she did not register the details, has forgotten them, or is now unable to retrieve them. The individual brings his or her imagination to bear in order to 'fill in the gaps'.

Quite normal people confabulate in this way. For example, you may not remember what you did between waking up and having lunch last Wednesday. You will do your best to remember, but at some point you will resort to your normal routine, the script (stereotyped action sequence) that you follow on weekdays or on Wednesdays, and fill in the gaps by giving this script detail. You might give an indication that you are doing this by saying something like *I must have...* or *I would have...*

Witnesses and suspects are likely to do the same. For example, a man arrested for causing death by dangerous driving, having pulled out of T-junction without apparently stopping, may not remember actions performed without thought. He may fill in the gaps in his experience by stating the script to be followed at T-junctions: *I would have stopped at the line...looked right...looked left...must have looked right again...and pulled out...and the guy just appeared and ran into me.*

Particular individuals are prone to fill in the gaps in their experience.

- **Anyone emerging from an extended period of coma (unconsciousness) following a traumatic head injury or physical assault.** The individual will have *anterograde amnesia*, inability to remember what happened in the period, perhaps for an extended period, prior to losing consciousness.

- **The developmentally immature (eg young children) and people with learning difficulties.** Such individuals are entirely able to give an accurate account. However, they are prone to confabulate if asked to give details that they cannot remember.
- **People with particular organic conditions.** For example, individuals who are suffering from any kind of dementia, brain damage arising from substance abuse, eg alcohol.
- **Pathological (compulsive) liars.** Such individuals are serial confabulators.

'Talking for effect'

This is also known as *blather*. Here the individual says things which may be imagined or not true in order to create an impression of being on relatively equal terms with whoever is asking him or her questions. It is very common amongst individuals—particularly young males—who:

- have a learning difficulty;
- are illiterate;
- have low self-esteem;
- are sensitive to their limitations and are blathering to hide these.

'Bullshitting'

Every reader of this text will have come into contact sometime with 'bullshitters'. Such individuals construct florid, grandiose accounts of their experiences, their deeds, their descriptions of themselves, in order to attract attention, gain a reputation, and command respect.

'Gilding the lily'

This refers to overstating particular detail, eg the individual gives an overblown description of what happened or his or her involvement. (In the police service there is a phrase that describes officers who do this: 'talking a good job'.)

4.5   Making sense of disclosed detail

4.5.1   The magic carpet

The individual presents you with a stream of visual information and auditory information—utterances spoken in the case of an average adult at about 180–220 words per minute. It is rather like a magic carpet of words and deeds that he or she is rolling out in front of you to examine (Figure 4.1). The interviewee weaves different kinds of detail into the carpet.

- **Background detail.** This includes information about people, places, locations, objects, routines, rituals, plans, intentions, and much more.
- **Narrative detail.** This is information concerning:
  — *events*: comprising actions, reactions, conversation, thoughts, decisions;
  — *episodes*: pieces of extended action, eg *Anna and Eric went shopping in Reading*. During this episode events will have taken place. If these events are not spontaneously mentioned the episode will need to be probed subsequently.
  — *continuous states*: a physical or mental state of affairs that continued to exist though the duration might not be stated, eg scene of accident—*a dead man was hanging from the car; dead man face down on ground in pool of blood beside driver's door*; interviewee's mental state—*I was out of it—unconscious*.

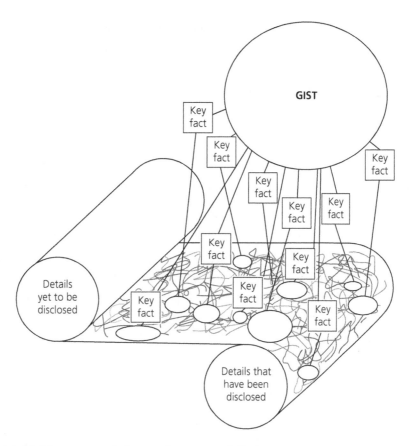

Figure 4.1 Making sense of the magic carpet of disclosure

- **Commentary**. These are observations that the individual makes about particular subject matter or the process of disclosing, eg *I'm finding it difficult to tell you about this bit.*

It is a magic carpet because the maker can overlay the existing material by weaving further material into it at any time.

You make sense of the material woven into magic carpet by using the same mental processes as a witness or suspect does when confronted with offence-related detail. Central to everything is your frame of reference (FOR) comprising:

- your knowledge of the case and this individual;
- your fund of 'general knowledge' (stereotype and script knowledge derived through experience);
- your hopes and aspirations;
- what you want to happen and to achieve.

Your FOR guides your attention, perception, and how you handle material in working memory. The auditory and visual information from the interviewee initially enters your immediate (sensory, or buffer) memory. You edit material that gets into your working memory:

- scanning for *key facts*;
- making the memory task easier by:
  — deleting the seemingly irrelevant;
  — compressing incidents with two or more events into an episode (a less specific notion);
- drawing conclusions: inferences and assumptions;
- gaining a 'gist'—overall—understanding of what the individual has disclosed.

What distinguishes the FOR of an effective investigative interviewer from that of an ineffective interviewer is commitment to pay maximum attention to detail.

4.5.2 Vigilance to detail

The genuine individual will have perceived from your Quadrant 4 assertive-empathetic management of the exchange thus far that:

- you are not the typical 'powerful person';
- this is a conversation in which the individual should not follow the 'less is best' strategy.

For the genuine individual, disclosing in detail will not be a problem. It will be for the would-be liar who is 'caught between a rock and a hard place':

- how to evade as much as possible and to be as non-specific as possible;
- how to deliver on the Expectations spelled out at the beginning of the interview ('it's all about detail', 'as much as possible', 'there can't be too much detail', 'take your time', 'there is no rush', 'think before you say something', 'think afterwards'): Expectations that the individual confirmed he or she understood, and in doing so 'signed up' to disclose in detail.

The requirement to listen and to look

It makes no sense to create the conditions for the interviewee to engage in maximum disclosure of detail if you do not pay maximum attention to the disclosed detail and the full range of behaviour—verbal and non-verbal—that occurs when this happens. It demands a lot.

- **Listening intently to the fine-grain detail (FGD) of the interviewee's disclosures**. This enables you to gain the fullest possible grasp of what the interviewee says, says non-specifically, or doesn't say at all.
- **Observing systematically the interviewee's non-verbal behaviour**. By continuously visually monitoring and actively listening to tone of voice and other vocal clues, you will be able to pick up clues to the individual's:
  — mood;
  — emotional state;
  — perceptions of you, the interview, and what is happening;
  — experience of increased physiological or psychological arousal: manifested as a 'hot spot' potentially linked to a particular topic.

Adopting this approach to detail is not easy. It requires the development of a good memory capacity as well as listening and observation skills. All these can be achieved using practical tools and established and maintained through practice. In Chapter 7 (Active Listening, Observing, and Assessing) we introduce you to BASELINES. This is a tool for monitoring behaviour and which we describe in more detail in the Reference Section.

The greatest barriers to paying maximum attention to the detail of an individual's account are motivational. It requires more effort and takes more time than the traditional inappropriate approach to making sense of disclosure: relevance filtering, editing, and compressing.

The traditional inappropriate response to the interviewee's disclosures

The interviewer may have managed the conversation in an appropriately assertive-empathetic (Quadrant 4) manner to set the interviewee up to disclose in detail. However, if the interviewer's response to the interviewee's disclosures is self-centred (Quadrant 1)—with behaviours evidencing that he or she is not disposed to pay attention and only wants confirmation of what he or she already 'knew'—this will rebound.

- The genuine interviewee who opened up initially, disclosing in relatively full detail, will:
  - — conclude that the interviewer has an 'agenda' in mind;
  - — revert to a 'less is best' strategy: not bothering to waste time and effort giving detail, enabling the process to end sooner.
- The liar will be thankful. Here is just the type of interviewer he or she wants:
  - — who does not pay attention to detail;
  - — who fails to register when the liar evades or says something non-specifically;
  - — who makes assumptions and draws unfounded conclusions that benefit the liar;
  - — who asks closed 'yes'–'no', leading, and option questions that are easy to answer: no mental effort is required to improvise untruthful detail.

4.6 Chapter summary

Interviewees' experience of 'powerful people' disposes them to say not a lot initially and to cope with inappropriate questions by giving no more detail than is necessary. Those who seek to deceive follow the same 'less is best' strategy: just not saying something, being non-specific, and giving thin, easily remembered, untruthful accounts and responses. Selective attention, relevance filtering, and desire for confirmation of what one knows—or believes—to be case constitute the mindset of many 'powerful people'. We all pay a high price for investigative interviewers who think this way. Much of the limited disclosure of interviewees goes unheeded or unremembered. Anomaly and potential clues to deception go undetected. Interviewees' accounts are neither fully nor faithfully represented. Information critical to the investigation is lost—in the case of interviews that are not electronically recorded—forever.

5

RESPONSE: Mindful Behaviours for Relationship Building

5.1 Chapter overview

This chapter examines in detail RESPONSE—the acronym of mindful conversational behaviours aimed at creating the basis of a working relationship with a witness, suspect and other key individuals.

5.1.1 Chapter objectives

This chapter will enable you to:

- understand each RESPONSE behaviour;
- appreciate the impact of RESPONSE behaviours upon the person with whom you are conversing.

5.2 RESPONSE behaviours: an overview

RESPONSE behaviours were briefly introduced in Chapter 1. They are a set of behaviours that are consistent with Quadrant 4 conversational behaviour, ie assertive-empathic, described in Chapter 3.

5.3 Respect

This is the fundamental behaviour from which all other RESPONSE behaviours emerge. It has three elements:

We are very sensitive to the issue of dignity, ie being worthy of respect and treatment as a fellow human being. In the case of interviewees, particularly suspects, you must communicate that:

- you have genuine respect for him or her as a person;
- your respect is unconditional, ie irrespective of the individual's status, or his or her actual or alleged behaviour and actions.

Being respectful is easily urged but sometimes hard to deliver on. Professionals who deal with humanity in less than pleasant circumstances are at risk of being adversely affected by their experience, becoming cynical and emotionally 'burned out', of depersonalizing the people they have to deal with.[1] They find it difficult to view some categories of people as worthy of respect, eg suspects with a history of violence, abuse, cheating, or anti-social behaviour; complainants who have put themselves and others at risk or have behaved irresponsibly. Such individuals are seen as an instance of a problem, an 'it'.[2] No one denies that experience can have this effect. However, one of the defining properties of professionalism when dealing with human beings is never to treat any of them as an 'it' and never to justify depersonalizing them by saying 'I'm only doing my job', or 'I haven't got time to do my job properly or to treat them properly'. The reason is simple. When that happens you yourself have ceased to be a person and become an 'it' dealing with an 'it'.

---

[1] Shepherd, E. (1982) 'Coping with the First Person Singular' in E. Shepherd and J. Watson (eds), *Personal Meanings*. Chichester: Wiley.

[2] Shepherd, E. (1993) 'Ethical Interviewing' in E. Shepherd (ed.), *Aspects of Police Interviewing Issues in Criminological and Legal Psychology, No 18*. Leicester: British Psychological Society.

Being a professional who has to interview less than attractive humanity regarding unpleasant circumstances requires reflection in the manner recommended at the end of Chapter 3. As a reflective practitioner, you should continuously remind yourself of two things.

- Everyone—even those that could be considered the very least in our society—warrants the same respect as you, or anyone known, or close, to you and who could find themselves at some time in a similar position.
- By being respectful to a less than pleasant suspect or a less than responsible witness does not mean that you are condoning the person's behaviour.

Respect is communicated in several ways.

5.3.1 Good manners

You should remain courteous at all times. There is no excuse for being ill-mannered.

5.3.2 Warmth

You should maintain an air of warmth—pleasantness—without attempting to be too amiable (friendly). You have to strike a fine balance between formality and friendship. The relationship loop on initial meeting (described in Chapter 3) sensibly signals warmth by:

- using the *consultative* form of self-address (eg *I'm Andy Griffiths from the Control Audit Team*);
- checking the individual's name (eg *Am I speaking to Dr Leggett?*);
- listening to the response and asking how the interviewee would like to be called (eg *How would you like me to call you?*);
- echoing back immediately the individual's preference, stating yours, and then moving seamlessly to what you need to say (eg *Dr Leggett I'm happy for you to call me Andy. Let me explain...*).

In the case of a vulnerable interviewee, eg someone who is very young, immature, or distressed, a greater degree of warmth (informality) is appropriate and helpful.

5.3.3 Sincerity

Sincerity is absence of pretence. People have a 'nose' for sincerity and quickly detect its absence. Children and individuals with learning disabilities or communication disorders are particularly adept at sensing insincerity. So be absolutely sincere at all times. If you fail in this you will fall in the estimation of the interviewee and any others involved in the interviewing process, eg legal adviser or appropriate adult.

Again, form of address matters here. In Chapter 3 it was pointed out that if the interviewee has requested that you use a less formal form of address when speaking to him or her, you must stick with this. If at a later point in the interview, eg when the interviewee has said things that do not match what you know or believe, you start using a more formal form of address, this will rebound. The interviewee will draw the conclusion that:

- you were being manipulative when referring to him or her less formally up to this point;
- you are addressing him or her more formally to put more 'distance' between you because you find what he or she has said as unacceptable.

5.3.4 **Being attentive**

You have to respect the detail of what the person is disclosing. This means making the effort to pay attention and not to listen randomly ('tuning out'–'tuning in') or selectively. You communicate attentiveness this by:

- engaging in SOFTENS behaviours (Box 5.1);
- verbal echoing, making statements, and asking questions—the content of which evidence you really have been listening.

S	Signs of sincerity	• A smile shows that you are receptive and open. • An appropriate facial expression shows that you understand the other's situation, eg looking concerned.
O	Open posture	• Keeping your hands away from your mouth and your arms uncrossed. • If seated, sitting comfortably (*not* slouching) rather than 'to attention'. • Works best if you are at the appropriate distance from each other: — sharing each other's *personal space* (3–4 feet between you) if standing; — if sitting, 3–4 feet between the middle of your shins and the middle of other person's shins. • [Note: You should not be in each other's *intimate space* or be too far away in *social space*.] • You should be appropriately orientated, particularly if sitting, ie chairs placed at 'ten-to-two on the clock face' angle (a little more than 90 degrees) rather than face-to-face, which some might feel was being 'pushy' or confrontational.
F	Forward lean	• Leaning slightly forward signals you are interested, listening, and want the person to keep talking. • Leaning slightly further forward at critical points signals empathy, eg when the other person discloses feelings.
T	Touch	• Shaking hands on meeting and departing. • Symbolic touching, ie raising your hand and touching the individual's shoulder in the visible profile that you have of the individual in your field of vision. • [Note: *Not* physical touch: this could be taken as inappropriate, unwanted touching and lead to a complaint or allegation.]
E	Eye-contact	• Look straight at the other person. • Maintain maximum eye-contact: but don't stare! • Sends the message that: • *I am listening.* • *I am paying attention.* • *I am interested.* • The other person should carry on talking.
N	Nods	• 'Guggling' at the key ideas that the individual stresses in his or her utterances sends the message that: • you are following what is being said; • you understand what is being said/the individual's position.
S	Supportive sounds and silence	• Helping the individual to talk—and keep talking—by: • saying supportive words, eg *I realize it's difficult* ^^ ^^; • making supportive noises, eg *Uh-huh.* ^^ ^^; • just listening rather than talking—creating a long pause, ie silence.

Box 5.1 SOFTENS: key conversation fostering behaviours

5.4   Empathy

Often the notions of *empathy* and *sympathy* are confused. Together with the word *apathy* they come from the Greek word *pathos*—feeling—and form a dimension.

- **Sympathy**. Human beings feel sympathy for the other person when they have had the same or similar experience, eg if they have been bereaved then they know the pain and difficulties involved.
- **Apathy**. This is being completely insensitive to whatever the person is, or could be, feeling.
- **Empathy**. This is midway between sympathy and apathy. When you empathize, you view things from the other person's perspective, bearing in mind:
  — how the individual is likely to be viewing circumstances;
  — what sense he or she is making of what has happened and is happening;
  — how he or she is probably or possibly feeling in all senses of the word;
  — the decisions and actions that he or she could be considering.

The 'problem' that you and the interviewee share is the difficult conversation that you must have. It is difficult for you. It is difficult for him or her. Empathizing is 'getting round to the other side of the circle' to look at the 'problem' from the other side. (Figure 5.1).

Making the effort to understand and bear in mind the individual's likely perspective on the investigation or the matter under question is a mental act and requires motivation. You have to make the continuous effort to keep unfailingly in mind the other person's perspective. Empathy is surprisingly difficult to achieve. We all have a strong tendency to advise, tell, agree, or disagree from our own point of view.

Empathetic people foster more disclosure. This is why empathy is a professional requirement. It is perfectly acceptable to feel sympathy, but it is important not to allow sympathy to take charge. The risk is of over-identifying with the individual, allowing strong feelings to influence your behaviour and cloud your judgement.

5.4.1   Knowledge of the individual

The greater your knowledge of the individual the greater your potential to get round to his or her side of the circle. This is why the conversation management approach to interviewing puts such emphasis upon researching the individual prior to the interview, in the

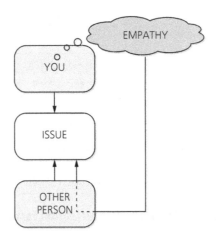

Figure 5.1 Empathy: 'getting round to the other side of the circle'

planning and preparation stage, the individual's personal attributes, background, well-being, and actual or potential vulnerabilities.

5.4.2 Expressing empathy

The entire range of SOFTENS behaviours signals empathy. It is essential to make particular well-chosen and sincere 'humanity' remarks, eg to a suspect *I realize you've been in detention a long time* ^^ ^^; to a witness or a parent acting as an appropriate adult, *I can understand if you feel a bit overwhelmed.* ^^ ^^ *I appreciate it's difficult.* ^^ ^^ *I know that it must be painful.* ^^ ^^

5.4.3 Explaining

In the brief description in Chapter 1 of the origins of the conversation management approach, it was pointed out that explanation pays a vital part in creating the working relationship. An empathetic interviewer knows that:

- interviewees are typically apprehensive, anxious, or fearful about what will happen in the interview;
- interviewees engage in the 'guessing game', trying to work out:
  — what are the interviewer's intentions;
  — what he or she will ask about;
  — the interviewer's expectations of the interviewee in the interview.
- the emotions aroused and the mental effort involved in the 'guessing game' are obstacles to spontaneous disclosure.

The word explanation comes from the Latin *explanare* 'to make plain'. It is a core skill in communicating, yet many 'powerful people', including interviewers, tend to neglect this essential task.[3] The health professions place major emphasis in training and in the workplace on the necessity to develop, and to apply continuously, the skill of explaining. The origins of conversation management are within this context, particularly the necessity to explain to someone confronted with a 'difficult conversation'.

A continuous commitment

PEACE follows the original GEMAC script in specifying a distinct stage for Explanation at the outset of the interview. It is important, however, to remember that explanation does not end at this point. Explanation is a commitment that extends across the entire interview.

- Whenever your sense of empathy tells you that whatever you are about to say, ask, request, or do needs to be made plain—explain.
- Whenever the interviewee or a third party asks you to make something plain, recognize this as feedback.

Sensibly checking comprehension

When you explain something never check comprehension by asking a closed confirmatory 'yes'–'no' question, eg *Do you understand that?* People will almost invariably say 'yes' even if they do not understand. The motivation for saying 'yes' in these circumstances can be varied.

---

[3] Hargie, O. and Dickson, D. (2004) *Skilled Interpersonal Communication: Research, Theory and Practice.* London: Routledge.

- The individual does not want to appear stupid. It is important to know that people who have learning disability know that they have such a disability and some will go to great lengths to disguise their problem.
- The individual does not want to take more of your time.
- The individual wants to get the interview over and done with as quickly as possible.
- The individual wants to please by appearing co-operative.

The only sensible way to check comprehension is to ask the individual to tell you his or her understanding, eg *It's important you understand what I've just said.* ^^ ^^ *So I need to check with you Noelle that I've made things clear.* ^^ ^^ *Tell me what you understand when I say 'There can't be too much detail'.* ^^ ^^

If the individual's explanation does not capture the key ingredients of what you were saying then repeat your explanation—and check back again in the appropriate way.

5.5 Supportiveness

It makes sense to engage in behaviours that help, sustain, encourage, or reassure the interviewee with a view to making disclosure of detail less difficult, if not less painful, for the interviewee.

5.5.1 Creating 'space' to talk

There is a saying in counselling and psychotherapy that is equally applicable to any investigative interview: when you are talking you are learning nothing. The brief description in Chapter 1 of the GEMAC model of investigative interviewing indicated the requirement, without creating the impression of submissiveness, to let the interviewee do most of the talking—some 80 per cent across the entire interview.

By occupying the listening turn for the greater part of the interview, you are also being respectful: respecting what the interviewee has to say. This distribution of access to the talking turn is achieved by observing the final element of SOFTENS behaviours—creating a longer pause. Simply saying nothing signals that you are comfortable with having the listening turn: if the individual has not spoken the talking turn is his or hers; if the individual has stopped talking momentarily, he or she can continue with the talking turn.

5.5.2 Supportive remarks

Again SOFTENS behaviours apply, particularly when you make remarks that reinforce (reward) the interviewee for engaging in the conversation.

Reward for participation

Given that this is a 'difficult conversation' for the interviewee, you should always reward for participation, eg *Trying to remember detail is always difficult* ^^ ^^ *and I can see you're trying hard.* ^^ ^^

Beware the use of approving remarks

If you respond by saying *Right* or a similar approving remark more than once in reply (*Right...right; Good...really good*), and you do this several times across the interview, whether or not you look approvingly when you do so, the risk is that you could shape—influence—the content of what the interviewee says. The interviewee might:

- think that your remarks mean that what he or she saying is 'correct': the kind of information you want to hear;
- say things to gain your approval which may not be the case, ie confabulate.

Compliant and suggestible interviewees are particularly vulnerable to approving remarks. You should make a point of never using such approving remarks when interviewing vulnerable individuals, eg the young, those with learning difficulties.

Excessive reinforcing

There can be too much of a good thing. If you reward the interviewee for almost every effort this:

- will diminish the impact of what you say;
- could come across as over-solicitous, gushing or, worse, insincere.

5.5.3 Take the pressure off

At the outset of the interview in the Explanation stage you spell out within the Expectations that:

- the interviewee should take his or her time—there is no rush, 'it isn't a race';
- taking time gives the interviewee plenty of time to think;
- you will give the interviewee plenty of time to think after you have mentioned or asked something, or the interviewee has said something.

Across the course of the interview you will need to restate these Expectations as appropriate, whenever the interviewee's behaviour indicates that he or she is struggling, eg *I'm finding it difficult to talk about the next bit*; frowning; glistening around eyes; tears; overt signs of distress.

If the interviewee becomes extremely distressed, rendering conversation impossible, you should:

- stop the interview for a moment to create a break for the interviewee to regain composure;
- if composure is not regained, the interviewee becomes incoherent, or both, you should end the interview completely.

5.5.4 Assist recall

Where applicable and appropriate, you should assist the interviewee's remembrance using the techniques described in detail in Chapter 10.

5.5.5 Give the individual non-verbal tools for describing experience

Some experience is very difficult to describe in words. You can help the individual to overcome verbal limitations by asking him or her to use the non-verbal techniques of:

- illustrators—finger and hand movements drawing something in space;
- enactment;
- drawing.

These techniques are described in Chapter 9, and detailed guidance on each technique is given in the Reference Section. The benefit of these techniques is that they very often trigger the individual to describe things verbally, something which was difficult if not impossible before engaging in the task.

5.6 Positiveness

Any interviewee expects to be guided in an interview and would be surprised by the absence of guidance across the course of the encounter. Interviewees expect the 'questioner' to be decisive: they understandably balk at being dominated.

In the conversation management approach to interviewing you are in effect both facilitator and gatekeeper of the interviewee's disclosures. It is of course a balancing act. Your facilitator role requires you to enable the interviewee to do most of the talking, being supportive in the ways described earlier. But you cannot abdicate—or surrender to the interviewee—the course and the content of the interview, ie allowing the interviewee to have complete control over what he or she says, when he or she decides to say it, and in what level of detail. You still have to exercise your gatekeeper role but you need to do this sensibly, sensitively, and skilfully.

5.6.1 Politeness

Balancing the two roles of facilitator and gatekeeper is not easy. When you switch, however fleetingly, into your gatekeeper role to guide the interview to achieving your aims and objectives, this demands politeness. It needs to be the right kind of politeness.

Solidarity politeness

You are of course required to engage in *solidarity politeness*: to be courteous and empathetic, eg *I know it's difficult* ^^ ^^ *and will not be easy for you to tell me.* ^^ ^^. Being polite in this manner lays down the groundwork for stating what is needed.

Deferential politeness

You must never be *deferentially polite*: subordinating your interview goals in order not to alienate, offend, upset, or distress the interviewee.

- Never give the individual the 'way out' should he or she not feel inclined to disclose on something, eg *You don't have to answer this if you don't want to.* ^^ ^^; *You may not be able to help me on this.* ^^ ^^
- Never apologise for mentioning, or questioning upon, an issue.

If you were deferentially polite in this manner it would not be an interview, ie a conversation with a purpose. Rather, you would be engaging in a conversation in which you were following wherever the individual decided to lead you. The interviewee, or any third party eg legal adviser, will quickly interpret deferential politeness as you not being in control because you are unsure, inexpert, or lack experience.

5.6.2 Techniques to help you be positive

Prior to the interview

In many instances you will have to deal with key third parties who will be fulfilling a particular role in the interview, eg the legal adviser, appropriate adult, interpreter, intermediary.

Prior to the interview, they need to be briefed in a positive, businesslike manner, telling them how you wish to conduct the interview. For example, if you are aware that the witness or suspect has not slept throughout the night before the interview, you will need to tell the requisite third party of your intention to keep the pace of the interview right down for the interviewee's benefit.

During the interview

The important issue is that you leave the interviewee in no doubt that you will be managing the conversation. You do this initially in the Explanation. Elements of this constitute devices that you can use to exercise control later.

- **The Route Map.** This not only overcomes the 'guessing game' but it makes quite clear to the interviewee what topics you wish to cover. If necessary, you can later draw his or her attention to a topic if this is not being addressed or disclosures go off course.
- **The Expectations.** The 'contract' is clear: what is expected of the interviewee, each ground rule being checked back with the individual and, where applicable, also with the third party. If the interviewee, or third party, does not observe the ground rule later in the interview, you can remind him or her about it, where necessary re-stating it and requesting a check back on comprehension.

In the case of a witness, and particular types of witness, the briefing will have different contents and format, but nonetheless the process of briefing signals that you are managing the interview—not the interviewee or any third party present.

There will always be occasions when the interviewee, or a third party, will behave inappropriately. This will often occur when you are requesting more detail, which necessarily will be sensed as pressuring. Furthermore, many people are unaware of their inappropriate, disruptive conversational behaviour, ie they unthinkingly overtalk, interrupt, rapidly change the topic, or don't listen to what has been said to them. Some people will attempt to sabotage your efforts to cover particular matters.

In all instances, you have to give the individual lots of 'rope' before giving corrective feedback using a technique called DEAL. This involves describing the inappropriate behaviour, explaining its effects, and spelling out the action required to solve the problem, and, as a last resort, stating the likely consequences. The technique is described in more detail in Chapter 11 (Responding to Inappropriate or Disruptive Behaviour and to Resistance).

Giving feedback in this manner will not produce an instant change in behaviour. You will have to repeat feedback for it to work.

5.7 Openness

Openness has to do with frankness and sincerity. You have to be honest and truthful in your dealings with the interviewee or any third party, eg legal adviser or appropriate adult, prior to, during, and at all times after the interview. This is logical. You are building up a reputation for being trustworthy. Put another way, you are building up a 'bank account' of trust on which you may well need to draw at some later time in this interview or at a later stage.

Chapter 16 gives specific guidance on the issue of openness when relating to the legal adviser.

5.7.1 Lack of knowledge of essential case information

It is still the case that many investigators interview without any knowledge of essential case information, eg they have no idea of the crime scene, other key locations, or where the suspect was arrested; they have not examined the scene; they have not viewed CCTV evidence. It is common practice for officers to bluff it out. This is a high-risk strategy that you should not embark on.

It becomes increasingly difficult to handle and to cope with an account or responses which bear upon matters that you know nothing about. It will become increasingly obvious to the interviewee or a third party that you have no idea about what is being referred to by the interviewee. When this happens, in addition to your trustworthiness, there is another casualty—your credibility.

If you have not had time to obtain the information during your planning and preparation prior to interview, you should turn your lack of knowledge to your advantage.

- Be open about the fact that you do not have the information, eg *I have not been to where it happened ^^ ^^ so I need you to describe it to me.*
- After obtaining a verbal description, ask the individual at an appropriate time to use one or more of the techniques described previously which make it easier to describe experience non-verbally.

5.7.2 Not understanding or not knowing disclosed detail

If you do not understand what the interviewee is saying or have no knowledge of detail mentioned by the interviewee, it is again a high-risk strategy to continue in the hope that things will 'fall into place'. As with ignorance of essential case information, should you be found out your trustworthiness and credibility will suffer. It is better to make a note—either mentally or jotted down—of what you do not understand or you do not know, and at an appropriate moment be open and resolve your ignorance: probe the interviewee about this matter.

5.8 Non-judgemental stance

From your involvement in the case and what you have learned additionally during your planning and preparation, you will have substantial case knowledge. Every bit of this knowledge comprises a preconception. In addition, like any human being, you may have a particular prejudice or prejudices concerning this type of offence and this type of offender. You might feel strongly about the circumstances of this particular offence, the victim and what has happened to the victim, and the suspect's behaviour.

The interviewee will quickly detect from your manner, what you say, and how you say it verbally and non-verbally that you are being judgemental. Children, including the very young, and individuals with learning difficulties are particularly sensitive to the attitude and emotional state of the 'powerful person'. If you are perceived to be judgemental, the individual is likely to become resentful and to retaliate by saying little or nothing, or refusing to participate.

No one denies that it is a hard fight to remain objective. Particularly if resource limitations require you to interview both the suspect and the person offended against. Remaining non-judgemental is especially draining if you know or believe that person is not telling the truth.

5.9 Straightforward talk

People are used to not paying too much attention and to being given relatively few ideas in what is said to them. Most people can only hold the content of two or three simple utterances in working memory. As we pointed out in Chapter 2, the evidence indicates that the digital age of TV and video has created successive generations suffering from 'attention deficit'. The practical implication is that whatever the age of your interviewee, or any third party, if you speak for any length the chances are that he or she will find it increasingly difficult to register and to remember the detail of what you are saying. Because you are straining his or her attention span and capacity to hold information in working memory, you risk losing the interviewee in more than one sense.

- He or she will not understand you.
- He or she will be increasingly 'turned off', putting less and less effort into paying attention and trying to make sense.

There are a number of ways in which you can make what you say uncomplicated, and therefore easier to grasp and to retain.

5.9.1 'Chunking' and pausing

You need to take account of the limited concentration span that people have in everyday life, particularly children, young people, and the elderly, that we described in Chapter 2. Get into the habit of delivering complete 'chunks' of information, ie sentences, divided by clear pauses (2–3 seconds, even more if you think the person needs it). The pause will allow the individual to register what you have said and you to consider what you are going to say next.

'Chunking' and pausing will ensure that you keep the pace down and also do not ramble.

5.9.2 Short sentences

Many interviewers utter sentences that are too long. Listen to recordings of your interviews. If you find that your sentences are more than 20 words long, you should definitely work on shortening your sentences.

- Aim to be as short as possible while making sense: try to get the average length down to around 10 words—the fewer the better! This will be hard but it is good discipline.
- Remember to use the pause: ^^ ^^. You will find that pausing will give you the 'space' to think of a shorter utterance, thus bringing your average sentence length down.

5.9.3 Not too much information in a sentence

Interviewers all too often deliver difficult sentences that contain too much information (or more precisely ideas that the individual needs to grasp). Their sentences typically combine 'subordinate' and 'main' parts: in effect welding the ideas of two sentences into one. The 'subordinate' section starts with a joining word, eg *Because...*; *Although...*; *As soon as...*; *When...*; *Before...*; *After...* etc, followed by detail that expands the ideas in the 'main' section that follows. For example, *Before I ask you about the fighting, I need know what you were doing.* Each successive element of a difficult sentence adds to the amount of information—the sum total of individual utterances—to be held in working memory. Each subsequent utterance has the potential to disrupt, distort, or to delete one or more prior utterances, and the logical links between utterances are prone to be lost.

People who are not inclined, or who struggle, to pay attention to detail for whatever reason are at particular risk of not wholly understanding or misunderstanding what has been said. The reason is that they failed to register sufficient detail in the 'subordinate' section. This is particularly likely to happen with individuals who have problems with working memory, eg:

- the developmentally disadvantaged—the young and the very old;
- those with literacy problems;
- those with learning disabilities;
- people who are fatigued, who have not slept;
- people who are distractible, perhaps due to the need to smoke, or who are excessively anxious or depressed.

Get into the habit of saying separate sentences instead of gluing two or more sentences into a long 'subordinate' + 'main' difficult sentence. A better alternative to the previous example would be: *First I need to know what you were doing.* ^^ ^^ *Then I'll ask you about the fighting.* ^^ ^^

5.9.4 Use simple words and phrasing

In the School of English at the University of Birmingham, researchers have collected material on the way in which police officers use language, labelling this 'Police speak'. As a working group, police officers tend to use:

- longer, more difficult words (with more syllables, often Latin in origin) than the shorter words (often Anglo-Saxon in origin) that people commonly use, eg *informed* vs *told*; *advanced towards* vs *came towards*;
- words with a meaning that is not common in the community, eg *attends*;
- 'legalese': phraseology not really understood by a large number of people, eg *in relation to*; *circumstances*;
- technical jargon and slang, eg *SOCO has examined the scene.*

Many factors have a potential to make it harder for an individual to understand what you are trying to say, eg:

- language use;
- intellectual ability;
- powerful emotions;
- fatigue;
- lack of sleep.

You should have a quiet attention to the words that the individual uses and the way he or she puts them together. These language clues will give you a good idea of the individual's:

- social background;
- language use;
- education;
- mental ability;
- mental state.

You can then use the same quiet attention to match your use of words and the way you put them together to those of the individual. Irrespective of the individual's ability and facility with language:

- don't sound more like a police officer than is absolutely necessary;
- use short, more widely understood words wherever possible and find easier ways of phrasing ideas.

You may feel that this advice is tantamount to 'talking down' to the individual, treating them as though they are incapable of understanding, and giving them cause to be offended. Expressing ideas in an uncomplicated way is not 'talking down'. It is the heart of being straightforward: ensuring the individual is absolutely clear. You can be confident that the person opposite will understand what you are wishing to say, and the significance of what you are saying.

5.9.5 Check comprehension

If you have to get across a matter or an issue that is critical or difficult, you should check back whether your attempt at being straightforward has been successful. Use the same approach described earlier in this chapter.

5.9.6 Use visual aids

On occasion, words alone are inadequate. When explaining or describing critical detail, or requesting a description or an indication of a location, if you use a visual aid, eg a map or a diagram, this makes your task and that of the individual so much easier.

5.10 Equals talking 'across' to each other

Given that your job is to interview to obtain information to progress the investigation and the interviewee knows that the expectation is that he or she will provide this information, there will always be a difference in relative power.

- You know things about the case and investigation that he does not.
- You have the authority and expertise to manage the interview, to guide its course, to influence what gets talked about, when, and in what detail.

It is by definition an 'up'–'down' relationship. However, your management of the talking turn, access to talking time, allowing the individual to talk freely and feel free to ask for an explanation or to make a request at any time, sends a powerful message. You want the interviewee to have the same view as you that this is an 'across' relationship: the two of you are equals, despite the difference in relative power.

5.11 Chapter summary

After your exchange with individual—irrespective of gender, age, or role—he or she will remember the impact of your conversational behaviour. Given that people have limited attention and concentration span, he or she may not remember you for the detail of what you actually said. For similar reasons, he or she may not remember you for what you actually did. One thing is certain, however. He or she will remember you for how you made him or her feel as the two of you conversed.

Such feelings born of your RESPONSE behaviours provide a firm foundation for the development of a working relationship.

6

Managing Information

6.1 Chapter overview

This chapter reviews the range of techniques that are available for managing investigative material. The techniques will enable you to capture comprehensively the fine-grain detail and to analyse and evaluate this detail systematically and rigorously. These are activities that are fundamental to a timely, professional investigative response prior to, during, and following the conversation managed interview.

6.1.1 Chapter objectives

This chapter will enable you to:

- listen more intently to the fine-grain detail in what people say;
- read documents more efficiently;
- develop as a skilled SE3R practitioner;
- use a Wants Analysis for investigative action planning;
- create key visual representations of locations and vehicles, and use Internet tools to assist investigation through access to geographical and aerial photographic representations;
- use grids to collate any kind of detail from single and multiple sources;
- apply an observer-participant plot to relate and evaluate detail of accounts of individuals located in different positions during an offence;
- create genograms to combine detail on links between people, descriptive detail, and location detail;
- use topic templates to manage the complexity of case material and to assist interview planning;
- use 'wheel of blobs' (WOB) mapping as a tool for managing information and questioning in an interview.

6.2 Vigilance to detail

Material gathered by investigators—from the time the offence came to notice—constitutes *case knowledge*. The material comes in many forms, eg:

- verbal briefings;
- handover notes;
- pocket books/incident report books;
- crime reports;
- information and evidence (Box 6.1) underpinning the:
  — allegation;
  — the line of logic—why the police believe this individual rather than anyone else committed the offence;
  — the police case (what it is believed has happened in the material time frame, ie leading up to, during, and following the commission of the offence.

In Chapter 1 we considered the mindset of defensive avoidance characterized by managing information to gain a partial grasp, rather than a comprehensive understanding, of detail by:

- operating on a single case theory;
- relevance filtering—attending selectively to what you think you need to know, ignoring the rest;

- Key location representations, eg sketches of the crime scene.
- Covert information on the suspect.
- Accounts and descriptions from police and police support staff.
- Accounts and descriptions from witnesses: initial version and subsequent formal statements/ video-recorded interviews; diagrams; first descriptions.
- Accounts and descriptions from co-accused: recorded interviews; subsequent formal statements; diagrams;
- House-to-house enquiries (responses to questionnaires).
- Films, video-recordings, and photographs released to the media.
- Identification by witnesses.
- Object evidence, ie material items of any kind: recovered from crime scene (including the victim) and in searches of the suspect, locations and vehicles associated with the suspect; recordings of any kind, eg CCTV, audio; still photography, eg from a security camera.
- Contact trace material (CTM), ie *fingerprints*—includes fingers and palms; *impressions*, eg made on a surface by footwear or an object (such as a tool) or by part of the body (such as an ear or teeth), and marks on clothing; *traces*, eg hair, natural and artificial fibres, shards of glass, wood, paint; *substances*, eg DNA, blood, semen, accelerant (used to set a fire), suspected drugs.
- Specialist opinion and testimony.
- Significant statements (including admissions) by, or silence from, the suspect.
- Relevant comments.
- Interviewing of the suspect to date, ie account(s) given; prepared statements handed in.
- Formal statements taken from the suspect.

Box 6.1 The range of information and evidence (after Shepherd 2004[1])

- excessive early editing—mentally deleting the apparently irrelevant, compressing information into 'bullet' points;
- engaging in confirmation bias—a variation on relevance filtering, ie scanning for, and asking questions to obtain responses, which buttress your interpretation.

We saw that defensive avoidance persists because it gives quick rewards to the investigator, including:

- rapid closure, ie a definite answer to the problem and the absence of ambiguity;
- quick resolution of the problem and the possibility of a quick result through:
  — quick processing of material (skim reading, extraction of 'bullet' points);
  — conducting a 'quick' interview.

Ignoring the seemingly irrelevant and compressing detail perceived as relevant turns out to be a 'rush to get it wrong'.

- A high proportion of investigatively significant detail within available information and evidence is never registered and, in the absence of any electronic recording, is lost forever.
- Contradiction, the easiest anomaly to detect, might be picked up but the prospects are poor of detecting the other eleven forms of anomaly (described in Chapter 4) in verbal disclosure, in a document, or a recording. Many of these anomalies concern what was not said or said peculiarly.

Managing information expediently in order to save time is actually a waste of time. Inadequate and inaccurate material is introduced into the investigative process. This slows

---

[1] Shepherd, E. (2004) *Police Station Skills for Legal Advisers: Accreditation Manual*. London: Law Society Publishing.

down, obstructs, and can render ineffective the entire investigative endeavour. Although expeditious, defensive avoidance when managing information diminishes and destroys your ability to provide a court with quality evidence to secure a conviction.

In Chapter 1 it was argued that vigilance to detail—the alternative mindset to defensive avoidance—is essential to the success of an ethical and effective investigation. The tools described in this chapter will enable you to operate ethically and effectively with this mindset. Vigilance to detail will always take more time than inattention. Good evidence takes time. If you find yourself saying 'I haven't got time to do this' it means 'I've only got time to do a quick job whatever the ultimate cost'.

6.3 Intent listening

Intent listening is an essential skill for any professional who engages in conversation management, who receives verbal briefings, and who has to work with electronically recorded material. Intent listening is a combined skill of registering comprehensively and remembering in great measure what has been said. It involves:

- **receptive listening**: capturing and remembering fine-grain detail and a sequence of details;
- **reflective listening**: comprehending central ideas, identifying logical links, and drawing inferences (conclusions based on a line of logic).

You can dramatically improve your intent listening performance by imaging, 'mental echoing', physically acknowledging key ideas, regulating the information flow, and developing your verbatim memory.

6.3.1 Imaging

People do not normally form mental images of what is being said to them. They simply hear sound. Consciously devote attention to creating an image in your mind's eye of:

- the activity, event, or episode described: 'acting it out in your head';
- the individual, location, and objects and the like—and the current and cumulative descriptive detail concerning these.

Storytellers across the world have used, like the Greek and Roman orators, the technique of imaging to remember what they had to say. By devoting conscious attention to creating the image, you will find:

- what you listen to more interesting;
- you will remember the detail, particularly as it is reinforced by one or more of the other techniques described here;
- you will instantly spot anomaly that requires investigation/probing: particularly the absence and non-specificity of detail, because your images will lack this information.

Some tips on imaging

When you image, stick simply to the detail given. If there is no detail you cannot image it. The fact that you can't should make this detail memorable enough to ask a probing question to obtain the detail you need.

Create simple mental models of whatever is described, adding the detail as it is disclosed.

Any room or building

Image this as a rectangle viewed from above. As more detail arrives just image the simple detail as a modification to the rectangle.

- All doors are two lines to represent the doorway. Don't anguish about the fact that you don't know its location. As soon as this information is given, you can modify the mental image.
- All windows are two lines with a W.

For example:

> I went down the **corridor**. The **room** was on the **left hand** side. I went through the **door** and saw a bed on the right hand side. Opposite the door standing in front of the window was a man.

Figure 6.1 shows the cumulative creation of an image from the content of these utterances.

A male, a female

If there is a mention of a man or a woman but not in a location, simply image the logos for male and female found on lavatory doors. Add to the image any descriptive detail as it is mentioned. Give every separate individual a separate identity. This ensures that you always keep track of individuals, something which does not happen if you just hear sound (or in traditional note-taking).

Hence the description 'I saw two men, one was white, the other was black' gives rise to:

- two male logos, each with a number—M1 and M2;
- M1 is labelled white;
- M2 is labelled black.

A group

Simply image a circle. When the constituents of the group are mentioned, place this detail in the circle. Hence *two men and a young woman* would be a circle with M1, M2, and YW annotated in the middle.

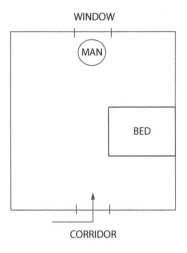

Figure 6.1 Imaging cumulative disclosed detail

Any vehicle

Image a rectangle looking down from above, with a wedge on the front to signify a bonnet. As seats are mentioned, image smaller rectangles within the vehicle rectangle. As people are mentioned, place these as circles in the stated location. If you cannot image where a person was located, this should trigger you to probe for this detail.

A note of warning

Imaging is not imagination, which is letting your mind run riot and going beyond the detail given. If the individual says *outside the hotel*, simply image a rectangle marked hotel with the person—as a circle—outside. Don't run riot by imagining the hotel to be the Holiday Inn, with large, beige awning and swinging door, with an adjacent swinging door. Restrict yourself solely to creating the simplest of images reflecting what the individual says, no more, no less.

6.3.2 'Mental echoing'

If you say silently to yourself—'mentally echo'—the words being used to describe detail, particularly that which is hard to image, eg a name, age, address, location, date, duration, this devotes a fraction more conscious attention to this information. As with imaging, this devotes a fraction more attention to the same benefit in terms of improved retention in working memory. You will remember it even more so if reinforced by any of the other techniques.

6.3.3 Physically acknowledging key ideas

In spoken utterances there is always a key idea or ideas. Speakers assist listeners to spot the key idea by stressing this, pushing it to the foreground of attention by using a difference in pitch, volume, and duration (Figure 6.2).

When we 'guggle' non-vocally by nodding our heads, we are in fact unconsciously signalling, a fraction of a second after the speaker's emphasized ideas, that we have noted and are following these.

The trick is to turn the unconscious into the conscious. Consciously spot the emphasized idea and 'guggle'. You will increase the likelihood of retaining this key idea in working memory and also have demonstrated that you really are actively listening. Get into the habit of spotting the key idea and 'guggling' when you are listening to or viewing a recording. It has the same registration-enhancing effect.

6.3.4 Developing your verbatim memory

Professional interpreters have very much better than average verbatim memory, ie ability to remember the actual words used by the individual speaking several sentences. They have

*There was a **small man** standing in the **shadow** . . . over by the*
***grassy** area. He looked **foreign**. . . On his own **just standing** there.*

Figure 6.2 An example of key ideas in utterances

Equipment required
- A video-recorder.
- Audio-recorder/dictaphone (digital or tape).

Training material

A video-recording of local news programme on the television, eg BBC 1 regional news at 6.30 pm.

Method

1. Record the local news programme. **Do not watch the programme**.
2. Rewind the video-recording.
3. Zero the video-recording at the point just before the first news announcer speaks.
4. Press *Play*. Listen to what the announcer says.
5. Press *Pause* as soon as your working memory capacity is reached.
6. Press *Record* on your audio-recorder. Say verbatim what you have just heard the announcer say.
7. Rewind both recordings.
8. Play the video recording up to the point where you stopped it. Press *Pause*.
9. Play your audio-recorder.
   - If you did not fully replicate what the announcer said this suggests that:
     — you were not listening intently, or
     — you tried to capture too much detail before you stopped the recording.

   Repeat the exercise, playing the next segment of the recorded programme, listening more intently, and stopping it earlier. This time you should have recalled the material verbatim. Then proceed as indicated in the next step below.
   - If you fully replicated what was said, repeat the exercise, taking the next segment of the recorded programme.

Gradually experiment, progressively extending the duration of the segment. If you fail to replicate the detail then revert to the duration which you were successful with. Continue the exercise.

A good target is the ability to hold about 30–40 words in working memory, ie about four or five short sentences.

Box 6.2 An exercise for developing verbatim memory (Shepherd, 2008[2])

to perform better than the average person, not only in terms of working memory capacity but also to remember in great measure the words actually spoken.

As part of their professional training, interpreters develop the capacity to hold what was actually said in working memory. Box 6.2 describes an exercise that is used by interpreters to develop this capacity. If you apply yourself diligently to this exercise with numbers of video recordings you will find that within a week to ten days your verbatim memory will have greatly improved. You may start receiving compliments for your very obvious attentiveness!

6.3.5 Regulating the information flow

The speed at which we think is some four to six times faster than average speech rate. Intuitively people should be much better processors of spoken detail than they are. The problem lies in the amount of information that we can comfortably and efficiently hold in working memory. Each successive utterance has a disrupting, displacing, or distorting effect upon prior utterances.

---

[2] Shepherd, E. (2008) *SE3R: A Resource Book*. Fourth edition. East Hendred: Forensic Solutions.

When instructed to listen carefully to a person who speaks for a single minute, people tend to remember only around a half of the key ideas. In one research study, even when listeners took notes, almost a third of all relevant information was not recorded.[3] In Chapter 2, and again in Chapter 5, we highlighted how most people can only hold the content of two or three simple utterances in working memory, and pointed out that the 'attention deficit' arising from living in the visual age of TV and video has created successive generations suffering from 'attention deficit'. Interviewers are as prone as any other individual to struggle with holding information in working memory.

It follows therefore that, where appropriate, you should regulate the flow of information that is disclosed to you to maximize your ability to register the detail and to process this in working memory.

Brief the individual to speak slowly

If a witness is about to give an account, particularly his or her initial free recall, you should explain the necessity to speak as slowly as possible, eg:

> *So you now understand that it's all about detail ^^ ^^ as much detail as possible ^^ ^^ And that there's no rush. ^^ ^^ Now because I've got to get my head round the detail that you give me ^^ ^^ I'm going to ask you to help me on this ^^ ^^ Can I ask you to speak as slowly and clearly as you can. ^^ ^^ As I said there is no rush. ^^ ^^ Taking me through things slowly ^^ and telling me things slowly ^^ will help you to remember the little details ^^ ^^ and also help me to get all the detail you give me in my mind ^^ ^^*

If you give this explanation, and all your communication, at a slower pace than normal conversation this will have a calming effect: the individual will be much more likely to deliver on your request to speak slowly.[4]

Brief the individual on the need to pause from time to time

During the free recall phase it is inappropriate to stop the person in mid-flow. However, it makes sense to stop the flow when necessary during:

- second free recall;
- detailed, lengthy responses in response to systematic probing.

For example:

> *When you take me through things again ^^ ^^ I might need to stop you from time to time ^^ ^^ to get my head round the detail you're giving me. ^^ ^^ When I come in to ask you to hold on for a moment ^^ ^^ I'll want you to hang on to whatever image you have in your head ^^ ^^ to stick with that image. ^^ ^^ So when I come in ^^ I'll say something like ^^ 'Just hold on to that image for a moment.'^^ ^^ As soon as I've got the detail in my mind I'll move my hand like this [demonstrate] to let you know that you can carry on. ^^ ^^ Or I might say 'OK. Got that.' ^^ ^^ That's the all clear to you to carry on talking. ^^ ^^ Can I check back with you that you are clear about what I've just said? ^^ ^^*

---

[3] Koehnken, G. Thuerer, C., and Zoberbier, D. (1991) *The Cognitive Interview: Are the Interviewers' Memories Enhanced Too?* Unpublished manuscript. University of Kiel. Cited in R. Fisher and R. Geiselman (1992) *Memory-enhancing Techniques for Investigative Interviewing.* Springfield, Ill.: Charles C. Thomas.

[4] Fisher, R. and Geiselman, R. (1992) *Memory-enhancing Techniques for Investigative Interviewing.* Springfield, Ill.: Charles C. Thomas.

The effect of intent listening techniques on the requirement to regulate the flow

If you develop skill at imaging, 'mentally echoing', and 'guggling' at key ideas, you will need to intervene to regulate the flow much less often than someone who does not use, or is not skilled in using, these techniques. Developing your verbatim memory will significantly reduce the number of times you ask the interviewee to pause.

6.4 Efficient reading

Most people leave school without having learned how to read efficiently. This has a knock-on effect for investigators and investigative interviewers whose role requires them to read often quite large amounts of information.

6.4.1 Patterns of inefficient reading

Two patterns of inefficient reading are widespread.

Skim reading while creating bullet notes

Here the individual, often under perceived or actual time pressure, reads the document quickly and superficially, scanning for 'key facts', ie detail deemed to be relevant and important in the light of the individual's current case knowledge. When detected, the 'key fact' is often, but not in every instance, transposed into written note form typically as a compressed 'bullet' point or note.

The risks of this strategy of rapid reading, relevance filtering, and rapid reduction of many words to a few 'bullet' points or notes are great. Much detail that may be now or later of potential or actual investigative significance is not registered and lost completely. Compression of detail into a note, if made, results in lack of specificity. There is no way of knowing or remembering the original detail that gave rise to the 'bullet' point or note.

Adopting this strategy, the reader emerges with a gist understanding, underpinned by an economical number of 'bullet' notes. However, the reader has very little chance of detecting the full range of anomaly.

Erratic reading while creating bullet notes

Here the individual, in addition to perceived or actual time pressure, has the additional pressure of anxiety and doubt that he or she is not obtaining a secure enough grasp of what is being read to register and to identify the 'key facts'. This induces the individual to read erratically, ie:

- reading a relatively small portion of text;
- experiencing anxiety and doubt about grasp;
- going back to the beginning of this portion;
- re-reading the material again—perhaps more than once—in order to understand and identify detail to be transposed as a bullet note.

Erratic reading is very time-consuming, yet the return on this extra effort is often very poor. The reader—who may even believe that he or she is skim reading—emerges with an inadequate, often incoherent grasp of what is said in the document and limited awareness of anomaly.

6.4.2 Efficient reading: the 'double-pass' plus mnemonics technique

Efficient reading involves a double-pass, an initial reading and a second reading, using a number of simple strategies to enable you to obtain a firm grasp of what is in the document and, critically, to identify the entire range of anomaly. It may sound more time-consuming but with practice you will find that you not only have a firmer grasp of the detail but achieve this relatively quickly.

Initial reading: reading to comprehend

Read the document in its entirety, ie from beginning to end, adopting the same techniques as intent listening.

- Regulate the flow, ie read the text in 'bite sized' chunks. If you find that you cannot engage in the next three techniques reduce the size of the chunk.
- Image.
- 'Mentally echo'.
- Identify the key idea—the word or words that would be stressed if the document was being read aloud—and reinforce your conscious awareness of this by non-verbally 'guggling' (nodding).

Don't divert or disrupt yourself in your comprehension task by:

- questioning what you are reading, ie don't go off at a tangent thinking about the implications, what needs to be done with this detail;
- attempting to memorize the detail: you will be returning to this detail a second time—that is how you will consolidate you remembrance of this detail, not by trying to rehearse detail now.

Going through the entire text using these techniques, and not falling into the trap of questioning and attempting to memorize, you will emerge with a gist understanding that is quite unlike gist understanding from the skim reading of defensive avoidance. Your gist understanding will:

- be relatively detailed, underpinned by images that you have created, the 'sounds' of mentally echoed descriptive detail, and your physical response to detected key ideas: all registered in working memory;
- be aware of anomaly—what was said peculiarly or not there at all.

Second reading: systematic extraction

The aim of the second pass is to capture the detail comprehensively so that you can work upon it, ie methodical analysis to enable a timely, targeted investigative response. When you read for the second time use the same techniques that you used for the first pass. This will:

- consolidate the detail in working memory;
- provide you with the basis to record this detail, and any anomalies you detected first time round or for the first time during this pass, using the techniques described in this chapter:

— an SE3R;
— a Wants Analysis;
— a visual representation;
— a grid;
— an observer-participant (O-P) plot;
— a 'wheel of blobs'—WOB—map.

6.5 SE3R

6.5.1 Traditional note-taking

Note-taking in lectures

Within the lecture, catching every word would be impossible and unnecessary. Your note-taking aim is to catch the key ideas in order to reconstruct later the material the lecturer prepared before the lecture and is now delivering. You listen carefully for, and respond to, clues:

- in the introduction: noting the listing of the topics to be covered;
- in the main body of the lecture: noting the nuggets—'signposts', their content, and what follows;
- in the final summary and conclusions: noting brief listing of topics covered, judgements, and opinions.

In the police context such lecture note-taking is an entirely sensible activity when attending a lesson or an operational briefing.

Note-taking in interviews

Interview note-taking is a widespread activity in the police service.

- **In witness interviews that are not electronically recorded**. The investigator takes notes to assist the drafting of a statement for signature.
- **In electronically recorded interviews of *significant* witnesses or *vulnerable and intimidated* witnesses**. The second investigator, or monitoring person, takes notes to ensure that all points are covered and to assist later drafting of a statement.
- **In electronically recorded interviews of *serious* complainants, eg of sexual assault**. The investigator, or where applicable the second investigator, takes notes to ensure that all points are covered and to assist the drafting of a statement for signature.
- **In suspect interviews**. The second investigator takes notes to ensure that all points are covered.

What interviewees disclose is extempore, relatively unstructured, and, in the case of an anxious, aroused, or distressed individual, liable to be 'all over the place' and may even verge on the incoherent. Even with the calm and collected interviewee, there will be hardly anything equivalent to the lecturer's conscious, deliberate 'signposting' to signal importance and relevance. Despite the total difference between spontaneous disclosure and the delivery of the planned and structured content of a lecture, investigators apply the only method they know for capturing spoken text: lecture note-taking.

We saw in Chapters 1 and 4 that the problem enters when the investigator's prior knowledge and notions of what is important and relevant determine what gets noted down in 'bullet' form. Research has consistently shown that a very large amount of material is never registered. The problem is compounded when the investigator drafts a statement based on selective remembrance of what the interviewee said, assisted by his or her 'bullet' notes.

The combination of relevance filtering, excessive editing, and selective remembrance all too often gives rise to handover notes, written notes, eg of initial conversations, and statements that are anomalous. Detail is missing. There are gaps, jumps, and 'non-barking dogs'. There is vagueness, ambiguity, and 'sidestepping'. All are unhelpful and potentially fatal to the investigation. Where there is no recording we have no means of recovering the lost detail, correcting the errors, or knowing whether the investigator influenced the interviewee's account and replies to questions.

Making notes from documents

Handover notes, written notes, and statements have a completely different character and content to the written texts of the educational system. They are typically skim read in the manner described in Chapter 1, the investigator scanning for, and noting down as 'bullet' points, key facts that fit with what is already known or needs to be achieved.

In effect, note-taking from written documents constitutes yet another stage of editing, compression, and deletion. Any new approach to note-taking that still relies on the investigator editing necessarily creates the same problems as traditional note-taking: potentially fatal relevance filtering.

6.5.2 Comprehensive capture and analysis of detail

SE3R (pronounced ESS, EE, THREE, AH) is a method for dominating detail to enable ethical and effective conversation management of investigative interviews. SE3R is an acronym for the steps of method:

- **S**: Survey
- **E**: Extract
- **R**: Read
- **R**: Review
- **R**: Respond

Applications of SE3R

SE3R can be applied to any form of document, audio- and video-recorded material, and even in interviews—face-to-face or on the telephone. It is not a form of note-taking, all of which rely upon selection and reduction of detail. SE3R is a 'catch it all' method that enables:

- the rapid, comprehensive capture of fine-grain detail;
- the rapid identification of, and timely response to, anomaly and issues requiring investigative action or probing in interview;
- the consolidation of this material in memory without making an active effort to do so.

SE3R gives you information in a rapidly accessible form that you are able to consult, refer to, and navigate around rapidly and easily when:

- planning;
- preparing;
- explaining and briefing;
- interviewing;

- evaluating;
- drafting a statement.

Defining features of SE3R

SE3Rs can be created on paper, on the computer, and on PC tablets (using software called *Storyboard*). Whatever the medium used, it has the same defining features.

Intent listening and efficient reading

The methodology incorporates key aspects of these skills.

Disentangling the weave of disclosed detail

SE3R disentangles the complex weave of the three different kinds of detail in disclosure that were described in Chapter 4 (Telling and Listening: Disclosing and Making Sense of Disclosed Detail).

- **Background knowledge detail**. Information that contributes to your stock of knowledge about people, locations, objects, relationships, routines, rituals, plans, intentions, explanations, and so on.
- **Narrative detail**. Chronological detail (day, date, time, place, duration); location of activity detail; events, ie actions, interactions, reactions, responses, utterances, verbal exchanges; episodes (extended or repeated activities) and continuous states (a mental or physical state, a state of affairs, circumstances).
- **Commentary**. The speaker's or writer's 'asides', ie observations made about the process of disclosing, about disclosing this particular detail, about the detail itself, about thoughts and feelings at the time and now, and qualifying remarks, eg concerning certainty or confidence concerning this disclosure.

Representation of detail from one or more sources in a memorable form

- **Visual representation of narrative detail**. Graphic Event Line representation of detail on chronological order of individual, multiple and recurrent events and episodes, duration, and material time frames. This detail can be expanded, connected, and transposed.
- **Cumulative collation of background knowledge detail**. In a readily used 'bin' format, akin to a collator card, collecting detail on each topic. 'Bins' are also used for drawings, eg of locations, objects, and 'ginger bread' people on which detail is collated.

An audit trail of disclosure

It captures all changes, all expansions, all explanations, and all versions, and identifies the stage of the interview when particular detail was disclosed.

Active response to detail

Anomalies, areas for action and probing, interpretation, and any other thoughts can be immediately recorded and located by the particular detail.

Maximum use of established notation methods

Abbreviations, symbols, different colours.

Easily shared and understood by people who know nothing about SE3R

The intuitive format and presentation of detail means the content of SE3Rs is easily and rapidly shared with, and immediately understood by, people who have never encountered SE3R format before.

6.5.3 Materials for creating a simple SE3R

Pens

- **Black pen**. The universal colour for an initial SE3R.
- **Coloured pens**. For example, when creating an SE3R in an interview or from a recorded interview: blue = probed detail; red = checking back/final probing; green = information provided by an external source.

SE3R format sheets

These have a standard layout: see Figure 6.3. If you do not have blank SE3R sheets, the format—two horizontal lines dividing the page into three sections of equal depth; four vertical lines dividing the bottom section into five boxes—can be drawn on:

- blank A4 sheets in 'landscape' view, ie rotated through 90° from normal 'portrait' view;
- A4 note-paper/pad in 'landscape' view.

6.5.4 Survey

This is your first straight through processing of the information.

- **Document**. Read the document from beginning to end.
- **Live interview/recording**. Listen to/observe from beginning to end.

When reading, listening, or observing during this first pass, you use the techniques of efficient initial reading and intent listening.

- imaging;
- 'mentally echoing';
- 'guggling' at stressed key ideas;
- regulating the information flow.

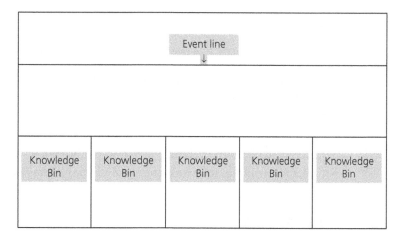

Figure 6.3 SE3R sheet layout

The result is a sound overall understanding, underpinned by substantial amounts of fine-grain detail and awareness of anomaly in your working memory.

6.5.5 Extract

This is your second pass at processing the information in the document or recording.

1. You read or listen to the material in 'bite sized' chunks.
2. You identify and enter detail in the appropriate area of the SE3R sheet which has a standard layout (Figure 6.3).
   - **Background knowledge detail**. You enter in the *Knowledge Bins* (KBs):
     — detail about people, locations, objects, relationships, routines, rituals, plans, intentions, explanations, and so on;
     — drawings and sketches.
   - **Narrative detail**. You enter on the *Event Line*:
     — chronological and location detail;
     — detail of events;
     — detail of episodes.
   - **Commentary**. You enter the individual's expressed attitude, disposition, and feelings concerning disclosure and particular detail, excuses, and justifications, and any qualifying remarks at the point it occurs or beside the detail being commented upon.
3. As you register and record the detail, annotate where applicable:
   - immediately revealed/detected anomaly;
   - topics requiring investigation or probing (expansion; explanation);
   - changes in BASELINES behaviours;
   - potential 'hot spots'.

The outcome is called an SE3R. At Figure 6.4 is an illustrative SE3R created from a statement by Eric Shepherd in which he gives an account of being attacked.

6.5.6 Read

You consolidate your grasp of the fine-grain detail and identify errors by:

- reading through all the KBs;
- then reading through the Event Line from beginning to end.

6.5.7 Review

You examine methodically the detail in the SE3R in order to identify and to annotate:

- the *material time frame* (MTF): circumstances leading up to, during, and following the commission of the offence;
- further anomaly and areas requiring investigation or probing (expansion; explanation) in interview;
- provisional order for probing material in the interview;
- topics for inclusion in your Wants Analysis and Route Map.

6.5.8 Respond step

You put your annotated SE3R to investigative effect, eg:

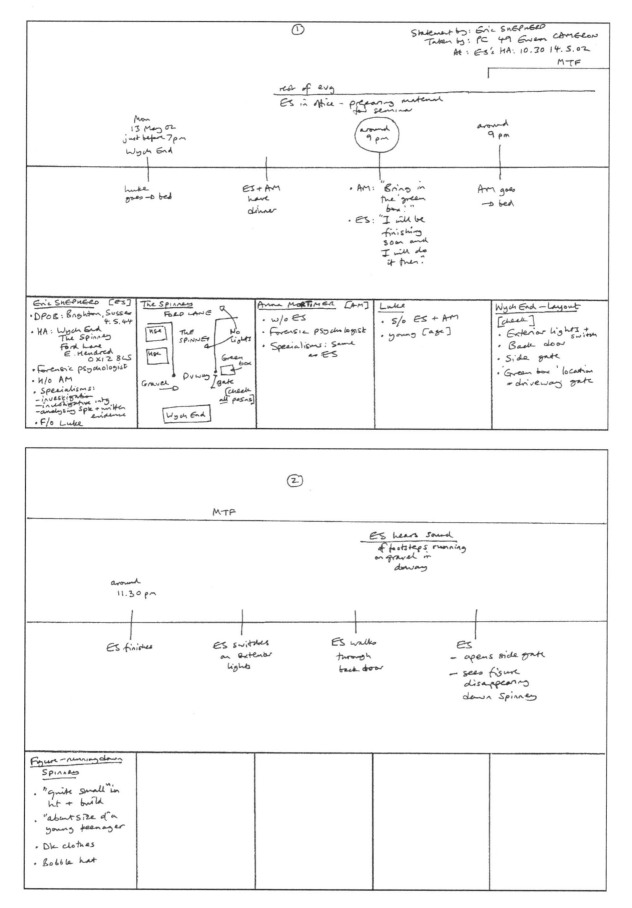

Figure 6.4 Illustrative SE3R created from a statement by Eric Shepherd

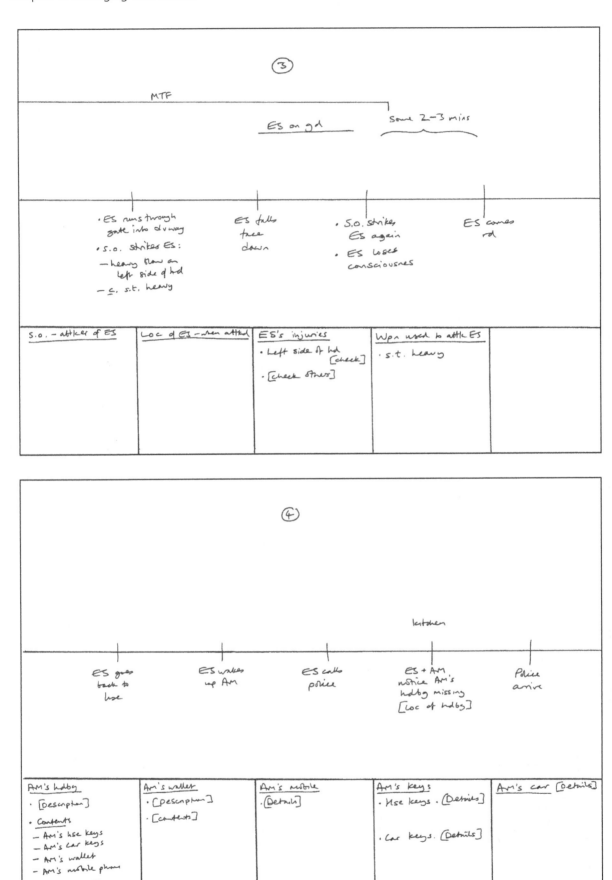

Figure 6.4 Illustrative SE3R created from a statement by Eric Shepherd (*continued*)

- contributing issues to your **Wants Analysis** (see section 6.6) that you wish, or wish others, to action through further investigation and investigative interviewing;
- transferring descriptive detail onto a grid in which you are collating detail (see **Grids** at section 6.8)
- creating a **composite SE3R**, ie this is a combination of individual SE3Rs into one SE3R. Each source is distinguishable either through annotation or use of different colours, eg X's detail in black, Y's in blue, Z's in green. You are able to see the total picture, what everyone says, with each individual being clearly identifiable. Composites immediately reveal differences in level of detail, match and mismatch, as well as the many other forms of anomaly.

6.5.9 Illustrative applications of SE3R

Individual SE3Rs

An individual SE3R can be created from any key document, eg handover note, witness statement, or electronic recording of an interview.

Composite SE3Rs

- **The Case SE3R**. This is a crucial composite SE3R. It presents a total picture of the police case, ie circumstances leading up to, during, and following the offence, by combining all the detail from every available appropriate and applicable source, eg:
  — key documents—handover and briefing material, telephone conversations with key individuals, SE3Rs, grids, sketches, and so on;
  — reporting;
  — results of forensic analysis.
- **Composite witness SE3R**. This brings together the detail of the accounts given by key witnesses. You might decide to have a composite that:
  — combines in KBs all the descriptive detail they give—but not bother combining the Event Line detail;
  — combines on an Event Line all the narrative detail—but not the KB background knowledge detail.

Live interview SE3Rs

These are particularly useful because they overcome the problems of traditional note-taking, eg:

- in a witness interview: the interviewer working alone can concentrate on the quality of interviewing, with the SE3R facilitating exhaustive probing;
- in a suspect interview: the second investigator is able to capture detail comprehensively, annotating observed BASELINES and potential 'hot spots'.

Statement creation

Box 6.3 describes the contents of a typical 'five part' statement and shows the source of material drawn from the SE3R.

Part 1
A very brief—one or two sentences—introduction indicating what the statement is about.

Part 2
Details of the witness and the key people known to the witness who will be mentioned in the statement, giving detail about his or her relationship with the witness. [**SE3R source**: detail in Knowledge Bins, including commentary.]

Part 3
Details of key locations which will be mentioned in the statement. Each one:
• comprising full physical description;
• supported by an annotated sketch plan.
[**SE3R source**: detail in Knowledge Bins, including commentary.]

Part 4
Detailed chronological narrative of events leading up to, during, and following the offence. [**SE3R source**: detail in Event Line, including commentary.]

Part 5
Detailed descriptions of people mentioned by the witness, starting with the suspect. [**SE3R source**: detail in Knowledge Bins, including commentary.]
In addition, declarations concerning:
• consent, eg during commission of the offence [**SE3R source**: detail in Knowledge Bins, including commentary]; forensic examination; taking of exhibits;
• monetary value, eg property damaged or stolen [**SE3R source**: detail in Knowledge Bins, including commentary];
• willingness to attend court [**SE3R source**: detail in Knowledge Bins, including commentary].

Box 6.3 Sections in a five-part statement

6.5.10 Finding out more about SE3R

Further guidance on creating SE3Rs is in the Reference Section and in *SE3R: A Resource Book*.[5]

6.6 Wants Analysis

A Wants Analysis is a simple tool to assist your investigative action planning. The layout of a Wants Analysis is shown at Figure 6.5. This is annotated to explain and to point to key features of this tool.

Using Microsoft Word or other software you can create a Wants Analysis document template. Alternatively you can simply use an A4 pad or book, drawing in and labelling the columns.

A Wants Analysis enables you to:

• collate issues that from your processing of the case material and in your judgement require investigative action;
• spell out your reasoning for this line of enquiry;
• specify the required action by you or another individual;
• assign a priority to this action: must do, should do, could do;
• record when the action was completed or when circumstances prevented action being carried out or completed.

---

[5] Shepherd, E. (2008) *SE3R: A Resource Book*. Fourth edition. East Hendred: Forensic Solutions.

What I Want (Issue)	Why I Want It (Rationale)	How I'm Going To Get It (Action)	M	S	C	When completed
1. Bus Station.	SP walked past this location prior to being robbed. There may be in existence other sources of information as yet unidentified. In particular CCTV and a search for other witnesses.	Visit station and assess scene for evidential potential.	✓			

Write here the issue you need to follow up, develop, or investigate.

Record every issue, no matter how minor or obvious, this may be the only detailed record of your investigative rationale.

You may need to record issues that you consider need following up, but are prevented from doing so by other factors eg budget or resources.

Write here your rationale for wanting to develop a particular issue. This is evidence of your decision-making process.

If you intend not to, or are prevented from following a particular issue record here the reasons.

Record the action needed to achieve the 'want'.

Then prioritize for the stage of the investigation you are currently in eg post-arrest, pre-interview the suspect.

M = Must do
S = Should do
C = Could do

Figure 6.5 Wants Analysis

Completing a Wants Analysis is sensible practice. In the context of police investigation a completed Wants Analysis is evidence of fulfilling the Criminal Procedure and Investigation Act 1996 (CPIA) requirement to consider all reasonable lines of enquiry.

Some forces train officers to create a Wants Analysis as part of the handover package to the next shift, enabling these colleagues to engage more effectively and rapidly in the tasks of investigation or interviewing.

6.6.1 Be specific

If you identify missing detail within a document, eg a witness statement or handover note, it is not enough to note on the Wants Analysis, *'Obtain another statement from X'* or *'Contact AO for details'*. Use your SE3R to specify the issues that need to be investigated when interviewing the witness.

6.6.2 Prioritizing

Figure 6.5 explains that you prioritize for the stage of the investigation that you are currently in, applying *must do*, *should do*, and *could do* criteria. Prioritizing is a matter of experience, knowledge of time available and available resource, and the stage of the investigation.

- It is essential to identify what *must* be actioned before interviewing takes place.
- As the investigation progresses you may need to revise the priority of an action.

6.7 Key visual representations

It is nonsensical to embark upon an interview of a witness or suspect if you have no idea of the physical reality of the location or vehicle in which:

- the offence took place;
- evidence was found;
- the suspect was found.

If you are ignorant of this detail, you have no means of making sense of what the interviewee says to you. You have no means of assessing the validity of anything that the interviewee asserts concerning the location or vehicle, eg relative positions, distance, direction of movement, objects touched or handled, marks made. You cannot tell if the individual is confabulating or engaged in active lying—representing an untruth as a truth.

If you attempt to interview when ignorant of this critical detail, your lack of knowledge will eventually be detected by the interviewee:

- You will immediately lose credibility in his or her eyes.
- The would-be liar knows that he or she is safe in making things up because you have no idea of what he or she is talking about.

6.7.1 'Flat pack' drawings

These can be drawn very easily and rapidly by you, or by someone else tasked by you in your Wants Analysis—with you giving some instruction on the method if he or she has never learned this useful method.

'Flat pack' drawing of a location

- Draw as if looking down from above: this gives you a *plan* view.
- Drop the walls down.
- Draw the detail that you see on the plan view, and on the walls.
- Annotate as required, eg labelling objects, using arrows to indicate points of entry or exit, and a cross ⊗ to show the location of a particular item or mark.
- If you need more space to expand the detail:
  — use white space in the margins of your drawing, connect the detail to the point on the drawing;
  — where there is a lot of detail needing to be expanded, use additional sheets, cross-referencing these to the drawing using letters or numbers in circles, eg ①, ②, ③.

Figure 6.6 shows an example of a 'flat pack' drawing of a room.

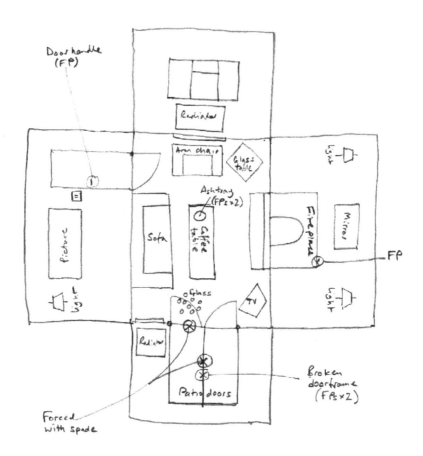

Figure 6.6 An example of a 'flat pack' drawing of a room

'Flat pack' drawing of a vehicle

The same technique applies to a vehicle as for a location. Figure 6.7 shows an example of a 'flat pack' drawing of a vehicle.

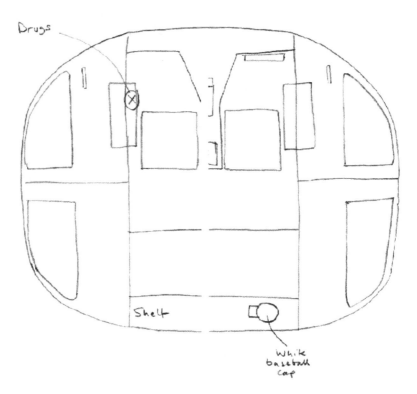

Figure 6.7 'Flat pack' drawing of a vehicle

Application

A drawing will enable you to validate what the witness or suspect are disclosing. In the case of a suspect, you will impress a legal adviser greatly if you are proactive, providing a suitably 'sanitized' drawing, ie not showing the location of evidence, before being asked whether you have a key location representation.

6.7.2 Relative position representations

You sometimes need to represent relative position, eg where items were found or an individual was seen. For example, a visual representation of where the suspect was arrested (eg at or near the scene of the offence) may be needed for planning and preparation (eg briefing a legal adviser), and to refer to when questioning in the interview. You have a number of options.

Make a drawing

For example, if a suspect was arrested near the scene of a fire in the dustbin area at the back of a Tesco's supermarket, a simple drawing will make life much easier for all concerned. You can annotate yours with the complete detail that you have to hand and can give the legal adviser a 'sanitized' copy.

Use the A–Z

If you have access to an A–Z:

- photocopy the page, using the enlarge facility if available;
- annotate the locations.

Use the Internet

Three websites are particularly useful to an investigator.

- <http://www.multimap.com>. Simply key in the postcode and this will give you access to a map showing the location in a highlighted circle, which even shows the side of the road the address is located. Multimap assists investigation in two ways.
  — it gives you clues to time and space, eg how long it might have taken a vehicle taken or used by a suspect to travel from A to B;
  — it gives you instant aerial photography, eg if you are investigating an attack on a person walking a dog across land which has footpaths a Multimap aerial photograph is able to show these.
- <http://www.streetmap.co.uk>. This is a useful adjunct site to use together with Multimap.
- <http://www.earth.google.com>. This is a remarkable website. You can locate a postcode and thereafter you can 'fly' over the location. You are able to zoom in and out, rotate, scroll, and tilt what you see, ie view from an angle. The downside is that, at the time of writing, not all areas of UK are covered.

6.8 Grids

6.8.1 The value of a grid

A grid—also called a matrix—is an excellent two-dimensional tool for organizing and analysing information. The *Practice Advice on Core Investigative Doctrine* recommends using a grid to perform a gap analysis (Figure 6.8) to assist you to identify areas that require further investigation. The grid enables you to identify conflicts (inconsistency and contradiction) and consistencies (convergence, similarity, or sameness).

When managing information, a grid enables you to collate, ie systematically collect and represent, detail from different sources (eg witness 1, witness 2, witness 3), focusing on specific subject matter (eg an event or a description) (Figure 6.9).

A grid is infinitely flexible. For each additional source, you simply add a column. For each additional focal issue, you add another row.

When using a grid to manage investigative material nothing is lost. Everything is immediately visible. This total picture enables you to identify:

- presence or absence of detail;
- varying level of detail provided by each source on a focal issue;

	What is known	What is not known	Conflicts	Consistencies
Who				
What				
When				
Where				
Why				
How				

Figure 6.8 Gap analysis matrix (ACPO Centrex 2005[6])

---

[6] ACPO Centrex (2005) *Practice Advice on Core Investigative Doctrine*. Cambourne: ACPO/Centrex.

	SOURCE 1	SOURCE 2	SOURCE 3
Focus 1 (event; description)			
Focus 2 (event; description)			
Focus 3 (event; description)			

Figure 6.9 An illustrative grid

Focus	Account 1	Account 2	Account 3
1	Detail	Detail (disagrees)	
2		Detail	Detail (agrees)
3	Detail		Detail (disagrees)
4	Detail		
5		Detail	Detail
6	Detail	Detail (agrees)	
7	Detail		Detail (disagrees)
8		Detail	
9			Detail

Figure 6.10 The evolution of a witness's account

- inconsistency, ie where detail given by a source does not fit with that given by another or others;
- contradiction, ie where there is a mismatch—sources give different versions.

Figure 6.10 gives a simple illustration of three accounts from a witness, eg an account given at the scene, a first statement, and a second statement, concerning nine areas of focus. These nine areas could be the MTF, with the detail drawn from the Event Line of the SE3R of each account. Or they could be descriptive detail concerning the offender. The grid reveals that the witness's account has evolved. Across the three accounts the witness has mentioned nine pieces of information, but the accounts are not consistent. They differ in terms of what the witness said and also what the witness did not mention.

You can use grids to collate descriptive detail or event detail. Indeed, grids are an alternative way of creating composite SE3Rs.[7]

6.8.2 Creating a grid by hand

The design of an SE3R sheet enables you to make grids quickly.

- Take an SE3R sheet and turn it on its side, ie portrait orientation (Figure 6.11).
- Draw lines across the page from the edges and the centre of knowledge bins, creating a grid of three columns and ten rows (Figure 6.12).
- If you need more columns, attach a similarly drawn up SE3R sheet to the first.
- When you have entered the detail, use the *reduce* facility on the photocopier to produce all the detail on a single A4 sheet.

Figure 6.13 shows an example of a grid used to collate descriptive detail from six witnesses concerning an offender, and the description of the suspect.

---

[7] Shepherd, E. (2008) *SE3R: A Resource Book*. Fourth edition. East Hendred: Forensic Solutions.

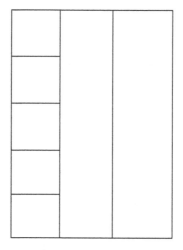

Figure 6.11 SE3R sheet in portrait orientation

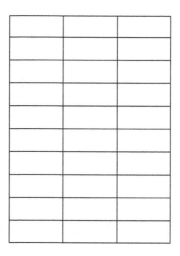

Figure 6.12 Grid created from SE3R sheet

6.8.3 Creating a grid on the computer

Grids can be created, and expanded infinitely, using a computer.

- Open **Word**.
- Click **Insert Table** on the Toolbar.
- Create a grid of the desired size.
- Number of sources + one extra column.
- Number of focal issues + one extra row.

Figure 6.14 shows the same detail as Figure 6.13, but created on a computer.

6.8.4 Using a grid to combine descriptions and actions

A grid is an excellent tool for combining multiple descriptions and actions. Figure 6.15 shows a grid collating material in the accounts of seven witnesses concerning a driver, front passenger, and rear passenger involved in a fight and who then drove off.

DESCRIPTOR	SUSPECT John PATTEN	Ronald BEALE	Christopher AYRES	Rowena ROBERTS	Edward HUGHES	William JOHNSON	Catriona CATHCART	Street lighting at time of attack
Age	19	About 18	21-ish	About 20	18-20	About 20	"early 20s"	Good
Height	5'11	Between 5'10-6'0		Approx 5'11 "same height as her boyfriend"	Not much more than 5'9	Around 6'0	6'0	
Build	Medium	Slim		Medium	Medium	Medium	Slim	
IC	1	1	1	1	1	1		
HEAD Hair	Dark brown		Dark		Dark			
Features	Unshaven			Stubbled face				
Eyes	Brown	"close set"		Large - "staring"				
Complexion				Slight tan				
CLOTHING Headgear	None	Baseball cap w. "some sort of logo" on front	Whitish baseball cap	"Dirty" white cap - possibly baseball	Creamy coloured baseball cap	Baseball cap "not sure of colour, possibly light"	White baseball cap	
Upper clothing	• Navy blue sweater w. four motif • yellow stain on left sleeve • Red T-shirt	Dark top	Casual gear		Dark - "something written on it, couldn't see clearly"	• (thinks) blue or black jumper • "not sure what was underneath"		
Lower clothing	Dark blue jeans w. bloodstains	Dark trousers		Cannot recall	• (thinks) darkish "jeans or casual trousers" • frayed at bottoms	Cannot recall	Dark tracksuit trousers	
Shoes	• Right grey trainer • Left grey trainer w. (appears) squashed chips in sole	"Not sure of colour"	"Looked light coloured"				Dark trainers	
ABILITY TO RECOGNISE		Possibly	Yes (definite)	Yes - "Looks like Johnny Depp"	Unsure	Yes	Yes	
PRIOR KNOWLEDGE			Yes (name NK but attacker went to same school)					

Figure 6.13 Grid of descriptive detail created by hand

DESCRIPTOR	SUSPECT: John PATTEN	SOURCE OF DESCRIPTION: Ronald BEALE	Christopher AYRES	Rowena ROBERTS	Edward HUGHES	William JOHNSON	Catriona CATHCART
Age	19	About 18	21-ish	About 20	18–20	About 20	'Early 20s'
Height	5'11	Between 5'10 – 6'0		Approx 5'11 – same height as her boyfriend	Not much more than 5'9	Around 6'0	6'0
Build	Medium	Slim		Medium	Medium	Medium	Slim
IC	1	1	1	1	1	1	
Hair	Dark brown		Dark		Dark		
Features	Unshaven			Stubbled face			
Eyes	Brown	'Close set'		Large – 'staring'			
Complexion				Slight tan			
Headgear	None	Baseball cap w. 'some sort of logo' on front	Whitish baseball cap	'Dirty' white cap – possibly baseball	Creamy coloured baseball cap	Baseball cap – 'not sure of colour, possibly light'	White baseball cap
Upper clothing	• Navy blue sweater ¾ w. **FCUK** motif ¾ yellow stain on left sleeve. • Red T-shirt	Dark top			Dark – 'something written on it, couldn't see clearly'	• (Thinks) blue or black jumper: • 'not sure what was underneath'	
Lower clothing	Dark blue jeans w. bloodstains	Dark trousers	Casual gear	Cannot recall	• (Thinks) darkish 'jeans or casual trousers' • frayed at bottoms	Cannot recall	Dark tracksuit trousers
Footwear	• Right grey trainer • Left grey trainer w. [appears] squashed chips in sole	'Not sure of colour'	'Looked light coloured'				Dark trainers
Able to recognize		Possibly	Yes (definite)	Yes – 'looks like Johnny Depp'	Unsure	Yes	Yes
Prior knowledge			Yes (name NK – but attacker went to same school)				

Street lighting at time of attack: Good

Figure 6.14 Grid of descriptive detail created on a computer

	WITNESS A	WITNESS B	WITNESS C	WITNESS D	WITNESS E	WITNESS F	WITNESS G
DRIVER							
Description							
Actions							

FRONT PASSENGER							
Description							
Actions							

REAR PASSENGER							
Description							
Actions							

Figure 6.15 Grid of descriptions and actions of three men given in the accounts of seven witnesses

6.9   Observer-participant plots

6.9.1   The value of an observer-participant (O-P) plot

There will be occasions when you have two or more accounts describing what they observed of one or more individuals participating in offence-related activity. You can create an observer-participant (O-P) plot, a visual representation that shows the physical position of people when they observed one or more participants engaged in offence-related activity. You are then able to create a grid in which you place adjacent observers in adjacent columns. This will enable you to:

- have realistic expectations concerning potential for agreement in the accounts of adjacent observers;
- identify and investigate the occurrence of anomalous inconsistency or contradiction.

6.9.2   Creating an O-P plot and grid

- Produce, or task others to produce, a line drawing of the location in which the offence took place. (Alternatively, if appropriate and applicable, you could create a 'blow up' of an A–Z page, or an Internet page of a map or aerial photograph.)

	WITNESS A (At bar)	WITNESS B (At bar near table 1)	WITNESS C (At table 1 by bar)	WITNESS D (At table 2 by door)	WITNESS E (By door)
Descriptions of males					
Actions observed					

Figure 6.16 Grid of an O-P plot of five witnesses to an assault

- Make multiple 'working copies' of the location drawing.
- Obtain, or task others to obtain, a drawing from each observer on which the individual locates himself or herself, those observed, and, where applicable, other observers.
- Then show, or ask others to show an unmarked 'working copy' of the location drawing and invite the observer to mark locations on the photocopy. (Doing this after the observer has drawn freehand is a low-key check on the validity of the witness's representation of locations.)
- Collate the positions onto a master 'working copy'.
- Label each observer, assigning letters sequentially, eg B the observer nearest A, C the observer nearest B, D the nearest to C, and so on.
- Where applicable, label each participant with a number, eg 2 the participant nearest to 1, 3 the participant nearest to 2, and so on.

Create a grid based on the positions of the observers. Figure 6.16 shows the grid of an O-P of five witnesses in a bar, who observed a violent attack by a white man (WM) on a Asian man (AM).

The grid translates the O-P plot into evidential reality. Because the letters represent adjacent positions, everything becomes clear. In the absence of a diagram, showing who was where will always struggle to:

- make sense of multiple accounts from people who observed one or more participants;
- comprehend and respond effectively to the accounts of the participants—who could easily exploit your lack of awareness of who was standing where and what could or could not be expected to be observed.

6.10 Genograms

6.10.1 Origins and applications

A genogram is technique that allows you to link different forms of detail visually:

- descriptive detail, eg age, occupation, location;
- links, eg past and present; frequency of contact;
- relationships, eg type; quality; history;
- behaviour patterns.

Genograms were originally developed for use in clinical settings by psychotherapists[8] working with families who needed to grasp the complexity of a family, the family 'tree', relationships,

---

[8] McGoldrick, M., Gerson, R., and Shellenberger, S. (1999) *Genograms: Assessment and Intervention*. New York: Norton.

and dynamics. They are now used by professionals working in wide range of contexts, including the criminal justice system. If you operate within a joint agency context you are likely to have come across genograms.

They are useful aids to summarizing, memorizing, and communicating a large amount of information on any grouping engaged in offending, eg:

- shoplifting;
- drug importation and dealing;
- vehicle 'ringing' and 'cloning';
- fraud;
- terrorism.

6.10.2 Creating a genogram

A genogram is created with simple standard symbols representing gender, various forms of line to illustrate links or relationships, and circles around symbols to represent where these individuals reside or work in the stated location. Figure 6.17 illustrates basic genogram symbols. You can annotate the genogram, its symbols, and circled areas in whatever way you wish. Genograms can be prepared by hand, using Draw in Microsoft Word. There are also computer programs for generating genograms.

6.11 Topic templates

The sheer amount of material that you have to work with can appear, and can be, daunting. Within the totality and the complexity, you have to identify a limited number of ingredients to form the basis for your interview planning. Within the UK police service there are two useful frameworks which we call *topic templates* to help you to see through the complexity: OHLAWTIPS and SPLATWIP-BC (Box 6.4 and Box 6.5).

Both topic templates do the same job, with the West Mercia one prompting the investigator to consider bad character. We do not know the names of the creators these valuable templates. They deserve all our thanks.

You can use these templates to take you from the mass of material to your interview Route Map and your opening question to trigger disclosure.

6.11.1 Initial analysis and action planning

Use the topic template to:

- help you analyse and annotate your Case SE3R;
- create your Wants Analysis.

6.11.2 Interview planning

Use the 'wheel of blobs' (WOB) mapping technique (see section 6.12):

- to clear your thoughts;
- to group material under particular headings.

Use the topic template to check that all material has been considered for inclusion in your grouped headings.

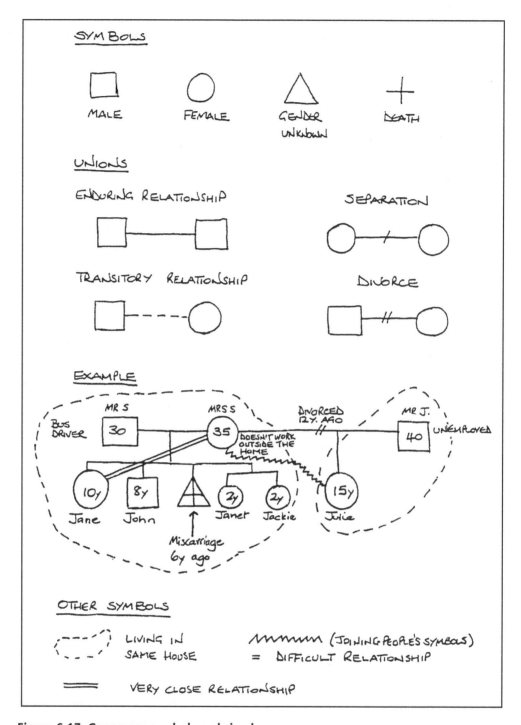

Figure 6.17 Genogram symbols and simple genogram

Use the WOB mapping technique to create:

- your interview Route Map;
- your map of investigatively important information, ie the detail that you will want to question about following the interviewee's spontaneous account and probing of this.

6.12 'Wheel of blobs' (WOB) mapping

WOB mapping is a simplified form of mind mapping that is particularly suited to the investigative context.

O	Offence	• Suspect's knowledge of the offence(s) under investigation. • Relevant case law with a bearing on this offence.
H	History	Suspect's account of: • antecedents; • previous incident(s); • precursor/precipitating event(s).
L	Locations	Suspect's explanation of: • presence at key location(s) material to the event(s) under investigation; • knowledge of key location(s) material to the event(s) under investigation.
A	Actions	Suspect's account of: • own actions, reactions, responses; • actions, reactions, responses of another/others; • key event(s)/sequences of events/episode(e)/continuous state(s).
W	Wounds/damage	Suspect's explanation of the nature and occurrence of: • all wounds; • all injuries; • all marks; • all instances of damage.
T	Times	Suspect's account of: • MTF(s); • time/timing of key events/event sequences/episodes.
I	Identification	Either: • suspect's knowledge of key person(s); • elements of *R v Turnbull*, eg distance from/visibility of key person(s). Or: Suspect's explanation of: • why witness(es) named the suspect; • why named/described by witness(es).
P	Possession	Suspect's explanation of: • material item(s)/matter involved in the event(s) under investigation; • tangible item(s)/matter linking the suspect to the events(s) under investigation, eg: — objects (property, weapons, clothing, forensics); — marks; — substances.
S	Speech	Words spoken by the suspect/another/others during the event(s) under investigation. • Content (What?) • Form (In what way?) • Message/meaning (What was the intended message/meaning?) Words heard by the suspect. • What was heard? • The content. The form? • What exactly was the message the hearer received? • What was their reaction to this?

Box 6.4 The 'Kent' topic template (Investigative Interview Training Team, Kent Police College)

6.12.1 Mind maps

Mind maps[9] (also called concept maps, spray diagrams, spider diagrams, spidograms, or spidergrams) were originally developed by Buzan in the late 1960s as a method for helping

---

[9] The term 'Mind Map' is a trade mark of the Buzan Corporation.

S	Speech
P	Possession
L	Locations
A	Actions
T	Times
W	Wounds and damage
I	Identification
P	Points to prove
BC	Bad character

Box 6.5 The 'West Mercia' topic template (Investigative Interview Training Team, West Mercia)

students to make notes that only used key ideas and images recorded.[10] Mind mapping is an extremely simple technique for capturing thoughts.

- Rotate an A4 sheet/pad into 'landscape' view. This gives you more space than normal 'portrait' view.
- Place your starting idea—central or main idea or topic—inside a box or circle in the centre of the page.
- As sub-ideas come to mind, draw lines radiating out from the start point to a 'node' point where you note the sub-idea. Leave space between the radiating lines: this gives you room to insert one or more extra lines later to new 'nodes'.
- As ideas subordinate to a sub-idea come to mind simply draw radiating lines from the sub-idea to 'nodes'.
- Lines, complete areas of branching, and one or more 'nodes' can be lassoed (a circumscribing line drawn around the entirety) and linked by a line to other areas of branching or 'nodes'.

Important rules when mind mapping.

- Stop trying to think linearly, ie don't rack your brains to work out what logically follows the next. Leave that line of thought if nothing comes to mind.
- 'Clear your mind' by mapping down the thoughts as they come to you. Ideas often come by doing this, which can turn out to be a solution to the problem that would not have arisen by trying to think logically.
- Don't anguish over the disconnected material. It's about getting your thoughts down, not being tidy or obsessive about layout and linkages. You can always:
  — modify the map later: testing for logic, amending, and expanding;
  — create a final 'fair' version—tidied up the way you wish.

There are many pieces of software available that you can use to create mind maps.

6.12.2 WOB maps

Mind mapping gives free rein to your ideas. They can get very full. With more and more branching and annotation the map can become very 'busy'. A point can come when there is so much branching and annotation that the simplicity of mind mapping is lost,

---

[10] Buzan, T. (1991) *The Mind Map Book*. New York: Penguin.

ie the map has become a mass of lines drawn at varying angles, with text crammed in and the entirety can be almost impossible to grasp—by you or by someone you are explaining it to.

WOB mapping is the use of mind mapping as a thinking tool but observing the KISS maxim: keep it simple and short. It is simply as many straight lines as you need to generate, each radiating from the central blob to peripheral blob. The result looks like the spokes of a wheel: hence the term 'wheel of blobs' and the acronym WOB map for ease of reference. Use the WOB as you would any mind map. If you want to branch out from a peripheral blob, just use that as the hub of WOB.

You can create a WOB by hand or very easily and rapidly on the computer using Microsoft Word drawing tools. The benefit of creating a WOB on the computer is that you can expand, amend, use the whole range of other tools, apply colour, and transmit your WOB electronically as an attachment.

6.12.3   Uses of WOB mapping

Initial interview planning

As already described, the WOB map technique enables you to group together topics methodically identified through the application of the OHLAWTIPS/SPLATWIP-BC topic template.

First pass

- Create centre blob.
- Clear your mind.
- Just put headings down as blobs at the end of lines radiating away from the interview aim blob. Don't try to be systematic or to prioritize at this stage.
- Create sub-blobs radiating away from topic blobs: each sub-blob is a potential questioning area within a topic, eg the heading *Communication* might have as sub-blobs:
  — mobile phone;
  — phone bill;
  — call to Alison.

Interview Route Map

It is a fundamental requirement in the planning and preparation phase to identify:

- your interview aim, eg to get X's 'side of the story';
- your interview objectives—the major topics that you want disclosure upon by the end of the interview;
- specific questions that need asking and to which you want focused answers.

Your WOB map of grouped headings will be a major aid. Other sources will be:

- intelligence and other evidence, eg results of forensic tests;
- directives, recommendations, and requests, eg from supervisors;
- inspiration and serendipity.

First pass

- Create centre blob = interview aim.
- Clear your mind.

- Just put topics/questions down as blobs at the end of lines radiating away from the interview aim blob. Each blob is a potential interview objective. Don't try to be systematic or to prioritize at this stage.
- Create sub-blobs radiating away from topic blobs: each sub-blob is a potential questioning area within a topic.

The result will be a WOB map that looks like Figure 6.18.

Identify logical sequence

- Sequence topics numerically...1, 2, 3, 4, and so on.
- Sequence questioning areas alphabetically...A, B, C, and so on.

The result will look like Figure 6.19.

Second pass

- Create a fresh WOB map.
- Place topics in the desired order.
- Place questioning areas for each topic in desired order.

Result: a WOB Route Map that looks like Figure 6.20.

WOB map of topics in the spontaneous account that require probing

Since the introduction of PEACE there has been a 'flight' from any form of note-taking by the interviewer:

- when questioning a suspect;
- when questioning a significant witness or a witness who is deemed to be vulnerable or intimidated.

By note-taking we do not mean taking down traditional notes of the kind described earlier in this chapter. The note-taking we are referring to is something akin to the technique that

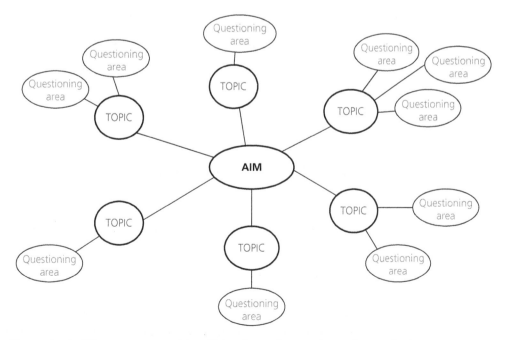

Figure 6.18 WOB Route Map: Identifying interview topics and questioning areas

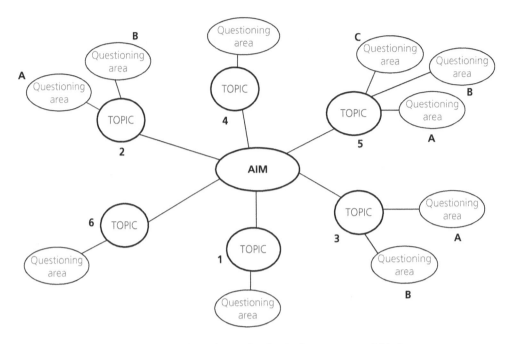

Figure 6.19 WOB Route Map: Identifying the logical sequence of blobs

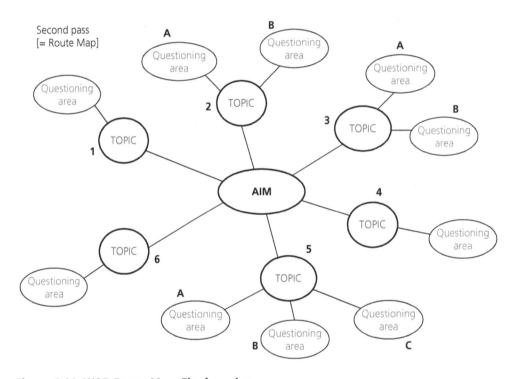

Figure 6.20 WOB Route Map: Final version

is so useful when we attend meetings: capturing essential information, marshalling material, and mapping out the way ahead.

- We listen to what is being disclosed by the other participant or participants.
- We make a rapid, physical note of:
    - emergent key issues—matters that required further exploration through conversation;
    - thoughts—reactions to, and possible ways of covering or addressing, a noted key issue;
    - actions—to be engaged in by the manager, another, or others after this conversation.

- We reflect rapidly on this physical note.
- Referring to the notes, we engage in the next stage of the conversation.

Chapter 9 raises the problem of keeping track of multiple topics raised by the content of the interviewee's spontaneous account that require probing. It recommends creating a WOB map of these multiple topics, ie:

- topics in blobs on spokes radiating from the centre of the wheel;
- blobs annotated as necessary;
- radiating sub-blobs for particular questioning areas;
- if you think it helpful, the blobs numbered in the questioning sequence that you think appropriate.

This will take hardly any time and will ensure that you do not forget to cover a topic.

WOB map of investigatively important information

It was pointed out in Chapter 1 that the Account stage of the basic PEACE model was expanded to specify three sub-stages: Account, Clarify, and Challenge. The Account and Clarify stages were further sub-divided to accommodate:

- the individual's spontaneous account and probing (clarification) of this;
- additional matters not raised in the individual's spontaneous account and material not disclosed to the individual that required investigation through questioning (clarification).

Trainers use different terms to describe additional matters requiring clarification. Some call these *interviewer areas*; others call them the *police agenda*. The problem with *agenda* is the negative connotations of this term in everyday conversation, particularly in the world of work and in contentious, potentially disputative contexts.

A third term, *investigatively important information*, is also used. We prefer this term because:

- it is more precise than *interviewer areas*;
- it loses the negative connotation of *police agenda*;
- it is applicable to witnesses and suspects.

It is cumbersome to say so we use the simple syllable-saving acronym I[3]—Investigatively Important Information. I[3] may include aspects of the case that you may not have disclosed or only alluded to in pre-interview disclosure, eg:

- information on key locations;
- prosecution evidence to do with this offence, ie also called *line evidence*:
  — covert information on the suspect;
  — accounts and descriptions from witnesses (including statements or recordings);
  — accounts or statement by co-accused;
  — identification by witnesses;
  — object evidence;
  — contact trace material;
  — specialist opinion and testimony;
  — significant statements by, or silence from, the suspect;
  — relevant comments;
- 'bad character' evidence: if you have planned to introduce this tactically at this stage rather than immediately, this interview has ended on a separate recording.

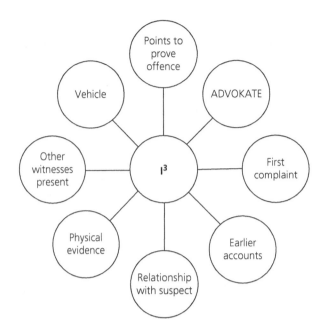

Figure 6.21 Illustrative WOB map of I³ (Investigatively Important Information)

In addition you need to question in order to address:

- points to prove;
- defences (legal and duress);
- negation of defences.

A WOB map of I³ is an excellent tool for use in the interview—so much easier than scanning a piece of paper with written headings. The blobs stand out and are easier to see and to navigate. You will be much less likely to overlook questioning on an item of I³. Figure 6.21 shows an illustrative WOB map.

WOB map of your FAIR review

Later in Chapter 15 we recommend that you conduct what is called a FAIR (Final Anomaly Investigation and Reasons to suspect) review as an appropriate way of bringing to the suspect's attention:

- unresolved anomaly in his or her account, and responses to probing of this and questions concerning I³;
- information that you have tactically withheld to the last.

It is helpful to create a WOB map of the FAIR review. As with any WOB map, these blobs will be easy to navigate and ensure that you cover everything.

6.13 Chapter summary

A professional investigation implies vigilance to detail, rather than defensive avoidance, when managing information prior to, during, and following an interview. This is not an easy option. Applying each tool described in this chapter is a separate skill, hard won through practice. Practice will enable you to apply these tools more confidently and more swiftly. However, compared to defensive avoidance and the 'rush to get it wrong', vigilance to detail will always take more time and effort. Good evidence does take time and certainly repays effort.

Active Listening, Observing, and Assessing

7.1 Chapter overview

This chapter examines three activities integral to a comprehensive understanding of the interviewee: what he or she says and the way it is said; his or her mental, emotional, and physical state; and potentially significant changes in his or her arousal level and condition from your first meeting onwards.

7.1.1 Chapter objectives

This chapter will enable you to:

- develop the skills of active listening;
- engage in systematic observation;
- use the BASELINES tool to identify potentially significant transient changes in the interviewee's level of arousal;
- respond appropriately to enduring changes in the interviewee's behaviour;
- assess and take appropriate action in respect of the interviewee's psychological make-up, physical, mental, and emotional state;
- use the ASSESS + tool to evaluate the features of an individual's account and behaviour when interviewed.

7.2 Active listening

7.2.1 The nature of active listening

Intent listening, ie listening to fine-grain detail, is a vital skill for managing information. It is integral to an even more demanding form of listening: *active listening*. Active listening is directed at detecting clues to what is going on inside the other person—in terms of his or her thoughts and, importantly, feelings—and doing something with this knowledge. Active listening is fundamental to effective conversation management.

People, and particularly 'powerful people', tend to hear what they want to hear, see what they want to see, and ignore the rest. Their personal agenda and self-focus deny them awareness of the verbal and non-verbal clues to what is going on inside the person. Hence they are surprised when the person acts, or reacts, 'unexpectedly' in a way that grabs their attention. The clues were there. They just failed to detect them.

7.2.2 Auditory clues

Words

There are a number of common verbal clues.

- **'Signposting'**. This is a form of commentary, eg *The first thing you need to know is...*; *You've got to understand that...*; *I'm finding it difficult to get my head round this...*
- **Repetition**. Saying the same utterance or utterances.
- **Order of mention**. What is mentioned first or last has significance.

Pausing

Pausing and waiting to establish mutual gaze, ie eye-to-eye contact, before going on to say something signals this is a potentially significant message, with feelings potentially involved.

'Tone of voice'

Change in rhythm, speed, volume, pitch (easily remembered as RSVP: Box 7.1) compared with manner of speaking up to this point in the conversation is a pointer to the individual's attitude or an emotional change—arousal.

Feature	Description	Detection
Rhythm	Irregular tempo or beat in delivery.	More difficult
Speed	Slowed speech; speeded up speech—particularly *cluttering* = abnormally fast rate, often with syllables running into each other.	Easy
Volume	Raised; lowered; mumbling.	Easy
Pitch	Higher or lower in tone compared to previous utterance.	Most difficult

Box 7.1 RSVP 'tone of voice' changes

Pitch is a change in the physical frequency of sound. It is an extremely good indicator of feeling. For example, a change of half an octave in a person's voice is a clear indicator to something going on inside. Females tend to perform better in detecting subtle variation in pitch. This is probably due to a combination of physiological difference, psychology, and practice.

In conversation, females characteristically spend much more time than males gazing at the other person, sustaining the other person in the talking turn. They tend to have an ear for detail, listening more intently to more of what is said. This gives them more information, enabling them to detect verbal and the entire range of 'tone of voice' emotional clues, including the hard one: pitch. The good news is that irrespective of your gender, it is possible to develop skill in this through practice in concentrated listening.

Visual clues

You don't need to look at, or even see, a person to detect verbal and vocal clues to the individual's feelings, attitude, emotional state, or level of arousal. You can pick these up when speaking to or interviewing an individual on the telephone or when listening to an audio-recording. You are, however, denied visual clues—non-verbal bodily movement and bodily change—that something is going on inside the person.

The implication is that one needs to look in order to detect these clues. People, and particularly 'powerful people', do not devote attention to what is happening before their eyes. It is true to say that both genders are unsystematic when looking. As pointed out earlier, men are at a disadvantage, they spend less time than women looking and listening. The adjunct skill of active listening is observation. This is addressed in a later section.

7.2.3 Evidencing active listening

You evidence your active listening, and enable further disclosure, by the way that you behave.

SOFTENS

In Chapter 3 you met SOFTENS (Box 7.2), key conversation fostering behaviours. Combining these behaviours with summarizing and reflection enables—and evidences—active listening.

S	Signs of sincerity	• A smile shows that you are receptive and open. • An appropriate facial expression shows that you understand the other's situation, eg looking concerned.
O	Open posture	• Keeping your hands away from your mouth and your arms uncrossed. • If seated, sitting comfortably (*not* slouching) rather than 'to attention'. • Works best if you are at the appropriate distance from each other: — sharing each other's personal space (3–4 feet between you) if standing; — if sitting, 3–4 feet between the middle of your shins and the middle of other person's shins. [*Note:* You should not be in each other's *intimate space* or be too far away in *social space*.] • You should be appropriately orientated, particularly if sitting, ie chairs placed at 'ten-to-two on the clock face' angle (a little more than 90 degrees) rather than face-to-face, which some might feel was being 'pushy' or confrontational.
F	Forward lean	• Leaning slightly forward signals you are interested, listening and want the person to keep talking. • Leaning slightly further forward at critical points signals empathy, eg when the other person discloses feelings.
T	Touch	• Shaking hands on meeting and departing. • Symbolic touching, ie raising your hand and touching the individual's shoulder in the visible profile that you have of the individual in your field of vision. [*Note: Not* physical touch: this could be taken as inappropriate, unwanted touching and lead to a complaint or allegation.]
E	Eye-contact	• Look straight at the other person. • Maintain maximum eye-contact: but don't stare! Sends the message that: • I am listening. • I am paying attention. • I am interested. • The other person should carry on talking.
N	Nods	'Guggling' at the key ideas that the individual stresses in his or her utterances sends the message that: • you are following what is being said; • you understand what is being said/the individual's position.
S	Supportive sounds and silence	Helping the other person to talk—and keep talking—by: • saying supportive words, eg *I realize it's difficult.* ^^ ^^; • making supportive noises, eg *Uh-huh.* ^^ ^^; • just listening rather than talking—creating a long pause, ie silence.

Box 7.2 SOFTENS: key conversation fostering behaviours

Eye-contact

Sustained gaze can be a problem.

- Men find it harder than women to engage in sustained eye-contact. In males, sustained gaze can be misinterpreted as threatening, aggressive, or sexualized behaviour.
- Sustained gaze is very straining on the eye muscles.
- The interviewee might think that you are staring and are not really paying attention, ie you've 'switched off', are not interested, are 'only going through the motions'.
- The very aroused, emotionally distressed, developmentally disadvantaged, and psychologically disordered are very sensitive to non-verbal behaviour.

We explained in Chapter 3 how you can 'soften' eye gaze and prevent eye-muscle strain by adjusting the focal length (depth) of your gaze.

- Make a common-sense judgement when to adjust the depth of your gaze.
- While still looking towards the interviewee's eyes, gaze at a spot further away behind his or her head for a couple of seconds then return to looking at his or her pupils.
- Next time you want to adjust the depth of your gaze, repeat the process, but this time gaze at a spot forward of the interviewee's eyes.
- Keep repeating this exercise as necessary.

Also, if the individual breaks eye contact, eg gazes down, seize the opportunity to close your eyes momentarily and to gaze fleetingly in another direction then quickly come back on target.

Supportive sounds and silence

Supportive sounds are essential. They are a form of reciprocity. You are acknowledging that you are following and understand, and also when you say something you are occupying the talking turn minimally. Your silence between these sounds sustains the individual in the task of disclosing. Making no sounds at all and remaining totally silent would be counter-productive.

- The interviewee might perceive you as detached or disinterested—particularly if you do not exhibit other SOFTENS behaviours.
- The interviewee might come to dominate the conversation such that you will struggle to get a word in and to influence topic selection and progression—both essential at the right time to enable you to manage the conversation to achieve your aims and goals.
- Linked to the previous point, the interviewee will conclude that you are extremely weak and able to be 'walked over'.

Summarizing and reflecting

Summarizing and reflecting are behaviours that evidence you have been and are intently and actively listening.

Summarizing

Summarizing is restating the key ideas that you have detected within the stream of detail disclosed by the person. It is manifest evidence that you have listened intently to and grasped the essentials of what he or she has said thus far.

Many people confuse summarizing with *replication*. Replication is the act of copying what has been produced. Interpreters and some kinds of psychotherapist train to develop their verbatim memory to enable them to retain more of what the individual said, more exactly. This is not replication. Any attempt at replicating—trying to state in as much detail as possible as many as possible of the details—is extremely risky. The likelihood of introducing errors of commission, ie inaccuracy, is very great. You run the risk of alienating the individual, who may interpret your unintended misrepresentation as proof that that you weren't really listening or, even worse, you have an agenda.

Reflecting

Reflecting—sometimes called a *feelings check*—is making a statement or statements about feelings, emotions, and thoughts that the individual may have struggled, perhaps unsuccessfully, to express. For example:

> *I sense you're having some difficulty in telling me about this.* ^^ ^ ^
> *It seems to me that you had reached the end of your tether.* ^^ ^ ^
> *I get the feeling that you want to tell me something.* ^^ ^ ^

Reflective statements are a very effective conversation management technique.

- They evidence that you are empathizing with the individual.
- They show that you are prepared to assist by attempting to label and to describe how he or she feels.
- They reduce the individual's level of arousal, lessening stress and tension.
- They give the individual confidence: in himself or herself, and in you.
- They foster further disclosure.

7.3 Observing behaviour

7.3.1 The nature of observation

Observation is the adjunct skill of active listening. It is the act of noticing. As pointed out earlier, people, and 'powerful people' in particular, are not very observant and are unsystematic in what they notice. Sensible, sensitive, and skilful conversation management is not possible without a continuing commitment to observe systematically.

7.3.2 Level of arousal

From a distance, then on first contact with the individual and thereafter, you should observe him or her closely. You need to examine methodically his or her non-verbal and vocal behaviour to arrive at an assessment of his or her level of arousal.

Arousal

We experience stress when we perceive that we are unable to control circumstances. The primary stress—or *flight or fight*—response occurs when we become aroused. Arousal has physiological (bodily) and psychological (mental and emotional) elements. Our brain goes on to 'red alert', preparing our body for action. Adrenalin and noradrenalin are released, triggering our nervous system to alter our body functioning to ensure maximum efficiency.

- Some physical processes increase, eg heart rate, breathing, blood pressure, blood flow, and perspiration.
- Other processes slow down or stop temporarily, eg digestion.
- Muscles tense.
- Our sphincter muscles close.
- The liver releases glucose.

Subjectively we sense increased alertness or tension. We may consciously sense a need to speak, act, or react to protect ourselves or our interests, perhaps engaging in damage limitation, or removing ourselves from the situation if this is possible. Chapter 2 explained how these perceptions narrow attention, influencing what detail is registered and potentially remembered.

Signs of arousal

There are visible clues and audible clues that a person is experiencing the primary stress response. We are able to control consciously some of these behaviours to a greater or lesser extent. Some are hard to control, eg lower limb movement. Others are easier to control if we concentrate on doing so, eg hand movements, speech rate. Some—reflexes—are impossible to control, eg blushing, pupil constriction.

The baseline, its status and significance

The pattern of non-verbal and verbal behaviours that you observe from a distance and then from first contact onwards constitutes a *baseline*: the individual's 'tick over' level of arousal. You cannot, of course, interpret the observed baseline as being the individual's characteristic behaviour pattern. You are observing the individual stressed by what has happened since the commission of the offence, by being in the role of witness or suspect, and by the prospect of being questioned.

The value of identifying a baseline is that you can monitor the interviewee's subsequent behaviour for transient changes—departures from the baseline—from now on.

- You will be able to gauge his or her reaction to circumstances prior to and during the interview.
- You will be able to detect 'hot spots', ie changes in behaviour occurring:
  — when a particular topic is being covered;
  — you are posing, or have just posed, a question;
  — the interviewee is answering, or has just answered, a question.

The individual's transient behaviour change around the 'hot spot' must not be construed as a 'lie sign'. When people are telling or have told lies they can, and do, become aroused. Some, but not all, will show this in their behaviour. People who are not lying but are experiencing strong emotion or embarrassment will exhibit behaviour that shows they are aroused. It follows that we cannot make a categorical—or self-serving—interpretation of 'hot spots'.

For example, the individual has given you a version of events. Later, when you probe, his or her behaviour departs from the baseline in parallel with:

- the individual having difficulty expanding detail or giving an explanation;
- giving an inconsistent or contradictory version.

Even in these circumstances you cannot narrowly interpret the change in behaviour as 'lie signs' indicative of deception. A detected 'hot spot' can only ever be an invitation to timely and considered probing.

7.3.3 BASELINES: a tool for monitoring potentially significant transient changes in behaviour

A very wide range of behaviours is liable to transient change when an individual is aroused. BASELINES (Box 7.3) is an acronym to assist you to develop expertise in monitoring behaviours subject to transient change. Commonly, but not always, transient change will occur in more than one behaviour.

In Box 7.3 one term—'inner dialogue'—requires explanation. The individual is silent, looking down, perhaps to one side, and may be exhibiting other transient behaviours such as adaptors, and lower limb movement ('leakage'). He or she is retrieving information from memory store, reflecting upon this (as well as the situation and his or her circumstances) in working memory, and engaging literally in an 'inner dialogue'—balancing up whether to say anything at all, or something—or something else—on this topic, or what to say, and how to say it. A fuller explanation of BASELINES behaviours is in the Reference Section.

7.3.4 Potentially significant enduring changes in the individual's behaviour

BASELINES is a useful tool for detecting transient change. However, you need to be alert, and where necessary act upon, potentially significant enduring changes in the individual's behaviour.

FOCUS OF ATTENTION		CHANGE AND TYPICAL CAUSATION
B	**Blink rate** **Blood vessels** [neck] **Blushing** **Body shift** **Breathing** **Brow**	Increases [= eg intense emotion; frustration; anger; hostility]. Swelling [= eg intense emotion; frustration; anger; hostility]. [= eg intense emotion; frustration; anger; hostility]. Orientation in sitting position to an angle away from direct view [= terminating the topic]. *Common parallel behaviour* Gaze aversion; pushing chair backwards; refusing to say anything else. Increased rate; shallow; difficulty in breathing [= eg intense emotion; frustration; anger; hostility]. Creasing ('omega') [= eg perplexity; disapproval; difficulty in remembering detail].
A	**Adaptors** [self-grooming; 'lint' picking; manipulating an item]	Increase in most people; decrease in some people [= eg intense emotion; frustration; anger; hostility].
S	**Shaking** **Sighing** **Sniffing** **Swallowing** **Sweating**	Body; limbs; hands [= eg intense emotion; frustration; anger; hostility]. Emission of deep, audible breath [= eg fatigue; impatience; growing frustration, annoyance or emotion]. *Common parallel behaviour* 'Glistening' in nostril/lip area. Movement of throat/gullet [= dryness of mouth throat due to intense arousal]. Brow; armpits; hands [= eg intense emotion; frustration; anger; hostility].
E	**Eyes** • **Gaze** • **Pupils** • **Tearfulness** • **Eyebrows**	• Upwards; sideways [= 'buying' thinking time—accessing material from memory]. • Downwards [= eg strong emotion; 'inner dialogue'] • Fixed—glaring or glowering [= eg dislike; frustration; anger; hostility]. • Aversion [= eg embarrassment; shame; guilt]. • Covering eyes [= eg embarrassment; shame; guilt]. *Common parallel behaviour* Failure to respond [= rejecting the 'talking turn']. Constriction [= eg intense emotion; frustration; anger; hostility]. 'Glistening'; actual tears [= eg distress]. 'Flashes' [= eg surprise; alarm; disapproval].
L	**Laughter** **Limbs** **Lips**	Inappropriate relative to topic [= eg anxiety, embarrassment, shame, guilt]. *Common parallel behaviour* Smiling. Leakage, ie movement of legs, feet, arms, hands [= eg intense emotion; frustration; anger; hostility]. Biting, licking, tightening, trembling [= eg anxiety, embarrassment, shame, anger, guilt].
I	**Illustrators** [demonstrative/emphatic this hand/finger movements]	Decrease in most people; increase in some people [= eg intense emotion; frustration; anger; hostility].
N	**Nods** [= non-vocal 'guggles']	Increase or decrease [= eg intense emotion; frustration; anger; hostility].
E	**Expressiveness** • **Words** • **Speech pattern** • **'Tone of voice'**	Increase or decrease [= eg intense emotion; frustration; anger; hostility]. Dysfluency, ie difficulty saying words [= eg intense emotion; frustration; anger]. **RSVP** [= **R**hythm; **S**peed; **V**olume; **P**itch] changes [= eg intense emotion; embarrassment; shame; guilt; frustration; anger; hostility].
S	**Silence** [= protracted pause] **Smiling** **Sneering** **Space**	• Before/during 'talking turn' [= eg difficulty marshalling thoughts; intense emotion]. • Failure to respond, ie rejecting the 'talking turn' [= eg intense emotion; hostility]. Inappropriate relative to topic [= eg anxiety, embarrassment, shame, guilt]. Derisive smiling; may occur prior to/when speaking as an extremely fast upward movement of the side of the upper lip, before a change to a 'normal' smile [= eg disdain, insincerity, deception]. Pushing chair backwards—disengaging by increasing distance [= eg intense emotion; frustration; anger; hostility]. *Common parallel behaviour* Gaze aversion; body shift; refusing to say anything else.

Box 7.3 BASELINES: potentially significant transient changes in basic behaviour

Distractibility

You must consider stopping the interview if the individual becomes and continues to remain distractible, eg his eyes, verbal behaviour, 'tone of voice' all indicate that you do not have his or her attention. This is a sign of extreme arousal. The individual is not following and therefore is unable to comprehend the significance of what you say or he or she says.

Shorter and shorter responses

These are indicative of:

- cumulative mental fatigue, and the individual 'closing down' mentally;
- a marked change in mood, ie a deep state of depression.

Extreme distress

If the individual loses composure, becomes uncontrollable, you will need to stop the interview temporarily. If the individual is unable to gain composure, you cannot effectively interview. Stop the interview.

7.4 Assessing the interviewee

7.4.1 Communication problems

It is fundamental to the administration of justice that when an individual is interviewed he or she should:

- understand the significance of the circumstances giving rise to the investigation and the interview;
- be understood;
- understand the significance of what is being put or said to him or her;
- understand the significance of his or her replies.

Central to the whole endeavour is comprehension and communication. Difficulties with comprehension and communication—whether expression, reception, or both—can have psychological origins, physical origins, or a combination of these.

Any interviewee who has a problem with comprehension and communication presents you with a problem. Whether a witness or a suspect, you have to take account of the interviewee's vulnerability.

Knowledge of a suspect's vulnerability

The custody system caters for the early identification of vulnerability. Those who attend to act as appropriate adults—whether relatives or care professionals—will be valuable sources of additional information.

Knowledge of a witness's vulnerability

The generality of witnesses

For the generality of witnesses who are interviewed outside the police station, you will typically not know that there is an actual or potential problem until you arrive at the interview location. There may be relatives and associates on hand, perhaps fulfilling a care role, to question if they have not volunteered information about the witness's 'problem'. Where there are no such informants, you have to assess whether there is a potential or actual problem.

Vulnerable witnesses defined under the Youth Justice and Criminal Evidence Act 1999 (YJCE) (as amended)

According to the Act, certain witnesses are potentially vulnerable due to:

- difficulty in communicating without assistance;
- difficulty in understanding questions or instructions;
- speech which is limited or difficult to understand;
- a short attention span.

Section 16 of the Act defines categories of vulnerable witness.

- **All child witnesses under 18.** They are readily identified. Home, school, and care contexts, and other professionals, are readily accessible informants concerning the individual and any specific vulnerability that presents a communication problem.
- **Witnesses with a mental disorder as defined by the Mental Health Act 1983 (as amended).** Many but not all will be known to have a disorder, ie a mental illness.
- **Witnesses with a significant impairment of intelligence or social functioning.** Many but not all will be known as being learning disabled. The individual's vulnerability will either be known or readily recognized on contact.
- **Witnesses with a physical disability or physical disorder.** The individual's vulnerability will either be known or readily recognized on contact.

ABE[1] training in the police service in England, Wales, and Northern Ireland prepares investigators to plan, prepare, and to interview individuals within these categories, mindful of their particular communication problems. *Vulnerable Adult and Child Witnesses*[2] provides a comprehensive coverage of the multiple issues involved.

7.4.2 **The requirement to assess**

Where you have prior information on the individual, this necessarily will assist your planning and preparation for the interview. It will always be the case, however, that whether or not you have information about potential or actual vulnerability, in every case you must assess the individual.

Your assessment is essential.

- It constitutes the critical first steps in fostering a working relationship.
- You are able to pitch your conversation to account for his or her frame of reference (FOR).
- You can manage the interview and the exchange of information mindful of the individual's:
  — psychological make-up;
  — physical, mental, and emotional state, and any changes in these;
  — communication disorder.

Where you have no warning of vulnerability, this presents you with a task of some significance and some difficulty. You are not expected to be a clinical psychologist or psychiatrist.

---

[1] Ministry of Justice (2011) *Achieving Best Evidence in Criminal Proceedings: Guidance on Interviewing Victims and Witnesses, and Guidance on Using Special Measures.* London: HMSO.

[2] Smith, K. and Tilney, S. (2007) *Vulnerable Adult and Child Witnesses.* Oxford: Oxford University Press.

Vulnerable and Intimidated Witnesses: A Police Service Guide

The guide[3] is the police service guide in England, Wales, and Northern Ireland for those dealing with witnesses encompassed by YJCE (as amended). It gives information in the form of 'prompts' about recognition of vulnerability. It has an appendix that gives short descriptions of common conditions that could affect communication. The guide stresses that:

- the 'prompts' are not diagnostic in the clinical sense;
- many of the characteristics and behaviours are just as likely to be the result of ingesting a drug or caused by stress.

Read in conjunction with this text and that of Smith and Tilney,[4] the guide will greatly assist you in your assessment task.

7.4.3 Psychological 'make-up'

The term psychological make-up refers to relatively enduring aspects of the individual: his or her social and mental functioning, language comprehension and use, and personality. A range of factors contribute to vulnerability in psychological 'make-up'.

- Illiteracy.
- Developmental disadvantage—intellectual disadvantage due to stage of development (being a child or of advanced age) or learning disability.
- Psychological disorder—current or past, treated and untreated.
- Long-term substance abuse or dependency.
- Disposition to acquiescence, compliance, and suggestibility.

7.4.4 Illiteracy

A very high proportion of the population has problems with literacy: ability to read and to write. Recent official reporting indicated that one in five young males leaving school have reading problems.

- Inability to read does not necessarily mean the individual is learning disabled, ie has a significant impairment of intelligence and social functioning.
- Illiteracy is a common denominator amongst individuals who are learning disabled and whose IQ is in the range of *dull normal* or of *borderline learning disability*.

Inability to read is associated with limited working memory—a crucial factor that you have to bear in mind when explaining anything (eg the caution in the case of a suspect; spelling out ground rules), stating information, and posing questions.

Clues to illiteracy

People are extremely sensitive about their illiteracy and will often go to great lengths to hide this fact.

The illiterate suspect

In the case of a suspect, illiteracy is more likely, but not guaranteed, to be detected by custody staff when the individual was being booked in.

---

[3] Ministry of Justice (2011) *Vulnerable and Intimidated Witnesses: A Police Service Guide.* London: Home Office.
[4] Smith, K. and Tilney, S. (2007) *Vulnerable Adult and Child Witnesses.* Oxford: Oxford University Press.

A useful clue to illiteracy is the individual's signature. Look at the Custody Record. All of the following are potential clues to illiteracy:

- signature all in capital letters;
- signature with interspersed upper case (capital) letters and lower case letters;
- child-like writing;
- different forms of the same signature in the three points of signing;
- a squiggle or flourish that has no correspondence with any letters—particularly initial letters—in the person's name.

It is also worthwhile asking the person who booked the suspect how long the suspect took to sign his or her name. If the suspect took a long time this is a very strong indicator of illiteracy.

The illiterate witness

Problems of literacy in the case of a developmentally disadvantage witness, eg a young child or an individual with a learning difficulty, will be already known. However, for an adult witness, matters have to be handled more sensitively. You have to establish whether there is a problem before you start interviewing. It would be extremely embarrassing for the individual, and you, to find out during the interview that he or she:

- cannot write, eg is unable to annotate a diagram;
- cannot read, eg is unable to read the statement that you have drafted.

7.4.5 Developmental disadvantage

The scope of developmental disadvantage

From birth onwards we all develop socially and intellectually. It is obvious that a very young child, one in the early years of the primary education, and one about to enter secondary education differ. The younger the child, the greater the difficulty—the disadvantage—he or she has in terms of self-care and safety, in comprehending what others are saying and doing, and expressing his or her experience through language.

Similarly, those who are suffering the degenerative effects of ageing, eg pre-senile and senile dementia, are disadvantaged by this stage of their development. About 5 per cent of people above 65 years of age, about 20 per cent of those over 80 years, and about 30 per cent of those over 90 suffer from Alzheimer's disease.

Also developmentally disadvantaged are those who are learning disabled. Through whatever causative factor or factors, eg genetic disorder, pre-natal, birth, or post-natal trauma, they have a significant impairment in social and intelligence (cognitive functioning).[5] About one in 50 in the population has a mild learning disability. Around one in 200 has a severe disability.

If the individual is a child, his or her problems are usually detected in the primary education system, where they are identified as having special educational needs. Identifying learning difficulty in adults who have passed through the education system is less straightforward. Severe learning disability is relatively easy to identify. Detecting mild and moderate learning disability is less easy.

Box 7.4 summarizes observable behaviours and background factors indicative of learning disability.

---

[5] Smith, K. and Tilney, S. (2007) *Vulnerable Adult and Child Witnesses*. Oxford: Oxford University Press.

Observable behaviours

Illiteracy

Inability to read or write.

Problems with comprehension

Obvious difficulty understanding what you are saying: explanations, requests, and questions—even when expressed in simple terms.

Slowness in thinking processes.

Difficulty concentrating.

Short attention span.

Problems with reasoning and expressing ideas

Remarks that do not make sense.

Logic, ideas, vocabulary, and descriptions out of keeping with the individual's actual age, eg use of children's words by an adult.

Speech and language use

Speech difficulties.

'Talking for effect', ie covering up for a lack of comprehension by using many words to say nothing.

Orientation problems

Problems telling the time, specifying the day of the week, giving dates.

Inability to say who he or she is or who you are.

Difficulty remembering personal details, eg date of birth, age, address, telephone number.

Background factors

Evidence of special educational needs (learning support assistance in mainstream school; attendance at a special school).

Attendance at institutions catering for learning disability, eg day centre, protected workplace.

Has support with daily living, eg carer, social worker.

Receives benefits for disability.

Box 7.4 Common indicators of learning disability

The more behaviours that you detect, the greater the likelihood that the individual is learning disabled. As pointed out earlier, illiteracy is a particularly significant alarm bell. Some learning disabled individuals may have particular abilities out of keeping with their disability, eg they may be quite articulate, making it difficult to spot the problems that they have with comprehension. You need to:

- listen intently to the fine-grain detail: what it is that they are *really* saying (as opposed to what you could all too easily assume they are saying);
- look out for superficiality in the way they express their thoughts.

7.4.6 Psychological disorder

There are many psychological disorders. This means that any attempt at simplification will fail to do justice to the breadth of psychological condition. For ease of explanation it is helpful to consider personality disorder, neurosis, and psychosis.

Personality disorder

There are many ways of classifying personality disorder. Most people know of the disorder called *psychopathy*, and another term *sociopathy*. This disorder is the one that people most associate with criminal activity and other anti-social behaviour, although there are others, eg *borderline personality disorder*. In the case of a suspect with a criminal record, his or her condition is likely to be known and, in the case of a serious offence, an interview strategy will be formulated using an external adviser.

In the case of a witness, in the absence of any information from a human source or accessible official records, you will not know that he or she has a personality disorder.

Neurosis and psychosis

These mental illnesses constitute the greater part of psychological disorder. A dramatic statistic that communicates the incidence of mental illness is that one in every three households has a family member with a disorder that is being treated or should be treated.

Depression and anxiety are forms of *neurosis*. Around one in six of the population is suffering at any one time from anxiety or depression that is being treated, or merits treatment. These are intense, disabling conditions distinct from the anxiousness, fears, and 'feeling down' that are experienced by everyone at some time. Anxiety conditions are characterized by panic, distractibility, excessive worrying, and fear. Depressive conditions are characterized by low spirits, crying, rumination, social withdrawal, and self-harm and suicidal thoughts.

Some individuals have a form of depression where they also show the signs and have the symptoms of *psychosis*: fragmented thinking, delusions and paranoia, hallucinations, inappropriate expression of emotion, hyperactivity, and inability to view their behaviour as abnormal.

An individual can be both highly anxious and deeply depressed.

Most people know the psychosis called *schizophrenia* that occurs in about one in 200 of the population. It is a condition that is particularly characterized by paranoia and very high levels of anxiety. (This is why so many schizophrenics smoke an excessive number of cigarettes.) There are many other forms of psychosis. One—cannabis-induced psychosis—is increasing steadily. Some forms of depression are characterized by psychosis.

Appropriate action

Where you know that the suspect is receiving treatment for a mental illness you need to liaise with the forensic medical examiner (police surgeon) to identify the best time to interview, ie at a time some time after and well before administration of any medication.

Similarly, if you are aware that a witness takes medication, to ensure that you interview at an appropriate time you should broach the subject. In the case of an individual who is a significant witness in a major investigation, timing will be part of the interview strategy and plan.

In the case of a suspect, unless he or she—or someone who knows the suspect—discloses current or past treatment, you will not know. You will find yourself in a similar situation in the case of a witness. You are left to look for signs.

- Extreme anxiety, agitation, and distractibility.
- Excessively underweight.
- Extremely low spirits.
- Extremely slow thought processes, long pauses between one utterance and the next, very slow reactions and actions—together called *psychomotor retardation*.
- Extreme withdrawal, lack of self-care, lack of attention to hygiene—appropriately called 'social hibernation'.
- Florid or manic behaviour—including pressure of speech.
- Grandiosity.
- Bizarre reasoning, ie leaps in logic without connection—'knight's move thinking' and 'derailment'.

- Strange vocabulary—'word salad'.
- Extreme suspicion.
- Not wholly engaged behaviour suggestive that the individual is not totally attending to you—because he or she is hearing voices talking, or giving instructions.

7.4.7 Long-term substance abuse or dependency

As with psychological disorder in the case of a suspect who has no previous contact with the police, custody staff should have questioned on this matter. Mostly, suspects will have disclosed their problem very soon after being brought to the police station.

Social circumstances are often a clue to whether a witness has a long-term history of substance abuse or dependency. It may be somewhat harder to detect this problem in an individual who has a reasonable income and standard of living.

Appropriate action

The same consideration concerning medication and time of interview applies here. In the case of a suspect, you will need to liaise with custody staff and the forensic medical examiner/police surgeon to ensure that you interview at a time after and well before administration of any maintenance medication.

7.4.8 Disposition

You will need to be alert for three aspects of an individual's make-up that could pose significant problems in interview: acquiescence, compliance, and suggestibility. An individual—witness or suspect—may manifest more than one.

Acquiescence

This is the tendency to respond unreflectively, ie without thinking, in the affirmative. Groups particularly at risk of being acquiescent are: children, particularly the very young; the learning disabled; females; ethnic minorities; anyone who wants to get the interviewing process over and done with as quickly as possible.

Appropriate action

If you suspect an individual is being acquiescent, take an earlier question that he or she said 'yes' to and phrase it in the negative. A 'yes' is evidence of potential compliance. Repeat the process later, reversing another previous question. If the pattern is repeated you have the proof that you need.

Compliance

Chapter 3 draws attention to the issue of *social desirability*, the individual pitches what he or she says to evokes a favourable response and avoid disapproval.

Some people want so much to be in your 'good books' that they will pay close attention to clues—demand characteristics—in what you say that point to what you might want to hear. The individual will then 'go along' with whatever you are saying, agreeing with or accepting this even when they know that what they are saying is not the case, ie untrue. In contrast to an acquiescent person a compliant person knows what he or she is doing.

Groups particularly at risk of being compliant are: children, particularly the very young; the learning disabled; females; ethnic minorities; people who have poor interpersonal skills; people who lack assertion skills; people with low self-esteem; anyone who wants to get the interviewing process over and done with as quickly as possible.

Compliance is something that 'powerful people' don't mind the person being! However, if you know that an individual is compliant and do nothing about it, your failure to act might rebound. If the individual's compliant responding is revealed at a later stage in the investigation, this could be fatal—even more so if it becomes an issue at trial.

In the case of a witness, his or her reliability could be cast into doubt. If his or her replies in cross-examination reveal your failure to act, this could cast into doubt your interviewing practice and integrity, and the individual might become a 'hostile witness'. In the case of a suspect, excessive compliance will almost always become an issue.

Appropriate action

If you are sensing that the individual is being compliant you should:

- draw it to his or her attention;
- explain its implications;
- ask the individual to stop.

Much more easily done with a witness than a suspect!

Suggestibility

A suggestible person has little or no remembrance of the issue that you are asking about. You have highlighted a gap in his or her episodic memory. He or she distrusts his or her memory concerning this matter. Chapter 9 points out that suggestible individuals are particularly vulnerable to misleading, leading, and option questions, which induce them to agree to something that was not the case.

For example:

Did you see the green car outside the flats? suggesting that:

- there was a car;
- it was green;
- it was outside the flats.

Did she have one or two children? suggesting that:

- she had children;
- no more than two.

His coat was leather, wasn't it? suggesting that it was leather.

Appropriate action

Of course the most appropriate action is not to ask leading or option questions. If you realize that you have asked such a question and the individual has accepted the content of what you have said, you should test whether the individual is suggestible.

- Return to this topic later.
- Stress that it is important that what the individual says is correct, so he or she should think really hard because you are going to ask the question again.
- Pose the question in exactly the same way as the first time.

- If the individual changes his or her answer, this is potentially indicative of suggestibility. Even if the answer is the same, concentrate on not asking any more counter-productive leading or option questions.

7.4.9 Situation-induced behaviour

Acquiescence, compliance, and to a certain extent suggestibility are aspects of a person's personality. Personality in the wider sense comprises those aspects of a person's behaviour that tend to occur across a range of differing situations. If a person consistently manifests the same behaviour in diverse situations you could be justified in saying that is an aspect of his or her 'personality'. If you only observe an individual's behaviour in a given situation you cannot attribute the behaviour to his or her 'personality'.

It follows therefore that if you are only seeing the interviewee in a particular, extremely unusual, situation in circumstances that are likely to be fraught, distressing, and even disturbing for the individual, it would be inappropriate and very unwise to construe his or her behaviour as personality. Much safer is to interpret the behaviour as being induced by the situation in which the individual finds himself or herself. The person could be putting on a 'face' or a 'façade'. You might be observing cocky behaviour, bravado, or hearing blather and 'bullshit'—forms of confabulation described in Chapter 4 (Telling and Listening: Disclosing and Making Sense of Disclosed Detail). These are often indicative of anxiety and a desire to create an impression.

Appropriate action

Whether the behaviour you observe is an aspect of the individual's personality or induced by the situation, it does not really matter. If the behaviour becomes excessive and disrupts you in achieving your interview aims and objectives, you will need to deal with such behaviour by following the advice in Chapter 11 (Responding to Inappropriate or Disruptive Behaviour and to Resistance).

7.4.10 Physical state

It is important to note overt signs of fatigue, especially due to lack of sleep. Others responsible for the well-being of the individual, eg carers in the case of a child and custody staff—or the custody record—in the case of a suspect, will have alerted you to the fact that he or she has had little or no sleep overnight or up to the time of the interview.

Lack of sleep is critical. Research has consistently shown that in the day following a night without sleep, an individual's working memory is significantly impaired. The individual struggles to pay attention, to follow, to comprehend, and to hold and manipulate material in working memory.

Fatigue, and in particular lack of sleep, compound problems arising from:

- psychological make-up in all its many components;
- mental or emotional state;
- communication disorder.

Appropriate action

In the case of a witness, delay the interview if possible. This will not be a realistic option for a suspect.

If you need to proceed with interviewing:

- get the individual to freshen up—at the very least having a face wash;
- give him or her to a hot drink, preferably sweetened—and keep prompting until it is consumed;
- explain you are aware of the individual's lack of sleep—and you will keep the pace right down, giving him or her plenty of time to think:
  — about what you say;
  — before answering and after answering.

7.4.11 Mental and emotional state

Again, others responsible for the individual's well-being and documentation, eg in the custody record in the case of a suspect, will provide you with information pointing to problems with the individual's current mental and emotional state that could affect the individual's ability to cope with the interview.

Whether or not you have such prior knowledge about the individual, you need to be alert to signs of significant anxiety and depression.

- Agitation.
- Distractibility.
- Acute 'anorexic' response, ie refusal of food and drink.
- Low spirits.
- Psychomotor retardation and 'social hibernation'—in particular not washing.
- Distractibility.

Appropriate action

In the case of a suspect, the forensic medical examiner can be involved. However, for a witness it is a case of advising that he or she consider medical help.

7.4.12 Communication disorder

If the suspect or witness has a communication disorder his or her reliance on communication systems will be well established.

Appropriate action

You will be working closely with a professional interpreter or intermediary.

7.5 Assessing the interviewee's account and disclosing behaviour

ASSESS + (Box 7.5) is an assessment tool that can be applied to a recording after the interview—in the Evaluate stage—or at any time afterwards. You collate your observations in seven areas.

- Account problems.
- Sense problems.
- Struggling to give detail.
- Evasion.

	FOCUS	EXPLANATION	INDICATOR
A	**Account problems**	Anomalies in the person's disclosures concerning everything that happened within the Material *Note*: The person's disclosures comprise: • his or her account(s) • his or her responses to requests for expansion and explanation of detail.	**Identifiable problems with detail** Missing detail. Gaps (= missing steps). Jumps (= big gap in time; sudden shift in location). Absence of reasonably expected detail (= 'non-barking dog'). 'Thin' story (= lacks detail throughout: 'agenda'-like account of 'what happened'). Non-specific (= vague or ambiguous). 'Sidesteps' (= passive verb use; 'not *really*...') Inconsistency (= doesn't 'fit' with prior detail). Contradiction (= different versions). Too 'pat' [**Note**: two versions compared] (= same wording, same order, little/no narrative reversal, too many descriptors). Narrative 'contrast' (= variation in detail). Other (specify).
S	**Sense problems**	The person's representation/ explanation of events does not make sense when considered objectively.	**Detail which questions validity** Improbable (= difficult to believe). Impossible (= counter to reality: can't occur/be done). Nonsensical Counter to reasonable behaviour. Other (specify).
S	**Struggling to give detail**	The person struggles, or is unable, to respond to the request for detail: even when reminded/ encouraged to take time and to think before speaking.	**When probed the person** Struggles to go beyond the original story. Repeats minimal or non-specific detail. Admits inability to give further detail. Other (specify).
E	**Evasion**	The person avoids disclosing detail.	**When probed the person** Tries to change the topic. Answers the question with a question. Gives measured/evasive responses. 'Blanks' an echo probe (= repeats minimal or non-specific detail). 'Sidesteps' (= passive verb use; 'not *really*...') Other (specify).
S	**Sabotaging behaviour**	The person obstructs the process of: • being briefed/informed • being assisted • being called upon to give reasonable detail.	**When briefed/probed the person** Argues. Becomes angry. Becomes abusive. Threatens. Refuses to be helped. Refuses to co-operate. Other (specify).
S	**Significant expressive behaviour**	The person's vocal behaviour changes indicating: • physiological and psychological arousal • difficulties thinking—or thinking twice—before and while talking.	**When probed the person's speech has** Marked dysfluencies (not occurring before). Marked pauses before/when answering. Changes in voice pitch. Changes from self-control to gabbling. Other (specify).
+	**Context factors**		

Box 7.5 ASSESS +

- Struggling to give detail.
- Significant expressive behaviour.
- Context factors.

Additional detail can be recorded on an accompanying piece of paper.

ASSESS + enables:

- assessment of the validity of the account and the individual's reliability;
- briefing of third parties without requiring them to view the recording;
- comparison with previous and subsequent assessments;
- planning for subsequent investigative and other actions.

A fuller explanation of the ASSESS + tool is in the Reference Section.

7.6   Chapter summary

If you actively listen and systematically observe, you will be able to make sense of what is going on inside the individual. Identifying a baseline of the individual's non-verbal and verbal behaviours is an invaluable aid to detecting change in his or her level of arousal. You will be able to detect 'hot spots' for probing in your interviewing of an individual that you assessed for the presence of barriers to comprehension and communication before and from first contact.

8

Right Person, Right Place to Interview, Right Time to Interview, and Right Duration of Interviewing

8.1 Chapter overview

This chapter and the next examine questioning, a core skill required to guide the interviewee's disclosures of offence-related detail. In this chapter we consider psychological and practical realities that constitute the context of questioning—the right match of people, the right place to interview, and the right time in terms of when interviewing takes place and for how long.

8.1.1 Chapter objectives

This chapter will enable you to:

- address the issues of interviewer suitability, the role of the second investigator, and working with an interpreter;
- make appropriate decisions concerning the interview location, time of interviewing, and duration of interviewing.

8.2 The right person

You have to ask yourself 'right person' questions about yourself and those with whom you need to work in the interview, and how you will work with these individuals.

8.2.1 You

Only you will know whether you have the appropriate knowledge, understanding, skills, attitude, and behaviours to fulfil the task of interviewing a witness or suspect concerning the type of offence that you have been tasked to investigate. Accepting that you fulfil these criteria, you have to consider *psychological contrast* that could render you unsuitable to interview this particular interviewee. The term psychological contrast refers to any difference between you and the interviewee that could inhibit him or her from disclosing freely or disclosing at all. There are a number of factors that you have to consider. In any given case one or more, perhaps several, will apply.

The offence

This may have an emotional component, eg if the offence is particularly horrendous and the victim was especially vulnerable. If so, it is a significant issue, immediately requiring you to consider sense of shame, dishonour, and embarrassment, and to take these reactions and their intensity relative to the other contrast factors described in the next sections.

Compatibility

Age

If there is a substantial difference between your age and the interviewee, assess the impact of this in terms of the alleged offences, eg sexual offending against boys. A significantly elderly man might have problems, eg embarrassment, dread of the impact, and implications of the investigation, and the same about going to court.

Gender

If you and the interviewee are of different gender, the nature of the offence is a critical consideration. A female witness or suspect may not want, and could find it impossible, to talk to a male interviewer, whatever his age. Similarly, a male interviewee might have problems, perhaps insuperable, talking to a woman interviewer of any age.

Culture and ethnicity

Certain cultures and groups have fundamental beliefs about conversation—especially concerning taboo matters—between members of the opposite sex. In other cultures, it is expected that a female will act subordinately to a male. In such circumstances, a male interviewer will get nowhere: a female interviewee has to be interviewed by a woman.

The only absolute barrier is forbidden contact between genders. Apart from this exception, if you are the only person available and circumstances are such that there is no-one else and that you must interview the individual despite the contrast, you will have to interview in a way that turns the negative into a positive. If you exhibit RESPONSE behaviours, evidence active listening, and question in the right manner, this will go a long way to achieving this none-too-easy task. It is all about not being afraid to disclose that you are aware of the potential difficulties and removing the other source of contrast perceptions: how you appear.

Appearance

Think through how formally the individual is likely to be dressed. If the answer is formal there is no problem: you are dressed smartly—to be otherwise would create a contrast. If the individual is dressed informally, then if you are formally dressed this could create, or heighten, perceptions of difference. These are likely to be very significant in the case of a suspect who has been detained overnight or for more than one day. He or she will feel anything but fresh and will be in the same clothes that they were wearing when brought to the police station. The solution is straightforward. Dress simply, neutrally, and consider ways of reducing formality, eg:

- if you are wearing a suit there is no need to wear the jacket in any of your dealings with the individual;
- don't wear brightly coloured or patterned, 'designer', ostentatious, or clearly expensive clothing or trappings, eg jewellery.

8.2.2 The second investigator

The need to control circumstances and behaviour

We experience stress when we perceive that we are unable to control circumstances and behaviour—our own and that of another or others. Once the interview is under way, it is a difficult task to keep appropriate control of the interviewee's behaviour and remain in control of yourself, your thoughts, and your own behaviour.

On some occasions a colleague may be present in the role of 'number two'. You may have been working collaboratively on the investigation with this colleague for some time, or he or she may have been assigned at very short notice to work with you as 'number two' in the interviewing process. Either way, you have the additional task of controlling your colleague's behaviour in the interview.

There is a tradition—particularly in the police and public sector context—of using the terms 'lead' interviewer and 'second' interviewer—the clear implication being that interviewing will be a joint responsibility. Again, traditionally the 'second' interviewer has three tasks:

- observing the interviewee's behaviour while the 'lead' does the interviewing;
- keeping track of the detail of the interviewee's responses and the exchange, perhaps taking notes;
- being a joint interviewer, ready to ask questions at some time on matters that the 'lead' (too preoccupied with asking questions!):
  — had failed to detect;
  — had failed to probe.

There are two common patterns of joint interviewing.

- **The 'second' has complete freedom to take the talking turn at any time.** This is a precarious arrangement. Unable to read the mind of the 'lead' interviewer, 'number two' is liable to disrupt the interview in any number of ways.
  — Starting to speak and in doing so destroying a pause deliberately created by the 'lead' to trigger disclosure or a response by the interviewee.
  — Overtalking and interrupting either the interviewee or the 'lead' interviewer.
  — Changing the topic abruptly, taking questioning off on a completely different tack.
  — Covering matters that the 'lead' interviewer did not want covered, or failing to cover matters that the 'lead' did want covered.
  — Behaving in a manner which adversely affects or even destroys the working relationship that the 'lead' interviewer has fostered with the interviewee.
  — Taking charge of the management of the interview, becoming the 'lead', and relegating the other to the role of 'number two'.

There are other problems.

  — If 'number two' fails to raise a required matter, or raises a matter inappropriately, or 'gets the wrong end of the stick', the 'lead' will have to question on these matters when he or she resumes the talking turn. This risks confusion, alienation, and, in the eyes of the interviewee, a diminution in your credibility and that of your colleague.
  — When 'number two' starts questioning how will the monitoring function (see later) be switched? Will it cease for the time being? What will you do if, much to your regret, the colleague interviews the individual at some length?
  — How are you going to keep track now you are functionally 'number two'? How will you remember the things that he or she might miss?

- **The 'second' is invited to ask questions.** A much more common pattern is for the 'lead' interviewer having either concluded questioning on a particular theme or topic, or prior to closing the interview, to ask 'number two' if he or she wishes to ask any questions. This is also a precarious arrangement. All of the shortcomings which apply to a colleague coming in will apply here. In addition, a sudden invitation to ask questions (*Is there anything you want to cover?*) all too often can reveal:
  — 'number two' was not monitoring as efficiently as he or she should;
  — 'number two's' attention had lapsed.

As a result, an embarrassed 'number two' often attempts to cope with the pressure to 'say something' by posing stumbling, banal, or even bizarre questions.

The common factor: loss of control

These situations do occur, frequently. No matter how well you know your colleague, no matter how often or how long you have worked together as team members or as a pair, managing conversation is inherently stressful because you have no means of knowing:

- what your colleague is thinking or feeling;
- what sense he or she makes of the interview thus far, the interviewee's behaviour, and disclosures;
- what your colleague wants to say, when they would like to say it, and how they want to say it.

If you give your colleague licence to come in at will or when invited to do so, and assume the talking turn in the interviewer role, you cannot predict what he or she will say, how it will be said, and for how long he or she will occupy the interviewing turn. Because you cannot read your colleague's mind and because—no matter how well you prepare and act appropriately—you cannot predict the course of the interview, the response of the interviewee, and the content of what he or she might disclose, for the period that your colleague is interviewing you have lost control of the interview.

The psychological pressure: the perception of 'two against one'

On commonsense grounds, where there is a second interviewer this will always be pressuring for the interviewee, whether he or she is a witness or suspect. The interviewee will inevitably perceive the arrangement as a case of 'two against one', however well-intentioned the interviewers might be and however appropriately they behave. Indeed, this was acknowledged officially some 30 years ago[1] and advocated as a means of pressuring the interviewee.[2] The interviewee has to cope with stress of conversing with and answering questions posed by two 'powerful people', ie two people who already know the answer, confronting the individual with double the conversational unpredictability. In the case of the suspect being questioned by two people occupying the questioning role, this might oppress, leading the interviewee to say things he or she would not say, or not to say things he or she otherwise would. It would be naïve in the extreme not to recognize that any witness—but most especially one who is vulnerable or deemed to be significant—confronted with two investigators, two powerful people, is likely to feel pressured and is at risk of greater acquiescence and compliance in what he or she says. This will always be the risk, no matter how well intentioned the presence, and verbal contribution, of the second investigator in an interview.

The working relationship

The working relationship with the interviewee is achieved through continuity of dialogue and observing the rules of conversation described in Chapter 3 (Conversation: From Everyday Talk to Ways of Relating and Changing Minds): the third rule being that once started you have to continue the exchange. As soon as your colleague talks to the interviewee, this is another dialogue, another relationship, which he or she has to establish and thereafter maintain with the interviewee when you cease—however briefly—with the interviewee. It is not, and can never be, the same dialogue or the same relationship that you have established and sought to maintain with the interviewee.

---

[1] Irving, B.L. (1980) *Police Interrogation: A Case Study of Current Practice*. Royal Commission on Criminal Procedure, Research Study No 2. London: HMSO; Irving, B.L. and Hilgendorf, L. (1980) *Police Interrogation: The Psychological Approach*. Royal Commission on Criminal Procedure, Research Study No 1. London: HMSO.

[2] Walkley, J. (1987) *Police Interrogation: A Handbook for Investigators*. London: Police Review Publishing.

It is unrealistic to assume that the interviewee will respond in the same manner to another 'powerful person' who has occupied the role of observer but has now taken the talking turn in order to make assertions, to give an explanation, and to ask questions with the expectation of receiving answers to these. There has been no continuity of dialogue with someone who up to this point has been a silent spectator. In the words of Steve Davies, a trainer and colleague of the first author, 'number two' in an interview is a stranger to the conversation: a stranger who confronts the interviewee with another conversation, and who wants to cover the stranger's 'agenda' of topics.

Furthermore, there is some basis for believing that at the point of the switch, you have broken the fourth rule of conversation by abruptly ending the exchange. You may think that it is not at an end and that you are only giving your colleague an opportunity to engage in a relatively short-lived exchange:

- to summarize what the interviewee has said;
- to cover issues that you might have missed;
- to resolve anomaly that you have not apparently noticed or fully resolved, eg missing detail, gaps, jumps, 'non-barking dogs', 'sidestepping', vagueness, ambiguity, detail that does not fit (inconsistency), or differing versions (contradiction);
- to put right misunderstanding or confusion that your colleague has detected;
- to cover topics that were agreed would be covered by the colleague.

To assume that the interviewee—again especially a vulnerable or significant witness—understands where you and your colleague are coming from and appreciates there are two interwoven conversations going on, neither of which has ended, is to miss the point. It is the interviewee's perceptions that matter: not those of you and your colleague. Completely different perceptions pose a fundamental threat to achieving your aim.

The decision

Aware of all these factors, it is a matter for you, your supervisor, or your manager to decide whether 'number two' will interview.

Where it is decided that the second investigator will not interview

This colleague's core task is to monitor. Monitoring is a full-time, mentally challenging task. It includes:

- systematically observing the interviewee's behaviour and, in addition, the interviewer's and that of any other third party;
- keeping track of the course of the interview—using SE3R or notes—keeping a record of the times of potentially significant disclosure or change in behaviour;
- using the 'working copy' composite SE3R to capture, note, and compare the interviewee's disclosures and responses to the detail and annotations in the SE3R;
- between interviews, and at the end of interviewing, briefing the interviewing officer on the outcome of the colleague's monitoring.

You will need to brief your colleague on the monitoring tasks you wish him or her to fulfil.

Where the decision is made to have a 'second interviewer'

If the second interviewer is to be allowed to combine monitoring with some interviewing tasks, you will need to:

- modify the Preamble to include an explanation that both you and your colleague will be asking questions;
- decide on the points, or the circumstances, when you will invite the second interviewer to ask questions;
- devise and agree a system for signalling to your colleague when you wish to take the talking turn, ie to resume the interviewer role.

8.2.3 The interpreter

The requirement for an interpreter

There will be many occasions when you need to identify, work with, and manage the contribution of, an interpreter to assist in overcoming an actual or potential communication barrier when the interviewee:

- does not have adequate command of English;
- does have an adequate command of English but wishes to be interviewed in a preferred language other than English;
- is a member of the Deaf community.
- is not a member of the Deaf community and is communicating through the use of an augmentative system, ie additional to speech, or alternative system, ie instead of speech.

Deafness

Deafness is a complex issue.[3] There are distinctions between the following.

- **The Deaf (with a capital D).** These are individuals who identify themselves as a community—hence the capital letter, like F is used when referring to the French. The Deaf community has the common experience of severe/profound hearing loss at an early age. This community uses sign language, for example British Sign Language (BSL) in the UK. For ease of explanation we will refer to BSL, but the same issues apply to the national sign language of all countries. BSL, like spoken English, has regional variations (difference in dialect) and differences in register (unique signs used within the individual's social group, eg family.
- **The deafened and the hard of hearing.** The deafened have acquired hearing loss. The hard of hearing are individuals who have a medical hearing loss, usually associated with increasing age. They are very unlikely to learn BSL. They get by through the use of hearing aids, and trying to make sense of what unaware hearing people are saying. They look at the speaker's lips for clues. There are myths surrounding such lip-reading. In fact, it is almost impossible to read lips because a significant proportion of English does not appear on the lips. Lip-reading is an activity in which the individual actually has a wide range of awareness: spoken language, body language, and contextual clues.

It follows that you need to know if the interviewee is Deaf or deafened/hard of hearing: the former needs a BSL interpreter, the latter are unlikely to do so. There are different levels of BSL competency. An interpreter should be above Stage III of the national system of awards.[4]

---

[3] Kyle, J. (2006) 'Witnesses who use British Sign Language' in A. Heaton-Armstrong, E. Shepherd, G. Gudjonsson, and D. Wolchover (eds), *Witness Testimony: Psychological, Investigative and Evidential Perspectives.* Oxford: Oxford University Press.

[4] Kyle, J. (2006) 'Witnesses who use British Sign Language' in A. Heaton-Armstrong, E. Shepherd, G. Gudjonsson, and D. Wolchover (eds), *Witness Testimony: Psychological, Investigative and Evidential Perspectives.* Oxford: Oxford University Press.

Communication disorders other than deafness

In line with the social model definition of disability, it makes sense to focus on the different ways of communicating rather than on the interviewee's impairment or condition.[5] At some point in your career you may find yourself having to work with a professional who is skilled in one of the many systems. For ease of reference I shall call these professionals 'interpreters'.

An interpreter's role

An interpreter performs the task of communicating verbally, giving an as accurate as possible rendering of what you or the interviewee are saying to each other. Although translator is used commonly as an alternative term, more precisely a translator works with documentary material. An interpreter is responsible for providing an accurate transfer of meaning from one language to another.

The interpreter must be allowed to intervene to ask for clarification, to request those present to collaborate to facilitate the interpreting process, and to alert you and the interviewee—and any other third party present—to possible misunderstanding and missed cultural inferences.

The distinction between interpreter and intermediary

There is much misunderstanding concerning the distinction between fulfilling the role of interpreter and intermediary. An intermediary explains the question to the interviewee and explains the interviewee's responses. Intermediaries who fulfil this role with witnesses come from a range of professional backgrounds, including speech and language therapy, psychology, education, and social work.[6]

It is not the task of an interpreter to act as an intermediary.[7] It is certainly the case that many interpreters on their own initiative take on the role of intermediary, and in doing so make the task of managing the interview very much more difficult.

The exception is an interpreter who is a specialist using a communication system which has limited capacity to express nuance of meaning. These professionals combine their expertise in interpreting with their experience of being an intermediary. This interpreter/ intermediary combination is the essential key to unlocking the interviewee's understanding and experience.

The suitability of the interpreter

Family and friends are often proposed as preferred sources of language support. Apart from procedural and evidential problems, family and friends will not usually be competent, or impartial, interpreters.[8]

Wherever possible, the interpreter should be qualified to fulfil this role using the force system. When the interpreter arrives you must establish whether he or she is the right person for the role.

---

[5] Marchant, R. and Gordon, R. (2001) *Two-Way Street: Communicating with Disabled Children and Young People.* Leicester: NSPCC.

[6] In the crime context in the UK, when the interviewee is a suspect the intermediary occupies the role of an appropriate adult under paragraph 1.7 of Code C to the Police and Criminal Evidence Act 1984.

[7] Office for Criminal Justice Reform (2006) *Intermediary Procedural Guidance Manual.* London: Office for Criminal Justice Reform.

[8] Corsellis, A. and Clement, A. (2006) 'Interpreters and Translators in the Criminal Justice System' in A. Heaton-Armstrong, E. Shepherd, G. Gudjonsson, and D. Wolchover (eds), *Witness Testimony: Psychological, Investigative and Evidential Perspectives.* Oxford: Oxford University Press.

Appropriate language match

Even though the system may show there is a language match, eg Arabic, this is not sufficient. Some languages, such as Arabic, are spoken in many countries and there may be differences in vocabulary and usage. You should question the interpreter about his or her awareness of the 'gap' between his or her type of this language and the language spoken in the interviewee's country.

Relevant qualifications

Professional interpreters hold qualifications such as the Diploma in Public Service Interpreting or an equivalent. A degree in the language is not a sufficient qualification in its own right.

In the case of BSL interpreters, there are different levels of BSL competency. An interpreter should be above Stage III of the national system of awards.[9]

Interpreting experience: non-police and police

It is essential to know what experience the individual has had in the interpreting task. Lack of experience is no justification for rejection, but awareness of limited experience will enable you to be particularly alert to the task of briefing and managing the interpreting process in the interview.

Potential barriers

As you did with yourself, you have to assess the issue of psychological contrast in respect of the 'differences' between the interpreter and the interviewee. The same factors apply: gender, ethnicity, and culture relative to the offence.

Briefing the interpreter

It is essential that you ensure firm management of the interpreter. All too often instances occur where the investigator loses control of the course, conduct, and even content of the interview. This must not happen. The interpreter must know from the very first meeting that you wish to take active control of the interview even though you do not speak the individual's language.

Form of address

Many interpreters attend police stations quite often, meeting the same investigators and other staff. They can in time start to address, and be addressed by, police colleagues in a collegial manner. Some witnesses and suspects come from countries where the police behave in inappropriate ways and whoever works for the police is part of the police, tarred with the same brush. Interviewees are very alert to any signs, eg use of first name/nickname either by the interpreter, you, or the custody staff, that the interpreter is a 'police person'. The suspect is likely then to be very inhibited in what he or she says to the interpreter.

Briefing

In Box 8.1 is a briefing sheet for use with interpreters.

---

[9] Kyle. J. (2006) 'Witnesses who use British Sign Language' in A. Heaton-Armstrong, E. Shepherd, G. Gudjonsson, and D. Wolchover (eds), *Witness Testimony: Psychological, Investigative and Evidential Perspectives*. Oxford: Oxford University Press.

I would like quickly to brief you as to how I would like us to work together. It may be helpful for you to take notes.

- **Please use the *direct approach* to interpreting.**

You may know what I mean by the *direct approach*. For both our benefits let me explain.

When I talk to [name of interviewee] I would like you to interpret as though I am speaking directly to [name of interviewee].

For example, if I say to [name of interviewee] *'I want you to answer these questions "yes" or "no"'* please say in [name of interviewee]'s language exactly what I have said, that is *'I want you to answer these questions "yes" or "no"'*. Please do not change what I have said into *'He said that he wants you to answer these questions "yes" or "no"'*.

When [name of interviewee] talks to me I would like you to interpret as though [name of interviewee] is speaking directly to me.

For example, if [name of interviewee] says to me in [name of interviewee]'s language *'I do not understand'* please say in English exactly what [name of interviewee] has said, that is *'I do not understand'*. Please do not change what [name of interviewee] says into *'He said that he/she did not understand'*.

Can I check that you understand how I would like you to interpret using the direct approach?

- **Please work with me to keep the pace of the exchange down.**

If we both work with [name of interviewee] to keep the pace, ie the speed, of the conversation down, this will help all three of us. If you find [name of interviewee] starts to speed up please ask him/her to slow down and tell me when you do this.

Can I check that you understand how we must work together to slow down the pace?

- **Please do not speak on [name of interviewee]'s behalf.**

By this I mean that if I ask a question please interpret and allow [name of interviewee] to answer. Please do not answer my question on behalf of [name of interviewee].

Can I check that you are clear on this matter of letting [name of interviewee] have his/her say?

- **Please do not engage in side conversations with [name of interviewee].**

By this I mean that I do not want a situation to occur where you and [name of interviewee] have a lengthy discussions—or private conversations—in [name of interviewee]'s language which I am not able to understand or to follow. If there is anything that requires discussion please tell me first. Then we will work together to solve any issues with [name of interviewee].

Can I check that you are clear on this matter of not engaging in side conversations?

- **Please do not talk at the same time as me or [name of interviewee].**

Only speak *after* I or [name of interviewee] has spoken. Please do not interrupt or overtalk either me or [name of interviewee].

Can I check that you will only speak after I or [name of interviewee] has spoken?

- **Please stop me or [name of interviewee] where necessary.**

It is essential that you stop me or [name of interviewee] immediately you need some time to think, to write a note, or to find the necessary words. It is better for us to stop us than for you to miss or misinterpret something.

Can I ask you to confirm that you will stop me and [name of interviewee] immediately you need time to think, to make a note, or to search for necessary words?

Box 8.1 Briefing the interpreter (after Shepherd 2004[10])

---

[10] Shepherd, E. (2004) *Police Station Skills for Legal Advisers: Accreditation Manual.* London: Law Society.

- **Always check if you are in any doubt as to what it is being said by me or [name of interviewee].**

It is essential that you speak directly to me or [name of interviewee] as soon as you have any problems about understanding. This means we can work on the problem. Then please explain to the other person listening in—[name of interviewee] or me—what the problem was.

Can I ask you to confirm that you know what to do if you are in any doubt about what is being said by me or [name of interviewee]?

- **Please do not compress or alter whatever is said by me or [name of interviewee]. Always let us know if there is a problem.**

It is *essential* that you do not edit or change what you hear. It is better for all of us if you say when you have missed something, do not understand something, or have forgotten what was said. Then I or [name of interviewee] simply have to say whatever you want to hear again. If then you cannot interpret for any reason we can work on the problem: I or [name of interviewee] can say things in another way until we find a solution.

Can I ask you to confirm that you will not compress or alter what we say and will always let us know if there is a problem?

- ☐ **Briefing [name of interviewee].**

When I speak to [name of interviewee] I will want to spell out some points on how we will work together with your help.
Do you have any questions?

Box 8.1 Briefing the interpreter (after Shepherd 2004) (*continued*)

Always use this sheet, and always confirm the interpreter's understanding of the key elements, ie the interpreter must:

- use the *direct approach* to interpreting;
- work with you to keep the pace of the exchange down;
- not speak on the suspect's behalf;
- not engage in side conversations with the suspect;
- not talk at the same time as you or the suspect;
- stop you or the suspect where necessary;
- check if he or she is in any doubt as to what is being said by you or the suspect—and let you know about this doubt;
- not compress or alter whatever is said by you or the suspect.

Finally, and crucially, on the task of actually interpreting, the interpreter must always let you or the suspect know if there is a problem, eg something missed or not understood.

Always position the interpreter to sit beside the interviewee—not beside you. If the interpreter were to sit with you this would run the risk of the interviewee misperceiving the interpreter as being part of the 'establishment'.

8.3 The right place to interview

The long-established view is that you should always interview on territory of your choosing and that if it's your own territory so much the better. The underlying rationale is that it is easier to control the environment, conditions, and circumstances on your ground.

8.3.1 Witness interviews

We have indicated elsewhere that in all investigative contexts, witness interviews, wherever they are conducted, should be electronically recorded. Increasingly, the demand and the requirement for transparency and accountability for the conduct of witness interviews will lead to legislation, regulation, and public and professional expectations that require electronic recording.

In the crime investigation context, operational or legal requirements will necessarily dictate that significant witnesses in major investigations and those who require special care interviewing[11] will normally take place in a dedicated suitably furbished location with electronic recording and monitoring facilities. Following cost-benefit, risk, and operational assessments, the decision may be made to interview the witness in his or her own home or equivalent location.

In the case of witnesses who are deemed not to require special care, the practicalities of availability and limited access to dedicated interviewing facilities dictate that the greater proportion of these will be interviewed at home or in another chosen location, eg at his or her workplace.

8.3.2 Suspect interviews

In the UK, the Police and Criminal Evidence Act 1984 requires that, unless exceptional operational or practical circumstances dictate otherwise, interviewing will take place in a designated police station with electronic recording and monitoring facilities. In many other countries there is a similar legal requirement. As with witness interviewing, increasingly the demand and the requirement for transparency and accountability for the conduct of suspect interviews will lead to legislation, regulation, and public and professional expectations that require electronic recording.

8.4 The right time to interview

8.4.1 Physical and psychological realities

Our bodies function according to the dictates of a biological 'clock'. This determines that for most of us our physiological systems and our thought processes:

- are less efficient in the earlier part of the normal waking day;
- become progressively less efficient from mid-evening onwards.

Between mid-morning and early evening is the optimum time window for interviewing. Of course circumstances may dictate that you have to interview outside this window. But it is essential to understand the risk that the physical and psychological realities created by the biological 'clock' apply to you, the interviewee, and any third parties, eg interpreter, intermediary, appropriate adult, or legal adviser, potentially prejudicing the quality of your respective performances and therefore the interview, and the outcomes.

8.4.2 Additional factors

Other factors occurring within, or outside, the optimum time window will influence your decision when to interview, eg:

---

[11] In England, Wales, and Northern Ireland these are defined as vulnerable or intimidated under sections 16 and 17 of the Youth Justice and Criminal Evidence Act 1999 (as amended).

- meal times;
- religious observance, eg the requirement to pray;
- time of medication, eg prescribed antidepressants or anxiolytics (anti-anxiety drugs)—the nearer the interview to the taking/administration of such drugs, the more likely the individual will become distractible and struggling to pay attention.

8.4.3 Urgent interviewing

In the case of a suspect, the circumstances of the case may require that urgent interviewing take place late at night and into the early hours of the morning. However, if there is no requirement for urgent interviewing and you still decide to interview, what may seem a convenient option now could well rebound if a court later rules that it was unfair and oppressive to do so and excludes evidence obtained in your interviews. A critical factor that a court would take into account when deciding on this matter is the amount of time you interviewed.

8.5 Right duration of interviewing

8.5.1 Paying attention in everyday conversation

A recurrent issue throughout this text is attention.

Chapter 2 highlights how people vary the amount of attention they devote to a particular task, influenced in this greatly by their frame of reference (FOR) and the circumstances in which they find themselves. In Chapter 4 we note how people in conversation selectively listen to what the other person is saying, editing the 'Magic Carpet' of incoming information, hearing what they want to hear and ignoring the rest. Chapter 7 points out that people don't pay attention to what they are looking at: because they don't observe from the outset and across the course of the conversation, they fail to register clues to the person's mental, emotional, and physical state.

8.5.2 Paying attention in investigative interviews

Everyday conversations are characteristically superficial and short-lived. Investigative interviews are not everyday events. They have significant personal implications for the interviewer, the interviewee, and any third party involved. Because of the implications, most interviewers and interviewees understand the necessity of paying attention for a protracted period of time, concentrating on what they say and the other person says, and trying to follow and remember this.

Questioning puts both participants under stress: both struggling to cope with a flowing, fundamentally *ex tempore*—spur of the moment—process. The interviewer has to think about what to ask and how to ask it, and to cope with the response. The interviewee is under pressure, frequently believing the questioner already knows the answer and is 'testing' to see how quickly the 'right' answer can be given.

Forty minutes is about the most that people can pay attention. They are at the limit of their capacity to concentrate and to cope with the course of events, the conduct of the other person and themselves, and the content of an exchange. As the minutes pass they become increasingly less efficient in processing information: crucially it gets harder and harder to hold and to manipulate detail in working memory. At the end of this period of time 'key facts'—personally defined as such—are likely to be remembered. But for the rest, the individual has a gist understanding, struggling to recall the detail of what was actually said or not said, at what point in the interview, and if said how and in what context.

Interviewers and interviewees typically find the drawn out mental effort of the interview experience to be:

- draining: mentally, emotionally, and physically;
- stress-inducing and distressing: reflecting perceptions of personal ability:
  — to control oneself;
  — to influence the other person and any materially involved third party;
  — to affect the course and content of the exchange.

Certain individuals will struggle more.

- **Interviewers under pressure**. The requirement to investigate with limited time and resource, inability to validate the contents of the crime file, and the press for 'results' necessarily affect an interviewer's mental performance in the interview.
- **Interviewees under pressure**.
  — The complainant making an allegation that involves substantial stress in the reporting and response to reporting process.
  — Those with limited capacity and capability in terms of memory, comprehension and language use, eg the developmentally disadvantaged.
  — The psychologically disordered.

Any of the following will affect an interviewer, interviewee, or third party.

- Limited or no sleep the night before the interview.
- Physical fatigue.
- Low blood sugar—due to not eating.
- Dehydration—due to not taking liquids or having ingested alcohol or other drugs.
- Nicotine addiction, eg a smoker who smokes ten or more a day.
- Distractibility, agitation, or both due to excessive arousal, fear, apprehension, anxiety, or need to use the toilet.
- Depressed mood.
- Requirement to communicate through an interpreter or an intermediary.

8.5.3 Duration of witness and suspect interviews

To continue interviewing beyond 40 minutes makes no sense—in every meaning of this word. The break in interviewing should be a real one:

- to allow all participants to attend to the demands of nature;
- to restore mentally and physiologically;
- to reflect:
  — if the interviewee is legally advised or there is a supporting third party, they and the individual can jointly consider what has happened thus far;
  — for your part, you are able to review the conduct, course, and critically the content of the interviewee's spontaneous disclosure, responses to questions, and material arising from techniques accessing non-verbal experience.

8.6 Chapter summary

Questioning is mentally demanding and inherently stressful for both you and the interviewee. Having removed or minimized any barrier arising from contrast between you and the interviewee and decided upon the second investigator's role, you are now in the appropriate location, at a time—and of a duration—that is mindful of psychological and physical frailties: yours as well as the interviewee's.

You are now at the point where you can progress to managing the course of the interview: giving the interviewee a comprehensive briefing and then posing the right questions in the right manner.

9

Right Start, Right Question, and Right Manner of Questioning

9.1 Chapter overview

This chapter reviews three areas of fundamental skill: explanation to start the interview in a manner which will enable you to manage the course of the interview, the conduct of the interviewee and any third party, and whatever the interviewee says or does; deciding upon the right question—productive or, where appropriate, risky—to elicit a full response; questioning in the right manner to facilitate maximum disclosure both verbally and non-verbally.

9.1.1 Chapter objectives

This chapter will enable you to:

- engage in explanation to maximize the interviewee's comprehension and to commit the interviewee to maximum disclosure of fine-grain detail;
- use the entire range of productive questions, framing and applying these to maximum effect;
- avoid the use of counter-productive questions;
- know how and when to use risky questions;
- understand and use the potential of pausing and pacing;
- trigger initial spontaneous disclosure;
- respond appropriately to inadequate disclosure;
- apply the interview spiral to probe matters mentioned and not mentioned by the interviewee;
- question on a number of same or similar events;
- respond to an admission or confession;
- use a range of techniques to access non-verbal experience;
- manage the contribution of the interpreter or intermediary.

9.2 Explanation

As pointed out in Chapter 1, within the conversation management approach to investigative interviewing your task is to explain from first meeting and thereafter to continue explaining for the entire period that you and the interviewee are in each other's company. The conversation management approach has also a distinct *Explanation* stage at the outset of the interview in which specific matters have to be addressed and made clear to the interviewee.

9.2.1 Explanation prior to beginning the interview formally

What is going to happen

Before you open the interview formally you should give the interviewee an idea of what is going to happen.

> *Let me explain what is going to happen* ^^ *when the interview starts.* ^^ ^^
> *I will say the day, date, and time.* ^^ ^^
> *Then I'll introduce myself.* ^^ ^^
> *Then I'll ask you to introduce yourself.* ^^ ^^
> [Where applicable: *I'll ask X/everyone else to introduce himself/herself/themselves.* ^^ ^^]
> *I will then explain the reason why I am interviewing you.* ^^ ^^
> *Then what we need to talk about.* ^^ ^^
> *Then I will tell you about how I/we will take notes* ^^ ^^ *and refer to material.* ^^ ^^

Then I will explain how you and I will work together ^^ ^^ *to get the details that I need.* ^^ ^^
Do you have any questions about that? ^^ ^^

Electronic recording

Where electronic recording is a legal or formal requirement or a standard operating procedure within your organization, you have to explain this.

- Explain that the interview will be recorded.
- Show or point out the equipment—including any cameras—to the interviewee.
- Reassure:
  — explain it is being used to ensure transparency;
  — explain the benefits to both the interviewee and to you;
  — explain what will happen to the recording;
  — explain access to, and entitlement to a copy of, the recording (Note: this will differ according to the investigative context).
- State that you are now switching on the recording device or that the recording is being operated remotely.

Then go straight into the Preamble.

9.2.2 Preamble

This is the formal opening to the interview.

- State the day, date, and time.
- State that the interview is being recorded.
- State who you are. Give your first and second name, and using detail according to your preference or formal requirements, state your designation/title, job, and institution.
- Invite the interviewee to state who he or she is and date of birth. [Depending on the interviewing context you may request further identificatory detail, eg role, address.]
- State the location of the interview, eg *This interview is taking place in...*
- Look to each third party in the interview room, and request that he or she states who he or she is, eg *Can I ask you please to give your name and to say why you are here?* ^^ ^^

9.2.3 Reason for the interview

As pointed out in Chapter 1, the interviewee has a right to know the reason why he or she is being interviewed. The only exceptions would be interviewing of some individuals under particular Special Circumstances: see Chapter 20.

9.2.4 Route Map

Spelling out the Reason for the interview and the Route Map overcomes the 'guessing game', that occurs when an individual is in the dark, most particularly as to what is going to be covered in the interview.

9.2.5 Routines

The Routines are the 'housekeeping' of the interview, eg referring to notes, note-taking, production of evidence. Explaining the Routines lessens the likelihood of the interviewee being distracted by, say, a colleague taking notes or you referring to your ring folder containing your interview plan, I³ WOB map, and other materials to which you might refer across the course of the interview.

9.2.6 Expectations: the 'contract'

As pointed out in Chapter 2, you should aim to deliver the 'contract'—Expectations—no earlier than five minutes into the interview. At this point the individual is entering a period of optimal focus which typically lasts for some 10 to 20 minutes. The individual is highly receptive to what you are saying and in a state of readiness to give a first account, hopefully in accordance with the contract, and thereafter to respond to your questions.

Organizations conducting investigations in different contexts will have different policies as to what to include in the 'contract'. As we pointed out in Chapter 1, there are essential 'ground rules' that apply in any investigative context.

'It's about detail'

> *I'd like you to tell me everything you can. ^^ ^^*
> *Tell me everything that comes to mind ^^ ^^*
> *in as much detail as possible. ^^ ^^*
> *Don't leave anything out. ^^ ^^*
> *Tell me the bits that seem obvious ^^ ^^*
> *that happened automatically ^^ ^^*
> *that you might think aren't important ^^ ^^*
> *Don't think that I already know something ^^ ^^*
> *that someone has told me anything ^^ ^^*
> *or that I might have seen ^^ or read ^^ something. ^^ ^^*
> *Using your hands can help ^^ ^^*
> *to show me positions ^^ movements ^^ directions ^^ and shapes. ^^ ^^*
> *As I said there can't be too much detail. ^^ ^^*
> *I've said a lot there ^^ I need to check back with you ^^ that you are clear about this. ^^ ^^*
> *What am I asking you to do? ^^ ^^*

This is a crucial 'rule' that some interviewees will not grasp on the basis of one explanation. Listen carefully to what the interviewee says. Note any omissions, misunderstandings, or where the interviewee is saying something that you did not say.

- If the interviewee has correctly fed back the detail of the 'ground rule' move to the next 'rule': *Take your time.*
- If the interviewee has omitted, misunderstood, or misreported the 'rule', explain that you will help to make matters clearer by taking him or her through it again, and checking back his or her understanding.

Once you have obtained feedback that is fully correct from the interviewee, if there is a third party present, eg a legal representative, an appropriate adult such as a relative, parent, guardian, or social worker, you must get his or her confirmation of comprehension of the 'rule'. This can be done by posing a simple confirmatory question, eg:

> *I just need to check with you Mrs O'Brien ^^ ^^ You're clear on that? ^^ ^^*

'Take your time'

> *Take your time. ^^ ^^*
> *There's no rush. ^^ ^^*

*It's not a race. ^^ ^^*

*If you take your time ^^ it will help you get the detail into your mind ^^ ^^*

*the little bits ^^ the obvious bits ^^ the bits that might not seem important. ^^ ^^*

*Don't worry if you can't remember everything. ^^ ^^*

*Tell me the bits that aren't too clear. ^^ ^^*

*Tell me the bits that you can't remember completely. ^^ ^^*

*Tell me if you're having a problem with something. ^^ ^^*

*As I said there can't be too much detail. ^^ ^^*

*So like before ^^ I need to check back with you. ^^ ^^*

*What am I asking you to do? ^^ ^^*

This is a relatively simple 'rule'. Most interviewees will correctly feed back the 'rule' allowing you to move to the next 'rule': *Think before, think after*. If the interviewee has not understood, explain the rule again, and check back his or her understanding.

If there is a third party present, check back on this 'rule' as you did with 'It's about detail'.

'Think before, think after'

*We'll work together to keep the pace down. ^^ ^^*

*I'll give you plenty of time to think. ^^ ^^*

*Think before you say something. ^^ ^^*

*Think after you've said something. ^^ ^^*

*When you are thinking ^^ ^^*

*or talking ^^ ^^*

*I won't interrupt to ask questions. ^^ ^^*

*I need to check back with you. ^^ ^^*

*What am I asking you to do? ^^ ^^*

This is a relatively simple 'rule', which most interviewees will correctly feed back upon, allowing you to proceed to the next 'rule': *I might need to ask you to slow down from time to time*. If the interviewee has not understood, explain the rule again, and check back his or her understanding.

Again, where applicable check back this 'rule' with the third party.

'I might need to ask you to slow down from time to time'

*Because you will be giving me a lot of detail ^^ ^^*

*I have to get my head round that detail ^^ ^^*

*[As will A (look at A as you name this person) ^^ ^^*

And B (look at B as you name this person) ^^ ^^]

*I might need to ask you to slow down from time to time ^^ ^^*

*Can I check with you ^^ that you are clear on that? ^^ ^^*

This is a simple 'rule' that most interviewees will give correct feedback upon, allowing you to move to the next 'rule': *I might need to stop you from time to time*. If the interviewee has not understood, explain the rule again, and check back his or her understanding.

Again, where applicable check back this 'rule' with the third party.

'I might need to stop you from time to time'

*As I said ^^ because you will be giving me a lot of detail ^^ ^^*

*I have to get my head round that detail ^^ ^^*

*[As will A (look at A as you name this person) ^^ ^^*

And B (look at B as you name this person) ^^ ^^]

I might need to stop you from time to time ^^ ^^
I'll say something like 'Stop there for a moment, keep what you have in your mind' ^^ ^^
and raise my hand like this (make a 'stop' gesture, slightly lifting and extending an almost horizontal hand)^^ ^^
When I've got my head round what you've told me ^^ ^^
I'll set you off again ^^ ^^
Saying something like 'Got that' ^^ ^^
And raise my hand like this (make a 'proceed' gesture, slightly lifting and extending a cupped hand) ^^ ^^
As you get more used to this ^^ ^^
I'll just use my hand to stop you and set you off ^^ ^^
I won't say anything. ^^ ^^
So again ^^ *I need to check back with you.* ^^ ^^
When I need to get my head round what you are telling me ^^ ^^
what will I do? ^^ ^^

This is a longer, more detailed 'rule'. Listen carefully to what the interviewee says. Note any omissions, misunderstandings, or where the interviewee is saying things that you did not say.

- If the interviewee has correctly fed back correctly then move to the next 'rule': *I might need to ask you to go over something again.*
- If the interviewee has omitted, misunderstood, or misreported, explain that you need to make matters clearer, take him or her through it again, and check back his or her understanding.

Again, where necessary check back this 'rule' with the third party.

'I might need to ask you to go over something again'

Because you will be giving me a lot of detail ^^ ^^
I have to get my head round that detail ^^ ^^
[*As will A* (look at A as you name this person) ^^ ^^
And B (look at B as you name this person) ^^ ^^]
I might need to ask you to go over something again ^^ ^^
So again ^^ *I need to check that you are clear about that.* ^^ ^^

This is a simple 'rule' that most interviewees will give correct feedback upon, allowing you to move to the next 'rule': *Tell me if you don't understand or need to ask something.* If the interviewee has not understood, explain the rule again, and check back his or her understanding.

Again, where necessary check back this 'rule' with the third party.

'Tell me if you don't understand or need to ask something'

It's important for you to know ^^ ^^
it's OK to ask. ^^ ^^
If you don't understand something ^^ *or need to ask something* ^^ ^^
at any time ^^ ^^
just tell me. ^^ ^^
I need to check with you ^^ *that you are clear about that.* ^^ ^^

This is a simple 'rule' that most interviewees will give correct feedback upon, allowing you to move to the next 'rule': *It's OK to say if you find it difficult to answer a question.* If the interviewee has not understood, explain the rule again, and check back his or her understanding.

Again, where necessary check back this 'rule' with the third party.

'It's OK to say if you find it difficult to answer a question'

*You need to know that it's OK to say ^^ ^^*
*if you find it difficult to answer a question.^^ ^^*
*Just tell me. ^^ ^^*
*So again ^^ I need to check you are clear about that. ^^ ^^*

This is a simple 'rule' that most interviewees will give correct feedback upon, allowing you to move to the next 'rule': *If you need something it's OK to ask.* If the interviewee has not understood, explain the rule again, and check back his or her understanding.

Again, where necessary check back this 'rule' with the third party.

'If you need something, tell me'

*You also need to know that if you need something ^^ ^^*
*just tell me. ^^ ^^*
*As before ^^ I need to check you are clear about that. ^^ ^^*

This is a simple 'rule' that most interviewees will give correct feedback upon, allowing you to round off with *Any questions.* If the interviewee has not understood, explain the rule again, and check back his or her understanding.

Again, where necessary check back this 'rule' with the third party.

The interviewee's demonstrated comprehension of the 'contract'—whether or not he or she accepted it—is a powerful tool for managing the interviewee's behaviour. Where the interview is recorded, the recording is tangible evidence of the interviewee demonstrating and confirming comprehension of the 'rules'—particularly to disclose in detail, to take his or her time, to think before and after saying something. If when questioning is underway the interviewee fails to deliver—gives a 'thin' response, rushes out a response, and does not think before saying something or after saying something, you have the means to control his or her behaviour—by drawing attention to the 'rules'.

Similarly, having checked back with any third party present, you will be able to manage any disruptions by this person that amount to a failure on his or her behalf to respect the 'ground rules'. For example, you can counter demands from a legal adviser 'to get a move on' or an objection/criticism that you are requesting too much detail from the interviewee.

In the PEACE model as currently taught in UK and throughout the world by serving and former UK police officers, it is the most important and least understood—and as a consequence most overlooked—element in the conversation management approach to investigative interviewing.

'Any questions'

This is yet another demonstration of your wish to ensure that your explanation has been registered and comprehended.

9.3 The right question

9.3.1 The qualities of a good question

Box 9.1 summarizes the qualities of a good question.

Relevant	Bearing upon the investigation and the individual's ability to contribute to this.
Respectful	Not oppressive, pressuring, or embarrassing.
Sensible	• Seeking new information.
	• Testing earlier, or other, information.
	• Checking on:
	— the individual's comprehension;
	— how the individual is coping.
Sensitive	Using words and constructing sentences mindful of the individual's ability to comprehend and to communicate given:
	• his or her current mental, emotional, and physical state;
	• his or her psychological make-up: literacy; level of intellectual functioning; stage of development; any psychological problem/disorder; disposition towards acquiescence, compliance, and suggestibility.
Short	As concise as possible.
Single	• Straightforward: to the point, not rambling, or 'all over the place'.
	• Unambiguous.
Simple	• Free from pretence or deceit.
	• Not misleading.
Sincere	

Box 9.1 Qualities of a good question

9.4 What makes a question?

Any question that you ask is composed of two elements.

9.4.1 The topic

This is the subject matter that you want to draw to the individual's attention and for him or her to think about, and to disclose upon.

9.4.2 The operator

Your non-verbal behaviour (vocal and non-vocal), your use of wording and types of word, alone or in combination, makes your utterance operate as a question, ie signalling to the individual that you wish a response—disclosure or action—concerning the topic. You can make your utterance operate as a question in several ways.

1. Stating the topic with a rising or falling cadence (intonation), then pausing.
2. Making a comment, then pausing.
3. Making an observation, then pausing.
4. Making a statement, then pausing.
5. Echoing—repeating something said by the individual—in effect stating the topic, then pausing.
6. Using a *minimal prompt*—a word, words, or a non-verbal movement—to trigger the individual to continue talking, then pausing.
7. Issuing an *instruction* to *tell*, *explain*, or to *describe*—whether or not preceded by request, eg *Could you...*—and then pausing.
8. Using a formal *interrogative*, eg a *wh-* question, whether or not preceded by request, and then pausing.

So you have a choice from eight ways of signalling that you would like the interviewee to tell you about a topic that you have in mind and that you would want him or her to think about. It is important for you to know about the several forms of posing questions for a number of reasons.

- It is likely that before reading this book you have been taught and therefore only ever used formal interrogatives to find out what the interviewee might have to say on the topic.
- Compared to interrogatives, the seven other ways of asking a question are all superior, *productive*, operators, ie they encourage the interviewee to think, give him or her greater latitude over what to disclose, and foster further disclosure.[1]
- While some interrogatives can be productive, many are counter-productive. They take you no further forward. They frequently hinder and prevent you finding out what is in the interviewee's mind.

9.5 Productive, counter-productive, and risky questions

The investigative potential of questions can be viewed as two overlapping spheres. Those in the productive sphere progress the investigation. Those in the counter-productive sphere add nothing new or even hinder. Risky questions—which may or may not progress matters—exist where the two spheres overlap (Figure 9.1).

9.6 Productive questions

Productive questions are just that. They take you forward, towards achieving your investigative aims, because they get the interviewee thinking and then disclosing his or her thoughts freely. Productive questions should be the only questions that you use.

9.6.1 Getting the interviewee thinking

Questions differ according to the amount of mental effort required to:

- search memory store (long-term memory) for the information;
- marshal thoughts, ie to select the appropriate information from what is available;
- think about how to frame a response based on this information;
- frame the actual response.

So questions can be classified according to the amount of effort required.

- **Process questions and extended recall questions.** These require more thinking time to perform a greater search of memory store, to marshal thoughts and to put together the answer.
- **Simple recall questions.** These are more focused demands for information, requiring much less time to search memory and to construct the answer. If you pause for too long after a simple recall question it risks an embarrassing silence. The interviewee can't think what else he or she could say, or be expected to say.

---

[1] MacKay, I. (1980) *A Guide to Asking Questions.* London: BACIE.

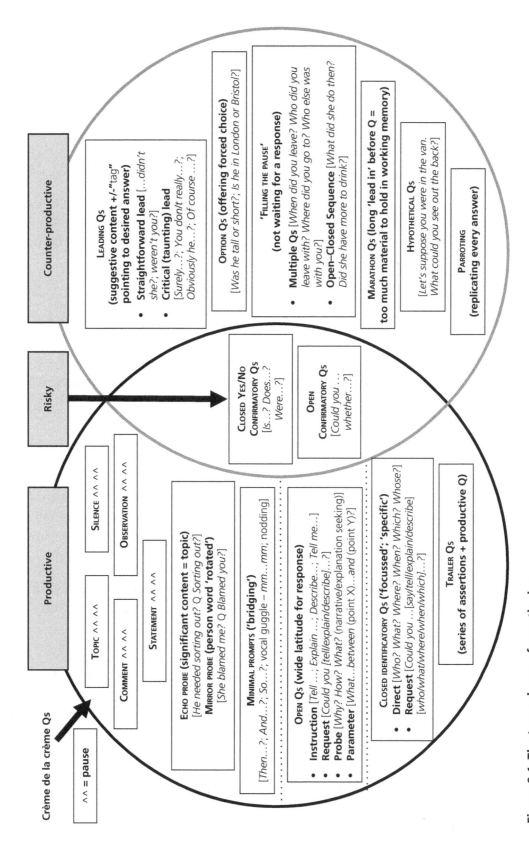

Figure 9.1 The two spheres of questioning

9.6.2   **Latitude of response**

In any question–answer setting, a questioner signals the extent to which he or she wishes to restrict the latitude—freedom—of the individual's response[2] in terms of:

- restricting the subject matter to be covered;
- restricting the individual's capacity to reply;
- indicating a response preferred by the questioner.

Productive questions differ according to the degree of latitude they give to the interviewee to decide the content of the response.

9.6.3   **Crème de la crème questions**

These productive questions are *crème de la crème* because they are the most overtly conversational, least interrogative forms of operator. They are also called 'indirect' or 'non-directive' questions because the interviewee is unobtrusively given the opportunity to:

- define the scope of the answer;
- say as much as he or she likes when answering.

Crème de la crème questions are the least used by professionals. Their experience has locked them into directive *wh-* questions. Crème de la crème questions are more demanding because:

- the content of the response is wholly unpredictable;
- the amount of detail disclosed may be very substantial—challenging ability to remember.

You should use crème de la crème questions whenever you possibly can because they are so unlike any other question because they are truly conversational.

Topic

In the case of a suspect interview, you will have laid out the Route Map of main topics that you want to cover in the interview. Having delivered the Routines and the Expectations, you merely need to re-state after a pause the first topic of the Route Map, eg:

> ^^ ^^ *Your relationship with Ruth.* ^^ ^^

When your are probing you are essentially putting to the foreground of the interviewee's mind a topic, and pausing to see what he or she will say spontaneously.

Echo probe and mirror probe

Actively listening enables you to identify the significant content—key idea—of the individual's response: echoing or mirroring this presents this as a topic to be disclosed upon.

    The person may 'blank' you, giving an immediate 'yes' or similar response, which is an anomaly because you would expect a fuller response to this crème de la crème question. Simply pause. Chances are that he or she might continue talking.

Statement, observation, or comment

Here a comment signifies something said that is more judgemental than an essentially neutral observation. The common denominator between these and a statement is that you

---

[2] Dillon, J.T. (1990) *The Practice of Questioning.* London: Routledge.

are sharing what is in your head, pausing and seeing if the interviewee will say something spontaneously on the issue, eg:

> *We need to know about your relationship with Ruth.* ^^ ^^
> *The video shows that you were clearly pleased by what was happening to him.* ^^ ^^

When interviewing a witness, a statement can trigger free recall, eg when engaging in context reinstatement (see Chapter 10, Assisting Remembrance of Offence-Related Detail):

> ^^ ^^ *I need to know everything that is in your mind* ^^ ^^ *and comes to mind* ^^ ^^

Silence

On occasions you will find that simply silence—saying nothing, observing closely, and actively listening with your 'third ear'—will have an extraordinary effect. The individual will keep talking, giving more details. Your silence—the final element of SOFTENS behaviours described in Chapter 3 (Conversation: From Everyday Talk to Ways of Relating and Changing Minds)—is the unstated request, creating more time and space for more disclosure. In Chapter 7 (Active Listening, Observing, and Assessing) we presented BASELINES—potentially significant transient behaviours—one of which is the individual not looking at you, typically gazing down and often to the side, indicative that he or she is engaged in an 'inner dialogue'. Your silence is the only proper response when this behaviour occurs.

Interviewers who are inexperienced, unaware, anxious, or any combination of these often find silence intolerable. Two to three seconds are sensed to be an eternity and when the question or response requires a longer silence, the stress can become extreme. They feel that they have lost control. They come in inappropriately to 'fill the pause' and often for a period to talk for effect (blather), saying something totally inconsequential or unrelated to the issue.

You have to be sensible. There is a clear difference between silence that creates the opportunity to search memory, marshal thoughts, and to frame a response, and silence that is oppressive: inducing the individual to say anything rather than nothing.

There is a simple relationship between the mental demand on the interviewee and the duration of the pause to allow this to happen.

- **Process questions and extended recall questions, and the response to such questions.** These should always be followed by a marked pause, ie silence, because they require more mental effort.
- **Simple recall questions and the response to these.** These should be followed by a normal pause ^^ ^^ and the next question posed. If you pause for longer it becomes an embarrassing silence because the interviewee can't think what else he or she could say, or be expected to say.

Minimal prompts

Sustaining prompts are an integral aspect of SOFTENS behaviours. When the individual is disclosing on a matter but the flow has temporarily stopped, 'bridging' by using a linking prompt continues the momentum to talk. Minimal prompts are also particularly useful when it is obvious that the individual has stopped talking completely, eg:

- the individual has stopped his or her narrative at a point short of where you wanted him or her to reach—a 'please complete' prompt will trigger the individual to continue the narrative;

- where you have stopped the interview briefly to allow the individual to compose himself or herself, eg after crying—'bridging' in the form of a 'please start again' prompt enables the individual to pick up and continue talking from where he or she stopped.

Box 9.2 lists common minimal prompts.

Sustaining prompt	Guggle, eg Uh-huh ...; nod.
Linking prompt	And ^^ ^^ Then ^^ ^^ And then ^^ ^^ Right ^^ ^^ Alright ^^ ^^ OK ^^ ^^
'Please complete' prompt	Please go on ^^ ^^ Carry on please ^^ ^^
'Please start again' prompt	It is difficult, I appreciate ^^ ^^ You were saying ^^ ^^ As you were saying ^^ ^^ You got to [state] ^^ ^^

Box 9.2 Common minimal prompts

9.6.4 Open questions

These are also called 'non-restrictive' questions. They are recognizable as an instruction, request, or question, albeit one offering substantial freedom of response.

Instruction: Tell, explain, describe (TED)

Tell, explain, describe are extremely useful instructions to the individual to disclose freely, expanding upon what he or she has said. The three instructions have a different potential impact.

- **Tell**. This is the least contentious instruction. It is simple and understood by even very young children. Particularly when said with a falling tone it can be used to great effect, signalling that you are really interested in what the individual has just said and you would like to know a lot more.
- **Explain**. You may well be seeking a straightforward *explanation*, ie for things to be made clearer. But the individual may take the instruction to mean that you want a *justification*, ie a reason or an excuse for acting in a certain manner. If you sense that there is a risk of the individual misinterpreting you should avoid using the instruction *explain* when you are wanting to know more about the individual's behaviour. Simply use *Tell* instead.
- **Describe**. *Describe* is not within the everyday vocabulary of some people who may be culturally or educationally deprived, or developmentally disadvantaged due to age or learning disability. *Tell* is much easier for them to understand.

Combining TED with a wh- *question*

There is a difference of view as to whether it is appropriate to combine TED with a *wh-* question. Our view is that there is nothing wrong in doing so. In fact, it would be rather stilted, unnatural, and arguably denying yourself essential flexibility not to combine TED with other forms of question.

Excessive use of instructions

There can always be too much of a good thing. As with any form of question, it is possible to overdo the use of TED instructions. If you use a very high proportion of TED instructions when you are questioning anyone, but particularly someone who is developmentally disadvantaged, acquiescent, or compliant, there are real risks.

• The interviewee is likely to perceive you as a 'typical' powerful person. Being the boss—in the superior, 'up' position—you are ordering the individual—in the subordinate, 'down' position—to do your bidding.

• If your response to the interviewee begins immediately with a TED instruction, this is delivered with all the force of the air coming from your lungs. People are sensitive to the tone of the initial utterance. TED—or indeed any *wh-* interrogative—can sound like, and can be sensed by the interviewee as, a verbal jab.

Excessive use of TED instructions, excessive use of *wh-* questions, or a combination of these, is *not* a conversation between equals. It is a question and answer (Q and A) exchange, in which the interviewee is cast in the role of being a 'question answering machine'. The interviewee could be forgiven for sensing the interview to be an interrogation.

Of course, it is possible to deliver a TED instruction in a non-forceful manner. However, even when delivered in soft tones, a high proportion of TED instructions still comes across and is sensed as a grilling! A simple technique for removing the jabbing effect of a TED instruction—or indeed any *wh-* question—is to deliver one or more utterances as a lead up to the instruction or question. Saying anything that is not overtly a question ensures the instruction emerges in a conversational tone at a much lower pitch, when there is much air being expended when delivering it. Compare the effects.

• **Jabbing: immediate use of TED.**

> INTERVIEWEE: *We didn't hit it off.* (silence)
> INTERVIEWER: *Tell me about that?*

• **No jabbing: conversational lead up to TED.**

> INTERVIEWEE: *We didn't hit it off.* (silence)
> INTERVIEWER: *You were together a long time.* ^^ ^^ *Take your time.* (lower pitch) ^^ ^^
>   *Tell me about that.* (much lower pitch) ^^ ^^

Other instructions

There are instructions other than TED that are entirely acceptable, eg:

> *Take me* as in *Take me through that.* ^^ ^^
> *Give me* as in *Give me some idea about that.* ^^ ^^

Request + instruction

You can lessen the cumulative, bossy effect of TED instructions by varying the way in which you deliver them:

- make it a request, eg *Could you tell me…?*
- better still precede the combination with a softening utterance, eg

> *I wasn't there ^^ ^^ and I need to know. ^^ ^^ So could you tell me how that happened?*

An interviewer who uses invitational questions is delivering on RESPONSE behaviours—being respectful and talking across as an equal—that foster a working relationship. The invitation also removes the jabbing effect of the instruction.

Some people believe that *Could you* or *Can you* is a closed 'yes'/'no' confirmatory question because it is possible to reply 'yes' or 'no'. They are, however, confusing matters. From very early on children, at nursery and reception stage, recognize that *Could you* is a request. The parent does not expect the child to state with a 'yes' that it is competent of fulfilling the request but does nothing towards this. This response would gain an immediate parental response of *Well go on then*. The child also appreciates that the answer 'no' would trigger the possibly less than patient parent to ask *And why not?* Soon into the schooling system the child also learns that when a teacher says *Could you* it is something more than a request—it is an instruction.

Taking these lessons forward into the world of conversation management, interviewees know that when you say *Could you* this is not an enquiry into physical or mental ability to relate something: it is a request-cum-instruction. If you get an inappropriate, blocking 'yes' or 'no':

- **Simply pause ^^ ^^.** Because you have not taken the talking turn the individual knows that he or she should start talking—to follow through the 'yes' by disclosing detail, or to explain the basis for refusing the request/instruction.
- **If the interviewee does not take the talking turn.** Adopt—sensibly and sensitively, with pausing—a caring response.
  — **To a 'yes':** *Take your time ^^ ^^ There's no rush ^^ ^^*
  — **To a 'no':** *I appreciate it might be difficult ^^ ^^ What's the problem?*

Explanation probe: Why

This is a contentious question because it has two potential meanings.

- You want an explanation involving extra detail concerning causation.
- You are seeking a special type of explanation: a justification or an excuse. The individual may draw the conclusion that what he or she did was in someway wrong, that you are now accusing him or her, and may become defensive or simply not answer your question.

Whenever possible avoid *why*. It can usually be replaced with an invitational TED question, eg:

> *Can you tell me the reason for…?; Take your time ^^ ^^ what was the reason for…?*

As a rule of thumb you should not use *why* when you are questioning anyone who is developmentally disadvantaged, acquiescent, or compliant.

Narrative/explanation probe: What

Also called a 'big' *what* question, this requests an account, eg:

> *What did you do after you left the nightclub?*

Parameter question

This is a particularly useful question because you are asking for an account of events between the two specified points, eg:

I'd like you to have a big think.^^ ^^Tell me what happened^^ ^^ from when you left the bank at four fifteen ^^ ^^ to when we arrested you at eleven o'clock?

The two points should be linked to your conclusions concerning the material time frame (MTF). It makes sense to set the first point immediately before the initial event of the MTF and the second point immediately following the last event. Unfortunately people get lazy when using parameter questions, particularly if they have not devoted time or thought to consider the MTF. So they will set the beginning point at time very far back, typically when the person woke up in the morning, eg:

Tell me everything that's happened ^^ ^^ from when you woke up this morning ^^ ^^ until quarter to midnight when we arrested you?

In this case, the interviewer could be laying himself or herself open to an account that covers some eighteen hours! The result will be a mass of detail—much of it irrelevant—of events, people, places, things, and so on for a protracted period up to the initial step of the MTF. This amount of detail challenges ability to remain attentive, and to register and hold this detail in working memory. Attention is bound to drift, detail will go unregistered, and anomaly unnoticed, eg *narrative* contrast—the difference in amount of detail prior to, during, and following the commission of the offence.

Keep the parameter points sensibly linked to the MTF. If you do need to extend later, ie backwards from the start point of the MTF, there will be no problem doing so.

9.6.5 Closed identificatory questions

These are also called 'focused', 'specific closed', or '*wh-*' probing questions. They cue the individual to recall detail and to identify people (*who*), objects and actions (*what*), possession (*whose*), locations (*where*), points in time (*when*), and alternatives (*which*).

9.6.6 Trailer questions

Trailer questions are extremely effective where you have a number of items of information—key facts—that are logically or sequentially related and warrant an explanation from the interviewee. They require planning prior to the interview and considered delivery within the interview.

- Identify the related items that you consider to be key facts.
- Normally restrict your trailer to no more than four key facts. Any more could overwhelm the interviewee's working memory. If there are more than four key facts these will require a much slower, more considered delivery.
- Wherever possible, the 'key facts' should be incontrovertible facts, eg forensic evidence. Unless backed up by objective evidence, eg CCTV, assertions by witnesses are controvertible. The trailer might not work or work as well as it could if the interviewee interrupts to argue the origin or status of the 'key fact'.
- Order the items in a logical or chronological sequence.
- On a sheet of A4 paper write a simple, concise description for each item. If your descriptions are too complex or long-winded the interviewee will not be able to hold the detail in working memory.
- Between each item leave some 'white' space to represent pausing.
- Complete the trailer with an appropriate question.
  - **Never a closed confirmatory 'yes'/'no' question.** You will have wasted the effort if the interviewee simply says 'no'.

— **Always a productive question followed by a pause.** Crème de la crème (eg *That needs to be explained.* ^^ ^^) or open (eg *How do you explain this?* ^^ ^^)

In the interview:

- Brief the interviewee that you are going to give him or her key information concerning the case, and then ask a question.
- He or she should listen to all the key information.
- He or she should not interrupt or disrupt you while you are giving the key.
- Deliver the key facts clearly and slowly, allowing proper pausing between each item.
- Pause after the last item.
- Ask the productive question followed by a pause.

You need to deliver the briefing and the trailer confidently. It is always sensible to practice saying the words out loud when you are preparing for the interview.

> *On Monday 10 February at 8 a.m. the computer reading showed your tanker was empty.* ^^ ^^
> *At 8.15 a.m. you drew off 54,000 litres of lead free at the supply point.*^^ ^^
> *At 10.45 a.m. you delivered to Rowstock Garage 54,000 litres of lead free, receiving a signature for this.*^^ ^^
> *Mr Jones checked the reading on the lead free tank.*^^ ^^
> *It showed only 51,000 litres had been delivered.*^^ ^^
> *How do you account for that?* ^^ ^^

9.7 Counter-productive questions

9.7.1 Leading questions

Sometimes known as a 'loaded' or 'provocative' question, the purpose of a leading question is quite clear: to prompt the desired answer. 'Powerful people' who already know, or assume they know, the answer use them a great deal, particularly when they feel under time pressure.

The content of all leading questions is suggestive, and may be combined with a 'tag' either at the beginning or the end, eg..., *didn't you?*; *Wasn't he...?*; *I suppose...?*;..., *I take it?*

In everyday life it is not uncommon for people to treat a leading question as if it were an open-ended question, eg *Didn't you go out on Saturday night? Yeah, had a great time. Went with Trish and the others to the King and Queen and spent hours on the slot machine. Both of us got really drunk, and I mean drunk* and so on. The problem is that individuals who want to please and be liked and suggestible individuals—who can't remember and distrust their memories— are particularly vulnerable to leading questions. They are especially disposed to agree to something that is, or was not, the case.

Straightforward lead

This is usually phrased in terms of clear-minded suggestive content and because of this is called the 'obvious' question, eg

> *Isn't it a fact that...?; You're not suggesting that...?; You tell the truth, I take it?*

Critical (taunting) lead

This relies for its effect on the minimum of sarcasm: denial would imply a lack of intelligence or irrationality, eg:

Surely you don't believe that...do you?; Surely you're not suggesting that...?; Do you really think that...?; Obviously...?; Anyone would...wouldn't they?

The compliant individual is particularly vulnerable to taunting leads.

Implication lead

This sets the individual up to implicate himself or herself, eg:

You've got to admit that...?; You knew that what you were doing was wrong, didn't you?

Again, the compliant individual is particularly vulnerable to such a question.

Justification lead

This minimizes, eg the gravity of the offence, or maximizes, eg the provocation, and thus justifies the action. For example:

You were only doing what comes naturally, weren't you?; Anyone could see that she had pushed you too far this time, hadn't she?

Leading questions that mislead

A leading question can contain accurate content. If Tom says he drove regularly to his friend Luke's along the High Street on which stands the village shop, the question *You would have driven past the village shop, wouldn't you?* is inappropriate because it leads but the content is not misleading.

However, a leading question can contain misleading content. *I take it you would've seen the display board outside at that time?* The use of the definite article *the* presupposes there was a display board outside at the time he drove past, when in reality there was no display board. The misleading content plus the prompt is likely to lead Tom, particularly if he distrusts his memory and is therefore suggestible, to recollect a non-present display board.

Never ask a leading question

It is senseless to ask a leading question. For every leading question there is always a better productive question, eg:

rather than
Isn't it a fact that you would have driven past the village shop on your way to Luke's?
a productive alternative could be
So the route you take Tom to Luke's ^^ ^^ *The buildings you pass on the High Street* ^^ ^^
If Tom doesn't start talking spontaneously on this topic at this point what about
I need to know about those. ^^ ^^ *Take your time.* ^^ ^^

9.7.2 Option questions

Also called 'forced choice' questions, these offer alternatives for the interviewee to consider. Option questions are potentially fatal to effective investigation.

- The offered alternatives:
  — may be meaningless, eg *Was he tall or short?*
  — may mislead because they are not valid, eg do not include all of the possible options. *Did he turn left or right?* is an invalid option if he could have gone straight on; *Was he black or white?* excludes the many other shades of humanity encountered;

— may be so numerous that they overwhelm the interviewee, particularly one with limited working memory capacity, eg *Was his jacket red, or white, or blue, or black, or grey?*

- The suggestible interviewee—who distrusts his or her memory—believes that one or other of the options must be correct, eg *Did he kick or punch the doorman?* implies that the man attacked the doorman and did so by either by kicking or punching.
- The interviewee who lacks assertion or the compliant interviewee—who just wants to please—may not believe either or any option applies but still endorses one.
- Often interviewers who can't think of an alternative deliver a 'trailing' or 'dangling' option, eg *Did she speak to him or…?* which is no option at all. The interviewee often reads this as a demand to say 'yes' and duly gives this response.

For every option question there is always a better productive question, eg:

> rather than
> *Was the knife in his right or left hand?*
> much more detail is accessed by saying
> *Take your time ^^ ^^ get the image in your mind ^^ ^^ describe how he was holding the knife.*

9.7.3 'Filling the pause'

Posing a question, not waiting for the interviewee to take the talking turn in order to answer, and removing the talking turn from the interviewee is very widespread and arises for a number of reasons.

- The interviewer interprets the interviewee's failure to answer immediately as evidencing no intention to respond, failure to comprehend, or lack of attention.
- Silence—which induces anxiety in apprehensive, under-confident, unprepared interviewers—is interpreted as a loss of control of the exchange. Taking the talking turn regains control either to ask the question another way or to ask a completely different question.
- The interviewer's head is 'buzzing' with questions. Rather than pausing to think the interviewer verbalizes a stream of questions, 'engaging mouth before engaging mind'.
- The interviewer asks an open question but does not expect, or is too busy to wait for, a full answer, or thinks he or she already knows the answer and immediately poses a narrower question. This is frequently a closed 'yes'/'no' question: creating yet another instance of the open–closed sequence so commonly delivered by parents and 'powerful people', eg *So why did you decide to do that? Was it because…?*

9.7.4 Marathon questions

These demonstrate a failure to deliver on the *short* and *simple* properties of a good question. The interviewer talks at length on matters, often in a rambling, incomprehensible manner, filling up the interviewee's working memory before delivering the question—to which the confused interviewee cannot give a sensible reply.

9.7.5 Hypothetical questions

The interviewee is being asked to conjecture rather than to talk about his or her own experience. Any competent legal adviser representing a suspect will immediately intervene if such a question is posed pointing out that it is an improper question and the interviewer must ask questions to do with fact not inviting the suspect to engage in speculation or supposition.

9.7.6 Parroting

Parroting occurs when the interviewer 'replicates' every answer as it is given. This was a very common behaviour prior to PEACE, because it assisted the interviewer to remember what the interviewee had said. It still occurs when interviewers 'summarize'—actually replicating the detail of responses—after posing only a couple or so questions on a topic before switching to another topic. The risks are that:

- the interviewer gives the impression of being a parrot—and a rather unintelligent one at that;
- it is very alienating to have your words constantly replicated;
- it takes the pressure off the liar who is making up the story as he or she goes along: replicating helps to consolidate the lie in memory store.

9.8 Risky questions

These are questions that can be either productive or counter-productive according to the interviewer's purpose.

9.8.1 Closed confirmatory 'yes'/'no' questions

Also called 'restrictive' or 'direct' questions, closed 'yes'/'no' questions supply the interviewer with a specific item or items of information.

Confirming information known or believed by the interviewer

Closed confirmatory 'yes'/'no' questions are extremely common because they are on face value easy to ask. Many interviewers believe that inviting the interviewee to confirm information known or believed by the interviewer saves time and effort, speeding up the investigation process. Such questions are fraught with problems.

- They require very little effort or thought by the interviewee. To use the tennis analogy, the ball is returned immediately and lands at the interviewer's feet.
- Paradoxically, confirmatory questions don't save effort. The pressure is on the interviewer to serve another ball—frame and deliver yet another confirmatory question, which is immediately returned.
- Research has shown that there is more of a tendency to say 'yes' rather than 'no'. The reasons for this are many, but clearly put the interviewer at risk of an interviewee who:
  — lacks assertion skills;
  — is acquiescent: unreflectively says 'yes';
  — is compliant: wants to please and says 'yes' to something that he or she knows not to be the case.
- Confirmatory questions take the pressure off the would-be liar, who is under no pressure to give a fuller response, and can 'cherry pick' which option fits.

Misleading confirmatory questions

A confirmatory question can contain accurate content. What the individual is being asked to confirm may well be the case. If Mary Cooper says she parked in Wantage town centre car park and is asked, *Did you see the statue of King Alfred?*, this question has within it a valid piece of information: the statue that is certainly in the town centre and is the hub of the car park.

However, a confirmatory question can be asked in a way that influences the content of the interviewee's reply, particularly if the individual is suggestible, ie distrusts his or her memory.

- By containing words or phrasing that influences the interviewee's perception of activity, eg *Did you see the car smash into the tree?* The verb *smash* implies the vehicle was travelling at speed at the point of impact.
- By containing factually incorrect information that the individual endorses as correct and incorporates into his or her account and stores this in memory, eg *Did you see anybody standing near her?* when in fact the observer only saw the lady but now is 'aware' that someone could have been near her.
- By presenting the interviewee with case knowledge, eg material from other witness accounts or on CCTV, that he or she endorses as correct and is taken—and even represented officially—as further corroborative evidence of the police case, eg *Did you see the blue car outside the flats around eight o'clock last night?* implies that:
  — there was a car;
  — it was blue;
  — it was outside the flats;
  — around eight o'clock.

For every closed confirmatory 'yes'/'no' question there is always a better productive question, eg:

> rather than
> *You said he attacked her. Did you see him punch her?*
> much more detail is accessed by saying
> *Take your time^^ ^^ get the image in your mind ^^ ^^ take me through how he was attacking her.*

Checking back

In a properly conversation managed interview, confirmatory 'yes'/'no' questioning does have a practical use: to check back with the interviewees that the interviewer has accurately summarized an account or a run of responses on a topic: see later.

Triggering spontaneous disclosure.

Closed confirmatory 'yes'/'no' questions are extremely common in everyday life. Indeed, they constitute around 80 per cent of questions posed in conversation between people who know each other, eg relatives, friends, and acquaintances, and who feel sufficiently confident to talk openly. They treat the closed 'yes'/'no' question as an open question, eg the response to *Did you go out on Saturday night?* is a 'yes' or a 'no' followed by a relatively free-flowing account.

It follows that you can use a closed 'yes'/'no' to 'test' whether you have the interviewee's confidence and whether he or she feels sufficiently confident to disclose freely. If you get a flowing response then you have a positive result. If you get a 'yes' or 'no' and after an appropriately long pause the interviewee has not spoken further:

- you know that you still have to work at the relationship;
- you can pose an appropriate productive question to develop the 'yes' or the 'no' with a subsequent productive question, eg:

> YOU: *Did you realize there was a problem?*
> INTERVIEWEE: *Yes.*
> YOU: *^^ ^^ I'd like to know about that ^^ ^^ I appreciate that it might be difficult ^^ ^^ Tell me about that. ^^ ^^*

9.8.2 Open confirmatory questions

Open confirmatory *whether* questions are relatively rare but can be very effective. They lack the 'fork' quality of a 'yes'/'no' confirmatory question, eg:

So you saw the man standing by the taxi cab. ^^ ^^ *Get a picture in you mind of what you could see* ^^ ^^ *Could you tell me whether there were other people around?* ^^ ^^

9.9 Pausing and pacing

9.9.1 Key messages

Pausing after your question is essential because it sends several messages.

- The talking turn has passed to the individual.
- There is no pressure to respond immediately: the question requires thought so he or she should take as much time as necessary to search, marshal thoughts, and frame a response.
- You are prepared to 'sit it out', ie to remain with the listening turn while the interviewee is thinking: you will not take the talking turn back, ie 'fill the pause' (see later).

9.9.2 Pausing is to the interviewee's benefit

Delivering on the contract

In the Explain phase of the Expectations stage you spelled out that you would give the interviewee plenty of time to think:

- to think about what you have just said;
- to think before answering;
- to think after answering.

When you deliver on this contract and pause, it sends simple but important messages.

- You want to listen not talk.
- You are interested in what the interviewee has to say.
- You don't have an agenda.
- You appreciate—and want the interviewee to appreciate—that this is a question that the interviewee needs to think about and needs time to do so.

The ethical, psychological, and practical bases for pausing

As pointed out in Chapter 1, conversation management has to be ethical: conversing with a two-sided logic, with self and other in mind. To this end it is a verbal and non-verbal demonstration of a commitment to co-operative talk by:

- using an appropriate conversational style;
- consciously orientating the individual as to the reason for the conversation, working to make the exchange mutual by sharing the talking turn and the talking time, balancing assertions—questions, statements, observations, comments—with responsive listening.

When you pause this ensures that you behave ethically, delivering on a commitment to share the talking turn and talking time.

Pausing also makes psychological sense. Chapters 6, 7, and 13 to 16 point to the necessity to research, to assess, and then to take account of every conceivable factor that might render the individual vulnerable by adversely affecting his or her capacity:

- to pay attention;
- to follow;
- to hold and process information in working memory;
- to grasp:
  — what is being put to him or her;
  — the significance of what is being asserted by way of a statement, request or question.

The individual's vulnerability increases with every additional factor. Such vulnerability is the psychological and practical justification to engage in conscious pausing, and to monitor the individual for:

- feedback, particularly guggling, while he or she is listening to what is being said, indicative that the individual is keeping track;
- behaviours indicative of problems with paying attention, following and grasping what is being said:
  — vacant expression ('empty gaze'), ie indicative that the individual is not aware of what is going on;
  — absence of guggling;
  — failure to remember the detail of something said by either you or the individual only a short while before.

Such vulnerability applies to individuals deemed to be 'normal'. Common sense argues that some categories of individual need more time to think, eg:

- the developmentally disadvantaged, ie children, particularly the very young, and the intellectually disadvantaged, ie individuals with learning difficulties;
- the elderly;
- those who do not use English as their first language.

For any individual who is vulnerable, your pausing behaviour is particularly critical. If you do not pause, pause, and pause again there is an extreme risk of you leaving the individual increasingly confused, tongue-tied, and distressed.

A useful notion is to think of every topic raised as a water lily on a pond. Moving to the next water lily (topic), nonetheless requires the individual to have remembrance of the water lily just left, and the lily before that. Characteristically vulnerable individuals struggle to remember even the most recent water lilies.

If while you are covering a particular topic you detect behaviour that indicates the individual is not paying attention, not following, and not grasping, you need to stop immediately and check out your concerns.

- Return to two 'clicks' back, ie what was being covered **before** the previous topic.
- Ask a non-threatening testing question to check, eg *Oh just before we continue with what we are talking about, I just need to be clear about something we covered earlier ^^ ^^ We were talking about* [state topic] *^^ ^^ Can you tell me* [pose the question].

9.9.3 **Pausing is to your benefit**

Cope with, and do not be panicked by, the occurrence of silence at any time in the interview. Let silence work for you. Silence signals to the interviewee that he or she still has the talking turn and that you are in no rush to take it back.

If the individual does not respond immediately do not jump in and start talking, ie taking back the talking turn. By the same token, if the individual **does** say something and then stops, do not immediately start talking. The individual might just have paused to take breath or to collect his or her thoughts before continuing—or both. If you take the talking turn immediately the individual pauses you will never know what he or she would have said—you have denied the individual and yourself the disclosure that might have occurred.

Pausing enables you to:

- concentrate, preventing your mind racing away on several things or in several directions;
- attend to and work with the fine-grain detail of what the individual is saying in the light of what he or she just said before or said earlier in the interview or even prior to interview;
- engage in SOFTENS behaviours while observing systematically the individual's behaviour, in particular that indicative of:
  — a 'hot spot';
  — vulnerability (covered in the previous section);
- identify the topic that needs to be brought to the individual's attention;
- think about how this topic could be raised;
- think about what you are going to say, ie preventing your mouth getting ahead of your mind;
- check yourself asking a counter-productive question—substituting this with a productive question.

These activities take up time: they create a pause.

Get used to responding to the absence of a response, or to any response, by *postponing*—delaying—the point at which you take back the talking turn:. Apply what we term the **POST** (pause + observe + SOFTENS + think) **formula**.

9.9.4 Pause duration

The longer the pause, the greater the pressure to speak

A two to three second pause after either you, the interviewee, or a third party has spoken is a natural mental break. With each additional, passing second the pressure grows to say something—to 'say anything'—and in so doing take the talking turn.

The duration of the pause and the type of question

We pointed out earlier that there is a link between the question you pose and the duration of the pause that the question 'buys' for the individual to think before responding, ie the thinking time required to process the question and to formulate a response.

- A 'high level' process—or long recall—question demands appreciable mental effort and 'buys' a long pause. Put empathy into effect here. To disclose in detail about a period of time—such as a matter of hours—or a significant issue—such as a relationship—will require a significant amount of material to be retrieved and brought into working memory. A good technique is to pause for however long you consider it would take you to answer a similar question, eg:

  Tell me what you did ^^ between the time you left work at six ^^ up to the point you were arrested just before midnight?—is asking the individual to disclose about a period of some six hours.

We need to know about your relationship with her—would be a big ask of anyone concerning a relationship.

- A 'low level' simple recall question 'buys' very little time, eg *Where did you go next?*

If your pause is longer than the time 'bought' by the type of question, there will be increasing pressure on both you and the interviewee. You will find differences in the pressure to talk. As the duration of the pause increases, adult interviewees typically experience a growing pressure to say something, ie to take the talking turn. In contrast, young children and individuals who are intellectually disadvantaged very often are able to 'sit out' pauses.

Common sense is the yardstick. If you create pauses that on common sense grounds are too long you could, in the case of a suspect, provide the basis for an argument that your questioning was oppressive.

Very long silences

Always avoid very long silences. The exception is the individual who is manifesting an 'inner dialogue'. As we explained in Chapter 7, this is when he or she is silent, looking down, perhaps to one side, and may be exhibiting other transient behaviours such as adaptors and lower limb movement ('leakage'). He or she is retrieving information from memory store, reflecting upon this (as well as the situation and his or her circumstances) in working memory, and engaging literally in an 'inner dialogue'—balancing up whether to say anything at all, or something—or something else—on this topic, or what to say, and how to say it.

It is essential to remain silent and not to interrupt when an individual is engaged in an 'inner dialogue'. If you start talking you risk disrupting the individual's retrieval of material or propelling the individual to make a decision which might be not to disclose detail or further detail. If there is a third party, look towards him or her and make a slight head movement (shaking it slowly), hand movement (lift an extended finger to your lips), or both, to signal 'It's OK. Let's sit this out. Please don't say anything.'

Practise pausing

Typically interviewers subjectively experience a pause as being much longer than it actually is. This 'speeding up' is explicable psychologically—a lot going on mentally—and physiologically—in terms of increased heart rate.

You need to develop three abilities necessary to pausing:

- bringing your heart rate down (breathe in slowly, and breathe out slowly—each time progressively increasing the duration of the inspiration and exhalation);
- judging the time 'bought' by different kinds question;
- judging the duration of a pause.

Work with a colleague, alternating in the role of interviewer and interviewee. Practise:

- posing process and simple recall questions;
- bringing down your heart rate;
- pausing for three, five, seven, ten seconds and even longer.

The longer pausing is good practice for dealing with an interviewee engaged in an 'inner dialogue': whoever is role-playing, the interviewee simply engages in 'inner dialogue' behaviour.

9.9.5 Absence of pausing and the pace of an interview

Rapid fire questioning as a tactic

It is a common misperception that rapid fire questioning of a suspect—asking questions at an extremely high rate, too fast for the individual to think let alone to give a full response—puts pressure on the individual. The logic for such questioning is that the individual does not have time to think up a lie and is unable to remember quickly enough what he or she has said earlier.

The reality is sobering.

- Some interviewees may attempt to keep up. However, insufficient time to search memory and rushing to give replies result in responses that become progressively shorter and less informative. Eventually the co-operative interviewee gives up trying to reply.
- The acquiescent interviewee simply agrees without thinking.
- The compliant interviewee simply agrees to keep the interviewer happy.
- Others realize that it is not worth bothering to reply—leaving the interviewer to talk to himself or herself. This is the simple strategy that the canny would-be liar adopts from the outset. He or she does not feel pressure because all he or she does is say nothing. This keeps the talking turn with—and the pressure upon—the interviewer, who has to think even more rapidly than had he or she been given a minimal response.

Most interviewers trying rapid fire questioning cannot think quickly enough to keep it up with the demand to frame and deliver a stream of questions. They eventually end up gabbling—breathlessly posing increasingly incoherent questions.

Rapid fire questioning to keep control of the interview

An interviewer may engage in rapid fire questioning not as a conscious tactic but simply by speaking immediately the witness or suspect has stopped speaking. This may give the interviewer a sense of controlling the talking turn but at great cost in terms of eliciting disclosure. Taking the talking turn immediately in this manner risks the same effect upon the interviewee as deliberate rapid fire questioning. The interviewee 'switches off': giving a minimal response or else saying nothing at all.

Conclusions drawn by the interviewee and the courts about the pace of questioning

Having indicated in the Expectations phase that you will give the interviewee plenty of time to think and that you will not jump in immediately he or she has stopped talking, your failure to do so will place a question mark over your sincerity. Also a pattern of excessively long pausing—irrespective of question type—is overtly burdensome.

Such inappropriate pausing—either not giving time to think or creating excessively long pressuring silence—places the entire interview at risk. In the case of a suspect, the defence will be able to cite case law when arguing that the interviewing should be excluded because the recording shows that the interviewer's behaviour was oppressive.

9.10 Triggering initial spontaneous disclosure

9.10.1 Questioning begins with your Route Map

Your Route Map lays out the main topics that you wish to cover in the interview. This creates an implicit understanding. When you raise the topic later, the interviewee understands that you want him or her to talk about that matter. You can harness this awareness to elicit spontaneous disclosure without even seeming to ask a question.

Sometimes your Route Map will only have one topic. This is not unusual. It can arise particularly when interviewing in extraordinary circumstances (see Chapter 20).

9.10.2 When interviewing a witness

Requesting a narrative

The initial—and in many cases principal—topic will be 'what happened'. You want the complainant or witness to give you the narrative of a key part of the MTF. Getting initial spontaneous disclosure is essentially a straightforward process.

- Where applicable and appropriate assist the witness's remembrance through context reinstatement (see Chapter 10).
- Ask a productive question to trigger a narrative response.
- Apply the POST formula, waiting two to three seconds.

Requesting disclosure on a specific topic

On occasions the interview will not focus on the commission of the offence but upon one or more specific areas of knowledge. Assisting remembrance may, or may not, be relevant here, depending upon the investigative circumstances. The triggering question should always be a productive one bearing upon a specific issue, followed by a pause.

If the witness does not respond immediately

Do not panic. You have asked a 'high level' process or extended recall (long narrative) question. Do not expect the witness to respond immediately, or even after a two- to three-second pause. Be patient. Let the witness think. Apply the POST formula—waiting a further two to three seconds.

In many instances the witness will start disclosing. Whenever he or she pauses for breath or to think, continue to apply the POST formula—waiting a further two to three seconds.

If the witness looks at you and continues to remain silent

The witness may remain gazing at you, saying nothing. This signals that the witness is not going to take the talking turn for whatever reason.

Engage in a sequence of reassuring comments and statements (conversational questions), ending the sequence with the POST formula, waiting a further two to three seconds, eg:

YOU: *I appreciate it is difficult to remember detail.* ^^ ^^ ^^ ^^

WITNESS: [Silence]

YOU: *Take your time.* ^^ ^^ ^^ ^^

WITNESS: [Silence]

YOU: *There's no rush.* ^^ ^^ ^^ ^^

In most cases the witness will start disclosing.

However, if the witness looks back at you and starts shaking his or her head—indicating an inability or unwillingness to disclose—you need to change the focus of your attention to the 'block' to disclosure. This requires you to adopt a **counselling** stance. You need to help the individual verbalize the 'block'.

YOU: *I sense that you're having some difficulty here.* ^^ ^^ ^^ ^^

WITNESS: [Silence]

YOU: *Let's put what I asked about to one side for a moment.* ^^ ^^ ^^ ^^ *Can you tell me about the difficulty you are having in telling me about that matter?* ^^ ^^ ^^ ^^

WITNESS: [Silence]

YOU: *Take your time.* ^^ ^^ ^^ ^^

WITNESS: [Silence]

YOU: *As I said, here's no rush.* ^^ ^^ ^^ ^^

The disclosure that emerges concerning the 'block' in many cases may be totally unexpected and investigatively important. Ethically you have to continue focusing on the 'block'. Time spent doing this is well invested. It will create an even stronger working relationship between you and the individual.

If the witness is not looking at you and remains silent

The witness is engaging is what is termed an 'inner dialogue'. He or she is going through matters mentally. Typically, when talking to himself or herself the witness will gaze downwards or to the side—associated with thoughts with an emotional connotation.

The witness may be running through the narrative rather like replaying a 'video' recording. He or she may be having an internal debate as to whether to disclose or not, or if he or she discloses, what to disclose, eventually arriving at the 'cusp', the point where he or she has to make a decision.

When the witness is engaged in an 'inner dialogue' you may detect other parallel behaviours, eg:

- adaptors (self-grooming);
- sideways head shaking (indicative of perplexity or arguing against disclosure) or nodding (indicative of agreeing with himself or herself that disclosure should happen);
- gazing for a short time upwards or away from you—and then down again;
- gazing towards you for a short while and then returning to sustained gazing away.

When the individual is engaged in 'inner dialogue':

- under no circumstances break the silence: keep applying the POST formula;
- be prepared to wait it out;
- don't become anxious if you have to wait what seems to you to be a very long time;
- if there is a third party present, he or she might become apprehensive and could disrupt the witness's thoughts by speaking. As pointed out earlier, look towards the third party and make a slight head gesture, hand, or both, to signal 'It's OK. Let's sit this out. Please don't say anything.'

Your patience will be rewarded in most cases: the individual will eventually look up and start talking.

Sometimes, after a protracted period of silence, the individual remains looking down—or away—and does not start talking. When this happens you need to gain the individual's attention.

- Softly but clearly say his or her name with either a rising or falling intonation (indicating it is a gentle request).
- If he or she does not look towards you, repeat his or her name.
- If this does not work, say his or her name with slightly more volume.

Eventually the witness will look at you.

Sometimes the witness may engage in a period of 'inner dialogue' then look towards you with a sustained gaze. This signals that he or she is not going to take the talking turn. Respond as suggested in the earlier section: *If the witness looks at you and continues to remain silent.*

9.10.3   When interviewing a suspect

In the case of a suspect there are many more facets to the basic matter of 'what happened'. There can never be a 'one size fits all' approach to triggering initial disclosure. You have a range of options.

Option: A closed 'yes'/'no' confirmatory question—then pausing

For example, in the police context where the suspect has been arrested and detained on suspicion of committing an offence: *Did you hit Frederick Forsyth in the King and Queen last night?*

In a non-policing context it is appropriate to ask: *Do you know why you are here?* or *Do you know why I need to interview you?* This option is not available in the policing context because as part of the preamble at the outset of the interview you will have spelled out the reason for the interview.

The suspect may respond immediately:

* saying *Yes*, continuing to disclose on the matter;
* saying *No*, explaining his or her denial;
* in the police context saying *No comment*, ie exercising his or her right to remain silent (see Chapter 17).

If the suspect does not respond immediately and remains silent

Be mindful of the multiple factors that might be affecting the individual's ability or desire to respond. The circumstances of the offence may have been emotive or the individual may be feeling particularly exposed, vulnerable, or defensive.

Respond in exactly the same way as you would with a witness who does not respond immediately and remains silent: apply the POST formula, waiting two to three seconds.

During the time that you are continuing to pause, the suspect may switch between looking at you, looking away, down or up, at you again, and away again. While this activity is going on say nothing. Be patient. The activity you are observing is indicative of potential turmoil going on inside the individual.

In many instances this extra silence triggers the suspect to say *Yes* or *No*—and often continue with spontaneous disclosure of detail, eg:

YOU: ^^ ^^ ^^ ^^
SUSPECT: *Yes, and I'll tell you why...*

In the police context the suspect might exercise his or her right to remain silent, ie saying *No comment* or remaining totally silent: see Chapter 17.

If, after extended pausing, the suspect continues to look at you and remains silent

The suspect clearly does not intend to take the talking turn. Engage in a sequence of crème de la crème question + the POST formula, culminating with a restatement of the closed 'yes'/'no' question.

YOU: *I appreciate it may be difficult to talk about this matter.* ^^ ^^ ^^ ^^

SUSPECT: [Silence]

YOU: *So take your time.* ^^ ^^ ^^ ^^

SUSPECT: [Silence]

YOU: *There's no rush.* ^^ ^^ ^^ ^^

SUSPECT: [Silence]

YOU: *Let me ask again.* ^^ ^^ ^^ ^^ *Did you hit Frederick Forsyth in the King and Queen last night?*

SUSPECT: *No. There's no way that I could. I was...*

This sequence often triggers an eventual spontaneous disclosure.

However, if the suspect looks back at you and starts shaking his or her head—indicating an inability or unwillingness to disclose—you need to change the focus of your attention to the 'block' to disclosure. You have to adopt a counselling stance, exactly in the same manner as described earlier when interviewing a witness. For example:

YOU: *I sense that you're having some difficulty here.* ^^ ^^ ^^ ^^

SUSPECT: [Silence]

YOU: *Let's put what I asked about to one side for a moment.* ^^ ^^ ^^ ^^ *Can you tell me about the difficulty you are having in telling me whether you hit Frederick Forsyth in the King and Queen last night?* ^^ ^^ ^^ ^^

SUSPECT: [Silence]

YOU: *Take your time.* ^^ ^^ ^^ ^^

SUSPECT: [Silence]

YOU: *As I said, here's no rush.* ^^ ^^ ^^ ^^

As with a witness, the suspect may start disclosing unexpected and investigatively important detail. Very often in doing so the suspect may actually provide the answer to the question you originally posed, or provide you with the basis for posing the trigger question again.

Despite your adoption of a counselling stance the suspect may:

- say *No comment*;
- remain totally silent.

Very few suspects remain totally silent in interviews. It requires significant will power and an ability to disengage mentally ('remote out' or 'switch off') from listening to what is being said. 'Remoting out' is hard work, very draining mentally and emotionally. It is very difficult to resist the pressure to take the talking turn when something is said or a question posed, followed by a pause. This pressure grows cumulatively with each successive statement, comment, observation, question, or pause.

To cope with the pressure to take the talking turn, individuals who 'remote out' adopt a strategy.

- They strive to occupy their minds, eg intently focusing on something else with their eyes or mentally going through a diversionary activity such as remembering something autobiographical in fine-grain detail about another time and another place.
- They avoid eye-contact.
- They physically turn away or even turn themselves, and where possible their chair, around placing their back towards you.
- They combine these activities in order to disengage from the conversation.

It follows that a suspect who is attempting to 'remote out'—or has done so—tends to be inert, exhibiting very little movement. This is readily detected.

When an individual 'remotes out' treat this in exactly the same way as a 'no comment' interview (see Chapter 17).

If the suspect is not looking at you and continues to remain silent

There are two explanations for this response.

- The suspect may be exercising his or her right to remain silent by remaining totally silent by 'remoting out'.
- The suspect may be engaging in an 'inner dialogue'.

Your observations will tell you which applies. Follow the relevant response described previously.

Option: State the topic—then pausing

This is a highly effective trigger. You have already told the suspect about the topic when you spelled out the Route Map. He or she is in no doubt as to the matter. For example: *So, her injuries,* ^^ ^^ ^^ ^^

The suspect may:

- respond immediately;
- in the police context say *No comment*, ie exercise his or her right to remain silent (see Chapter 17).

If the suspect does not respond immediately and remains silent

Stating the topic is by its very nature posing a 'high level' process question. It 'buys' therefore significant thinking time for the suspect—particularly so if the topic is extremely emotive or the suspect feels particularly exposed, vulnerable, or defensive.

Follow the same approach that you would with no response to a 'yes'/'no' question: apply POST, waiting two to three seconds. Look for behaviours indicative of potential turmoil going on inside the individual.

In many instances this extra silence triggers the suspect to disclose on the topic. However, in the police context the suspect might:

- say *No comment*;
- remain totally silent.

If, after extended pausing, the suspect continues to look at you and remains silent

Engage in a sequence of crème de la crème question + the POST formula, culminating with a restatement of the topic. For example:

YOU: *I appreciate it may be difficult to talk about this matter.* ^^ ^^ ^^ ^^
SUSPECT: [Silence]
YOU: *So take your time.* ^^ ^^ ^^ ^^
SUSPECT: [Silence]
YOU: *There's no rush.* ^^ ^^ ^^ ^^
SUSPECT: [Silence]
YOU: *Her injuries.* ^^ ^^ ^^ ^^.

In most cases the suspect will start disclosing.

However:

- if the suspect's behaviour indicates an inability or unwillingness to disclose, adopt a counselling stance described earlier;
- if the suspect is inert and continues looking at you, this suggests that he or she is 'remoting out', treat this as the suspect exercising his or her right to silence.

If the suspect is not looking at you and continues to remain silent

Your observation of the suspect will enable you to decide whether the suspect:

- is engaged in an 'inner dialogue'; or
- is attempting to 'remote out'.

Whichever applies, follow the suggested responses described earlier.

Option: A parameter question—then pausing

For example, *What did you do between* [point X] *and* [point Y]*?* ^^ ^^ ^^ ^^

This is a very common, safe, and in many cases an investigatively productive trigger.

As when you pose a closed 'yes'/'no' question or state a topic, the suspect may respond immediately:

- disclosing on the matter;
- in the police context saying *No comment*, ie exercising his or her right to remain silent (see Chapter 17).

However, as with any other trigger question, the suspect:

- may not respond immediately and may remain silent;
- after extended pausing may look at you and may continue to remain silent;
- may not look at you and may remain silent.

Whichever applies, follow the suggested responses described earlier.

Option: A trailer question—then pausing

The cumulative items of information, each followed by a pause to allow the suspect to register the detail, present a sequence of events/actions/activities or a set of circumstances that he or she is called upon to account for or to explain. This makes a trailer followed by a pause, a very effective trigger to disclosure.

The suspect may respond immediately:

- disclosing on the matter;
- in the police context saying *No comment*, ie exercising his or her right to remain silent (see Chapter 17, Interviewing the Suspect who Exercises the Right to Silence).

However, as with any other trigger question, the suspect:

- may not respond immediately and may remain silent;
- after extended pausing may look at you and may continue to remain silent;
- may not look at you and may remain silent.

Whichever applies, follow the suggested responses described earlier.

9.11 Responding to initial disclosure

Within the PEACE model the spontaneous disclosure of a witness is called *free recall* and that of a suspect an *account*. As the dictionary definition of account means both 'narration' and 'description', for ease of reference this term will be used to cover such disclosure by witnesses and suspects.

9.11.1 Responding to an account that has no bearing upon what you are investigating

If the interviewee digresses this presents you with a problem. You have to intervene but this must be done calmly, tactfully, and skilfully. Normally, intervening to put the interviewee 'on track' will occur during the topic selection and probing phase. In exceptional circumstances you may need to intervene during the first account stage when it becomes patently clear that the interviewee is completely 'off beam' and is disclosing on matters that are wholly unconnected with the focus of the interview.

- You must be patient. You must listen sufficiently long to have the evidence that the interviewee is substantially digressing. To intervene earlier would be bad manners and would risk losing the interviewee's co-operation.
- When you have sufficient evidence of digression 'come in' gently but positively.
- Make a non-verbal gesture that attracts the interviewee's attention and signals you would like to take the talking turn in order to say something, eg move your chair, raise your hand slightly, lean forward.

Return the interviewee to topic in a socially skilled manner, eg:

> *Can I just come in there.* ^^ ^^ *That's just the kind of detail that I need.* ^^ ^^ *Could I ask you to give me that detail a little later.* ^^^^*So can we come back to that later.* ^^^^ *Could I take you on to [state].* ^^ ^^*It would be a big help for you and me to take me back to what you were saying about [state].*

9.11.2 Responding to a 'yes' or 'no' followed by silence

If the suspect says 'yes' or 'no' but does not expand immediately upon his or her response

Apply the POST formula, waiting two to three seconds. During the time that you are continuing to pause, the suspect may switch between looking at you, looking away, down or up, at you again, and away again. These are signs of inner turmoil.

This may trigger him or her to continue with spontaneous disclosure of detail, eg:

SUSPECT: *And I'll tell you why...*

- If the individual eventually remains looking down—indicative of engaging in an 'inner dialogue'—respond in exactly the same manner as if the suspect were a witness.
- If the suspect looks at you and continues to remain silent, follow the procedure suggested earlier (**If, after extended pausing, the suspect looks at you and continues to remain silent**).

For example:

YOU: *He's now in intensive care.* ^^ ^^ ^^ ^^
SUSPECT: [Silence]

YOU: *I appreciate your situation.* ^^ ^^ ^^ ^^
SUSPECT: [Silence]
YOU: *Take your time.* ^^ ^^ ^^ ^^
SUSPECT: [Silence]
YOU: *There's no rush.* ^^ ^^ ^^ ^^
SUSPECT: [Silence]
YOU: *So I have to ask again.* ^^ ^^ ^^ ^^ *Did you hit Frederick Forsyth in the King and Queen last night?*

Very often at this point the suspect will:

- respond;
- say *No comment* or remain totally silent. If this happens respond in the way suggested in Chapter 17.

If the individual says 'yes'

Engage in a sequence of crème de la crème questions, applying the POST formula, eg:

YOU: *OK. Over to you.* ^^ ^^ ^^ ^^
SUSPECT: [Silence]
YOU: *Tell me about her injuries.* ^^ ^^ ^^ ^^
SUSPECT: [Silence]
YOU: *Take your time.* ^^ ^^ ^^ ^^
SUSPECT: [Silence]
YOU: *There's no rush.* ^^ ^^ ^^ ^^

The individual is highly likely to continue disclosing.

If the individual says 'no'

Adopt a counselling stance.

YOU: *I sense that you're having some difficulty here.* ^^ ^^ ^^ ^^
SUSPECT: [Silence]
YOU: *Let's put what I asked about to one side for a moment.* ^^ ^^ ^^ ^^ *Can you tell me about the difficulty you are having in telling me about that matter?* ^^ ^^ ^^ ^^
SUSPECT: [Silence]
YOU: *Take your time.* ^^ ^^ ^^ ^^
SUSPECT: [Silence]
YOU: *As I said, there's no rush.* ^^ ^^ ^^ ^^

9.11.3   Responding to a relatively full account

If you judge that the interviewee has delivered on the contract to disclose in detail then you need to demonstrate a sound grasp of his or her account, evidencing that you have been actively listening. You do this by summarizing the essential details. As pointed out earlier, summarizing is not replicating: were you to attempt to replicate this would create problems:

- putting you under some degree of pressure, and at risk of introducing inaccuracy, especially if there is a large amount of detail involved;
- helping a would-be liar to overcome the problem of remembering detail that he or she had made up as he or she was going along.

If the individual has referred to a location, positions of people and objects, relative positioning, and activity occurring within this location, you have a choice.

- To access a non-verbal disclosure of this location now through the use of illustrators and/or an enhanced drawing (see section 9.16) before proceeding:
  — in the case of a witness to a second account;
  — in the case of a suspect to *clarification*, ie topic selection and probing.
- To defer accessing non-verbal disclosure:
  — until the witness has given his or her second account;
  — to a suitable point or points across the process of clarifying the suspect's account.

9.11.4 Responding to a problem first account

A 'thin' account

A thin account is any narrative or description that lacks detail throughout. It has the character of an 'agenda'.

- A limited number of steps.
- Each step described in minimal detail.
- No detail concerning what happened between the steps.

In the Explanation stage you spelled out in the Expectations the ground rule 'to disclose in detail'. When the interviewee gave—and confirmed—his or her understanding of this ground rule, this constituted a verbal 'contract'. A 'thin' account is a failure to deliver on this contract. This failure could be the behaviour of a genuine person or a would-be liar.

- It could be a genuine person following the 'less is best' strategy who:
  — either does not realize that this does not apply in this conversation; or
  — is so unused to disclosing in detail to 'powerful people' that it is a difficult task; or
  — for some reason does not want to disclose in detail.
- It could be a person who wants to deceive and is engaging in passive lying, ie avoiding giving detail.

Whatever the reason for its emergence, were you to accept a thin account this would:

- take the pressure off of the interviewee;
- put the pressure upon you—to engage in the mentally demanding task of framing questions to get more detail;
- send the message to the interviewee who, for whatever reason, does not want to respond in detail that there is a likelihood that he or she will get away with thin answers to your questions.

You should therefore never accept a thin account. Always get the individual to have 'another go'.

- **Explain the 'problem'.**

    Thanks for that. ^^ ^^ *You've given me detail as a run of steps* ^^ ^^ *this step* ^^ ^^ (hold your hand upright in 'chopping' position immediately in front of you at waist height, slightly off to your right; then make a small up and down chopping movement as you say 'this step'; then move your hand slightly across to your left, signifying a move from the first step to the second) *and this step* ^^ ^^ (repeat the up and down chopping movement when you say 'this step'; then move your hand slightly across to your left, signifying a move from second step to the third) *and this step* ^^ ^^ (repeat the chopping and lateral movement actions for this step) *and the other steps.* ^^ ^^ (Quickly make the chopping and lateral movements two or three times as you say this.)

- **Raise the issue of detail**.

   But you haven't given me any detail about the steps ^^ ^^ *you haven't given me any detail about this step.* ^^ ^^ (Slowly rotate your index finger round the point in space where you signified the first step.) *You haven't given me any detail about what happened between this step* ^^ *and this step.* ^^ ^^ (Using your index finger slowly draw a line from the point in space of the first step to the point in space of the second step.) *You haven't given me any detail about this step.* ^^ ^^ (Slowly rotate your index finger round the point in space of the second step.) ^^ ^^ *You haven't given me any detail about what happened between that step* ^^ *and the next step.* ^^ ^^ (Using your index finger slowly draw a line from the point in space of the second step to the point in space of the third step.) *And you haven't given me any detail about this step.* ^^ ^^ (Slowly rotate your index finger round the point in space of the third step.) ^^ ^^ *You haven't given me any detail about what happened between that step* ^^ *and the next step.* ^^ ^^ (Repeat index finger movement; then repeat the process for a couple more steps.)

- **Go over the ground rules again**.

Repeat the Expectations and get the individual to check back his or her understanding about detail and taking time. In effect you have made the contract crystal clear.

- **Trigger 'another go'**.

   I'd like you to take me through [state] *again* ^^ ^^ *this time give me as much detail as possible* ^^ ^^ *there can't be too much detail* ^^ ^^ *take your time* ^^ ^^ *it will help you to remember the little bits of detail that we need.* ^^ ^^

A 'pat' account

Two forms of anomaly are potential indicators that an initial account is a 'pat' account, one which has been learned by a would-be liar.

- **Events described in chronological order with little or no narrative reversal**. It is highly unusual to tell a complete narrative without narrative reversal.
- **Too many descriptive words preceding a critical item, person, or location described**. For example: *it was a shiny, black, hooded, bomber jacket.* Usually people put no more than two descriptive words in front of what is being described, eg *a shiny bomber jacket.* Often people use just one, eg *a bomber jacket.* They describe in reverse, typically tacking on descriptive words, eg *a bomber jacket...shiny...black...with a hood...*

You will never know if an account has been learned 'pat' on the basis of one telling. As soon as you consider that the individual has given you a 'pat' account:

- don't summarize: if the account is 'pat' you would be helping the individual to consolidate his learned lies;
- get the individual to go through the account once more.

   Thanks for that. ^^ ^^ *That's just the kind of detail I need.* ^^ ^^ *There was a lot of it.* ^^ ^^ *So to help me get my head round it,* ^^ ^^ *I'd like to ask you to take me through it again.* ^^ ^^ *Just like before with as much detail as possible,* ^^ ^^ *taking your time.* ^^ ^^

Listen intently to the 'second go'. You can reasonably conclude that this is likely to be a 'pat' account if:

- there is still little or no narrative reversal;
- there are still too many words preceding a critical item, person, or location;
- this account has the same or similar words and phrases as the first.

Don't summarize the 'second go' since this would merely help the individual to consolidate his or her remembrance of the 'pat' account. Proceed to probing.

An account that does not accord with what you know

If the account does not fit with your case knowledge, say nothing about this: simply summarize and proceed to probing.

9.12 Keeping track of numerous topics that require probing

9.12.1 Creating a WOB map of topics

If the interviewee's account has produced a substantial number of topics that need probing, consider creating a WOB map of these multiple topics. This will ensure that you do not forget to cover a topic. The WOB map can be easily referred to and navigated, enabling you to manage the content and course of the conversation through confident, effective probing.

- Explain.

    That's a lot of detail you've given me Jason. ^^ ^^ *I'm going to make a couple of notes before we move on.* ^^ ^^

- Quickly create a WOB map.
    — Topics in blobs on spokes radiating from the centre of the wheel.
    — Blobs annotated as you wish.
    — Radiating sub-blobs for particular questioning areas.
    — If you think it helpful, the blobs numbered in the questioning sequence that you think is appropriate.

There is a benefit to having a WOB map. You can respond flexibly to whatever the suspect says. If the suspect introduces, or raises, a topic that you had not, or could not have, anticipated it is a simple matter of noting this on your WOB map together with any issues radiating from this new 'node'. In sum:

- Having a WOB map ensures that you do not forget to address all the issues while flexibly responding to what the suspect raises.
- Not having a WOB map risks not remembering to address a topic.

9.12.2 Noting other issues on your WOB

A second benefit of creating a WOB map at this point is that you can use it to note down:

- issues that have struck you as potentially significant;
- actions to be taken following the interview.

9.13 Probing the account: the Interviewing Spiral

Within the PEACE model, probing—asking questions to obtain expansion and explanation of selected detail—is termed *clarification*. There is much more to probing than simply asking a question to obtain more information. Your questioning must be systematic if you are to achieve your investigative aims and objectives. This requires conscious attention to four activities:

- opening up a topic you want the interviewee to disclose further upon;
- probing the topic methodically and exhaustively;
- summarizing the key issues that you have learned;
- stating a logical link to the next topic you want the interviewee to disclose further upon.

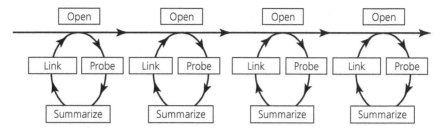

Figure 9.2 The Interviewing Spiral

The entire process constitutes the *interviewing spiral* (Figure 9.2) that you apply to all the topics requiring expansion and explanation.

The interviewing spiral is a flexible tool. According to circumstances—the content and the quality of the interviewee's spontaneous disclosures—you may judge it appropriate not to summarize, moving immediately from probing on a particular topic to linking with the next topic.

9.13.1 Topic selection

The available options

The topic that you select for probing—expansion and explanation—may have:

- a focus upon narrative: you have identified a section of the narrative, an event, episode. or continuous state;
- a focus upon material fact, ie an aspect of a person, location, or object.

The risks of returning to the topic

In Chapter 1 we saw that Principle 6 of the seven principles of investigative interviewing, endorsed by the National Investigative Interview Steering Group, says that a police interviewer is not bound to accept the first answer given. Questioning is not unfair merely because it is persistent.

Persistent has a positive and negative form.

- **Positive persistence is *tenacity*.** You will not be stopped from doing your job of probing just because the interviewee or a third party does not want you to ask for details concerning this matter.
- **Negative persistence is *perseveration*.** Your repeated questioning on the topic has become unreasonable and excessive because the same response has been given each time.

You have to keep on asking yourself, and be able to explain in this interview or later at court, your reason to question on this topic yet again. There are only two reasons for persistent questioning.

To resolve an anomaly through expansion or explanation

Your return to question on this topic again has an investigative aim.

1. An earlier response is deficient, eg:

- is missing critical detail, has apparent gaps and jumps, and lacks detail that could be reasonably expected to be there ('non-barking dogs');
- is non-specific, vague, or ambiguous;
- manifests 'sidestepping'—disclosure is avoided by using the passive or 'not really' responses.

2. The earlier response is internally inconsistent or contradictory, ie does not fit with or, is at odds with, what the interviewee has said earlier in the interview.

3. The interviewee's responses on this topic in this interview are *internally consistent*—there is no mismatch—they are at odds with the police perspective on matters.

- They are *externally* inconsistent, ie they do not fit with or contradict case knowledge on this topic—the police case and the prosecution evidence.
- Where the interviewee is a suspect, they are at odds with:

  — the current case theory (what the police believe happened);
  — the line of logic for believing that this individual committed the offence rather than anyone else.

Persistent questioning is always hazardous.

- **It coaches the interviewee to give the same answer.** If the individual confabulated or told an active lie, it has a 'rehearsal' effect, akin to learning something off rote.
- **It becomes wearisome and alienating.** It is increasingly likely to evoke a negative response from the interviewee, or a third party, eg a supporter (carer; appropriate adult) or a legal adviser.
- **It can produce change that you don't want.** Vulnerable individuals will interpret repeated questioning on a topic as saying indirectly 'you're giving me the wrong answer'. Whether an adult or developmentally disadvantaged, the following are highly likely to change their answer, potentially making your life even more difficult.

  — **Compliant interviewees**: who want to 'go along with' you, and to please you but conclude that they have not.
  — **Suggestible interviewees**: who distrust their memories, and are constantly looking for any clue to the correct answer. The repeated questioning on the topic signals that they need to look closer at your question for the 'right' answer.

To induce the interviewee to give responses that accord with the police perspective on matters

Persistent questioning here is not to obtain expansion or explanation but to get the interviewee to abandon his or her position on matters, ie to say thing that he otherwise would not, or not to say things that he otherwise would. This constitutes oppression[3] and the aim of the interview is unlawful.

- If the suspect is legally advised, he or she should intervene if you go over something for a third or fourth time when a suspect's replies have been consistent.
- If the suspect is not legally represented and changes his or her response in the face of repeated questioning and subsequently makes incriminatory disclosures, at court the defence will argue:
  — these disclosures were coerced;
  —the evidence should be excluded under the Police and Criminal Evidence Act section 76 (oppression) or section 78 (unfairness).

If you ask the wrong kind of question

On occasions every interviewer poses a question that he or she immediately recognizes as not appropriate eg an unproductive question or a productive question but one which buys you too little pause. You need to correct the error by what is termed 'repairing':

---

[3] *R v Prager* [1972] 1 All ER 1114; *R v Priestley* [1965] 51 Cr App R 1; *R v Fulling* [1987] 85 Cr App R 136.

acknowledging that you need to express the matter in a different, better, manner and then doing so, eg: Let me put that another way. ^^ ^^—then pose the more appropriate question.

Don't ask the same question repeatedly

If you have gone through the information and evidence that you have, and return to the material to repeat the question, this is entirely acceptable. Where the suspect is legally represented, the legal adviser will not normally intervene when there is repeated questioning in a 'no comment' interview. If the suspect has said 'no comment' to questions that have been posed three or more times, it is highly likely that the legal adviser will intervene:

- to ask you to stop while the legal adviser consults his or her notebook;
- having counted the number of same responses have been given
  - to ask why you are repeating your questions on this topic yet again
  - to point out that your behaviour constitutes oppression, perhaps citing appropriate case law[4] eg:

    Officer, that is the [number of times] *you have asked that question. It is clear that you have rehearsed all the evidence. Nothing new is now emerging. My client is consistent in exercising his/ her right to silence. Oppression has been defined as behaviour that is likely to induce an individual to say things that he otherwise would not, or not to say things that he otherwise would. Please accept my client's decision not to answer this question and please do not repeatedly ask it again.*

Even if the legal adviser does not intervene, if the suspect is charged, it is likely that at court the defence will argue that:

- repeated questioning was oppressive;
- the legal adviser was in error.

9.13.2 Probing: questions born of answers

When you pose a question concerning a topic and the interviewee gives an answer to this, common sense argues that you should listen intently to the answer. Within the detail of this answer there will be a key issue: something new not previously disclosed that you will want to know more about. So you ask a question about this key issue. The key issue within the answer to this question gives rise to your next question, and so on until you judge that you have sufficient information about topic. You will then want to move to another topic.

Lines of questioning

Systematic questioning involves following *lines of questioning*: each line a logically linked sequence of questions born of answers—Q-A-Q-A-Q, or familiarly called 'quack-quack' by conversation management practitioners and trainers (Figure 9.3).

Following a logical line of questioning enables you to gain a breadth and depth of knowledge on a topic by applying two skills: intent listening and adept questioning.

- Open up the topic, using a productive question.
- Register the fine-grain detail of the answer.
- Identify the key issue within the answer.
- Frame the question.

---

[4] *R v Prager* [1772] 1 All ER 1114; *R v Priestley* [1765] 51 Cr App R 1; *R v Fulling* [1787] 85 Cr App R 136.

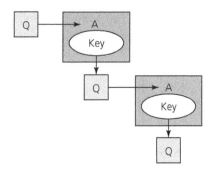

Figure 9.3 Systematic questioning: Q-A-Q-A-Q ('quack-quack')

- Deliver the question.
- Register the fine-grain detail of the answer.
- Identify the key issue within the answer.
- Frame the question.
- Deliver the question…and so on.

Skilled, productive questioning involves conscious, considered movement along a 'general' to 'specific' dimension, reflecting the degree of latitude implied in the question.

- At the extreme of the 'general' end of the dimension are crème de la crème questions— ways of asking a question without seemingly asking a question—giving most latitude to the interviewee.
- Further along the dimension are open-ended questions allowing substantial latitude of response.
- Moving towards the 'specific' end there are closed identificatory questions with their stated focus.
- At the extreme 'specific' end are closed confirmatory 'yes'/'no' questions.

We have to remember, however, that putting closed confirmatory 'yes'/'no' questions at the specific end of the spectrum is a simplification. As pointed out earlier, the relationship between you and the interviewee determines whether he or she treats your 'yes'/'no' question:

- as an invitation for confirmation, ie consistent with being the most 'specific' response of all;
- as an invitation to speak freely, ie as if asked an open-ended question towards the 'general' end of the dimension.

Navigating the 'general' to 'specific' dimension of questioning

Wherever possible you should keep towards the 'general' end of the dimension. This does not mean that you should not use closed identificatory questions or, where appropriate, closed confirmatory 'yes'/'no' questions. Once you have received the required detail in the response to a focused question, or a 'yes' or a 'no' to a confirmatory question, you should as a matter of skilled professional practice follow this answer with a crème de la crème or open question. By moving towards the 'general' end of the dimension, the greater latitude of response increases the potential to learn new information.

Accessing and probing non-verbal experience

If you judge it appropriate, access non-verbal experience through illustrators, enactment, and enhanced drawings: see later in this chapter at section 9.16 and the Reference Section on these three investigative tools. Where applicable, this experience should be probed.

'Hot spots'

When you detect a 'hot spot' you will need to judge if, and when, you will act upon it.

For example, you may observe a number of changes in BASELINES behaviours potentially indicative of a 'hot spot' as you are posing a question, during the interviewee's response, and during pause preceding and following the interviewee's response. If you judge that now is the right time to use this awareness, you may decide to pose a crème de la crème question, eg an observation such as:

> *I sense that you are not very comfortable with us talking about this.*

Common sense is necessary. Never describe the behaviour you are observing to the interviewee. It is alienating and bizarre to say something like:

> *I see that you sweating; for the purposes of the tape ^^^^ Ian is trembling. ^^ ^^*

'Topic hopping'

Probing systematically by following a line of questioning in which questions are born of answers:

- encourages coherent disclosure;
- shows you're really listening to what is said to you;
- helps you to remember the fine-grain detail of the interviewee's responses;
- enables you to detect anomaly: what the interviewee says oddly—or doesn't say at all.

Unsystematic probing is called 'topic hopping', which you met earlier in Chapter 3, ie switching without warning and with no apparent logic from the current topic to another topic (Figure 9.4).

'Topic hopping' is entirely self-defeating. It prevents you achieving your investigative aims.

- It discourages disclosure: because it challenges the interviewee's ability to keep up logically and conversationally. As Figure 9.4 shows, his or her replies—the As—get less and less informative as the interviewee disengages more and more.

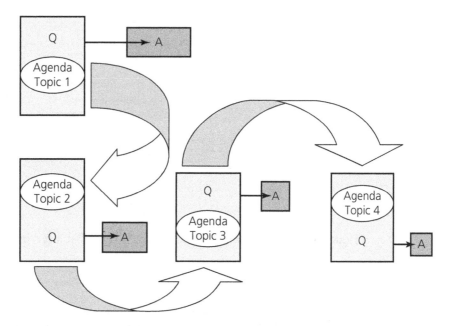

Figure 9.4 Unsystematic questioning: 'topic hopping'

- It destroys the working relationship with the interviewee. He or she rightly concludes that you are following your 'agenda', ie you are only interested in what you want to know.
- If you 'hop' from one topic to another it makes it difficult for you to:
  — organize your thoughts logically;
  — remember the detail of what you said and what the interviewee said in reply: no one issue is ever thought about sufficiently;
  — spot anomaly.
- You could fail to ask about matters that the suspect later relies upon in his evidence. There has to be a direct question to create the conditions to mention—or to fail to mention—something later relied upon at court.[5]

Structure of an interview

The increased use of technology (audio and visual recording) has increased scrutiny on the product of witness interviews. Whereas, previously, only a written statement would be created as a record, now lawyers—both defence and prosecution—have access to the recordings of both vulnerable and significant witnesses. The use of recordings as evidence as chief[6] has highlighted the poor structure that is evident in some interviews where key evidence is intermingled with irrelevant topics. This has resulted in fresh guidance[7] being issued on the ideal structure of a visually recorded interview (see Figure 9.5).

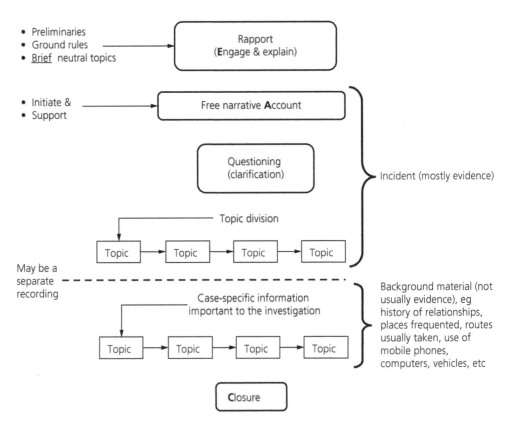

Figure 9.5 The ideal structure of a visually recorded interview (ACPO, 2010)

---

[5] *R v Hillard* (2004) CA 2/3/2004 Unreported. Document No AC9800288.

[6] Youth Justice and Criminal Evidence Act 1999 (as amended).

[7] ACPO (2010) *Advice on the Structure of Visually Recorded Interviews* available at <http://www.acpo.police.uk/documents/crime/2011/20110418%20CBA%20Advice%20on%20the%20Structure%20of%20Visually%20Recorded%20Witness%20interviewsAug2010.pdf>.

Questioning about an image

You have to sustain the individual's mental imagery by remaining with the reporting modality. For example, in this response the interviewee is reporting a visual experience:

INTERVIEWEE: *I saw there was something in his hand when he turned round.*

Image compatible questioning

An appropriate productive question to probe this visual imagery would be an echo probe, eg:

YOU: ^^ ^^ *Something in his hand* ^^ ^^.

(Note, by the way, the sensible pause before the echo probe. If you come in immediately with an echo probe, this could actually snatch the talking turn from the interviewee who is just taking a moment to draw breath and to think before continuing to disclose on this issue. As a rule of thumb, always pause before delivering an echo probe: you might find that very often the individual says spontaneously what your intended echo probe was seeking to elicit!)

Image incompatible questioning

An inappropriate image incompatible question guaranteed to disrupt the individual's line of thought, to destroy focused concentration, and to confuse would be:

Try hard to think about anything said at that point.

Rather than sticking with the visual key issue—the 'something in his hand'—the interviewer has 'hopped' onto topic in the auditory modality: words said!

9.13.3 Summarizing

This is a restatement of the critical factual ideas within the key issues (Figure 9.6).

So let me pull together what it is that you're saying ^^ ^^ *Tell me if I'm right in what I say* ^^ ^^ *or if I'm not quite right, put me right.* ^^ ^^ *If I've missed something,* ^^ *or you want to add something* ^^ *just speak up.*

Benefits of summarizing

The benefits of summarizing are substantial. It helps you to remember the critical detail in the responses to a line of questioning. If it is an extended run of questioning you should judge points at which you should deliver a *stage summary*—or more than one such summary—of the critical detail thus far, and then continue with the line of questioning. Mindful of the issues concerning variation in attention that we describe in Chapter 2, stage summarizing is particularly helpful as it has the effect of refocusing and refreshing attention.

Summarizing is not replication

As pointed out previously, summarizing is not replication. Replication puts you at risk of introducing error, which the unassertive interviewee may not feel it 'right' to correct. It also potentially assists the would-be liar. If the interviewee goes along with your erroneous summary and you continue questioning upon it being correct this could:

• in the case of a suspect, lead to the interviewing being excluded as evidence;
• in the case of a witness, undermine his or her reliability in the eyes of the court.

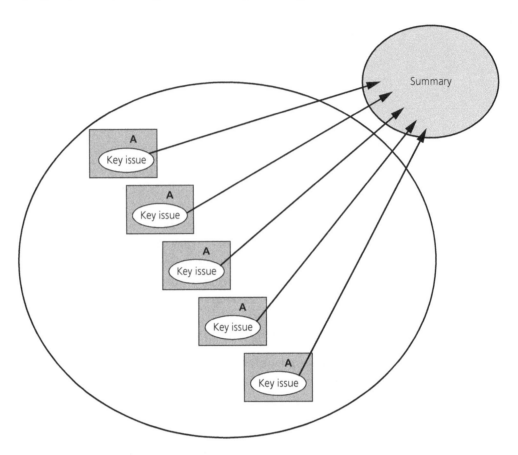

Figure 9.6 Summarizing: restating the critical detail of the key issues

Your summary must be accurate

Introducing inaccuracy into a summary puts at risk you, the interviewee, and the interview as evidence. If you probe on the basis of an inaccurate summary and the interviewee is compliant, ie goes along with your inaccuracy, then this response and any other disclosure issuing from this has no investigative worth. The interview is a waste of time, giving rise to information that inevitably misinforms, misleads, hinders, or can even destroy your investigation. It is almost inevitable that the court will rule the content of the interviewee's responses inadmissible.

If the interviewee disagrees with your summary

If the interviewee says that your summary is incorrect, respond constructively, eg

> *Thanks for that.* ^^ ^^
> *Can you please tell me what part of what I have said is incorrect.* ^^ ^^

Listen, then re-summarize, and move on.

If there is a significant difference you should consider stopping the interview to examine the recording.

When not to summarize

There are circumstances when summarizing is inappropriate.

- **Where there is just too little detail to summarize.** If the responses to the line of questioning are extremely thin, it makes no sense to summarize. To do so would sound like a parrot. Parrotting is a form of counter-productive questioning. It grates and signals the interviewer cannot remember detail. Better to pause for moment, to consolidate the detail in your working memory, and then move on.

- **After a short sequence of responses.** It might make things easier for you but:
  — it sounds odd;
  — it could lead to the interviewee thinking that you are unable to hold information in your head;
  — if done repeatedly it is very alienating: it is parrotting albeit at length.
- **Where the individual has disclosed detail that is inconsistent with, or contradicts, earlier detail.** The interviewee may give detail which does not fit or contradicts what has been said in this line of questioning or earlier in the interview, or before the interview. Summarizing might alert the individual to this and lead to a change in response: the interviewee attempting to negate the earlier inconsistent, or contradictory detail, eg *That's it. Sorry! What I said earlier wasn't right on that.*

9.13.4 Linking to the next topic

If you were to move directly from your summary to opening up the next topic this would amount to 'topic hopping'. You need to explain the transition:

- **either** striking a logical link, eg:

    I've got a clear idea now of what happened how the two of you ended up in the bedroom. ^^ ^^
    I need to get things clear about what happened next. ^^ ^^

- **or** explaining the shift to an unconnected topic, eg:

    That's covered what happened up to the time you left. ^^ ^^ *I'd like to move now to the taxi.* ^^ ^^

9.13.5 Questioning on investigatively important information (I³)

In Chapter 6, we recommended that you create a WOB map of I³ as part of your preparation for the interview. Referring to your WOB map you are able to engage in the interviewing spiral for each topic, and any topic raised by the interviewee's responses that requires probing.

9.14 Questioning about a number of same or similar events

If there have been a number of the same or similar events, it is difficult for the interviewee to distinguish between them. You have to help him or her disentangle the detail and also need to bear in mind how memory deteriorates and changes over time. Furthermore, if the event happened on several occasions it will be difficult for the individual to remember a specific instance. This is indicative that the frequency has created a script memory, ie a stereotypic representation of what happened.

9.14.1 Create a tangible representation

You can turn each event or episode into something real that can be seen as distinct from the others, and discussed. All you need is a set of coloured pens, eg the four that you use for SE3R, plus pencils, biros etc.

9.14.2 Work to overcome the script memory

Explain the use of the pens which you are going to lay out in an Event Line type way, with a short distance between each pen, eg:

> *Right Sandy ^^ ^^ You said you went to your dealer three or four times ^^ ^^ over the last couple of months.^^ ^^ I'm going to use these different coloured pens ^^ ^^ in a way that will help us both and stop us getting confused. ^^ ^^ This black pen* (pick up) *stands for the last time you went to your dealer.* (place on table) ^^ ^^ *This blue pen* (pick up) *stands for the time before that.* (place on table) ^^ ^^ *And this red pen* (pick up) *was the time before that.* (place on table) ^^ ^^ *This green pen* (pick up) *is the first time you went.* (place on table) ^^ ^^

Move the most recent event (pen) away from the others, ie getting the interviewee to focus on this event, eg:

> *So Sandy ^^ ^^ Let's take the last time you went to your dealer. ^^ ^^ About a week ago you said ^^ ^^ Let's concentrate on that. ^^*

You will find that very often concentrating on the last occasion actually enhances ability to remember the one before that. This enhances the quality of the remembrance of the time before that, and so on.

Sometimes it makes sense to start from the first occurrence, if this was notionally the most memorable, eg the first sexual assault. You take that farthest point and the corresponding pen and concentrate on getting the maximum detail for that. You will have to bear in mind that if this is very elderly in relative terms, although it may be vivid it may not be accurate.

9.15 Responding to an admission or a confession

Irrespective of the investigative context, interviewees make admissions and confessions, disclosing detail that is personally damaging.

An admission is not the same as a confession. Suspects and witnesses are liable to make admissions. The individual voluntarily discloses—and acknowledges—detail to be the case and that is inconsistent with, or contradicts, the account that he or she has given. A confession is an acknowledgment—admission—of guilt in any investigative context. In the main it will be suspects who confess, but on occasions a witness may surprise by making a spontaneous admission of guilt.

It is uncommon for an individual to give spontaneously a fully detailed admission or confession. Typically it emerges as an initial shred—a partial disclosure. Arguably this is a reflection of the individual being on the cusp, ie the point where he or she is beginning to accept the necessity of making a personally damaging disclosure. Your task is to facilitate a spontaneous flow of increasing disclosure.

9.15.1 Spot the clues

You have to be alert to the signs that the individual is on the cusp. For example, the individual is engaged in an 'inner dialogue' or making remarks, punctuated by pauses and accompanied by vocal non-verbal clues (eg sighing, long inhalation) and non-vocal non-verbal clues (eg facial movement, placing his or her face in cupped hands with extended fingers covering eyes, slowly shaking or nodding his or her head)—indicative of self-questioning and acknowledgment that something has to be confronted.

Say nothing.

9.15.2 Respond appropriately to the emergent disclosure

When the individual discloses the initial shred, stops talking, and looks away/down

Say nothing: apply the POST (pause + observe + SOFTENS + think) formula.

If the individual remains silent, continuing to look down/away

Say nothing: apply the POST formula.

If the individual remains silent and looks towards you

Say nothing: apply the POST formula.

- If he or she does not resume the talking turn, trigger further disclosure by using a crème de la crème question, eg an echo or mirror probe; an observation (such as *I appreciate it's difficult*); a minimal prompt (such as, *And...*).
- If he or she resumes the talking turn, keep listening and observing, applying the POST formula whenever he or she falls silent.

Probing

Never interrupt to probe. To do so would be not only unprofessional, it risks rendering him or her aware of what has been said and its potential implications, and making the decision to stop disclosing.

Wait for the individual's **verbal sign off**—an utterance—indicating that he or she has finished disclosing, eg *So that's it. I know that I should have said earlier. But now I've told you.*

At this point it is appropriate to start probing the disclosed detail.

9.16 Accessing non-verbal experience

9.16.1 The limitations of language

In Chapter 2 we drew to your attention the fact that most people have a very limited vocabulary to describe people, particularly faces, and how they use illustrators—drawing in the air using their fingers and hands. In Chapter 5 we indicated that it is very supportive to the interviewee to be allowed to use illustrators, making disclosure of detail less difficult, if not less painful, for the interviewee.

People resort to illustrators to describe almost anything non-verbally:

- augmenting their verbal description; or
- overcoming:
  - their lack of words altogether;
  - inability to find words at this moment: the words escape them.

In addition to illustrators, Chapter 5 recommends two other techniques to help interviewees to communicate their experience non-verbally: enactment and drawing.

All three techniques overcome the limitations of language. From an investigative interviewing perspective they have two enormous benefits.

- The process of illustration enactment and drawing commonly triggers, or facilitates, verbal disclosure for the first time or adds to previous disclosure, eg:
  - actions/reactions;

— words said;

— other modality detail, eg smell, touch;

— commentary, eg At this point I was panicking.

- They enable a form of validation—a check on the reality or accuracy—of what has been said earlier:

— verbally without resort to using these techniques;

— using one of these techniques.

9.16.2   Illustrator representation

Illustrators

Illustrators are simple movements of a finger, fingers, a hand, or hands to show—illustrate—the 'reality' of the speaker's 'mental picture' (image) of visual, felt, or otherwise sensed experience, eg:

- shape;
- dimension: length, width, height, depth;
- orientation;
- relative position;
- relative distance;
- relative height;
- location;
- direction;
- trajectory/direction of movement;
- route travelled;
- point of contact/impact;
- force of contact/impact;
- rhythm/tempo.

The value of illustrator representation of offence-related detail

They help the interviewee

- Illustrators are a physical form of focused retrieval and assist further context re-instatement.
- They can supplement—or reinforce—the verbal description.
- They substitute for words, relieving the pressure to find words where for whatever reason these are lacking.
- They overcome the common difficulty of using units of measure accurately, eg hands held a distance apart to show the length of a knife blade remove the necessity to express verbally the length in terms of centimetres or inches.

They help you

- You can 'see' the reality of the experience being described physically, something that words and your imaging alone could never achieve.
- You can check whether the observed illustration corresponds with external reality, eg your personal knowledge of the location; any visual representation (eg 'flat pack' drawing, plan, photograph) in your case material.
- You can return later to request a further demonstration to validate the representation. If the illustration is the same then it has been internally validated.

- Markedly imprecise, gross, or sweeping movement are a potential anomaly: a possible indicator of the interviewee not having experienced what he or she is describing.

Obtaining an illustrator representation is not a substitute for drawing. It is an essential intermediate stage between verbal account and drawing.

Guidance on obtaining illustrator representations

Guidance is in the Reference Section.

9.16.3 Enactment

Enactment is a simple but invaluable investigative tool. The interviewee represents crucial detail by:

- moving or positioning his or her body/limbs (solo enactment);
- moving or positioning your body/limbs or those of a third party;
- engaging in an action sequence involving the interviewee and you, and where applicable a third party.

Enactment allows representation of multiple facets of experience, eg:

- posture;
- orientation;
- relative position;
- relative distance;
- hold or how something was held;
- trajectory/direction of movement;
- direction of gaze;
- point of contact/impact;
- force of contact/impact.

Props

Providing the interviewee with a 'prop', eg a ruler to represent a knife, can generate detail that would have been impossible to describe in words.

When not to request an enactment

Common sense has to be exercised. There will be occasions when it would be wholly inappropriate to ask an individual to enact an experience, eg intimate touching or body contact of a sexual nature.

Guidance on obtaining enactment

Guidance is in the Reference Section.

9.16.4 Enhanced drawing

Drawing gives you access to an extremely rich source of non-verbal experience concerning:

- objects and locations (irrespective of actual size);
- shape;

- dimension—length, width, height, depth;
- orientation;
- position and relative position;
- direction;
- trajectory/direction of movement;
- route travelled;
- point of contact/impact.

Drawing is an extremely rich source of additional verbal disclosure. When drawing, many individuals spontaneously 'talk aloud':

- saying what they are attempting to draw—which may or may not be capable of being visually represented;
- providing an insight into the individual's thoughts, feelings, and even actions at the time or now at the time of drawing.

However, providing the individual with drawing materials and asking him or her to draw something does produce some problems, eg:

- individuals are characteristically anxious about their 'ability' to draw;
- you potentially have no control over the size of the drawing;
- an individual who is developmentally disadvantaged, illiterate, or who does not have command, or sufficient command, of English may not be able to annotate the drawing to indicate what a particular representation signifies;
- by using only one pen or pencil—a single colour—it is impossible for anyone inspecting the drawing to know:
  — what detail was disclosed, ie drawn, initially;
  — what detail was added or corrected in response to a request for expansion or explanation.

The technique of *enhanced drawing* overcomes problems.

Core techniques of enhanced drawing

Enhanced drawing involves:

- specific instructions to manage the interviewee's anxiety and manage the scale of the drawing;
- instructions to the interviewee to access thoughts and emotion;
- requesting illustrators (*Show me*) to augment the drawing;
- additional non-verbal experience, ie you drawing in parallel a copy of what the interviewee is drawing:
  — enables you to annotate your copy with anything that he or she says by way of labelling or commentary;
  — enables you to annotate anomalies and areas for probing;
  — overcomes the inability of the interviewee to label his or her drawing;
  — creates a very positive 'working together' experience: rather than the interviewee 'doing all the work' and feeling self-conscious while being observed;
- the use of different coloured pens to provide an 'audit trail' of the stage at which the detail was drawn: implementing the SE3R 'industry standard' sequence, ie:
  — initial spontaneous disclosure in black;
  — disclosure in response to probing (requests for expansion and explanation) in blue;
  — disclosure to later probing in red.

Guidance on enhanced drawing

Guidance is in the Reference Section.

9.16.5 The non-verbal disclosure 'staircase'

It is not a case of choosing one technique or another. It does make sense to combine techniques. An extremely practical way of using all three is to take the individual up a 'staircase' of non-verbal disclosure that combines all three, in a way that allows progressive validation yet prevents rehearsal.

- Obtain initial disclosure verbally at an appropriate point, eg following the first or second account.
- Request an initial illustration/enactment.
- At a later point in the interview request a further illustration/enactment: constituting a check on the validity of the earlier illustration.
- At a later point in the interview towards the closing stages engage in enhanced drawing.

However, you have to be flexible. On occasions you will want to move from an illustrator to a subsequent enhanced drawing. Circumstances may argue that a move directly from verbal disclosure to enhanced drawing is appropriate. This said, given that illustrator representation is natural, everyday behaviour—and drawing is not—illustrators:

- are the most productive, first non-verbal approach to disclosing experience that challenges ability to describe in words;
- assist the use of subsequent non-verbal techniques.

9.16.6 Writing

You may at some time want an individual to write out a particular word or words in order to see whether the individual replicates idiosyncratic spelling or script that was found in a key location.[8]

9.17 Chapter summary

Skilled explanation, most particularly of the 'ground rules' to gain the interviewee's acceptance of the 'contract', is vital to managing the disclosure process across the conversational exchange. Productive and, where appropriate, risky questions are the chosen key to the door of disclosure. However, it is the manner in which you question—pausing, pacing, triggering disclosure, and responding to disclosure—the way you turn the key in the lock that will open the door to the interviewee's experience—both verbal and non-verbal.

---

[8] *R v Nottle* [2004] EWCA Crim 599.

10

Assisting Remembrance of Offence-Related Detail

10.1 Chapter overview

This chapter presents the range of techniques to facilitate the interviewee's remembrance of offence-related detail.

10.1.1 Chapter objectives

This chapter will enable you to:

- appreciate the benefits and risks of assisting an interviewee's remembrance of detail;
- have a sound understanding of the techniques for assisting remembrance;
- make practical decisions concerning the implementation of these techniques.

10.2 Assisting remembrance: the benefits and the risks

As pointed out in Chapter 3, people's remembrance is significantly more action than description focused, and they have a limited vocabulary to describe features. Based upon extensive examination of memory research, Fisher and Geiselman[1] provided investigative interviewers with an invaluable toolkit of *cognitive*—mental—memory techniques that can assist an individual to search for and to report memory for material on a specific episode, ie remembrance of actions and, to a lesser extent, descriptive detail.

Every interviewer should know about these techniques that have the potential to enhance an individual's recall and should develop expertise in helping interviewees to use them.

These techniques work by enabling the individual to give significantly more detail than would be the case by simply asking 'what happened' and then extensively probing. You have to exercise judgement when considering the use of these techniques, taking into account past retrieval by the individual, the risks of relevance filtering and contamination, confabulation, the limitations of the interviewee, and the price of repeated retrieval.

10.2.1 Past retrieval by the individual

It is essential to know the 'disclosure history' of the individual. If the individual has disclosed detail concerning the offence on a number of occasions, whether to the police or to some other individual, eg a counsellor or relative, he or she will have necessarily a relatively well-established account that he or she has accessed repeatedly. Repeated accessing has a rehearsing effect. There is no sense in using techniques to assist remembrance in these circumstances. You would only be expanding an over-learned account.

It makes sense, therefore, to check with the interviewee at the outset his or her 'history' of disclosing detail to people since the offence.

10.2.2 The risk of relevance filtering and contamination

Wherever possible you should enter the interview with as little knowledge as possible about 'what happened', or what this individual or others have said about the material time frame. You should have sufficient information, eg about key locations and the identities of key individuals, to be able to appropriately focus the individual's attention and to understand

---

[1] Fisher, R. and Geiselman, R. (1992), *Memory-enhancing Techniques for Investigative Interviewing: The Cognitive Interview.* Springfield, Ill: Charles C. Thomas.

what he or she is talking about when disclosing detail. Prior knowledge poses risks to you and the interviewee: inducing you to relevance filter, ie to register detail that fits and ignore detail that doesn't, and to contaminate the individual's account by introducing or putting a slant upon detail that he or she did not mention.

10.2.3 Confabulation

The techniques for assisting remembrance require the individual to think about matters in great detail, and to reflect upon this detail at some length. These are behaviours that are not normal in everyday life. It follows that the techniques will necessarily create a point where the individual recognizes a gap in his or her experience. At this point you and the interviewee are extremely vulnerable.

As explained in Chapter 2, individuals build up a body of general knowledge based on first-hand (directly experienced by the individual) and second-hand experience (gained through observing other individuals, or through media representations). We therefore end up with very large numbers of *scripts*, ie stereotypic representations of what our experience tells us happens normally or usually. In the case of offence-related detail there is always a risk that the individual is not reporting what happened but disclosing the contents of a script of such circumstances, eg an armed robbery or an assault. Similarly, individuals have stereotypic notions of people—and their descriptions—involved or engaged in a given activity.

You have to be alert, therefore, to clues that the individual is on the extreme limit of *episodic* memory—retrieving detail concerning this particular incident—and is now on the margins of confabulation, accessing *script* memory.

- **Commentary**. This is when the individual makes a comment which qualifies or 'hedges' what he or she is saying, eg ***I must have*** then gone to check the baby; I was coming up to the *T-junction and* **as I always do** *I would have* looked right and left. Such commentary is a clue that the individual has reached the margins of valid recall and is now in the realms of script memory.
- **Absence of narrative reversal**. If the individual describes a sequence of events with little or no narrative reversal, this rings an alarm bell. A second run is necessary. If the same pattern emerges, it is a potential indicator of this being a script memory.

10.2.4 Lying

In Chapter 4 we see that the greater part of deception involves passive lying, ie just not saying something. Active lying—representing an untruth as the truth—constitutes a lesser part, and the storylines tend to be thin because they are easier to remember. Techniques to assist the remembrance of a truthful person may well reveal the would-be deceiver who is unable to make things up. It could be equally argued that the self-pacing, essentially reflection- and repetition-based, character of memory-enhancing techniques assist the liar to create and to commit to memory detail that expands his or her storyline.

10.2.5 Limitations of the interviewee

The techniques rely upon the individual engaging fully in the process, devoting maximum mental effort and attention to the task. Common sense argues that you should take into account any limitation of the interviewee's mental functioning that would affect his or her ability to engage in this way.

Temporary impairment

If an individual's mental functioning is sub-optimal due to extreme exhaustion or the continuing effects of alcohol or any other drug, whether taken recreationally or prescribed, his or her ability to retrieve and to hold material in working memory is fundamentally impaired. Different drugs have differing effects upon an individual's mental functioning and 'body clock', eg alcohol, opiates, anti-anxiety, and anti-depressant drugs slow these down, amphetamines and ecstasy speed them up.

While an individual is impaired in this manner, it may be appropriate to obtain the fullest possible spontaneous account and to probe this. It makes no sense to devote valuable time and effort to using memory-enhancing techniques to assist his or her remembrance. You need to ask the interviewee a direct question about potential sources of temporary impairment. If it emerges that there is potential impairment you should not attempt to use these techniques, even if the individual says that he or she is 'perfectly OK'.

Long-standing impairment

If an individual has a long-standing impairment that affects his or her intellectual functioning, eg developmental disadvantage, this will necessarily present an obstacle to using techniques to assist remembrance. As a rule of thumb these techniques should not be used with children under the age of about seven, or with an individual of any age with significant intellectual impairment. The common sense criteria that you are applying when making judgements are:

- Will this individual understand what is being asked of him or her?
- Will this individual be able to engage fully in the process?
- Will the techniques do more harm than good, ie affect the content of disclosure in a way which undermine the individual's reliability?

Physical trauma and coma

Chapter 2 describes circumstances in which information is never registered or consolidated, eg when physical trauma results in extended coma. Techniques to assist remembrance exploit 'memory pegs': if there is no memory peg, then there is nothing to enhance! The individual will have a complete blank for a period up to the point of sustaining the physical injury that resulted in coma. He or she will be extremely vulnerable, suggestible to anything you say—whether intended or not—about the incident and likely to respond to suggestion by confabulating, giving you the contents of script memory.

You should not attempt to enhance the recall of an individual who has been in coma for a significant period as a result of head injury. The only sensible question that you can ask is *What is the last thing that you can remember?* Then, taking a start point that is a suitable distance in time before the last remembered thing, create a parameter question, eg:

> *What I'd like you to do Terry ^^ ^^ is to take me through everything that you can remember happening between* [start point] *^^ ^^ and* [last remembered point].

Intoxication at the time of the event

Chapter 2 points out that alcohol or drug intoxication affects the registration of detail. Again, assisting remembrance is counter-productive. An appropriate sequence of questioning would be:

- The individual's remembrance of the first thing when he or she came round.
- The individual's remembrance of the last thing before losing consciousess.

- Take a start point a suitable distance in time before the last remembered thing.
- Ask a parameter question.

10.2.6 Repeated retrieval in this interview

You have to exercise a fine balance, judging the point at which you should stop memory enhancing. The more often in this interview the individual accesses and reports the contents of episodic memory, the greater the rehearsal effect mentioned earlier. Going over something again and again produces two effects.

- A *mass practice* effect. This is how people remember lines in a play or revise for a test or examination. It becomes so established that it becomes a form of script.
- A *freezing* effect. It can constitute as a hard 'fact' something which is not the case.

In either case the result increasingly becomes a 'pat' account. Look out for clues that this is likely to be happening.

- Little or no narrative reversal.
- The individual is saying the same thing using the same or extremely similar words and phrases.

To continue beyond this point risks undermining the investigative and evidential value (validity) of the individual's account and the reliability (trustworthiness) of the individual.

10.3 Techniques for assisting remembrance

10.3.1 Engage in RESPONSE behaviours

RESPONSE behaviours are described in Chapter 5. They incorporate SOFTENS, conversation-enhancing behaviours, including attention to seating positions, ie chairs placed in a consultative position at 'ten-to-two on the clock face' angle.

10.3.2 Orientating explanation

A simple, straightforward explanation that orientates the individual is essential for assisting the individual to retrieve and to report as much offence-related detail as possible. This should include:

- the reason for the interview;
- your roles;
- the Route Map;
- Expectations.

In effect you are removing the mental obstacle of the 'guessing game', ie the interviewee being distracted by trying to work out what's happening, what is due to happen, and what's expected.

It is useful to have two laminated cards—one for you, one for the interviewee—that shows:

- the Route Map and the Routines on the front;
- Expectations on the reverse.

If the interviewee is unable to read, you should give the laminated card to whoever is accompanying the individual.

Reason for the interview

This has to be clearly stated to overcome the guessing game. A useful technique that you can use with witnesses but not suspects is to open with a closed confirmatory 'yes'/'no' question—*Do you know why I want to speak with you today?*—then to develop the response with productive questions.

Roles

This is where you indicate that the interviewee, and what he or she remembers, will determine in great measure what happens.

Your job

I'm here to help you to remember the detail of [state] ^^ ^^ *to help you to get things back from your memory* ^^ ^^ *giving you some tools—some techniques—to help you to remember* ^^ ^^ *and to tell me as much as you can of what you're remembering.*

The interviewee's job

As you were there and I wasn't ^^^^ *it means that you're the important one: not me.* ^^ ^^ *What happens and what gets talked about is very much down to you* ^^ ^^ *to what you remember.* ^^ ^^ *You will need to concentrate really hard* ^^^^ *and keep on concentrating* ^^^^ *to get things back from your memory.* ^^^^ *This is hard work, so I'll be working as hard as I can to make it less difficult for you.* ^^ ^^

Route Map

This gives the interviewee a clear understanding of the stages that will be followed.

- Using some techniques to help remembrance.
- Free recall.
- Using more techniques to help remembrance.
- Questions.
- Checking back.

These bullet points are listed in suitably simple language on the laminated card.

Routines

Matters that need to be covered here include:

- where applicable, electronic recording;
- referring to notes/laminated card;
- how you and/or the second investigator will be recording whatever the interviewee discloses;
- you might ask the interviewee to describe something using his or her hands;
- you might ask the interviewee to draw something.

These matters are listed in suitably simple language on the laminated card.

Expectations

These are the ground rules for working together. The headings shown in bold in the list that follows should be listed on the reverse of the laminated card.

- **Think hard.**

  I will be asking you to think hard—to concentrate—and to keep doing that. ^^ ^^

- **Plenty of time to think.**

  We'll work together to keep the pace down. ^^ ^^

  I'll give you plenty of time to think ^^ ^^

  after I've said something ^^ ^^

  before you say something ^^ ^^

  after you've said something. ^^ ^^

- **Report everything.**

  I'd like you to tell me everything you can. ^^ ^^

  There can't be too much detail. ^^ ^^

  Tell me everything in your mind ^^ ^^

  and everything that comes to mind ^^ ^^

  in as much detail as possible. ^^ ^^

  Tell me in words ^^ ^^

  if you can use your hands to show me positions, directions, and shapes. ^^ ^^

  Tell me and show me everything. ^^ ^^

  Don't leave anything out. ^^ ^^

  Tell me the bits that you might think are not important. ^^ ^^

  Don't think that someone has told me anything or that I might have read something. ^^ ^^

  Don't worry if you can't remember everything. ^^ ^^

  Tell me bits that aren't too clear. ^^ ^^

  Tell me the bits that you can't remember completely. ^^ ^^

  Often a little bit can work out to be worth a lot. ^^ ^^

  As I said, there can't be too much detail. ^^ ^^

  I'll give you some ways to help you to remember this detail. ^^ ^^

- **It's OK to say you can't remember something.**

  If you can't remember some detail ^^ ^^

  don't worry. ^^ ^^

  Just tell me if you're having a problem with something. ^^ ^^

- **It's OK to say you're not sure.**

  If you can't be sure about something ^^ ^^

  don't worry. ^^ ^^

  Just tell me if you're not sure ^^ ^^

  and what you are not sure about. ^^ ^^

- **Don't guess.**

  If you can't remember something ^^ ^^

  please don't guess. ^^ ^^

- **Take your time.**

  It's very important that you take your time. ^^ ^^

  It's not a race. ^^ ^^

  If you take your time ^^ ^^

  it will help you to think ^^ ^^

  to concentrate ^^ ^^

  and get all that detail into your mind. ^^ ^^

- **Saying things slowly helps.**

  If you say things slowly ^^ ^^

  it can help you to think ^^ ^^

  to concentrate ^^ ^^

  and get all that detail out. ^^ ^^

- **I won't interrupt to ask questions.**

  When you are thinking ^^ ^^

  or talking ^^ ^^

  I won't interrupt to ask questions. ^^ ^^

- **I might need to stop you from time to time**.

  If there is a lot of detail ^^ ^^

  I might sometimes have to ask you to stop ^^ ^^

  to keep what you have in your mind ^^ *for a moment* ^^ ^^

  while I get my head round what you've said. ^^ ^^

  Then I'll ask you to go on. ^^ ^^

- **OK to ask for something**.

  If you need something, ^^ *or need to ask something,* ^^ ^^

  at any time ^^ ^^

  just say. ^^ ^^

- **Any questions**.

Check back with the interviewee his or her understanding of each ground rule.

10.3.3   'Think hard': focused retrieval

It is a fact of life that trying to remember something is hard work. It requires concentration, directing all your attention or mental ability on the task. It follows that you should explain this, inviting the interviewee repeatedly to think hard.

Good and poor rememberers

Concentrating is mentally, and physically, demanding. You will find that many individuals find it difficult to achieve or to maintain focused attention. Fisher and Geiselman[2] talk of poor and good rememberers.

- **The poor rememberer**. Often those with a 'poor memory' will let you know very quickly about their problem remembering, eg *I've got a terrible memory. My memory is not good at the best of times.* In everyday life people do not exercise their memories too much, or for any period of time. It follows that when called upon to remember offence-related detail they stop putting in effort relatively quickly. Typically, poor rememberers will attempt to think about the episode for a matter of seconds before:
  — concluding that they are unable to remember;
  — ceasing to exercise their minds in trying to retrieve detail from long-term memory.
- **The good rememberer**. People may not say they have good memories, some saying that their memory is not that good. However, these individuals tend to work hard at remembering, continuing to do so because successful retrieval encourages them:
  — to continue concentrating;
  — to keep on trying.

This 'success experience' increases their chances of retrieving further information.

Ways of helping the individual to concentrate

A number of common sense steps will assist in getting the individual onto, and staying on, 'target'.

- **Continuously reward and encourage effort**. This will ensure that the individual does concentrate and feels good about working so hard.
- **Closing eyes**. By closing his or her eyes, the interviewee immediately removes sources of visual distraction.

---

[2] Fisher, R. and Geiselman, R. (1992) *Memory-enhancing Techniques for Investigative Interviewing: The Cognitive Interview*. Springfield, Ill: Charles C. Thomas.

- **Focus on a neutral spot**. If the individual is not comfortable closing his or her eyes, then visual distraction can be reduced by looking at a spot on the floor or on the wall.
- **Avoid direct eye contact with the interviewee during retrieval**. Direct your eye gaze slightly down and to the side, or to the lower part, of the interviewee's face.
- **Remove physical sources of distraction**. Wherever possible ensure that there are no distractions, eg in the case of a witness being interviewed at home, TV and radio switched off, children not in the same room as you.
- **No psychological distractors**. Ensure that there are no concerns or issues that will make the individual increasingly distractible, eg children needing to be collected.
- **Don't destroy the individual's concentration**. Resist the urge to:
  — say something;
  — ask a question.

Apply the **POST** (pause + observe + SOFTENS + think) **formula** described in Chapter 9.
A number of BASELINES behaviours are clues that the individual is concentrating.

- Infrequent blinking.
- Furrowing of the brow.
- Narrowing of eyes.
- Gazing into the middle distance or at a fixed point.
- Pupil dilation.
- Reduction in gross body movements.
- Tensing of body posture.
- Slowing in speech rate.
- Pausing and periods of silence.

10.3.4 Keeping the pace down

The witness is likely to be anxious and aroused, particularly if the interview is taking place soon after the experienced offence. You need to reduce these negative emotions through modelling calm behaviour, explicit instruction, and, if necessary, taking the witness through a calming exercise.

Modelling calm behaviour

Behaviour is contagious. If you appear keyed up, stressed, or anxious, this will affect the witness, cancelling out the value of any instruction to the witness to calm down. Conversely, if you conduct yourself in a calm, relaxed manner then this will be picked up by the witness, who will be himself or herself correspondingly calmed. Engage in SOFTENS behaviours, particularly concentrating on talking slowly and using plenty of pause.

Explicit instruction

You need to reinforce your original 'working together to keep the pace down' and 'plenty of time to think' instructions, extending these by inviting the witness to speak as slowly and clearly as possible, eg:

> *So you now understand that it's all about detail ^^ ^^ as much detail as possible ^^^^ And that there's no rush.^^ ^^ Now because I've got to get my head round the detail that you give me ^^ ^^ can I ask you to help me on this? ^^ ^^ Please can you speak as slowly ^^ and clearly ^^ as you can. ^^ ^^ As I said there is no rush. ^^ ^^ Taking things slowly ^^ and telling me things slowly ^^ will help you to remember the tiny details ^^ ^^ and also help me to get all the detail you give me in my mind ^^ ^^.*

Calming exercise

If the witness becomes excessively anxious or aroused, use a simple relaxation exercise that clears the mind, gets oxygen to the brain, and brings down heart rate by progressively extending the count of inhaling and exhaling air.

- Talk slowly to the witness, giving instructions in the exercise:
  — to breathe in to the count of three;
  — to breathe out to the count of four;
  — to breathe in to the count of five;
  — to breathe out to the count of six;
  — to continue extending the count till the witness reaches his or her maximum capacity to breathe in and then start over again at three, and so on.
- Tell the witness that you will do the exercise together.
- Perform the exercise.
- Reassure the witness once you have brought his or her heart rate down.

10.3.5 Report everything

You want the individual to retrieve everything he or she can from episodic memory—imaging this in his or her mind—and then to report everything about this image and everything else that comes to mind. Your Orienting Explanation included this as a key ground rule, spelling itself out in great detail and sending a critical message: a little can work out to be worth a lot.

In Chapter 9 we described the value of using illustrators:

- to extend what has been said;
- to validate disclosure;
- to facilitate further verbal disclosure.

Follow the guidelines on illustrators in the Reference Section.

10.3.6 Context reinstatement

Chapter 2 demonstrates that a highly effective way of cueing recall is reinstating the context *mentally*. The individual thinks back, reliving now in his or her mind that point in time: the circumstances and his or her experience of:

- the original event;
- the immediate environment surrounding the event, eg the weather, the time of day, the location;
- his or her thoughts, emotions, and physical state at the time;
- what he or she could see;
- what he or she could hear;
- what he or she could smell;
- even the ambient conditions, eg illumination, temperature, weather.

Reinstating the context that the individual was experiencing at the time of an episode is the most powerful aid—or *cue*—to recall and to retrieve detail. Context reinstatement accounts for the major part of additional detail remembered compared to an interview in which no attempt is made to assist remembrance.

Current sensory, particularly visual, input can distract when we are trying to think. Just before the first author typed this idea into the computer he reduced the visual input by putting his forehead in his cupped left hand, and closing his eyes to consider carefully what he wanted to say and how to say it. When we are trying to cast our minds back, to remember, reducing visual input can similarly help. We need to suggest ways of doing this, eg cupping a hand over the eyes, closing eyes, looking at a fixed, neutral point.

Instructing an individual to reinstate contextually

Helping an individual to reinstate memory is a skill, but one that can be developed so long as you bear in mind the difficulty of the remembering task and that pulling back detail from long-term memory into working memory is a gradual reconstruction task: going back and forth, looking for, locating, picking up, and bringing into conscious attention more and more detail.

It makes sense to frame simple instructions, and deliver these at a slow, deliberate pace. Create plenty of pause—significantly extended silence—between one instruction and the next. This will give the individual the time to go back to long-term memory, obtain the detail, and place this in awareness.

To make things clearer—and to emphasize the need for long pauses—the instructions in this following example are spaced out.

> *I'd like you to think back now.* ^^ ^^ ^^ ^^
> *Cast your mind back* ^^ ^^ *to the time you saw what happened.* ^^ ^^ ^^ ^^
> *Get in your mind's eye* ^^ ^^ *the place where you were at that time.* ^^ ^^ ^^ ^^
> *You might find it easier to do this if you close your eyes* [demonstrate]. ^^ ^^
> *Or you might want to cover your eyes with your hand* ^^ *like this* [demonstrate forehead in cupped hand with eyes closed]. ^^ ^^
> *If you're not comfortable with either of these* ^^ ^^ *try looking at a spot on the floor* [demonstrate]. ^^ ^^
> *So try one of those now* ^^ ^^ *to get in your mind's eye the place.* ^^ ^^ ^^ ^^
> *Now bring back from your memory* ^^ ^^ *every bit of detail you can.* ^^ ^^ ^^ ^^
> *The lighting at the time,* ^^ ^^ ^^ ^^
> *what could be seen.* ^^ ^^ ^^ ^^
> *The weather* ^^ ^^ ^^ ^
> *the temperature.* ^^ ^^
> *Anything within view.* ^^ ^^
> *Anything that you could sense.* ^^ ^^
> *Any person.* ^^ ^^
> *Any object.* ^^ ^^
> *Anything going on* ^^ ^^
> *around you* ^^ ^^
> *in the background.* ^^ ^^ ^ ^ ^
> *What you were thinking about at the time* ^^ ^^
> *your thoughts,* ^^ ^^
> *your feelings.* ^^ ^^
> *Just concentrate* ^^ ^^
> *on all that detail.* ^^ ^^
> *Concentrate* ^^ ^^
> *as hard as you can.* ^^ ^^

Helping the individual to locate the detail in time

If and when necessary the individual is helped to locate the detail in time using 'time anchors' or 'landmarks'.

- **Anchoring to a significant event**. Ask the individual to think whether the occasion was near a significant event, eg birthday, Christmas, Easter, during the summer holidays, half-term.
- **For an event in the distant past, anchoring to biographical detail**. Ask the individual what he or she was doing at the time, eg employment, study, or where he or she was living at the time.
- **For an event in the near past, anchoring to a media event**. Ask the individual whether the incident coincided with a publicized film or a particular programme on television.

Molar and molecular context reinstatement

Context reinstatement is not an 'all-or-none' technique. You need to continuously call upon the interviewee to context reinstate.

- **Molar reinstatement**. Context reinstatement at the beginning of the interview is called *molar* reinstatement: you are getting the interviewee to create a mental replication of the entire experience that is as comprehensive as possible.
- **Molecular reinstatement**. Later, when questioning on specific issues—rather like researching the molecules of a chemical—you will need to get the interviewee to engage in *molecular* reinstatement.

Accessing non-verbal experience

It is important to note that reporting involves using illustrators to access non-verbal experience: drawings in space that can:

- extend what has been said;
- validate disclosure thus far;
- facilitate further verbal disclosure.

Backing illustrators up at the right time with enactment (where applicable and appropriate) and enhanced drawing immeasurably extends the breadth and depth of the individual's account and responses.

10.3.7 The importance of a 'success experience'

Context reinstatement, assisted and done properly, enables the individual—even the one professing a poor memory—to retrieve detail and to report this progressively and cumulatively. Because human beings respond particularly well to success, this success at remembering increases their chances of retrieving further information.

Practising context reinstatement and reporting everything

Instructions to focus attention, to report everything, and to reinstate context provide explicit guidelines to enable the individual to succeed in retrieving and disclosing detail. However, there are barriers to the individual delivering the detail. You are not the typical 'powerful person'. You invite the individual to behave in a completely alien manner: to abandon the 'less is best' strategy for disclosing to powerful people.

If you proceed immediately from instructions to inviting the individual to recall, there is a risk that he or she will nonetheless give a relatively thin account because:

- he or she has never 'gone into detail' when disclosing to a powerful person;
- he or she is still unsure about the level of detail you require.

A useful technique to overcome these barriers is to select an episode experienced by the interviewee and use this episode to practise:

- focused concentration;
- reporting everything (including using illustrators);
- context reinstatement.

The choice of practice episode

Views differ on this. Some consider it best to practise using a neutral episode, ie that was not memorable, such as a period from everyday life; others prefer practising on an ostensibly memorable episode, eg previous Christmas, birthday.

We tend to take the middle course, choosing an experience that is out of the ordinary but not perhaps so biographically located, eg when the individual last arrived home, from the point of walking towards the door up to a point of having been inside for about five minutes.

The practice sequence

- Explain that it helps to practice remembering and describing in detail, eg:

    It often helps to have a practice at remembering and describing in detail what you have brought to mind. ^^ *Let's spend a bit of time on this.* ^^ *You having a practice at remembering detail and telling me everything that you have in your mind.*

- Identify the practice episode.
- Spell out the Expectations again.
- Instruct in the manner described to reinstate contextually and then trigger recall, eg:

    I'd like you to take yourself back to [state a point in time = start point]. ^^ *Now concentrate really hard.* ^^ *I'd like you to tell me every little bit of detail that you remember.* ^^ *Tell me everything that's in your mind's eye.* ^^ *What you see,* ^^ *what you hear,* ^^ *what you smell,* ^^ *what you touch,* ^^ *what thoughts were going through your mind,* ^^ *what you were feeling,* ^^ *even how you felt physically.* ^^ *Don't hold back on telling me every bit of detail.* ^^ *Don't hold back detail that strikes you as obvious.* ^^ *Don't hold back detail that you think anyone would know.* ^^ *Don't hold back detail that you think I might already know.* ^^ *There can't be too much detail.* ^^
    There's no rush. ^^ *Take your time.* ^^ *Tell me everything that you remember from* [restate the start point] *up to* [state end point]. ^^

- Practise the individual in:
    — use of illustrators;
    — where applicable, enactment;
    — enhanced drawing.

10.3.8 Post-practice context reinstatement

If you have conducted a practice at context reinstatement and reporting everything on a non-offence-related episode, you will need to facilitate reinstatement of the context of the offence experience using the approach described in section 10.3.6.

10.3.9 Trigger Free Recall

Having facilitated reinstatment of the context of the offence it is now a matter of triggering Free Recall, eg:

Now, tell me ^^ *in as much detail as possible* ^^
every bit that's in your mind, ^^
every bit that comes to mind, ^^

*taking your time, ^^*
*there's no rush. ^^*
*Tell me everything ^^*
*everything you have in your mind ^^ and comes to mind. ^^ ^^*
*about what happened. ^^ ^^*

10.3.10   Multiple retrieval

It is essential to encourage the individual to engage in multiple attempts at retrieving the detail. In every instance you should:

- reward the individual for his or her concentration and effort, and the outcome of this;
- explain that going through matters again helps in remembering more detail.

Second Free Recall

Asking the interviewee to take you through the episode again from beginning to end in as much detail as possible has two significant benefits.

- It increases the likelihood of further detail being retrieved.
- It enables you to capture the detail using SE3R, the second recall being the basis for the Extract stage, ie generating an SE3R using a black pen, annotating immediately:
  — anomalies;
  — 'hot spots', ie potentially significant changes in BASELINES behaviours, indicating that this memory needs to be probed using varied retrieval techniques: see later;
  — areas requiring probing.

Recalling in reverse order

Recalling events in reverse order is a useful technique when you have concerns that the individual is confabulating, presenting the contents of script memory (the general knowledge stereotype of what normally happens) rather than episodic memory.

Sustained reverse order recall is hard mental effort. Try it yourself. Starting with reading this book, go back a step at a time trying as hard as possible to concentrate on stating the step in front, ie consciously attempting not to slip into describing things moving forwards in time. You will find that this is very difficult to keep up. In everyday life we do not relate our experience backwards.

Many individuals struggle with reverse order recall, especially those who are developmentally disadvantaged, are extremely tired, or who are extremely aroused. Many individuals will do their best, but for some the mental effort will overwhelm. The individual starts getting tangled, moving forwards, then jumping back to continue with the reverse order narration. Such difficulties can potentially dishearten, frustrate, or alienate. You must be alert to signs of difficulty and clues that this technique is becoming counter-productive.

Some have unjustifiably interpreted inability to recall in reverse order as indicative of deception.

- The individual is able to give a learned version of events in first and second recall.
- The individual is 'caught out' because he or she cannot give this learned version in reverse order.

The only sensible conclusion to be drawn from inability to give a reverse order account that remains flowing or mismatch between this account and one given in chronological order is that this aspect of the narrative must be systematically probed.

Changing perspective

This technique can *only* be applied if the individual describes another person as also being involved in witnessing what happened but who is not available to give his or her own account, eg being dead, unconscious, or untraceable having left the scene. It is not a case of asking the individual to put himself or herself in a location other than the one that he or she actually occupied.

You invite the individual to engage in an act of empathetic imagination:

- putting himself or herself in that person's 'shoes'
- describing what the other person would have observed—but being careful not to guess at information when doing this.

The ongoing debate

There is an ongoing debate about this technique.

- Advocates of this technique say that so long as you tell the person 'not to guess at information' it is acceptable if it triggers more detail from the interviewee's perspective or generates potential investigative leads.
- The counter-argument is that as soon as you attempt to see things from another's perspective—even though you saw this person—when you are giving a view of what this person was likely to have witnessed:
  — it can only be conjecture, ie a guess;
  — a conjecture has no evidential status and could be a spurious investigative lead.

Caveat on use

The *change perspective* technique should not be used with children aged seven and under.

10.3.11 Overcoming the effects of script memory

Chapter 2 raises the issue of an interviewee who is being asked to disclose an instance of a repeated occurrence, for example, a victim of abuse that has occurred frequently over a period of time or an individual who has committed multiple, serial, or repeated offences. The individual may have difficulty differentiating a particular instance in time, struggling to describe the actual sequence of offending behaviour, instead reporting a stereotyped sequence: a script memory.

You can facilitate an individual to dis-embed a particular instance from a series of repeated occurrences, and thus decrease the potential for reporting a script memory by using a simple technique.

The logic for the technique

The aim is to differentiate progressively each instance of offending by identifying:

- the first and last instance of offending;
- how often—if only an approximation—the offending has occurred;
- an instance or instances perceived as salient: standing out as particularly significant, easier to remember, or conversely harder to forget;
- focusing methodically on the first instance, the most recent instance, and the instance—or each instance—reported as standing out.

The first instance

The individual may well have a clear remembrance of the circumstances surrounding and what happened during the first instance. In effect, it may well have remained etched as a totally 'one off' episodic memory. The individual may have reported that this instance is one that stands out, but there is no guarantee that this will be the case.

The initial offence may have occurred a long time ago—many months or even years during which repeated offending occurred—or offending has occurred repeatedly within a compressed period of time. The further back in time the first instance occurred, the sheer frequency of offending since, or both, may render it difficult for the individual to remember the first instance. As explained in Chapter 2, sheer repetition has established a stereotypical 'pattern' in the form of a script memory. The individual may therefore have difficulties dis-embedding this event, and struggle to remember the detail of the first instance.

It is therefore a judgement call.

- Having located the first instance, if the individual is able to disclose spontaneously detail about this event, then common sense argues that this should be the focus of attention. If probing evokes similar spontaneous disclosure then you should continue probing. At particular points it might be appropriate to use the techniques described in this chapter to assist remembrance.
- If the individual experiences difficulty, perhaps disclosing problems recalling or differentiating the initial occurrence from others, it is best not to focus on obtaining detailed disclosure of this instance. Continued probing or using the techniques to facilitate remembrance described in this chapter increases the likelihood of the individual confabulating, ie reporting the content of script memory for the offence.

Many investigators have a mindset that disposes them to think linearly. Having focused on the first event they go into 'auto pilot', they work forward in time, focusing on the next instance, and the next, and so on up to the most recent instance. A moment's reflection points to this approach as likely to be rather unproductive and even frustrating for both the individual and you, particularly if the successive offences occurred a long way back in time, there was a high frequency of offending, or both. The individual may struggle to remember the actual details of the second instance, the third, and successive instances coming forward in time. Far better to bring the individual forward in time to the most recent instance of offending.

The most recent instance

The individual may have reported the most recent instance as the one—or one amongst others—that is salient. However, whether or not the individual reports this instance as standing out, the explanation of memory in Chapter 2 indicates why you should focus on this instance. Being the most recent, there is the potential for the individual to disclose the content of episodic memory—idiosyncratic detail—as opposed to the content of a script memory. This will be particularly so if the offence occurred hours, days, weeks, or months prior to the interview.

Even if the offence occurred a very long time before the interview, if it was the concluding instance of an extended, or compressed, run of offending, the detail of this occurrence is likely to be memorable. There is a distinct likelihood that the individual will be able to describe spontaneously the particular details of this instance rather than providing the content of script memory. Similarly, the individual is more likely to respond with detail when probed about the occurrence.

If the individual declares difficulty in remembering, given the nearness in time or the significance of the most recent occurrence, you should facilitate recall by using the techniques described in this chapter.

Dis-embedding and reporting the particular detail of the most recent occurrence very often triggers remembrance of the *preceding instance*: remembrance that, if not spontaneous, can be assisted by the techniques described in this chapter. The experience of dis-embedding and reporting the particular detail of this preceding occurrence facilitates remembrance of the instance before this.

Memorable instances

Some individuals perceive a particular instance or instances of an occurrence as salient. Particular detail of the occurrence renders it more memorable, much more of a 'one off'. The individual is much more likely to disclose idiosyncratic features that distinguish it from other instances of offending. Thereafter, working backwards in time, focusing on each preceding memorable instance provides the best chance of accessing the particular detail of each instance.

The method

Equipment

Several biros, pencils, or marker pens with shafts of different colours, eg white, black, blue, red, green, yellow, orange, and so on. Each biro, pencil, or marker pen constitutes an instance of offending. For ease of reference we will call them **event markers**. Following the logic of SE3R representation of events as **stems** on a horizontal Event Line, each marker is a stem on a notional sequence of offending over time. (You can use this technique in combination with SE3R recording. There is no requirement to do so, however.)

Establish the parameters—the first and last instances of offending.

- Produce one **event marker**, eg a black stem.
- Lay the black stem down in a horizontal (upright) orientation, explaining that it represents the first instance of offending.
- Produce another event marker, eg a white stem.
- Lay the white stem down in a horizontal (upright) orientation some 40 cms (15 inches) to the right of the first stem, explaining that it represents the last instance of offending.

Establish the number of instances of offending in the period between the two stems

- If the individual is able to specify the number of instances, lay the requisite number of event markers between the first and last instance.
- If the individual is unable to state the number of instances—because offending has been prolific and has occurred either over a long period or within a compressed period—do not press the matter.

Where the individual is able to specify the number of instances, he or she may volunteer anchoring detail for these, eg dates, times, locations, individuals involved, surrounding circumstances. You should note these.

Ask if any particular instance stands out, or instances stand out, as particularly significant, easier to remember, or conversely harder to forget. You should note these.

Do not start probing the detail of instances following upon the first occurrence. Similarly, do not focus at this time on the most recent instance.

The first instance

Move the event marker for this occurrence away to the left of the subsequent markers. This action signals visibly and psychologically the significance of the event as you remind the individual that this is the first instance of offending and the focus of attention.

Invite disclosure concerning the first instance.

- If the individual discloses freely, then continue focusing on this instance, probing at the right time to obtain further spontaneous disclosure, expansion, and explanation. At particular points it might be appropriate to use the techniques described in this chapter to assist remembrance. When you have concluded probing on this instance, move the event marker to the right—back to its original position—and switch to the most recent instance.
- If the individual struggles to disclose spontaneously from the outset concerning the first instance, do not persist. Move the event marker to the right, back to its original position, and switch your focus to the most recent instance.

The most recent instance

Move the event marker for the most recent occurrence away to the right of the preceding markers. This action signals visibly and psychologically the significance of the event as you remind the individual that this is the most recent instance of offending and the focus of attention.

Invite disclosure concerning this instance.

- If the individual discloses freely then continue focusing on this instance, probing at the right time to obtain further spontaneous disclosure, expansion, and explanation. At particular points it might be appropriate to use the techniques described in this chapter to assist remembrance.
- If the individual struggles to disclose spontaneously, use the techniques described in this chapter.

Decision point

At this point you have to make a decision.

- To work progressively back in time from the most recent occurrence—this makes sense if the individual has not disclosed an instance, or other instances, as salient. Move the event markers apart to highlight this instance visually and psychologically.
- To focus on the most recent instance deemed by the individual to be salient, moving the event markers to make it stand out. Then where there are other salient instances, to focus progressively on each one, working backwards in time, moving the event marker to make it stand out.

10.3.12 Jogging memory for specific detail (mnemonics)

Remembrance of a name

Box 10.1 based on Fisher and Geiselman[3] summarizes memory jogs to assist remembrance of a name.

---

[3] Fisher, R. and Geiselman, R. (1992) *Memory-enhancing Techniques for Investigative Interviewing: The Cognitive Interview*. Springfield, Ill: Charles C. Thomas.

Focus of attention	Jogging question/instruction	Accessing non-verbal experience
Beginning letter	Go through the alphabet starting at *a*: • say the letter • test the 'fit' with what you heard/saw.	Have written alphabet to hand (= checklist for the interviewee who may not know all the alphabet)
Length	Short? Long? How many syllables?	Tapping the sound pattern (= syllables: technical word may not be understood, demonstrate with your names)
Stress pattern	Which syllable was stressed?	Soft-loud tapping (louder = more stress, demonstrate with your names)
Speaker saying the name	Think about the speaker's voice.	
Pleasantness	Pleasant sound?	
Visual pattern	Image the handwriting.	
Physical location	Image: • position of name on the page; • position of speaker saying the name.	
Frequency	Common? Unusual?	
	Characteristic of an ethnic or national group?	
Similarity	Sounded like name of someone known to you?	
Affiliation/ association	Reminded you of an occupation, group, activity?	
Other names	Other names mentioned?	

Box 10.1 Jogging remembrance of a name (after Fisher and Geiselman, 1992)

Remembrance of an individual

Box 10.2 based on Shepherd[4] summarizes memory jogs to assist remembrance of an individual.

Remembrance of number and letter sequences

Box 10.3 based on Fisher and Geiselman[5] memory jogs to assist remembrance of an individual.

---

[4] Shepherd, E. (1996) *Police Station Skills for Legal Advisers: Becoming Skilled.* London: Law Society.

[5] Fisher, R. and Geiselman, R. (1992) *Memory-enhancing Techniques for Investigative Interviewing: The Cognitive Interview.* Springfield, Ill: Charles C. Thomas.

Focus of attention	Jogging question/instruction	Accessing non-verbal experience
Physical appearance	• Reminds you of someone? • Height? • Build? • Body shape? Proportion? • Complexion? • Head? Size (relative to body)? • Hair? Presence/absence? Colour? Thickness? Type? Length? Parting? Style? Hairline? • Facial hair? Presence/absence? • Sideburns (length)? • Eyes? Colour? Shape? Size? Location (distance from centre of nose)? Anything prominent? • Eyelashes? Anything prominent? • Eyelids? Anything prominent? • Eyebrows? Shape? Size? Location (distance from eye)? Anything prominent? • Ears? Size? Shape? Lobes? Anything prominent? • Nose? Size? Shape? Nostrils? Coloration? Anything prominent? • Mouth? Size? Line of mouth? Lips? Anything prominent? • Teeth? Anything prominent? • Chin? Shape? Proportion? Anything prominent? • Hands? Shape? Proportion? Anything prominent? • Nails? Shape? Proportion? Anything prominent?	Illustrators (indicate with finger movement) Enhanced drawing
Clothing	• General appearance? • Reminds you of someone? • What kind of clothes (= style)? • How smart? • Describe 'tip to toe'. • Any prominent item? • Any peculiarities?	Illustrator Enhanced drawing ('gingerbread person')
Verbal behaviour/ expression	• Remind you of someone? • What kind of reaction did the voice evoke? • Accent? (manner of talking) Indicative of geographical origin? Indicative of education/'class'? • Dialect? (regional difference in vocabulary, phrasing; Creole; slang) • Quality (rhythm; speed; volume; pitch)? • Anything peculiar in speech?	
Gestures	Any noticeable: • facial movement? • body movement? • limb movement?	Enactment
Way of walking (gait)	• Remind you of someone? • Any peculiarities?	Enactment
Way of standing (posture)	• Remind you of someone? • Any peculiarities?	Enactment
Indexical detail	• Smell? Pleasant? Unpleasant? Anything prominent? Remind you of any smell you know? • Any objects on or about person?	Illustrators Enhanced drawing

Note: Always follow up a closed confirmatory question with a productive question, eg *Can you tell me about that.*

Box 10.2 Jogging remembrance of an individual (after Shepherd, 1996)

Focus of attention	Jogging question/instruction	Accessing non-verbal experience
Length	How many characters? Long or short sequence?	Draw a dash for each character
Order	Digits in ascending or descending order? Letters in alphabetical order?	
Mixture	Only numbers? Only letters? Mixed?	Draw a dash for each character Locate position of letters/digits (even if actual letter/digit not recalled)
Repetition	Any digits or letters repeated?	Draw a dash for each character Locate repetition
Odd/even	Mainly odd or mainly even digits?	
Magnitude	Large or small numbers?	
Letter type	Mainly vowels or mainly consonants?	Draw a dash for each character Locate vowels and consonants (even if vowel/consonant not recalled)
Pronounceability	Can letter groups be pronounced, eg DAT vs DTA	Draw a dash for each character Locate pronounceable letters
Meaningfulness	Word or associated idea, eg DNA, BBC, PTE	Draw a dash for each character Locate meaningful word/associated idea
Partial letter/digit formation	Ascending? Crossing? Curving?	Draw a dash for each character Illustrator Draw partial letter/digit
Relative location of letter/digit		Draw a dash for each character Locate letter/digit

Note: Always follow up a closed confirmatory question with a productive question, eg *Tell me about that.*

Box 10.3 Jogging remembrance of number and letter sequences (after Fisher and Geiselman, 1992)

10.3.13 Image compatible questioning

All of the memory-enhancing techniques require you to be sensitive to the modality of the individual's reporting. It follows that you must engage in *image compatible* questioning—also called *witness compatible* or *witness focused* questioning. This is described in Chapter 9 as a particular form of 'topic hopping'. For example, the interviewee says:

I heard...grunting

The only sensible image compatible question is a productive question that sticks with the auditory modality, eg an echo probe:

^^ *grunting* ^^.

An image incompatible question would change the modality and 'hop' to a different topic, eg

Try hard here ^^ *tell me what you could see at this point.*

10.4 Putting the techniques into effect

10.4.1 The range of techniques to be used

Two key factors will determine the range of techniques used to assist the witnesses here: available time given the stage of the investigation, and the current circumstances. This will determine the extent of memory-enhancing technique you will apply in combination with others in a conversation managed interview aimed at getting the individual to:

- retrieve detail of actions and descriptions within one or more episodes;
- report everything experienced in every sensory modality.

Most of the retrieved detail is generated through context reinstatement and second free recall. Reverse order recall and the contentious changing perspective generate much less. Research comparing interviews with and without these two techniques showed the practical value of a shorter interview, which included only context reinstatement and second free recall.[6] This permits a practical distinction to be drawn between a *standard memory assistance* interview and a *full memory assistance* interview.

10.4.2 Standard memory assistance interview

This does not include reverse order recall or change perspective technique. It will typically apply when investigating volume crime or crime of low or intermediate level of seriousness.

Training

All the techniques other than reverse order recall and change perspective should be taught as standard practice for interviewing any witness.

Recording

You should record the interview as comprehensively as possible:

- electronically;
- using SE3R—because:
  - unlike notes, you edit nothing out so nothing gets lost;
  - there is a clear audit trail shown by colours as to what was said or asked, and when.

Sequence

- Brief on context reinstatement, focused retrieval, reporting everything.
- Practice recall of neutral episode.
- First free recall of offence-related episodic memory.
- Second free recall of offence-related episodic memory.
- Access non-verbal detail: using illustrators, enactment, and enhanced drawing.
- Systematic probing.
- Memory jogging (mnemonics).

---

[6] Davis, M., McMahon, M., and Greenwood, K. (2004) 'The Efficacy of Mnemonic Components of the Cognitive Interview: Towards a Shortened Variant for Time-critical Investigations'. *Applied Cognitive Psychology, 19,* 75–93.

10.4.3 Cognitive Interview/Enhanced Cognitive Interview

In Chapter 1 we brought attention to the fact that ABE recommends the CI/ECI as an optional approach to interviewing a vulnerable victim or witness

Cognitive Interview (CI)

Geiselman, Fisher, and their associates researched the psychology literature and devised an interviewing approach that incorporated four instructions that could facilitate remembrance of detail:

- Report everything.
- Mentally reinstate the context.
- Recall events in a variety of different temporal orders.
- Change perspective.[7]

We commented earlier on the problematic nature of changing perspective, and the debate surrounding this.

Enhanced Cognitive Interview (ECI)

Geiselman and Fisher noted that police interviewing lacked the psychology of interpersonal communication. They developed the ECI, which is essentially an interview in which the interviewer engages in conversation management as the vehicle to bring into use selected memory-enhancing techniques.

ABE points out that the ECI is not an 'all-or-nothing' affair. Interviewers are not obliged to use all the techniques. It is preferable to use one technique well rather than all techniques poorly.

Consistent with our views on complexity and flexibility, the necessity to assess and be responsive to the individual is a question of asking:

- Which technique to use?
- With whom should each technique be used?
- When should each technique be used?
- How should each technique be presented?[8]

10.5 Chapter summary

The evidence is incontrovertible that assisting a witness to remember offence-related detail is a cost-effective investigative interviewing activity. There is a cost in terms of time but, in the case of a standard memory assistance interview, this is not substantially more than an interview that does not offer such help to the interviewee. There are also risks that have to be taken into account. However, the potential return on investment of your time is enormous. Detail critical to the progress and success of your investigation—that, in the absence of your skilled effort to assist the interviewee to remember, would otherwise have remained beyond the individual's awareness—is rendered accessible.

---

[7] Fisher, R.P. and Geiselman, R.E. (1992) *Memory-enhancing Techniques for Investigative Interviewing: The Cognitive Interview.* Springfield, Ill: Charles C. Thomas.

[8] Ministry of Justice (2011) *Achieving Best Evidence in Criminal Proceedings: Guidance on Interviewing Victims and Witnesses, and Guidance on Using Special Measures.* London: HMSO. Annex H.

11

Responding to Inappropriate or Disruptive Behaviour and to Resistance

11.1 Chapter overview

This chapter examines inappropriate or disruptive behaviour and resistance. If not responded to, or responded to ineffectively, these can frustrate and even destroy your best efforts to manage conversation to achieve your goals.

11.1.1 Chapter objectives

This chapter will enable you to:

- understand the nature of inappropriate or disruptive behaviour and the nature of resistance;
- understand the three domains of skill necessary to manage behaviour which is inappropriate or disruptive and to manage resistance;
- use the DEAL technique to manage inappropriate and disruptive behaviour;
- cope with resistance.

11.2 Inappropriate or disruptive behaviour and resistance

These are challenging behaviours that confront you when you are interviewing witnesses and suspects. They constitute barriers to the achievement of your investigative aim and objectives. The challenge is: will you face up to them? As with everything in life, not everything that is faced up to can be changed, but nothing can be changed until it is faced up to.

When you do face up to them you will need to bring to the three core conversation management skills described in Chapter 3:

- influence;
- persuasion;
- negotiation.

11.2.1 Inappropriate and disruptive behaviour

This is disruptive talking and poor listening by the interviewee or a third party, eg legal adviser or appropriate adult, which makes it difficult to progress the interview. Typical inappropriate and disruptive behaviours include:

- attempting to deny you the talking turn, talking at the same time as you (overtalking), and forcing you to stop talking;
- cursorily acknowledging or dismissing what you have said;
- ignoring totally what you are saying or have said;
- claiming to know what you are about to say before you say it;
- finishing your sentences for you;
- taking what you are saying in a wholly selective manner and not in the way that you intended.

Very often these behaviours are outside the individual's control. They are part of the individual's psychological 'make-up'. He or she has poor interpersonal skills, and has behaved in this manner for most of his or her life. Typically, such people will be unaware, and not care, that they are behaving inappropriately or disruptively.

Inappropriate and disruptive behaviour can be caused by stress. The process of being interviewed, a line of questioning, a topic, or the content or particular details of something that you have said or a question that you have posed:

- has aroused the individual psychologically, physically, and emotionally;
- has triggered the subjective experience of inability to control matters.

It follows that stress will compound any shortcomings arising from lack of interpersonal skills.

Inappropriate or disruptive behaviour may, however, be a conscious tactic to take control of the interview and to determine what gets talked about, when, and in what level of detail.

11.2.2 Resistance

Resistance is verbal, emotional, and even physical behaviour of the interviewee that blocks your efforts to create and sustain a co-operative relationship that enables achievement of your investigative aims and objectives.[1] Resistance can occur in many forms:

- Evasion.
- Sabotaging behaviour.
- 'Putting down'.
- Exercising the legal right to remain silent.

The two dimensions of resistance

We saw in Chapter 1 that the traditional perspective was that suspects resist and witnesses co-operate. This reflected a one-dimensional view of resistance, where the interviewee is located somewhere along a continuum of *willing–unwilling to talk*. The degree of unwillingness to converse, to enter into a working relationship, and to disclose facts of the matter is taken to be indicative of having something to hide, of guilt arising from culpability or indiscretion, and of feelings caused by consciousness of guilt, such as shame, embarrassment, or remorse.

Unwillingness to talk can stem from extreme psychological stress and distress, from strong emotions—such as anger, apprehension, anxiety, fear (especially of the unknown), dread, or depression—and from antipathy or a decision not to engage in the interview process.

These factors certainly play their part in the emergence of resistance. However, resistant behaviour originates from the interaction of the degree of willingness to talk with the degree to which the individual is able to tell—to disclose detail that will progress the investigation (Figure 11.1).

Inability to tell can arise because:

- the individual never had the information, failed to register detail, or has forgotten detail;
- post-event information has overwritten the original detail;
- the individual is now unable to retrieve the information that the interviewer is seeking to obtain.

---

[1] Shepherd, E. (1993) 'Resistance in interviews: the contribution of police perceptions and behaviour' in E. Shepherd (ed.), *Aspects of Police Interviewing. Issues in Criminological and Legal Psychology, No. 18*. Leicester: British Psychological Society.

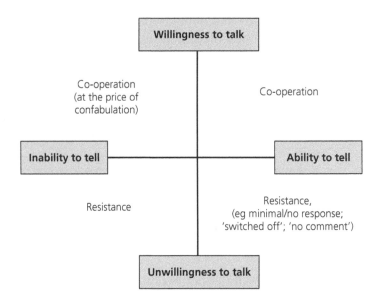

Figure 11.1 The two dimensions of interviewee resistance

Being intellectually and developmentally disadvantaged, mentally or physically fatigued, and the same factors that affect willingness to talk place additional constraints upon the individual's ability to tell.

Considering the two dimensions together highlights the risks for the unaware interviewer.

- Failing to distinguish the co-operative who disclose potentially valid information from the co-operative who confabulate.
- Misconstruing the interviewee who is unwilling to talk and unable to tell as having something to hide or guilty knowledge.

An interviewer can create or compound resistance.

- Denying the interviewee 'space' to talk—by monopolizing the talking turn, failing to pause, and dominating the talking time.
- Being excessively controlling and assertive: signalling an 'up'–'down' relationship.
- Talking disruptively: overtalking, interrupting, minimally responding, and rapidly changing the topic ('topic hopping').
- Listening disruptively: not paying attention, being an assumer, or wordpicking.
- Having an inadequate and/or inaccurate grasp of the fine-grain detail of the case.
- Alienating the interviewee by labelling the interviewee's account, responses, or a given response, as inconsistent or contradictory, or calling the interviewee a liar.

11.3 Dealing with inappropriate or disruptive behaviour

11.3.1 Inappropriate and disruptive behaviour

This is behaviour by the interviewee or a third party, eg legal adviser or appropriate adult, which makes it difficult to progress the interview. Very often such behaviours are part of the person, ie he or she has poor interpersonal skill or has behaved in this manner without feedback for most of his or her life. Importantly they are unaware that they are behaving in such a destructive way.

Typically the behaviour involves disruptive talking and poor listening, ie:

- Not allowing you to have your say or to finish what you are saying by:
  — monopolizing the talking turn;
  — overtalking (talking at the same time as you);
  — interrupting (forcing you to stop).
- Paying no attention to what you are saying by:
  — minimally responding (making a cursory acknowledgement);
  — being a 'non-attender' (not listening to what you are saying);
  — being an 'assumer' (knowing what you are about to say before you say it, even finishing your sentence for you);
  — being a 'word picker' (taking what you are saying in a wholly selective manner and not in the way that you intended).

11.3.2 Responding to inappropriate or disruptive behaviour: rewarding and informing

Ignoring inappropriate and disruptive behaviour

In any relationship in which you are involved—personal or professional—as a matter of principle you should never reward any pattern of inappropriate or disruptive behaviour. There is a very good reason why. The person engaging in the inappropriate behaviour will do it again.

However, if you responded immediately to correct every single instance of inappropriate or disruptive behaviour you would earn the reputation of being overly reactive, too sensitive, touchy, inflexible, or a martinet—a strict disciplinarian.

This is different to responding to a pattern, ie something that the person does repeatedly. You have to ignore the behaviour while gathering the evidence that the behaviour *is* a pattern. Ignoring inappropriate and disruptive behaviour is sometimes not what the person wants. For example, if the person tries to provoke you and you ignore the provocation, he or she did not get rewarded: the person might not try it on again. If the behaviour does happen again, and you do not 'rise to the bait', the behaviour might stop.

If the behaviour happens a third time this is definitely a pattern. To allow the pattern to continue would make it impossible for you to have a mutually respectful relationship. It would be an 'up'–'down' relationship: the other person in the superior position, dominating or abusing you with his or her behaviour; you in the subordinate position being submissive and abused. You have to deal with the behaviour: asserting yourself and giving feedback in order to extinguish the behaviour and put the relationship on an equal footing.

The problem is that giving an individual feedback on behaviour that is very established, ie it is their 'personality' or 'interpersonal style', is unlikely to work immediately. It is unrealistic to believe that telling them once about his or her behaviour will bring about a change.

11.3.3 DEAL: a technique for countering inappropriate or disruptive behaviour

DEAL (Box 11.1) is a technique for responding systematically to inappropriate behaviour. DEAL is based upon:

- giving the person the benefit of the doubt, ie he or she is unaware of engaging in the inappropriate behaviour;
- three times is a pattern;
- the recognition that giving feedback once will not change behaviour.

Step		Objective	Example
Qualify your assertion		Give him/her the benefit of the doubt = he/she is unaware of the behaviour.	*I need to tell you about something that you may not be aware of,* ^^ ^^
D	**Description**	Describe the behaviour.	*I need to point out that every time that I ask a question,* ^^ ^^ *you interrupt me.* ^^ ^^
E	**Explanation**	Explain the actual or potential effects of the behaviour.	*This makes it difficult to progress matters.* ^^^^ *It will take even longer to cover the issues that I must cover.* ^^ ^^
A	**Action required**	Spell out the action needed to correct the behaviour.	*Please do not to interrupt me when I am talking.* ^^^^ *Allow me to finish what I am saying.* ^^ ^^ *I will pay you the same courtesy.* ^^ ^^
L	**Likely consequences**	Spell out what will happen if the requested action does not occur.	*If you persist in this behaviour after my repeated requests* ^^ ^^ *I will have no option other than to [specify consequence].*

Box 11.1 DEAL: steps to countering inappropriate or disruptive behaviour

The first cycle: ignore, ignore, respond

Deliver a qualifying remark

The aim here is to lessen the sting that the person might feel by being given feedback on something that they are doing unconsciously. Many people do not know that they are behaving inappropriately. Often this is because it has been tolerated—rewarded—so they have never received corrective feedback on its unacceptability. You have to give the individual the benefit of the doubt, ie he or she does not know what they are doing.

Deliver the first three steps: D, E, and A

Say what needs to be said (Box 11.2) simply, concisely, and in a calm, even manner. The aim is to pre-empt an emotional or explosive reaction.

D	**Description**	Describe the behaviour.	*I need to point out that every time that I ask a question,* ^^ ^^ *you interrupt me.* ^^ ^^
E	**Explanation**	Explain the actual or potential effects of the behaviour.	*This makes it difficult to progress matters.* ^^ ^^ *It will take even longer to cover the issues that I must cover.* ^^ ^^
A	**Action required**	Spell out the action needed to correct the behaviour.	*Please do not to interrupt me when I am talking.* ^^ ^^ *Allow me to finish what I am saying.* ^^ ^^ *I will pay you the same courtesy.* ^^ ^^

Box 11.2 DEAL: Responding to the first cycle of inappropriate or disruptive behaviour

The second cycle: ignore, ignore, respond again

Deliver D, E, and A again (Box 11.3), as before simply, concisely, and in a calm, even manner.

D	**Description**	Describe the behaviour.	*A while back I pointed out that every time that I ask a question, ^^ ^^ you interrupt me. ^^ ^^*
E	**Explanation**	Explain the actual or potential effects of the behaviour.	*I explained that this makes it difficult to progress matters. ^^^^ It will take even longer to cover the issues that I must cover. ^^ ^^*
A	**Action required**	Spell out the action needed to correct the behaviour.	*I must ask you again, please do not interrupt me when I am talking. ^^^^ Allow me to finish what I am saying. ^^ ^^ I will pay you the same courtesy. ^^ ^^*

Box 11.3. DEAL: Responding to the second cycle of inappropriate or disruptive behaviour

The third cycle: ignore, ignore, respond again

The individual has behaved inappropriately or disruptively nine times. You have to respond. Deliver D, E, A and this time L—likely consequences—as well (Box 11.4).

D	**Description**	Describe the behaviour.	*I need to point out yet again that every time that I ask a question, ^^ ^^ you interrupt me. ^^ ^^*
E	**Explanation**	Explain the actual or potential effects of the behaviour.	*As I have said twice now, ^^ ^^ this makes it difficult to progress matters. ^^^^ I have explained twice ^^ ^^ that it will take even longer to cover the issues that I must cover. ^^ ^^*
A	**Action required**	Spell out the action needed to correct the behaviour.	*For the third time of asking, please do not to interrupt me when I am talking. ^^^^ Allow me to finish what I am saying. ^^ ^^ I will pay you the same courtesy. ^^ ^^*
L	**Likely consequences**	Spell out what will happen if the requested action does not occur.	*You have persisted in this behaviour after my repeated requests. ^^ ^^ If it happens again I will have no option other than to [specify consequence].*

Box 11.4 DEAL: Responding to the third cycle of inappropriate or disruptive behaviour

Implement the consequences if the behaviour re-occurs

If the individual behaves inappropriately or disruptively again, implement the consequences.

- Don't take what is happening personally.
- Don't react in anger.
- Stop the interview.
- Take the action that you stated you would do.

- Review:
  — calm down;
  — reflect on the course of the interview and the 'journey' to the action that you took.

11.4 Coping with resistance

11.4.1 Responding to resistance

'I shall not be stampeded'

The core issue is not to allow the interviewee to stampede you into responding. In all cases 'keep your cool' and bring your heart rate down.

- Don't rush to respond. Pause after the individual's utterance or utterances. Then pause again! The interviewee who does not want to talk may well continue talking.
- Breathe slowly, gently, and at some length in through your nose, and then breath out through your partly opened lips (just sufficiently open without being visibly so to the interviewee. Breathe in slowly, and so on.

It is essential that you remain, and evidence that you are, prepared to listen, to remain open minded, and to resist being sucked into being judgemental, showing impatience, and finding it hard not to raise your voice or lose your temper. This means:

- distancing yourself from your preconceptions, prejudices, and strong feelings;
- being a detached participant observer: tolerant, emotionally uninvolved, and unaffected by the details he or she asserts: becoming emotional will cloud your judgement and affect the way in which you relate to the individual;
- in the case of a suspect, not treating him or her as guilty.

Continued denials

If the individual denies knowing or doing something, you or, where applicable, the second investigator should discreetly keep a tally of the number of denials. If the individual denies something an excessive number of times, you should consider stopping the interview to check the validity of what you are asserting. It could be that this has not been established and the person may well be justified in denying until you have validated what you know or believe to be the case.

Evasion

This is potentially passive lying.

Answering a question with a question

Treat as a rhetorical question. Don't reply. Pause. Pause again. If the interviewee does not take the talking turn, restate the question. For example:

INTERVIEWEE: *So what do you want to know?*

YOU: *^^ ^^ ^^ ^^ I'll ask the question again Derek. ^^ ^^ Take your time. ^^ ^^ Think before you speak. ^^ ^^ Tell me about…*

Treat moral indignation, eg *Now would a man in my position do something so foolish?* in the same manner.

Changing the topic

Bring the individual back to your topic. Treat as for answering a question with a question. For example:

INTERVIEWEE: *Rather than asking me about what I did why don't you ask me what she did?*

YOU: ^^ ^^ ^^ ^^ *I may do that* ^^ ^^ *But not until we know what you did.* ^^ ^^ *I'll ask the question again Tracy.* ^^ ^^ *Take your time.* ^^ ^^ *Think before you speak.* ^^ ^^ *Tell me why you…*

'Passing the buck'

If the interviewee tries to 'pass the buck', handle in the same way as an attempt to change the topic/answer a question with a question.

INTERVIEWEE: *You need to ask* [named person]. *She'll know better than me.*

YOU: ^^ ^^ *I will talk to her later.* ^^ ^^ *At this moment I need to hear what you have to say.* ^^ ^^ *You tell me what you know.*^^ ^^

Giving measured responses

Here the interviewee gives sufficient to answer your question but no more. It includes 'blanking', ie saying *yes* and no more in reply. Create a long pause after the *yes*: the interviewee may start talking. If this does not happen, restate the ground rules for disclosure, eg:

YOU: *So you sat with the man in the pub* ^^ ^^ *and did the deal.* ^^ ^^ *Describe the man to me.*

INTERVIEWEE: *He was small.* ^^ ^^

YOU: ^^ ^^ ^^ ^^ *Small?* ^^ ^^

INTERVIEWEE: *Yeah* ^^ ^^

YOU: ^^ ^^ *Take your time.* ^^ ^^ *Think before you speak.* ^^ ^^ *Describe him to me.* ^^ ^^

'Putting down'

The individual—the interviewee or a third party present in the interview, eg a lawyer, union representative—attempts to snub you by questioning your credibility, eg *You haven't been doing this job long, have you?*

The intention is to intimidate, make you feel uncomfortable, undermine your confidence, and disrupt your ability to manage the conversation and follow your interview plan. Neutralize this tactic by:

- recognizing it for what it is: 'sticks and stones';
- ignoring the question: don't rise to the bait and never waste time giving a response;
- pausing: don't give any indication that you are ruffled, maintain eye-contact, don't fidget or move paper around, think clearly about what you are about to say;
- continuing with what you were doing before the snub, eg repeating the question *I'll say that again. How do you account for that?*

Arguing

Remember that it takes two to have an argument. Don't engage, ie 'bite'. If you do, the individual will know immediately that he or she has 'pressed the button' and will continue pressing. Ignore the argument. Wait for the interviewee to stop talking, and then reintroduce the question.

Never try to smother arguing by overtalking or interrupting. It creates what is called the 'dialogue of the deaf': neither party is listening to the other.

Becoming emotional

This includes indignation, hostility, anger, raising the voice, becoming abusive. Strong emotions are difficult to control and are infectious.

Detect the emotion early

You should monitor the interviewee's non-verbal behaviour—physical and non-vocal, especially tone of voice—actively listening to detect early clues to frustration, annoyance, and anger (the 'rumblings of rage').

Ask yourself what are the possible triggers of the rumbling, eg The topic? Why is the interviewee so sensitive to this? The question born of the last answer? The interviewee's mental or physical state (such as tiredness, lack of sleep) requiring a break? Is it you?

When you detect gradual emotional change, use reflection to lower the temperature and also to add value to your investigation, eg:

> *I can sense you are getting keyed up ^^ ^^ and are unhappy talking about [X]. ^^ ^^ Shall we take a step back? ^^ ^^ I'd like to know the reason for your unhappiness about what we are covering. ^^ ^^*

Don't allow the emotion to infect you. It is important that you do not get sucked into the emotionality.

- Think and act paradoxically. As the interviewee gets more aroused, consciously think more and more relaxed.
- Complement the behaviour, don't mirror it.
- Never smile when a person is getting angry.

When the emotion breaks through

- Allow the individual to *ventilate*, ie express the emotion.
- Listen and observe his or her BASELINES behaviours.
  Ventilating strong emotions burns up energy. The individual will tire and eventually become subdued. At this point return to what you were originally saying.
  Should the individual begin to cry, or be overwhelmed with emotion, stop talking and remain silent. When the individual has composed himself or herself, continue with what you were originally saying. Should the interviewee start crying again, create the space— the silence—to allow him or her to regain composure. Be prepared to stop the interview if the interviewee breaks down and a further period to regain composure does not work.

11.5 Chapter summary

Police officers are necessarily frustrated that training does not equip them to deal with inappropriate behaviour and resistance. This has produced past and present generations of investigative interviewer who actually create and compound these behaviours. Attention to your own conversational behaviour and dominating the detail of the case will enable you to employ the DEAL technique confidently and competently, and not to allow yourself to be stampeded by resistant behaviour.

Evaluation: The Last Piece of the Jigsaw

12.1 Chapter overview

This chapter reviews evaluation—a key stage in the ACCESS model of investigation, in the GEMAC framework for investigative interviewing, and in the PEACE model for investigative interviewing. We examine evaluation from two perspectives: investigation-focused evaluation and evaluation to enhance practitioner performance.

12.1.1 Chapter objectives

This chapter will enable you to:

- recognize the difference between evaluation, review, and assessment;
- understand the concepts of experiential learning, reflection, and reflective practice;
- appreciate organizational barriers to the implementation of the evaluation stage of the PEACE model;
- distinguish between evaluation conducted immediately after the interview to progress the investigation and planned events where performance is examined as a basis for developing skills;
- have a sound grasp of the when, the what, the who, the how, and the outcomes of investigation-focused evaluation and of planned events to develop practitioner performance.

12.2 Review, evaluation, and assessment

The terms *evaluation, review*, and *assessment* are widely used—often interchangeably—in investigative and training contexts. They have common features. All three involve resource deployed to engage in systematic examination that enables learning from experience—essential to progression whether of the investigation or the individual practitioner.

12.2.1 Review

A review is a *historical* activity conducted *after* the event, often to learn lessons for the future. The focus of the post-hoc review is usually on the issue of process. The advantage of a review is that its precise timing can be chosen to have maximum effect, eg to consider other factors, or to allow the impact of other events to be included. Reviews can have a thematic basis, or address organizational or broader issues.

In an investigative context, a review can assist with identifying areas for improvement based on what was learned.

12.2.2 Assessment

An assessment is also a post-hoc activity. It differs from a review in that:

- the focus is usually directed at *performance*;
- typically, there is a notion of a standard, and the potential to achieve, surpass, or fall below this;
- there is an aspiration to be, if not an achievement of being, objective in judging performance:
  — when examining information (evidence);
  — when applying criteria;

— when using tools and metrics (measurement devices);
— when arriving at an 'assessment', eg pass or fail, outstanding, exceeding expectations, good, below expectations;

- assessment typically occurs within a controlled environment, eg a training unit or department, which enables assessors to hold the world stable. This is necessary to eliminate compounding variables, which would render judgements problematic and prone to excessive subjectivity. The aim aspired to is objectivity and realistic focus, eg selecting particular issues or variables to be assessed, ie put to the test.

Assessment provides information for improving learning. It can be done alone, ie self-assessment, but of greater value is assessment that includes exchange with another person. This person can be a peer, trainer, mentor, supervisor, or manager—but with the requisite knowledge, understanding, awareness, and skills to facilitate and to guide examination of the individual's performance. The aim is to identify aspects of performance where there is a need for skills development. Assessment enables the creation of an action plan to develop the skill in question.

12.2.3 Evaluation

As pointed out in Chapter 1, investigation is a form of problem solving. The ACCESS model constitutes a problem-solving cycle: common stages in a continuous process of:

- formulating the problem and specifying actions;
- collecting information;
- systematically examining the outcome—the *product*—of the collection process;
- weighing up this product;
- placing the product within the context of already existing knowledge;
- summarizing the totality in a graspable form;
- incorporating this into re-formulating the investigative problem, ie starting the problem-solving cycle anew.

In keeping with the ACCESS model, it is necessary to look back at any investigative interview in order to identify and evaluate the product—emergent *information* in achievement of the interview objectives and, even better, information adding value in the form of unexpected disclosures.

Where appropriate, evaluation focuses additionally on the *processes* that gave rise to the product:

- Value added information may be gained by identifying particular conversational behaviours manifested by the interviewee, the interviewee's responsiveness, or changes in his or her behaviour when particular topics were raised, which are potential indicators of the interviewee's state of mind, emotional state, attitude, or disposition, as well as potential 'hot spots' requiring investigation, probing in a subsequent interview, or both.
- Across the course of the verbal exchange, the conduct of the interviewee, the interviewer, or both may indicate a 'clash of personalities'. In such circumstances decisions are necessary: what changes the interviewer needs to make in his or her behaviour, or whether a better solution is to assign another interviewer to conduct the next interview with the individual.

Evaluation must also focus on the extent to which the conduct of the interviewer accorded with the law, regulations, or any other formal directives, guidelines, or policies.

Evaluation of an investigative interview to *progress the investigation* is entirely distinct from evaluation of the interview to *develop the skills of the practitioner* who conducted the interview. The former is *operational evaluation*, the latter is *developmental evaluation*.

12.3 Reflection and reflective practice

Both operational evaluation and developmental evaluation require *reflection*, which is integral to engaging in *reflective practice*.

12.3.1 Reflection

Kolb[1] described learning from what one has done as *experiential learning*, a cyclical process (Figure 12.1) involving, in the interviewing context:

- **Concrete experience.** The interviewer preparing and planning for, and then conducting the interview.
- **Reflective observation.** Self-reflection by the interviewer. This may be paralleled by a third party (tasked with subsequently giving feedback), contemporaneously observing the recording or live via a link.
- **Abstract conceptualization.** Consideration of observations and feedback, leading to the formulation of changes to be made, eg greater attention to explanation, reduction in controlling behaviours, adoption of a different questioning style.
- **Active experimentation.** The interviewer incorporating the specified changes into the next concrete experience, ie the next interview.

The cycle then begins again.

This model is sometimes incorrectly associated solely with a learner's experience that enables *development of skill* in the formal training environment, or mentoring and coaching in the workplace. In fact, reflection is essential in the process of evaluation. It enables learning

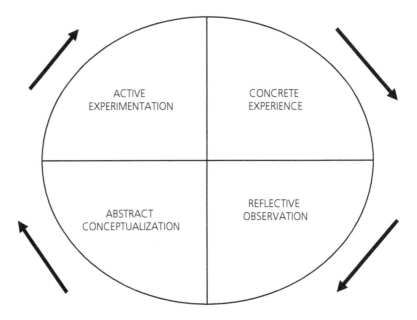

Figure 12.1 The experiential learning cycle

---

[1] Kolb, D. (1984) *Experiential Learning: Experience as the Source of Learning and Development.* New Jersey: Prentice-Hall.

that has *operational* worth, recognizing information gained—or insufficiently or not at all—across the course of the interview.

Kolb's experiential learning cycle is complimented by the work of Schön,[2] who describes the process of *reflection in* action: the professional dealing with a unique situation (and every interview is unique) by applying a combination of learned theories and experience in order to solve the problem (in this case to maximize interview effectiveness). Akin to Kolb's abstract conceptualization, Schön's model includes the formulation of a fresh hypothesis after reflection on the issue at hand ('I think if I spend longer building rapport in my next interview I will get a better account'). The revised hypothesis is then tested by applying it to the next situation (next interview = concrete experience). Reflective practice is an appropriate way to learn from thinking about personal performance. However, it is equally applicable to 'learning' from a reflective examination of the output of the interview—essential to progressing the current investigation.

12.4 The PEACE experience

Evaluation is the final stage of the PEACE model (Figure 12.2).

The earliest PEACE text pointed out that:

> *if you are to* improve and develop as an interviewer, it is essential that you **reflect** on the way you conducted the interview.[3]

According to the official training text the *Practical Guide to Investigative Interviewing*, evaluation is an integral part of the interview process.[4] Its purpose is to:

- *examine whether the aims and objectives for the interview have been achieved.*
- *review the investigation in the light of information obtained during the interview.*
- *develop interviewing skills by evaluating how you performed and setting goals for the future.*[5]

In effect, practitioners were being invited to carry out both operational evaluation and developmental evaluation.

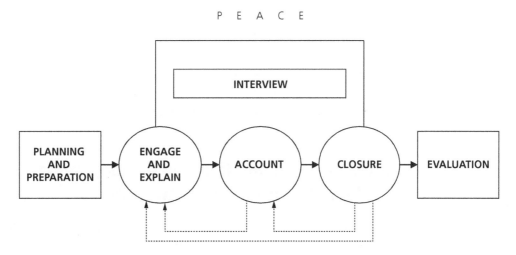

Figure 12.2 The PEACE model

---

[2] Schön, D.A. (1991) *The Reflective Practitioner*. Farnham: Ashgate.

[3] CPTU (1992) *Investigative Interviewing: The Interviewer's Guide*. Harrogate: CPTU (p. 38, emphasis added).

[4] Centrex (2004) *Practical Guide to Investigative Interviewing*. Bramshill: Centrex.

[5] Centrex, *Practical Guide to Investigative Interviewing* (p. 110).

Arguably, the police service is a pragmatic profession. Management and trainers alike recognize the necessity for, and the benefits to be derived from, reflection upon work done—in this case investigative interviewing. Official texts such as the *Practical Guide to Investigative Interviewing* constitute the 'formal code' of practice: what is expected, and should be, done. However, the way in which work is organized and done, availability of resource, the requirement for rapid response to demand, and where 'three crimes only two officers' is a commonplace, create the reality of the 'informal code' of practice that render reflection if not a perceived irrelevance then an infrequent practice, and for many something that is never really done in any systematic way.

Given the hierarchical structure of the police service, supervisors were expected to oversee the engagement of practitioners in dual tasks of evaluation following interviews.[6] The service is becoming, but is not as yet, reflective, with practitioners feeling ready, willing, and able to take responsibility for professional development through reflective practice. The same applies to supervisors. Research conducted soon after the introduction of PEACE revealed that supervisors saw their task of overseeing the evaluation of interviews as a low priority. They failed to recognize the need to physically manage interview skills, with a consequent effect on interview quality.

The supervisors voiced resource and time pressures as the reason why this activity was not seen as important. In other words, evaluation of investigative interviews was less important than competing, tasks. This pointed toward cultural and leadership issues.

- Supervisors, unconvinced of the value of the activity and nervous about whether they possessed the skills to evaluate officers' interviews used excuses not to do it.
- Leaders in the organization did not give explicit instructions that this was an important activity and must be completed, and did not ensure the correct staff had the skills to carry it out.

A later national post-implementation review[7] of the PEACE programme found that in some forces supervisors were still not prioritizing this activity. In those forces where it was treated as an important supervisory task, there was a positive correlation between this and the standard of interviewing.

It appears, then, that despite being promoted as an integral part of the PEACE model, many forces have yet to enable evaluation—a 'learning' activity that is vital to the progression and effectiveness of the investigation, even if there is no attention to the actual performance of the individual.

This situation reflects a mismatch between the senior leadership of the police (who had launched the PEACE programme) and junior management (in charge of making it happen). It underlines the importance of physically managing all parts of change including culture.

12.5 Operational evaluation and developmental evaluation: a practical framework

Common sense argues that in any investigative context evaluation should take place immediately or as soon as practicable after the interview. Even if we put lack of motivation to one side, practical constraints—time and workload—are strong disincentives to doing something that people rarely do and many have never done. As soon as practitioners

---

[6] Stockdale, J. (1993) *Management and Supervision of Police Interviews*. London: Home Office.

[7] Clarke, C. and Milne, B. (2001) *National Evaluation of the PEACE Investigative Interviewing Course*. London: Police Research Award Scheme.

recognize the payback from reflection upon the output, this will motivate them to evaluate following every interview.

This said, it is unlikely that the majority of practitioners in any investigative context will view reflection on personal performance after each interview as worthwhile. Far better for the institution to create a continuous professional development and performance management infrastructure which:

- makes regular reflective practice—individually and collaboratively with a supervisor—an explicit responsibility, ie stated as specific responsibility in the individual practitioner's and supervisor's job description;
- actually provides the conditions for reflective practice to take place, ie as a planned and scheduled development event occurring, say, once a month or tailored to the individual's needs.

Box 12.1 presents a practical framework for post-interview investigative evaluation and planned skills development events.

	Primary focus	
	Operational evaluation	**Developmental evaluation**
When	• Immediately post interview • Between interviews (inter-interview) • During interview (intra-interview) (only in critical circumstances)	• Planned event • Frequency tailored to development needs and organizational capacity
What	• **Product**: Information and evidence • **Process**: Relationship/behaviour change • **Conduct**: Rule compliance/ effectiveness	**Interviewer selected interview** • 'Most recent'; 'Best since last evaluation'; 'Problematic' **Evaluator selected interview** • Interview contains behaviours requiring development
Who	• Interviewer • Second investigator • Interview adviser • External adviser	Interviewee with: • peer • supervisor • mentor (eg interview adviser) • trainer
How	**Output evaluation tools** • Mental replay • Replay of recording • Interview plan • Real time SE3R • Real time GQM	**Performance evaluation tools** Macro • Interview plan • WOB map • Combined checklist and rating scale (training) • Recording/transcript • SE3R Micro • Interview product • Recording • GQM • SE3R
Outcome	• Contribution to investigative re-assessment, action planning and further investigative actions • Formal product: transcript/statement/ summary • Investigative/intelligence report	• Behaviour-focused development plan • Training needs requirement • Organizational feedback

Box 12.1 A practical framework for interview evaluation and skills development

Box 12.1 reflects our views on the issue of evaluation. The primary focus of evaluation is the investigation: how did the interview progress the investigative process? It is not about performance—skills—development. Practitioner skills development occurs in planned events in which illustrative recordings permit real reflection and feedback.

12.6 Operational evaluation

This type of evaluation:

- begins the planning process for future interviews;
- should be clearly focused;
- to achieve its objectives must be relevant, objective, and not too time-consuming: criteria that are achievable using the appropriate techniques and tools described later;
- is assisted by planning documents for the interview (principally the interview aim and objectives and, where applicable, the I^3 created prior to the interview;
- should not be bureaucratic;
- should include an impact assessment on the investigation as a whole. This is focused document: it is not a review.

When there are multiple interviews with the same interviewee, there are a number of interviews as part of the same enquiry (eg where a group of suspects are arrested following an investigation, or there are a number of witnesses to an event) and evaluation should be in two stages.

- The first stage must deal with the interview as a single entity.
- The second stage deals with how information from other interviews should be incorporated (or not) into the next interview.

A key consideration here is that the requirement to evaluate must not conflict with other issues, such as custody time limits, or inconveniencing a witness for the sake of a detailed development discussion relating to an interviewer.

12.6.1 When?

Evaluation must be an integral part of the investigative interview process.

Unless there are wholly extraordinary circumstances, evaluation should take place immediately after the interview. Chapter 2 indicated the precariousness of memory. The longer the delay between the end of the interview and the commencement of evaluation the greater the disruptive effect of intervening activity, information exchanged, received, or processed upon ability to retrieve memory of interview detail.

If there is to be a follow-on interview—or the interview just completed is in a planned run of interviews with this interviewee—this is all the more reason to carry out an immediate interview evaluation. This will maximize the potential to assist planning and preparation for the next interview. Such *inter-interview* evaluation is vital.

On occasions—in critical circumstances—evaluation will have to occur during the interview. In practical terms such *intra-interview* evaluation involves technology—remote monitoring and, where applicable and practicable, in-the-ear microphones worn by the interviewer and the second investigator.

This rule also applies where there are multiple interviews with the same interviewee, or with a number of interviews as part of the same enquiry. In these circumstances the evaluation should be in two stages—the first dealing with the interview as a single entity, the second dealing with how information from other interviews should be incorporated (or not) into the next interview.

A key consideration here is that the requirement to evaluate must not conflict with other issues, such as custody time limits, or inconveniencing a witness for the sake of a detailed development discussion relating to an interviewer.

12.6.2 What?

Product

As pointed out earlier, the detail disclosed in the interview constitutes the product of the investigative encounter. Whether the interview involved a witness or a suspect, the interviewer will have embarked upon the encounter with an interview plan—reflecting a definite investigative aim and specific objectives (topics to be covered)—and an I^3 (investigatively important information) 'shopping list'. These will of course differ from case to case, and in a sequence of interviews, for each interview.

Process

Chapter 3 raised the issue of process: the dynamic aspect of a conversation in terms of changes in behaviour across the course of the encounter.

- 'Hot spots' that required probing—which now in hindsight can be judged as having been appropriately responded to or inadvertently gone unprobed.
- Transient changes occurring indicative of emotional reaction, stress, distress, or an 'inner dialogue'—which the interviewer may or may not have detected and handled appropriately.
- Inappropriate behaviour and resistance—which may or may not have been managed with appropriate assertion.
- Clues indicative of a change in the relationship—positive or negative—between the interviewee and the interviewer, or with a third party.

Conduct

By this we mean:

- the interviewer's (and where applicable the second investigator's) ethical conduct:
  — respect for the truth—identifying actual instances of misrepresentation obligation to respect the interviewee—manifested in mindful RESPONSE behaviours;
  — engagement in appropriate assertion (Quadrant 4);
  — persuasion that did not oppress;
  — negotiation that did not oppress;
- the interviewer's observance of the requisite law, regulations, instructions, policy, and guidelines;
- effectiveness—the extent to which the interviewer's (or second investigator's) behaviour was effective.

12.6.3 Who?

Where the interviewer is managing the case alone, he or she will be evaluating the interview. If a second investigator was present, he or she must be involved—contributing his or her remembrance and perspective.

In serious cases where the investigative team includes an interview adviser, he or she may have been remotely monitoring the interview and will have much to contribute to the evaluation process. Similarly, in cases where an external adviser has been brought in to assist, he or she will necessarily be invited to participate in the evaluation in which he or she will bring to bear his or her expertise and perspective and give expert opinion.

12.6.4 How?

Output evaluation

This involves examining the interview in terms of information arising from the conversational exchange. This examination should combine reflection based upon remembrance, replaying of the recording, and the application of appropriate aids to identification, collation, and decision-making.

Mental replay

By this we mean closing your eyes and running through the entire encounter your mind, imaging (in your mind's eye) and also 'hearing' the vocal exchange again (in your mind's ear): akin to replaying a video recording or going over in your mind a programme that you have just watched on television.

What you will find is that your replay will be akin to moving from one salient event/episode (landmark) to the next salient event/episode (landmark). You will in effect be unconsciously 'fast forwarding' the recording between these landmark points. As you become more practised at mentally replaying interviews, you will find (in the same way that other professionals such as counselors and psychotherapists do) that you will become increasingly better at remembering more and more salient episodes (landmarks) and the detail within these.

The first author has blank SE3R sheets to hand. When a key point, behaviour or behaviour change, utterance, response, disclosure, remark, observation, or item of detail crops up in the replay—comes to mind—he opens his eyes and quickly notes the detail down on the SE3R: as an event, a continuous state, an item of detail in a knowledge bin.

Mentally replaying your remembrance of the encounter has multiple benefits. The detail is as fresh in your memory as it can possibly be, bringing with this increased likelihood of accurate recall. Replaying in this way puts the detail in your working memory (which will be for the second time, since its original occurrence was the first time) and this is a very useful form of appropriate memory consolidation. Also you are much more likely to retrieve a greater amount of detail by 'going through' the total mental video than if you started to focus on a particular point of the interview, topic, or behaviour.

Mental replaying of the interview is useful even if it was electronically recorded.

Replay of the recording

This makes total sense. If time permits it is well worth replaying the entire recording. However, if time is restricted you can navigate around the recording with the assistance of your remembrance of key episodes in the interview.

You will find that recordings reveal the operation of the editing rules that we described in Chapter 4:

- what you did not register that disclosed detail, behaviour change, and potential 'hot spots';
- instances where you have generalized or compressed disclosed detail;
- instances where you assumed something.

The recording will also reveal:

- instances of anomaly, eg missing detail, gaps, jumps, 'non-barking dogs', 'pat' disclosure, vagueness, ambiguity, inconsistency, contradiction, that you may or may not have detected and responded to;
- instances of insufficient probing;
- instances of failure to listen to the detail of a response of disclosure.

Topic transition times (TTTs)

At the pause created between the completion of one topic and the start of the next, the first author annotates the time (visible in the digital recorder display window) on his WOB interview plan. If he subsequently returns to the topic he puts that time also by the topic. Each notation is a *topic transition time* (TTT). Making a note of TTTs enables you to navigate rapidly around the recording. TTTs have one enormous benefit: you are able to replay all the detail disclosed on a given topic. If there is a second investigator he or she can also note TTTs.

Electronic tagging

There is now technology that allows electronic tagging (bookmarking) of key points/TTTs in the recording across the course of the interview.

Interview plan

Your interview plan (whether this is a WOB map or a list) has two significant uses.

- It helps you to navigate around the recording (if you noted TTTs or used electronic book marks).
- It enables a *gap analysis*—a systematic comparison of your stated objectives with the detail within the recording (or if there was no electronic recording, your remembrance and, where applicable, that of the second investigator, interview adviser, external adviser.

Real time SE3R

If there was a second investigator, he or she may well have created a real time SE3R of the interview, annotating this where necessary (including TTTs!). This will show the course of the interview and the content of the interviewee's disclosures.

Real time Griffiths Questioning Map (GQM)

We describe this monitoring tool later in the sections on practitioner skills development. It can be used in real time by an adept colleague, in the remote monitoring location.

12.6.5   The outcome

The primary focus of this 'instant' evaluation should be:

- generating tangible product of the interview;
- identification, where applicable, of key process information.

Interview product

One method of evaluating the interview product is by asking a series of questions linked to the preparation for that interview.

- Was the aim of the interview achieved, eg has a complete account of X's relationship with Y been obtained?
- If not, what further interview activity is required/possible?
- Have all interview objectives been achieved, eg:
  — Has X been asked to account for abusive texts sent to Y?
  — Has X been asked why he was overheard to threaten Y?
- If not, what further interview activity is required/possible?
- Was the interviewee's account obtained for all relevant matters, including those that arose within interview? (Check against SE3R/WOB.)
- Were all relevant topics examined in sufficient detail? (Check against SE3R, WOB.)
- (Suspect only) Were all legal points necessary covered in order to prove the offence?
- (Suspect only) Were all defences available in law covered?

In relation to the broader investigation:

- What information known prior to the interview has been corroborated by, negated by, contradicted by, or is inconsistent with, information disclosed in the interview?
- How does this affect the investigation?
- What actions are now necessary?
- What evidential product needs to be prepared as a result of interview?

It is then useful to divide the evaluation into a two-part discussion.

- A consideration of:
  — the evidence gathered (unless a non-evidential special circumstance interview (see Chapter 20);
  — how this should be presented (preparation of statement, transcript);
  — other information gathered (intelligence, further complaints of crime), and how to address these.
- Concluding the product evaluation by focusing on:
  — what affect the interview has had on the overall investigation;
  — what other interviews are now required;
  — what action is required to investigate information obtained.

Interviewer conduct

This is an operational evaluation and as such the product of the interview is the primary focus. Consistent with this focus, examination of interviewer conduct should identify anything said or done by the investigation likely to undermine the admissibility of the product or the success of any subsequent interview.

Interviewer conduct becomes an issue if:

- the interviewer has displayed unacceptable behaviour;
- the interviewer's conduct has failed to observe a legal or procedural requirement;
- the interviewer's behaviour has adversely affected the interviewee, the interviewee's willingness to participate, and degree of disclosure.

These are operational matters and will need to be addressed.

Of course, when examining the interview there may be aspects of the interviewer's performance that merit complimentary comment. However, identified shortcomings in performance present a difficulty. Giving feedback after the interview on an area of weakness could adversely affect—rather than improve—the individual's next performance: even more so if there are shortcomings in a number of areas of skill.

A solution is to make a note of the area of shortcoming and the interview in which this occurred. Outside the confines of the investigation—optimally when it has been completed—the note should be shared with the individual and become part of the planned event in which evaluation focuses on the development of the individual's practitioner skills.

12.7 Developmental evaluation

As pointed out earlier, the requirement is for practitioners to engage in planned events to develop their interviewing skills. These events should:

- have an emphasis on performance; and
- follow a more formal assessment tools based approach.

12.7.1 When?

Events to facilitate development of practitioner skills should occur:

- as part of the *performance management system* on a planned, regular basis in the workplace;
- during *formal training*, when the individual attends an investigative interviewing course.

The frequency of events can be set by the organization as part of the practical implementation of practitioner development.

By their very nature, planned evaluation events require time and effort, both in the preparation and debrief. Therefore, it is not realistic to attempt to include within the review every interview that the individual has conducted since the previous evaluation event. More practicable is to target a selected interview or interviews *beforehand*: interviews which highlighted particular areas for skills development (eg coping with a suspect exercising the right to silence; a legal adviser who constantly interrupts). This approach allows development and indicates what behaviours require monitoring in future interviews.

This type of evaluation can also fit into organizational performance strategies for investigative interviewing. Results can be aggregated for:

- discussion at supervisory level over broader performance;
- identification of organizational issues;
- development of professional development training programmes.

The timing of this evaluation should be based on both logistical and investigative considerations. The balance here is to carry out such evaluations where sufficient time has elapsed to allow mature consideration of the issues, but not so much that the memory of what took pace has faded so that events are not clear and the evaluation becomes speculative.

12.7.2 What?

Either the individual brings to the 'one-to-one' evaluation event an interview that he or she has selected for examination and discussion, or the supervisor (or mentor/trainer) selects an interview conducted by the individual. Common criteria for personal selection include 'my most recent' or 'best interview since my last evaluation', or a 'problematic interview'. A supervisor, mentor, or trainer may select the interview because it contains evidence of behaviours that require development.

Once basic competence has been achieved, ie legal compliance and delivery of the interview plan, developmental evaluation is akin to sports coaching, observing, raising awareness, and making adjustments to established technique.

Developmental evaluation should always be individually focused. Only necessary alterations to technique should be recommended, using an individual's characteristics to develop their personal style. It should not seek to cement wooden and robotic adherence to theoretical models. The goal should be increased efficiency through skills development.

It is not feasible or necessary to examine or to assess all interviewer behaviours. A targeted approach should be adopted, based on previous plans or discussion with the interviewer. It makes no sense to consolidate strengths by complimentary feedback when other areas requiring development are overlooked.

As outlined earlier, the use of a series of questions will assist this process.

- How productive was the working relationship between interviewer and interviewee?
- How could it be more productive (rapport/questioning style/pace)?
- How could the interviewer improve effectiveness (topic coverage/question style/use of exhibits)?
- How did the interviewer deal with vagueness/resistance?

12.7.3   Who?

We view developmental evaluation as integral to the performance management system. Any effective system specifies regular 'one-to-one' meetings between the individual and his or her supervisor/team leader/manager. For ease of reference we will refer to this person generically as the individual's supervisor.

In the investigative interviewing context the regular, planned developmental evaluation event is in effect a 'one-to-one' that focuses on improving the individual's skills through examination of evidence of the individual's behaviour within a selected interview or interviews.

There is no natural link between general supervision skills and the ability to evaluate an interview. From our commentary earlier about the shortcomings of supervision within the implementation of the PEACE model, it is obvious that in any context of investigation the organization must equip supervisors with the necessary knowledge, understanding, and skills not only in respect of investigative interviewing but in terms of giving feedback to interviewers appropriately and effectively.

This situation highlights the difference between examining practitioner performance and evaluating the content of an interview in order to progress the investigation and to perform an evidential review. Individuals with knowledge of the law, eg police supervisors and lawyers, will be competent to look at the *product* of an interview and determine:

- what else needs to be investigated;
- whether it contains sufficient evidence to lay charges against a suspect.

Their competency stems from training in the definition of particular offences and real life experience in dealing with those offences.

Circumstances may be such that there is insufficient supervisory resource to conduct developmental evaluation events as regularly as they should occur. If this is the case then the organization must create the opportunity for practitioners to work together in peer evaluation events.

Where interviewing is practised as a team activity, generally within dedicated investigation teams, peer reviewing is very practicable and effective. A team member who was, say, involved in preparation and planning the interview, or was tasked with remote monitoring of the interview, is extremely well placed to fulfil the role of collaborative peer evaluation.

Collaborative peer evaluation implies a meeting of minds and perspectives made possible by self-evaluation and evaluation by the peer. This demands objectivity and maturity from those involved, particularly where both parties work together often. Harsh, subjective feedback must be avoided; otherwise evaluation becomes a criticism loop where the performance of both interviewers will suffer through a downward spiral of negative feedback.

In an organization where there are interview advisers—with extra skills and training in investigative interviewing—these individuals are wholly capable of acting as professional mentors. They are another resource, able to engage with practitioners in a planned collaborative evaluation of a selected interview or interviews.

In the context of a formal training course in investigative interviewing, it is a clear and reasonable expectation that the trainer has the requisite knowledge, understanding, and skills to fulfil the task of professional evaluator—working as the 'expert' with the individual in the reviewing of a selected interview or even interviews.

12.7.4 How?

It will assist if we first review methods that are commonly used to evaluate performance.

Checklists

It is unfortunately too common to see checklists in circulation and for these to be associated with evaluation. It should be clear that a basic checklist with space for tick box marking next to specified elements of the investigative interview model has no place in the process of evaluation.

- There are very few elements that must appear within every investigative interview beyond simple, legal requirements such as name of interviewer and provision of legal rights and so the yes/no approach is of little use in improving interview effectiveness and quality.
- A tick or a cross (binary marking) has no focus on quality, and merely encourages an observer to look for the presence or absence of an element.
- The checklist provides no assistance to the interviewer in considering improvements to his or her performance.

We do not recommend the use of checklists.

Rating scales

Rating (also called Likert) scales are appropriate for use in training assessment as they provide consistency when used in controlled circumstances. Although superior to checklists, there are still some issues with rating scales.

- If the rating scale is, for example, from 1 to 5 then rater consistency immediately becomes a factor. Inconsistency devalues the feedback. This issue can be overcome in a training environment. Consistency is increased by using a restricted number of raters and a common standard of training.
- The need to attach a numerical value to the performance of an interviewer can distract an observer into considering comparisons on a 'best case' basis, ie trying to identify another situation that was most similar and then comparing what they are observing with that occurrence.

- A pure numerical assessment, even where used correctly, only provides a score. In the absence of a stated reason for the score, the number does not assist with improvement.
- Rating scales, either with or without total scores or averages can encourage an inappropriate competitive mindset, with interviewers either striving to improve their own or colleagues' 'scores', ignoring the fact that every interview is different, and cannot be directly compared in this manner.

We do not recommend the use of simple rating scales as a developmental evaluation tool.

Written narrative feedback

Long-hand or abbreviated note style feedback is at the opposite end of the scale from the previous two methods. This method has significant drawbacks.

- It risks being purely subjective, with the added risk of interviewers 'word picking' on either seemingly positive or negative judgements, and missing other important feedback.
- It lacks the clarity and order of more formatted approaches that can be cross-referenced with areas of the interview model. Key points can be lost in the narrative.
- It is not time efficient.
- If prepared without reference to the particular context and circumstances of an interview, it can appear purist and unrealistic.

Narrative feedback can assist in providing the reader with contextual as well as factual data, eg in the form of accompanying diagrams, tables, or charts. However, the key drawback with this type of feedback is the lack of interaction that renders it much less effective as a medium for developmental evaluation.

Combined rating scale and narrative

This combines a score with an accompanying rationale. The format of the document organizes the feedback into defined areas that are easier for the interviewer to absorb, remember, and reflect upon. It is also a useful aide-mémoire to the person giving the feedback. Sheets completed at different times can be compared, enabling change in performance across time. Figure 12.3 shows an example of combined rating scale and narrative sheet.[8]

This type of document is appropriate for a training environment as it can be tailored to the specified competencies. Its effectiveness for a performance management meeting is limited because the scale is linked to a standard—or comparison with other interviewers—as opposed to reflecting the actual dynamics of the interview selected for evaluation. In addition, feedback provided in this manner tends to encourage interviewers to focus on the scores rather than the actual behaviour that gave rise to the score.

Appropriate performance evaluation

The person working with the interviewer is there to fulfil the role of a *coach*. The role of the coach is to help the individual to perform to his or her best, not judging the individual's performance from a perfectionist perspective. Therefore the coach must wherever possible refrain from directive feedback and not sound like a doctor diagnosing an ailment. The aim is to guide the interviewer, wherever possible, to self-identify behaviours that are areas of strength and areas requiring reflection with a view to improvement.

---

[8] Our thanks to Sussex Police (UK) for allowing the reproduction of these training materials.

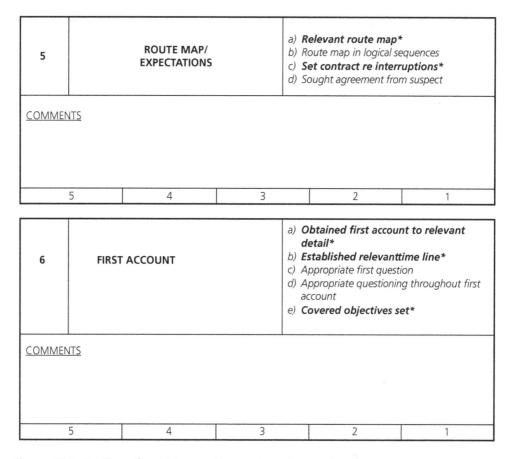

5	ROUTE MAP/ EXPECTATIONS	a) *Relevant route map** b) Route map in logical sequences c) *Set contract re interruptions** d) Sought agreement from suspect
COMMENTS		

5	4	3	2	1

6	FIRST ACCOUNT	a) *Obtained first account to relevant detail** b) *Established relevanttime line** c) Appropriate first question d) Appropriate questioning throughout first account e) *Covered objectives set**
COMMENTS		

5	4	3	2	1

Figure 12.3 Section of combined rating scale and narrative sheet

Placing the interviewer at the centre of the process empowers the interviewer to manage his or own development and increase technical efficiency. There will, of course, be areas where the coach will need to take a greater role and intervene to a greater extent, either correcting technical faults, or encouraging the interviewer to consider other areas in their self-reflection.

Remember, there is no such thing as the perfect interview in real life. Feedback, dependent on the skill level of the interviewer, may include significant development points, or a number of smaller issues.

Performance evaluation, as a planned activity, needs to be worthwhile and deliver a return for the investment of time. Sessions should adopt a two-level approach.

Macro level

This involves a 'top down' perspective on the selected interview. It generally includes attention to the stages of the interview, evaluating each in global terms.

The tools commonly used to assist a macro level evaluation include:

- the interview plan;
- WOB maps;
- a combined rating scale and narrative (more applicable in training);
- recording and/or transcript (also applicable at micro level);
- real time SE3R (also applicable at micro level).

Micro level

The amount and reliability of information obtained in an interview are directly correlated to two essential areas of skills that are central to any developmental evaluation.

- Skill in asking appropriate and productive questions.
- Skill in selecting and covering relevant subject matter.

Skill in these two areas, coupled with observance of relevant legal, regulatory, or similar protocols, are the defining qualities or the key components of a competent performance. They can be visually portrayed (Figure 12.4).

$$(\text{Question use} \times \text{subject choice}) + \text{Legal compliance} = \text{INTERVIEWER SKILL}$$
$$\text{All phases of interview}$$

Figure 12.4 Key components of investigative interview

Evaluation of these areas at a micro level necessitates accuracy and attention to detail. Therefore use of interview products as basic tools is essential.

Interview transcript

If there is a transcript, this can be a useful aid to navigating around the recording of the interview. It can also be annotated with alternative ways of doing things.

A statement derived from a witness interview, in the absence of a recording, is less useful but does enable the identification of areas that could have been questioned in more detail and areas that were not covered.

The recording of the interview is extremely valuable since it is evidence of what actually happened, of what topics were covered, of what questions were or were not asked, in what way, and of the interviewer's response to interviewee's disclosures.

Interview recording

This can be replayed and particular questions examined and discussed. Where there are topic transition times (TTTs) or there was electronic tagging (bookmarking) this greatly assists navigation of the recording.

As well as these basic tools, other bespoke tools are valuable in this process.

SE3R

SE3R is explained in Chapter 6. If a real time SE3R is created during the interview, this assists in navigating around the recording and examining the question and the response that gave rise to the entry in the SE3R.

12.8 Griffiths Question Map (GQM)

In this section we introduce and describe an innovative tool that has been designed to capture and evaluate two core indicators of interviewer skill—questioning and topic coverage. Further information is given in the reference section.

12.8.1 Rationale

Conventional methods of question type frequency analysis do not offer the ability to improve officers' practical questioning ability other than by reference to techniques previously excluded by the courts, ie *what not to do*. Neither the courts nor the academic world have proved particularly useful in *improving* the practical interview ability of police officers in real life situations. Apart from providing an abundance of information that quantifies what is wrong with officers' technique, there has been little to assist officers to improve practically.

Performance in a practical environment is more than demonstrating the ability to follow theoretical models outside of a training course, or simply achieving legal compliance in real life interviews. Practical effectiveness is demonstrated by the successful adaptation of theoretical concepts into varying real life situations, and requires the ability to translate knowledge into practical application. Evidenced feedback supported by reliable yet pragmatic analysis is a key tool in this aspect of evaluation.

12.8.2 Questioning

Well-established theory governs a hierarchy of question types across productive to counterproductive categories (see Chapters 8 and 9). However, it is possible to conduct an interview asking appropriately worded productive questions, but for that interview to still be ineffective, due to the point made in the previous paragraph Ineffective questioning arises where questions are not used appropriately, ie with due consideration to the interviewee's circumstances such as reluctance, resistance, or developmental disability.

Effective practical questioning occurs when the various productive question types are worded, sequenced, and combined appropriately in order to obtain, negate, confirm, or corroborate an account.

The evaluation of effective questioning requires a method that goes beyond the standard academic approach of frequency, scoring the different question types as they occur in an interview as a measure of interview quality (see Figure 12.5 below).

The shortcoming of this approach is that while it does show how many productive or unproductive questions occurred in this interview, it does not assist with where in the interview these occurred (eg earlier/later in the interview or throughout), or why this might be happening (eg particular subjects or phases). Therefore, frequency scoring of question types as an evaluation tool is inadequate on all but the most basic of levels.

12.8.3 Topic coverage

Interviewers must enquire beyond the points to prove and defences to a particular offence, and cover all relevant topics, in order to obtain both information and evidence. However, topics within an interview will have varying degrees of importance, and need to be prioritized accordingly.

For example, if an interviewer extensively probes an account provided by a murder suspect that he struck out with a knife in self-defence, in an attempt to reconcile this with post mortem evidence that the deceased suffered one deep stab wound in his side, then this would be effective and appropriate. However, if an interviewer spends 10 minutes of an interview asking questions to obtain a detailed description of an individual, where that individual is already identified or of peripheral interest, then this would be ineffective.

Question Type/Area	Topic 1	Topic 2	Topic 3
Open	4	5	5
Probing	13	9	8
Closed Yes/No	3	1	0
Leading	2	0	0
Force Choice	3	1	1
Multiple	1	4	0
Opinion	0	0	0
TOTAL	26	20	14

Figure 12.5 Frequency of question types across three topics of an interview

Consider the following very simple example.

> The interviewee is being questioned about an allegation that he assaulted another motorist in an empty car park, after an initial altercation at a set of traffic lights two streets away. It is known that the interviewee made a call to his employer immediately after the incident.

Basic consideration of this interview identifies four topics. These are shown in Box 12.2.

Topic 1	Topic 2	Topic 3	Topic 4
Journey from home	Argument at traffic lights	Fight in car park	Telephone call to employer

Box 12.2 Topics selected for interview coverage

These topics cover the basic timeline of the incident, including the period before, the initial incident, the actual assault (the crime?), and contact with the suspect's employer. However, the individual topics have varying degrees of importance.

Although Topic 3 (T3) relates to the physical contact, it is T2 and T4 that could both potentially reveal key information. Many interviewers would focus extensively on T3, because it covers the moment where the alleged crime occurred.

However, in a case like this, with non-fatal injuries, no likelihood of expert medical evidence to support or negate blame on either party, and no witnesses (remember, the car park was empty), this area of questioning is unlikely to produce conclusive evidence. T2 and T4, conversely, could provide valuable information. T2, if probed effectively, could produce additional information, for example the exact location, allowing a search for CCTV or independent witnesses. T4 may contain relevant statements made to the first person the suspect spoke to after the incident. However, it is not possible to tell from the simple table records the topics covered to evaluate the interviewer's approach and how effective their topic coverage was.

It follows, therefore, that evaluation of topic coverage must extend beyond a list of the subjects that the interviewer questions about, and must include the prioritization and depth of interest.

12.8.4 GQM defining features

The GQM can be applied to a live interview, electronic recording, or transcript of an interview. When completed the GQM displays:

- the complete chronology and frequency of question usage across an interview;
- all details of topic choice and coverage;
- the relationship between these aspects.

The design and simplicity of the GQM are distinct attributes.

- It captures the questioning used by an interviewer, in a unique graphic map-like form (Figure 12.6).
- It displays the sequencing and types of question employed by the interviewer using pragmatically defined productive and counter-productive question types.
- It records the subject matter and duration of the topics covered (Figure 12.7).
- It can be cross-referenced with other interview documents such as SE3R, the interview plan WOB, or the I³ WOB.
- It categorizes both effective and ineffective interview strategies.

- It holds demographic information for identification of individual interviews, and thematic or personal comparison.
- It is both intuitive and logical to use by those with an understanding of investigative interviewing.
- It can be used across all or part of an interview, as desired, in either training or real life environments.
- It is easy to interpret with a minimum of instruction and allows quick and practical evaluation of both product and performance.
- It is applicable in any language.

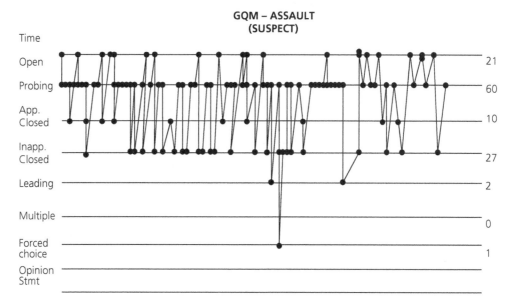

Figure 12.6 Question map segment of GQM showing series of questions plotted across time

Account – 10m	T1 – relationship with wife – 8m	T2 – argument on 2nd May – 5m	T3 – argument on 3rd May – 6m	T4 – fight on 3rd May – 8m
T5 – hospital attendance – 5m	T6 – arrest – 2m			

Figure 12.7 Topic segment of GQM showing account and six topics

12.8.5 Steps

The GQM can be completed 'live' as an interview progresses, or post-interview using the interview product, either recording or transcript. In both contexts the operator:

- needs to fulfil this one task, ie not be expected to fulfil another parallel task;
- should not be subject to distractions.

In paper form, the operator needs to equip him or herself with a supply of blank GQMs, at least one pen, and a ruler.

- Once the interview commences, and proceeds beyond the introductions, the operator notes the various topics by brief title, as introduced by the interviewer, and their time duration (the Route Map can serve as a useful guide as to what is coming at the start of the interview).

- During each identified topic, the operator then plots each question as per the agreed definition (see Reference Section for full explanation) and marks the GQM question area with a line denoting the start and completion of each topic.
- Irrelevant speech (eg about meal breaks, comments from any third party present) is not included and should be marked with a symbol to denote the use of time.

As the interview progresses, the map of questions and topic progression develops, producing a reference map of all topics and questions asked during the interview.

12.8.6 Giving feedback

The GQM is an extremely effective tool for giving feedback.

Question strategy

- What combination of questions did the interviewer adopt?
- Did the interviewer use productive questions throughout?
- How effective was that questioning?
- Did the interviewer tailor the questioning style to the circumstances?
- Did the interviewer consider the interviewee in their questioning?
- What learning is there for the interviewer?

Topic coverage

- What topics were covered?
- How were those topics prioritized?
- How did this compare to the interview plan?
- Was the interviewee's account examined effectively?
- What learning is there for the interviewer?

12.8.7 GQM example analysis

This section provides an example of the application of this type of analysis to a real life murder case as part of an organizational review by New Zealand police.[9] Figure 12.8 shows the question and topic selection of an interview with a suspect in this case, completed from a written transcript of the interview, from which times were noted.

It is with one of four suspects, alleged to have been involved in a burglary that resulted in the rape and subsequent fatal shooting of a woman. The interviewee, not legally represented, has admitted going to the house to steal a gun, prior to interview, but is alleging that the main offender acted alone when he assaulted then shot the victim. The aim of this interview is to obtain and test that account, in order to establish any culpability for the more serious offences.

Question style

This interview lasted 1 hour 44 minutes (104m) and contains 143 questions (94 productive; 49 unproductive). The questioning is random and unstructured, with frequent use of unproductive questions. The majority of unproductive questions were either 'yes'/'no' or leading. The interviewee was compliant, wanting to put forward his account, and so

---

[9] Schollum, M. (2005) *Investigative Interviewing—The Recommendations*. Wellington: Police National Headquarters.

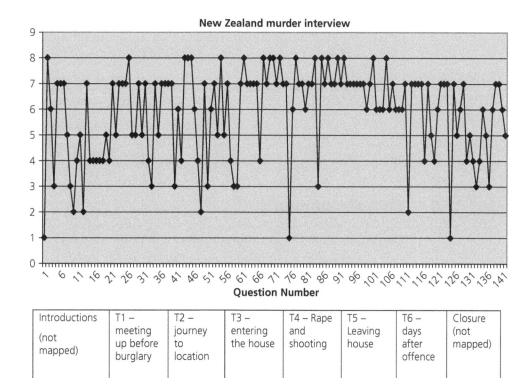

New Zealand murder interview

Introductions (not mapped)	T1 – meeting up before burglary	T2 – journey to location	T3 – entering the house	T4 – Rape and shooting	T5 – Leaving house	T6 – days after offence	Closure (not mapped)
6m	15m	18m	20m	13m	9m	15m	8m

Figure 12.8 New Zealand GQM interview analysis

responded to the majority of questions with an answer that exhibited apparent co-operation, but the interviewer frequently followed an open question with either a closed 'yes'/'no' or leading question using assumed knowledge from the crime scene, limiting the amount of detail obtained by the interviewer and compromising the aim of the interview.

For example, after being asked, *Tell me about the 'firearms and stuff'?* the interviewee replies *We were just gonna have a look around in the house for firearms.* The interviewer then asks *Yeah, alrighty, um, okay, so, you thought that you'd go through the house for firearms first, is that right?* The interviewee rejects this, by saying *Oh, not me, it was ******'s decision.* The difference in who was the originator of the idea is critical to the overall culpability of this interviewee.

The apparent co-operation of the interviewee was an opportunity to ask open questions and save cognitive capacity for active listening and probing key topics later in interview (see the Reference Section for an example of this approach). However, it appeared that the interviewer saw this co-operation as a reason to seek confirmation of points rather than an objective examination.

Topic selection

This crime involved four suspects so obtaining and comparing their accounts is important in solving this crime. The topics covered followed a chronological theme and did reflect the offence timeline. This was acceptable as a basic approach. However, there were key topics that required prioritization. Given the circumstances and the suspect's stance, the amount of time spent on T4 was insufficient, especially when compared to T2 and T6. In addition, there was no dedicated topic relating to the interviewee's relationship with ******, vital where duress has been put forward as a defence to the rape and murder. Box 12.3 shows a summary of feedback points.

Areas of strength	Development needs identified
Some use of productive questions	Knowledge of productive question types
Covered timeline chronologically	Application of appropriate question sequences
	Interview preparation—identification of relevant topics
	Interview planning—prioritization of key topics

Box 12.3 Summary of feedback points in murder interview

12.9   Chapter summary

The ACCESS model of investigation locates evaluation as a key step in a problem-solving cycle. Its outcome is placed in context (surveyed), expressed in a more condensed form (summarized), and becomes part of the totality of material available for assessment—the antecedent to further action planning and investigation effort. Evaluation is currently the least attended to stage of the PEACE model. If PEACE was conceived not as a linear model but as a problem-solving cycle, like ACCESS, those learning the model and applying it in the workplace would better understand the link between evaluation and planning and preparation, and perhaps see the advantage in taking time to evaluate (Figure 12.9).

PEACE arguably asks too much when it says the interviewer should examine the interview from an investigation perspective and from a personal performance perspective. We advocate immediate post-interview evaluation that focuses solely on the output and its impact upon the investigation, with attention to performance only in cases of unacceptable behaviour by the interviewee. In contrast to investigation-focused evaluation, the institution must create the working conditions to ensure there are regular planned events to focus on performance and which:

- are aimed at developing practice;
- involve the practitioner in self-reflection;
- involve a trainer or in the workplace a supervisor ready, willing, and able to facilitate reflection and to formulate a development plan.

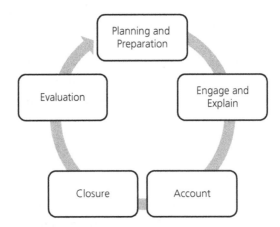

Figure 12.9 Circular PEACE model

Applications

Interviewing the Witness: Key Considerations

13.1 Chapter overview

This chapter starts by considering the many categories of witness: ranging from those who need specialist interviewing through to the majority interviewed outside police locations. We examine how you can reduce the risks posed by case knowledge, and plan effectively for an interview in which you will prepare the witness to disclose in detail, probe the history of the witness's disclosures, and, where applicable, probe mindful of the *Turnbull* criteria.

13.1.1 Chapter objectives

This chapter will enable you to:

- appreciate the different categories of witness and the form of interview each requires;
- reduce the risks of prior case knowledge;
- appreciate common ingredients in a witness strategy or plan;
- question appropriately on the history of the witness's disclosures;
- apply the ADVOKATE checks.

13.1.2 Interview maps

Figure 13.1 and Figure 13.2 (pp 304–7) show the maps for a standard memory assistance interview and a full memory assistance interview.

13.2 The different categories of witness

13.2.1 The victim–witness distinction

The *Code of Practice for Victims of Crime*[1] defines victims who have suffered the effects of crime and witnesses who give evidence in court. Not all victims are witnesses and not all witnesses are victims.

13.2.2 Vulnerable and intimidated witnesses

Vulnerable Witnesses: A Police Service Guide[2] provides definitions of both categories of witness.

Vulnerable witnesses

Under section 16 of the Youth Justice and Criminal Evidence Act 1991 (as amended by the Coroners and Justice Act 2009) vulnerable witnesses are:

- all child witnesses under 18;
- any witness whose quality of evidence is likely to be diminished because:
  — they have a significant impairment of intelligence or social functioning, ie are learning disabled;
  — they have a physical disability or suffer from a physical disorder;
  — they suffer from a mental disorder as defined by the Mental Health Act 1983.

---

[1] Home Office (2005) *Code of Practice for Victims of Crime*. London: Home Office.
[2] Ministry of Justice (2011) *Vulnerable Witnesses: A Police Service Guide* available at <http://www.justice.gov.uk>.

All these need *special care interviewing*: interviewing that is mindful and takes account of their specific disadvantage. This text identifies *developmental disadvantage* as the common theme that unites:

- children;
- children with a learning disability;
- adult witnesses who are learning disabled;
- children and the learning disabled with a communication disorder;
- adults who are dementing.

These are the vulnerable witnesses with whom you will most frequently work. Chapter 14 examines factors that you need to consider when interviewing the developmentally disadvantaged. Chapter 15 looks at particular aspects of the interview process.

Intimidated witnesses

Under section 17 of the Youth Justice and Criminal Evidence Act 1999 (as amended) intimidated witnesses are witnesses who are vulnerable because the quality of their testimony is likely to be diminished by reason of fear or distress, through:

- the nature and alleged circumstances of the offence;
- the age of the witness, for example those that are elderly or frail;
- where relevant:
  — the social and cultural background and ethnic origins of the witness;
  — their domestic and employment circumstances;
  — any religious beliefs or political opinions;
- any behaviour towards the witness by:
  — the accused;
  — members of the accused's family or associates;
  — any person likely to be the accused or witness to proceedings.

In addition, complainants to certain sexual offences and all witnesses to gang and gun crime are automatically defined as intimidated—unless they opt out.

Other witnesses that may be regarded as intimidated are victims and witnesses in cases of domestic violence or hate crime. The *Code of Practice for Victims of Crime*[3] has added the families of homicide victims to the definition of intimidated witnesses.

13.2.3 Significant witnesses

Also referred to as 'key' witnesses, significant witnesses are individuals:

- who witnessed an indictable or triable either way offence, or part of this, or events closely connected to it—but are unlikely to have their video-recorded interview admitted as evidence-in-chief;
- who stand in a particular relationship to the victim or who have a central position in the investigation into an indictable offence;
- who are adults alleging abuse in their childhoods who do not meet the criteria to be considered an intimidated witness.[4]

---

[3] Office for Criminal Justice Reform (2005) *Code of Practice for Victims of Crime*. London: Home Office.
[4] Ministry of Justice (2011) *Achieving Best Evidence in Criminal Proceedings: Guidance on Interviewing Victims and Witnesses, and Guidance on Using Special Measures*. London: HMSO.

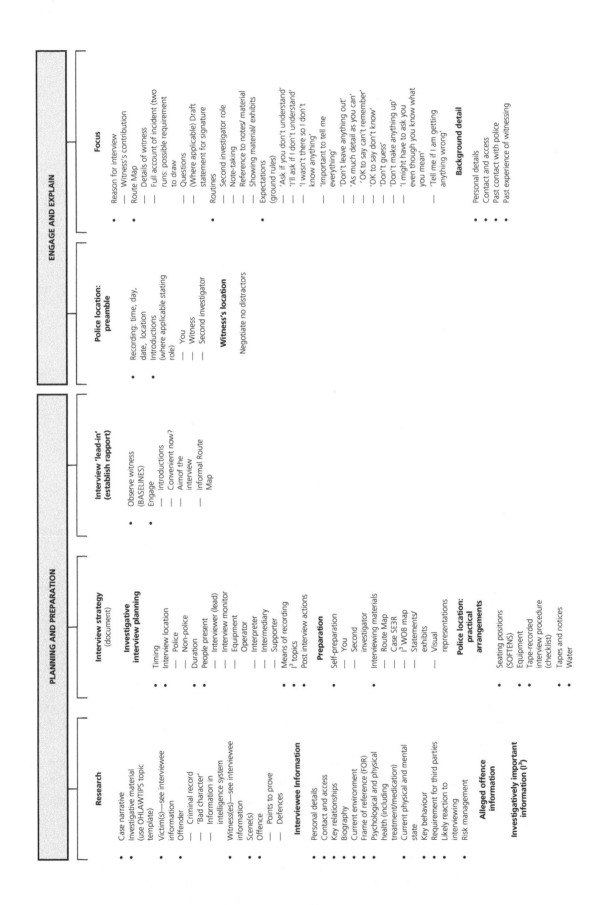

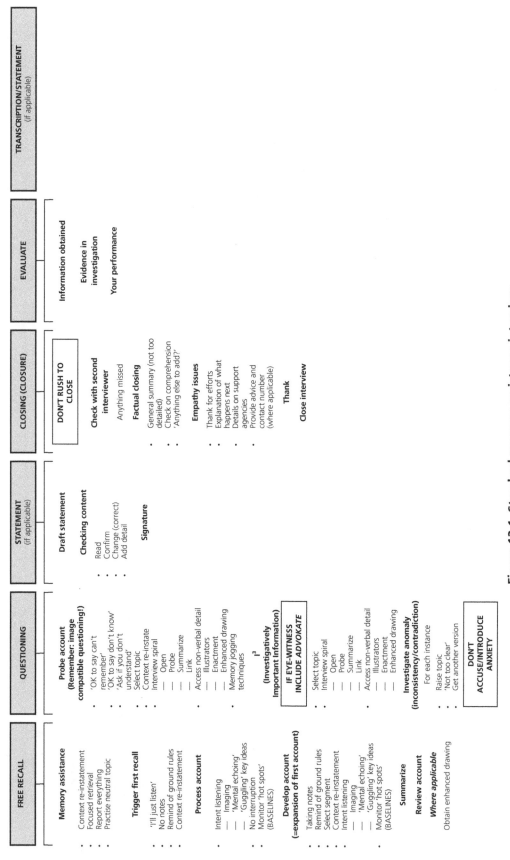

Figure 13.1 Standard memory assistance interview

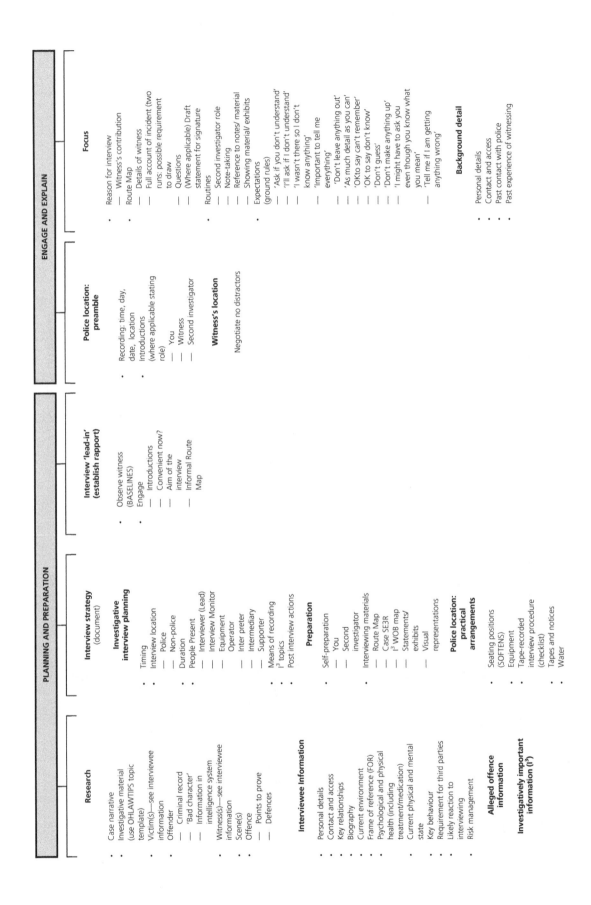

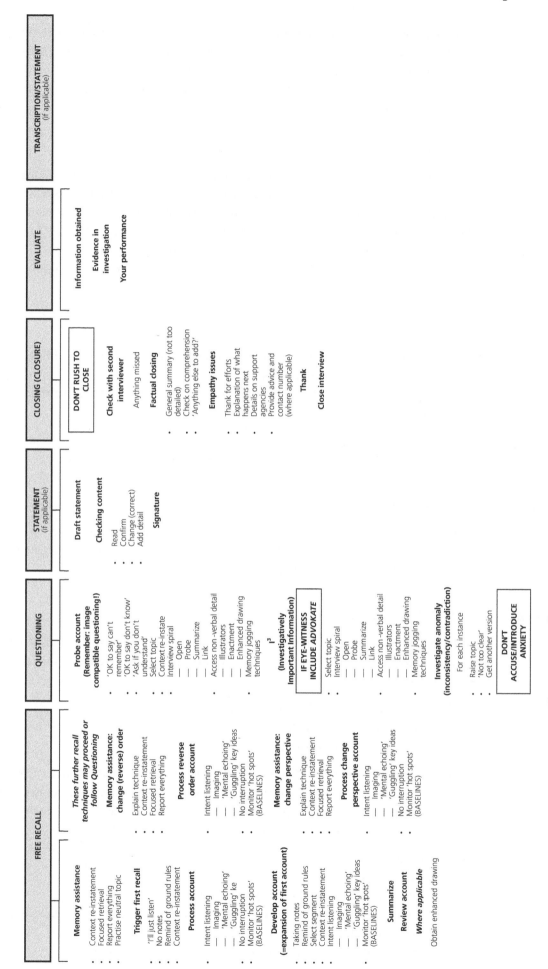

Figure 13.2 Full memory assistance (enhanced cognitive) interview

The purpose of recording the interviews of significant witnesses is to demonstrate that the interviewing was properly conducted. Again, where there are many such witnesses the SIO may decide on resource grounds to restrict video-recording of interviews.

Where the interview has been recorded, there are two options for turning the witness's account into evidence.

Option 1

- As soon as possible after the interview the witness makes a brief section 9 Criminal Justice Act 1967 statement confirming that what he or she said in the interview is an accurate account of his or her evidence. The statement should not include the detail of what he or she said, because this is in the transcript.
- A transcript of the interview is prepared and checked for accuracy.
- The section 9 statement and the transcript constitute the evidence. The recording is 'unused material'.

Option 2

- Using the recording, a full Criminal Justice Act statement is prepared. The witness is not required to be present when this is done.
- The statement is treated in the traditional manner, ie the witness checks the statement, makes alterations and additions, and signs.
- The statement is the evidence. The recording is 'unused material'.

The Association of Chief Police Officers have stated that Option 2 will be used.

13.2.4 The generality of witnesses to crime

The majority of witnesses of crime will not fall into any of the categories described. Currently their interviews are not recorded and culminate in the drafting of a statement for checking, alteration, addition, and signature.

13.2.5 Reluctant witnesses

The reluctant witness is reluctant to become involved in the investigative process. A reluctant witness could be in any of the preceding categories of witness. Possible reasons for this reluctance include:

- adverse perceptions of the police or the justice process;
- concern about the response of others;
- concern about their identity being revealed.

The witness should be interviewed to create the conditions for an informed choice whether to become involved in the investigative process. The interview record can be either notes or electronic (audio or video) recording. No pressure should be placed on the individual, with the interview following a relationship building/informing process.

- Establish rapport.
- Establish the reasons for the reluctance.
- Outline the offence, withholding details of the allegation.
- Outline reason for believing that the individual is a witness, withholding details of what is alleged to have been witnessed.
- Obtain the witness's decision in the light of what has been explained.

13.2.6 Hostile witnesses

The hostile witness is opposed to the investigative process. The reasons for this could be, eg, his or her lifestyle, a close link to the alleged offender, or an intention to be a defence witness. Such witnesses may refuse to co-operate or, if they allow themselves to be interviewed, may give false information.

If the individual does agree to be interviewed, the interview must be recorded, on video, unless he or she objects.

13.3 Prior case knowledge

13.3.1 The threat to the witness's disclosures

You are very aware of the threat posed by prior case knowledge to the integrity of any witness's account and responses through:

- relevance filtering;
- excessive editing;
- confirmation bias;
- contamination.

You can take a number of precautions to ensure that you do not put the integrity of the witness's disclosures at risk.

- You only have the minimal amount of case knowledge.
- Where there are two or more witnesses you only interview one, and remain in the dark as to what the others have disclosed.
- If you interview the victim you do not interview the suspect.

It is not a perfect world. You will therefore find yourself in contexts where these eminently sensible precautions cannot be fulfilled either partially or at all.

13.3.2 The compromise

Research the witness

The actual breadth—scope—of your research and depth—degree of detail you seek—will be determined by the nature of the offence, available resource (especially time and investigative capability), and the availability of sources of information. Box 13.1 gives an illustrative, not exhaustive, range of research areas in respect of an adult witness. You will find other illustrative checklists for child witnesses in *Vulnerable Witnesses* and *Achieving Best Evidence* (ABE).

Such research is essential to interview planning, and provides you with the awareness that will enable rapid fostering of a working relationship.

Wherever possible you should restrict yourself to your awareness of what this witness, other witnesses, and the suspect have said. This should always apply when you are interviewing a vulnerable or significant witness.

If the plan is to conduct a cognitive interview of the witness you should:

- know the chronology of his or her disclosing, ie at what points he or she has given accounts, been formally interviewed, made statements;
- not know what he or she said in any prior account;
- in the Explanation stage, be able to say with absolute honesty that you do not have any knowledge of what he or she has said to others.

Personal details
- Name and preferred name.
- Age.
- Gender.
- Sexuality (relevant if the offence has a bearing upon this, eg homophobic crime).
- Race, ethnicity, culture.
- First language.
- Employment.
- Communication disability/disorder.
- Information from crime/intelligence databases.

Contact and access
- Contact details: address (home/employment); telephone numbers.
- Availability/accessibility.
- Restrictions on mobility.

Key relationships
- Relationship/link with alleged offender.
- Family.
- Friends/associates.

Biography
- Significant stressors, eg loss of significant relationships (through such events as bereavement, family break-up, separation and divorce, imprisonment); hospitalization.
- History of contact with social services and police.

Current environment
- Current lifestyle.
- Social support, eg family and non-family relationships, friends, acquaintances, and position within the home and non-home context, links to community including ethnic and religious groups.
- Care and living arrangements—including safety.
- Sources of stress, eg micro stressors (continuing sources of stress including financial situation, family problems, relationship problems—infidelity, continuing arguments, and violence—and sources of threat and fear) and significant life stress events occurring over the past year.

Frame of reference (FOR)
- Strong feelings, attitudes, beliefs, values, prejudices.
- Expectations particularly of other people, communicated needs.
- Sense of shame, guilt, remorse.

Psychological and physical
- Illiteracy.
- Level of intellectual functioning.
- Psychological problems—diagnosed and treated.
- Disposition to acquiesce, compliance and suggestibility.
- Personality.

Current physical and mental state
- Ill-health.
- Injuries and wounds.
- Continued effects of ingested recreational drugs, including alcohol.
- Medication/treatment and its effects.
- Counselling/therapy.
- Degree of fatigue.
- Lack of sleep.
- Emotional state, eg degree of apprehension, fear, dread.
- Evidence of extreme anxiety/extreme depression.
- Distractibility due to external concerns, worry, substance dependency, pain.

Key behaviour
- Social behaviour when interacting eg level of social skill, degree of assertiveness, emotional responsiveness, tendency to explosive behaviour, reaction to authority.

Box 13.1 Researching the witness

- Coping behaviour and marked changes in this when under stress: 'acting out', attention seeking, anger, verbal abuse, destructiveness, violence, self-harm, suicidal thoughts, suicidal gestures, attempted suicide, depressive reactions, addictive behaviours, substance abuse, excessive sexual activity.

Requirement for third parties

Where applicable:
- Interpreter.
- Intermediary.
- Supporter/carer.

Likely reaction to interviewing
- Co-operative.
- Reluctant.
- Hostile.

Risk management
- Risk attending witness's location v. witness attending police station.
- Requirement for second officer/backup.

Box 13.1 Researching the witness (*continued*)

Research the alleged offence

Wherever possible, you should restrict your knowledge of the alleged offence to, eg:

- the type of offence;
- the approximate time and location of the offence;
- the scene of the offence—enough to enable you to comprehend what the witness is talking about;
- how the offence came to attention.

Investigatively important information (I³)

You should have a detailed understanding of all the required I³ issues. The topic templates in Chapter 6 provide a good framework for identifying these. *Vulnerable Adult and Child Witnesses*[5] and ABE[6] provide illustrative I³ issues in the context of interviewing a child witness.

In the case of the ADVOKATE checklist of descriptive detail:

- plot a grid of all disclosures on each element;
- create a blank final column, enabling you to drop detail into this in the interview.

Where there is detail from more than one source, eg the witness's first description at the scene, and notes taken down later by an officer, you need to look for error or an inconsistency and contradiction.

13.4 Interview planning

13.4.1 Interview strategy or interview plan?

An *interview strategy* is a 'higher' level plan that places the interview of this individual, or all interviewing, in the context of the overall investigation.

---

[5] Smith, K. and Tilney, S. (2007) *Vulnerable Adult and Child Witnesses*. Oxford: Oxford University Press.

[6] Ministry of Justice (2011) *Achieving Best Evidence in Criminal Proceedings: Guidance on Interviewing Victims and Witnesses, and Guidance on Using Special Measures*. London: HMSO.

As a general yardstick, interview strategy creation is a requirement in any investigation that has any degree of seriousness or complexity and involves team working, including external advisers and agencies, and is headed by an SIO. It is essential to construct and to apply a tailored, 'one-off' strategy for any vulnerable, intimidated, or significant witness—particularly if traumatized.

If you are investigating an offence of intermediate or lower level of seriousness and/or complexity—particularly if you are working alone—your interview plan is all that is necessary.

13.4.2 The content of your interview strategy/plan

The aims of any interview strategy and interview plan converge in considering factors to:

- maximize the amount of information disclosed, consciously and unconsciously, in the interview;
- enhance the investigative and evidential potential of this information.

Both need to specify practicalities.

- Behaviour outside and within the interview location.
- Contrast factors, eg age, gender, ethnicity, dress.
- Layout of the interview location, ie relative seating position—orientation and management of personal space.
- Time and duration of interview.
- Form of address.
- Overcoming barriers to communication and comprehension: working with an interpreter and/or intermediary.
- I^3 topics.
- Considered selection of, reference to, and showing of information and evidence during the interview.

Where the interview is likely to be held in a non-police location, eg the witness's home, your planning must include:

- a risk assessment of attending the location;
- provision for a second officer/backup.

13.5 The interview aim

You interview aim will very often be to obtain a free recall account: as detailed as possible narrative of 'what happened'.

However, in some instances you will not want a narrative. You have to be flexible and act according to the requirements of the investigation. For example, in, say, a fraud investigation, if the witness and the suspect are known to each other and work together in joint positions of trust, your Route Map topics might be the witness's knowledge of the suspect and the manner in which they work together, rather than remembrance of an event.

13.6 Practise context reinstatement and recalling in detail

Many witnesses will be bemused by your request to reinstate the context of their offence-related experience. Some will be puzzled and may even be anxious about what you are asking them to do or about their ability to 'do well' at the task. Furthermore, the theme throughout this text is that in everyday life people do not disclose in detail to 'powerful people'. They are unused to being asked, or allowed, to tell in detail. Some have extremely limited experience in ever disclosing in detail, either being denied the opportunity or through the constraints imposed by their personality, eg extreme introversion, extreme timidity, poor expressive ability.

You should reinforce just how different this encounter is by setting the witness up to succeed: giving him or her the opportunity to practise context reinstatement, focused retrieval, and describing in detail. It will add time to the interview but it will repay handsomely in terms of the quantity and quality of disclosed detail, and the evidential value of the individual's contribution. The common aim is to give practice by remembering and describing a neutral topic. Experience shows that using a recent episode, preferably hours prior to the interview, means that the witness has a greater chance of remembering and telling more. This is the aim: to get him or her to think back and tell you lots.

- Identify a timeframe, eg the individual's movements today or yesterday.
- Select an episode from this timeframe.
- Identify a start point and an end point
- Brief for a practice run at retrieving and reporting detail on this episode.
- Trigger recall.

For example:

> *I think it would be helpful if you had a practice at remembering detail and telling me everything that you have in your mind.*
>
> *I'd like you to take yourself back to* [state a point in time = start point] *Now concentrate really hard. ^^ ^^ I'd like you to tell me every little bit of detail that you remember. ^^ ^^ Tell me everything that's in your mind's eye. ^^ ^^ What you see, ^^ ^^ what you hear, ^^ ^^ what you smell, ^^ ^^ what you touch, ^^ ^^ what thoughts were going through your mind, ^^ ^^ what you're feeling ^^ ^^ even how you felt physically. Don't hold back on telling me detail. ^^ ^^ Don't hold back detail that strikes you as obvious. ^^ ^^ Don't hold back detail that you think anyone would know. ^^ ^^ Don't hold back detail that you think I might already know. ^^ ^^ There can't be too much detail. ^^ ^^*
>
> *There's no rush. ^^ ^^ Take your time. ^^ ^^ Tell me everything that you remember from* [re-state the start point] *up to* [state end point] *^^ ^^*

13.7 Audibility

Audibility is the key issue that you need to consider when questioning an earwitness.

- The distance between the witness and the witnessed sound.
- The presence of obstacles and surfaces, eg walls, doors, and windows, between the witness and the source of the sound.
- The physical properties of the obstacle or surface and the effect on the audibility of the noise being described.
- The presence of background noises, and the levels of these, at the time of hearing the described sound.

13.8 The chain of disclosure

13.8.1 The need to know

The witness's account is akin to an item of evidence and raises the same issue of the chain of continuity. Every time he or she has spoken to someone, or been spoken to, about it this is akin to more than one hand holding the item. On each occasion the material is liable to be contaminated.

13.8.2 Lines of questioning

You need to know in as much detail as possible—reminding the witness of this:

- who the witness has spoken to—or attempted to speak to: when, where, how long, why;
- who has spoken to—or attempted to speak to—the witness: when, where, how long, why.

SE3R is well suited to capturing, probing, and checking back this detail.

- The Event Line is totally flexible. You drop each exchange into the requisite point in the narrative as it is actively recalled or comes to mind.
- You create knowledge bins for people and locations.

13.9 Inconsistency and contradiction

The development of PEACE introduced challenging into the Account stage. While many have viewed this as an issue that has to be considered when interviewing a suspect, there is understandably discomfort at the thought of challenging inconsistency and contradiction in a witness's disclosures.

In Chapter 15 the concerns about the negative connotations of challenging and relationship-destroying potential of a challenge are explained, particularly if not done adeptly. We recommend that in the case of suspect interviewing you consider conducting what is called a FAIR (Final Anomaly Investigation and Reasons to suspect). You can perform a similar anomaly investigation process with a witness whose account or responses are inconsistent or contradictory.

The investigation involves three steps for most witnesses, but for vulnerable witnesses only Step 1 and Step 2 apply.

- **Step 1.** Draw the witness's attention to things that are 'not quite clear'.
- **Step 2.** Use appropriate questioning that requires the suspect to take you through the detail again, without impugning the suspect's character, ie not telling him or her that you consider his or her response to be untruthful.
- **Step 3.** Allude to the existence of the anomaly without implying the witness is a liar and get a final version. Note, however, that you should not tell the witness that the versions don't fit or how many versions he or she has given.

For example:

> *I'm not too clear about the detail of what you did between [A] ^^ ^^ and [B]. ^^ ^^ I need to get my head round that. ^^ ^^ I'd like you to take me through that again ^^ ^^ in as much detail as possible ^^ ^^ taking your time. ^^ ^^*

When the inconsistency or contradiction endures or is added to:

> *You've taken me through more than once about what you did between [A] ^^ ^^ and [B]. ^^ ^^ Each time the detail doesn't marry up. ^^ ^^ So I want to be fair to you. ^^ ^^ I want you to think really hard ^^ ^^ really hard about what you did between [A] ^^ ^^ and [B]. Now I want you to take me through that ^^ ^^ for one last time ^^ ^^ in as much detail as possible ^^ ^^ taking your time. ^^ ^^*

13.10 Descriptions from eyewitnesses

13.10.1 The ADVOKATE checks

Eyewitnesses' descriptions of key individuals and events are of fundamental investigative importance. We see in Chapter 2 the factors which affect the registration of such crime-related detail. PEACE requires investigators to check through direct questioning the basis for descriptions from eyewitnesses. The framework for this questioning is the mnemonic ADVOKATE (Box 13.2). These are a series of checks that reflect the *Turnbull*[7] guidelines for assessing such witness testimony.

A	AMOUNT OF TIME UNDER OBSERVATION	How long did the witness have the person/incident in view?
D	Distance	What was the distance between the witness and the person/incident?
V	Visibility	What was the visibility at the time? Factors include time of day, street lighting.
O	Obstruction	Were there any obstructions to the view of the witness?
K	Known or seen before	Did the witness know, or had the witness ever seen, the person before? If so, where and when?
A	Any reason to remember	Did the witness have any special reason for remembering the person/incident? Was there something specific that made the person/incident memorable?
T	Time lapse	How long has elapsed since the witness saw the person/incident?
E	Error or material discrepancy	Are there any errors or material discrepancies between descriptions in the first and subsequent accounts of the witness?

Box 13.2 The ADVOKATE checks

Instances will occur when the witness only heard, and did not see, that which he or she is attempting to describe. They are earwitnesses. ADVOKATE must still be applied but with an auditory focus. For ease of reference, unless a specific point concerning auditory experience needs to be made, the term witness will be used to refer to eyewitnesses and earwitnesses.

13.10.2 Applying ADVOKATE

Aided vision and hearing

A significant proportion of the population has some form of visual impairment, requiring correction in the form of spectacles or contact lenses. Many do not know they are impaired. Of those that do, many for cosmetic reasons choose to limit the time, and occasions, when they wear spectacles. The implications are obvious. You have to ask the witness about these matters.

---

[7] *R v Turnbull* [1976] 63 Cr App R 132.

- Whether the individual has aided vision or hearing.
- If the answer is 'yes', whether the individual was wearing his or her spectacles or contact lenses (or hearing aid in the case of an earwitness) at the time he or she observed the individual or event.

Amount of time under observation

People are extremely poor at judging time and even poorer at estimating duration. Any estimate is extremely problematic and is unlikely to be accurate. This inability to give an accurate estimate is no justification for questioning the witness's reliability.

For certain individuals their experience at the time of the observation will have the potential to distort their judgement of duration. Chapter 2 points out that extreme emotion and fear for one's physical or sexual integrity, attention to means of escape, thoughts about what is being experienced, can profoundly affect the processes of attention and quality and amount of registered detail. This is why it is so essential not to edit or compress what the witness describes and why the total rationale of SE3R is to catch-it-all. Using SE3R will enable you to:

- capture all the disclosed experience, including 'commentary', ie the observations made by the witness about how he or she was feeling and the thoughts going through his or her head;
- make much more sense of what the witness is describing, and to understand how the effects of inner experience are likely to have distorted judgement of duration.

Distance

Whether they do not need visual aids or are wearing their spectacles or contact lenses, people are notoriously poor at judging distance. The same issues concerning the potentially distorting effect of the witness's experience at the time apply here.

Things are further complicated because people use seemingly precise terms such as *feet, yards,* and *metres,* often with great confidence. As always, you cannot assume that they mean the same as you when using these terms. Also, without being offensive, large numbers of police officers have poor distance judgement, never having been trained to do this, unlike, say, a soldier in the infantry. So these officers will be wholly unreliable. The only solution is to validate.

Wherever possible carry out some simple validating checks of the individual's ability to judge distance. On completion of the interview carry out simple validating checks outside the interview location, eg standing in a corridor, outside the house looking down the garden or across the road.

For example, where Mrs Cooper has said the man was 'about 15 feet away':

OK Mrs Cooper. ^^ ^^ *Because we all differ in our estimation of distances* ^^ ^^ *I just need to get some idea of the distance that you said the man was from you.* ^^ ^^ *We'll use the garden to help me on this.* ^^ ^^ *I'd like you to look down the garden.* ^^ ^^ *I'm now going to walk away from you slowly* ^^ *and I'd like you to tell me to stop* ^^ *when I reach the same distance that he was away from you.* ^^ ^^

Visibility

Be mindful of facts of life concerning constraints on visual performance.

Illumination

Vision at night is markedly reduced. Whilst movement continues to be detectable, actual detail is much harder to make out. The distance over which detail can be distinguished and people recognized reduces markedly. However, people are overconfident in their ability to see and to recognize despite these physical constraints.

In terms of recognition of an individual:

- At 30 feet/approximately 10 metres, a person is recognizable in bright moonlight.
- At 100 feet/approximately 30 metres, in good illumination, a person who is not well known to an observer is recognizable.
- At 150 feet/approximately 45 metres, in good illumination a person who is well known to an observer is recognizable.
- At 300 feet/approximately 90 metres, in good illumination, a person in distinctive clothing or with a distinctive manner, eg peculiar gait, is recognizable.

Colour perception

Colour vision is progressively affected as illumination reduces such that at night, in the absence of a light source, colours cannot be distinguished: only shades of lightness and darkness can be discriminated. What people report in terms of colour is internally driven by expectation, eg pupils of eyes which are seen in very low light or near darkness are reported as being dark brown. They are erroneously extrapolating colour from brightness.

It is also very important to bear in mind colour-blindness.

- Some three per cent of the population are colour-blind.
- They are overwhelmingly male, because colour blindness is carried on the male chromosome.

Obstruction

Chapter 9 recommends you to take the individual up a 'staircase' of non-verbal disclosure. This is particularly important when obtaining descriptions about obstruction.

- Obtain initial disclosure verbally at an appropriate point, eg following the first or second account.
- Request an initial illustration.
- At a later point in the interview request a further illustration. This constitutes a check on the validity of the earlier illustration.
- At a later point in the interview towards the closing stages engage in enhanced drawing. This is a validation check on the illustrators.

You can then validate these disclosures by:

- showing the witness a photocopy of a 'blown up' section from an A–Z or map (from whatever origin);
- inviting the witness to mark where he or she, and others to whom he or she referred were standing;
- where applicable and appropriate, after the interview validate the descriptions by examining the physical location.

Known or seen before and any reason to remember

Disclosed knowledge or acquaintance

You will need to probe this.

- Circumstances of knowledge/coming to attention.
- Relationship between person and witness.
- History of contact between person and witness.
- Quality of relationship between person and witness.

Basis for remembrance

You can extend the value of ADVOKATE by using the mnemonic—memory jogging—techniques described in Chapter 10. Bear in mind, as indicated in Chapter 2, the longer a facial image is in store the more likely it is to undergo change.

Time lapse

Chapter 2 points out that people tend to report action and activity happening much more recently than it did.

Error or material discrepancy

It is essential to be methodical. Deal with one inconsistency or contradiction at a time.

- Don't reveal that there is an inconsistency or contradiction.
- Explain the problem, eg:

  I'm not to clear about something. ^^ ^^ *Can I ask you to take me through* [spell out the general area of the description, not the 'problem' detail] *again?* ^^ ^^

13.11 Getting the witness to endorse your SE3R

Having checked back your SE3R with the witness:

- Place a dated one-liner concerning the truth and accuracy of the material at the top right or top left of each sheet.
- Get the person to sign.
- Take the SE3R away and translate the wealth of material into a high quality statement that the individual will sign.

13.12 Statement drafting and signature

If there is a need to obtain a statement, do a time appreciation. If the interviewing has lasted more than 40 minutes take appropriate action.

- Stop interviewing and take a natural break.
- Consider drafting the statement at the police station and returning later for this to be signed by the witness.

If a later return is not possible, eg detention clock issues leading the OIC to want a statement now, use your SE3R to assist you in drafting a statement—following your particular force's guidelines as to statement format.

13.3 Chapter summary

Prior to the introduction of PEACE little thought was given the diversity of witnesses, their vulnerabilities, and how to interview them to enable them to give best evidence. As the number of categories has grown so have the factors that you and others have to take into consideration: when researching and planning, and establishing the history of their disclosing and the evidence of their eyes and ears.

14

Interviewing the Developmentally Disadvantaged Witness: Key Considerations

14.1   Chapter overview

This chapter seeks to enhance your practice of interviewing developmentally disadvantaged witnesses by:

- examining barriers to disclosure by such witnesses;
- explaining how you can use this knowledge to help these witnesses to disclose as much detail as they can.

14.1.1   Chapter objectives

This chapter will enable you to:

- understand why awareness of the constraints on children—with or without learning disability—can inform your practice when interviewing developmentally disadvantaged adults;
- appreciate the problems confronting children when called upon to disclose detail;
- recognize the problems children confront us with when they disclose detail;
- know how to overcome barriers to disclosure.

14.2   Developmentally disadvantaged witnesses

14.2.1   Children

It is helpful to divide the generality of children into three groups.

- **Young children**. Those under school age.
- **Children**. Those aged between 5 and 7.
- **Older children**. Aged 7 and above.

When considering the child's ability to disclose, and to comprehend your attempts to facilitate his or her disclosure, age is only an initial benchmark.[1] Children, like adults, vary enormously. This is why you have to spend time on the process of orientation and assessment before you ever embark upon offence-related interviewing to arrive at an understanding of his or her actual or potential to disclose and to comprehend what you are driving at.[2] We consider some key issues in orientation and assessment in Chapter 15.

14.2.2   Children with learning disability

Children with learning disabilities are usually identified during the primary school years as having special educational needs.

- You need to adjust everything you say and do to accord with the degree of limitation that the child exhibits.
- The child needs more time to register, to handle information in working memory, and to put together a response.

---

[1] Aldridge, M. and Wood, J. (1998) *Interviewing Children: A Guide for Child Care and Forensic Practitioners*. Chichester: Wiley; Wilson, C. and Powell, M. (2001) *A Guide to Interviewing Children: Essential Skills for Counsellors, Police, Lawyers and Social Workers*. London: Routledge.

[2] Smith, K. and Tilney, S. (2007) *Vulnerable Witnesses*. Oxford: Oxford University Press.

• The duration of the interview should be shorter and interviewing may need to take place over more than one day because the mental demands on the child are greater and are cumulative.

14.2.3 Adult witnesses who are learning disabled or dementing

The challenges confronting children in disclosing their experience are in many ways qualitatively the same as those experienced by adults with learning disability and those who are suffering from dementia. Both are developmentally disadvantaged, although the origins of this are different. No offence is intended in making this observation. Nor is it to be taken that we should treat adults who are learning disabled or dementing as if they are children.

• Your RESPONSE behaviours should be exactly the same as for any adult you are relating to.
• You are bringing to bear your awareness of the difficulties of those who are developmentally disadvantaged due to young age to assist you and this individual to work together.

14.2.4 Children with communication impairments

All of the issues within this chapter apply, with the added requirement to be mindful of this child's means of communicating. There are very many communication options:

• British Sign Language (BSL).
• Blissymbolics.
• Braille.
• Chailey Communication System.
• Cued Speech.
• Deaf Blind Manual Alphabet.
• Fingerspelling (or standard manual alphabet).
• Lipreading.
• Makaton Language Programme.
• Mayer Johnson PCS Symbols.
• Moon.
• Objects of reference.
• Paget Gorman Signed Speech.
• Picture Exchange Communication System (PECS).
• Photographs.
• Rebus Symbols.
• Signalong.
• Signed English (SE)/Sign Supported English (SSE).
• Symbols.

The problem with communication boards (with symbols and pictures) is their limited vocabularies. It can be difficult to discuss certain topics. They can be augmented with other symbol systems and personalized.[3] Most particularly you will be required to:

• research the nature of the child's impairment—consulting with key figures on this;
• assess its actual or likely impact upon the child's potential to disclose;
• work closely with the interpreter/intermediary and carer on how you will work together when communicating with the individual prior to, during, and after each interview.

---

[3] Marchant, R. and Gordon, R. (2001) *Two-Way Street: Communicating with Disabled Children and Young People.* Leicester: NSPCC.

14.3 Problems confronting children when asked to disclose detail

Even very young children can disclose their experience very competently. However, what they say reflects that their minds are not developed. They do not see the world through the eyes of an adult. We have to be mindful of a child as the interviewing progresses from rapport, through the free recall phase, and subsequently to the questioning phase.

14.3.1 Processing information

Capacity and speed of processing

Children have much less efficient working memories than adults.[4]

- They do not cope with multiple ideas.
- A 5- to 7-year-old takes twice as much time to process information as an adult. A younger child requires even more time to think.

With each passing year, through to adolescence, capacity and speed of processing improve. For individuals with learning disability progress is slower and ceases earlier.

Language comprehension

Children are a different culture than adults. Among themselves, they think and talk about their world and their experiences in a completely different way to adults. 'Powerful people' talk a different language to children. Much of what adults say and how they say it is incomprehensible to the child with its limited language competency.[5]

Concrete thinking

Children are concrete thinkers.

- They interpret language very literally.
- They need concrete examples.

Box 14.1 explains some of the basic building blocks of language. For children, particularly young children, each of these blocks is a block in the sense of being a barrier to comprehension. Some blocks are considerable.

Verbs

Very difficult for children are *verbs* that have more than one meaning. A good yardstick of difficulty is how many meanings the verb has in the dictionary. Children also struggle with verbs that refer to mental or expressive processes. Examples of difficult verbs, many not fully understood until after 7 years of age, are:

- 'ask' and 'tell';
- 'explain', 'describe';
- 'know', 'think', 'guess';

---

[4] Baker-Ward, L. and Ornstein, P. (2002) 'Cognitive Underpinnings of Children's Testimony' in H. Westcott, G. Davies, and R. Bull (eds), *Children's Testimony: A Handbook of Psychological Research and Forensic Practice*. Chichester: Wiley.

[5] Walker. A. (1999) *Handbook on Questioning Children: A Linguistic Perspective*. Washington: American Bar Association.

Building Block	Definition	Examples
Adjective	A word or group of words describing a noun.	*nice, funny, green, older, smaller, five*
Adverb	A word or group of words describing an adjective, a verb, or another adverb.	*very, much, often, sometimes*
Conjunction	A word connecting words, phrases, and clauses.	*and, but, for, or, so, yet*
Interrogative	A word asking a question.	*Who? What? Where? When? How? Why? Whether?*
Noun	***Concrete noun***	
	A word naming what your senses can detect.	*mother, father, school, bedroom, camera*
	Abstract noun	
	A word naming something your five senses cannot experience.	*truth*
Preposition	A word indicating physical location and location in time.	*above, in, behind, at midnight, in the Spring, during the day*
Pronoun	A word replacing a noun.	*he, she, it, this, that, neither, either, another, each, any, anyone, anything*
Verb	***Action verb***	
	A word expressing something that a person, animal, force of nature, or thing can do.	*to play, to tell, to eat, to say*
	Linking verb	
	A word connecting the subject to additional information.	*to be, to seem* (confusingly some verbs can be action and linking depending on the sense, eg *to look, to feel*)

Box 14.1 Basic building blocks of language

- 'remember', 'forget';
- 'promise';
- 'make', 'let'.

Adjectives

Adjectives that have many meanings are very confusing for children, eg *big*.

Adverbs

Adults use these to add shades of meaning to verbs (eg *always*, *never*), and adjectives (eg *rather*, *really*). Nuance is lost on children still at the stage of concrete thinking.

Pronouns

Adults use pronouns (eg *he, she, it, this, that*) to refer back or forward to a noun. This saves time and effort, and avoids redundancy—repeating the noun again and again. Adults understand the pronoun and job that it is doing. Children have to develop this skill. Pronouns confuse them.

Prepositions

These are difficult concepts for children.

- They confuse prepositions that locate objects and people physically, eg *in* with *between*, *on* with *above*, *ahead* with *behind*.
- Location in time is very challenging. Awareness of time is a later aspect of development.

Interrogatives

Children's comprehension of interrogatives follows a developmental sequence:

- *what* is mastered earliest followed by *who*;
- *where*, *how*, and *why* are understood much later: before this they are commonly confused with *what* and each other; in due course children become sensitive to *why* used as a rebuke or accusation.

We shall return to problems with questions in a later section.

Children's comprehension: a health warning!

The basic building blocks of language are potential barriers to the child understanding what you are saying or what you mean. It is essential that you remain continuously aware of the health warning concerning children's comprehension: Box 14.2.

- Children, particularly young children, do not know that they do not understand what an adult is saying.
- Children know that adults want them to say *something*.
- They will say *anything* rather than *nothing*.
- Only exceptional, and older, children give adults feedback, ie *I don't understand*.
- You have to check comprehension.
- It is useless to ask *Do you understand?*
  — Get the child to tell you what he or she thinks you mean.
  — Continuously check across the course of the interview.

Box 14.2 Does this child understand me?

14.3.2 Retrieving information from memory

Children have sufficient ability to retrieve information from long-term memory to give an adequate account containing:

- core (central) rather than peripheral detail: though in Chapter 2 we learn that there are large individual differences in what people perceive as core detail;
- events experienced personally rather than as an observer.

All the evidence points to the fact that, when allowance is made for the individual's stage of development, he or she can give a valid and reliable account.

- We should be interviewing as soon as possible after the events that we want the child to tell us about.

- We must not have unrealistic or overly high expectations of the child. Inconsistency (later detail not fitting with earlier detail) and contradiction may occur, particularly with young children and the passage of time.

14.4 Problems children confront us with when they disclose detail

14.4.1 The *quantity-quality* problem with free narratives

Quantity

Children's free narratives are typically short and incomplete.

- Young children provide very little information compared to older children and adults.
- The amount of information increases with the age of the child.

Quality

Children do not know what information to include in a free narrative and struggle to organize the detail that they do include. As a result, their accounts are 'empty' of narrative detail, and can be difficult to grasp.

- They have a beginning and an end, but little or no middle: detail of 'what happened' is missing or at best very scanty.
- Their narratives are liable to be jumbled, out of sequence, and incoherent.

Origin of the quantity-quality problem

The child's experience of conversing with 'powerful people'

When you—as a powerful person—invite a child to disclose information to you in as much detail as possible—and just listen, not coming in relatively quickly to ask questions—this is a completely unfamiliar experience to most children. In Chapter 3 we see that from baby days onward children learn how to behave in interactions they have with powerful adults.

- **Taking the talking turn.** Even very young children know that when a powerful adult—any powerful adult—stops talking the child is expected to start talking.
- **Gaining approval.** The pursuit of *social desirability* leads children to behave in a way that the adult will approve. Children learn that powerful people seem already to 'know the answer' and will ask questions to get the child to give the desired answers. To gain the adult's approval, children learn to follow a script, a stereotyped way of conversing:
  — say as little as possible: follow the 'less is best' strategy;
  — wait for questions that inevitably follow;
  — give the answers that the adult wants.

The child's level of language skill

The child's level of language competency strongly affects what he or she retrieves from memory store. Under the age of 7 children have particular language limitations.

- **Location.** Because children do not understand prepositions, they leave physical location detail out of their narratives.

- **Chronological detail**. Time is a late aspect of development. There are large individual differences. On average children can tell the time around the age of 7. Days of the week and seasons of the year are learned around 8. Few children disclose spontaneously any chronological information.
- **Measurement**. Age, height, weight, frequency are all difficult concepts which are understandably absent from children's spontaneous accounts.
- **Linking events**. Children focus on particular features of events (called *centring*) rather than on linking these features, or whole events, together (called *chaining*). Chaining is essential to narrative flow. Children who have not mastered *conjunctions* (eg *so*, *but*) struggle to give a coherent account.
- **Commentary**. Adults engage in commentary when disclosing detail, ie they make observations about what they are describing, eg *I'm not too sure about this bit*. Commentary is useful because it can pre-empt questioning. Commentary starts to appear in older children's accounts.
- **Expressive skill**. As children mature they acquire greater skill at expressing themselves through language. They learn more words and ways of saying things. They learn how to use these in more and more contexts. They become more adept at providing specific information.

Emotional or motivational blocks

A child may have an emotional or motivational block, or a combination of these, that prevent him or her disclosing too much detail, if any detail, of a particular kind. Such blocks include.

- shyness;
- embarrassment;
- fear of a negative or angry response from significant people;
- fear of consequences: what might happen if particular detail is disclosed;
- observing the instruction by a significant person—who may or may not be the offender—not to disclose.

14.4.2 Counter-productive disclosure

The more disadvantaged the individual, the more likely the following counter-productive forms of disclosure are to happen.

Acquiescence

Children are very prone to acquiesce, ie to agree unreflectively to questions. They will say *yes* without thinking about what they are saying.

Compliance

Compliance is an aspect of *social desirability*. The child wants to please and be approved so follows a ritual:

- examining what the adult says;
- working out what the adult appears to want to hear: called by psychologists the *demand characteristics*;
- giving this response even though the child knows this to be incorrect.

Suggestibility

The child may distrust his or her memory, or be unable to recall detail. He or she may be suggestible, ie:

- reasoning that the correct answer lies in the content of your question;
- giving you the answer derived from your question.

It is possible to be acquiescent or compliant as well as suggestible.

Confabulation

The younger a child is the more likely that he or she will tell the truth. Children learn to lie. By the age of 2 they engage in deception. Ability to deceive and to detect deception occur around the age of 4 to 6 years when they typically:

- appreciate that lying is morally wrong;
- consider any untrue statement to be a lie whether or not the teller intended to deceive.

A more developed understanding of the intention to deceive and ways of deceiving begins around the age of 8. For example, a child of this age asked whether he has washed his or her hands after visiting the toilet will say 'yes' even though he or she clearly has not. The child works on the basis that you will not check to see whether his or her hands are damp!

Chapter 4 explains that people confabulate. They 'fill in the gaps' of their experience—imagining detail—and assert things which are not true—blather and 'bullshit'—to create a favourable impression and to gain the respect of the other person. Children are no exception, but are more prone to confabulate. Their confabulation is not lying. It is not a deliberate intention to deceive. We have to accept that amidst the accurate recall confabulation can occur.

Perseveration

When they do not understand what is being asked in a run of questions, some children will *perseverate*, unreflectively continue to give the same or very similar response—word, phrase, or gesture—to each question.

14.5   Creating a working relationship

Investigative interviewing is not a natural form of conversation. Nothing underlines this fact of life more than when you are faced with interviewing a child. The reason for it happening and the formalities involved mean that you can never instil it with the quality of an everyday conversation.

The child will always see you as a 'powerful person': you are an adult, your 'job' is about asking the child questions, and you want the child to 'tell you'—a bit like a teacher.[6] However you want the child to know that:

- you are a very different kind of 'powerful person';
- 'less is *not* best'—'more is best';
- you are mindful of the difficulties facing him or her in disclosing detail;
- you will help the child to say as much as it can to the best of its ability about its experience.

---

[6] Mortimer, A. and Shepherd, E. (1999) 'The Frailty of Children's Testimony' in A. Heaton-Armstrong, E. Shepherd, and D. Wolchover (eds), *Analysing Witness Testimony: A Guide for Legal Practitioners and Other Professionals*. Oxford: Oxford University Press.

You can achieve this through:

- conversational behaviour centred upon the child's perspective;
- considered, considerate questioning behaviour and question use.

14.6 Conversational behaviour centred upon the child's perspective

14.6.1 Use the child's name consciously and consistently

Children, like adults, are particularly attentive, and sensitive, to their name. You should consciously attend to using the child's name consistently across the course of the interview. Particular points when you should use the child's name are:

- when moving from one issue or topic to another;
- to attract the child's attention, eg if the child becomes distractible;
- when explaining something;
- when reassuring the child.

14.6.2 Be courteous

Children respond particularly well to good manners. They are as sensitive as adults to being treated respectfully or being taken for granted. Don't interrupt the child while he or she is talking. Interruption 'turns off' children as it does adults.

- The child thinks that you don't want him or her to say too much because you are busy, already know the answers, or both.
- The child loses confidence in talking with you.

14.6.3 Pausing

Don't be afraid of pause. Resist the pressure within you to talk and to reduce your anxiety by mouthing irrelevancies. Pausing gives you time to observe the child, to think what you want to say, and to think how to say it.

- Pausing is very productive. It gives child chance to process what you are saying/have said. The more developmentally disadvantaged the individual, the greater, and more frequent, the need to pause.
- Always pause before making an utterance and after the utterance.
- Get into the habit of pausing at least one or more seconds between your utterances. Also pause after the child has spoken. Resist the urge to come in immediately!
- Pausing is the best cue for the child to carry on talking and the prime evidence that you are indeed a very different kind of 'powerful person'.
- Pause duration that would induce anxiety in adults does not faze children.
- There is a qualitative difference between a sensible one or more seconds pause and pro-tracted silence which is likely to make the child feel that 'something is wrong'. There are common sense 'clues' that the pausing has gone on for too long.
  — The child looks at you with a sustained gaze—signalling that he or she does not want to take the talking turn.
  — Having said something, the child gives you a sustained gaze, signalling that he or she has passed the talking turn to you.
  — The child breaks eye contact, and may become restless or distractible.

14.6.4 Pacing

If you pause, then this will keep the pace of the conversation down. The greater the individual's disadvantage, the greater the need to keep the pace down.

14.6.5 Be mindful of the child when you express yourself and your ideas

If you want to gain access to a child's experience, you must mirror the child's way of talking and thinking in the way you express yourself and your ideas. The core idea is to minimize the mental demand on the child.

Speak clearly

Slow down your rate of speech and try to speak as clearly as possible.

Simple vocabulary

You must use simple, common, everyday English words and phrases. Words of Anglo-Saxon origin are usually easier than those that come from Latin. It makes no sense, particularly to the child, if you unthinkingly use jargon or technical words.

Short sentences and minimum ideas

We saw earlier that children need much more processing time and cannot handle too many ideas. In any utterance that you make, ie statement, observation, comment, request, or question, it is essential that:

- you keep the number of words to a minimum;
- you keep the number of 'ideas' in your utterances to a minimum.

The younger the child, the shorter your sentences should be and the fewer the ideas they should contain.

This is quite hard to do.

The only sure way is to slow down and 'engage mind before mouth'. Think consciously what you want to say, think how this needs to be said, and then say it. The child will not be disconcerted by such considered behaviour: not least if what you say emerges as understandable to the child. Indeed, you will come across as a very different kind of 'powerful person': one who is considerate, who seems to see things from the child's perspective—making things easy for the child to grasp and making it easier for the child to have its say.

Avoid complex sentence structure

Adults tend to *embed* in one big sentence other sentences—called *subordinate* or *qualifying*—which provide additional information. There are two very common patterns of embedding detail.

- **'Front loaded' embedded detail.** We say one or more sentences providing additional information, *before* saying the main sentence with the key information. In the following examples the 'tack on' prior information is underlined.

  When you came into the room, you saw something in the corner.
  After Nan left the house, I made a cup of tea.

This form of sentence structure is difficult for a child, particularly a young one. The child struggles to keep track of the front loaded information and to retain this in working memory. Hence the child only partially understands or misses this detail completely.

- **'Follow on' embedded detail.** We say the main sentence with the key information and follow this with one or more sentences providing additional information.

  You saw something in the corner <u>when you came into the room</u>.
  I made a cup of tea <u>after Nan left the house</u>.

This sentence structure is notionally easier to follow. Indeed by the age of 4 children produce simple 'follow on' embedded sentences. This structure still poses a memory challenge, especially for children in the earlier years at school. They struggle to keep track and hold detail in working memory:

— if there are too many 'follow on' sentences;
— if the main sentence is too long.

Having identified in your mind what you want to say there are two ways in which you can make things easier for the child.

- **Deliver the information in separate sentences.** This is the best option because it avoids embedding completely. It is suitable for most children, especially the very young.

  *You came into the room. ^^ ^^ You saw something in the corner. ^^ ^^*
  *Nan left the house. ^^ ^^ I made a cup of tea. ^^ ^^*

- **State the main sentence first, pause, and then state the 'tack on' (subordinate/qualifying) sentence or sentences.** This is suitable for older children with potentially more effective working memory.

Keep pronouns and prepositions to a minimum

In adult conversation we avoid being repetitious by using particular words to refer to someone, something, or some location that we have already mentioned. We use these words to avoid being *redundant*, ie repeating a name, object, or location more than once.

- **We use pronouns to substitute for people**

  *Then James came in. **He** was very upset.*
  *I saw Anna and Luke. **They** were crossing the road.*
  *Grace picked up the toy. **It** was broken*
  *Toby hit Andrew. **He** said he was a naughty boy.*

This last example demonstrates how language can be very confusing: which *he* was doing the accusing?

- **We use prepositions to substitute for locations**

  *George went into the kitchen. He was **there** for a long time.*
  *This is the kitchen. We have our meals in **here**.*

Because young children are confused by pronouns and prepositions, make redundancy—repetition—in what you say a virtue.

- Repeat the name, the object, or the location.
- Keep on repeating it.

  *You told me James came in. ^^^^ You said James was very upset. ^^^^*
  *You told me Toby hit Andrew. ^^ ^^ And Toby said Andrew was a naughty boy. ^^ ^^*
  *You said that Grace went to John's house. ^^ ^^ Did John ask other children to go to his house? ^^ ^^*
  *This is called the interview room. ^^ ^^ Have you been in the interview room before? ^^ ^^*

Nominalization

The technical term *nominalization* refers to the way in which we use a single word to replace two or more words, or even a complete sentence.

You remember <u>telling</u> me a moment ago about...

Here *telling* substitutes for *that you told*. Nominalization makes utterances potentially shorter but it requires more mental capacity to understand than the longer version. This is taking the requirement to keep things short too far. Try to avoid nominalization. If you find that you have used a nominalization and the child is likely not to have understood, simply 'repair', eg:

I was not too clear there. ^^ ^^ I wanted to say...

Avoid using abstract words and phrases

Adults frequently use abstract words, eg 'thing', and abstract phrases in conversation, eg:

These things might have made you sad.
That's not a nice thing to do.
*I'd like to know if there **was a time** when you felt unhappy.*

Because children, particularly young children, think concretely, they don't understand this usage of the word 'thing'.

If you find that you have not expressed yourself as simply as you should don't panic. The important point is that you have realized you've done so. Now you can do something about it by 'repairing' your use of language.

*I wasn't very clear when I said that. ^^^^ I will say that another way. ^^^^*

14.6.6   Explain and keep on explaining

Explain about sharing information

Young children do not understand what you are trying to do. It makes sense to explain in the simplest of terms that the two of you are sharing information. It helps to do this visually. Many years ago, when the first author was working with an autistic girl who had major learning difficulties he explained what he was trying to do by drawing two matchstick people with their heads together, explaining that one matchstick person was him and that the other was her. Then he moved his finger from his head into her head on the drawing to show what was happening when he said something. Then when she spoke, he held her finger and moved it from her head to his head on the drawing.

Whatever you use, a drawing or a felt board showing your head and the child's head, you need to get across to the child what's going on: the transmission of detail from the one to the other.

'It's OK to say you don't understand'

You must pass on this key message. However, it is vital to remember that, even though you have said this, the child will probably be like all other children and will not let on that he or she does not understand. It is no use operating in the hope that the child will act out of character with the ethos of a child's world. You must never assume that the child is holding in working memory or understands what you are saying, or remembers or understands what you have said earlier—no matter how many times you have said it.

Signpost

Signposting means letting the child know what you would like the two of you to talk about or do next.

14.6.7 Reward for participation

The child wants to be socially desirable so you should send messages that reward for participation.

- Be sincere, eg *That is a help.*
- Do not say words such as *Right* or *Good*, or excessively praise: this will lay you open to the allegation that you coached the child.
- Engage in SOFTENS behaviours.

14.6.8 Never take anything for granted

As soon as you assume something to be the case you have made a fatal step. Consciously guard against assuming that you know what the child means when he or she says something vague or ambiguous. Let the child know that you have not understood and simply request the child to make it simpler for you.

14.6.9 Check your meaning and the child's understanding are the same

As an investigator, you are never allowed to assume. However, people commonly make assumptions when engaged in everyday conversation. You have to guard consciously against assuming that your meaning and the child's understanding are the same. Across the course of the interview you should regularly check that the two of you mean the same thing, especially if the topic or issue is extremely significant or has serious implications.

> *I think I'm a bit mixed up about X.* ^^ ^^ *I need your help.* ^^ ^^ *Tell me what an X is.* ^^ ^^
> *You said that John used a Y.* ^^ ^^ *What does a Y do?* ^^ ^^

14.6.10 Positiveness

There will be occasions when a child goes off at a tangent. When this happens you must be patient, but eventually you must act positively to bring the interviewing back on course. If you do not, the interview aims will never be achieved, you will get frustrated (and this will be hard to hide), and even worse, the reliability of the child as a witness will be brought into question by the defence.

14.6.11 Non-judgemental

You have to be even-handed. You may have extensive case knowledge, eg concerning family circumstances, past offending behaviour by significant people, previous allegations. You cannot put this detail out of mind because it is the context in which the allegation is being made. The child may be extremely challenging, showing very little respect for you or what you are trying to do.

Being open-minded in such circumstances is difficult and only checked by you consciously reminding yourself when you are slipping into being judgemental.

14.7 The right question

14.7.1 Single questions

The reference material on *Questioning* explains that all questions should be single, ie you should only ever ask one question at a time.

Adults are confused by multiple questions—when an interviewer asks:

- more than one question rolled into one joined by the word *and*, eg:

  Did you go out with Jo and did anyone else go as well?

- a sequence of questions, not allowing the interviewee time to respond and 'filling the pause' with the next question, eg:

  What do you like doing at school? Do you like painting? Or do you like other kinds of lesson?

Asking a child a number of questions in succession:

- challenges the child's ability to keep up mentally and to hold the separate pieces of information in working memory;
- confuses the child;
- frustrates because it serially denies the child the talking turn.

Children cannot cope with multiple questions. Those who are significantly disadvantaged cannot cope.

14.7.2 No double negatives

Earlier it was pointed out that children, particularly young children, have problems with negatives. Adults often have to do a 'double take' when they are confronted with a *double* negative, eg *Did Jane not let you know that she was not going to collect Cameron?* Double negatives are a step too far. If you find yourself asking a double negative then 'repair' the situation: telling the child that you will say it another way, then say it more simply.

14.7.3 The ABE hierarchy of questioning

ABE[7] spells out the hierarchy of questioning in a phased interview.

- Open-ended questions.
- Specific-closed questions.
- Forced-choice questions.
- Leading questions.

14.7.4 Open-ended questions

It is unrealistic to expect that simply because you pose as many open-ended questions as you possibly can that the child will respond to your best efforts. You will have to judge when to switch from open-ended to specific questions.

---

[7] Ministry of Justice (2011) *Achieving Best Evidence in Criminal Proceedings: Guidance on Interviewing Victims and Witnesses, and Guidance on Using Special Measures.* London: HMSO.

Crème de la crème questions

Older children may respond to *crème de la crème* questions, ie:

- you raise a topic by making a statement, observation, or comment, or making an echo or mirror probe;
- you pause appropriately, creating the 'space' for the child to talk.

Developmentally disadvantaged individuals respond well to echo and mirror probe questions. These questions show that you are listening and have helped their thought processes by bringing the key idea in what they have said to the fore.

Skilled echo probing requires you to pause before echoing or mirroring, eg:

CHILD: *He said if I told anyone I would get into trouble.*
YOU: ^^ ^^ *You would get into trouble.* ^^ ^^

Tell, explain, describe (TED)

The three TED words—*tell, explain, describe*—are extremely useful questions but you have to be careful in their use.

- **Tell.** This is the least contentious instruction. It is simple and understood by even very young children. Particularly when said with a falling tone, it can be used to great effect, signalling that you are really interested in what the child has just said and you would like to know a lot more.
- **Explain.** The problems with this instruction mirror those of the question word *why*. The child may take the instruction to mean that you want a *justification*, ie a reason or an excuse for acting in a certain manner. Given this risk, you should avoid using the instruction *explain* when you want to know more about the individual's behaviour. Simply use *Tell* instead.
- **Describe.** This is a difficult instruction for a child, particularly a young one. Avoid it completely when conversing with children: *Tell* is much easier for the child to understand.

Don't overdo the use of a TED instruction—you are at risk of coming across as a 'typical' powerful person driving the conversation by directing the individual to disclose detail. Lessen the cumulative, bossy effect of TED instructions by varying the way in which you deliver them.

- Make TED a request, eg:

  Could you tell me what happened next?

- Precede TED with a softening utterance followed by the usual required pause. Some examples:

  I wasn't there. ^^ ^^ *Tell me what happened.* ^^ ^^
  I've not been to X. ^^ ^^ *Could you tell me about X?* ^^ ^^
  I haven't seen the man. ^^ ^^ *I'd like to know about him.* ^^ ^^ *Tell me about the man.* ^^ ^^

Narrative questions

- **Narrative *What*.** eg:

  What did you do when you went out with Uncle Fred?

- **A parameter question.** eg:

  I'd like you to have a big think. ^^ ^^ *Tell me what happened* ^^ ^^ *from when Billy came into your room* ^^ ^^ *to when Billy left.*

While young children may have problems with parameter questions, those in reception class and beyond will have increasing ability to give an answer.

Why

Children experience great difficulties with *why*. It has two potential meanings.

- **The questioner is seeking an explanation involving extra detail concerning causation.** This is a substantial conceptual challenge for the child. Very young children are likely to confuse *why* with *where* or *what*. A child who lacks the capacity to explain can effectively blank the question, eg saying *because they do* or *because it is*.
- **The questioner is seeking a special type of explanation: a justification or an excuse.** The child senses that the adult does not hold an entirely neutral position on what is being asked about. An apprehensive child who is sufficiently developed to understand this use of why, who is reticent, feels pressured, or thinks that he or she has been 'bad', may blank the question by remaining silent.

As a rule of thumb avoid asking *why*. If you consider it unavoidable then you should precede it with sensitive statements to remove perceptions of blame or being bad.

14.7.5   Specific-closed questions

Some children, particularly the very young, may not respond to an initial invitation to *Tell me* or a parameter question. In such circumstances you will need to ask a specific-closed question

What, who, where, when, which

This set of questions, including 'small' *what*, are asking the child to identify specific detail. They are good workaday questions but have implications if the question produces a vague or incomplete response.

- Consider asking a closed confirmatory 'yes'/'no' question mindful of the risks (see later).
- Do not repeat the question in the same form because the child:
  — may think that his or her response does not satisfy you;
  — may try to please you by changing his or her answers to the repeated question.

Closed confirmatory 'yes'/'no' questions

Closed confirmatory 'yes'/'no' questions are extremely common in everyday conversation. They direct the individual's attention onto a specific matter, eg *Did you have any bruises after he hit you the second time?* They have benefits.

- They make less of a demand upon the individual's mental and verbal capacities.
- If the one on the receiving end feels sufficiently confident to talk openly, he or she will treat the closed 'yes'/'no' question as an open question.

However, there are drawbacks.

- They restrict the individuals' latitude of response.
- The individual feels under pressure to say something.
- Research has shown that people are more likely to answer *yes* than *no*—particularly in order to 'help' the questioner.

- In the case of a child, where social desirability matters so much, the risk is that the child will say *yes* in order to gain your approval.
- Having said *yes* to one confirmatory question, the risk is that the child does not follow this up by saying something spontaneously.
- Asking further confirmatory questions risks:
  — the child perseverating continuing to answer *yes* to each question;
  — generating nonsensical agreement, damaging the child's credibility and reliability as a witness.

Confirmatory questions risk undermining the child's reliability as a witness. Whatever the response—relatively full or a simple *yes* and nothing else—you should revert to:

- open-ended questions:

  I would like to know about that. ^^ ^^ [= statement]
  You can... ^^ ^^ [= mirror probe of child saying an utterance containing the key idea *I can*]
  Can you tell me about that? ^^ ^^ [= invitational instruction]

- where appropriate, specific-closed questions.

The more open confirmatory question—*whether*—is more suited to an older child who has demonstrated a more secure grasp of language.

14.7.6 Forced-choice questions

If specific-closed questions do not succeed you have to ask a forced-choice question. These questions are potentially counter-productive.

- They suggest the possible options.
- Children under the age of 6 very often select the last option—attributable to the *recency effect* in memory, ie they remember last piece of information arriving.
- The child may not subsequently expand upon the option that he or she chose.
- The suggestible child—who distrusts his or her memory or has no remembrance of either option—resolves the problem by guessing the 'correct' response from the suggested alternatives.

For this reason you must adopt two safeguards.

- Never use option questions to probe core (central) detail that is likely to be in dispute at court.
- If you decide to ask a closed option question always remind the child that it is 'OK to say no'. However, the child may ignore your reminder since, as pointed out earlier, children are not disposed to let on that they do not know something.
- It is essential that as soon as the child chooses an option you revert to:
  — open-ended questions;
  — where appropriate, specific questions.

14.7.7 Leading questions

If a forced-choice question does not succeed in triggering disclosure, asking a leading question is your last resort. We see in Chapters 4 and 8 that these are extremely common in everyday conversation and are used extensively by powerful people to get the answers that they want.

The 'tag' of the question prompts the child to answer in a way that confirms what you know or believe to be the case. The question is wholly risky.

- The 'tag' is liable to induce the child to agree with you: particularly a child who is acquiescent, compliant, suggestible, or any combination of these.
- As the response is almost invariably *yes*, you have still yet to get the child into the 'habit' of answering your questions more fully.
- Children, particularly young children, and individuals who are intellectually disadvantaged are more likely to acquiesce to these questions than any other.
- A suggestible child will agree:
  — if the question concerns peripheral/poorly retained detail rather than core, salient memorable detail;
  — if he or she has no remembrance whatsoever.
- The accepted content constitutes *post event information* contaminating the suggestible child's remembrance of matters.
- The acquiescent or suggestible child is likely to give anomalous responses, ie inconsistent, contradictory, or nonsensical.
- If the child's response becomes a matter of dispute at court, parts of—or the entire—interview may be ruled inadmissible.

For these reasons your leading question is a gamble. The child's answers to some leading questions will not be challenged at court if the content is not contested by the defence, eg the child is led to agree to personal information or factual detail that is not in dispute. However, the Crown will find it difficult to counter the argument that the child's account is tainted because you put the idea into his or her head.

It is therefore essential that as soon as the child says '*yes*', you proceed immediately to an open question or, where necessary, a specific-closed question.

14.8 The 6 to 7 shift

From around the age of 6 to 7 onwards children tend to answer questions more accurately than younger children: though there are large individual differences.

14.9 Children's strategies for dealing with difficult questions

Young children use strategies when asked difficult questions.

- If they don't understand the question they give an answer to a question whose form they do understand, eg if asked *when*, the child gives an answer as if the question was *where*.
- If they do not understand the whole question, they give an 'answer' to the bit that they do understand.
- If they do not understand the question at all, they give a stereotypical response, ie repeat the same answer given to an earlier question: as described earlier, they perseverate.

Children of all ages are liable to block a difficult question by saying *I don't know* or *I can't remember*. They may even sabotage further questioning by perseverating with this blocking response.

14.10 Chapter summary

The number of factors that we have to take into account when we invite a child at a given stage of development—as an exemplar of developmental disadvantage—to disclose offence-related detail are numerous and potentially daunting. This chapter has sought to give you the foundation of awareness and understanding to engage in the processes of planning, preparation, and then conduct of orientation and assessment interviewing and investigative interviewing.

15

Interviewing the Developmentally Disadvantaged Witness: Orientation and Assessment (O & A) and Investigative Interviewing

15.1 Chapter overview

This chapter assumes that the decision has been made to interview. It reviews the distinct demands of orientation and assessment (O & A), and investigative interviewing. It takes you through the transition from O & A and uses a dialogue between an investigative interviewer and a child to examine and consider key issues.

15.1.1 Chapter objectives

This chapter will enable you to:

- appreciate the importance of time spent on O & A;
- engage skilfully in the transition between O & A and investigative interviewing;
- cope with common problems encountered in the investigative interviewing stage.

15.1.2 Interview map

Figure 15.1 shows the map for interviewing a developmentally disadvantaged witness.

15.2 Orientation and assessment (O & A) and investigative interviewing

15.2.1 The scope of special care interviewing

Achieving Best Evidence (ABE)[1] explains that every interview of a vulnerable witness comprises two elements:

- **A social element.** A witness, particularly one who is vulnerable, will only disclose detail if the witness feels at ease with and trusts the interviewer.
- **A cognitive element.** Being interviewed is a mental challenge, testing the witness's memory, capacity to process information, and language ability.

Where a witness is developmentally disadvantaged ABE recommends *phased interviewing* to take into account these elements:

- establishing rapport;
- free narrative recall;
- questions;
- closure.

Attempting to fulfil all phases within one interview poses real problems for, and places great pressure upon, the child, you, and everyone else involved in the interviewing process. There are just too many procedural objectives to be performed. Each successive step confronts an individual acknowledged to be vulnerable mentally with yet more information to be attended to, held in memory, and worked upon. This risks impacting negatively upon the performance of the child in the already emotionally and practically challenging task of disclosing in detail to a 'powerful person' in a strange environment.

---

[1] Ministry of Justice (2011) *Achieving Best Evidence in Criminal Proceedings: Guidance on Interviewing Victims and Witnesses, and Guidance on Using Special Measures.* London: Home Office.

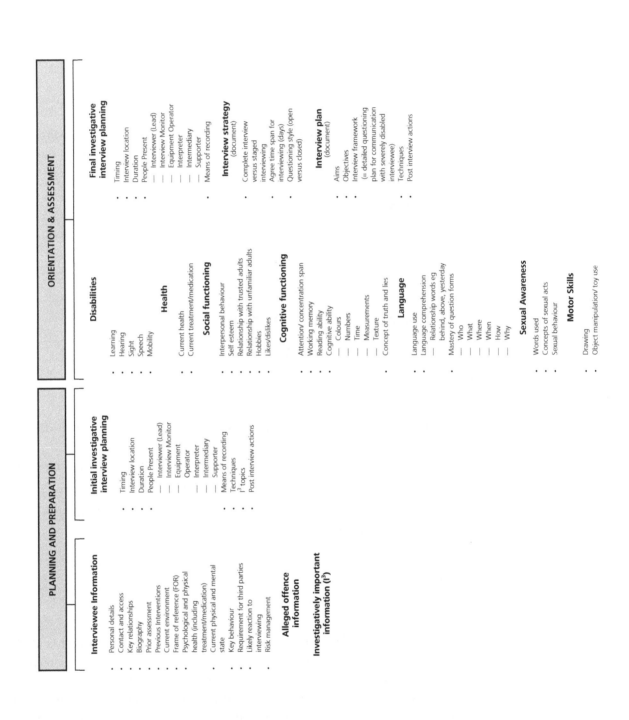

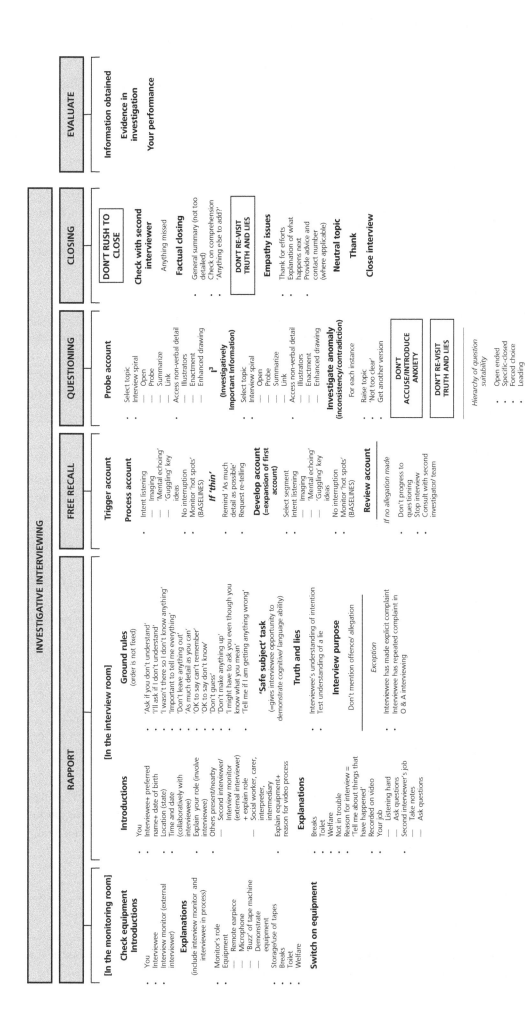

Figure 15.1 Map for interviewing a developmentally disadvantaged witness

343

To do justice to the child and his or her testimony, and to achieve best evidence for justice to be done, we need to recognize that we have to spend much more time in orientating—and in parallel assessing—the child. This will achieve best evidence and enhance the process of investigation.

15.2.2 Orientation and assessment (O & A) interviewing

Wherever you talk to the child you are interviewing, ie conversing with the child to achieve specific aims. Although your way of talking will be conversational, what you are engaged in is focused work—it is not a chat. It explicitly does not focus on the allegation or offence. However, if the child starts spontaneously disclosing you should not stop this disclosure.

Orientation

Orientation means bringing the child, yourself, and others—and other different elements—into a clearly understood position or relationship. A range of necessary explanation orientates the child to the task of working together with, and disclosing in detail to, you and colleagues. This is true rapport, as explained in Chapter 1: overcoming the guessing game, sharing goals, understanding respective responsibilities, and through reciprocity fostering an emotional bond. It reduces the child's eagerness to please.

Assessment

At the very moment you are explaining something, you are assessing the child: monitoring for clues to his or her capacity, or motivation, to pay attention, to follow, and ability to comprehend. You both benefit.

- The child has the opportunity to practise disclosing in detail, albeit on non-offence matters.
- The child provides evidence of his or her stage of development, language comprehension, and language use.
- You are able adapt to the child, consciously adopting a way of talking which matches the child's social and cognitive functioning.

15.2.3 Investigative interviewing

This focuses on obtaining from the child the fullest possible disclosure concerning:

- his or her offence-related experience;
- investigatively important information (I^3).

It harnesses the working relationship that you have fostered in your O & A interviewing. It builds upon the child's secure understanding of the ground rules, and his or her positive experience of disclosing in detail to a 'powerful person' on non-offence related material.

15.3 O & A interviewing

15.3.1 Location

Orientation and assessment interviewing is best started in the child's home location. As the child becomes accustomed to you, and you to the child, you are able to gather baseline material.

- **A baseline of the child's 'tick-over' level of emotional arousal.** Applying BASELINES you will be able to detect change indicative of potential stress when the child is inside and outside the child's home, en route to the interviewing location, in the monitoring room, and in the interview room.
- **Social behaviour.** You are able to gain an insight into the child's behaviour and the context in which it happens.
    — The style and quality of interaction, eg how the child and those surrounding him or her talk to each other.
    — The way the child uses language to express his or her experience within and outside his or her home.
    — The nature of the relationship between the child, carers, and siblings.

At some point, O & A interviewing switches to the interview location. This is best done as a separate visit rather than as a preliminary to immediate investigative interviewing. The focus of this visit—or stage—is to explain and to reduce stress and anxiety by getting to know the facilities, the equipment, key people, and their jobs.

15.3.2   Duration

Duration of O & A is practically linked to the nature of the offence, the course of the investigation, and the practicalities of availability and resource. The more time you spend on O & A the better.

- The greater the potential to foster a working relationship that has a 'history' and a 'future': the next interview.
- The greater your understanding of the child and the child's ability to understand.
- The greater confidence all round.
    — A self-confident child, ready, willing, and able to confide to you and your colleagues because you have his or her confidence.
    — You feel confident in fulfilling your tasks.

The challenge of communication disability: an exercise in joint learning

If the child has a communication disability, both of you need more time to learn. For your part it is going to be a steep learning curve!

The communication keys

You have to find out how the child usually communicates: the communication keys. Very often individuals with a communication disability use a combination of methods. You need to learn, and gain facility with, the child's anchor vocabulary and phrases, eg:

- *Yes, No, Not sure, Don't know, Maybe.*
- *I don't understand.*
- *I want.*
- *Please* and *Thanks.*
- *What, who, where.*
- *I'm thirsty* and *I'm hungry.*
- *I want the toilet.*
- *I'm tired* and *I want to stop.*

In a severely disabled individual, high-frequency messages—like a need for the toilet or a desire to stop—are a typical movement of the head, a limb, or body part. There is heavy reliance upon *yes* and *no* signalling. This necessarily requires you to plan for an interview where the closed confirmatory question is the norm, not the exception that must be immediately followed by a crème de la crème or open question.

Learning to communicate and relate across a wider spectrum

You can engage in activities in which the child is likely to be much more relaxed and able to communicate, eg play, drawing, creating a model, engaging in the child's hobbies. A useful aid that you can take along is a bag or folder for the child to look through and play with in your presence, while the two of you converse. The contents you adjust to the child's age and understanding, calling upon the advice of the child's carer beforehand.

Creating working relationships with key people

Where the carer is involved, you need to negotiate clear ground rules on how the carer will assist rather than give his or her views on matters. You should have an easier task negotiating ways of working together with the interpreter or intermediary. They are crucial because they will let you know the limitations imposed on the child by his or her disability and the communication systems that he or she uses. In Chapter 14 we explained that communication boards have limited vocabularies and it can be difficult to discuss certain topics.

15.3.3 Recording

O & A interviewing must be recorded in writing and electronically where this is possible, eg when O & A extends into the interview room. The record of O & A interviewing evidences that no investigation of the offence took place. If the child spontaneously discloses when not in the interview room, ensure that you make the fullest written record.

15.3.4 Interview planning

Your O & A interviewing will enable you to construct an interview plan that is tailored to the child, taking into account what you know about his or her social and cognitive performance, and his or her frame of reference (FOR). Some children are too disadvantaged to give a spontaneous account, eg those who:

- are developmentally unable: too young or so severely learning disabled;
- have a severe communication disability: reliant on 'yes'/'no' signing or use of a limited vocabulary communication board.

In such circumstances your interview plan should include a specific *questioning framework*. Use your knowledge of the allegation to pre-plan and to construct questions that are adjusted to the child's communication difficulties.

Using a grid format you can create pre-planned and pre-constructed lines of questioning. You should also include in the framework questions covering I^3 topics.

15.4 The transition from O & A interviewing to investigative interviewing

15.4.1 A child with a communication disability

You have to manage two aspects of the child's communication.

Idiosyncratic speech or communication pattern

You have to work with the child, his or her intermediary, or carer, to put on the record the 'vocabulary' that the court would otherwise not understand. This can be done in a socially skilled manner, and is best done as you go along rather than having a mini-session on 'this means this'.

A child with limited movement

You have to be alert to the evidential implications of the use of a computer, another form of communication equipment that is accessed by finger, or pointing to a board or other means. The child must move or point himself or herself. If a third party is involved in the moving and pointing process, this evidence will be ruled inadmissible.

15.4.2 Managing the transition

In the following sections we will consider aspects of the dialogue recorded on video at the start of the investigative interviewing stage. It is a transition phase in which:

- the child demonstrates his or her level of cognitive and social functioning;
- the child is confronted with the ground rules, the issue of truth and lies, and a descriptive task before being invited to disclose his or her offence-related experience.

You will read—and 'hear'—the conversation between Anna, a child protection officer, and Eric the child. Next door in the monitoring room is Ashley, the second investigator, fulfilling the role of interview monitor.

Note how the interviewer Anna involves Eric in the process:

- providing the court with evidence of Eric's level of functioning;
- ensuring that she does not do all the talking.

For the sake of brevity only small fragments of the dialogue are represented to illustrate the issues.

15.4.3 Reference to notes

As pointed out from the outset of this text, self-disclosure is a form of reciprocity. It fosters disclosure by the other person. If you have a note pad or a checklist, then, like Anna, this is a perfect opportunity to engage in self-disclosure.

> **Anna:** *See this book that I've got here* [show], ^^ ^^, *there's lots of writing on it.* ^^ ^^ *I need to go through this list.* ^^ ^^

15.4.4 Refer to all previous meetings

Reference to the continuity of dialogue between the child and you, and other colleagues, is a requirement for the court. Anna states how many times she and Eric have met and the conversation immediately before coming into the interview room.

> **Anna:** *Now my book says that,* ^^ ^^ *today is the third time we have met.* ^^ ^^ *I came to your house last Friday* ^^ ^^ *and on the Tuesday before that.* ^^ ^^
> *And this morning* ^^ *we've just come from the room next door* ^^ ^^ *where Ashley is with the machines.*

15.4.5 Introducing yourself and your job

This may sound an easy and obvious task. How it is done matters. If done expertly, you can achieve more than one objective, including giving the court an insight into the child's perception of your role.

> **Anna:** *I need to tell you who I am.* ^^ ^^ *Then I'm going to ask you to tell me who you are.* ^^ ^^ *So can you remember what my first name is?*
> **Eric:** *Anna.*
> **Anna:** ^^ ^^ *And my second name is Mortimer.* ^^ ^^ *And I'm a police officer here at [name of location].* ^^ ^^ *You won't see police officers in uniform here.* ^^ ^^ *We wear clothes that are just like your Mum and Dad's.* ^^ ^^
> *So Eric,* ^^ *As I said, I'm a police officer.* ^^ ^^ *Can you tell me what types of things police officers do?*
> **Eric:** *You catch baddies.*
> **Anna:** ^^ ^^ *What else do police officers do?*
> **Eric:** *Help people.*
> **Anna:** ^^ ^^ *That's what I do. My job is to help children and young people like you with things that have happened, things that have upset them.*
> *I've told you about me so I'd like to know about you. What's your name?*

Notice the pause that Anna creates after Eric replies. This keeps the pace of the interview down, and helps her as well—she can look down, register the next item, and frame what she wants to say before saying it.

15.4.6 The time, day, and date

Anna puts her O & A knowledge to good effect. She knows Eric can read the time so he shares in the task of 'date stamping' the interview.

> **Anna:** ^^ ^^ *I have to make a note of the time Eric.* ^^ ^^ *Can you tell the time?*
> **Eric:** *Yeah.*
> **Anna:** ^^ ^^ *If you look on the wall just there.* ^^ ^^*There's a clock.* ^^ ^^ *What time is it?*
> **Eric:** *It's twenty to ten.*
> **Anna:** ^^ ^^ *That's it.* ^^ ^^ *twenty to ten.* ^^ ^^ *Can you tell me what day of the week it is?*
> **Eric:** *Monday.*
> **Anna:** ^^ ^^ *Yes, it's Monday.* ^^ ^^ *Can you tell me what the date is?*
> **Eric:** *Second of April.*
> **Anna:** ^^ ^^ *Monday the second of April.* ^^ ^^ *And what about the year?*
> **Eric:** *2013.*
> **Anna:** ^^ ^^ *So it's twenty to ten on Monday, the second of April 2013* ^^ ^^

Never correct the child if he or she makes an error in any element. A skilful way to get the right detail on record would be to look down at your watch or note pad and then use a simple 'no-attribution' device, eg:

> **you:** ^^ ^^ *I'll get the workman to check that clock.* ^^ ^^ *My watch says [states correct time].*
> **you :** ^^ ^^ *Let me look at my watch just to make sure.* ^^ ^^ *My watch shows the date.* ^^ ^^ *Oh!* ^^ *It says today is [states correct day].*

15.4.7 Monitoring the interview and the equipment

> **Anna:** ^^ ^^ *You met Ashley before we came in.* ^^ ^^ *She's still next door* ^^ *in the room with the machines.* ^^ ^^ *Ashley will be watching us from in there.* ^^ ^^ *She's listening to you and to me* ^^ ^^ *and she's writing some notes.* ^^ ^^ *And she might tell me through this* [points to

earpiece] ^^ *to ask you a question. ^^ ^^ She will be looking at us through the cameras. ^^ ^^*
So how many cameras is she using?
Eric: *Two*
Anna: ^^ ^^ *She's using two cameras. ^^ ^^ Can you point to me where the cameras are?*
Eric: *There* [points to camera one] *and there* [points to camera two].

Anna has also achieved something else. She has used this very early topic to introduce the notion of pointing, ie using an illustrator. She can harness this later if she decides to ask Eric to use an illustrator to describe non-verbally a relative position.

15.4.8 The toilet

Anna: ^^ ^^ *Now there are two doors. ^^ ^^That one we came in. ^^ ^^That one there is to the toilet. ^^ ^^ I showed you that just before we came in. ^^ ^^That's not locked. ^^ ^^ If you want to go to the toilet at any time ^^ ^^ just tell me and then go through that door. ^^ ^^*
So Eric, ^^ what do you have to do if you want to go to the toilet?
Eric: *Tell you and go through that door.*
Anna: ^^ ^^ *That's it. ^^ ^^ And when can you tell me you want to go to the toilet?*
Eric: *Anytime I want to go.*

Anna has used this again to more than one effect. She is setting in train the 'habit' of Eric telling her what his understanding of her explanation.

15.4.9 Need for a break

Anna: ^^ ^^ *If you need a break at any time ^^ ^^ Just tell me and we'll stop. ^^ ^^*
So Eric, ^^ what do you have to do if you want to stop?
Eric: *Tell you.*
Anna: ^^ ^^ *That's it. ^^ ^^ And when can you tell me you want to stop?*
Eric: *Any time I want.*

15.4.10 'Not in trouble' and the reason for the interview

Anna: ^^ ^^ *So I'm a police officer. ^^ ^^ I want to say Eric that you mustn't worry. ^^ ^^ You haven't done anything wrong. ^^ ^^ You're not in trouble. ^^ ^^ My job is to help you.*
So Eric, ^^ The reason that you are here today ^^is so that you can talk to me in a little while ^^ ^^ about what happened that made you unhappy.

This is a crucial message to get over to the child. You will have made it clear in your O & A contacts from the outset, but it is something that cannot be said too often. Many children do feel implicitly that they have done something wrong and it weighs heavily on them.

15.4.11 The ground rules

You have the difficult task of explaining, and the child the difficult task of understanding and holding in working memory, several ground rules. Let's look at some of these.

'There are rules here'

Anna: ^^ ^^ *Just like there are rules at home ^^ and at school, ^^ ^^ there are some rules here Eric. ^^ ^^ There are rules for both of us. ^^ ^^ Rules about how you ^^ and I will do things.*

^^ ^^ *I'm going to tell you the rules now.* ^^ ^^ *I'll tell you when it is a rule for me* ^^ ^^ *and when it's a rule for you.*

Anna has been self-disclosing again. She has made it clear to Eric that he is not alone: there are rules for her.

'Listen hard' rule

Anna: *The first rule is that you must listen hard.* ^^ ^^ *I need you to listen very, very carefully to what I say,* ^^ ^^ *and listen very carefully when I ask you a question.* ^^ ^^ *So Eric* ^^ *what's the rule for listening?*
Eric: *I've got to listen.*
Anna: ^^ ^^ *And what have you got to listen to Eric?*
Eric: *What you say and when you ask me questions.*

Anna has been self-disclosing again. She has made it clear to Eric that he is not alone: there are rules for her.

'OK to say you don't understand' rule

People learn not to admit when they do not understand. At school it becomes more and more the imperative not to 'let on' to anybody your lack of understanding—even though many present may also fail to grasp. To admit is to draw attention to 'failing', and the risk of inviting ridicule. You have to overcome this totally defeating behaviour.

Anna: ^^ ^^ *Yes.* ^^ *And if you don't understand what I say Eric* ^^ ^^ *I want you to stop me right away* ^^ *and tell me.* ^^ ^^ *Tell me that you don't understand.* ^^ *I won't be upset when you stop me.* ^^ ^^ *I will be pleased* ^^ *because I want you to understand what I say.* ^^ ^^ *So, Eric,* ^^ *Can you tell me what the rule is* ^^ *when you don't understand what I say?*
Eric: *I've got to stop you and let you know. And you'll be happy when I stop you.*
Anna: ^^ ^^ *Yes.* ^^ *And I have to follow the rule as well Eric.* ^^ ^^ *If I don't understand what you say I have to tell you.* ^^ ^^ *I have to stop you and tell you that I don't understand.* ^^ ^^

The previous chapter explained that we can never assume that the child understands our words. Anna decides to reinforce the rule that it is OK to say you don't understand an adult.

Anna: *Sometimes children don't understand* ^^ *when adults try to explain* ^^ ^^ *and when adults ask questions.* ^^ ^^ *Adults sometimes say words* ^^ *that children don't understand.* ^^ ^^ *I want you to tell me* ^^ *when you don't understand any of my words.* ^^ ^^ *and when you don't understand a question.* ^^ ^^ *It's OK to say if you don't understand what I say.* ^^ ^^ *So what must you say Eric* ^^ *when you don't understand my words?*
Eric: *I tell you I don't understand.*
Anna: ^^ ^^ *And a question that I ask*
Eric: *I tell you I don't understand what you are saying.*
Anna: ^^ ^^ *And when do you stop me to tell me you don't understand?*
Eric: *Right away.*

Notice how Anna used a crème de la crème question—*and a question that I ask*—a topic extending the previous question. She has established that Eric can cope with such a question.

'OK to say you don't know' rule

Children, like adults, view being questioned as a test that has to be passed. Adults do not like saying that they do not know, particularly if they feel that they ought to know something. Children are no different.

Anna: *Now you won't know the answer to every question I ask Eric. ^^ ^^ If you don't know the answer to a question ^^ ^^ I want you say that you don't know. ^^ ^^ It's OK to say that you don't know. ^^ ^^*
*So Eric ^^ I need you to tell me when you don't know the answer ^^ ^^ I don't want you to guess an answer. ^^ ^^ I don't want you to make anything up. ^^ ^^*
So if I said to you, ^^ 'What's the colour of the front door of my house?' ^^ ^^ What would you say?
Eric: *I would say that 'I don't know'.*
Anna: *^^ ^^ You don't know Eric because you have never been to my house. ^^ I need you to tell me when you don't know something. ^^ ^^ I don't want you to guess an answer. ^^ ^^ I don't want you to make anything up. ^^ ^^*

Like Anna, you have to make it clear that you understand already that the child will not have an answer for every question. We have to give the child licence to say 'I don't know' without each instance making the child feel as though he or she is failing himself or herself, or you.

Anna's approach to the issue of not knowing, and before that not understanding, has reduced the likelihood of Eric confabulating.

15.4.12 Get the child naming and describing in detail

The aim is to get the child naming and describing things in as much detail as possible, eg a piece of furniture, the room, fittings, or clothing—yours, any third party, or the child's.

Anna: *When I ask you a question, Eric ^^ ^^ I want you to tell me as much as you can. ^^ ^^ The little bits. ^^ ^^ The more little bits you tell me the better. ^^ ^^ You can't tell me too many little bits. ^^ ^^ And you don't have to rush. ^^ ^^ So don't rush to tell me all the little bits. ^^ ^^ You stop ^^ and have a think. ^^ ^^ I am happy to wait Eric. ^^ ^^ There's no rush.*
So what's the rule then Eric ^^ ^^ when you answer a question?
Eric: *You want me to say lots.*
Anna: *^^^^ And?*
Eric: *I can stop if I want.*
Anna: *^^ ^^ And?*
Eric: *If I stop that's OK with you.*
Anna: *^^ ^^ Let's have a go. ^^ ^^ What I'd like you to do Eric ^^ is look at the room in which we are sitting. ^^ ^^ Have a good look. ^^ ^^ When you are ready, ^^ tell me as much as you can about it.*

Anna knows that children are able to respond to crème de la crème questions: the skill is creating the conversational setting for the child to demonstrate that he or she is on the same 'wavelength'. Having just before given Eric a topic to respond to, now she is seeing whether he can cope with minimal prompts. She used *and* to sustain Eric describing, and she succeeded in this. Of course, if Eric had not coped with the topic earlier, or the minimal prompt, Anna would have paused and then moved along the dimension towards open ended questioning, eg:

Anna: *^^ ^^ And a question that I ask*
Eric: [silence]
Anna: *^^ ^^ What do you say when you don't understand a question?*

Or in the case of a minimal prompt

Eric: *You want me to say lots.*
Anna: *^^^^ And?*
Eric: [silence]
Anna: *^^^^ What did I say about stopping?*
Eric: *I can stop if I want. I can stop to think.*

She is achieving something important in the way she is talking with Eric. She is setting in train the 'habit' of Eric telling her his understanding of matters, in this case her explanation in which she includes essential 'keys' to the task of disclosing.

15.4.13 Raising awareness about the interviewing spiral

Anna proceeds to making Eric aware of what we know to be the interviewing spiral—summarizing and linking to a logically connected topic, then opening that up, and probing.

> **Anna:** *So Eric you've told me it's square, ^^ ^^ it's got two lights, ^^ ^^ two cameras, ^^ ^^ and that it's nice. ^^ ^^ The furniture, Eric, ^^ that's in the room. ^^ ^^ Can you tell me about that?*

When Eric has finished disclosing spontaneously on the topic of the furniture, she engages in QAQAQ, practising him in answering specific probes constituting a line of questioning about a topic.

> **Anna:** *^^ ^^ And how many doors?*
> **Eric:** *Two.*
> **Anna:** *^^^^ And the colour of the doors?*
> **Eric:** *White.*
> **Anna:** *^^^^ And the colour of the table?*
> **Eric:** *Browny.*
> **Anna:** *^^^^ And when you touch it ^^ ^^*
> **Eric:** *It's hard 'cos it's wood. Wood is hard.*

Notice how Anna used an open question and then moved towards a sequence of yet more crème de la crème questioning. The benefit of developing the child's response to crème de la crème questions is that it makes the interview much more conversational and less of a *wh*-questioning process.

Because summarizing is an 'odd' behaviour that does not happen in everyday life, it is worth making it feel 'natural' in your conversation with the child. Appreciating this, Anna summarizes again, to share what the two of them have done together.

> **Anna:** *Eric what we've done together is ^^ ^^ I asked you a question, ^^ ^^ you told me something, ^^ ^^ I asked a question ^^ ^^ and you said some more. ^^ ^^ You told me a lot ^^ ^^ and I learned a lot. ^^ ^^*
> *Also when you told me a lot ^^ ^^ I said back to you what you told me. ^^ ^^ This helps us both. ^^ ^^ You might remember a lot more. ^^ ^^ You can tell me more. ^^ ^^ And you can tell me if what I say is wrong.*

15.4.14 Truth and lies

In Chapter 14 we see that around the age of 4 to 6 years children typically:

- appreciate that lying is morally wrong;
- consider any untrue statement to be a lie whether or not the teller intended to deceive.

A more developed understanding of the intention to deceive and ways of deceiving begins around the age of 8. You should try to establish first whether the child has grasped the abstract notion of honesty. Then you should present an example of deceptive behaviour, allowing you to probe the issue of intention.

> **Anna:** *We have to talk about honesty Eric. ^^ ^^ Can you tell me what I mean by honesty?*
> **Eric:** *Telling the truth. Not telling fibs.*

Anna: ^^ ^^ *Fibs?*

Eric: *Yeah. Not telling the truth. Er ^^ lies.*

Anna: ^^ ^^ *So there's a difference between truth and lies. ^^ ^^ Can you tell me the difference?*

Eric: *Telling the truth is good. And lies get you into trouble.*

Anna: *To make sure that you understand the truth Eric ^^^^ I'm going to tell you a story about a boy called Johnny. ^^ ^^ It is a story about telling the truth ^^ and telling lies. ^^ ^^ When I have finished telling the story ^^ ^^ I will ask you some questions about the story. ^^ ^^ Johnny is a little boy ^^ ^^ who is football mad. ^^ ^^ He loves playing football. ^^ ^^ He is always kicking a ball. ^^ ^^ He kicks the ball whenever he can. ^^ ^^^ He keeps kicking the ball everywhere he can. ^^ ^^ His mum tells him not to. ^^ ^^ But he still keeps kicking the ball around indoors. ^^ ^^*

One day Johnny's mum is outside hanging out the washing. ^^ ^^ Johnny is inside kicking the ball. ^^ ^^ The ball hits the kitchen window and it smashes. ^^ ^^ Johnny's mum comes in and asks Johnny, 'Have you been playing football?' ^^ ^^ And Johnny said, 'No'. ^^ ^^ So by Johnny saying 'No. Mummy I haven't been playing football. ^^ ^^ And I did not smash the window', ^^ ^^ what did Johnny do?

Eric: *He told a lie.*

Anna: ^^ ^^ *Why did Johnny lie to his Mum?*

Eric: *Because he didn't want to get in trouble with his Mum. He didn't want to be 'grounded'.*

Anna: ^^ ^^ *So what should he have done?*

Eric: *Should've told her the truth. He should have said, 'Yes, it was me. Sorry Mum.'*

Anna: ^^ ^^ *So sometimes people don't tell the truth ^^ because they don't want to get into trouble. ^^ ^^ But as you said it's important that people tell the truth. Eric. ^^ ^^ I want you to tell me the truth Eric ^^ ^^ and I will do the same.*

There are endless variations that you can develop on the Johnny story line, adjusting the content to the child and his or her interests that you have established during your O & A interviewing.

Some learning disabled children may have problems with truth and lies. They may grasp that it is 'bad' to say something that is not the case, but may not be able to put the label *lie* to it. Similarly they may have little or no understanding of intent.

15.5 Free narrative recall

15.5.1 Making the focus of the interview clear

This is always a difficult task. You are not allowed to specify the nature of the offence. At court the defence would argue that this was excessively leading. However, if the child has made a complaint and he or she repeated the complaint in an earlier O & A conversation you can refer back to it.

Remember that you want child's memory of the incident(s) that gave rise to the complaint, not what child remembers telling someone else, although this is useful.

15.5.2 Triggering disclosure

Remind the child of your perspective

You should remind the child about key issues before posing the triggering question.

- The child has done nothing wrong.
- No one is going to get angry.
- You want the child to tell you the whole story.

- You have heard lots of children tell you about what made them sad and upset.
- The child should not be afraid.
- The child should not be embarrassed.
- You don't know what happened.

You could say that these are a seamless lead up to the triggering question. Logically, however, they could follow an attempt to trigger disclosure that has not apparently worked! The point is that there is no programmatic approach. To use a psychotherapy adage concerning the process of eliciting disclosure, 'push where it gives'. The 'it' of course is not the person you are conversing with but the sense that his or her response or pattern of responding is telling you that now is the time to move forward by saying something or asking a particular question. The Greeks had a word for this special sense of time, *kairos*, which means the 'right time' to do or to say something. Guidelines are about the other Greek word for time, *chronos*, the procession of time and the world of sequences.

It is often the case that after you have covered truth and lies, many children are at the point of disclosing spontaneously. They feel it is *kairos*. If you sense that the child wants to disclose, that it is the 'right time', then don't stick slavishly to the checklist. If something procedural needs to be covered later then this can happen. ABE is clear on this matter. You have to use professional judgement.

The triggering question

One of the most frequently used triggering questions is *Can you tell me why you are here today?* ABE gives some excellent other examples of triggering questions. It is not a criticism, just a fact, that triggering questions define the conversation as being difficult. Our question is emotionally difficult for the child, but the sensitivity of the subject—the alleged offending—casts us into the thicket of difficult words: *why*, *something* or *things*. It is no easy task thinking up ways of communicating a difficult subject in a simple way. In Chapter 16 we will meet the same problem when we think about explaining the caution to suspects, particularly those who are learning disabled.

> **Anna**: *Sometimes Eric ^^ ^^ we get sad and unhappy at what happens to us.* [Changes occurring in Eric's BASELINES behaviours.] *^^ ^^ We look for someone to talk to. ^^ ^^ To talk to about what has happened ^^ ^^ and has made us sad and unhappy. ^^ ^^ We can be so sad and unhappy sometimes ^^ ^^ that we find it hard to talk to someone. ^^ ^^*
> *You remember Eric that I said my job was to help. ^^ ^^ I help children who feel sad and unhappy ^^ ^^ sad and unhappy about what has happened to them. ^^ ^^ I listen when they tell me what has happened to them. ^^ ^^ Can I help you like that?*
> **Eric**: [nods—more changes in BASELINES behaviours.]
> **Anna**: *^^ ^^ Tell me what has happened to you Eric ^^ ^^ to make you sad and unhappy.*

Triggering recall from a child with severe communication disability

Implement your interview framework contained in your interview plan.

15.5.3 Respond appropriately

Concentrate on the detail

Engage in SOFTENS behaviours, and listen intently: image, 'mentally echo', and 'guggle' at the key idea in the child's utterances. Work hard at listening actively, with your 'third ear', trying to detect the emotion behind the message.

Help the child over embarrassment

Because it is a difficult conversation for the child, embarrassment is very likely to be a barrier. If the child's demeanour and struggle with words tell you that he or she is feeling self-conscious or awkward, come in gently with some 'softening' techniques.

Child looking away

> **Anna:** *Sometimes Eric ^^ ^^ it is very difficult to look at a person ^^ ^^ when we tell them what has made us sad or unhappy. ^^ ^^ Some children look away from me ^^ ^^ when they find it difficult to say something. ^^ ^^ You can do that if you want. ^^ ^^ Do you want to try that?*

You looking away

> **Anna:** *Sometimes Eric ^^ ^^ children ask me to look away from them ^^ ^^ when they find it difficult to say something. ^^ ^^ You can do that if you want. ^^ ^^ Do you want me to look away?*

Writing down

> **Anna:** *Sometimes Eric ^^ ^^ children find it easier to write down words ^^ ^^ words that they don't like saying. ^^ ^^ You can do that if you want. ^^ ^^ There's a pencil and some paper on the table there^^ ^^right beside you. ^^ ^^ Do you want to write the words down?*

15.5.4 If the child's account seriously deviates

At some time you are bound to meet a child who seriously deviates from what you have asked him or her to tell you about. You must be patient and resist the urge to intervene in order to refocus matters.

- Continue to listen intently to what the child is saying, even though it has no bearing upon the matters you wish to investigate.
- Don't give the child the impression—through inattentive non-verbal behaviour—that you are not paying attention.

The child may bring itself back on track. If this does not happen, then at some point you have to intervene. This requires fine judgement. You must allow the child to talk a sufficient length of time to provide you with enough evidence to conclude that the child has irretrievably drifted away from matters that are the focus of your investigation. When you have the necessary evidence, intervene.

- Wait for an appropriate break in the child's stream of talk, ie when the child has completed an utterance and is pausing for breath.
- Attract the child's attention if necessary, eg by moving forward.
- Take the talking turn to refocus the disclosure, eg:

> **Anna:** *That's really helpful Eric. ^^ ^^ We can talk a bit more about what you have told me in a moment. ^^ ^^ I wonder, ^^ ^^ before then can you help me ^^ ^^* [returns Eric back to topic].

If the child deviates yet again, you must decide whether to continue with the interview or to stop the interview to discuss the way ahead with colleagues and other third parties. If you decide to stop the interview, then you must close the interview appropriately, ie thanking the child and explaining that it would be good to take a break.

15.5.5 **If the child gives an account which addresses the investigative issues**

When the child has finished his or her account you should thank the child in the normal way and move on to the second recall.

15.6 Second recall

15.6.1 The value of a second recall

Although ABE does not specifically mention second recall, it is always the case that going over something again generates more detail. We do this for witnesses who do not require special care questioning, to assist their remembrance. You will see in the chapters that follow that for suspects we facilitate second recall through a process of questioning to expand their spontaneous disclosure: a process called *developing the first account*.

In the case of a child the object of second recall is twofold.

- It enables the child to expand upon its first recall. You will recall the quantity–quality problem. Children's first attempt at 'telling' usually produces a 'thin' account. Often they can tell more but they are performing true to form, ie giving the 'powerful person' just enough to enable the person to ask the questions. By asking the child to go over it again, the child can spontaneously add the detail that he or she could have disclosed first time round.

- As with any interviewee, the absolute value of a second version is that you can compare its fine-grain detail with that of the first version. You are able to make a sensible, grounded judgement as to what is potentially core detail (common to both versions), or peripheral (mentioned on one but not the other), and other anomalies and areas that require probing.

However, children are sensitive to being asked something again. Let's see how Anna handles this.

> **Anna:** ^^ ^^ *That must have been very difficult for you Eric.* ^^ ^^ *And you told me such a lot there Eric.* ^^ ^^ *A lot about what made you unhappy and sad.* ^^ ^^ ^^ ^^ *Sometimes children can't say everything all at once Eric.* ^^ ^^ *They find it easier to tell me a second time.* ^^ ^^ *The second time they can say a lot more.* ^^ ^^ *They find it gets easier.* ^^ ^^ *They have a think.* ^^ ^^ *Then they tell me more* ^^ *have another think* ^^ ^^ *and tell me more about what made them sad and unhappy.* ^^ ^^ ^^ ^^ *Let's try that.* ^^ ^^ *You tell me again what has made you sad and unhappy* ^^ ^^ *and tell me more and more.* ^^ ^^ *I will just listen.* ^^ ^^ *And remember that rule: you don't have to rush.* ^^ ^^ *When you are ready to talk,* ^^ *off you go.* ^^ ^^

15.6.2 Helping the child to expand its first recall

Sometimes the child may not present information in a logical order. It helps the child, and the evidential value of the child's testimony, to provide the child with some guidance before inviting a second recall.

- From the first recall identify an appropriate *start point* and, if contained within the account, a suitable *end point*.
- Explain to the child that it will help to take you from the start point to the end.

> **Anna:** ^^ ^^ *You can help me if you tell me everything from* [specify start point] ^^ ^^ *and tell me what happened up to* [specify end point].

15.6.3 If the child's account deviates

If the child deviates follow the procedure described earlier.

15.7 Questioning

15.7.1 You are requesting information

The interview is a sustained request for information. All of your questions are requests.

'Could you...'

As pointed out in Chapter 8, the words *Could you...* or *Can you...* do not determine that this is a closed confirmatory 'yes'/'no' question. *Could (Can) you pass the salt?* is not asking whether the person has the competence to pass the salt. It is a request. Even before entering reception class at school children know this and that *Could (Can) you* is a mild instruction. Certainly once in school this lesson is reinforced.

Saying *Could you* reinforces that you are requesting information. In the dialogue between Anna and Eric you will have seen how often she uses invitational, or requesting, questions. If the child does appear to misinterpret your invitation or request and says *Yes*, and then nothing else, don't panic. Pause to see if the child does start talking. If he or she does not continue talking then 'repair': simply ask a TED question or any other kind of open-ended question.

Again as pointed out in Chapter 8, saying a couple of words like *Could you* lets air out of your lungs so that the subsequent *wh-* question is not so jabbing as an interrogative.

'Thank you'

Get into the habit of saying *thank you* when the child grants your request for significant information. Where the disclosure has implied a lot of effort and potential difficulty for the child you should accompany your thanks with a suitably empathic statement, eg *I know how hard it was to tell me what Uncle Jack did to you.*

15.7.2 Raising the topic and inviting disclosure

Raising the topic and pausing is crème de la crème questioning. It is an extremely effective questioning technique when interviewing adults. Children, even very young children, can and do disclose in detail if:

- you draw their attention to a topic;
- you pause to allow the child to register this information and to think;
- you invite the child to tell you everything he or she can about the topic.

Anna had already practised Eric with crème de la crème questions. She can build upon this.

> **Anna:** *You told me about X. ^^ ^^ I'd like to know some more about X ^^ ^^ Have a think about X ^^ ^^ and let me know as much as you can about X. ^^ ^^*

15.7.3 Echo or mirror probing

Developmentally disadvantaged individuals respond well to echo a mirror probing. This is because you show that you are listening and have helped their thought processes by bringing the key idea in what they have said to the fore.

> **Eric:** *He said that it was a secret between us.*
> **Anna:** ^^ ^^ *A secret?*
> **Eric:** *Yeah. I wasn't to tell anyone. He said it was like in Pirates of the Caribbean. I would be punished.*
> **Anna:** ^^ ^^ *You'd be punished?*
> **Eric:** *He went on about him visiting me at night…*

Of course you have to be careful about echo and mirror probing. Don't use too many in a sequence, lest you sound like a parrot.

15.7.4 Don't 'topic hop'

Developmentally disadvantaged individuals need the help of the interviewing spiral. You should avoid 'topic hopping', moving rapidly from one topic to another. Get into the habit of:

- following a line of questioning on a topic: not just asking one or two questions;
- summarizing;
- linking to the next issue, ie focused signposting.

Concentrate on ensuring that the link is explicit. If it is not the child will fail to understand why you have switched from one topic to something totally unrelated.

15.7.5 Keep checking comprehension

Even where you and the child have extremely good rapport, and the child has confirmed his or her grasp of the *'OK to say you don't understand'* rule, you must keep checking that he or she understands across the entire interview.

15.7.6 Be prepared to 'repair'

Even the most skilled and adept practitioner can fail to pause, creating a very long utterance, use inappropriate words and phrasing, or ask a counter-productive question. The important issue is to recognize when you do this and do something about it immediately. You cannot expect the child to respond to an explanation, assertion, or question that confuses or is beyond the capacity of his or her working memory or ability to comprehend.

'Repair' the problem by being self-disclosing about what you've done and have another go, eg:

> **Anna:** Sorry *Eric.* ^^ ^^ *I have got myself mixed up there.* ^^ ^^ *I'll have another go.* ^^ ^^

If you do not 'repair' this is bad for the child. It can be fatal to the child's testimony if, in his or her efforts to cope with the problem, he or she confabulates to give a response rather than no response.

15.7.7 Repeating the question

You should avoid repeating a question because repetition creates problems.

- The child could perceive you as being intimidating, ie:
  — he or she is failing because he or she has not given you the 'correct' answer;
  — you want a different answer.
- They have a leading effect—inducing the individual to comply, ie to go along with you.

Rather than repeat a question be honest, explain the problem, and then use an open-ended prompt, eg:

Anna: You told me about Y.^^ ^^ I need to know some more about Y. ^^ ^^ Can you tell me anything more about Y.

15.7.8 Revisiting topics

Returning to a topic raised earlier is unavoidable when interviewing. However, if you revisit a topic, particularly if this happens more than once, the child is likely to think that:

- you are not happy with the answer;
- he or she was wrong, ie not saying what you wanted to hear.

Each and every time you return to a topic you must explain to the child:

- why you have returned to the topic;
- that what he or she said earlier was not wrong;
- that you need to be very clear about what the child is saying.

15.7.9 Probing repeated events

If the child discloses repeated events there is a risk that the described experiences have acquired the status of script, ie a stereotype in memory. The most recent event is more likely to be remembered as a discrete episode. The first occurrence could also have retained its uniqueness. There can, of course, be no guarantees.

- Ask the child which of the events stands out most, eg:
  Anna: You've told me that Tom did nasty things lots of times, Eric. ^^ ^^ It is hard to remember one time when there have been lots of times. ^^ ^^ I'd like you to think really hard. ^^^^ In those lots of times when Tom did nasty things ^^ think and tell me about a time that you really remember a lot.
- Ask about the most recent time, eg:
  *Anna: I'd like you to think really hard ^^ ^^ about the last time Tom did nasty things. ^^^^ Tell me as much as you can ^^ ^^about that time. ^^*
- Ask about the first time, eg:
  *Anna: I'd like you to think really hard ^^ ^^ about the first time Tom did nasty things. ^^^^ Tell me as much as you can ^^ ^^ about that time. ^^*

Whichever event you probe, probe this exhaustively. Don't inadequately probe and topic hop from one event to another, and find yourself returning to an insufficiently probed event that you now want to know more about.

15.8 Accessing information non-verbally

15.8.1 Illustrators and enhanced drawing

Illustrators and enhanced drawing are excellent techniques to access information non-verbally, and in so doing facilitate yet more verbal disclosure. Enactment is, of course, inappropriate for describing physical acts of a sexual kind.

15.8.2 'Ninety-degree' drawing

This is a simple, effective technique that can assist disclosure by a young child concerning a key location, eg the bedroom in which alleged abuse took place. It is a variation of enhanced drawing, where you trigger disclosure through your own drawing.

You need A3 size (ie double A4) photocopying paper, two black pens or felt-tips (one for you, one for the child). Have to hand more paper and, out of sight, blue and red pens.

- Be sitting at right angles to the child, eg sitting on the floor or at a table.
- Take a piece of paper, and your black pen.
- Explain what you are about to do, eg:

    I feel like doing some drawing Charlie. ^^ ^^ *I'm going to draw my house.* ^^ ^^ *Tell you what,* ^^ *I'm going to fly over it like a helicopter.* ^^ ^^ *I'm going to take the roof off* ^^ ^^*and I'm going to draw what I can see inside* ^^ ^^ *as I look down from my helicopter.*

- As the child looks on, continue explaining and talking to the drawing as you draw, ie you don't look at the child.

    There's the stairs. ^^ ^^ *At the top, there,*^^ ^^*on that side,* ^^ ^^ *is the bathroom.* ^^ ^^ *Here's the door.* ^^ ^^ *I'm going to open it.* ^^ ^^ *That's the way it goes in,* ^^ ^^ *that way.* ^^ ^^ *There's the bath.* ^^ ^^ *And the sink.* ^^ ^^ *And the loo.* ^^ ^^ *Here's the brush by the loo.* ^^ ^^

- Engage the child's attention and contribution by asking questions as you draw, eg:

    You can see we've got three rooms, ^^ ^^ *that's the bathroom as I said.* ^^ ^^*That's our bed-room,* ^^ ^^ *that's our little boy's.* ^^ ^^

- Look up from your drawing, push a piece of paper and a black pen towards the child, and invite participation, eg:

    I've got lots of paper here Charlie ^^ ^^ *and here's another pen.* ^^ ^^ *Tell you what* ^^ *you fly over your house in your helicopter* ^^ ^^ *and take the roof off like I did* ^^ ^^ *and draw what you can see* ^^ ^^ *looking down from your helicopter.* ^^ ^^

- Continue drawing in parallel, but switch roles to you being observer, commentator and questioner of what the child is drawing.
- Gradually and naturally move to other rooms, and then the bedroom. Don't rush this stage.
- Because your drawing and the child's will be relatively full of detail, take a new piece of paper and give one to the child.
- Talk about your bedroom, trigger the child to draw his or her own.
- Then comment positively on the drawing and justify you copying what the child draws.
- Continue as for an enhanced drawing: adjusting the instructions on this technique in the Reference Section to the comprehension and communication ability of the child.

This technique can be adjusted according to the offence circumstances, the child, and can be applied to any location in which an alleged offence took place, eg you draw your car looking down, explaining what you are doing then invite the child to draw the car in question.

15.9   Inconsistency and contradiction

You should never challenge a witness, least of all a vulnerable witness. It would destroy the relationship, and lead the individual to disclose less, or even to stop disclosing completely.

- **Step 1.** Draw the witness's attention to things that are 'not quite clear'.
- **Step 2.** Appropriate questioning that requires the witness to take you through the detail again, without impugning the witness's character, ie not telling him or her that you consider his or her response to be untruthful, eg:

Anna: *I'm not too clear, Eric, about what he did between [A]* ^^ ^^ *and [B].* ^^ ^^ *It will help me a lot if I could hear again what he did* ^^ ^^ *telling me as much as you can.* ^^ ^^ *Don't rush.* ^^ ^^ *Have a think.* ^^ ^^ *Tell me as much as you can.*

When the inconsistency or contradiction endures or is added to, just accept it. Move on to the next topic.

15.10 Chapter summary

Interviewing a developmentally disadvantaged witness is a challenging conversation management task. It is a difficult conversation with an individual who has to cope with limited working memory, intellectual disadvantage, limited language comprehension, limited capacity to express his or her experience, and poor past experience of conversations with 'powerful people'.

ABE acknowledges the necessity for rapport and preparation before interviewing begins in earnest. Our view is that more emphasis must be placed on orientation and assessment, and more conscious attention to developing a conversational relationship with the child. This must, and will, take time. The return to this investment of time will be best evidence: yet another confirmation that quality evidence takes time.

16

Interviewing the Suspect: Key Considerations

16.1 Chapter overview

This chapter examines key issues that you have to consider in order to effectively manage the interview of any suspect: legal advice, interview planning, pre-interview disclosure to the legal adviser, practical preparation, the initial meeting with the suspect, the suspect's comprehension of the caution, his or her registration of any material presented to him or her, reactions to your questioning on 'bad character', your response to disclosures by the suspect that do not accord with what you know, and interviewing beyond the current interview.

16.1.1 Chapter objectives

This chapter will enable you to:

- foster a working relationship with the legal adviser based on a comprehensive understanding of legal advice to suspects;
- engage in interview planning that is matched to the circumstances of the case and the suspect;
- plan and prepare for using an applied psychological approach to pre-interview disclosure that creates a positive impression on the legal adviser, enhances your credibility, and increases your ability to manage the forthcoming interview;
- implement the applied psychological approach to pre-interview disclosure;
- make appropriate practical preparations for the interview;
- increase your ability to manage the forthcoming interview by using your initial meeting with the suspect to assist assessment of the individual, to make initial steps to developing a working relationship, and to attend to vulnerability factors;
- explain the caution mindful of individual differences in suspects' ability to comprehend;
- understand the rationale for the legal adviser's notification of the suspect's decision concerning his or her response to police questions;
- increase further your ability to manage the interview by obtaining the legal adviser's acknowledgement of the interview ground rules;
- respond appropriately to a request from the legal adviser or the suspect to stop the interview;
- fulfil Court of Appeal requirements concerning the presentation of material to the suspect for comment;
- understand the 'no comment' response to questioning on 'bad character' evidence;
- plan and prepare to use the FAIR review: a constructive approach to challenging anomalous disclosures and responses;
- conduct a FAIR review;
- consider what you will say in the closure stage about future interviewing.

16.2 Legal advice to suspects

16.2.1 The right to free legal advice

Under section 58 of the Police and Criminal Evidence Act 1984, all suspects have a right to free legal advice in private at any time.

16.2.2 The legal adviser

The individual who gives the suspect legal advice is generically termed a *legal adviser*. A legal adviser may be:

- a qualified solicitor;
- an accredited or probationary representative of the solicitor included on the register of representatives maintained by the Legal Services Commission.

The status of the accredited or probationary representative

Representatives are bound by exactly the same professional code as qualified solicitors.[1] It is important to note that paragraph 6.12 of Code C to the Police and Criminal Evidence Act 1984 states that representatives are solicitors for the purposes of the Code.

Some unprofessional investigators seek to 'put down' the legal adviser by misrepresenting the status of the legal adviser, telling the suspect that the individual is a legal representative and 'not a solicitor'.

- 'Putting down' is wholly inconsistent with a working relationship.
- The officer is implying the legal adviser is not qualified to act in the role of solicitor, and therefore the advice given is not competent.

Incompetent legal advisers

The legal adviser who behaves in a grossly incompetently manner presents a significant problem. The two key words are *behaves* and *incompetently*.

- **Behaviour not advice**. The advice that the adviser gives is not the issue. It is the behaviour outside the closed confines of the private consultation, eg when in the interview room, or attending an identification procedure with the suspect.
- **Incompetently not improperly**. The legal adviser's behaviour must reflect knowledgeability about police conduct, procedures, and what constitutes the required and the improper, unacceptable and illegal. How else could he or she be relied upon to defend the suspect? Incompetent behaviour is quite different to improper behaviour, eg disruptive conduct that renders you unable to put questions to the suspect, answering questions on the suspect's behalf, or providing written replies for the suspect to quote. Improper behaviour is covered by paragraph 6.9 of Code C to the Police and Criminal Evidence Act 1984. Incompetent behaviour risks sabotaging the police case. If the suspect is charged, a court might rule inadmissible that evidence obtained—or even facilitated—by this incompetence because the suspect did not receive his or her right to advice under section 58 of the Police and Criminal Evidence Act 1984. There have certainly been cases where courts have ruled in this way.[2]

If the legal adviser's behaviour is blatantly incompetent you should take the following action.

- Say nothing to the adviser, the suspect, or the appropriate adult. This would make matters worse not better.
- Pay particular attention to fulfilling every legal and procedural requirement to the letter. Do not attempt to turn the legal adviser's incompetence to your advantage.
- Make a note of the legal adviser's incompetent behaviour, brief your superior/manager and the Crown Prosecution Service (CPS) who will be able to advise.

---

[1] Solicitors Regulation Authority (2011) *SRA Code of Conduct*. London: Law Society Publishing.
[2] eg *R v Mankda* (1997) Preston Crown Court. Unreported.

16.2.3 The role of the legal adviser

The legal adviser represents the side of the defence:

- from receiving the initial request to attend the police station;
- to the final CPS/police decision concerning the case against the suspect.

The Court of Appeal made it clear that the legal adviser's sole task is to defend actively and skilfully, continuously protecting the suspect and the client's legal interests *at all times*.[3] Note 6D to Code C to the Police and Criminal Evidence Act 1984 says:

> The solicitor's only role in the police station is to protect and advance the legal rights of the client. On occasions this may require the solicitor to give advice which has the effect of the client avoiding giving evidence which strengthens a prosecution case. The solicitor may intervene in order to seek clarification, challenge an improper question to their client or the manner in which it is put, advise their client not to reply to particular questions, or if they wish to give their client further legal advice.

16.2.4 The legal adviser's aims

The legal adviser has seven aims which are summarized in Box 16.1.

To fulfil these aims the legal adviser will build a *case narrative*, a cumulative picture of 'what's happened' in respect of the case, including police contact with the suspect and the police investigation (Box 16.2).

Action when requested to attend

Typically when informed that a suspect is in custody and wishes to be legally represented the legal adviser will seek to cover a number of tasks.

---

1. To investigate:
   — the allegation;
   — the line of reasoning, ie why the police believe the suspect rather than anyone else committed the alleged offence;
   — the police case;
   — the prosecution evidence;
   — the police investigation;
   — all police contact with, and conduct towards, the suspect.
2. To assess the extent of the suspect's:
   — vulnerability;
   — ability to comprehend, to cope, and to communicate to best effect in any police interview.
3. To identify the **safest defence** for the suspect:
   — to remain silent; or
   — to provide a written statement; or
   — to answer police questions.
4. To influence the police to accept the suspect is not guilty.
5. To influence the police not to charge the suspect.
6. To influence the police to make the most favourable case disposal decision for the suspect: the most constructive alternative to charging relative to the circumstances of the case and the suspect.
7. To create the most favourable position for the suspect if he or she is charged.

Box 16.1 The legal adviser's seven aims (Shepherd, 2004[4])

---

[3] *R v Miller, Paris and Abdullahi* [1993] 97 Cr App R 99.

[4] Shepherd, E. (2004) *Police Station Skills for Legal Advisers*. London: Law Society Publishing.

Topic	Examples of detail	Potential source of information
Circumstances leading up to the offence	• Lead up to incident. • Police already *in situ* (eg proactive investigation: acting on information received; police surveillance.)	***Main*** Consultation with Investigating Officer (IO). ***Subsidiary*** Call from third party (re: lead up to incident). Call from the suspect (re: lead up to incident). Consultation with the suspect (re: lead up to incident).
Occurrence of the offence	• Offence(s). • The suspect's involvement. • Other persons involved.	***Main*** Consultation with IO. ***Subsidiary*** Call from third party. Call from the suspect. Consultation with the suspect.
How the offence came to police attention	• 999 call to police. [Note: This could be the point where the *first description* is given.] • Officers at or near scene.	***Main*** Consultation with IO. ***Subsidiary*** Call from third party. Call from the suspect. Consultation with the suspect.
Initial police response to the offence	• Despatch of police (by Control Room). • Immediate police intervention.	***Main*** Consultation with IO. ***Subsidiary*** Call from third party (re: police intervention). Call from the suspect (re: police intervention). Consultation with the suspect (re: police intervention).
Initial police actions at the crime scene	Identification of, and contact with: • victim; • eyewitnesses.	***Main*** Consultation with IO. ***Subsidiary*** Call from third party. Call from the suspect. Consultation with the suspect.
Immediate police contact with other officers/police locations via radio	• Content of situation report transmitted. • Circulated description of the offender or offenders. [Note: This is typically the point of *first description*.]	Consultation with IO.
Subsequent police actions at the crime scene	• Interviewing of victims and witnesses. • Recording of scene and vicinity (sketches; photography; video-recording). • Physical searches of scene and vicinity. • Identification of material locations. • Discovery of *object evidence* (items and objects; video- and audio-recordings; still photography) • Discovery of *CTM* (fingerprints, human marks, non-human marks, body-derived substances and traces, non-human substances and traces). • Securing the scene. • Identification of further witnesses (by 'house-to-house' enquiries).	***Main*** Consultation with IO. ***Subsidiary*** Call from third party. Call from the suspect. Consultation with the suspect.

Box 16.2 The case narrative (Shepherd, 2004)

Topic	Examples of detail	Potential source of information
Police contact with the suspect—prior to, at the time of, and after the offence	• Tracking, observation, and detention of the suspect (including location if not the crime scene). • Questioning and arrest of the suspect (or the request to attend the police station). • During the journey to the police station. • Whilst being booked into custody. • Comments (ie significant statements; relevant comments).	*Main* Consultation with Custody Officer (CO). Consultation with IO. *Subsidiary* Call from the suspect. Custody record. Consultation with Appropriate Adult (AA). Consultation with the suspect.
Interviewing of the suspect	• At or near the scene of the offence. • At another location (eg the suspect's home). • En route to the police station. • Following arrival at the police station. • Comments (ie significant statements; relevant comments).	*Main* Consultation with IO. *Subsidiary* Call from the suspect. Consultation with CO. Custody record. Consultation with AA. Consultation with the suspect.
Identification procedures	• Type of procedure. • Modality examined (visual; auditory).	*Main* Consultation with CO. Custody record. *Subsidiary* Consultation with IO. Consultation with AA. Consultation with the suspect.
Taking of fingerprints, photographs, samples, swabs, and impressions		*Main* Consultation with CO. Custody record. *Subsidiary* Consultation with IO. Consultation with AA. Consultation with the suspect.
Physical examination of the suspect by forensic medical examiner (police surgeon)/ custody nurse		*Main* Consultation with IO (access to clinician's/ nurse's report(s) and observer notes). Consultation with CO (access to custody record entries). *Subsidiary* Consultation with AA. Consultation with the suspect.
Subsequent police investigation	• Interviewing of the victim or witnesses. • Taking, or making, of formal statements. • Attendance by crime scene attender/ SOCO. • Searches of locations and vehicles. • Submission of items for forensic analysis.	*Main* Consultation with IO. *Subsidiary* Consultation with CO (re: searches). Custody record (re: searches). Consultation with AA (re: searches). Consultation with the suspect (re: searches).
Other contact between the suspect and police officers since detention	• Requests by the suspect to 'talk with an officer'. • Off-tape interviewing, eg in cell; in interview room; in a police vehicle). • Taking the suspect to the scene.	*Main* Consultation with the suspect. *Subsidiary* Custody record (re: periods in custody of an officer for unspecified reason). Consultation with IO (re: taking to crime scene). Consultation with the suspect.

Box 16.2 The case narrative (*continued*)

- Talk with the custody officer concerning detention and custody record matters.
- Talk with the suspect. The legal adviser will explain that the suspect should not answer the adviser's questions freely but to answer 'yes' or 'no' until such time as the legal adviser says that it is appropriate to answer freely. This is a safeguard against the conversation being overheard.
- Attempt to speak with the investigating officer, but will not press the issue if no contact can be established.

Action on arrival at the police station

On arrival at the police station the legal adviser will examine the custody record carefully. In particular he or she will examine and note:

- the details of the arrest;
- the suspect's details;
- critical timings in terms of the 'detention clock';
- the signatures by the suspect—to identify potential clues to illiteracy and associated vulnerability;
- the narrative entries in the record, eg all police staff contact with the suspect, examinations, indications that the suspect slept little or not at all throughout the night, taking (and refusal) of refreshment;
- matters to do with property—looking out for such matters as medication.

Pre-interview disclosure

The legal adviser will then request pre-interview disclosure. The Law Society guidelines[5] on advising the suspect have a checklist for obtaining disclosure (Box 16.3). Many officers are surprised that the checklist covers many more issues than are contained in the pre-interview disclosure document that they produce.

Meeting with the interpreter, appropriate adult, or reader

If there is an interpreter, appropriate adult, or reader (under paragraph 3.20 of the Police and Criminal Evidence Act 1984) involved, the legal adviser will explain that whatever passes between the legal adviser and the suspect is legally privileged (see later) and explain what this means. The adviser will then ask if the individual:

- will respect the confidentiality of any exchange between the adviser and the suspect;
- will give an undertaking not to pass on to the police anything said in the consultation.

If the individual refuses, the legal adviser will explain that the individual cannot be present during the adviser's consultation with the suspect. In the case of an interpreter, the Legal Aid Fund will cover the cost of an alternative interpreter found by the adviser.

Consultation with the suspect

The legal adviser will then consult with the suspect in private. During this consultation the legal adviser will follow a standard sequence of actions.

- Establish if there are any concerns that prevent the suspect concentrating on the matters to be covered.
- If possible, reassure that everything will be done to address these concerns.
- Take personal details.

---

[5] Cape, E. (2006) *Police Station Advice: Advising on Silence.* London: Law Society.

Seek disclosure regarding the alleged offence(s).
- Respond appropriately to the serving of a written disclosure document.
- Comprehensively record initial disclosure.
- Assess initial disclosure.
  — The allegation against the client.
  — The line of reasoning that leads the police to believe the client rather than anyone else committed the offence.
  — The 'special knowledge' that the police attribute to the client concerning the circumstances before, during, after the offence.
  — The police case.
  — The prosecution evidence.
  — The police investigation.

If the disclosure equates to 'no disclosure' or minimal disclosure
- Make representations.
- If necessary, make a position statement.

If the evidence is complex or relates to an old offence(s)
- Ask for full disclosure.
- Press for time to consider disclosure.

In all cases
- Probe the case narrative.
- Obtain information held by the police concerning:
  — the client—including information on 'bad character';
  — the client's potential vulnerability;
  — any medical examination of the client.
- Probe the crime scene and any other key location(s).
- Probe systematically every form of potential prosecution evidence.
  — Covert information on the client.
  — Accounts and descriptions from victim and witnesses (initial version and subsequent formal statements/video-recorded interviews; first descriptions).
  — Accounts or statements by co-accused.
  — House-to-house enquiries.
  — Films, video-recordings, and photographs released to the media.
  — Identification by witnesses.
  — Object evidence (ie material items of any kind: recovered from crime scene or in searches; video- and audio-recordings; still photography).
  — Fingerprints, impressions, traces, and substances.
  — Specialist opinion and testimony.
  — Significant statements by, or silence from, the client.
  — Interviewing of the client to date (account(s) given).
  — Formal statements taken from the client.
- Obtain detail on outstanding investigations.
- Obtain detail on intentions concerning other investigatory procedures.
- Obtain the investigating officer's assessment of the prosecution evidence.
- Identify the purpose of interviewing the client—including intended coverage of 'bad character'.
- Obtain detail on proposed interviewing arrangements.
- Obtain the investigating officer's view on case disposal.

Box 16.3 Law Society checklist for obtaining police disclosure (Cape, 2006[6])

- State what was said to the legal adviser in pre-interview disclosure in terms of:
  — the allegation;
  — the line of reasoning, ie why the police believe the suspect rather than anyone else committed the alleged offence.

---

[6] Cape, E. (2006) *Police Station Advice: Advising on Silence*. London: Law Society Criminal Law Committee.

- Explain in terms that are pitched towards the suspect's apparent level of comprehension:
  — the definition of the alleged offence;
  — the points to prove the offence;
  — available defences in law.
- State what was said to the legal adviser in pre-interview disclosure in terms of the police case, ie what the police believe were the circumstances leading up to, during, and following the commission of the offence.
- State what evidence was disclosed to the legal adviser.
- Give the suspect the legal adviser's assessment of the strength of the case based on the content of pre-interview disclosure.
- Explain that the suspect should give his or her version of events, telling the truth, describing matters in as much detail as possible, and without rushing.
- Listen to the account:
  — some will take notes or create an SE3R while this account is being given;
  — others will just listen then ask for a second telling in which they will take notes or create an SE3R.
- Examine the account to identify anomalies.
- Probe anomalies.
- Check back the account, inviting correction and expansion.
- Identify the safest defence, noting this in his or her legal notebook.
- Inform the suspect of the options: safest to least safe.
- Invite the suspect to decide, note the decision with the date and time, and get the suspect to sign.
- Explain the ways of responding to questions, according to the choice made by the suspect.
- Typically give the suspect some 'role play' practice in being questioned and the correct way to respond according to the chosen response to police questions.

A detailed description of this process is in *Police Station Skills for Legal Advisers*.[7]

16.2.5 The contractual relationship between the legal adviser and the suspect

In technical terms the legal adviser receives *instructions* from the suspect, who is his or her client. It is important to realize the following constraints on the legal adviser.

Legal privilege

The legal adviser has a professional contract with the suspect. Whatever the suspect says to the legal adviser is a matter of legal privilege.[8] The legal adviser can tell no other person anything about what was said and done when the suspect was consulting with the legal adviser. It is solely the suspect's decision as to whether he or she wishes to waive legal privilege, thus allowing the legal adviser to disclose material from the consultation.

The legal adviser has to accept what the suspect says

Whatever the suspect asserts to be the case, eg his or her explanation or description of events leading up to, during, and following the offence, the legal adviser has to accept. The legal adviser has no means of validating—checking—what the suspect asserts. Even if the legal

---

[7] Shepherd, E. (2004) *Police Station Skills for Legal Advisers*. London: Law Society.
[8] Solicitors Regulation Authority (2011) *SRA Code of Conduct*. London: Law Society Publishing.

adviser thinks that what the suspect is asserting is improbable, impossible, unbelievable, or nonsensical, there is nothing that he or she can do if the suspect insists this is the truth.

The legal adviser has to accept what the suspect decides

The legal adviser cannot decide for the suspect. If the suspect has decided to do something that he or she will regret later, or renders the suspect vulnerable now, the only thing that a legal adviser can do is to advise strongly.

16.2.6 Identifying the safest defence

The *safest defence* is the response to police questioning that does the suspect least harm if he or she is charged and goes to court.

The suspect has three options.

- To exercise the right to silence, ie to respond to police questioning concerning the allegation by saying 'no comment'.
- To answer questions concerning the allegation.
- To produce a prepared defence statement and thereafter respond to police questioning concerning the allegation by saying 'no comment'.

Identifying which of these options is the safest defence is a methodical process.

Assessing information that has been gathered

The legal adviser will have gathered information covering seven factors.

The amount of police disclosure

Disclosure covers:

- the allegation;
- the line of logic, ie why the police suspect this individual rather than anyone else;
- the police case, ie an account of circumstances leading up to, during, and following the commission of the offence;
- the prosecution evidence—comprising information and actual evidence.

The strength of the prosecution evidence

If there has been little or no disclosure then it will be extremely difficult to assess this. Even where evidence is lacking, an indirect, approximate assessment can be made of whether there is a persuasive case against the suspect based on:

- the existence of a clear allegation;
- a reasonable line of logic for believing the suspect committed the offence;
- an appropriately detailed police case that does not exhibit any of the anomalies described in this text.

The suspect's age and maturity

Immaturity is not always associated with age. A teenager may behave immaturely, eg displaying inappropriate bravado and engaging in confabulation, eg talking for effect or 'bullshitting'. Some adults behave in such an immature manner and are similarly a risk to themselves.

The suspect's experience of custody and questioning. As pointed out in Chapter 1, it has long been recognized that being in police custody is extremely stressful. We experience stress whenever we cannot control circumstances, and this certainly describes the suspect's position in the police station. Although a suspect might have been in police custody many times and could be deemed to 'be used to it', there will always be unique stress attached to this particular instance of being in custody. The same psychology applies to individuals who have been to prison many times. They may know what to expect but it does not make this particular period without liberty any easier—and in many ways makes it harder—to bear.

The suspect's psychological vulnerability

Like you, the legal adviser has to take into account and assess the overall impact of all the suspect's potential or actual sources of vulnerability.

- Current physical and mental state.
- Exposure to stress-inducing adverse personal circumstances and significant life events.
- Other sources of individual pressure, eg from the suspect's family, and social and cultural groups of which he or she is a member.
- Being within a mentally vulnerable category as defined in Code C to the Police and Criminal Evidence Act 1984.
- Having a source of vulnerability in his or her psychological 'make-up' not recognized in Code C, eg, lack of self-esteem, poor interpersonal skills, lack of assertion skills, excessive shyness or timidity.

The suspect's case

The suspect may have an innocent explanation. As pointed out earlier the legal adviser has to accept this even if he or she considers it to be improbable, impossible, nonsensical or counter to reasonable behaviour.

Alternatively the suspect may say that he or she committed the offence. The legal adviser has no means of validating this and cannot know the motivation for admitting the offence, eg:

- the suspect wants to protect the true offender;
- the suspect is deeply depressed at the enormity of what has happened eg the death of a child or a passenger in a car driven by the suspect;
- the suspect is overwhelmingly embarrassed or guilt-laden, eg wants to confess even though the 'crime' being admitted is not that which exists in legal terms.

Even if the indicators are that the suspect committed the offence, there has to be an advantage to making an admission. Even with the provision in section 144 of the Criminal Justice Act 2003 concerning possible sentence reduction for an early admission of guilt, there can never be any guarantee of reduction. Indeed, this would be unlikely if the suspect had a record of violent offending or was 'caught red-handed'.

If the suspect does not have an innocent explanation and says that he or she will make up a story, the legal adviser cannot allow this to happen (see later).

The suspect's personal reasons for remaining silent

The suspect might say that he or she knows who committed the offence. Although every citizen has a civic duty to assist the police, this is not a statutory requirement. The legal adviser has to take into account the substance of this personal reason for silence.

Identifying the safest option

The legal adviser has to balance the risks by combining all the assessments on the seven critical factors.

- **The risk of the court drawing an adverse inference under section 34 of the Criminal Justice and Public Order Act 1996 if the suspect remains silent**. The risk is low if at court the defence can show that at the time the legal adviser advised the suspect the following circumstances applied to such an extent, or in such a combination, as to have made it reasonable for the suspect to remain silent and not to mention a fact upon which he or she relies.
  — There was little or no disclosure.
  — The offence and the evidence was complex or the allegation was dated, but the suspect was not given time to assimilate or to reflect upon the material.
  — The disclosed evidence was weak being fundamentally lacking, fundamentally flawed, or both.
  — The suspect was extremely psychologically vulnerable at the time of the interview.
The risk is higher if these circumstances applied to a lesser extent, or in lesser combination. The risk is higher still if these circumstances only applied to a limited extent.
- **The risk of the suspect performing badly in interview and failing to do justice to his or her case**. The defence can argue at court that remaining silent was reasonable given that there was a high risk of the suspect performing badly in the interview due to significant inability to comprehend or to communicate coherently or circumspectly. Both are obvious pre-requisites to doing justice to one's case. Significant disadvantage necessarily stems from any of the following:
  — Little or no disclosure of the police case and the prosecution evidence.
  — Lack of experience of police custody and questioning.
  — Extreme psychological vulnerability arising from problems in respect of extreme immaturity, personality, psychological functioning, current physical and mental state, exposure to stressors, and adverse personal circumstances.
  — A combination of these factors.
The degree of disadvantage defines the degree of potential risk.

Figure 16.1 shows a decision-making template that enables the legal adviser:

- to map his or her assessments of these seven dimensions;
- to identify the degree of risk posed to the suspect by the interviewing process;
- to identify the safest defence to police questions.

The safest defence route

A suspect can revise his or her defence decision at any time and go down another route in terms of the safest defence given the evolving circumstances Figure 16.2 shows the safest defence routes available to the suspect as he or she progresses from one interview to the next.

Prior to the commencement of interviewing the legal adviser, and therefore the suspect, will not know if your intention is to conduct one interview or more than one. The safest defence for the initial—and perhaps only—interview is therefore critical.

Not all the seven decision-making factors have the same weight. The most significant dimension is degree of disclosure. The legal adviser is very likely to conclude that the safest defence is to exercise the right to silence if you do not communicate convincingly to the legal adviser that there is a grounded allegation, ie a persuasive case against the suspect. The clues that the case is not persuasive are:

- your line of logic for concluding that the suspect rather than anyone else committed the offence is tenuous or lacking;
- your account of the police case is anomalous, ie is 'thin' with few events and lacking detail throughout, is non-specific, or both;

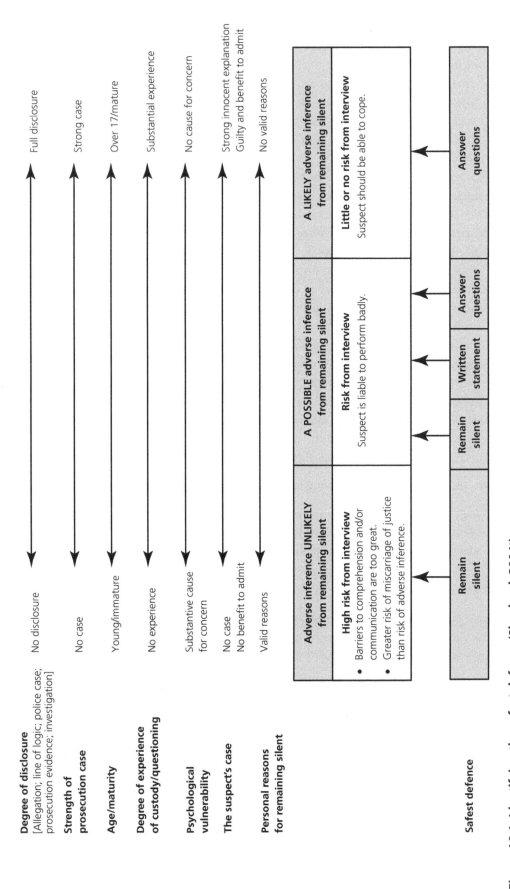

Figure 16.1 Identifying the safest defence (Shepherd, 2004[9])

[9] Shepherd, E. (2004) *Police Station Skills for Legal Advisers*. London: Law Society Publishing.

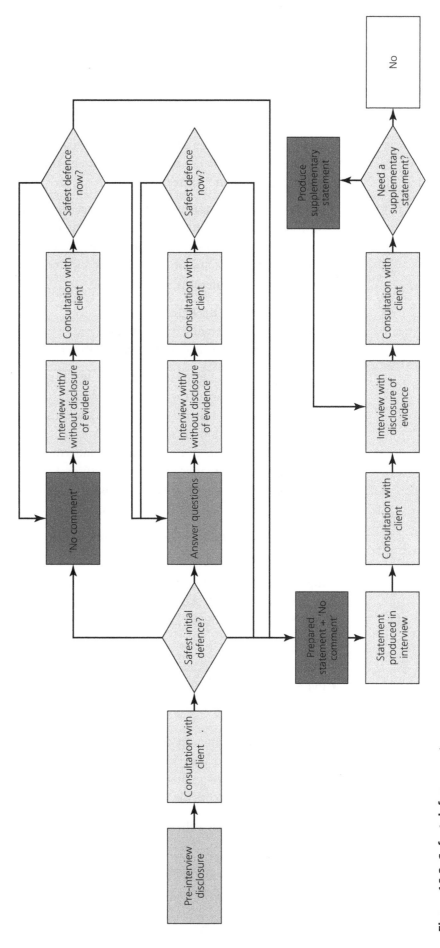

Figure 16.2 Safest defence routes

- you have disclosed little or no prosecution evidence: not even as to the type of evidence underpinning the allegation, line of logic, and the police case.

In contrast, if you have communicated to the legal adviser that there is a persuasive case, you have effectively created the circumstances in which the Court of Appeal has said that society expects an early innocent explanation if the suspect claims innocence to his or her legal adviser.[10] There are only two options available to the suspect, either to:

- answer questions, giving an innocent explanation; or
- produce a written defence statement containing the innocent explanation, and exercising the right to silence thereafter.

If you gave little or no disclosure and the suspect remains silent in the initial police interview, your questioning will provide pointers to your line of logic for suspecting the individual, the police case, and the prosecution evidence. After this interview the suspect can, following further consultation and advice, decide on the next step in the safest defence route, ie in the next interview, either to:

- continue exercising the right to silence; or
- switch either to answering questions; or
- produce a prepared defence statement and thereafter remain silent.

The risk after the initial interview is that you will decide that further interviewing is inappropriate or unnecessary. If the decision is made to charge the suspect, the court could well draw a section 34 adverse inference from the suspect's silence in the single interview. If the suspect has asserted innocence in consultation, at charge the legal adviser will produce a prepared defence statement containing the innocent explanation.

If there is a second interview in which the suspect continues with 'no comment' and no substantive evidence emerges, the legal adviser will conclude that taking the risk to continue exercising the right to silence has paid off.

- The likelihood is that there is no substantive evidence.
- The risk of charging is low.

If the suspect has responded 'no comment' and there is a third interview, the suspect has *three* options available. If substantive evidence emerges in this interview—or indeed in any interview—the legal adviser can always request interviewing stop to enable the giving of legal advice in private:

- whether to answer questions; or
- to produce a prepared defence statement and continue to remain silent.

If charged, the court:

- will focus on what the suspect said or did not say:
  - after switching to answering questions; or
  - in his or her written statement;
- will have little or no interest in 'no comment' responses in earlier interviews.

Whatever point at which the suspect answers questions, he or she has only *two* options thereafter, either to:

- continue answering questions; or
- produce a prepared defence statement and thereafter remain silent.

---

[10] *R v Howell* [2003] EWCA Crim 1.

The suspect cannot change from answering questions to 'no comment' in response to offence-related questioning. To switch in this manner would be to engage in *mixed responding*. This risks an almost inevitable section 34 adverse inference, with the court concluding that the suspect could not provide an answer to those questions responded to with 'no comment'.

Where the suspect in consultation tells the legal adviser that he or she will lie

Instances occur where the suspect tells the legal adviser that he or she will make up a 'story', ie lie in the interview. There are two circumstances in which this might happen.

The suspect admits guilt but intends to lie

The legal adviser cannot knowingly and actively assist a client to mislead the police. This rule derives from two sources and applies to any legal adviser, ie solicitor or solicitor's representative.

The Solicitors Regulation Authority Code of Conduct[11]

Principle 1:

> You must uphold the rule of law and the proper administration of justice.

Principle 2:

> You must act with integrity.

A known deception when defending at this stage has the potential to give rise to a deception of a court should the suspect be charged.

Criminal Law Act 1967, section 4

This states:

> Where a person has committed an arrestable offence, any other person who, knowing or believing him to be guilty of an offence…does without lawful authority or reasonable excuse any act with intent to impede his apprehension or prosecution, shall be guilty of an offence.

The legal adviser must advise the suspect of the key issues.

- The suspect must not lie in the police interview. The only option open to the suspect is to remain silent. It is neither unethical nor an offence to give this advice.
- If the suspect is unable to accept this advice, ie still intends to lie, the adviser has no alternative other than to withdraw now, ie without giving the reason, to inform the custody officer that another legal adviser must be found for the suspect.
- If the suspect accepts the advice now but gives responses in interview that the adviser knows to be untrue, the adviser will ask the officer to stop the interview to allow a private consultation with the suspect. This will protect the suspect but, in the consultation, the adviser will explain the situation.
  - The suspect has said things in the interview that the adviser knows to be untrue.
  - The adviser explained earlier that if the suspect said things to the police that the adviser knew to be lies, the adviser must cease representing the suspect.

---

[11] Solicitors Regulation Authority (2011) *SRA Code of Conduct*. London: Law Society Publishing.

— If the suspect will not take the advice on this matter, the legal adviser must withdraw immediately, ie without giving the reason, to inform the custody officer that another legal adviser must be found for the suspect.

— The legal adviser is unable to say what sense the police will make of the adviser withdrawing at this point.

— The police will know that one reason for a legal adviser withdrawing is when a client says things that the legal adviser knows to be untrue.

— The legal adviser will ask the suspect for a final time whether he or she is prepared to follow the advice on this matter.

— If the suspect still intends to lie, the legal adviser will withdraw immediately.

The suspect asserts innocence but an intention to confess

The legal adviser must:

- probe the suspect's reasons for confessing even though he or she asserts innocence;
- attempt to dissuade the suspect;
- if the adviser's counsel is rejected, respect the suspect's assertion even though this is not in the suspect's best interests.

The adviser must explain that once a confession has been made it is remarkably difficult to retract. It is almost impossible to convince a court that the confession is false. If the court does accept that it is false then the suspect is liable to prosecution for wasting police time or perjury. Having explained this the adviser must:

- advise the suspect that there are far safer options;
- ask the suspect to allow the adviser to take him or her through these options.

If the suspect rejects these efforts, the adviser should explain that what the suspect intends to say is, in effect, a lie and an attempt to mislead the police. The suspect must understand that this puts the adviser in an impossible situation. The adviser may decide that he or she should respond in the same way as though the suspect is stating that he or she will lie to the police, as described earlier. However, this is a thorny problem. If the suspect is adamant there is no obligation upon the adviser to withdraw at this point. Many legal advisers are unwilling to withdraw given the greater risk to the client if he or she 'goes it alone'.

The implications

- As the exercise of the right to remain silent is likely to be advised in very many cases and for a wide variety of reasons, it is common sense to anticipate, to plan, and to prepare for a 'non-comment' initial interview in every case.

16.2.7 Constructing a 'defence'

Many police officers hold the view that a significant proportion of legal advisers make up, or help the suspect to make up, a 'defence'—an untruthful constructed narrative—giving a purportedly innocent explanation to account for the circumstances and information given in pre-interview disclosure. This perception is particularly the case in the context of high-volume crime, and crimes of low to medium seriousness.

As pointed out in Chapter 4, the second hurdle facing a would-be liar is the construction of a storyline, or script. Most would-be liars keep the memory demand to the minimum by constructing a script with a limited number of steps and a limited amount of detail. They are typically 'thin' accounts.

Any 'defence' constructed by, or with the assistance of, an unethical legal adviser will of necessity be a 'thin' account given the mental functioning of many suspects. Three clinical psychologists assessed suspects in two police stations over three months. Their findings were sobering.[12]

- The average IQ of suspects was 82. This is very low, given that an IQ of 100 is general population average.
- Forty-two per cent of suspects had an IQ between 70 and 79: the range of score called *borderline learning disability*, formerly *borderline mental handicap*.
- One third of all suspects assessed were mentally impaired.
- About 35 per cent of suspects were not in a normal mental state due to:
  — extreme distress;
  — mental disorder;
  — being under the influence of drugs.
- About 20 per cent of suspects were suffering from an unusually high level of anxiety and distress.

A suspect with a constructed defence is struggling as soon as probing starts. He or she has to cope with the third hurdle to lying—making up detail as he or she goes along. The story will collapse in the face of an interviewer who reveals the lies because he or she:

- remembers what the suspect says;
- detects the anomalies;
- responds with systematic questioning.

The suspect is then in an even worse situation. Having answered questions, the option of acceptable 'no comment' cannot apply because this would be mixed responding. The constructed 'defence' has set the suspect up for an adverse inference to be drawn at court.

The vast majority of legal advisers know the realities. Constructing a 'defence' is against the rules of professional conduct, it is unethical and illegal, and harms the client. The only sensible advice to give to a suspect who does not have an innocent explanation that will pass muster, and for whom an admission offers no benefit, is to exercise the right to remain silent.

16.3 Interview planning

16.3.1 Right person

Wherever possible, you should not interview both the victim of a serious alleged offence and the alleged offender—otherwise it will be extremely difficult for you to engage in the essential RESPONSE behaviour of being non-judgemental. Everything that you hear will be through a filter of what you know or believe to be the case.

16.3.2 Interview strategy

Interview strategy is reviewed in some detail in Chapter 11.

When planning and preparing your interview strategy to interview a suspect, you need to consider the same kinds of factor. These are summarized in Box 16.4.

---

[12] Gudjonsson, G., Clare, I., Rutter, S., and Pearse, J. (1993) *Persons at Risk During Interviews in Police Custody: The Identification of Vulnerabilities*. Royal Commission on Criminal Justice. London: HMSO.

Detailed analysis of the offence

Includes:

- injuries to the victim;
- body deposition;
- verbal communication by the offender to the victim—with a particular view to the identification of a 'signature' or characterizing pattern.

Suspect's 'biography'

Includes significant life events in the journey from infancy to the present, eg:

- time spent in 'care' contexts;
- bullying, abuse;
- special education;
- disrupted education;
- periods of hospitalization;
- loss of significant relationships (through such events as bereavement, family break-up, separation and divorce, imprisonment);
- contact with the police;
- acquisition of a criminal record.

Suspect's current 'environment'

Includes:

- *current social support*, eg family and non-family relationships, friends, acquaintances, and position within the home and non-home context, links to community including ethnic and religious groups;
- *domestic circumstances*, ie the setting in which the suspect lives;
- *sources of stress*, eg micro stressors (continuing sources of stress including financial situation, family problems, relationship problems—infidelity, continuing arguments and violence—and sources of threat and fear), and significant life stress events occurring over the past year.

Suspect's current physical and mental state

Includes:

- physical state—including any injuries and wounds;
- continued effects of ingested recreational drugs, including alcohol;
- effects of medication;
- degree of fatigue;
- lack of sleep;
- emotional state, eg degree of apprehension, fear, dread;
- evidence of extreme emotion: anxiety, depression;
- distractibility due to external concerns, worry, substance dependency, pain.

Suspect's frame of reference (FOR)

Includes:

- strong feelings, attitudes, beliefs, values, prejudices;
- expectations, particularly of other people, communicated needs;
- sense of shame, guilt, remorse;
- fantasies (thoughts, feelings, and behaviours—particularly sexual, violence- and pain-associated—linked to particular types of individual, context, activity, events).

Suspect's psychological 'make-up'

Includes:

- cognitive competencies including language use and working memory, illiteracy, level of intellectual functioning (high, average, or low);
- past and present psychological problems/diagnosed and treated conditions indicators to self-esteem (high, average, low valuing of himself or herself), need for respect, attention, affection, sympathy;
- need to exercise power and control;
- disposition to acquiescence, compliance, and suggestibility;
- personality, ie habitual ways of behaving such as introversion, extraversion, impulsiveness (acting without thinking).

Suspect's past and present behaviour

Includes characteristic patterns of:

- social behaviour—and marked changes in this—when interacting with others, eg level of social skill (high, average, or low ability to relate to and communicate with other people), degree of assertiveness (dominant, appropriately assertive, submissive), emotional responsiveness, tendency to explosive behaviour;

Box 16.4 Suspect interview strategy: relevant factors

- coping behaviour and marked changes in this when under stress: 'acting out', attention seeking, anger, verbal abuse, destructiveness, violence, self-harm, suicidal thoughts, suicidal gestures, attempted suicide, depressive reactions, addictive behaviours, substance abuse, excessive sexual activity.

Requirement for third parties

According to the needs of the suspect, eg:
- interpreter;
- reader of documentation;
- appropriate adult.

Box 16.4 Suspect interview strategy: relevant factors (*continued*)

Scope and degree of research required

The generality of suspects

Researching the offence should present no problem nor should the descriptive detail concerning the suspect. However, researching the suspect's 'biography', current 'environment', past and current behaviour may be limited to:

- police sources with knowledge of the suspect;
- data systems containing detail from previous contact with the police;
- intelligence systems.

The custody record can provide information on the suspect's current physical and mental state, and any communicative disorder. They may not have much to contribute on psychological 'make-up' other than the suspect:

- disclosing mental or psychological problems;
- providing evidence, eg reading and signing the custody record that the suspect has a learning disability or is unable to read.

Neither they nor you are expected to be clinical psychologists. The only requirement is common sense, and observation in the way described in Chapter 7. You have to remain alert to the manifest. The research cited earlier found that about 20 per cent of suspects clearly required an appropriate adult, whereas custody staff only identified 4 per cent as needing this support.[13]

Individuals suspected of extremely serious offences

In cases involving extremely serious offences and where the suspect has particularly significant attributes (eg a history of such offending, a diagnosis of personality disorder), the interview has all the potential to be an exceptionally difficult conversation. The Senior Investigating Officer (SIO) will have a team to assist in determining the most suitable interview strategy.

- The assigned interview adviser.
- Assigned interviewers.
- Colleagues who know the suspect and who have had contact with the suspect recently or in the past.
- Very often an external adviser, eg a forensic psychologist or forensic psychiatrist, will be part of the advisory team.

---

[13] Gudjonsson, G., Clare, I., Rutter, S., and Pearse, J. (1993) *Persons at Risk During Interviews in Police Custody: The Identification of Vulnerabilities*. Royal Commission on Criminal Justice. London: HMSO.

The content of the interview strategy

The content of the interview strategy for interviewing all suspects will reflect the entire range of issue covered in previous chapters.

- An assertive, empathetic (Quadrant 4) pattern of conversational behaviour (Chapter 3).
- Observing the range of RESPONSE behaviours (Chapter 5).
- Attention to the issues of right person, right place, right time, right question (Chapter 8).
- Attention to the right manner of questioning (Chapter 9).

Where interviewing involves an exceptionally difficult conversation with a 'one-off' character, the content of the interview strategy will need to cover particular topics.

- **Arrest strategy, where the suspect has yet to be arrested.** Typical issues will be:
  - timing;
  - how the arrest will be done;
  - the gathering of as much information as possible from any exchanges between the suspect and the arresting officers, and those transporting him or her to the police station, and custody staff from arrival onwards.
- **How police and police staff employees should relate to the suspect during detention.** This needs to cover:
  - all points of contact between the suspect and staff, outside and within the interview room;
  - form of address.
- **Contrast factors.** Achieving the 'best', least contrasting match.

16.3.3 Where the case involves complex evidence or is elderly

The Court of Appeal has ruled[14] that a suspect should be given time to consider matters where the evidence is complex or a substantial period of time has elapsed between the offence and the requirement to interview the suspect. A sensible approach is to draw up a timetable, ie:

- initial briefing;
- interval of sensible duration to enable the legal adviser and the suspect to consider disclosure;
- initial interview.

16.4 Planning and preparing pre-interview disclosure

16.4.1 The key: communicating a grounded allegation

The perspective of the Law Society and practitioner texts on advising suspects in the police station is clear.[15] In the light of *R v Howell*, if the suspect asserts innocence to the adviser and the police have communicated a grounded allegation—a persuasive case—a 'no comment' response to police questions will actually harm the suspect should he or she be charged. A grounded allegation has four elements.

Element 1. Clear allegation

Communicating this should present no problem.

---

[14] *R v Roble* [1997] Crim LR 449.

[15] Cape, E. (2003) *Defending Suspects at Police Stations: The Practitioner's Guide to Advice and R.* London: Legal Action Group; Keogh, A. (2006) *CLSA Duty Solicitor's Handbook*. London: Law Society Publishing; Shepherd, E. (2004) *Police Station Skills for Legal Advisers*. London: Law Society Publishing.

Element 2. Rationale for suspecting the individual

This might be difficult to verbalize if, for whatever reason, you are unwilling or unable to allude to even the type of evidence underpinning the allegation.

Element 3. Detailed police case

Your Case SE3R ensures that you are able to draft a suitably explicit, but not over-detailed, account that is sanitized (no mention of evidence *source*), is convincing, and anomaly-free.

Element 4. An indication of the prosecution evidence

What you describe and in what level of detail is a matter of professional judgement. There are categorical views within the service, not necessarily held by all officers, concerning disclosure of evidence.

- The case of *R v Imran and Hussein*[16] confirmed that police officers do not have to disclose the existence of evidence. Some officers 'don't do' disclosure, ie they only ever give minimal or no disclosure.
- Prior to the first interview some officers will not disclose evidence as a tactic. Their view is, 'Let's hear what the suspect says first'.
- Some officers never disclose or allude to 'golden nugget' or 'trump card' evidence, particularly fingerprints, DNA, and CCTV. They withhold this to the last.

All these views rest upon a wholly invalid assumption: the legal adviser will advise the suspect to answer questions in these circumstances. From all that you have read earlier, it is clear that it is highly unlikely that the legal adviser will give such advice.

If you allow applied psychology to inform your practice of pre-interview disclosure, you will be able to deliver on Element 4 in a way that will increase the likelihood of the legal adviser concluding that there is a persuasive case against the suspect.

16.4.2 Applying psychology in pre-interview disclosure

You and the legal adviser want something that is not the same but very akin.

- You want the legal adviser to advise the suspect—whether asserting innocence or seeing a benefit in admitting culpability—to do this rather than remaining silent. With the 'detention clock' ticking in the background 'no comment':
  — is wasteful of investigative time and resource;
  — is potentially harmful to the progress of the investigation.
- The legal adviser wants you to give him or her sufficient information to identify the safest defence for the suspect, ie:
  — if the suspect asserts innocence to the adviser, he or she should give an early innocent explanation;
  — if the suspect admits culpability to the adviser and there is a benefit to admitting culpability, he or she should admit this and perhaps others in interview.

There is a gap between your position and that of the legal adviser.

The gap

There are always two points of view when two people talk to arrive at a mutually acceptable decision, eg concerning a holiday to be taken, or the potential for a pay increase. Each party

---

[16] *R v Imran and Hussein* [1997] Crim LR 754.

has an *opening position*: what each is prepared to state to the other, inviting the other to accept this. A *gap* between these positions is entirely natural: it is not very common for people to have the same view, or 'take', on matters.

Negotiation is the gradual process of narrowing the gap. It involves each party showing an ability to adjust his or her position to get round to the other person's side of the 'problem' and to take into account some, but not all, of the other person's perspective. You will recognize that this is empathy: one of the key RESPONSE behaviours described in Chapter 5, and an essential ingredient of active listening, ie listening with the 'third' ear.

All negotiators have what is called their *final*—or *'walk away'*—*position*. This is the point at which the individual is unwilling to make any further accommodation to the other's perspective.

Progressing from opening position through stages of gradual accommodation, the aim is for both parties to end up with final positions which achieve an outcome in which:

- neither party feels that he or she has 'lost' and the other 'won';
- both parties feel that it is a 'win'–'win'.

The 'win'–'win' outcome of pre-interview disclosure is:

- the legal adviser is persuaded that there is a grounded allegation such that:
  — if the suspect asserts innocence, he or she gives an early explanation either by answering questions or producing a prepared written defence statement;
  — if the suspect admits guilt to the adviser, and there is an advantage in making an admission, the suspect makes an admission in interview;
- you have a suspect who does not waste valuable time, frustrate your investigation, and add to your cumulative caseload by answering 'no comment'.

In any negotiation, if either party's final, 'walk away' position is the same as his or her opening position then he or she is saying from the outset, 'Take it or leave it'. If your opening position on disclosure is also your final position then it creates what sociologists call a *self-fulfilling prophecy*: virtually guaranteeing that the legal adviser will advise the suspect to exercise the right to silence in the knowledge that there is minimal risk of an adverse inference from silence at this stage.

Closing the gap

Planning and preparing to apply the psychology of seeing each other's position, narrowing the gap between these to achieve a 'win'–'win' outcome, offers a realistic prospect of avoiding automatic 'no comment'.

Your opening position on prosecution evidence

There will always be cases in which you cannot give even an indication of the prosecution evidence, eg it may be the outcome of covert investigation, sources need to be protected, or there are public interest immunity issues. In these cases a 'no comment' response is to be expected. For the majority of cases, however, you are able to exercise your professional judgement.

There is only one imperative when disclosing evidence: you must not deliberately lie. Deliberately lying includes misleading,[17] overstating,[18] and telling an untruth,[19] ie representing something to be the case that it is not. There are practical as well as ethical reasons for not

---

[17] *R v Miller, Paris and Abdullahi* [1993] 97 Cr App R 99.
[18] *R v Mason.* [1987] Crim LR 757.
[19] *R v Heron, Daily Mail,* 22 November 1993. See Wolchover, D. and Heaton-Armstrong, A. (1996) *Wolchover and Heaton-Armstrong on Confession Evidence.* London: Sweet and Maxwell.

telling lies. In all your dealings with the legal adviser, the suspect, and any third party, they are assessing you in terms of integrity: can you be trusted. You are building up a 'bank account' of trustworthiness. As soon as it becomes clear that you have deliberately lied you have overdrawn your 'bank account'. The relationship between you and the adviser, the suspect, and the third party will radically change for the worse. No one listens to an untrustworthy police officer. Your untrustworthiness will live on, being remembered and affecting all that you seek to do the next time you have to relate to that legal adviser or suspect.

It makes sense to consider a minimum opening position that might convince the adviser that there is a persuasive case. This minimal position would be to state simply the *type* of evidence that you have.

Progression from your opening position to your final position

For each type of evidence you can use a grid (Box 16.5) to plan the steps that you can take from your opening position, through additions to your opening position, to your final position.

If the adviser does not ask a question beyond a particular point then leave it at that. You do not need to disclose something unless you are asked a question.

You can collate all the progressive disclosure positions for the different types of evidence on a simple one- or two-page document, ie one complete grid or separate grids for each evidence type.

Opening position	Fingerprint evidence.
Addition 1	More than one print.
Addition 2	Prints in separate locations.
Addition 2 + Final Position	Locations are material to the offence.

Box 16.5 Opening position–additions–final position grid

16.5 Delivering pre-interview disclosure

16.5.1 Electronic recording

Across the country the practice of recording pre-interview disclosure is still unevenly applied. It is not clear why some practitioners—police officers and legal advisers—cling on to the practice of not recording. What we do know is that without a recording either or both parties have no means of evidencing:

- whether something was or was not disclosed spontaneously;
- the content of requests and questions asked and the responses to these.

The Law Society recommends that the legal adviser should use his or her own recorder if the police officer does not record.[20]

16.5.2 The significance of pre-interview disclosure

Adversarial does not have to mean combative and antagonistic

The UK has an adversarial legal system. Prior to the Court of Appeal ruling in *Miller, Paris and Abdullahi*[21] it was uncommon for solicitors to engage in active defence of their clients

---

[20] Shepherd, E. (2004) *Police Station Skills for Legal Advisers*. London: Law Society Publishing.
[21] *R v Miller, Paris and Abdullahi* (1993) 97 Cr App R 99.

in the police station, and particularly in the interview room. Solicitors viewed the task of defending the client as beginning after charge, in the adversarial setting of the courtroom. Now legal advisers must defend their clients continuously from the moment they are summoned to the police station and especially in the interview. From the legal adviser's perspective, this destines the investigating officer and the adviser to occupy adversarial roles in the legal sense: the officer representing the prosecution and the adviser the defence.

The basis for this perspective is worth thinking about.

- When the police arrested the suspect, they believed it was more likely than not that he or she had committed the offence.
- This assessment was inherited and endorsed by the custody officer when he or she authorized the suspect's detention to obtain evidence through questioning, and the detention of the suspect to gather evidence through questioning.
- The police are building a police case against the suspect which will, upon charge, become the contents of the prosecution case.
- Withholding detail concerning evidence is a tactic to prevent the guilty suspect constructing an untrue version of events to account for disclosed detail.
- Where a suspect says something that does not accord with withheld detail, there is a significant psychological and practical pressure to construe the suspect as the one not telling the truth.

Of course, common sense argues that neither police officers nor advisers should view adversarial as meaning—and giving licence to be—combative, hostile, or antagonistic. Consider the court room where the Crown prosecutor and the defence lawyer fulfil their adversarial roles without being aggressive or acrimonious, or abusing each other. In fact, they make a point of being courteous and, to the extent that they have to, they work together on their separate but nonetheless collaborative tasks.

Managing the conversation with the legal adviser

Your task is to manage the conversation with the adviser: the conduct of a conversation that extends from first contact through pre-interview disclosure up to the point of final contact concerning case disposal. How the two of you relate as persons and in your conversations will affect your management of each and every interview with the suspect. As with any conversation that you have to manage, it will require attention to reciprocity and evidencing RESPONSE behaviours to foster a constructive working relationship.

Simple gestures

Often simple gestures give birth to what eventually emerges as an entirely positive working relationship. Engaging in a relationship loop, shaking hands, and the offer of a tea or a coffee are all that it needs, eg:

> *Hello. Mr Herity isn't it?* ^^ *My name is Alan Marshall,* ^^ *I'm the duty CID officer working on the case involving your client* ^^ *John Carter.* ^^ *Sorry you've had to wait out there for a while.* ^^ ^^ *It's pandemonium here today as I'm sure you've seen and heard!* ^^ ^^ *I'm just about to get a cup of coffee before we go to the room where I'll brief you.* ^^ ^^ *I can fix you one it's no bother. What would you like?* ^^ ^^

Impression management

You want to create in the mind of the legal adviser a positive assessment of you as a person and as a professional. You acquire credibility in two stages: *initial* and *derived*.

Initial credibility

Your initial credibility stems from the immediate impression that you make.

- You should always be smart, well groomed, and never give the appearance of being the worse for wear as a consequence of your non-working life prior to coming on duty.
- You should be assured without being over-confident, and courteous without being deferentially polite in the manner described in Chapter 5.

Derived credibility

Being smart, alert, and assured is important. However, derived credibility is critical. It derives from your manifest knowledge, understanding, skills, attitude, and behaviour. From your first meeting the legal adviser will be assessing your credibility in terms of:

- your demonstrated grasp of the detail of the case;
- your demonstrated knowledge of every aspect of the suspect;
- your management of the investigation thus far;
- your demonstrated awareness of the legal adviser's role and what this involves;
- you awareness of the Law Society's guidelines and disclosure checklist.

Minimizing misunderstanding and intervention in the interview

If you do not pay attention to creating a working relationship with the legal adviser in pre-interview disclosure, both you and the adviser enter the interview room as strangers, neither very much interested in the other, both acting defensively and wary as to what the other is doing and why. The legal adviser is likely to be excessively primed to intervene to:

- question what you are doing;
- request the interview be stopped to allow consultation with the suspect.

You can avoid this situation if you put your mind, and devote conscious effort to making clear:

- your intended conduct of the interview;
- your intended management of the process of questioning and the exchange of information;
- your reasons for managing it in the way you describe.

16.5.3 The legal adviser signals that there is too little disclosure

In the Law Society's disclosure checklist (Box 16.3) you will see that the adviser should make representations, ie to make it apparent that there is a problem and inviting you to go some way to resolving it.

Whenever your opening position is the same as your final position, the legal adviser is likely to follow the Law Society's advice and make a *position statement* citing the case of *R v Roble*.[22] The wording will differ from one adviser to another. The following example captures the key issues.

> *I have pointed out that I have not spoken to my client yet. I also pointed out that what you have said to me does not constitute a grounded allegation. I have asked you to be flexible and to give me some more information to convince me that there is a persuasive case against my client. You have indicated*

---

[22] *R v Roble* [1997] Crim LR 449.

that you will not be flexible on this matter. I therefore have to let you know that unless you are prepared to revise your position on this, my client may well exercise the right to remain silent. I will remind you that in R v Roble *the Court of Appeal ruled that one of the reasons that a court might not draw an adverse inference from silence is where a legal adviser has so little information that he or she cannot usefully advise the suspect. I am saying that we have such a situation. I would therefore ask you to reconsider your decision and let me have at the very least some more information that would enable me to conclude that there is a grounded allegation upon which I can usefully advise.*

Don't panic. Just accept this feedback and be appropriately assertive and empathetic, eg:

Thank you. ^^ *I appreciate you position on this matter.* ^^ *If the matter does go to court it will be for the court to decide on these matters.* ^^ ^^

16.5.4   Disclosing what you know about the suspect

An extremely effective aspect of creating a positive impression on the legal adviser is to be proactive in disclosing about the suspect. Rather than wait for questions reflecting the Law Society checklist, get in first by providing appropriate information.

Descriptive detail concerning suspect

It is very professional for you to provide the adviser with a suitable summary version of what you know about the suspect. Even though you may not be considering questioning in respect of the suspect's 'bad character', it would be perverse not to let the adviser know details of the suspect's history of contact with the police and the police record.

The suspect's actual or potential vulnerabilities

Again, it is professional to let the legal adviser know of any actual or potential vulnerability the suspect has and that you are aware of. Vulnerability here, of course, means the entire spectrum including:

- the continuing effects of ingested drugs/alcohol (dehydration, lassitude, distractibility, problems with attention and working memory);
- behaviour since being detained that gives you cause for concern, eg:
  - the suspect has not slept throughout the night (indicative of high anxiety and distractibility—which will affect his or her attention and working memory in the interview);
  - the suspect has refused food and drink (indicative of an acute anxiety and/or depressive reaction which will affect attention and memory);
  - the suspect has not taken the opportunity to freshen up (again indicative of severe depression and social withdrawal).

Giving very simple explanations will ensure that the legal adviser does not inappropriately intervene to ask you to speed up the interview.

Effects of alcohol

You will have seen from the Custody Record ^^ *that John was brought in the worse for wear.* ^^ *He's slept it off* ^^ *but you'll see when you meet him that he is still pretty rough.* ^^ *We need to get some fluid into him.* ^^ *I don't know if you've brought in your attendance kit anything for him to drink.* ^^ *If you haven't* ^^ *I'll fix you up with a couple of hot drinks to take into your consultation.* ^^ ^^ *Also we'll have water in the interview room.* ^^ ^^

*In the interview I appreciate that John might find it difficult to concentrate. ^^ So I will keep the pace of the interview right down. ^^ I'll give him plenty of time to think about what I say or ask, ^^ and plenty of time to think before he says anything, ^^ and plenty of time after he's said something. ^^ ^^*

Lack of sleep

*You will have seen from the Custody Record that Wayne has not slept throughout the night. ^^ Of course that's a matter of concern for both you and me. ^^ In the interview I appreciate that Wayne might find it difficult to concentrate,^^ to keep track of what is being said and done and to hold information in his head. ^^ So I'll keep the pace of the interview right down. ^^ I'll give Wayne plenty of time to think about what I say or ask, ^^ and plenty of time to think before he says anything, ^^ and plenty of time after he's said something. ^^ ^^*

Refusal of refreshment

*You will have seen from the Custody Record^^ that Joanna has not accepted any offer of refreshment since she was brought in last night. ^^ Of course that's a matter of concern for both you and for me. ^^ I don't know if you've brought in your attendance kit anything for her to eat and drink. ^^ If you haven't ^^ I'll fix you up with a couple of drinks to take into your consultation. ^^ I would ask you to encourage Joanna to eat anything that you might have brought with you ^^ or what we offer her after your consultation. ^^ When I meet Joanna prior to interview I will ensure that I have another hot drink ready. ^^ In the interview I appreciate that she might find it difficult to concentrate, ^^ to keep track of what is being said and done ^^ and to hold information in her head. ^^ So I'll keep the pace of the interview right down. ^^ I'll give her plenty of time to think about what I say or ask, ^^ and plenty of time to think before she says anything, ^^ and plenty of time after she's said something. ^^ ^^*

Refusing to freshen up

*Andy has refused the offer to wash and freshen up this morning. ^^ Of course that's a matter of concern for both you and me ^^ because we want him to be as alert as possible. ^^ I would ask you to encourage him to take up the offer after your consultation. ^^ When I meet Andy prior to interview I will ensure that the offer is made again. ^^ In the interview I appreciate that he might not be that alert, ^^ and find it difficult to concentrate, to keep track of what is being said and done and to hold information in his head. ^^ So I'll keep the pace of the interview right down. ^^ I'll give him plenty of time to think about what I say or ask, ^^ and plenty of time to think before he says anything, ^^ and plenty of time after he's said something. ^^ ^^*

Medical examination of the suspect

Common sense dictates that you give the legal adviser all the detail that you have on this matter. Doing so before being asked is again demonstrative of your credibility.

16.5.5 Disclosing on key locations

An extremely effective aspect of creating a positive impression on the legal adviser is to be proactive on the issue of key locations. Provide the legal adviser with suitably sanitized drawings and other key location representations before being asked for these, eg *Here is a diagram which shows the entrance to the night club, the adjacent taxi rank, and where the group was standing when the attack happened.*

This is a tangible aid for the legal adviser, for which he or she will be grateful. It will be something that makes it easier to consult with the suspect. In giving what is not really a lot, you demonstrate reciprocity yet again, contributing further to the development of a working relationship.

16.5.6 Disclosing on evidence

At this point you should cease to be proactive and become reactive to the legal adviser's questioning. Some advisers will give you a mini-briefing framed upon the suggested content for such a briefing in *Police Station Skills for Legal Advisers*.[23]

> *I would now like to ask questions about evidence in this case. I am working from a standardized checklist. This means that some of the types of evidence may not apply in this case. Only you will know this.*
>
> *For each type of evidence I will therefore ask if it is an issue in this case. You may think that it is irrelevant or strange to ask about a particular type of evidence given the nature of the alleged offence, what you know, and what you have told me so far in your disclosure. However, I request your forbearance on the matter and your recognition that it is my professional duty to cover all types of potential evidence.*

Thereafter, where you are able, and consider it appropriate, to disclose on a particular type of evidence you can adopt the negotiation—opening position-additions-final position—approach to disclosure. As pointed out earlier, if the adviser does not ask a question beyond a particular point then leave it at that, ie you do not need to disclose something unless you are asked a question.

16.5.7 Disclosing on outstanding investigations

Disclosing on these matters is all part of communicating a persuasive case. If you give a succinct but suitably detailed description, this will add further to your credibility.

16.5.8 Disclosing on intended coverage of 'bad character' evidence

The legal adviser will be interested at what point in the interview you intend to introduce 'bad character' evidence. Don't be fazed by this. It is a reasonable question.

16.6 Practical preparations

16.6.1 Collate your interview materials

Set yourself up to navigate smoothly around your materials in the interview.

- Put your interview management materials, ie Route Map, Case SE3R, and WOB map of I[3] in a separate folder. Placing items in 'polyslip', 'see through' pockets is very helpful.
- Label individual items in your folder with a Post-It so that you can quickly look down, locate, and register the contents.
- Put any evidential items to which you will want to refer, eg diagrams, in a separate plain folder. You do not want them on view as a visual distraction.

---

[23] Shepherd, E. (2004) *Police Station Skills for Legal Advisers*. London: Law Society Publishing.

16.6.2 Always prepare for a 'no comment' interview

You must dominate the detail that you have.

- Read your Case SE3R.
- Examine any individual SE3Rs, grids, observer-participant plots, and genograms.
- Examine any key location representations.
- Examine your Route Map.
- Examine your WOB map of I^3.

16.6.3 Setting up the room

- Organize the layout: bearing in mind particular elements of SOFTENS—seating positions, orientation of chairs, and distance from suspect.
- Have your folders to hand.
- Keep evidential items out of view until you want to work with them.
- Work on an 'empty' desk basis, putting no materials in a position where the suspect can be distracted by them, or attempt to read upside down.
- Make sure that there is water.

16.6.4 Personal preparation

- Don't drink alcohol in the 12 hours before you interview. Interviewing is like being a pilot or an authorized firearms officer: alcohol impairs your attention, concentration, ability to register detail, and your ability to hold and to handle detail in working memory.
- Don't drink large amounts of fluid before the interview. It will have the expected biological effect. You will become distracted by your need to visit the toilet.
- Freshen up. In every interviewing context in which the authors have worked, they have always had a toothbrush and toothpaste to hand. Cleaning your teeth before an interview makes you feel enormously alert.
- Before meeting the suspect in the custody suite area visit the toilet as the last act of preparation.

16.7 Meeting with the suspect

16.7.1 Closely observe and monitor the suspect's demeanour and behaviour

If possible hold back a moment to observe the suspect's demeanour and behaviour. As pointed out in Chapter 7, this is like an initial 'snapshot', which is a sensible basis for subsequent monitoring and for making sense of the suspect's observable behaviour. Go methodically through the elements of BASELINES. Then approach the suspect.

From now on continue applying BASELINES and listen with your 'third ear', to the vocal clues to the suspect's 'feelings', ie emotional state and attitude to you, the current topic, and the conversation.

16.7.2 Establishing contact

Your task is to manage the conversation with the suspect from this point on: a conversation that will extend up to the point of final contact concerning case disposal. As with any conversation that you have to manage, it will require attention to reciprocity and evidencing RESPONSE behaviours to foster a constructive working relationship. The suspect will be assessing you in terms of the impression you create, in particular how caring you seem, and your credibility.

Take with you two hot drinks or two cups of water. Engaging in a relationship loop, shaking hands, and the offer of a tea or a coffee are all that it needs, eg:

> *Hello.* [extending hand] *My name is Alan Marshall* ^^ *I'm the duty CID officer working on the case* ^^ *and you are…?* [Shaking hands; wait for reply; echo reply] *John Carter.* ^^ *How would you like to be called?* [Wait for reply; echo reply; stop shaking the suspect's hand; release] *John. OK John.*^^ ^^

16.7.3 Attend to physical needs and vulnerability

You don't want the interview to start and then have the suspect being distracted by the need to go to the toilet. In addition to ensuring that the suspect uses the toilet, you must attend to any vulnerability issues to do with not drinking, eating, or not freshening up. You can to this very neatly by combining the requirements, eg:

> *I'm a bit concerned, John, that you've not taken anything we've offered you to drink* ^^ ^^ *I'm a coffee person* ^^ *So I'm off to get a drink of coffee before we go to the interview.* ^^ ^^ *I can fix you one it's no bother. What would you like?* ^^ ^^ [Suspect indicates his or her preference.] *Now while I'm doing that* ^^ *it will be a help for you to go to the toilet* ^^ ^^ *and also to freshen up with a quick face wash.*^^ ^^ *That'll set you up well* ^^ *for when we talk to each other in the interview room.* ^^ ^^

16.7.4 Smoking

People who are addicted to nicotine are highly vulnerable. Nicotine is both a stimulant and a relaxant. Individuals with psychological conditions in which an extremely high level of anxiety and distractibility are symptoms, eg schizophrenia and anxiety states, are typically very heavy smokers. These individuals need nicotine.

Nicotine patches can help but they do not work for everyone. Also some forensic medical examiners (police surgeons) are unwilling to prescribe such patches because of potential side effects.

16.8 The caution

16.8.1 Comprehension and delivery of the caution

Since its introduction, the caution has been a cause of enormous problems for police officers and those on the receiving end. The Home Office asked psychologists to produce a simplified version. After some 60 attempts they gave up. The problem lies in the fact that the caution is too long, it contains too many concepts, and is a nightmare in terms of lexicon (the actual words), the grammar (the construction of words, phrases, and sentences), and the syntax (the way the ideas are connected).

Research has shown that the assumption that people in the street, ie presumed not to be intellectually disadvantaged, would understand the caution is without foundation. One hundred and nine people were stopped in the street and taken through the caution, and their understanding checked at each stage when listened to twice. They were asked to point to a card to identify their highest educational attainment level and a check was made on their reading ability (reading age), an indirect indicator of IQ.

- On average, people claimed that about half of the caution made sense.
- When delivered as a whole, about one in eight actually understood the second, long, 'difficult' element.
- Even when the caution was repeated, and said as separate sentences, still only about one in four understood this element (Box 16.6).
- Also worrisome was the fact that eight out of ten people perceived the second element to be pressuring, many viewing it as a threat that they would be in trouble if they did not answer questions.

Police officers learn the caution as a lifeless script: difficult wording and words to be remembered and rattled off by rote. They become so used to it that they say it quickly and without stressing the key ideas. They have missed the point. It is a formality, but it is something that is extremely important for the person on the receiving end to understand. It is not just a series of words that the 'job' requires to be dumped on the individual.

This is not solely an aspect of police behaviour. Call centre workers who have to deliver similar scripts with important information behave in the same manner. Listen the next time that you renew an insurance policy. You will often be given a script in insurance 'jargon' (eg *I have to advise you…*). Typically, this will be read too quickly for you to keep up with, and in a completely 'flat' voice, ie with no emphasis on key ideas. You will recall in Chapters 3 and 7 that it was explained that when people speak naturally they place emphasis on key ideas. This helps the listener to keep track and to identify and to comprehend. Police officers, like call centre staff, fail to appreciate that although they know the script by heart and can rattle it off without thinking, it is thoughtless and a waste of time if the individual on the receiving end fails to understand the important messages. For the recipient to understand the script, or in your case the suspect to grasp the caution, you must put your awareness of the issues into effect.

- Give an alerting statement, eg *Now I'm about to say something.* ^^ ^^ *It's called the caution.* ^^ ^^ *It is very important that you understand it.* ^^ ^^ *It has a lot of information in it.* ^^ ^^ *So please listen to it as closely as you can.* ^^ ^^
- Because this is an interview—as opposed to a situation of pressure, eg an arrest on the street—you should deliver the caution twice. Let the suspect know this, eg *I'm going to go through the caution twice* ^^ ^^ *because it is important* ^^ ^^ *and because it does have a lot of detail in it.* ^^ ^^
- Deliver the script, in 'bite-sized chunks', pausing between each chunk to enable the suspect to:

	Number who correctly understood when caution delivered as a whole	Number who correctly understood when caution delivered as separate sentences	Remarks
You do not have to say anything.	27%	92%	
But it may harm your defence if you do not mention when questioned something which you later rely on in court.	14%	39%	Strong association with educational level and reading ability.
Anything you do say may be given in evidence.	35%	87%	

Box 16.6 The caution: comprehension in the general population (Shepherd, Mortimer, and Mobasheri, 1995[24])

[24] Shepherd, E., Mortimer, A., and Mobasheri, R. (1995) 'The Police Caution: Comprehension and Perceptions in the General Population. *Expert Evidence*, vol 4, 60–7.

— register the detail;
— place the detail in working memory;
— pull knowledge from long-term store in order to understand what you have just said;
— make sense of this bit of material in the context of everything said before this bit.

> *You do not have to say anything.* ^^ ^^ *But it may harm your defence* ^^ ^^ *if you do not mention* ^^ ^^ *when questioned* ^^ ^^ *something which you later rely on* ^^ ^^ *in court.* ^^ ^^ *Anything you do say* ^^ ^^ *may be given in evidence.* ^^ ^^

• Take the suspect through the caution again:
— delivering it a chunk at a time;
— checking back the suspect's understanding: not by asking a closed confirmatory 'yes'/'no' question but by inviting the suspect to explain his or her understanding of the chunks.

16.8.2 Explaining the caution

Explaining is an attempt to give understanding:[25] in this case to the suspect concerning the caution. All explaining involves four elements.

• Understanding the knowledge and characteristics of the person who needs to understand.
• You having a complete grasp of the 'problem', what needs to be explained.
• The process of explaining.
• The outcome, ie establishing whether you have succeeded in your task of explaining.

Understanding the knowledge and characteristics of the suspect

You cannot take anything for granted. You will recall in Chapter 1 that particularly those with the investigative mindset of defensive avoidance make assumptions: they 'beg the question' rather than ask the question, never checking whether something is or is not the case. The *Practice Advice on Core Investigative Doctrine*[26] urges investigators to adopt the ABC—*assume nothing, believe nothing, challenge everything*—approach when investigating, ie treating all material as possibly wrong and regarding all sources of material as potentially misleading. This is a variation on a long-established CID heuristic: *assume nothing, believe no-one, check everything*.

You cannot assume that even someone who does not appear to have a comprehension problem will actually understand the caution. Six out of ten people still don't understand the second element even when read a second time. It follows that many with 'normal' comprehension will not understand the caution if they are affected by:

• the stress of extreme emotion, apprehension, fear, dread, anxiety, depression;
• fatigue;
• little or no sleep the night prior to being questioned;
• distractibility, eg thoughts and concerns elsewhere, worrying about other matters; a heavy smoker who desperately needs nicotine;
• a vulnerable psychological 'make-up', eg is acquiescent, compliant, suggestible;
• any combination of these points.

A suspect's grasp of the caution will be limited to say the least if he or she is vulnerable in terms of developmental disadvantage through young age, old age, or being learning disabled. His or her understanding will be even more tenuous if any of the other factors that affect 'normal' comprehension apply.

---

[25] Brown, G. (2006) 'Explaining' in O. Hargie (ed.), *A Handbook of Communication Skills*. London: Croom Helm.
[26] ACPO/Centrex (2005) *Practice Advice on Core Investigative Doctrine*. Cambourne: ACPO/Centrex.

You have to see the 'problem' through the eyes of the suspect. If you know the suspect is vulnerable, it makes sense to refresh your awareness of the issues concerning developmental disadvantage covered in Chapter 14.

The process of explaining

You can know the subject but still be a poor explainer. Your colleagues working in criminal justice administration units will be able to show you evidence of this. Police service staff—those transcribing records of interview—typically keep memorable examples of failure to explain the caution in simpler terms.

Effective explanation rests upon identifying what are termed 'keys': key ideas that you consider the individual on the receiving end needs to grasp in order to unlock his or her understanding.[27] In practical terms the process of explaining is:

- turning each 'key' into an explanatory statement;
- joining the 'keys' up using linking explanatory statements.

It would be inappropriate for the authors to provide you with an explanation 'crib', ie a 'here's what to say to explain this key idea'. It would be counter-productive because any explanatory 'keys' would be pitched at a person with a particular degree of vulnerability or disadvantage. The 'keys' would be inherently inappropriate for someone who had a lesser or greater degree of vulnerability or disadvantage. The answer is to:

- assess the level at which the suspect is functioning in terms of his or her manifest thought processes, ie:
  — listen with your 'third ear' to his or her way of talking and describing;
  — look closely at his or her demeanour and the responsiveness observable in his or her reactions and non-verbal behaviour;
- take into account the factors described earlier, ie:
  — his or her circumstances;
  — all the evidence that points to potential or actual vulnerability or disadvantage;
- pitch your explanation of each 'key' to his or her need.

In almost every instance you will need to get some basic concepts across before attending to the actual wording of the caution. We would suggest that you—at the very minimum—address the individual's understanding of the following key ideas which may seem straightforward to you but could be meaningless to a vulnerable or disadvantaged suspect. Wherever possible, draw a sketch to help you to help the individual visualize what you are talking about, eg the police station, the court, the judge.

- Harm.
- Defence.
- Mention.
- Mentioning something.
- Rely on.
- Court.
- Evidence.

We all have to face up to the fact that comprehension of these basic building blocks of the caution is fundamental. Consider the alternative.

---

[27] Brown, G. (2006) 'Explaining' in O. Hargie (ed.), *A Handbook of Communication Skills*. London: Croom Helm.

- Stating to the individual an extract from the caution which has the key idea or ideas embedded in it.
- Then saying the sentence another way, ie trying to change the words, the wording, and the sentence structure to make the key ideas in the original extract 'simpler'.

Even if you do this slowly, the result is that the individual's chances of grasping are actually less rather than more. You have filled up his or her working memory with:

- the original words, wording, and sentence structure of the extract caution;
- your subsequent words of 'simplifying' explanation.

The outcome: checking the suspect's understanding

In effect you are receiving feedback on the worth of your explanation. You may have explained the caution to the suspect, but if he or she does not understand it despite your efforts, your explanation was not an explanation after all.

Following the ABC heuristic, you should believe no-one who answers 'yes' to a closed confirmatory 'yes'/'no' question concerning comprehension. As pointed out in Chapter 5 concerning the Empathy element of RESPONSE and the need to check comprehension, the motivation for saying 'yes' can be varied.

- The individual does not want to appear stupid. It is important to know that people who have a learning disability know that they have such a disability and some will go to great lengths to disguise their problem.
- The individual does not want to take more of your time.
- The individual wants to get the interview over and done with as quickly as possible.
- The individual wants to please by appearing co-operative.

There is only one sensible way to check the suspect's comprehension.

- Get the suspect to prove that he or she has understood the 'key', eg *So I need to check with you Tom that you are clear about that.* ^^ ^^ *Take your time* ^^ ^^ *Don't rush.* ^^ ^^ *Tell me what you understand I've just said.* ^^ ^^
- If the suspect's explanation does not capture the key ingredients of what you were saying, repeat your explanation—and check back again in the appropriate way.

16.9   **The notification of the suspect's decision**

The legal adviser should notify the suspect's decision when you invite the legal adviser to introduce himself or herself. Strictly speaking the legal adviser should use the present tense, eg *My suspect is deciding to exercise his/her right to silence.* If the adviser uses the past tense— *has decided*—this is technically a breach of the suspect's legal privilege by making public his or her advice to the suspect.

In exceptional circumstances the legal adviser will give a reason for the suspect's decision, eg:

- when no sensible pre-interview disclosure has been made;
- when the case is elderly/complex and the suspect and legal adviser have been given insufficient—or in the case of urgent interviewing—no time to examine personal documentation (in the case of an elderly case) or to consider the evidence (in a complex) case;
- when the interview is taking place late at night/very early in the morning;
- when the legal adviser is prevented from sitting beside his or her suspect—the justification being given while standing by the suspect and the adviser remaining there until a seat is provided.

16.10 Spelling out the ground rules

After checking back each ground rule with the suspect you should get the legal adviser to 'sign off' his or her comprehension—and acknowledgement—of the rule. Keep this 'signing off' exchange to a minimum using a closed confirmatory question to do this, eg *Are you clear about that* [name of legal adviser]*?*

16.11 Responding to a request to stop the interview

16.11.1 A request from the legal adviser

The suspect's right under section 58 of the Police and Criminal Evidence Act 1984 to free legal advice in private at any time is sacrosanct. As we saw earlier, Note 6D to Code C to the Police and Criminal Evidence Act 1984 says the legal adviser may intervene if they wish in order to give their suspect further legal advice.

The only proper response

If the legal adviser intervenes to request the interview be stopped so that he or she can advise the suspect, you have to stop the interview. It is important to recognize that the request is based upon the adviser's assessment of the suspect's legal situation in the light of all that has transpired up to that point.

Improper responses

Attempting to nullify the legal adviser's intervention

Some officers attempt to nullify the adviser's intervention by asking the suspect if he or she wishes the interview to stop. It is because the suspect needs to know his or her legal position and is no judge of this at the moment that the adviser is intervening.

Refusing the request or delaying the point at which the interview will be stopped

You cannot refuse the adviser's request, eg by asserting that the legal adviser has had his or her chance to advise before the interview. Nor can you say that you will stop at a point convenient to you.

The legal adviser's management of an improper response

Whether or not the suspect says that he or she does not wish the interview to stop, the legal adviser must:

- insist on the interview stopping to advise the suspect;
- point out that:
  - the suspect's right to free legal advice in private at any time is being denied;
  - the adviser is obliged to advise in public to exercise the right to silence until legal advice can be given in private;
  - the recording will provide evidence for the court concerning the improper response to the request to stop the interview.

16.11.2 A request from the suspect

If the suspect asks to speak to the adviser in private, or to use the toilet, you have to stop the interview.

16.12 Presenting material for comment

Following *R v Hillard*[28] it is a requirement not to present to a suspect more information for comment than he or she can reasonably be expected to hold in working memory. The common sense answer is to read the material twice:

* the first reading—in 'bite sized' chunks, to allow the suspect who should simply listen and say nothing, concentrating on getting a grasp of the content from beginning to end;
* the second reading—a line at time—to allow the suspect to listen and then to comment after each line.

Brief the suspect on how the two of you will be working together, eg:

> *I'm going to read what* [X] *has said.*
> *This will give you the opportunity to comment upon what* [X] *says about what happened.* ^^^^
> *I'm going to read to you what* [X] *has said **twice**.* ^^^^ (Stress ***twice***.)
> *The **first** time I read it,* ^^*I will do this a bit at a time.* ^^ ^^ (Stress ***first***.)
> *This will give you a clear idea of everything that* [X]*is saying.* ^^^^
> *When I'm reading* ^^ ^^ *just **listen**.* ^^^^ (Stress ***listen***.)
> *Don't say **anything** out loud at this stage.* ^^^^ (Stress ***anything***.)
> *Save any thoughts you have at this stage* ^^^^
> *Just **listen*** ^^^^ *and wait until I've finished.* ^^ ^^ (Stress ***listen***.)
> *Then I'll read what* [X] *is saying for the **second** time.* ^^^^ (Stress ***second***.)
> *I will again do this a bit at a time.* ^^ ^^
> *I'll only say a few words*^^^^ *then I'll stop.* ^^^^
> *When I stop then it's over to you* ^^ ^^ *to have your say* ^^ *about the bit that I've just read to you.* ^^ ^^
> *Then I'll read the next bit and then stop.* ^^ ^^
> *Again it will be over to you* ^^ ^^ *to have your say* ^^ *about that bit.* ^^ ^^
> *And so on.* ^^^^
> *Can I just check back with you that you are clear about this?* ^^ ^^

Listen to the suspect's explanation of his or her understanding and correct any misunderstanding, checking back again.

You may consider it useful to have *R v Hillard* instructions on a laminated sheet. If you are working with a recording—or a CCTV clip—amend your wording to accommodate the different medium.

16.13 Questioning tactically on 'bad character' evidence

If the suspect has been legally advised and you introduce 'bad character' evidence tactically, this will evoke either a 'no comment' response from the suspect or an intervention by the legal adviser.

---

[28] *R v Hillard* (2004) CA 2/3/2004 Unreported. Document No AC9800288.

16.13.1 'No comment' response

The legal adviser will have advised the suspect on 'bad character'.

- There is no risk from exercising the right to silence when 'bad character' is raised because the suspect will not be relying on this information in any defence that he or she might give in interview or at court. Hence no adverse inference should be drawn from a failure to answer questions about 'bad character', eg disposition to behave in a reprehensible way; past convictions.
- There is a risk from answering questions on 'bad character'. The suspect might:
  — remember matters erroneously;
  — say things that a court would view negatively, eg asserting being 'whiter than white' when this is not the case; maligning the conduct of complainant/victim, a witness or a co-suspect.

In the light of this advice the suspect will automatically say 'no comment' to any questions about 'bad character'.

16.13.2 Intervention by the legal adviser

The legal adviser may have some concerns about your introduction of 'bad character' at this stage, ie in the light of other matters that you have introduced and questioned upon up to this point.

- The legal adviser may ask:
  — whether you have introduced all the 'line evidence' or if there is more to come after questioning on 'bad character';
  — what is the purpose of introducing 'bad character' evidence at this stage rather than after all line evidence has been covered.
- In the light of your responses the legal adviser will:
  — either request the interview be stopped to allow a consultation with the suspect;
  — or remind the suspect to exercise the right to silence when questioned about his or her character.

16.14 FAIR review

16.14.1 The negative connotations and response to challenging

It was pointed out in Chapter 1 that the Account stage of the basic PEACE model was expanded to specify three sub-stages: Account, Clarify, and Challenge. The Challenge stage was introduced to accommodate the need to respond to:

- contradiction within the interviewee's account and responses, and when these are compared to the accounts of others;
- inconsistency—an absence of fit—between the interviewee's account and the information and evidence in the investigator's possession.

It was acknowledged that challenging would:

- normally apply to a suspect's account;
- on occasions might apply to a witness's account.

Challenge is an unfortunate word. It has even more negative connotations than *persistent questioning* that we considered in Chapter 9. It is inextricably woven with:

- the summons—the throwing down of a gauntlet—to take part in a contest, a fight, trial of strength, or a duel to decide who is superior;
- the summons—or provocation—to prove or justify something;
- the act of criticizing, disputing, or denying the validity of a statement or claim.

Challenging necessarily plays to the vulnerability of an investigator who is morally indignant, frustrated with an individual who is giving a 'flawed' account and responses, which do not match what the investigator knows or believes. Challenging in such circumstances is much more likely to tip towards:

- posing questions in a combative and accusatory manner;
- taking a delight in 'disproving' the suspect's version;
- asserting that the suspect is not telling the truth or, more baldly, lying;
- accusing the suspect.

As soon as you do any of these, you no longer have a working relationship. Whether genuine or lying the suspect will become indignant. It has become a matter of 'face' rather than 'fact'.

This text advocates an approach—a review—which enables you to think and act in a professional, psychologically and evidentially constructive manner. The review achieves the same aims as challenging but without the fighting and reproving connotations, and the loss of 'face'. The elements of the review are captured by a mnemonic FAIR, which captures the spirit of the process: *Final Anomaly Investigation* and *Reasons to suspect.*

16.14.2   Final anomaly investigation

The aim is not to resolve the 'problem', ie to draw to the suspect's attention the words that he or she used, and to invite him or her to 'solve' the mismatch or to say which version does he or she want. Rather it is to see whether:

- the suspect generates yet another inconsistent or contradictory version;
- the suspect gives a version that accords with one of the earlier versions: still leaving the matter open as to the emergence of the version that is not replicated.

Put simply, if the suspect is lying or confabulating we want more—not less—lies and confabulation. The electronic recording of these lies and confabulation are vital evidence that can be put before the court.

The investigation involves:

- drawing the suspect's attention to things that are 'not quite clear';
- appropriate questioning that requires the suspect to take you through the detail again, without impugning the suspect's character, ie not telling him or her that you consider his or her response to be untruthful.

This requires a detailed, accurate knowledge of the anomaly in the suspect's account and responses.

16.14.3   Reasons to suspect

This involves presenting the suspect with the basis for your suspicions.

- Where applicable, reminding him or her of the information and evidence that was disclosed in pre-interview disclosure.
- Where applicable and appropriate, disclosing information and evidence that you have withheld.

- Where applicable and appropriate, questioning on 'bad character' if not covered before.
- Where applicable and appropriate, issuing a Special Warning.

This requires a detailed, accurate knowledge of the police case and the information and evidence underpinning this.

16.14.4 Planning and preparing a FAIR review

You should normally stop the interview to enable you plan and to prepare a FAIR review. It is unwise to move from questioning on I^3 or tactically on 'bad character' to addressing the issue of anomaly.

Anomaly awareness

Reflect on what has emerged

Examine closely the content of:

- the suspect's account and responses to probing of this;
- the suspect's responses when questioned about I^3.

Where time and resource permit, and offence seriousness requires, it is essential to check the accuracy of your remembrance and representation of the suspect's account and responses.

- Replay of the recording.
- While replaying, where applicable, check the accuracy of the contemporaneously created SE3R of the suspect's accounts, showing the inconsistency and contradiction.

Collate the material

- For each inconsistency or contradiction plot the detail:
  — **either** as a grid: with different columns for each version and rows for the key detail: highlighting the detail that does not fit (inconsistency) or is a mismatch (contradiction);
  — **or** onto a composite SE3R.
- Create a WOB map: a blob for each instance of inconsistency and contradiction.

Investigation

Plan how you will:

- question on the anomaly without alerting the suspect, eg:

  *Sean I'm not too clear about the detail of what you did between [A] ^^ ^^ and [B]. ^^ ^^ I need to get my head round that. ^^ ^^ I'd like you to take me through that again ^^ ^^ in as much detail as possible ^^ ^^ taking your time. ^^ ^^*

- finally reveal the existence of anomaly without implying that the suspect is a lying, eg:

  *Sean you've taken me through more than once about what you did between [A] ^^ ^^ and [B]. ^^ ^^ Each time the detail doesn't marry up each time. ^^ ^^ So I want to fair to you. ^^ ^^ I want you to think really hard ^^ ^^ really hard about what you did between [A] ^^ ^^ and [B]. Now I want you to take me through that ^^ ^^ for one last time ^^ ^^ in as much detail as possible ^^ ^^ taking your time. ^^ ^^*

Reasons to suspect

Concentrate on gaining a secure grasp of the other material that you have decided to:

- remind the suspect about, ie pre-interview disclosure that you made;
- question the suspect about, ie:
  — further information and evidence that you have withheld;
  — 'bad character' evidence;
- to issue a Special Warning.

16.15 Conducting a FAIR review

If interviewing was stopped to allow a break and to enable the FAIR review, the standard administrative and legal procedures must be observed at the beginning of this interview.

16.15.1 Anomaly awareness and investigation

For each anomaly you follow the same sequence.

- Raise awareness, obtain another version.
- Reveal anomaly without calling the suspect a liar.
- Move on to the next anomaly.

16.15.2 Reasons to suspect

- Remind of information and evidence produced in pre-interview disclosure.
- Where applicable and appropriate, disclose and question about information and evidence that you have withheld.
- Where applicable and appropriate, question on 'bad character'.
- Where applicable and appropriate, issue a Special Warning.

16.16 Closure

This will normally include:

- the suspect now has an opportunity to consult with his or her legal adviser;
- you have yet to decide whether further interviewing will take place.

You may decide that it is appropriate to let the legal adviser know that there may not be another interview.

16.17 Chapter summary

Conversation management of the interview of a suspect begins well before you enter the interview room. It rests greatly upon a sound understanding of legal advice, the role of the legal advisers, their identification of the safest defence, their perspective, and their behaviour in police stations. This knowledge enables you to apply psychology in pre-interview disclosure, to generate a positive impression, to communicate credibility, and to create a working relationship that enhances your management of the forthcoming interview. Having attended to practical preparations, you are able to use psychology in the initial meeting with the suspect to assess and to act upon actual or potential vulnerability. You are in a position to explain the caution appropriately, mindful of barriers to the suspect's comprehension. You can cope with the suspect's 'no comment' response to 'bad character' evidence. Engaging in a FAIR review will give you the means to respond to anomaly in a way that does not mean a loss of 'face' for the suspect.

Interviewing the Suspect who Exercises the Right to Remain Silent without Handing in a Defence Statement

---

17.1   Chapter overview

This chapter examines the reasons for a suspect exercising the right to remain silent, ie to say 'no comment' in response to questions concerning the offence and the effective, ethical, and professional conversation management of an interview following this very common decision.

17.1.1   Chapter objectives

This chapter will enable you to:

- understand the suspect's logic for exercising the right to silence;
- know what questions the suspect can answer in a 'no comment' interview;
- understand why legal advisers usually give no reason for the suspect's decision;
- have a clear understanding of your aim in a 'no comment' interview;
- appreciate the necessity to be in total control of the pace of the conversation and the exchange of information;
- pay special attention to explanation of Routines and Expectations;
- question systematically I³ topics without disclosing underpinning information and evidence;
- plan and prepare a FAIR review;
- conduct the FAIR review;
- respond appropriately to a suspect who starts answering questions;
- appreciate the logic and behaviour of different types of suspect who are not legally represented and exercise the right to silence.

17.1.2   Interview map

Figure 17.1 shows the map of appropriate interviewing when a suspect exercises the right to remain silent.

17.2   The decision to exercise the right to silence

17.2.1   The logic for exercising the right to silence

There are at least 13 different reasons why a legal adviser might advise a suspect, and a suspect accept the advice, that the safest defence is to exercise the right to silence.

1. Whether the suspect has told the legal adviser that he or she is innocent or guilty, the legal adviser considers that:
   - answering questions now would constitute a risk to the suspect because you have disclosed so little detail that he or she cannot usefully advise the suspect;
   - the conditions of *R v Roble*[1] apply: a court knowing of the inadequacy of pre-interview disclosure would not draw an adverse inference from the individual's silence in interview.
2. The suspect has told the legal adviser that he or she is innocent but the legal adviser has concluded that an early innocent explanation is not required[2] because your pre-interview

---

[1] *R v Roble* [1997] Crim LR 449.
[2] *R v Howell* [2003] EWCA Crim 1.

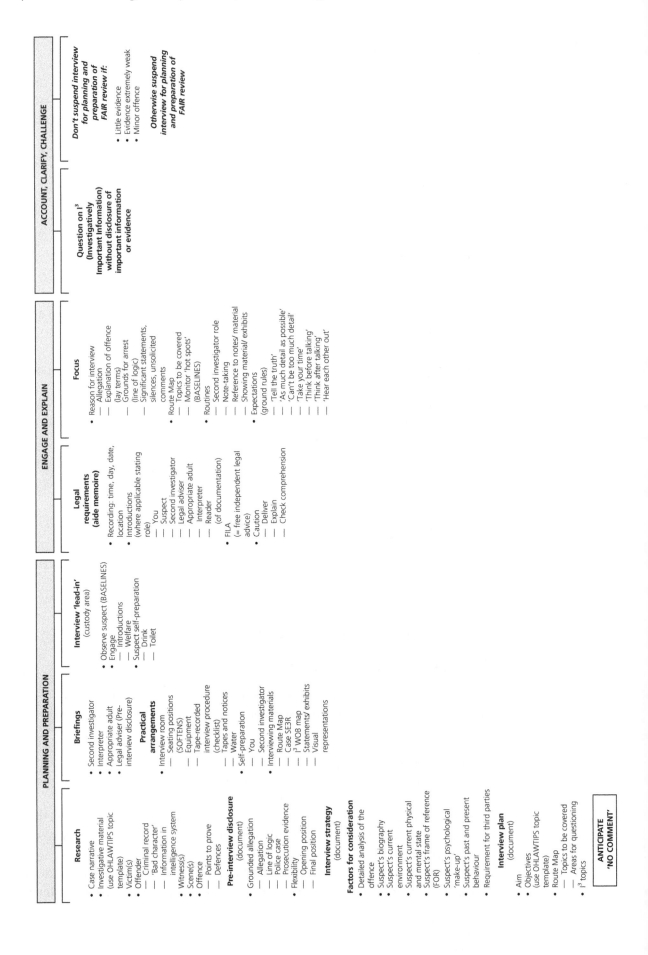

PLANNING AND PREPARATION

Research
- Case narrative
- Investigative material (use OHLAWTIPS topic template)
- Victim(s)
- Offender
  - Criminal record
  - 'Bad character'
  - Information in intelligence system
- Witness(s)
- Scene(s)
- Offence
  - Points to prove
  - Defences

Pre-interview disclosure (document)
- Grounded allegation
  - Allegation
  - Line of logic
  - Police case
  - Prosecution evidence
- Flexibility
  - Opening position
  - Final position

Interview strategy (document)

Factors for consideration
- Detailed analysis of the offence
- Suspect's biography
- Suspect's current environment
- Suspect's current physical and mental state
- Suspect's frame of reference (FOR)
- Suspect's psychological 'make-up'
- Suspect's past and present behaviour
- Requirement for third parties

Interview plan (document)
- Aim
- Objectives (use OHLAWTIPS topic template)
- Route Map
  - Topics to be covered
  - Areas for questioning
- i³ topics

ANTICIPATE
'NO COMMENT'

Briefings
- Second investigator
- Interpreter
- Appropriate adult
- Legal adviser (Pre-interview disclosure)

Practical arrangements
- Interview room
  - Seating positions (SOFTENS)
  - Equipment
  - Tape-recorded interview procedure (checklist)
  - Tapes and notices
- Self-preparation
  - You
  - Second investigator
- Interviewing materials
  - Route Map
  - Case SE3R
  - i³ WOB map
  - Statements/ exhibits
  - Visual representations

Interview 'lead-in' (custody area)
- Observe suspect (BASELINES)
- Engage
  - Introductions
  - Welfare
- Suspect self-preparation
  - Drink
  - Toilet

ENGAGE AND EXPLAIN

Legal requirements (aide memoire)
- Recording: time, day, date, location
- Introductions (where applicable stating role)
  - You
  - Suspect
  - Second investigator
  - Legal adviser
  - Appropriate adult
  - Interpreter
  - Reader (of documentation)
- FILA (= free independent legal advice)
- Caution
  - Deliver
  - Explain
  - Check comprehension

Focus
- Reason for interview
  - Allegation
  - Explanation of offence (lay terms)
  - Grounds for arrest (line of logic)
  - Significant statements, silences, unsolicited comments
- Route Map
  - Topics to be covered
  - Monitor 'hot spots' (BASELINES)
- Routines
  - Second investigator role
  - Note-taking
  - Reference to notes/ material
  - Showing material/ exhibits
- Expectations (ground rules)
  - 'Tell the truth'
  - 'As much detail as possible'
  - 'Can't be too much detail'
  - 'Take your time'
  - 'Think before talking'
  - 'Think after talking'
  - 'Hear each other out'

ACCOUNT, CLARIFY, CHALLENGE

Question on i³ (Investigatively Important Information) without disclosure of important information or evidence

Don't suspend interview for planning and preparation of FAIR review if:
- Little evidence
- Evidence extremely weak
- Minor offence

Otherwise suspend interview for planning and preparation of FAIR review

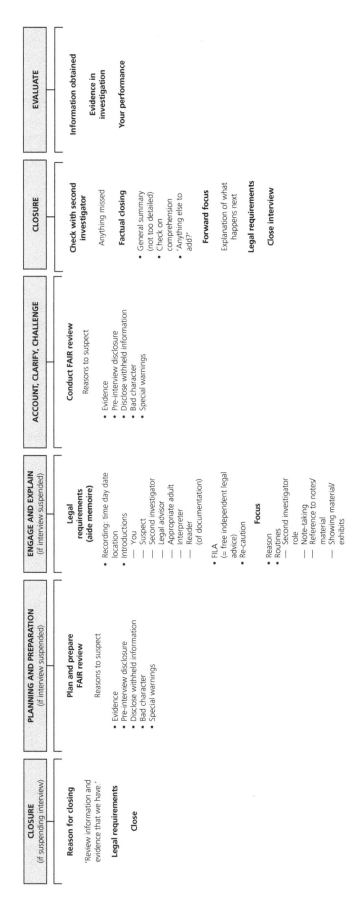

Figure 17.1 Map for interviewing a suspect who exercises the right to remain silent

disclosure failed to convince that there was a persuasive case—a grounded allegation—against the suspect. Pre-interview disclosure failed to convince on one or more of the following criteria.

- allegation, ie this was unclear;
- your line of logic, ie you failed to justify your belief that the suspect rather than anyone else committed the offence;
- the police case, ie your description of circumstances leading up to, during, and following the commission of the offence—including police actions and investigation to date, ongoing and planned—was anomalous, eg:
  — 'thin';
  — lacked detail—including representations of key locations;
  — manifested gaps, jumps, and non-barking dogs (NBDs);
  — was non-specific, vague, ambiguous;
  — was inconsistent;
  — had narrative contrast;
- the prosecution evidence, ie little or no indication was given of the information and actual evidence—not even the type of evidence—underpinning the allegation, line of logic, and police case.

3. The suspect has told the legal adviser that he or she is innocent but the legal adviser has concluded that the suspect's account is:
   - implausible in the light of detail disclosed by the police;
   - lacks sufficient detail to withstand close questioning.

4. The suspect has informed the legal adviser that he or she is guilty but the legal adviser concludes there is no benefit in admitting the offence at this stage because you have not convinced the legal adviser that there is a persuasive case.

5. You have convinced the legal adviser that there is a persuasive case, the suspect has informed the legal adviser that he or she is guilty, but the legal adviser assesses that there is little likelihood of a sentence reduction under section 144 of the Criminal Justice Act 2003 for an early admission in interview to the police given:
   - the circumstances of the offence;
   - the suspect's past history of offending and convictions.

6. Whether or not you have convinced the legal adviser that there is a persuasive case, the suspect:
   - knows who committed the offence; and
   - wishes to protect this person.

7. Whether or not you have convinced the legal adviser that there is a persuasive case, the suspect:
   - indicated to the legal adviser that he or she would lie in response to police questions;
   - the suspect has accepted the advice that he or she cannot do this following the legal adviser's reasons for this advice.
     — Once the interview was underway the legal adviser would not know whether the suspect was telling the truth or lying.
     — The legal adviser would be in contravention of his or her professional code of conduct[3] if he or she were to knowingly allow a client to tell lies to the police.
     — The legal adviser would be technically party to an offence.
     — The police are professional interviewers and will easily detect that the suspect was lying and take appropriate action to reveal this in interview.

---

[3] Solicitors Regulation Authority (2011) *SRA Code of Conduct*. London: Law Society Publishing.

— If the suspect started to tell lies, the legal adviser would have to stop the interview at some time in order to remind the suspect of his or her advice on this matter and to explain that if the client did not accept advice now to remain silent the legal adviser would have to withdraw, ie the suspect would have to find another legal adviser.

8. The legal adviser assesses that:
   - the suspect is too vulnerable, ie would not cope with the mental, emotional, and physical demands of robust interviewing;
   - there is a greater likelihood of a miscarriage of justice arising from answering questions than one occurring at court should an adverse inference be allowed from remaining silent in interview.

9. The legal adviser has had previous negative experience in interviews conducted by you and/or the second investigator in which:
   - there was limited disclosure, the suspect answered questions, was charged, and it emerged that there was little or no evidence;
   - there was inappropriate police conduct, representations were made, and these were ignored.

   The legal adviser has concluded that given this 'track record':
   - answering questions could result in a miscarriage of justice;
   - a court would be likely to accept that it was reasonable to remain silent, ie no adverse inference should be drawn.

10. It is an elderly or complex allegation but the legal adviser is unable to advise on the safest defence because you have refused the legal adviser the time to:
    - examine the material; or
    - access and examine relevant documentation held by the suspect or others.

11. It is late at night/in the early hours of the morning and you wish to interview the suspect even though:
    - common sense argues that the suspect, you, the legal adviser, and anyone else present will be tired;
    - the circumstances of the case do not warrant an urgent interview.

12. The legal adviser has concluded that you are introducing 'bad character' to buttress weak or inadequate evidence.

13. The legal adviser is physically separated from his or her client, ie is unable to fulfil the basic requirement to sit beside the client and give advice at any time.

Nearly half of these reasons have the same theme: little or no disclosure of the police case and the prosecution evidence prior to interview. Exercising the right to silence in these circumstances will eventually oblige the police to disclose, progressively, information that is being withheld.

17.2.2 The benefits and the risks of exercising the right to silence

The benefits

By exercising the right to silence the suspect forces the police to respond by moving from a position of little or no pre-interview disclosure of the police case and prosecution evidence to disclosing more and more of the withheld information on these matters.

If nothing of substance is disclosed in response to the suspect's reply 'no comment'

The process has revealed that:

- the allegation is currently founded upon little or no evidence—and what evidence there might be is neither strong nor sufficient enough to warrant charging or another form of disposal;
- it was the correct decision to exercise the right to silence.

If a detailed case and substantive evidence is disclosed in response to the suspect's reply 'no comment'

The process has revealed that:

- the case is persuasive;
- if the suspect has a case, ie is asserting innocence, depending upon the legal adviser's assessment of the circumstances the suspect should either answer questions, or produce a prepared statement and continue exercising the right to silence;
- if the suspect does not have a case, ie is guilty, but there is no benefit to admitting the offence to the police, the safest defence for the suspect is to continue with 'no comment'.

The risk

If, following interviews in which silence was exercised, the suspect who asserts innocence now answers questions or produces a prepared statement there will be no risk attached to having changed from 'no comment' to either of these decisions. The reasoning is straightforward. If the suspect is charged the court will be interested in what he said, or failed to say, when answering questions: not in his or her 'no comment' responses in earlier interviewing.

The risk of 'no comment' interviewing is that there is no subsequent interviewing in which the suspect can answer questions or produce a prepared statement, ie there is a move from 'no comment' interviewing to charging. If the suspect later at court asserts innocence, his or her failure to do so in the police station will lead to a section 34 Criminal Justice and Public Order Act 1996 adverse inference direction.

17.3 Questions that the suspect should answer

The exercise of the right to silence only applies to questioning concerning the offence and any matter related to it. The legal adviser will have explained to the suspect that he or she should:

- answer questions of an administrative nature, eg when asked for his or her name, to confirm that he or she has understood the caution;
- where a significant statement is delivered, indicate whether the record is *inaccurate*: not to say anything more than this, ie to say 'no comment' to any other questions concerning the content of the statement or the circumstances in which it arose.

17.4 The notification of the suspect's decision

The usual point for notifying the suspect's decision should be when the legal adviser is invited to introduce himself or herself. Strictly speaking, the legal adviser should use the present tense, eg *My client is deciding to exercise his/her right to silence.* Using the past tense—*has decided*—is technically a breach of legal privilege because the legal adviser is making public his or her advice to the suspect.

Only in exceptional circumstances will the legal adviser give a reason for the suspect's decision, eg:

* when no sensible pre-interview disclosure has been made;
* when the case is elderly/complex and the suspect and legal adviser have been given insufficient or—in the case of urgent interviewing—no time to examine personal documentation (in the case of an elderly case) or to consider the evidence (in a complex) case;
* when the interview is taking place late at night/very early in the morning;
* when the legal adviser is prevented from sitting beside his or her client.

17.5 Your aim in a 'no comment' interview

Chapter 16 points out that exercising the right to silent remains the safest defence. Even if you are never given the reasons for the suspect's decision, you know that almost half of the reasons stem from insufficient disclosure and the legal adviser not being convinced that there is a persuasive case against the suspect. In the vast majority of cases you will never know upon which of the 13 possible reasons the suspect's decision was based.

It follows that your two-fold aim is to:

* provide the court with a comprehensive record of:
  — your assertions and questions concerning the allegation, the police reasoning for suspecting this individual, the police case, the prosecution evidence, and the police investigation;
  — the suspect's silence in the face of these assertions and questions;
* persuade the suspect and legal adviser that this is indeed a grounded allegation:
  — if the suspect is innocent it is less risky in subsequent interviewing to answer your questions or to produce a prepared statement;
  — if the suspect is guilty there may be benefit to be gained from making an admission.

17.5.1 The ethical and professional response

The only proper response is to:

* acknowledge and respect the suspect's decision—even though you may consider it to be ill-advised;
* manage the interview to achieve your two-fold aim.

This is the only rational course of action given that:

* there are at least 13 possible reasons for the decision;
* only in the minority of cases will the reason be disclosed by the legal adviser.

17.5.2 The unethical and unprofessional response

Common aim, same message

Improper responses to a suspect's decision to exercise the right to silence have a common aim: to induce the suspect to abandon the decision to exercise the right to silence and to answer questions in this interview. They send the same message: 'Silence is the wrong answer. Start talking now.'

All reflect:

- an indifference to creating a working relationship with the legal adviser prior to the interview and now during the interview;
- a narrow interpretation of 'no comment', ie the breadth of reason is either unknown or not a matter of interest;
- a failure to recognize that little or no pre-interview disclosure will inevitably generate 'no comment' because:
  — there is no grounded allegation;
  — exercising the right to silence represents no risk to the suspect in these circumstances;
- an attempt to oppress the suspect: behaving in a manner that induces the suspect to say things that he or she otherwise would not, and not to say things that he or she otherwise would.

Any improper response is liable to:

- spur the legal adviser to intervene;
- draw adverse comment from the CPS and the court;
- prejudice the admissibility of the interview as evidence either in part or whole.

Frequently occurring improper responses

Misrepresenting the status of the legal adviser

Some unprofessional investigators seek to 'put down' the legal adviser:

- telling the suspect that the individual is 'not a solicitor': he or she is a 'legal representative';
- raising doubts in the suspect's mind about the competence of the adviser and the advice given.

These investigators are lying to the suspect. Under the Police and Criminal Evidence Act 1984, legal representatives are solicitors. As representatives, acknowledged to be solicitors in the eyes of the law, they are subject to the same professional guidelines as solicitors.[4]

Pointing out that the legal advice does not have to be accepted if the suspect is innocent

Some investigators misguidedly point out to the suspect—perhaps citing *R v Howell*[5]—that:

- if he or she is innocent it is best to give an innocent explanation now;
- he or she does not have to accept legal advice to remain silent.

The investigator is unaware of the reasons that led the adviser to advise an innocent suspect to exercise the right to silence, principally that:

- pre-interview disclosure has not communicated a persuasive case against the suspect;
- even if there has been acceptable pre-interview disclosure, to answer questions would pose an even greater risk to the suspect than remaining silent.

Asserting in these circumstances that, if innocent, the suspect does not have to accept legal advice is exploitative and disingenuous.

---

[4] Solicitors Regulation Authority (2011) *SRA Code of Conduct*. London: Law Society Publishing.
[5] *R v Howell* [2003] EWCA Crim 1.

Pointing out that the legal advice is incorrect

An investigator who asserts the advice given as incorrect is implying that the investigator has a more informed grasp of the suspect's legal position than the legal adviser. The investigator is acting *ultra vires* and attempting to deny the suspect the legal right to independent legal advice.

- He or she is assuming the role of a legal adviser giving advice under section 58 of the Police and Criminal Evidence Act 1984.
- In this unlawfully assumed role of legal adviser, he or she is giving advice that:
  — disagrees with lawful advice given to the suspect;
  — is not independent but favours the investigator's narrow interpretation that will facilitate achievement of the investigator's aims and objectives.

Offering an inducement to answer questions

It is improper to represent verbally, or through the use of a locally produced form, that under section 144 of the Criminal Justice Act 2003:

- if the suspect makes an early admission of guilt he or she 'will be entitled to a reduction in sentence';
- the earlier the suspect 'admits responsibility the greater the reduction will be'.

In reality, a sentence reduction is not an entitlement and cannot be guaranteed. Hence these assertions are an inducement. Like the form, they are bogus and not endorsed by the CPS.

Repeated administration of the caution

Some investigators try to pressure the suspect into abandoning 'no comment' by repeatedly administering the caution within the interview. It will be extremely difficult for the investigator at court to defend repeated cautioning, ie to give to a court a credible justification for re-administering the caution at this point, and every other point.

17.6 **Totally in control**

In a 'no comment' interview, because the response is so short and quickly delivered, you are necessarily in the conversational spotlight. You want to come across as, and actually be, totally in control.

17.6.1 **Pausing and pacing**

Intuitively, a 'no comment' interview might be expected to be a relatively short-lived event, and the legal adviser and suspect would rather hope this would be the case, your task is to keep the pace of the interview down. Even though the suspect says 'no comment' and relinquishes the talking turn, this does not mean that you have to abandon the listening turn immediately.

Don't immediately take the talking turn when the suspect has said 'no comment'.

- If you unreflectively respond instantaneously this will cumulatively put more and more pressure on you.
- If you create suitably long pauses after the 'no comment' response of at least two or three seconds—^^ ^^ if not more ^^ ^^ ^^ ^^—this will enable you to:

— keep the pace of the interview, and your heart rate, down;
— observe the suspect;
— refer to your WOB map of I^3, your Case SE3R, or any material item;
— take your time in identifying the particular information you want to work with;
— take your time considering the particular information you want to work with;
— think what you want to say;
— frame the words that you want to ask;
— observe the suspect before delivering your words.

17.6.2 Totally in control of information

As the pace of the interview is much slower than an interview in which a suspect answers questions, you need to be well organized. You don't want to be shuffling around looking for something that you wish to consult or refer to when questioning the suspect. Pay particular attention to:

• having a list of items to hand;
• be working on or referring to no more than one or two items at any one time: only in exceptional circumstances have more on view;
• keeping all other items out of the suspect's view until you want to work with or refer to them;
• putting an item back in its folder when you have finished with it.

17.6.3 Coping with interruption and disruption

If the suspect overtalks you—saying 'No comment' while you are talking

• Stop talking. ^^ ^^
• Repair, eg *I have to be fair* ^^ ^^ *and make sure that you hear what I say.* ^^ ^^ *So I'll [say that] [start] again.* ^^ ^^
• Continue with what you were saying.

If the suspect overtalks you more than three times in succession

Use DEAL to:

• remind of the ground rule to 'hear each other out';
• request no interruption while you are talking.

The suspect adopts the 'Shipman Response'

Even though you are looking at the suspect's back:

• don't be diverted: continue in the same way as you would were the suspect to be looking at you;
• increase the pause: this ensures the court will conclude reasonably that the suspect had every opportunity to understand and to reply.

If the legal adviser interrupts to intervene while you are speaking

• Stop talking. ^^ ^^
• Let the legal adviser finish talking. ^^ ^^

- Respond as applicable to the legal adviser's intervention.
- If the behaviour is repeated, use DEAL to require that he or she does not interrupt you while you are talking—and you will do the same for him or her.

If the legal adviser intervenes appropriately but frequently

- Respect and, as applicable, respond professionally to the intervention.
- Don't 'lock horns' because:
  — this will prejudice the working relationship;
  — this could undermine your credibility if the suspect construes the assertive legal adviser as putting you in your place.

If the legal adviser intervenes to request or require you to speed up

The legal adviser might draw the conclusion that the interview is going too slowly, perhaps to the disadvantage of the suspect. The appropriate response is to:

- respect the intervention;
- remind the legal adviser of the Routines and Expectations that you spelled out at the outset;
- continue with your questioning in the manner that you have.

If the legal adviser requests that the interview be stopped

- Ask why the legal adviser is making the request. (Don't be pressured if you get no explanation.)
- Explain that interviewing will re-commence following the consultation with the suspect.
- Stop the interview.

17.7 Question on investigatively important information (I³) without disclosing information or evidence

17.7.1 An 'audit trail' of questioning

All too often interviewers move directly into questioning in a manner that discloses the information, evidence, and the source of this investigative material, eg *CCTV outside the Snell's Hall Club shows you arriving at 8 o'clock*. What do you have to say to that? You have to be more subtle. You certainly want to cover I³—topics that you want an account or explanation for—but need to:

- do this in a way that does not disclose the source;
- create an 'audit trail' of questioning that a court:
  — will grasp and appreciate as a totally comprehensive presentation of the issues and the case;
  — draw evidence-based conclusions concerning the 'no comment' response to critical questions, should the suspect not decide at some point after this interview to answer questions or to produce a prepared statement and thereafter continue exercising the right to silence.

17.7.2   Creating the 'audit trail'

Questioning on topics in your WOB map

Work your way methodically through the topics in your WOB map applying the interviewing spiral:

- raise the topic from your WOB;
- probe: ranging from 'general' to 'specific'—keeping as much as possible to the 'general' end;
- treat the 'no comment' as the answer to be probed by your next question;
- don't summarize: there is no purpose to summarizing a sequence of 'no comment' responses to a line of questioning;
- make a linking remark to the next topic;
- raise the next topic from your WOB.

Be extremely systematic

Always look at the suspect when you are talking or asking a question.

- Look down at your WOB map. ^^ ^^
- Identify the detail to be delivered. ^^ ^^
- Register the topic and area of questioning within this that you wish to cover. ^^ ^^
- Tick this in red. ^^ ^^
- Think what you want to say—in particular the question that you will ask. ^^ ^^
- Frame your words mentally. ^^ ^^
- Look up. ^^ ^^
- Monitor the suspect for 'hot spot' behaviours (BASELINES). ^^ ^^
- Deliver the question. ^^ ^^
- Look at the suspect for 'hot spot' behaviours. ^^ ^^
- Register mentally, don't react visibly or verbally to the 'no comment': simply monitor the suspect for 'hot spot' associated behaviours (BASELINES). ^^ ^^
- Look down at your WOB map... and so on.

Concentrate on your questioning behaviour

Vary your questions, using the 'general' to 'specific' hierarchy to maximum effect.

- **Crème de la crème questions.**
  - Statement/comment, eg *It's about a serious assault last night.* ^^ ^^
  - Topic, eg *Your movements last night.* ^^ ^^
  - Silence after raising a topic, or after the suspect has said 'no comment' is by far and away the best question.
- **TED instructions**, eg *Could you tell me about that?* ^^ ^^; *Take me through...* ^^ ^^
- **Open questions.**
  - Parameter, eg *Can you tell me what you did between leaving your house until we arrested you at two this morning?* ^^ ^^
  - 'Big' (narrative) 'what', eg *It will help all concerned if you can tell me what happened then?* ^^ ^^
  - 'How', eg *There's no rush, can you tell me how you got to Owen's where we arrested you?* ^^ ^^
  - 'Why' or a suitable alternative, eg *We need to know why you went to Owen's.* ^^ ^^

- **Closed identificatory questions**. 'Who?', 'What?', 'Where?', 'When?', 'Which?', 'In which way?'
- **Closed confirmatory questions**.
  — 'If' or 'whether', eg *Can you tell me if you were intending to go out last night?*
  — Closed confirmatory 'yes'/'no', eg *I want you to think about this.*^^ ^^ *It is very important.* ^^ ^^*Take your time.* ^^ ^^ *Do you know Ian McCaffery?* ^^ ^^

Link pause duration to the mental demand of the question

When the suspect says 'no comment', you should create a pause after this response, the duration of which is linked to the mental demand of the question had the suspect been answering this question.

- A longer pause 3 to 4 seconds—^^ ^^ ^^ ^^ should follow a process/extended recall question.
- The usual 2 to 3 second pause—^^ ^^—should follow a simple recall question.

If you ask the wrong kind of question

Take appropriate action if you ask the wrong kind of question, eg a productive question but one which buys you too little pause; an unproductive question.

- *Let me put that another way.* ^^ ^^
- Pose the more appropriate question.

Don't ask the same question too many times

Where the suspect is legally represented, the legal adviser will not normally intervene when there is repeated questioning in a 'no comment' interview. If you ask the same question three or more times expect the legal adviser to intervene. Follow the advice given in Chapter 9 on this.

An illustrative extract

The suspect is Liam Hudson who has been arrested for the attack on Eric Shepherd. The SE3R of Eric Shepherd's statement is the example of an SE3R in Chapter 6.

> **You:** [Look up from WOB map. Look at Liam. ^^ ^^ Monitor BASELINES] *We need to talk about your movements last night* (= introduce topic)
> **Liam:** *No comment.*
> **You:** [Monitor BASELINES] ^^ ^^ ^^ ^^ *between half past eight* ^^ ^^ *and midnight.*
> **Liam:** *No comment.*
> **You:** ^^ ^^ ^^ ^^ *Take your time* ^^ ^^ *I'd like to know about your movements,*
> **Liam:** *No comment.*
> **You:** [Monitor BASELINES] ^^ ^^ ^^ ^^ *between those times.*
> **Liam:** *No comment.*
> **You:** [Monitor BASELINES] ^^ ^^ ^^ ^^ *Take me through your movements.*
> **Liam:** *No comment.*
> **You:** [Monitor BASELINES] ^^ ^^ ^^ ^^ *Think about them*
> **Liam:** *No comment.*
> **You:** [Monitor BASELINES] ^^ ^^ ^^ ^^ [Look down at your WOB map. ^^ ^^ Register area of questioning within this that you wish to cover. ^^ ^^ Tick this in red. ^^ ^^ Think what you want to say—in particular the question that you will ask. ^^ ^^ Frame your words mentally. ^^ ^^ Look up. ^^ ^^ Monitor BASELINES. ^^ ^^ ^^ ^^] *So* ^^ ^^ *where did you go?*
> **Liam:** *No comment.*

You: [Monitor BASELINES] ^^ ^^ ^^ ^^ [Look down at your WOB map. ^^ ^^ Register area of questioning within this that you wish to cover. ^^ ^^ Tick this in red. ^^ ^^ Think what you want to say—in particular the question that you will ask. ^^ ^^ Frame your words mentally. ^^ ^^ Look up. ^^ ^^ Monitor BASELINES. ^^ ^^ ^^ ^^] *Cast your mind back ^^ ^^ to any person ^^ ^^ to any people ^^ ^^ that you saw.*

Liam: *No comment.*

You: [Monitor BASELINES] ^^ ^^ ^^ ^^ *We need to know ^^ ^^ who did you see?*

Liam: *No comment.*

You: [Monitor BASELINES] ^^ ^^ ^^ ^^ *As I said ^^ no rush about this ^^ ^^^^^^ who were you with?*

Liam: *No comment.*

You: [Monitor BASELINES] ^^ ^^ ^^ ^^ [Look down at your WOB map. ^^ ^^ Register area of questioning within this that you wish to cover. ^^ ^^ Tick this in red. ^^ ^^ Think what you want to say—in particular the question that you will ask. ^^ ^^ Frame your words mentally. ^^ ^^ Look up. ^^ ^^ Monitor BASELINES. ^^ ^^ ^^ ^^] *And ^^ think now ^^ ^^ ^^ ^^ what did you do?*

Liam: *No comment.*

You: [Monitor BASELINES] ^^ ^^ ^^ ^^ [Look down at your WOB map. ^^ ^^ Register area of questioning within this that you wish to cover. ^^ ^^ Tick this in red. ^^ ^^ Think what you want to say—in particular the question that you will ask. ^^ ^^ Frame your words mentally. ^^ ^^ Look up. ^^ ^^ Monitor BASELINES. ^^ ^^ ^^ ^^] *I want you to not rush on this next question. ^^ ^^ It is important. ^^ ^^ The far side of East Hendred village ^^ ^^ ^^ where there are no lights ^^ ^^ ^^ ^^ Ford Lane ^^ ^^ ^^ ^^ the little road ^^ ^^ ^^ ^^ just off Ford Lane ^^ ^^ ^^ ^^ it's called The Spinney. ^^ ^^ ^^ ^^ Were you in that road last night?*

Liam: *No comment.*

You: [Monitor BASELINES] ^^ ^^ ^^ ^^ [Look down at your WOB map. ^^ ^^ Register the next topic that you wish to cover. ^^ ^^ Tick this in red. ^^ ^^ Think what you want to say—in particular your linking statement and the question that you will ask following this. ^^ ^^ Frame your words mentally. ^^ ^^ Look up. ^^ ^^ Monitor BASELINES. ^^ ^^ ^^ ^^] *I want to leave your movements for a moment ^^ ^^ ^^ ^^ to talk about a key person ^^ ^^ ^^ who lives in the Spinney ^^ ^^ ^^ ^^ down the far end of that little road ^^ ^^ ^^ in the last house ^^ ^^ ^^ ^^ the owner of that house ^^ ^^ ^^ ^^ Eric Shepherd. ^^ ^^ ^^ ^^ Take your time ^^ ^^ ^^ ^^ tell me about Eric Shepherd.*

Liam: *No comment.*

You: [Monitor BASELINES] ^^ ^^ ^^ ^^ *How do you know Eric Shepherd?*

Liam: *No comment.*

You: [Monitor BASELINES] ^^ ^^ ^^ ^^ *What contact have you had with Eric Shepherd?*

Liam: *No comment.*

You: [Monitor BASELINES] ^^ ^^ ^^ ^^ *Where did you last see Eric Shepherd?*

Liam: *No comment.*

You: [Monitor BASELINES] ^^ ^^ ^^ ^^ *When did you last see Eric Shepherd?*

Liam: *No comment.*

You: [Monitor BASELINES] ^^ ^^ ^^ ^^ *Describe Eric Shepherd to me.*

Liam: *No comment.*

And so on.

17.8   Decision-making concerning a FAIR review

17.8.1   The logic for stopping to plan and to prepare a FAIR review

In any investigation that involves an offence of any degree of seriousness or complexity, even where a suspect exercises the right to remain silent you should as a matter of routine stop the interview to plan and prepare for a FAIR review.

In the FAIR review you will want to:

- ask direct questions about key material in your Case SE3R;
- where applicable and appropriate, question about:
  — pre-interview disclosure that you made;
  — further information and evidence that you have withheld;
  — 'bad character' evidence;
- issue a Special Warning.

Stopping at this point is sensible because it fulfils other requirements.

- Mindful of the advice in Chapter 8 about interview duration, if the interview has lasted for 40 minutes or more you need to stop the interview anyway to allow everyone to attend to the demands of nature.
- The suspect is able to consult with the legal adviser or any other third party.

17.8.2 The logic for not stopping to plan and to prepare a FAIR review

There are circumstances when it may not be practical or appropriate to stop a 'no comment' interview to conduct a FAIR review.

- If you have little evidence.
- If the evidence is extremely weak.
- If is a minor offence.

17.8.3 Closing the interview to plan and to prepare a FAIR review

If you are closing the interview:

- give a simple explanation of your decision;
- don't give an overall summary of the interview thus far;
- invite questions;
- close.

For example, in the interviewing of Liam:

Right Liam ^^ ^^ I'm now going to stop the interviewing for the time being. ^^ ^^ This will enable everyone to take a natural break. ^^^^ During the break you will be able to talk with [name of legal adviser; name of appropriate adult]. *^^ ^^*

When you and [name of legal adviser; name of appropriate adult] *talk with each other you will be able to think about what I've talked about ^^ ^^ and asked you about ^^ ^^ in this interview.*

*While you are doing that I [and my colleague] will be looking at the information and evidence that [I] [we] have. ^^ ^^*

I will let [name of legal adviser; name of appropriate adult] *know when we are ready to start interviewing again. ^^ ^^*

*So before we switch off the recorder Liam ^^ ^^ can I just check whether you have any questions? ^^ ^^*

17.8.4 Continuing to interview

If you decide that circumstances do not warrant stopping the interview to plan and to prepare a FAIR review, you should proceed—where appropriate and applicable—to **Investigation**: see section 17.10.3.

17.9   Planning and preparing a FAIR review

The FAIR review will not include anomaly awareness because the suspect's responses have contained no information—anomalous or otherwise. It will include **Investigation** and **Reasons to suspect**.

17.9.1   Investigation

You should examine the Case SE3R to put you in a state of readiness to question directly on material in the Event Line (material time frame) and in your Knowledge Box (KB).

17.9.2   Reasons to suspect:

Concentrate on gaining a secure grasp of material that you have decided it is applicable and appropriate to question about, eg:

- pre-interview disclosure that you made;
- further information and evidence that you have withheld;
- 'bad character' evidence;
- special warning material.

Create a WOB map with radiating blobs for each of these areas.

17.10   Conducting the FAIR review

If you stopped to allow a break and to enable planning and preparation of the FAIR review, you will need to observe the standard administrative and legal procedures at the beginning of this interview.

17.10.1   Where the legal adviser notifies a change in the suspect's response to questioning

The legal adviser may state that his or her client has chosen no longer to exercise his or her right to silence.

If the legal adviser indicates a decision to answer questions

Follow the advice in Chapter 18.

If the legal adviser indicates a decision to produce a prepared statement

Follow the advice in Chapter 19.

17.10.2   Explanation

As always in any conversation managed interview, you give an explanation to overcome the 'guessing game'.

Reason

> OK Liam ^^ I have had a chance to look over the information and the evidence that we in this case.
> ^^ ^^ I want to go through with you now important matters to do with the allegation. ^^ ^^

Route Map

*I will take you through the case we have ^^ ^^and I will ask you direct questions about this. ^^ ^^In the light of your responses I will make a decision as to what to do next. ^^ ^^*

Routines

*As you are continuing to exercise your right to silence ^^ ^^ I need to remind you about my job. ^^ ^^ My job is to ensure that you have every opportunity to comment upon the information in this case ^^ ^^ and evidence ^^ ^^ and to give your version of matters. ^^ ^^ To make sure that nothing is missed ^^ ^^ I will be referring to notes that I have prepared. ^^ ^^ If necessary I will also refer to other information ^^ ^^ and to other material ^^ that are relevant to our investigation ^^ ^^ and that to be entirely fair to you ^^ ^^ you need to know about. ^^ ^^*

Expectations

As before, pay particular attention to the ground rules of 'taking time' and you stopping from time to time.

17.10.3 Investigation

Work from your Case SE3R, being extremely systematic and asking direct questions.

- Always looking at the suspect when you are talking or asking a question, follow the same sequence of questioning:
  — looking down;
  — identifying and registering the topic;
  — ticking off the topic;
  — thinking what to say and framing the words;
  — looking up;
  — delivering the question.
- Concentrate on pausing.
- Monitor for BASELINES changes.

For example, an extract of the focused questions of Liam.

> **You:** [Monitor BASELINES] ^^ ^^ ^^ ^^ *So last night Liam ^^ ^^ where did you go?*
> **Liam:** *No comment.*
> **You:** [Monitor BASELINES] ^^ ^^ ^^ ^^ *How long did you spend in The Wheatsheaf pub in East Hendred last night?*
> **Liam:** *No comment.*
> **You:** [Monitor BASELINES] ^^ ^^ ^^ ^^ *Who did you leave The Wheatsheaf with at eleven o'clock?*
> **Liam:** *No comment.*
> **You:** [Monitor BASELINES] ^^ ^^ ^^ ^^ *What were you doing at the junction of Ford Lane and The Spinney around quarter past eleven last night?*
> **Liam:** *No comment.*
> **You:** [Monitor BASELINES] ^^ ^^ ^^ ^^ *When you went down The Spinney ^^ ^^ ^^ ^^ what was you reason for doing this?*
> **Liam:** *No comment.*
> **You:** [Monitor BASELINES] ^^ ^^ ^^ ^^ *When you went into the drive of Wych End ^^ ^^ ^^ ^^ what was you reason for that?*
> **Liam:** *No comment.*

> **You:** [Monitor BASELINES] ^^ ^^ ^^ ^^ *When you saw Eric Shepherd* ^^ ^^ ^^ ^^ *at the side gate* ^^ ^^ ^^ ^^ *what did you do?*
>
> **Liam:** *No comment.*
>
> **You:** [Monitor BASELINES] ^^ ^^ ^^ ^^ *When you struck Eric Shepherd* ^^ ^^ ^^ ^^ *it was with something heavy* ^^ ^^ ^^ ^^ *what was that?*
>
> **Liam:** *No comment.*
>
> **You:** [Monitor BASELINES] ^^ ^^ ^^ ^^ *When you struck Eric Shepherd* ^^ ^^ ^^ ^^ *where did you strike him?*
>
> **You:** [Monitor BASELINES] ^^ ^^ ^^ ^^ *When Eric Shepherd was on the ground* ^^ ^^ ^^ ^^ *and he was struck again* ^^ ^^ ^^ ^^ *how was that done?*
>
> **Liam:** *No comment.*

And so on.

17.10.4 Reasons to suspect

Present information and evidence produced in pre-interview disclosure and withheld till now

If you consider it appropriate and applicable at this stage, present the information and evidence that you wish to cover. A skilful approach is to state the source, state the detail, ask the question—wherever possible a trailer, eg:

> *CCTV evidence shows two men* ^^ *leaving the Wheatsheaf pub* ^^ *in East Hendred* ^^ *at eleven o'clock last night.* ^^ ^^
>
> *One is wearing a distinctive white hoody* ^^ ^^ *with a New York logo.* ^^ ^^
>
> *More than one witness reports seeing two men* ^^ ^^ *one in a white hoody* ^^ ^^ *with a New York logo* ^^ ^^ *at the junction of Ford Lane and The Spinney* ^^ ^^ *around quarter past eleven last night.* ^^ ^^
>
> *You have a distinctive white hoody* ^^ ^^ *with a New York logo.* ^^ ^^
>
> *Think carefully* ^^ ^^ *What have you to say?*

'Bad character' evidence

Question about 'bad character' at this point if you consider, preferably after consulting the CPS advice, this is the appropriate point to do this.

Special Warning

Issue a Special Warning under the provisions of the Criminal Justice and Public Order Act 1996 if you have decided to do this before closing the interview.

17.11 Responding to the suspect unexpectedly switching to answering questions

17.11.1 Interpretation

An actively defending legal adviser will intervene:

- if the suspect lapses from 'no comment' to remind the suspect of the suspect's decision;
- to request the interview be stopped to advise the suspect in private:
  - if the suspect dissents and says that he or she wants to answer questions;
  - if the suspect repeatedly lapses from 'no comment'.

It is important that a request to stop the interview at this stage does not necessarily mean that the legal adviser is being obstructive. It could be that:

- what the suspect is saying is not the account given to the legal adviser;
- the suspect had indicated that he or she would lie, then accepted the legal adviser's arguments against this, and is now delivering something which the legal adviser knows to be a lie.

An indifferent, incompetent legal adviser will do nothing if the suspect starts talking.

17.11.2 Act professionally

If the legal adviser intervenes to remind the suspect of the 'no comment' decision, remain quiet while this happens. Don't act unprofessionally in the ways described earlier, ie do not:

- misrepresent the status of the legal adviser;
- point out that the legal advice does not have to be accepted;
- point out that the legal advice is incorrect;
- offer an inducement to answer questions.

17.12 Closure

This will normally include:

- the suspect now has an opportunity to consult with his or her legal adviser;
- you have yet to decide whether further interviewing will take place.

Where applicable and appropriate, you may decide that it is appropriate to let the legal adviser know that there may not be another interview.

17.13 The suspect who is not legally represented and exercises the right to silence

The suspect who is not legally advised and exercises the right to silence is likely to be aware of this right:

- **either** through previous experience of custody and being legally advised;
- **or** vicariously, ie has never had contact with the police but knows—probably through television—that one can say this to avoid answering questions.

17.13.1 Previous experience of being detained and questioned

The individual is exercising the right to avoid answering questions with a particular intention.

- To remain silent irrespective of whatever information or evidence is produced or put to him or her. The suspect knows, eg because of previous offending, there is no benefit to be had in answering questions or making admissions.
- To remain silent until persuasive information or evidence is produced. He or she then has to decide either to answer questions or continue to remain silent.

Such individuals are likely to be able to:

- withstand an interview which has plenty of pauses and is suitably paced;
- avoid lapsing from 'no comment'.

17.13.2 No previous experience of being detained and questioned

This individual is likely to be motivated in the same way as an individual with experience of being detained and questioned. However, such individuals:

- are much less likely to cope with saying 'no comment' as a tactic to avoid answering questions;
- often find that they cannot keep up 'no comment';
- switch to answering questions during the interview.

17.14 Chapter summary

'No comment' is a very common initial response to police questioning, frequently but not always born of a failure to communicate that there is a persuasive case—a grounded allegation—against the suspect. Having anticipated that the suspect will exercise the right to silence and planned accordingly sets you up to manage the interview in the manner described in this chapter. The aim is to put before the courts an 'audit trail' of failure to answer critical questions. It will hear silence in response to your questioning on key topics with no indication of the information source. Then it will hear silence as you conduct your FAIR review: 'no comment' to your direct questioning without revealing information and evidence, and then to your invitation to comment upon the reality of the information and evidence, including where appropriate, 'bad character'. You will have achieved your aim.

18

Interviewing the Suspect who Answers Questions

18.1 Chapter overview

This chapter examines the reasons for a suspect answering questions concerning the offence and key stages in the effective, ethical, and professional conversation management of an interview following this decision.

18.1.1 Chapter objectives

This chapter will enable you to:

- understand the logic for the suspect answering questions;
- appreciate the implications for the suspect of answering questions;
- decide which form of question to use to trigger a spontaneous account on the initial and any subsequent topic on your Route Map;
- know how to develop the spontaneous account;
- conduct an effective review of the spontaneous account;
- probe the account systematically, including accessing non-verbal experience;
- question on investigatively important information (I^3);
- understand and respond to barriers to investigation arising from probing of the suspect's account and questioning on I^3;
- plan and prepare a FAIR review;
- conduct a FAIR review.

18.1.2 Interview map

Figure 18.1 (p 428–9) shows the map of appropriate interviewing when a suspect answers questions.

18.2 The decision to answer questions

18.2.1 The logic for answering questions

The rationale for answering questions stems from you having successfully communicated to the legal adviser that there is a persuasive case against the suspect requiring an early innocent explanation.[1]

Where the suspect has given the legal adviser an innocent explanation

The legal adviser will have closely questioned the suspect's innocent explanation, ie mimicking what any competent police interviewer would do. On the basis of the suspect's total pattern of behaviour, his or her responses and manner of responding in the consultation with the legal adviser, the adviser has concluded the safest defence is to answer questions.

- The suspect has a good case, ie an innocent explanation that:
  — he or she will rely upon if charged and the case go to court;
  — is plausible in the light of what the police have disclosed thus far;
  — is sufficiently detailed to withstand questioning;
  — there is a strong possibility of an adverse inference under section 34 of the Criminal Justice and Public Order Act 1996 if not disclosed now.

---

[1] *R v Howell* [2003] EWCA Crim 1.

- The suspect could cope with questioning because:
  — there are no indications that the suspect is psychologically vulnerable;
  — the suspect has coped with the legal adviser questioning closely the detail of the suspect's account.

Where the suspect has admitted committing the offence to the legal adviser

The legal adviser will have closely questioned the suspect's admission, as above. The legal adviser has concluded that making an admission in interview is the safest defence having assessed that:

- the suspect's admission is probably true: an assessment based on the suspect's total pattern of behaviour, his or her responses and manner of responding when questioned about the admission;
- there is a benefit in making an admission now either:
  — because police management have approved an alternative to charging in this case; or
  — the legal adviser considers the suspect's record and the circumstances of the offence are not a barrier to reduction in sentence for making an early admission to the police: under section 144 of the Criminal Justice Act 2003.

18.3 The implications for the suspect of answering questions

18.3.1 Answering questions is extremely risky

Answering questions is the hardest option for the suspect to manage. In effect, it is a 'rolling' or continuously emerging defence, comprising the suspect's first account and the sum of all responses that follow this. Once the suspect has given a spontaneous first account, he or she has little or no control over the course or content of the interview. Answering questions is therefore risky because the suspect is at a continuing disadvantage.

- The suspect may give responses that do not fit with the case information and evidence that you have not disclosed to the legal adviser:
  — in pre-interview disclosure;
  — during this or any previous interview.
- The suspect may not be able to cope with questioning—particularly searching and robust questioning—that arises from:
  — the introduction of evidence;
  — anomaly detected within the content of his or her account and responses to questions.
- Having decided to answer questions concerning the offence the suspect cannot then change to exercising the right to silence to avoid:
  — giving detail on a particular issue;
  — searching and robust questions.

To do so would constitute *mixed responding* and risk an adverse inference being drawn at court.

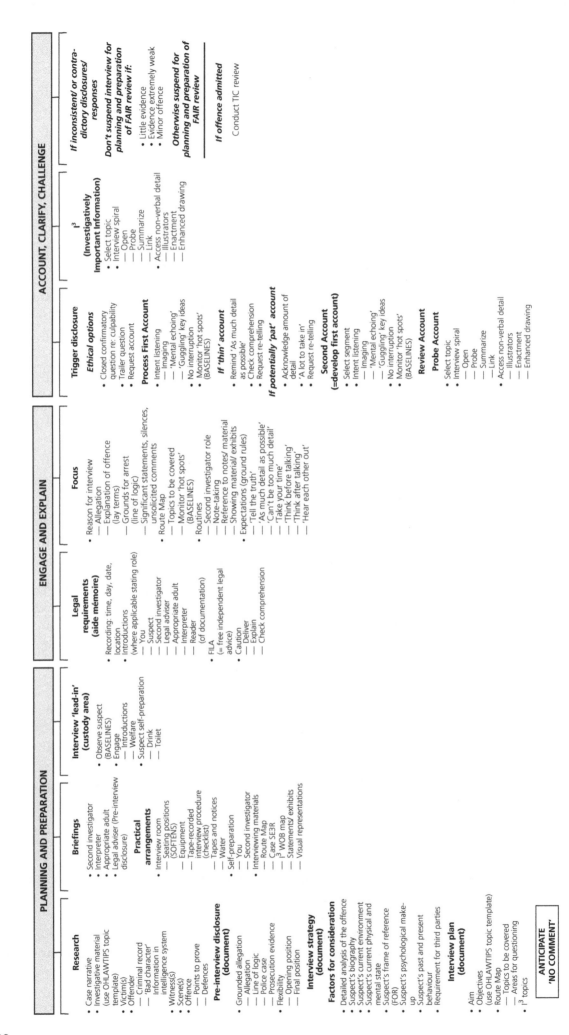

PLANNING AND PREPARATION

Research
- Case narrative
- Investigative material (use OHLAWTIPS topic template)
- Victim(s)
- Offender
  - Criminal record
  - 'Bad character'
  - Information in intelligence system
- Witness(es)
- Scene(s)
- Offence
  - Points to prove
  - Defences

Pre-interview disclosure (document)

Interview strategy (document)

Factors for consideration
- Grounded allegation
  - Allegation
  - Line of logic
  - Police case
  - Prosecution evidence
- Flexibility
  - Opening position
  - Final position

- Detailed analysis of the offence
- Suspect's biography
- Suspect's current environment
- Suspect's current physical and mental state
- Suspect's frame of reference (FOR)
- Suspect's psychological make-up
- Suspect's past and present behaviour
- Requirement for third parties

Interview plan (document)
- Aim
- Objectives
- Route Map (use OHLAWTIPS topic template)
  - Topics to be covered
  - Areas for questioning
- I³ topics

ANTICIPATE 'NO COMMENT'

Briefings
- Second investigator
- Interpreter
- Appropriate adult
- Legal adviser (Pre-interview disclosure)

Practical arrangements
- Interview room
  - Seating positions (SOFTENS)
  - Equipment
  - Tape-recorded interview procedure (checklist)
  - Tapes and notices
- Self-preparation
  - You
  - Second investigator
- Interviewing materials
  - Route Map
  - Case SE3R
  - I³ WOB map
  - Statements/ exhibits
  - Visual representations

Interview 'lead-in' (custody area)
- Observe suspect (BASELINES)
- Engage
  - Introductions
  - Welfare
- Suspect self-preparation
  - Drink
  - Toilet

ENGAGE AND EXPLAIN

Legal requirements (aide mémoire)
- Recording: time, day, date, location
- Introductions (where applicable stating role)
  - You
  - Suspect
  - Second investigator
  - Legal adviser
  - Appropriate adult
  - Interpreter
  - Reader (of documentation)
- FILA (= free independent legal advice)
- Caution
  - Deliver
  - Explain
  - Check comprehension

Focus
- Reason for interview
  - Allegation
  - Explanation of offence (lay terms)
  - Grounds for arrest (line of logic)
  - Significant statements, silences, unsolicited comments
- Route Map
  - Topics to be covered
  - Monitor 'hot spots' (BASELINES)
- Routines
  - Second investigator role
  - Note-taking
  - Reference to notes/ material
  - Showing material/ exhibits
- Expectations (ground rules)
  - 'Tell the truth'
  - 'As much detail as possible'
  - 'Can't be too much detail'
  - 'Take your time'
  - 'Think before talking'
  - 'Think after talking'
  - 'Hear each other out'

ACCOUNT, CLARIFY, CHALLENGE

Trigger disclosure

Ethical options
- Closed confirmatory question re: culpability
- Trailer question
- Request account

Process First Account
- Intent listening
  - Imaging
  - 'Mental echoing'
  - 'Guggling' key ideas
- No interruption
- Monitor 'hot spots' (BASELINES)

If 'thin' account
- Remind 'As much detail as possible'
- Check comprehension
- Request re-telling

If potentially 'pat' account
- Acknowledge amount of detail
  - 'A lot to take in'
- Request re-telling

Second Account (=develop first account)
- Select segment
- Intent listening
  - Imaging
  - 'Mental echoing'
  - 'Guggling' key ideas
- No interruption
- Monitor 'hot spots' (BASELINES)

Review Account

Probe Account
- Select topic
- Interview spiral
  - Open
  - Probe
  - Summarize
  - Link
- Access non-verbal detail
  - Illustrators
  - Enactment
  - Enhanced drawing

I³ (Investigatively Important Information)
- Select topic
- Interview spiral
  - Open
  - Probe
  - Summarize
  - Link
- Access non-verbal detail
  - Illustrators
  - Enactment
  - Enhanced drawing

If inconsistent/ or contra-dictory disclosures/ responses

Don't suspend interview for planning and preparation of FAIR review if:
- Little evidence
- Evidence extremely weak
- Minor offence

Otherwise suspend for planning and preparation of FAIR review

If offence admitted
- Conduct TIC review

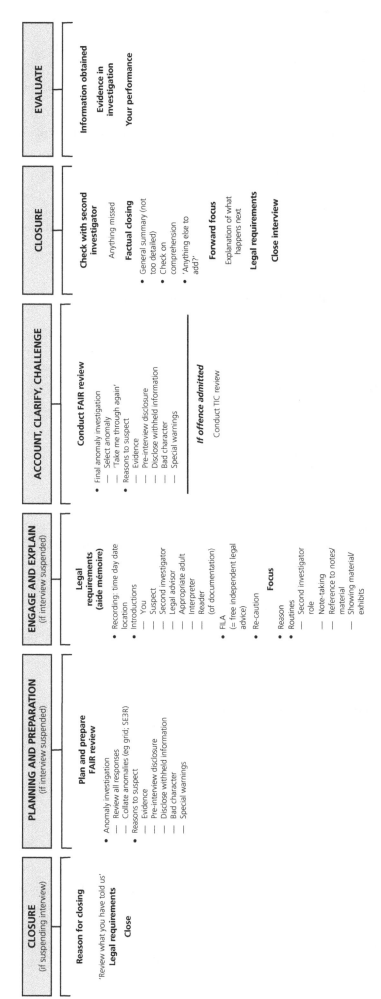

Figure 18.1 Map for interviewing a suspect who answers questions

18.3.2 Not all questions have to be answered

The suspect can exercise the right to remain silent and reply 'no comment' to questions that:

- have no bearing upon the offence because they are irrelevant from the viewpoint of the defence that the suspect will rely upon at court;
- concern 'bad character' evidence because remaining silent:
  — does no harm should the case go to court
  — prevents the suspect from making assertions about his or her character;
  — prevents the suspect from making assertions about the character of the complainant/victim or other co-defendants.

18.3.3 The suspect cannot give an account that is inconsistent with or contradicts the version given to the legal adviser

The suspect cannot give an account and responses to questions that are inconsistent with the version of events given in consultation with the legal adviser. The legal adviser must at some point intervene to request the interview be stopped to advise the suspect that lying is not permissible for the reasons explained in Chapter 16.

18.4 Capturing the suspect's disclosures

18.4.1 Working alone

You should use the standard methods for maximizing capture of fine-grain detail: imaging, 'mental echoing', identifying—and 'guggling' to—key ideas. When progressing beyond the first account you should be prepared, where appropriate, to regulate the flow of detail.

18.4.2 Working with a second investigator

The most effective means of capturing the detail of the suspect's disclosures is a contemporaneous SE3R.

18.5 Triggering a spontaneous account

18.5.1 Ethical approaches

There are three ethical approaches to triggering a spontaneous account.

- A closed confirmatory question concerning culpability.
- A trailer question, ie a number of key facts followed by a productive question.
- A productive question requesting an account, ie disclosure of narrative detail for a specified period, or detail concerning a specified topic.

The productive question requesting an account is the least risky option. But it may not be the most suitable if the allegation is particularly well grounded in terms of the detail of the police case, and in particular the information and evidence that you have. A trailer question might be appropriate here. However, you might judge a closed confirmatory question concerning culpability to be the most suitable opener given the circumstances. In sum, there is no 'one size fits all' question applicable in all circumstances. You have to consider the case that you have and the situation in which you are investigating the offence, including practical constraints such as the time of day and 'detention clock'.

18.5.2 Unethical approaches: inducements

The Oxford English Dictionary provides a clear definition for the term inducement: *an attraction that leads one on.* An inducement is a lure, bait, carrot, spur, or incentive. The matter is clear. Anything that you do or say, offer, or promise, as an actual or potential benefit to the suspect for making an admission, eg a reduction in sentence under section 144 of the Criminal Justice Act 2003 (which is a decision that is made by the court not you):

- is an inducement;
- is likely to render the recording of the interview inadmissible evidence.

Never offer any form of inducement. It will come back to haunt you. Why throw away all your hard investigative work by acting unethically and having the case thrown out at court?

18.5.3 Closed confirmatory question concerning culpability

This gets to the heart of the matter. It can be asked in a more open *whether* form or 'yes'/'no' form, eg:

> Now you are clear about the reason for this interview Jason ^^^^ I need you to tell me [whether you stabbed] [did you stab] your flatmate Kevin Jones?

Whatever the response, it should be immediately followed either by:

- a trailer question; or
- a productive question to trigger a spontaneous account.

18.5.4 Trailer question

As indicated in Chapter 9, a trailer question is a series of key facts—not too many—delivered with pauses and followed by a productive question, eg:

> This afternoon witnesses heard you and Kevin Jones arguing in your flat. ^^^^
> You were heard to leave the flat, slamming the door. ^^ ^^
> Minutes later Kevin Jones collapsed on the landing with serious stab wounds. ^^ ^^
> You have blood on your shirt and a slashed hand. ^^^^
> I need to know Jason ^^ how do you account for these things?

Whatever the response, it should be immediately followed as appropriate by either:

- a productive question to trigger a spontaneous account; or
- a closed confirmatory question concerning culpability.

18.5.5 A request for an account

It will be recalled that the term *account* refers both to a narrative and to a description or explanation concerning particular subject matter. The request for the account was heralded in your Route Map, being the first of the topics you specified.

Assisting remembrance

Where the suspect is deciding to answer questions there is no reason why, if you think it applicable and appropriate, you should not assist his or her remembrance. Follow the guidance in Chapter 10, ie brief on:

- focused retrieval;
- reporting everything, including use of illustrators;
- context reinstatement.

Initiating disclosure

The suspect is aware of the topic about which you wish him or her to disclose. Initiating disclosure is simply a matter of using productive process questioning and appropriately long pauses to allow for thoughts to be collected and the response to be framed.

- Open with a crème de la crème question.
- If no response is forthcoming, work your way down from crème de la crème to open.

For example.

> *So, Jason ^^ it's about the stabbing of Kevin Jones this afternoon. ^^ ^^ ^^ ^^*
> *Over to you. ^^ ^^ ^^ ^^*
> *(If no response) Take your time. ^^ ^^ ^^ ^^*
> *There's no rush. ^^ ^^ ^^ ^^*
> *(If no response) We need to know about the stabbing. ^^ ^^ ^^ ^^*
> *Could you tell me about that? ^^ ^^ ^^ ^^*

and so on.

18.6 Responding to an admission

Admissions vary in their fullness of content: from a very non-committal allusion to culpability (eg *I might have ...*) through partial admission to a full account of culpable action, the triggering circumstances, and the suspect's state of mind at the time.

Whether alluding to guilt, partially admitting, or speaking at length about culpability, your task is to obtain the fullest possible spontaneous admission. You must resist any internal pressure to start developing the account. If you switch too early to developing the admission you run the risk of pre-empting and preventing the suspect giving you detail that he or she might have given you had you not come in to probe.

The key is to exercise self-control, coping with the differing degrees of admission by following the sequence outlined in Box 18.1.

Suspect's disclosure	Your response
Allusion to guilt	• Remain silent. • Don't interrupt. • Monitor BASELINES. • Look for 'hot spots'. • Engage in SOFTENS behaviours.
Suspect then remains silent	• Remain silent. • Engage in SOFTENS behaviours. • Monitor BASELINES—be alert to 'inner dialogue'.

Suspect's disclosure	Your response
Suspect continues to remain silent	• Remain silent. • Engage in SOFTENS behaviours. • Monitor BASELINES—be alert to 'inner dialogue'.
Partial admission	• Remain silent. • Engage in SOFTENS behaviours. • Monitor BASELINES—be alert to 'inner dialogue'.
Full admission	• Remain silent. • Engage in SOFTENS behaviours. • Monitor BASELINES—be alert to 'inner dialogue'. • Don't close down the interview. • Treat the admission as a separate topic. • Develop the admission as a spontaneous account.

Box 18.1 Coping with admissions

18.7   Developing the suspect's spontaneous account

18.7.1   Respond to problematic spontaneous disclosure

'Thin' account

If the suspect's account is 'thin'—like an agenda with a few steps but no detail about the steps or what happened between one step and the next—follow the advice in Chapter 9.

- Don't summarize.
- Explain to the suspect the lack of detail.
- Take the suspect through the 'it's about detail' ground rule again.
- Check back the suspect's understanding of the ground rule.
- Take the suspect through the 'taking your time' ground rule again.
- Check back the suspect's understanding of the ground rule.
- Ask the suspect to take you through his or her account again—this time:
  — giving as much detail as possible: there can't be too much detail;
  — taking his or her time: taking time will help him or her to remember the detail that's needed.

Think of the requested account as inviting an individual holding a closed, compressed accordion to release the securing catch and open the instrument to view. The 'thin' account is no more than releasing the catch and a token gesture at opening.

If the result is another 'thin' account

It is pointless to summarize. Go straight to developing the account.

If it is an acceptably full account

Summarize the key issues and go to developing the account.

'Pat' account

If the suspect's account has features pointing to it being potentially a 'pat' account (little or no narrative reversal; too many descriptors before a subject, eg person, item, or location) follow the advice in Chapter 9.

- Don't summarize.
- Reward the suspect for the quality and quantity of detail given, eg:

  That's just the kind of detail we need Jason. ^^^^ *Lots of it too.* ^^ ^^

- Explain the information processing demand, eg:

  There's a lot there to get my head round. ^^ ^^

- State the solution, eg:

  To help me to do that ^^ *I'm going to ask you to take me through that detail again.* ^^ ^^

- Ask for another telling, eg:

  So taking your time Jason ^^^^ *take me through that again* ^^ ^^ *in as much detail as possible.* ^^ ^^

If the result indicates this is likely to be a 'pat' account

If there is still little or no narrative reversal, there are still too many descriptors before particular subject matter, and the suspect uses the same words and phrases as the first 'pat' account:

- don't summarize—it would help the individual to consolidate the potentially learned detail in his or her memory;
- go straight to developing the account.

If the account no longer has 'pat' features

Summarize the key issues and go to developing the account.

18.7.2 Developing the account

Where applicable you should acknowledge the account and the amount of detail given, eg:

  That's been helpful. ^^ ^^ *That's the kind of detail we need.* ^^ ^^

Then explain the need to expand the account, eg:

  I will need you to give me more of that kind of detail. ^^ ^^

The options

There are two options. Both have advantages and risks.

Going back over the entire account

Let's go back to the image of the first account as being like an accordion that the suspect has opened out. Open to view are some but not all of the bellows and the ribbing around the exposed bellows. If you ask the suspect to take you through the account, this time including even more detail, the suspect opens out the accordion further and further, to reveal more and more of its construction and structure.

The risk is that going through the account in its entirety could be counter-productive:

- it is wearisome;
- it is potentially alienating, ie the suspect might protest that he or she has given substantial detail already;
- the extra disclosure concerning the entire narrative could strain your working memory capacity and that of the suspect.

Expand selected key segments

This option makes less mental demand on working memory.

- **'Fan' approach.** In this very common approach the first selected segment typically includes the period during which the offence was actually committed. Depending on the circumstances the next segment might be a period of time preceding the first segment. The third similarly might be the period following the first. The fourth might be the period preceding the second. The effect is akin to a fan being opened out: hence the name.
- **'Opening the book' approach.** This is a 'select where it makes sense to question' approach, selecting key topics. Akin to going to a chapter in a book, a section in the chapter, a sub-section within this, a paragraph within this.

Whether moving from segment to segment on a back and forth chronological basis or on a 'makes sense' basis there is an obvious risk of 'topic hopping'.

Assisting the suspect's remembrance of offence-related detail

Whatever the approach you decide upon to expand the account, if you have a co-operative suspect, who has given a relatively full account, you should consider assisting his or her remembrance of fine-grain detail.

18.8 Reviewing the spontaneous account

In this stage you need to consider the topics that you wish to probe, ie to have expanded or explained in fine-grain detail. It makes sense to pause for a moment to create a WOB map if:

- there are many issues that require probing;
- you have had some thoughts of issues that might be significant;
- you have identified actions that need to be taken after the interview.

18.9 Probing the account

18.9.1 Applying the Interviewing Spiral

As explained in Chapter 9 this involves:

- opening a topic;
- probing by following a line of questioning—'questions born of answers' not 'topic hopping';
- where applicable, summarizing the key issues in the run of responses: never attempting to replicate the detail;
- linking to the next topic—either by striking a logical link or stating a need to switch to another (unconnected) issue.

Concentrate on your questioning behaviour

Vary your questions, using the general to specific dimension to maximum effect.

- **Crème de la crème questions**
  - Statement/comment, eg *You were seen leaving your house at quarter past five.* ^^ ^^
  - Topic, eg *We need to know about what led you to leave the house.* ^^ ^^
  - Silence after raising a topic, or after the suspect has given his or her response, is by far and away the best question.

- **TED instructions**, eg *Could you tell me about that?* ^^ ^^; *Take me through…* ^^ ^^
- **Open questions**
  - Parameter, eg *Can you tell me what you did between leaving your house until you entered Yates's Wine Bar at seven?* ^^ ^^
  - 'Big' (narrative) 'what', eg *It will help me if you can tell me what happened then?* ^^ ^^
  - 'How', eg *There's no rush, can you tell me how you got into town from your house?* ^^ ^^
  - 'Why' or a suitable alternative, eg *We need to know why you went into the Wine Bar?* ^^ ^^
- **Closed identificatory questions.** 'Who?', 'What?', 'Where?', 'When?', 'Which?', 'In which way?'
- **Closed confirmatory questions**
  - 'If' or 'whether', eg *Can you tell me if you were intending to go out this evening?*
  - Closed confirmatory 'yes'/'no', eg *I want you to think about this.* ^^ ^^ *It is very important.* ^^ ^^ *Take your time.* ^^ ^^ *Did you hit John McCaffery?* ^^ ^^

18.9.2 Respond to anomalies

Appropriate responses

Your response will depend on the type of anomaly.

Absence of detail

You should continue to probe systematically as a line of questioning when the response is characterized by anomalies indicative of evasion:

- missing detail, gaps, jumps, 'non-barking dogs';
- evasive behaviour—'sidestepping', answering a question with a question, referring you to someone else, vagueness, or ambiguity;
- narrative contrast.

If your probing does not resolve these shortcomings:

- summarize;
- move to the next topic;
- return at a later point to obtain further expansion and explanation.

'Pat'

If the responses are indicative of being 'pat'—little or no narrative reversal; too many descriptors before an item; same words and phrasing—don't alert and don't summarize. Note the 'pat' indicators and move to another topic.

Inconsistency and contradiction

If the responses are inconsistent with or contradict those given earlier:

- don't alert the suspect to the inconsistency or contradiction;
- make a judgement whether to summarize or not: the risk is that a deceptive suspect will twig that he or she has given an inconsistent or contradictory response and move to give an account for the lack of fit or mismatch, eg:

  Oh, just to let you know why I said first off that…;

- move to the next topic;
- return at a later point to obtain further disclosure on the anomalous material.

Inappropriate responses to the suspect's disclosures

Repeated questioning on a topic

As indicated in Chapter 9, you have to keep on asking yourself, and be able to explain in this interview to the legal adviser or later at court, your reason for questioning on this topic yet again. Your only reason for your persistence must be investigative: to resolve an anomaly. It must never be to induce the suspect to abandon his response on this matter.

If you probe and ask essentially the same questions three or more times, the legal adviser should intervene to:

- ask you to stop while the legal adviser consults his or her notebook;
- having counted the number of same responses have been given:
  — ask why you are repeating your questions on this topic yet again;
  — point out that your behaviour constitutes oppression, perhaps citing appropriate case law[2] eg:

  Officer, that is the [number of times] you have asked that question. Nothing new is now emerging. I have consulted my notes and I am confident that the recording of this interview will show that my client has been consistent in his/her replies on this matter. I need to point out that, in the absence of you producing any evidence to counter my client's account, your questioning on this matter constitutes oppression. Oppression has been defined as behaviour that is likely to induce an individual to say thing that he otherwise would not, or not to say things that he otherwise would. Please accept my client's consistent responses on this matter, please do not ask the question again, and please move onto another matter.

If the suspect is not legally represented or if the legal adviser does not intervene, as explained in Chapter 9, should the suspect make incriminatory disclosures the defence at court will argue that these were coerced and the evidence should be ruled inadmissible.

Repeatedly administering the caution

This is a widespread inappropriate behaviour. If you repeatedly administer the caution the legal adviser should intervene to:

- ask why you are re-administering the caution;
- if no sensible explanation is forthcoming, point out that your behaviour constitutes oppression, perhaps citing appropriate case law.[3]

You have to be able to explain to the legal adviser—or later at court in the case of an unrepresented suspect—your reason for administering the caution on several occasions in the interview. It will be difficult to convince that your re-cautioning was not linked to:

- dissatisfaction with the suspect's replies;
- attempting to induce the suspect to change his or her response, ie to abandon his or her version and give you different detail—that fitted with what you knew or believed to be the case.

---

[2] *R v Prager* [1972] 1 All ER 1114; *R v Priestley* [1965] 51 Cr App R 1; *R v Fulling* [1987] 85 Cr App R 136.
[3] *R v Prager* [1972] 1 All ER 1114; *R v Priestley* [1965] 51 Cr App R 1; *R v Fulling* [1987] 85 Cr App R 136.

Unethical responses

All the following are unethical responses.

- Questioning on the matter of motive when the suspect has yet to admit culpability.[4]
- Minimizing the seriousness, or stating the understandability, of the offence.[5]
- Engaging in emotional blackmail.[6]
- Engaging in amateur psychologizing, eg *it will help if you get it off your chest.*[7]
- Questioning about the individual's sexuality if this has no bearing on the offence.[8]
- Misrepresenting evidence, including overstating and being disingenuous.[9]
- Claiming that witness accounts are independent unless you are sure they are.[10]
- Telling active (actual) lies about what you know to be the case or asserting the existence of information or evidence that does not exist.[11]

18.9.3 Obtaining non-verbal disclosure

Use the guidance in the Reference Section to assist you in obtaining non-verbal disclosure. Remember not to verbalize what the suspect is:

- showing you with his fingers or hands (illustrators);
- acting for you, or getting you or others to act under his or her instructions (enactment);
- drawing (while you are drawing in parallel).

In many cases you will simply need to progress steadily up the 'staircase'.

- Illustrator representation—move on to other topics.
- Second illustrator representation—to 'validate' the first—then move on to other topics.
- Enactment—move on to other topics.
- Second illustrator representation—to 'validate' the first—then move on to other topics.
- Enhanced drawing—as the final stage.

However, you will need to be flexible. Sometimes you will need to proceed from illustrators to enhanced drawing, or even straight to an enhanced drawing.

18.10 Obtaining disclosure on other topics in your Route Map

Where your Route Map includes two or more major topics to be covered, work through these systematically.

- Link to the second major topic—reminding the suspect of your Route Map of things that needed to be covered.
- State the major topic.

---

[4] *R v Heron, Daily Mail,* 22 November 1993. See Wolchover, D. and Heaton-Armstrong, A. (1996) *Wolchover and Heaton-Armstrong on Confession Evidence.* London: Sweet and Maxwell.

[5] *R v Miller, Paris and Abdullahi* [1993] 97 Cr App R 99.

[6] *R v Miller, Paris and Abdullahi* [1993] 97 Cr App R 99.

[7] *R v Miller, Paris and Abdullahi* [1993] 97 Cr App R 99.

[8] *R v Heron, Daily Mail,* 22 November 1993.

[9] *R v Mason* [1987] Crim LR 757.

[10] *R v Miller, Paris and Abdullahi* [1993] 97 Cr App R 99.

[11] *R v Heron, Daily Mail,* 22 November 1993.

- Trigger spontaneous disclosure on this topic.
- Develop the spontaneous account on this topic.
- Review.
- Probe the account.
- Link to the third major topic.
- State this topic.
- Trigger spontaneous disclosure on this topic...and so on.

18.11 Questioning on investigatively important information (I³)

The range of I³ will differ widely according to the circumstances of the case. Your WOB of I³ will reflect the particular issues in this investigation.

18.12 Barriers to investigation arising from probing the suspect's account or questioning on I³

18.12.1 Assertions of innocence and denials

You must keep a track—a simple tally—of how many times the suspect asserts innocence or denies culpability or involvement in the offence. Clearly this could be a guilty person making multiple denials. However, as pointed out in *R v Miller, Paris and Abdullahi*,[12] repeated denials are a warning bell.

If a large number of assertions of innocence or denials occur in a short space of time, you should consider:

- closing the interview;
- re-examining:
  — the police case;
  — the information and evidence that you have;
  — the line of logic that leads you to consider that this suspect rather than anyone else committed the offence.

18.12.2 'I don't understand' assertions

You must keep a tally of the number of times a suspect says that he or she does not understand. Clearly this could be a guilty person trying to avoid answering your questions. However, you have to treat repeated assertions of inability to understand as a serious matter.

If you assessed the suspect as not being mentally vulnerable

- Assess the potential significance of the assertions, taking into account his or her behaviour, eg signs of extreme arousal, distress, fatigue.
- Given that the more indicators you identify the greater the risk, in the event of a significant number:
  — stop the interview;
  — do not wait for the legal adviser to intervene, ie requesting the interview be stopped.

---

[12] *R v Miller, Paris and Abdullahi* [1993] 97 Cr App R 99.

If the suspect does not have English as a first language but was deemed not to require an interpreter

Stop the interview and consult with the custody officer to arrange for an interpreter.

18.12.3 The suspect cries or breaks down

Be professional and proactive. Don't wait for the legal adviser or appropriate adult to tell you that there is a 'problem'.

If you judge the behaviour to be actually or potentially genuine

- Tell the suspect, and where applicable the legal adviser or appropriate adult, that you are stopping the interview to allow the suspect to compose himself or herself.
- Stop the interview.
- Observe the suspect closely—looking for BASELINES behaviours, particularly:
  — shaking;
  — sustained, genuine inability to control tears;
  — expressiveness problems, eg incoherence, wailing, shouting, screaming.
- If the behaviours persist, the suspect is clearly unable to regain composure and you should stop the interview to take a break.

If you judge the behaviour to be potentially bogus

- Tell the suspect, and where applicable the legal adviser or appropriate adult, that you are stopping the interview to allow the suspect to compose himself or herself.
- Stop the interview.
- Observe the suspect's behaviour closely. Where there is no interaction and it is silent, it is very difficult to sustain:
  — shaking;
  — tears;
  — incoherence, wailing, shouting, screaming.
- If your observation leads you to believe the suspect is shamming, be open about this:
  — give the suspect the opportunity to reply;
  — observe the suspect's verbal and non-verbal behaviour—particularly vocal—for signs that the suspect has composed himself or herself to protest the genuineness of the tears and the breakdown.
- If your suspicions are confirmed:
  — state this;
  — continue with the interview.
- If your suspicions are not confirmed, stop the interview.

18.12.4 The suspect engages in sabotaging behaviour

Chapter 11 explains that there are many behaviours with the potential to sabotage the interview and obstruct you in achieving your investigative aim and objectives.

- 'Putting down'.
- Being abusive.

- Arguing.
- Being indignant or angry.
- Threatening.
- Seeking to speak to someone else
- Refusing to be helped.
- Refusing to co-operate.

These may be exhibited by the suspect, by the legal adviser, or more rarely by the appropriate adult.

In each instance follow the advice given in Chapter 11. In sum this involves the following steps.

- Give the individual the benefit of the doubt, ie he or she is unaware of engaging in the inappropriate behaviour.
- Remember that simply giving feedback once will not change behaviour.
- Follow the 'rule of three'.
- To extinguish the behaviour and to put the relationship on an equal footing follow the DEAL technique:
  — to assert yourself;
  — to give feedback;
  — ultimately, to spell out the consequences of the behaviour.

18.12.5 The relationship deteriorates

If the evidence is clear that there is a 'personality clash' between you and the suspect, follow the guidance in Chapter 11 which involves the following steps.

Spot the problem as early as possible

- Try to tackle the problem early on, before it really gets to you.
- Don't take what is happening personally.
- Don't react with overt frustration, sarcasm, or anger.

Stop the interview

The judge in *R v Timothy John West*[13] said that the interviewing should stop immediately to allow both, or either of the parties to cool off or to hand over interviewing to another investigator.

Review the situation

- Reflect on:
  — the course of the interview;
  — the emergence to the personality clash.
- Look at the two sides of the clash: asking hard questions.
  Did my reactions wind him or her up?
  Are my reactions a reflection of my stress due to:
  — *workload;*
  — *pressure for results;*
  — *not having the time;*

---

[13] *R v Timothy John West* (1988) Gloucester Crown Court. Unreported.

> — *not having secure knowledge of the case;*
> — *shortcomings in evidence;*
> — *being unprepared;*
> — *personal circumstances?*
> *What reactions by the suspect wound me up?*
> *What are his or her reactions a reflection of?*

- Identify the solution.
  - Having calmed down, recommence interviewing and use appropriate assertion (DEAL) to manage further inappropriate behaviour by the suspect.
  - Get another investigator to take on the interviewing task.

18.12.6 The suspect switches from answering questions to exercising the right to silence

This is *mixed responding*.

If legally advised, the suspect's the legal adviser should ask you to stop the interview so that he or she can consult with the suspect. The legal adviser must do this because a court:

- could reasonably conclude that the suspect was:
  - unable to give responses on matters to which he or she said 'no comment';
  - was hiding behind the right to silence;
- would almost inevitably allow an adverse inference to be drawn under section 34 of the Criminal Justice and Public Order Act 1994.

A suspect who is not legally advised will not realize the implications of making this change.

18.13 Decision-making concerning a FAIR review

18.13.1 The logic for stopping to plan and to prepare a FAIR review

You should as a matter of standard practice stop the interview to plan and to prepare a FAIR review if there are anomalies—particularly inconsistency and contradiction—in the suspect's:

- spontaneous account and responses to probing of this account;
- responses to questions on I^3 topics.

In the FAIR review you will want to:

- question about the anomalies without alerting the suspect;
- where applicable and appropriate, question about:
  - pre-interview disclosure that you made;
  - further information and evidence that you have withheld;
  - 'bad character' evidence if not already covered;
- issue a Special Warning.

Stopping at this point is sensible because it fulfils other requirements.

- Mindful of the advice in Chapter 8 about interview duration, if the interview has lasted for 40 minutes or more you need to stop the interview anyway to allow everyone to attend to the demands of nature.
- The suspect is able to consult with the legal adviser or any other third party.

18.13.2   The logic for not stopping to plan and to prepare a FAIR review

However, there will be circumstances when you may consider it impractical or inappropriate to stop to conduct a FAIR review.

- Where the evidence is extremely weak.
- It is a minor offence.

18.13.3   Closing the interview to plan and to prepare a FAIR review

If you are closing the interview:

- give a simple explanation of your decision;
- don't give an overall summary of the interview thus far;
- invite questions;
- close.

For example:

> *Right Tim ^^ ^^ I'm now going to stop the interviewing for the time being. ^^ ^^ This will enable everyone to take a natural break. ^^^^ During the break you will be able to talk with [name of legal adviser; name of appropriate adult]. ^^ ^^*
>
> *When you and [name of legal adviser; name of appropriate adult] talk with each other you will be able to think about what I've talked about ^^ ^^ and asked you about ^^ ^^ in this interview.*
>
> *While you are doing that I [and my colleague] will be looking at the information and evidence that [I] [we] have. ^^ ^^*
>
> *I will let [name of legal adviser; name of appropriate adult] know when we are ready to start interviewing again. ^^ ^^*
>
> *So before we switch off the recorder Tim ^^ ^^ can I just check whether you have any questions? ^^ ^^*

18.13.4   Continuing to interview

If you decide that circumstances do not warrant stopping the interview to plan and prepare a FAIR review, you should proceed—where appropriate and applicable—to **Anomaly awareness and investigation** at section 18.15.3.

18.14   Planning and preparing a FAIR review

The FAIR review will include **Anomaly awareness, investigation** and **Reasons to suspect.**

18.14.1   Anomaly awareness

When you interview next your task will be to draw the suspect's attention to things that are 'not quite clear'. You must have a total grasp of inconsistency and contradiction within his or her account and responses to questions.

Reflect on what has emerged

You must review the content of:

- the suspect's account and responses to probing of this;
- the suspect's responses when questioned about I^3.

Where time and resource permit, and offence seriousness requires, it is essential to check the accuracy of your remembrance and representation of the suspect's account and responses.

- Replay of the recording.
- While replaying check the accuracy of contemporaneously created SE3Rs.

Collate the material

- Where applicable create radiating sub-blobs for each instance of inconsistency and contradiction.
- For each inconsistency or contradiction plot the detail **either:**
  — as a grid: with different columns for each version and rows for the key detail: highlighting the detail that does not fit (inconsistency) or is a mismatch (contradiction); **or**
  — onto a composite SE3R of the suspect's account and responses: with a legend to explain the use of different colours for different versions.

18.14.2 Investigation

In the interview your task will be to get the suspect to take you through the anomalous material again without impugning the suspect's character, ie not telling him or her that you consider his or her response to be untruthful. You must plan how you will:

- question on the anomaly without alerting the suspect: 'not too clear' about particular detail, request to be taken through again;
- finally reveal the existence of anomaly without implying that the suspect is a lying.

18.14.3 Reasons to suspect:

Concentrate on gaining a secure grasp of the other material that you have decided to:

- question about:
  — pre-interview disclosure that you made;
  — further information and evidence that you have withheld;
  — 'bad character' evidence;
- issue a Special Warning.

Create a WOB map with radiating blobs for each of these areas.

18.15 Taking the suspect through the FAIR review

If interviewing was stopped to allow a break and to enable the FAIR review, the standard administrative and legal procedures must be observed at the beginning of this interview.

18.15.1 Where the legal adviser notifies a change in the suspect's response to questioning

The legal adviser may state that his or her client has chosen to produce a prepared statement. Follow the advice in Chapter 19.

18.15.2 Explanation

An explanation is necessary to overcome the 'guessing game': the suspect trying to work out what is coming next.

Reason

> *I have had a chance to look over what you've said to me ^^ ^^*
> *and the information in this case. ^^ ^^*
> *I want to go through these with you now. ^^ ^^*

Route map

> *I've made a note of the matters I want to cover. ^^ ^^*
> *First I want to ask some questions ^^ ^^ to make sure that I've understood ^^ ^^ exactly ^^ ^^*
> *what you've said to me about certain matters. ^^ ^^*
> *Then I'm going to take your through information that I have ^^ ^^*
> *and ask some questions about this. ^^ ^^*

Routines

As normal.

Expectations

Recapitulating the ground rules, ensuring that the suspect gives his or her understanding of each ground rule.

18.15.3 Anomaly awareness and investigation

Raise awareness, obtain another version

For example, where the suspect in a sexual assault allegation has given two versions concerning the removal of clothes.

- Consult the Anomaly blob on your FAIR map.
- Look at the grid/composite SE3R in which the contradictory versions are side by side.
- State the topic:
  > *You described how you and X ended up without any clothes. ^^ ^^*
- Make aware of the problem, and then pose the question, eg:
  > *I'm still not clear about that ^^ ^^ about what happened ^^ ^^ from the time you went into the bedroom ^^ ^^ until both of you were without clothes. ^^ ^^ We need to clear that up. ^^ ^^ So I'm going to ask you to take me through that again, ^^ ^^ describing what happened, ^^ ^^ from the time you went into the bedroom, ^^ ^^ until both of you were without clothes. ^^ ^^ Taking me through everything ^^ ^^ in as much detail as possible. ^^ ^^ There can't be too much detail. ^^ ^^ Taking your time. ^^ ^^ There is no rush. ^^ ^^ Use your hands to help you to show me ^^ ^^ what happened ^^ ^^ and what's in your mind's eye. ^^ ^^ If it helps ^^ ^^ close your eyes ^^ ^^ to help you to concentrate. ^^ ^^ OK then ^^ ^^ over to you. ^^ ^^*
- Listen intently, observe closely.
- Image, mentally echo, guggle, and if necessary regulate the flow.
- Capture—and compare—the detail in the grid/SE3R.

Reveal anomaly without calling the suspect a liar

When all anomalies have been covered, reveal these one at a time without impugning the suspect.

Continuing with the example.

> *I've got to be fair to you.* ^^ ^^ *You have given me more than one description of what happened.* ^^ ^^ *And that has happened a number of times.* ^^ ^^ *I'm not saying that you are not telling the truth.* ^^ ^^ *But you need to clear things up* ^^ ^^ *once and for all.* ^^ ^^ *So this last time* ^^ ^^ *think very hard,* ^^ ^^ *describe to me what happened,* ^^ ^^ *from the time you went into the bedroom,* ^^ ^^ *until both of you were without clothes.* ^^ ^^ *Taking me through everything* ^^ ^^ *in as much detail as possible.* ^^ ^^ *There can't be too much detail.* ^^ ^^ *Taking your time.* ^^ ^^ *There is no rush.* ^^ ^^ *Use your hands to help you to show me* ^^ ^^ *what happened* ^^ ^^ *and what's in your mind's eye.* ^^ ^^ *If it helps* ^^ ^^ *close your eyes* ^^ ^^ *to help you to concentrate.* ^^ ^^ *OK then* ^^ ^^ *over to you.* ^^ ^^

Irrespective of what the suspect says—even if it is yet another version—this is the end of the matter.

- In any case where anomaly endures or grows at this stage, this will have an impact upon case disposal.
- If the suspect is charged it must be for the suspect to explain to the court the giving of inconsistent or contradictory accounts on this matter.

At this point you need to progress to the next anomaly on the Anomaly blob.

- Thank the suspect, eg:

  > *Thanks for that.* ^^ ^^ *Now I have a clear idea of what you are saying* ^^ *about how the two of you ended up without clothes.* ^^ ^^

- Consult the Anomaly blob on your FAIR map.
- Identify the next inconsistent/contradictory disclosure for questioning.
- Link, eg:

  > *I want to take things forward to when you said you started heavy petting.*

- State the next topic, eg:

  > *You described how this began and what brought it to an end.* ^^ ^^

- Pose the question.

and so on...progressing through all the anomalies on the Anomaly blob.

18.15.4 Reasons to suspect

Present information and evidence produced in pre-interview disclosure and withheld till now

Present the source, state the detail, ask the question—wherever possible a trailer, eg:

> *I want you to listen to some key bits of information that I have.* ^^ ^^
> *I'll then ask you a question about them.* ^^ ^^
> *Hear me out as I tell you all the bits.* ^^ ^^
> *Please don't interrupt me as I tell you the bits of information.* ^^ ^^
> *Wait for the question.* ^^ ^^
> *The hotel lobby CCTV shows X was barely able to walk.* ^^ ^^
> *Shows you propping her up.* ^^ ^^
> *You said 'Good night' to the night porter.* ^^ ^^
> *He says she was visibly unconscious.* ^^ ^^

You said X tore your clothes off you. ^^ ^^
Take your time. ^^ ^^ *How do you account for that?* ^^ ^^

Question on 'bad character' evidence

If the suspect is legally represented as soon as you start questioning on 'bad character', you should expect the legal adviser, as pointed out in Chapter 16, to follow the advice of the Law Society's Criminal Law Committee, ie to remind his or her client to exercise the right to silence on these matters. If the suspect starts answering questions, the legal adviser should request the interview be stopped in order to advise his or her client.

Issuing a Special Warning

If you have decided to issue a Special Warning, do so at this point, following your force guidelines.

18.16 Closure

This will normally include:

• the suspect now has an opportunity to consult with his or her legal adviser;
• you have yet to decide whether further interviewing will take place.

Where applicable and appropriate, you may decide that it is appropriate to let the legal adviser know that there may not be another interview.

18.17 Chapter summary

Answering questions is the most risky option because the suspect cannot anticipate what you will say and does not know what you know. It is the defence in which the competent legal adviser will be actively defending. You can expect him or her to intervene at every perceived risk posed by your systematic approach to eliciting a spontaneous first account, developing and probing this, addressing other topics, questioning on I^3, and conducting a FAIR review. If you follow the guidance in this chapter, a court will not find your conversation management exploitative, the risk of the interview being ruled inadmissible will be correspondingly low, and the unresolved multiple anomaly created by the suspect extremely significant evidence.

19

Interviewing the Suspect who Produces a Prepared Statement

19.1 Chapter overview

This chapter examines the issues involved when a suspect has accepted the legal adviser's advice that the safest defence is the production of a prepared statement. Prepared statements are very common, the 'bare bones' variety much more so than the 'full'. Both have major implications for you in terms of processing their contents and subsequent effective, ethical conversation managed interviewing of the suspect.

19.1.1 Chapter objectives

This chapter will enable you to:

- anticipate a prepared statement based on the three scenarios in which a statement is likely to emerge;
- understand the logic for producing a 'bare bones' or 'full' prepared statement and the risks to the suspect;
- understand the timing of the statement—when it is produced—and its legal status;
- appreciate the risks in enquiring prior to the interview whether a statement is to be produced;
- respond to the production of the statement within an interview;
- process systematically the content of the prepared statement;
- decide which strategy to adopt for the interview in which you draw matters to the suspect's attention;
- plan for and conduct pre-interview briefing of the legal adviser and any other third party;
- manage effectively the interview in which you draw matters to the suspect's attention.

19.1.2 Interview map

Figure 19.1 shows the map of appropriate interviewing when a suspect produces a prepared statement.

19.2 The decision to produce a prepared statement

If the suspect has an innocent explanation he or she may accept the advice of his or her legal adviser that the safest defence to police questioning is the production of a prepared statement. There are three scenarios where a legal adviser would consider this to be the safest defence.

- The suspect is yet to be questioned about the offence. You have disclosed sufficient information and evidence to convince the legal adviser that the suspect should give his or her innocent explanation. However, the legal adviser assesses that giving this in an interview involving answering questions would pose a significant risk to the suspect.
- The suspect has been questioned about the offence and has answered your questions. However, the legal adviser now considers that continuing to do so puts the suspect at increasing risk.
- The suspect has been questioned about the offence and has exercised the right to remain silent. In response to this you have disclosed further information and evidence sufficient to convince the legal adviser that the suspect should give his or her innocent explanation. However, the legal adviser assesses that giving this in an interview involving answering questions would pose a significant risk to the suspect.

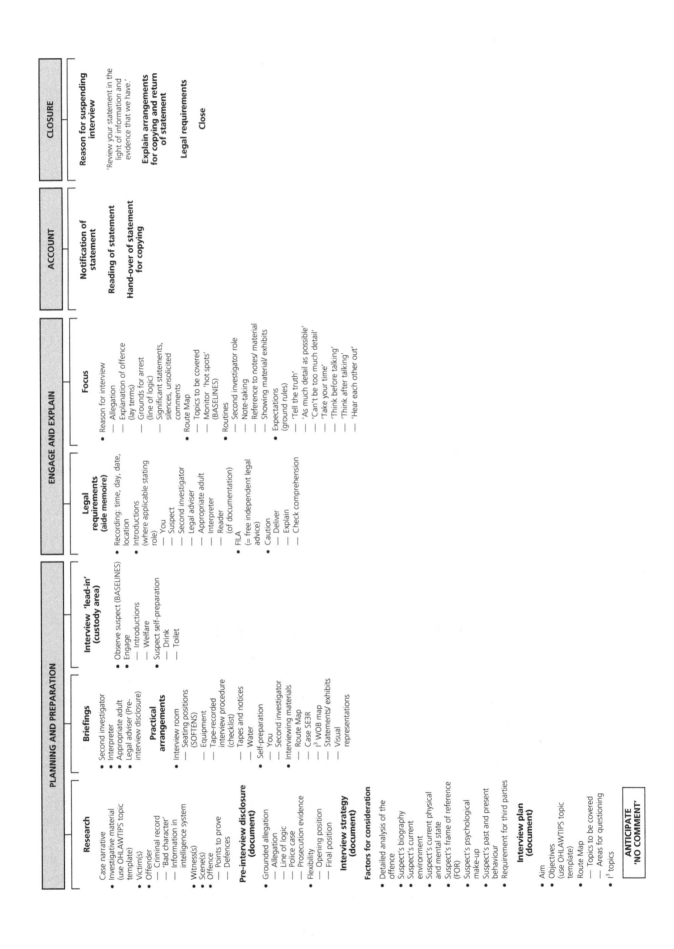

PLANNING AND PREPARATION

Research

Case narrative
- Investigative material (use OHLAWTIPS topic template)
- Victim(s)
- Offender
  - Criminal record
  - 'Bad character'
  - Information in intelligence system
- Witness(s)
- Scene(s)
- Offence
  - Points to prove
  - Defences

Pre-interview disclosure (document)

- Grounded allegation
  - Allegation
  - Line of logic
  - Police case
  - Prosecution evidence
- Flexibility
  - Opening position
  - Final position

Interview strategy (document)

Factors for consideration

- Detailed analysis of the offence
- Suspect's biography
- Suspect's current environment
- Suspect's current physical and mental state
- Suspect's frame of reference (FOR)
- Suspect's psychological make-up
- Suspect's past and present behaviour
- Requirement for third parties

Interview plan (document)

- Aim
- Objectives (use OHLAWTIPS topic template)
- Route Map
  - Topics to be covered
  - Areas for questioning
- I³ topics

ANTICIPATE 'NO COMMENT'

Briefings

- Second investigator
- Interpreter
- Appropriate adult
- Legal adviser (Pre-interview disclosure)

Practical arrangements

- Interview room
  - Seating positions (SOFTENS)
  - Equipment
  - Tape-recorded interview procedure (checklist)
  - Tapes and notices
  - Water
- Self-preparation
  - You
  - Second investigator
- Interviewing materials
  - Route Map
  - Case SE3R
  - I³ WOB map
  - Statements/exhibits
  - Visual representations

Interview 'lead-in' (custody area)

- Observe suspect (BASELINES)
- Engage
  - Introductions
  - Welfare
- Suspect self-preparation
  - Drink
  - Toilet

ENGAGE AND EXPLAIN

Legal requirements (aide memoire)

- Recording: time, day, date, location
- Introductions (where applicable stating role)
  - You
  - Suspect
  - Second investigator
  - Legal adviser
  - Appropriate adult
  - Interpreter
  - Reader (of documentation)
- FILA (= free independent legal advice)
- Caution
  - Deliver
  - Explain
  - Check comprehension

Focus

- Reason for interview
  - Allegation
  - Explanation of offence (lay terms)
  - Grounds for arrest (line of logic)
  - Significant statements, silences, unsolicited comments
- Route Map
  - Topics to be covered
  - Monitor 'hot spots' (BASELINES)
- Routines
  - Second investigator role
  - Note-taking
  - Reference to notes/ material
  - Showing material/ exhibits
- Expectations (ground rules)
  - 'Tell the truth'
  - 'As much detail as possible'
  - 'Can't be too much detail'
  - 'Take your time'
  - 'Think before talking'
  - 'Think after talking'
  - 'Hear each other out'

ACCOUNT

Notification of statement

Reading of statement

Hand-over of statement for copying

CLOSURE

Reason for suspending interview

'Review your statement in the light of information and evidence that we have.'

Explain arrangements for copying and return of statement

Legal requirements

Close

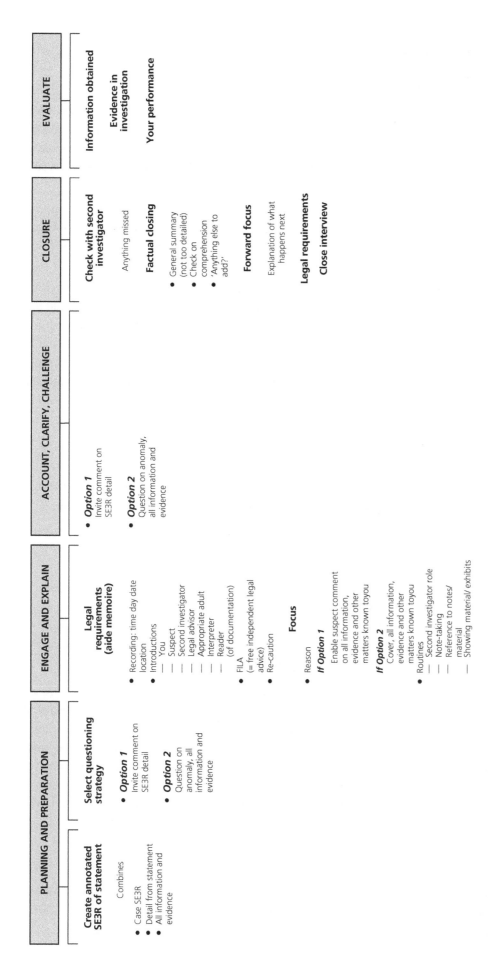

Figure 19.1 Map for interviewing a suspect who produces a prepared statement

19.3   Types of prepared statement

19.3.1   A McGarry 'bare bones' prepared statement

This is a prepared statement which gives very little information, normally a few lines of text setting out in very simple terms an innocent explanation to the allegation. It is called a *McGarry* statement after the Court of Appeal ruling[1] concerning a 'bare bones' statement produced at the beginning of an interview concerning an altercation outside a club. The statement read:

> *I agree that I was present at the Bamford Squash Club on the date in question. I had an altercation inside the club with the complainant. I agree that I left the club at about ten past one. As I was walking up the path towards the pavement the complainant was at my left hand side. He said something to me and lunged forward with his right hand at which point I punched him in self-defence. I have nothing further to say.*

Thereafter, as should always happen when a prepared statement is produced in interview, McGarry answered 'no comment'. The judge directed the jury that, although they did not have to draw any adverse inference from the lack of detail in the defence contained in a statement, they might wish to take it into consideration. McGarry was convicted and at appeal his conviction was overturned. The Court of Appeal held that if a prepared statement gave the 'bare bones'—failing to mention detail later relied on at court—and the judge did not consider this failure warranted an adverse inference, it was wrong for the court to draw adverse conclusions about the unmentioned detail.

When a 'bare bones' statement is most likely to be prepared

A 'bare bones' statement is most likely to be prepared if the suspect asserts innocence to the legal adviser who has doubts about the persuasiveness of the allegation and the basis for this.

- **Your line of logic.** Why you believe the suspect, rather than anyone else, committed the offence.
- **The police case.** The quantity and quality of detail in your description of:
  — the circumstances leading up to, during, and following the commission of the offence;
  — investigation undertaken by you or others up to this point and ongoing investigation.
- **The prosecution evidence.** You have either given insufficient or no detail concerning the prosecution evidence, ie the information and actual evidence that underpins the allegation, your line of logic, and the police case.

Inadequate disclosure does not pose a risk to the suspect. Answering questions—giving an innocent account and responding to probing of this account—does put a client at risk if there has been inadequate disclosure. The legal adviser must necessarily assume that once the suspect has given his or her defence as a spontaneous account and answered your questions, you might 'ambush' him or her with evidence that this defence did not cater for, was inconsistent with, or contradicted.

The legal adviser has therefore advised the suspect that the interview poses a risk to the suspect.

The risk of a 'bare bones' prepared statement

A prepared statement 'fixes' the suspect's defence. However the legal adviser will have reasoned that the risks are relatively low.

---

[1] *R v McGarry* [1998] 3 All ER 805.

- **There are shortcomings in disclosure**. These potentially indicate that this is not a per-suasive case, in particular that the police lack sufficient—or sufficiently strong—evidence to justify a decision to charge.
- **The absence of detail in the prepared statement is a benefit**. Not saying too much means that the suspect's account may well be able to accommodate, or not be harmed by, the detail of any subsequently disclosed evidence.

Where appropriate, the legal adviser may consider that the prepared statement is too 'thin' and may produce a *supplementary prepared statement* that expands the 'bare bones' to account for detail contained in other evidence disclosed subsequent to the production of a prepared statement.

The risk remains, however. If the suspect is charged, when the case goes to court the judge may consider that it was reasonable to expect the suspect to have given more detail in his or her innocent explanation. The judge might well allow an adverse inference given that the lack of detail points to:

- the individual recognized that, following a first account, he or she would struggle to give responses that could withstand close scrutiny;
- the individual used the prepared statement as a device—disclosing as little detail as possible and then hiding behind subsequent 'no comment' responses.

19.3.2 A *Knight* 'full' statement

This is a prepared statement which gives substantially detailed information. It is called a *Knight* statement after the Court of Appeal ruling[2] concerning a 'full' statement produced at the beginning of an interview. Knight had taken the 10-year-old daughter of a friend for a walk in a wood. Afterwards the child complained to her mother that Knight had twice put his hand down her trousers. Knight was arrested.

Knight's legal adviser had concerns that Knight was psychologically vulnerable. Knight's demeanour suggested that he would not be able to cope with the pressure of being subjected to rigorous, robust questioning. At the beginning of the interview Knight's solicitor read a prepared statement that gave a full account in which Knight denied touching the girl in the way described by the police. Knight then consistently answered 'no comment' to questions.

At trial Knight did not depart from the content of the prepared statement. However, the judge directed that the jury might draw an adverse inference from Knight's refusal to answer questions after the production of his prepared statement. The Court of Appeal overturned the conviction indicating that:

- making a prepared statement does not give automatic immunity against adverse infer-ences under section 34 of the Criminal Justice and Public Order Act 1994 (CJPOA);
- at court Knight did not depart from the content of his full prepared statement;
- it was wrong for the judge to direct an adverse inference could be drawn from Knight's 'no comment' responses to questions because:
  — the purpose of section 34 was to obtain early disclosure of the suspect's account;
  — it was not the purpose of section 34 to allow the police to subject a prepared state-ment to cross-examination, ie scrutiny and test through questioning, or else the law would have been written otherwise.

When a 'full' statement is most likely to be prepared

A *Knight* 'full' prepared statement is more likely to be produced where:

---

[2] *R v Knight* [2003] EWCA Crim 1977.

- there has been a significant amount of disclosure of evidence, in particular the detail contained in the account of the complainant or of one or more significant witnesses;
- the client gives the legal adviser a detailed version of events that constitutes an innocent account;
- the legal adviser concludes there are factors which suggest the interview would pose a threat to the client, ie he or she would not be able to cope with the pressure of being subjected to rigorous, robust questioning;
- a 'bare bones' prepared statement would be inappropriate: given the circumstances, in particular the evidential detail, the court might receive an adverse inference direction.

The risk of a 'full' prepared statement

A 'full' *Knight*-type statement is risky because it 'fixes' the suspect's defence. Given the circumstances that give rise to a 'full' statement, the risk of 'fixing' is arguably less than for a 'bare bones' statement.

- The suspect's statement is already inconsistent with, or contradicts, the detailed account of the complainant or a significant witness revealed in pre-interview disclosure or subsequently if the suspect was exercising the right to silence in previous interviewing.
- The suspect's statement will of necessity be inconsistent with, and contradict, other evidence disclosed subsequent to the production of the prepared statement: evidence which further corroborates the account of the complainant or significant witness.

19.3.3 Supplementary prepared statements

An additional *supplementary prepared statement* may be produced if, following production of the prepared statement:

- interviewing of the suspect reveals potentially significant new evidence;
- the legal adviser assesses that:
  - the prepared statement's failure to account for this evidence risks an adverse inference;
  - the defence disclosed in the prepared statement must be expanded to account for this new evidence.

19.4 The point at which the prepared statement is produced

The legal adviser has to judge the appropriate point to produce a prepared statement, either:

- at the outset of the interview, immediately after the preamble; or
- at the end of the interview; or
- at the point of charge.

19.5 The status of a prepared statement

The document is in the suspect's property. In effect its production is a decision by the suspect to allow you to know legally privileged material. It is a matter of choice whether the suspect allows you to have the document in order to make a photocopy. The Law Society

Criminal Law Committee guidelines on advising on silence[3] in the police station state that this should normally be the case.

It is a common misconception that the prepared statement is documentary evidence that belongs to the police, ie that they are entitled to it take from the suspect, if necessary by force. The electronic recording of the contents of the statement read aloud in the interview room is the police evidence, not the document.

19.6 Enquiring about a possible production of a prepared statement

You may feel that it is advantageous to ask the legal adviser ahead of the interview whether the suspect is considering or will be producing a prepared statement. Your reasoning may be that if you know that a prepared statement is likely to be or will be produced you can prepare for a 'no comment' interview. Such reasoning raises two issues.

19.6.1 Breaching legal privilege and breaking professional code of conduct

Questioning the legal adviser prior to the interview about the likelihood of a prepared statement being produced in the forthcoming interview is likely to produce a rebound response from an actively defending, articulate legal adviser.

- What is the purpose of the question?
- It is an improper question revealing that you are unaware that legal advisers are bound by legal privilege and a professional code of conduct.
- The legal adviser can tell no one about what a client has said, or decided, when receiving free legal advice in private.
- You are inviting the legal adviser to breach his or her client's legal privilege and to contravene his or her code of conduct.
- The legal adviser will inform you of what his or her client is deciding to do during the interview not before.

19.7 Responding to the statement when produced in interview

19.7.1 The legal adviser's role in the interview

Having decided to accept the advice to produce a prepared statement, in legal terms the suspect has given implied instructions to the adviser:

- to inform the police that the suspect wishes to produce a prepared statement;
- because the suspect is exercising his or her right to silence, to answer questions on the suspect's behalf concerning the prepared statement.

A competent legal adviser will have advised the suspect that:

- the suspect should not answer any questions concerning the creation of the prepared statement, or respond to any invitation to read the statement aloud;
- the suspect should reply 'no comment' to any question or invitation to read the statement;

---

[3] Cape, E. (2006) *Police Station Advice: Advising on Silence*. London: Law Society.

- the legal adviser will intervene to ensure that questions are directed to the legal adviser not the suspect on matters to do with the creation, or the reading aloud, of the prepared statement.

19.7.2 When the legal adviser indicates the intention to produce a prepared statement

Who should be questioned about the statement?

Given the points made earlier, it makes no sense to talk directly to the suspect on matters to do with the prepared statement. If you should attempt to engage the suspect in conversation concerning the statement, the legal adviser will put you straight on these matters, eg:

> *Officer, following my client instructions I shall answer any appropriate question concerning my client's prepared statement. Please address your questions on these matters to me.*

Whose wording and who wrote the statement?

It also makes no sense to ask whose words are contained in the statement or who wrote the statement. An articulate legal adviser is likely to put on record the realities of policing and legal advising, eg:

> *Officer, I need to remind you that witnesses do not write their statements. Nor do witnesses dictate their statements to police officers. Police officers do not transcribe what the witness says. Police officers are the authors of witness statements. Police officers listen to the witness and take notes of the key details in what the witness says. They then draft the statement for the witness to approve as an accurate and acceptable representation of what the witness said. The words, phrases, sentences, and sequencing of ideas of this drafted statement are not those of the witness. They are the police officer's. Police officers do not reflect the individual's way of talking. They draft an account in formal written English suitably constructed to make it easy for everyone in the criminal justice system to understand.*
>
> *In taking and writing my client's prepared statement I have worked in exactly the same way as a police officer in taking and writing a witness's statement. I think that we should move on.*

Who should read the statement?

It is a proper question to ask if it is intended to read the prepared statement aloud.

If the legal adviser says it is not intended to read the statement

Ask why the prepared statement will not be read aloud. Note the response but do not get involved in a discussion as to the merits of the decision not to read it aloud.

Ask if the suspect will allow you to read the statement aloud so that it may be recorded electronically.

If the legal adviser says it is intended to read the statement

Ask who will be reading it. The legal adviser, following the Law Society guidelines on police station advice,[4] will explain that he or she will read the statement aloud.

---

4 Cape, E. (2006) *Police Station Advice: Advising on Silence.* London: Law Society.

Do not invite—or even worse direct—the suspect to read the statement aloud. Although section 34 of the CJPOA was intended to encourage the giving of an early defence, it does not say that:

- this defence must be delivered verbally;
- when the defence is contained within a prepared statement:
  — this must be read aloud;
  — the suspect must do this.

It is also nonsensical and unethical to call upon a suspect to read a document in formal English when:

- you know or believe that he or she is potentially or actually unable to read due to educational or intellectual disadvantage;
- the allegation, the offence, and the circumstances of the offence are a potential source of distress to the suspect.

A request, or a direction, to the suspect to read the statement will inevitably produce an intervention from the legal adviser drawing your attention to:

- the law on this matter;
- your insensitivity to obvious issues.

Listening to the statement

Just before the legal adviser starts reading the document, make a written note of the time shown on the recorder. If the legal adviser does not give you the statement for copying, you still have the recording to work upon. Having noted the time, you will be able to go straight to that part of the recording.

Pay close attention while the legal adviser reads the statement:

- Do not take notes. This will reduce your ability to register the fine-grain detail of the statement.
- Listen intently.
- Observe closely. Be alert to the legal adviser annotating the document. If this happens it is a clue that the legal adviser has spotted an error of omission—detail left out—or commission—an inaccuracy—that must be corrected. The prepared statement must be pristine, ie have no amendments, insertions, or deletions. Such changes would give a negative impression to the court should the suspect be charged. If the document requires amendment, the legal adviser must have a further consultation with the suspect to allow the legal adviser to prepare a pristine statement.

When the legal adviser stops reading the document, make a written note of this time on the recorder.

Requesting permission to copy the prepared statement

Ask the legal adviser if the suspect will allow you to copy a prepared statement, returning the original to the legal adviser once this is done.

If the legal adviser says 'no'

Do not trigger an exchange about the reasons for this decision or its appropriateness. Let the legal adviser know that:

- you respect the decision;
- the decision not to allow you to make a copy of the statement will extend the time before interviewing recommences, eg:

> *I respect your client's decision. In a moment I will be stopping this interview. I will need to re-interview your client when I have examined your client's prepared statement in detail and considered its contents. Because your client is unwilling to allow me to copy the document I must replay the interview tape and transcribe what you have just read out. This will of course take more time than photocopying the document. Given this, you might want to advise your client to reconsider and to allow me to photocopy the statement.*

It would be an exceptionally contrary legal adviser, who did not care about his or her client's continued detention, not to give you the document at this stage.

If the legal adviser says 'not at the moment'

This is a clue that the legal adviser had detected errors which requires a production of a pristine statement.

- Ask the legal adviser when he or she will be able to provide a statement for copying.
- When the legal adviser says, *After I have advised my client* or words to this effect, this is confirmation that a pristine statement needs to be produced.

If the legal adviser says 'yes'

Ask the legal adviser when you can have the document.

- If the legal adviser says, *Now*, and hands you the document:
  — thank the legal adviser;
  — take it.
- If the legal adviser says, *After I have advised my client* or words to this effect, this is confirmation that a pristine statement needs to be produced.

19.7.3 Closing the interview

Explain.

- You will now end the interview.
- **If applicable:** You will copy the document and return it to the legal adviser.
- **If applicable:** You will await the legal adviser while he or she advises the suspect who will then give you the document for copying and return.

Close the interview in the normal manner.

- After you have examined the statement, you will brief the legal adviser on the next steps.
- Ask the suspect if he or she has any questions.
- Ask the legal adviser if he or she has any questions.
- Ask any supporter present, eg appropriate adult, if he or she has any questions.
- Observe the legal requirements for closing an interview.

19.8 Processing the content of the prepared statement

19.8.1 Document or recording

In most cases you will have copied the statement to work upon. In the event of the legal adviser retaining the statement in order to rewrite a pristine statement, you are still able to work upon the recording of the statement for which you have start and finish times of the reading. This will not require transcription. You will be transforming it into an SE3R.

In the case of a 'bare bones' statement, there will be very little information to be transformed and this will not occupy too much time.

In the case of a 'full' statement there will be a substantial amount of information and transforming this into an SE3R will take longer. The advantage is that you already 'know' the material, having listened to it once already. Nonetheless it makes sense to regularly check with the legal adviser to establish if the prepared statement is now ready for copying.

19.8.2 Processing a 'bare bones' statement

Processing a 'bare bones' statement is relatively easy and quick. There is so little detail that it does not merit a separate SE3R of the statement. It is a straightforward matter of assessing the limited detail of the prepared statement in the context of:

- **Your Case SE3R.** The composite SE3R of accounts concerning the police case, particularly the MTF, which incorporates other relevant information and evidence.
- **Other relevant information and evidence.** For example, exhibits, reports.

The steps

- **If you have a Case SE3R.** Photocopy this to produce a working copy which you will be writing upon.
- **If you do not have a Case SE3R.** Create one now.
  — Photocopy this to produce a working copy composite. You will be writing on this working copy.
- **Enter onto the working copy of the Case SE3R relevant additional information.** Using a green pen (the industry standard colour for external source material incorporated into an SE3R), note this information, eg:
  — descriptive detail and actions shown on CCTV;
  — information from SOCO;
  — results of forensic analyses.
- **Drop into the working copy of the Case SE3R the few bits of detail contained in the prepared statement.** Most of this will be Event Line detail.
  — There will be minimal Knowledge Bin material.
- **Analyse the working copy of the Case SE3R.** Identify and annotate anomalies, in particular shortcomings in the detail of the prepared statement, eg missing detail, vagueness, inconsistency, contradiction. Using square brackets—the industry standard format for annotating SE3Rs—record:
  — the nature of the anomaly;
  — the source of the information that does not square with that of the prepared statement, any observation you consider appropriate.

19.8.3 Processing a 'full' statement

Working with the minimal detail of a 'bare bones' statement, you are able to drop this into a working copy of your Case SE3R. In the case of processing a 'full' statement you:

- create an SE3R of the detail in the prepared statement, ie a PS SE3R;
- drop into a working copy of the PS SE3R detail from your Case SE3R.

The steps

- **Create an SE3R from the prepared statement (PS SE3R).** Allow plenty of room between events and between episodes on the Event Line. You will need this space to accommodate:
  — detail from the Case SE3R;
  — other relevant additional information.
- **Make a photocopy of the PS SE3R.** This is your working copy of the PS SE3R. You will be dropping detail on to this and annotating this.
- **If you have a Case SE3R.** Using a green pen, transpose detail from this on to the working copy of the PS SE3R.
- **If you do not have a Case SE3R.** Create one now.
- Using a green pen, transpose detail from this on to the working copy of the PS SE3R.
- **Enter onto the working copy of the PS SE3R other relevant additional information.** For example, using a green pen note:
  — descriptive detail and actions shown on CCTV;
  — information from SOCO;
  — results of forensic analyses.
- **Analyse the working copy of the PS SE3R.** Identify and annotate anomalies, in particular shortcomings in the detail of a prepared statement, eg missing detail, vagueness, inconsistency, contradiction. Use square brackets—the industry standard format for annotating SE3Rs—to record:
  — the nature of the anomaly;
  — the source of the information that does not square with that of the prepared statement, any observation you consider appropriate.

19.9   Selecting your questioning strategy for the interview

19.9.1   Your interview aim

Your aim is to confront the suspect with the detail in the composite SE3R, highlighting the anomalies, ie:

- information known to you but not accounted for in the prepared statement;
- missing detail, gaps, 'non-barking dogs', vagueness, ambiguity, inconsistency—what the suspect says does not fit with or contradicts what is known to you.

The recording of this process will provide the court with a complete picture of:

- everything known to the police and everything in the prepared statement;
- the suspect's responses to having this detail and all the anomalies drawn to his or her attention: to which the suspect can only say 'no comment'.

19.9.2   Drawing matters to the suspect's attention

Detail in the composite SE3R

You have a choice between two ways of presenting the detail in the composite SE3R, ie two strategies.

- **Strategy 1.** Invite the suspect to comment on the detail.
- **Strategy 2.** Question the suspect concerning each anomaly.

The advantage of Strategy 1 is that it pre-empts the legal adviser referring you initially—and thereafter repeatedly across the course of the interview—to the Court of Appeal rulings in *Knight*[5] and *Turner*.[6]

Both rulings state that it was not the intention of CJPOA to permit police officers to submit a prepared statement to scrutiny or question. It is a matter of debate amongst trainers whether questioning to expand the statement—to obtain missing detail—or to explain matters raised by the statement and missing detail—constitutes subjecting the statement to scrutiny. This debate will continue in the absence of an appeal and a ruling on these issues. Until then strategy choice must remain a matter of personal, professional preference.

Other material to be presented the suspect

You may need to present other material to the suspect, eg:

- the statement of the complainant or a significant witness;
- electronic recording, eg CCTV;
- photographic evidence;
- key visual representation, eg of the crime scene;
- annotated observer-participant (OP) plot.

19.10 Pre-interview briefing

19.10.1 Briefing the legal adviser

Brief the legal adviser on what you intend to do so that he or she can advise the suspect.

- You have examined the prepared statement in detail.
- You have made detailed notes of all the information, evidence, and other matters that are known to you.
- You intend to interview the suspect.
- **If you are adopting Strategy 1 (inviting comment):**
  — You will be *bringing to the suspect's attention* information, evidence, and other matters known to you.
  — To help everyone you will be using the statement as a framework to do this.
- **If you are adopting Strategy 2 (questioning):**
  — You will be *covering* information, evidence, and other matters known to you.
  — To help everyone you will be using the statement as a framework to do this.

Awareness of *R v Knight* and *R v Turner*

The legal adviser might cite *Knight* and *Turner* concerning the fact that CJPOA does not permit police officers to submit a prepared statement to scrutiny.

- Do not get sucked into a discussion over the legality of what you intend to do.
- Respect the legal adviser's opinion, re-state your intention, and close the issue, eg:
  I understand your position. I will nonetheless be interviewing you client about these matters. Should your client be charged it will be for the court to decide on the appropriateness of my decision.

---

[5] *R v Knight* [2003] EWCA Crim 1977.
[6] *R v Turner* [2003] EWCA Crim 3108.

19.10.2 Briefing other third parties

Brief other third parties (eg the interpreter, appropriate adult, reader) in the same manner that you briefed the legal adviser.

19.11 Managing the interview

19.11.1 Pausing and pacing

Even though you know that the suspect will say 'no comment' and relinquish the talking turn, this does not mean that you have to instantly abandon the listening turn. Never take the talking turn immediately after a 'no comment' response.

- If you unreflectively respond instantaneously this will cumulatively put more and more pressure on you.
- If you create suitably long pauses of at least two or three seconds after the 'no comment' response this will enable you to:
  — keep the pace of the interview, and your heart rate, down;
  — observe the suspect;
  — refer to your SE3R;
  — take your time in identifying the particular information you want to work with;
  — think what you want to say;
  — frame the words that you want to ask.

19.11.2 Essential materials

Have to hand:

- the annotated working copy of the PS SE3R;
- a red pen—which you will use to ensure that you cover each item of detail (information, evidence, anomaly), ticking off the item once it has been covered;
- any material that you intend to present to the suspect.

19.11.3 Explain the reason for the interview

Having re-cautioned the suspect explain the reason for the interview, eg:

> *I need to explain the reason for this interview.^^ ^^*
> *I will do this in the same way that I explained matters earlier to* [name of legal adviser].^^^^
> *You have produced a prepared statement.^^ ^^*
> *I have examined this in detail.^^ ^^*
> *I have made detailed notes of all the information, ^^ all the evidence ^^ and all other matters ^^ that I know.^^ ^^*

If you are adopting Strategy 1

Explain the reason for the interview and what will happen, eg:

> *I am going to give you the opportunity to have your say, ^^^^ to comment, ^^ ^^ upon all the information, ^^ all the evidence ^^ and other matters ^^ that I know.^^ ^^*

Look to the legal adviser,

Is that how I explained matters to you earlier [name of legal adviser]*?*

The legal adviser may respond by citing *Knight* and *Turner* for the first time, or again if he or she cited them in the pre-interview briefing.

- Do not get sucked into a discussion over the legality of what you intend to do.
- Respect the legal adviser's opinion.
- Re-state your intention.
- Close the issue.

Check back with the suspect his or her comprehension of the reason for the interview and what will happen, eg:

> *I need to check back with you that you understand what I've just said to you.* ^^ ^^ *I'd like you to tell me what you understand I am going to do.* ^^ ^^

If you are adopting Strategy 2

Explain the reason for the interview and what will happen, eg:

> *I am going to cover all the information,* ^^ *all the evidence* ^^ *and other matters* ^^ *that I know.*^^ ^^

Look to the legal adviser,

> *Is that how I explained matters to you earlier* [name of legal adviser]*?*

The legal adviser may respond by citing *Knight* and *Turner* for the first time, or again if he or she cited them in the pre-interview briefing.

- Do not get sucked into a discussion over the legality of what you intend to do.
- Respect the legal adviser's opinion.
- Re-state your intention.
- Close the issue.

Check back with the suspect his or her comprehension of the reason for the interview and what will happen, eg:

> *I need to check back with you that you understand what I've just said to you.* ^^ ^^ *I'd like you to tell me what you understand I am going to do.* ^^ ^^

19.11.4   Conduct the interview according to your chosen strategy

Strategy 1. Inviting comment from the suspect

Chunking, pausing, and pacing

Take the suspect at a very slow pace through your annotated copy of the PS SE3R.

- Be mindful of *R v Hillard*[7] (where the Court of Appeal underlined the need to take account people's ability to hold material in working memory) and deliver the detail in 'bite-sized' chunks:
  - preferably one or two sentences at a time containing detail (as opposed to instructions such as *Take your time on this*);
  - more than three is likely to be too great a demand.
- Pause to create the space for the suspect to say 'no comment'.

---

[7] *R v Hillard* (2004) CA 2/3/2004 Unreported. Document No AC9800288.

- When the suspect says 'no comment' create a different duration of pause after this response linked to the mental demand of the material that you have placed in the suspect's working memory:
  — a longer pause 3 to 4 seconds^^ ^^ ^^ ^^—linked to two or three or sentences containing detail;
  — the usual 2 to 3 second pause—^^ ^^—to a single sentence.

Working from your SE3R

Be systematic. Always look at the suspect when you are talking or delivering detail.

- Look down at your SE3R. ^^ ^^
- Identify the detail to be delivered. ^^ ^^.
- Register the item of detail (information, evidence, anomaly) and tick this in red. ^^ ^^
- Think what you want to say. ^^ ^^
- Look up. ^^ ^^
- Look at the suspect for 'hot spot' associated behaviours (BASELINES). ^^ ^^
- Deliver the detail. ^^ ^^
- Pass the talking turn to the suspect, eg:
  — *Over to you for comment.* ^^ ^^
  — *And your comment on this.* ^^ ^^
  — Making a non-verbal gesture—a cupped hand, fingers extended, lifting this towards the suspect, opening the fingers when doing so.
- Register mentally, don't react visibly or verbally to the 'no comment': simply observe the suspect for 'hot spot' associated behaviours (BASELINES). ^^ ^^
- Look down at your SE3R...and so on.

You will soon get into a rhythm. You will find that you do not have to keep inviting comment verbally, and that a simple hand gesture will suffice.

Strategy 2. Questioning the suspect

Working from your SE3R

Work your way methodically through the working copy of the PS SE3R:

- applying the Interviewing Spiral;
- treating the 'no comment' as the answer to be probed by your next question;
- ranging from 'general' to 'specific'—keeping as much as possible to the 'general' end.

Be systematic. Always look at the suspect when you are talking or asking a question.

- Look down at your SE3R. ^^ ^^
- Identify the detail to be delivered. ^^ ^^
- Register the item of detail (information, evidence, anomaly) and tick this in red. ^^ ^^
- Think what you want to say—in particular the question that you will ask. ^^ ^^
- Frame your words mentally. ^^ ^^
- Look up. ^^ ^^
- Look at the suspect for 'hot spot' behaviours (BASELINES). ^^ ^^
- Deliver the question. ^^ ^^
- Look at the suspect for 'hot spot' behaviours. ^^ ^^
- Register mentally, don't react visibly or verbally to the 'no comment': simply observe the suspect for 'hot spot' associated behaviours (BASELINES). ^^ ^^
- Look down at your SE3R...and so on.

Concentrate on your questioning behaviour

Vary your questions, using the 'general' to 'specific' hierarchy to maximum effect.

- **Crème de la crème questions.**
  - Statement/comment, eg *You were seen leaving your house at quarter past five.* ^^ ^^
  - Topic, eg *We need to know about what led you to leave the house.* ^^ ^^
  - Silence after raising a topic, or after the suspect has said 'no comment' is by far and away the best question.
- **TED instructions**, eg *Could you tell me about that?* ^^ ^^; *Take me through . . .* ^^ ^^
- **Open questions.**
  - Parameter, eg *Can you tell me what you did between leaving your house until you entered Yates's Wine Bar at seven?* ^^ ^^
  - 'Big' (narrative) 'what', eg *It will help me if you can tell me what happened then.* ^^ ^^
  - 'How', eg *There's no rush, can you tell me how you got into town from your house?* ^^ ^^
  - 'Why' or a suitable alternative, eg *We need to know why you went into the Wine Bar?* ^^ ^^
- **Closed identificatory questions.** 'Who?', 'What?', 'Where?', 'When?', 'Which?', 'In which way?'
- **Closed confirmatory questions.**
  - 'If' or 'whether', eg *Can you tell me if you were intending to go out this evening?*
  - Closed confirmatory 'yes'/'no', eg *I want you to think about this.* ^^ ^^ *It is very important.* ^^ ^^*Take your time.* ^^ ^^ *Did you hit John McCaffery?* ^^ ^^

Link pause duration to the mental demand of the question

When the suspect says 'no comment', create a different duration of pause after this response linked to the mental demand of the question had the suspect been answering questions:

- a longer pause of 3 to 4 seconds—^^ ^^ ^^ ^^—linked to a process/extended recall question;
- the usual 2 to 3 second pause—^^ ^^—to a simple recall question.

Presenting material to the suspect

If in addition to taking the suspect through your annotated copy of the PS SE3R, you have decided to present material to the suspect for comment observe *R v Hillard*, ie that you have to take account of people's ability to hold material in working memory. When reading a statement to a suspect as part of Strategy 1 to invite the suspect to comment upon its content, adopt a dual pass approach, eg:

> *In a moment I'm going to read to you what X has said about what happened* ^^ *so that you can have your say about what X says.* ^^ ^^
> *As there is a lot of detail I'm going to take you through it twice.* ^^ ^^
> *First time through* ^^ *I'm going to read it in 'bite sized' chunks* ^^ *so you get an overall understanding of everything X has said.* ^^ ^^
> *I'll read a bit,* ^^ *then I'll stop so that you can get you head round what I've read.* ^^
> *Don't say anything when I stop.* ^^ ^^ *Keep that to later* ^^ *when I read through for a second time what X has said.* ^^ ^^
> *When I read through for the second time* ^^ *I'll take it a line at a time.* ^^ ^^ *I'll read a line,* ^^*then it will be over to you* ^^*to say what you want.* ^^ ^^ *When you've said that,* ^^ *I'll read the next line,* ^^ *then stop to let you say what you want,* ^^ *and so on.* ^^ ^^
> *I just need to check that you're clear on that.* ^^ ^^ *Tell me what I'm going to do and what you need to do.* ^^ ^^

If you are showing video-recorded material, simply substitute 'show' for 'read'.

19.11.5   **Coping with interruption and disruption**

If the suspect says 'No comment' while you are speaking

- Stop talking. ^^ ^^
- Repair, eg *I have to be fair and make sure that you hear what I say.* ^^ ^^ *So I'll [say that][start] again.*
- Continue with what you were saying.
- If the behaviour is repeated, use DEAL to remind of the ground rule to 'hear each other out' and to request no interruption while you are talking.

If the legal adviser interrupts to intervene while you are speaking

- Stop talking. ^^ ^^
- Let the legal adviser finish talking. ^^ ^^
- Respond as applicable to the legal adviser's intervention.
- If the behaviour is repeated, use DEAL to require that he or she does not interrupt you while you are talking—and you will do the same for him or her.

If the legal adviser intervenes appropriately but frequently

- Respect and, as applicable, respond professionally to the intervention.
- Don't 'lock horns' because:
  — this will prejudice the working relationship;
  — this could undermine your credibility if the suspect construes the assertive legal adviser as putting you in your place.

If the legal adviser intervenes to request or require you to speed up

The legal adviser might draw the conclusion that the interview is going too slowly, perhaps to the disadvantage of the suspect. The appropriate response is to:

- respect the intervention;
- remind the legal adviser of the Routines and Expectations that you spelled out at the outset;
- continue with your questioning.

If the legal adviser requests that the interview be stopped

- Ask why the legal adviser is making the request. (Don't be pressured if you get no explanation.)
- Explain that interviewing will re-commence following the consultation with the suspect.
- Stop the interview.

19.11.6   **Close the interview**

- Ask the suspect if there is anything further that he or she wishes to say.
- Ask the suspect if he or she has any questions.

- Ask the legal adviser if he or she has any questions.
- Ask any supporter present, eg appropriate adult, if he or she has any questions.
- Observe the legal requirements for closing an interview.

19.12 Chapter summary

Prepared statements have their risks but are commonly produced because they are a sensible safe defence when the legal adviser has doubts about the persuasiveness of the case against the suspect who has an innocent explanation, or has concerns that there are risks to answering questions and to 'no comment' (either from the outset or continuing to do so).

Having a sound understanding of 'why', 'what', 'when', and 'how' of the two types of statement, knowing how to use SE3R to represent and to analyse their contents in the light of your case knowledge, and using this tool to conduct a comprehensive interview of this material, enables justice to be done—in the interview room and at court, should the suspect be charged.

20

Interviewing in Special Circumstances

20.1 Chapter overview

This chapter examines investigative interviewing in special circumstances—encounters that fall outside the ambit of conventional reactive or proactive investigation. These encounters highlight the limitations of linear goal models such as PEACE and ABE, useful as they are in other circumstances. Special circumstances demand flexibility and attention to the fundamentals of set induction, relationship, and skilful monitoring and assertion to enable the practitioner to impact positively upon the individual, to exert appropriate influence necessary to engage in ethical persuasion, and, in some circumstances, ethical negotiation.

20.1.1 Chapter objectives

This chapter will enable you to:

- consider what constitutes *special circumstances*;
- recognize the relevance of using the conversation management approach to investigative interviewing in diverse special circumstances;
- understand how applying the GEMAC framework will enable you to create appropriate set induction and to monitor and to assert appropriately to facilitate maximum disclosure.

20.2 What constitutes 'special circumstances'?

In Chapter 1 we describe how in 1983 the first author:

- advocated the use of the term 'investigative interviewing' to describe a purposive encounter with a witness or suspect to achieve a definite aim and objectives;
- designed a conversation management approach to these encounters.

Thirty years later, the world of policing is considerably more complex.

- The term *police* now embraces a wider range of institutions whose practitioners may or may not have a warrant that was the defining attribute of a police officer. These practitioners have extremely diverse professional qualifications, specialist knowledge and skill sets commensurate with working in an environment that is data-rich and involves extensive use of information technology.
- Governments now manage a wide range of threats that require 'law and order' to be maintained by diverse institutions—both police forces and other agencies granted specific statutory powers, eg in the UK the Border Agency and the Environment Agency. There is accountability for practitioner conduct within these institutions, although the requirement for—and practicability of—technology to enable monitoring and scrutiny varies according to operational context.
- Increased public access to the Internet, telephony, and other technology poses a threat in terms of exposing and compromising investigations conducted, and tactics used, by 'law and order' institutions.

We are now in an era in which there is a requirement to conduct purposive encounters with individuals in circumstances that are outside the bounds of conventional investigation. We term these *special circumstances*. On face value the circumstances differ wildly. In some instances there is compulsion to co-operate and to disclose information. Investigators and court officials have powers to compel the individual to disclose financial information, eg in the contexts of criminal asset confiscation, recovery of lost tax revenue, and removing incentives for acquisitive crime.[1] In some jurisdictions there are powers to summons and to compel witnesses to give evidence, eg in scrutiny enquiries.[2]

In others there is a compulsion to engage in conversation: failure to so will result in unwanted outcomes, eg:

- refusal to allow entry and immediate deportation;
- loss of liberty in the case of a certain categories of dangerous offender living in the community[3] who must participate in monitoring interviews to enable assessment of the risk that the individual poses.

20.3 The relevance of investigative interviewing using the conversation management approach

At the outset of this text in *How to use this book* we explained that the conversation management approach to investigative interviewing was applicable in any investigative context, whether the investigation was reactive or proactive. We spoke of the core demands to face up to complexity and to be flexible when applying this approach. Interviewing in special circumstances is certainly complex. It certainly demands flexibility. Conversation management is wholly suited to any special circumstance that brings with it the task of conducting an ethical conversation and facilitating the individual's involvement by:

- attention to professionalism in planning and preparation prior to the encounter;
- impacting favourably on the individual;
- communicating respect and creating a positive relationship through reciprocity and mindful RESPONSE behaviours;
- creating a working relationship through continuous attention to explanation;
- monitoring—observing and listening intently and actively;
- appropriate assertion—telling the truth, asking the right question in the right manner, responding constructively to inappropriate behaviour and resistance;
- attention to evaluation following the encounter.

We saw how many special circumstances are special because they pose risk: to the individual, the interviewer, and even beyond these two. Appropriate conversation management of the encounter has the additional potential to mitigate risk.

In many situations the special circumstances in which the interview occurs are such that there is no transparency afforded by technology. This is the case in order to protect the individual, to preserve confidence in the product of the exchange, or because electronic recording is impracticable. Adherence to the ethical principles that underpin conversation management—respect for the person and the obligation to tell the truth—means that the practitioner has the responsibility to keep an accurate record.

Rather than addressing the very wide range of special circumstances, we have chosen three contexts that demonstrate the universal applicability of the conversation management approach to investigative interviewing.

---

[1] Proceeds of Crime Act (as amended by Serious Crime Act) 2007, ss 357–62.
[2] Australian Crime Commission Act 2002, s 28; Police (Complaints and Conduct) Regulations 2013.
[3] Criminal Justice Act 2003, ss 325–327B.

- Securing the assistance of offenders facing serious criminal charges—called *assisting offenders*.
- The recruitment and handling of informants.
- Countering terrorism by examination of travellers at border entry points—termed *port examination*.

20.4 Assisting offenders

Assisting offenders[4] are individuals:

- who are already facing serious criminal charges;
- who are approached to provide information about, and to give evidence against, other criminals in return for improvement of their own position, eg mitigation of their own situation or tariff reduction of sentence;
- who must admit all of their own criminality as part of the process.

Put simply, due to the value of the information known by the offender, he or she is offered an inducement: something explicitly forbidden under the Police and Crminal Evidence Act 1984 (PACE).[5]

This situation presents opportunities.

- The offender may be highly motivated by the chance to improve his or her own situation.
- As long as the practitioner is speaking to the correct criminal, the practitioner is able to gain accurate, timely information against either criminals that are currently contesting charges, or those that are actively involved in serious criminal activity.
- The benefits are both substantial and attractive: from the accuracy of the knowledge—given as it is by a witness close to the events—to the potential savings on the long-term investigations usually required to catch these types of determined criminal.

The risks, however, are correspondingly high.

- The offender's motivation is to improve the offender's own situation. This may spur the individual to give false information.
- Desperation may also lead the individual to:
  — provide information that places the offender himself or herself, or those around the offender at risk of physical harm;
  — orchestrate further criminal acts enabling the offender to disclose about these.
- The process requires the offender to disclose his or her own criminality, bringing with this the risk of further prosecution.
- The danger to the assisting offender continues after trial.
- The assisting offender may face the prospect of segregation in prison or being taken into a witness protection scheme.

20.5 Informants

Informants are defined as a special circumstance because in their conversations with their handlers, they:

- are treated akin to adult witnesses;
- but have the potential to self-incriminate.

---

[4] Serious and Organised Crime Prevention Act, 2005 ss 71–5.
[5] *R v Fulling* [1987] 2 All ER 65.

There are key issues concerning informants and the conversations—investigative interviews—that handlers engage in with informants.

- An informant typically has numerous meetings with his or her handler.
- There is no mandatory recording of interviews.
- There is no independent third party tasked with monitoring the process and with ensuring the informant's welfare or legal rights.
- There is no control over the duration of the interview.

The lack of immediate scrutiny provided in a conventional investigative interview context by, eg, a legal adviser or custody sergeant, means that the informant has limited protection in his or her interaction with his or her handler. There is a very real risk of exposure of, or physical harm to, the informant should confidentiality be breached.

This said, there is increased regulation over police handling of criminal informants. Informant handlers are required to:

- keep records of all contacts;
- inform courts where cases originate from, or are supported by, intelligence from informants;
- warn the informant accordingly if, in the process of giving information to the handler to prevent serious crime or catch criminals, the informant discloses his or her own criminality.[6]

This situation also creates opportunities.

- A skilled handler can maximize disclosure through greater freedom of location, timing, conversation, subject matter, while still respecting the rights and safety of the informant.
- Handlers can discuss issues that may affect the motivation and reliability of the informant, as well as the information they may impart, as extra tests of its reliability and provenance.
- The nature of the interaction allows negotiation: something not possible in the suspect or witness environment. Negotiation provides an extra dimension to both the planning and interaction, and the context allows numerous interactions to achieve investigative goals.

20.6   **Port examinations**

Legislation is now commonplace across jurisdictions to counter international terrorism. One protection is assertive prevention powers: to discourage and to discover terrorist activity. In England, Wales, and Northern Ireland those tasked with securing entry points, generically termed *ports*, have the power to detain and to conduct an *examination* of selected travellers.[7]

Port examination constitutes a special circumstance in which the individual must be questioned. The purposive encounter is not occasioned by criminal offences that have been, or are about to be, committed.

- Suspicion is not a pre-requisite for the decision to detain and to conduct an examination— in effect a screening investigative interview.

---

[6] Regulation of Investigatory Powers Act 2000.
[7] Terrorism Act 2000, s 7.

- The traveller can be detained for up to 9 hours in order for the examination to take place.
- To ensure that the detained traveller does not present a terrorist threat, he or she is compelled to:
  — answer all reasonable questions put to him or her;
  — submit to physical search;
  — surrender items for examination.[8]
- Failure to co-operate and to fulfil these obligations results in repatriation.
- The traveller's disclosures will result either in release with no consequences or arrest on suspicion of involvement in terrorism.

Port examinations pose particular challenges.

- The legislation, and the derived powers to stop, examine, and to repatriate, are more far-reaching than those for the prevention of crimes. They are deprecated by many, particularly by sections of the community most likely to be subject to these powers.
- Given these negative perceptions in the community, practitioners must conduct the examination in a manner that does not alienate and lend weight to these negative perceptions.
- In most cases the practitioner will have minimal information about the individual prior to the examination.
- At the very moment the practitioner is attempting to gain information, he or she faces an extra challenge: to ensure that he or she does not disclose information to a person who may be involved in terrorism.

The practitioner has to operate within a coercive situation that endows him or her with extraordinary powers but has to develop and maintain a working relationship with a subject over, potentially, an extended period equivalent to a full working day.

20.7   Planning and preparation

Practitioners acknowledge that planning is a key skill for interviewers in conventional interviews.[9] However, interviewing in special circumstance presents discrete challenges. The legal framework is by definition very different: there is no legally defined offence, no specific points to prove, and no available defence within statute law.

20.7.1   Assisting offenders

Assisting offender interviews are directed at gaining a distinct evidential or intelligence product that will eventually be used to judge the amount of credit the offender will receive for giving the information. Credit will range from a reduction in sentence to complete immunity from prosecution.[10] The situation is precarious.

- The offender must admit the full extent of his offending as part of the process.
- The interviewer jeopardizes the whole process should any offences deemed in scope by the prosecutor be omitted from the investigative interviewing process.

---

[8] Terrorism Act 2000, s 7.

[9] Cherryman, J. and Bull, R. (2001) 'Police Officers' Perceptions of Specialist Investigative Interview Skills. *International Journal of Police Science and Management*, 3, 199–212: Soukara, R., Bull, R., and Vrij, A. (2002) Police Officers' Aims Regarding their Interviews with Suspects: Any Change at the Turn of the Millennium? *International Journal of Police Science and Management*, 4, 100–14.

[10] Serious and Organised Crime and Police Act 2005, ss 71–5.

Planning is therefore of paramount importance. However, it is rare to know at the start of the process exactly—or the totality of—what the assisting offender has done. This information will emerge over several meetings as negotiations proceed to define the detail of the agreement with the assisting offender.

When planning and preparing for interviews, the interviewer has a large task—collecting and collating typically a very large amount of information and evidence, which will enable the formulation of an interview strategy and interview plans for what will be a long run of interviews. The interviewer is able to use the entire range of tools described in Chapter 6: from efficient reading through a Wants Analysis and grids to SE3R and WOB maps. A grid is a particularly useful tool to enable mapping of all the offender's known crimes prior to each interview. This ensures:

- all offences are covered;
- key elements of the offender's culpability are covered.

Box 20.1 shows one example of a grid.

The grid can be combined with WOB mapping to develop the subjects to cover, questioning areas, and chronology, and with SE3R within the interview to ensure comprehensive accounts are obtained, detail is contemporaneously analysed, and responded to in a timely manner.

Assisting offender interviews routinely require a number of days or even weeks to complete. The interviewer has to prepare to deliver an explanation to the interviewee that:

- the interviews will take place over a period, at set times each day;
- there will be allowance for sufficient rest periods;
- spells out the range of topics to be covered.

	Offence 1	Offence 2	Offence 3	Offence 4
What	Robbery	Car theft	Car theft	Assault
When	17 December 2000	17 December 2000	1 January 2001	February 2004
Convicted/status	Yes	No/Suspect	No/Suspect	Yes
Plea	Not Guilty			Guilty
Co-defendants	No	No	No	Yes
Other suspects	Yes	No	No	No
Property	£500 recovered	Audi £5000 not recovered	BMW X5 £75,000 not recovered	N/A
MO	Entered bookmakers, brandished axe, demanded money, made off, chased and caught by customers.	Entered house, took keys, and removed car. Seen by victim, identified by photograph. Not identified at ID parade.	Entered house, took keys, and removed car. Linked crime series, no witnesses.	Argued with another in pub during football broadcast, punched victim, broke nose. Remained at scene. Arrested. Admitted offence in interview.

Box 20.1 Interview preparation grid for interview of assisting offender

20.7.2 **Informants**

All meetings with informants require extensive logistical work to avoid compromise and ensure safety. There is very little that can usually be done in the formal sense before an initial meeting with a potential or new informant. This said, even though meetings with informants are naturally more diverse than conventional witness or suspect interviews and there is a lack of a crime to focus upon, before the initial—and any subsequent—meeting the handler must identify a clear aim and objectives. The aim may be tightly focused and the objectives equally so or perhaps broader. A WOB map enables these to be crystallized. Two examples are given here.

The first interview plan (Figure 20.1) shows that the aim is to establish the informant's knowledge of the local drug market as an overall aim. The specific objectives are identified as topics, each of which would produce questioning areas.

The second interview plan (Figure 20.2) shows the aim as developing knowledge of the informant.

The topics are broader, in keeping with the wider investigative aim. For example, by questioning on the topic of 'principles', the handler wishes to facilitate maximum

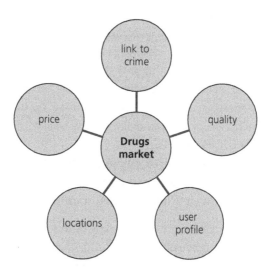

Figure 20.1 WOB map of informant interview plan (drugs)

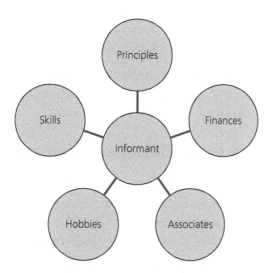

Figure 20.2 WOB map of informant interview plan (background knowledge)

disclosure concerning the informant's attitudes to certain types of crime, such as fraud, sex crimes, or burglary.

- Understanding this will assist the handler in assessing the informant's motivation.
- This information, when cross referenced with knowledge about the informant's ability to give information on certain crime types, will enable appropriate tasking of the informant—considerably enhancing his or her efficiency as a source of criminal intelligence.
- Information about the informant's background will also assist in logistical planning for meetings, crucial to the success of the working relationship. It is pointless, for example, through lack of knowledge, arranging to meet an informant in a cafe where he is well known, or has previously worked. In the worst case scenario, the informant will simply not show up, or will turn up, feel uncomfortable, and be unable to concentrate on the purpose of the meeting.

20.7.3 Port examinations

The detailed work with information ahead of an interview with an assisting offender represents the extreme end of the spectrum of planning and preparation. At the other extreme is the port examination of a detained traveller. Here the practitioner is unlikely to have much, if any, information about the detainee before the examination begins.

Furthermore, time is against the practitioner, who only has a maximum of nine hours within which to conduct the entire examination process. He or she *must* achieve the investigative aim within this period. The only way that further time can be gained is by progression to an arrest for terrorist offences. This time pressure contrasts with, say, conventional interviewing under PACE which allows up to a maximum of 96 hours: a period within which there is freedom to choose the time of interviews, balancing investigative needs with other considerations.

In the case of port examination, the solution is *preparedness*—as opposed to preparation. Preparedness encompasses a wide range of antecedent knowledge, organization, and ability to engage in an activity without warning.

- Up-to-date knowledge of relevant terrorist threat assessments.
- A good knowledge of systems for researching information.
- Cultural awareness and a sound knowledge of the customs of diverse groups of travellers.
- Standard operating procedures and teamwork drills, with each member clear, proficient, and rehearsed in his or her role.
- A total grasp of the physical layout of the examination facilities.
- Logistical support able to cater for basic rights, needs, and requirements of individuals—mindful again of cultural, ethnicity, gender, and age factors.

This is contingency planning and preparation: ensuring readiness to apply rapidly and with confidence information management tools across the course of an examination to enable skilful conversation management.

20.8 Back to the basics of conversation management

The diverse demands of investigative interviewing in widely differing special circumstances underlines the fact that the conversation management approach is a framework—a way of thinking and behaving captured in the mnemonic GEMAC—rather than a linear goal-defined model such as PEACE. All of the steps in GEMAC apply in any set of special circumstances.

- How the practitioner greets the individual and subsequently explains the Reason for the encounter, the Route Map (what the practitioner needs to cover/achieve), the Routines (what the practitioner will be doing by way of 'housekeeping' activities across the encounter), and Expectations (the 'contract' as flexibly framed to the particular circumstances)—all constitute essential social and cognitive set induction. This lays down the foundation for the rapid development of a working relationship between the individual and the practitioner—whose whole manner of communication from initial meeting has sent a congruent message:

— *I am a professional with a job to do.*
— *I'd like a positive 'across' relationship to exist between us.*
— *You can rest assured that I will behave ethically—at all times respecting you as a person and obliged to tell the truth—and will not behave dishonestly or seek to trick or exploit you.*

- How the course of the interview, the conduct within it, and the content disclosed by the individual rests upon the practitioner's ability to engage in the mutual activities of monitoring and assertion.

Given the explanation stage will differ according to the circumstances that require the conduct of an investigative interview, in the following sections we focus on the mutual activities of monitoring and assertion.

20.9 Monitoring the individual's behaviour

In every instance of investigative interviewing in special circumstances there is the same requirement, as in a conventional investigative context, to monitor the behaviour of the individual. Close observation—aided by the BASELINES template—and active listening are essential to identify:

- a relatively enduring pattern—'baseline'—of vocal (verbal and non-verbal) and non-vocal, non-verbal behaviour indicative of mental, emotional and even physical state (see Chapter 7);
- observable transient changes in behaviour (departures from the 'baseline') potentially indicative of:
  — emotional and attitudinal change;
  — a 'hot spot'—a particular issue raised by the practitioner or the individual that needs to be focused upon and developed further at the right time, ie when the practitioner judges it to be the best point to return to this issue.

20.9.1 Assisting offenders

Assisting offenders can be anticipated to react stereotypically in most circumstances. Typically the individual will be conflicted, experiencing stress and strain, as he or she struggles to make the decision whether or not to protect themselves and maybe those close to them by informing on others.

We have explained that the journey of relating to an assisting offender is a long one—typically involving many encounters. The lengthy nature of assisting offender interviews, in particular, requires continuous, systematic monitoring of the individual's behaviour. Throughout, the interviewer can use BASELINES to identify departures from the individual's fundamental 'music' ('baseline') indicative of a change in mood, motivation, or both. Recognizing the change is vital, enabling conversation to be developed to overcome the incipient, or actual, psychological block.

We have also pointed out that these interviews have numerous inherent risks, not least fatigue resulting in impaired concentration, inability to follow, and problems recognizing the significance of what is being put to the individual and of the individual's responses. Put simply, observation is vital to detecting when the individual is not fit to interview further. Failure to spot the signs is likely to render derived evidence as inadmissible at trial.

20.9.2 Informants

Informants typically experience a wide range of strong emotions prior to, during, and following the decision to give information. It is essential to remember this and that informants often feel guilty as explained by Tony:[11]

> *Informants generally are not at peace with themselves. If they have a conscience, a heart and a soul, it's very difficult to live with … you will have nightmares about that continuously.*

For such reasons, informants are precarious individuals. The relationship between handler and informant is often likely to be pragmatic rather than one founded upon a positive psychological bond. (This said, very often across time strong bonds can, and do, emerge between informants and handlers. So much so that both parties are put at risk by the other: both vulnerable to losing a sense of proportion, and forgetting the frailty of the relationship and the circumstances that gave rise to the relationship.)

In an earlier career, the first author was a handler of informants. He did not have the benefit of BASELINES (developing this monitoring tool nearly two decades later), but was always alert to vocal (verbal and non-verbal) and non-vocal, non-verbal behaviour indicative of a change in the potential (or actual) informant's mental state, disposition, and appetite to proceed further.

The logical and easily remembered elements of BASELINES provide the handler with a template for focusing attention across the course of the encounter. Transient changes can be mapped onto particular issues, eg pointing to a disinclination to talk about this individual, location, or activity.

Using BASELINES to assist your monitoring the informant closely will enable assessment—ahead of post-encounter evaluation—of:

- the credibility of information disclosed by the informant;
- the informant's cognitive capabilities, ie:
  - ability to register, store, retrieve, and recall detail;
  - comprehension of past tasking and present tasking;
  - resilience to cope with the psychological strain of being an informant.

20.9.3 Port examinations

The life cycle of the relationship with the detained person is short. The practitioner has to hit the ground running in terms of being totally alert to the individual's vocal (verbal and non-verbal) and non-vocal, non-verbal behaviour. Systematic monitoring aided by BASELINES starts from first meeting and continues across the period taken up with the examination.

20.10 Assertion

20.10.1 Quadrant 4 behaviour: appropriate assertion

Research has shown that even well-trained interviewers are liable to be disposed to exert excessive control within conventional interviews.[12] Special circumstances are characterized

---

[11] *Inside the mind of a Snitch: An interview with Tony* at <http://www.pbs.org/wgbh/pages/frontline/shows/snitch/etc/tony.html>—accessed 23 April 2013.

[12] Griffiths, A., Milne B., and Cherryman J. (2011) A Question of Control? The Formulation of Suspect and Witness Interview Question Strategies by Advanced Interviewers. *International Journal of Police Science and Management*, 13(3).

by implicit or explict coercion. For this reason it is vital that the practitioner does not fall victim to this very source of power, ie behaves in an overly controlling way.

The practitioner has no option other than to manifest a Quadrant 4—appropriately assertive—behaviour pattern described in Chapter 3. He or she will come across as assertive, but by engaging in RESPONSE behaviours this balances the requirement to control and to manifest concern: essential to fostering and sustaining a positive working relationship.

In contrast, a practitioner who manifests a Quadrant 1—dominant and self-centred—behaviour pattern is over-controlling and locked into his or her agenda. This should not happen. Furthermore, the obligation to reply to reasonable questions is likely to trigger the detained traveller to exhibit Quadrant 1 behaviours or Quadrant 2 behaviours (going through the motions). If the interviewer meets the detained traveller with Quadrant 1 behaviours, the result will be a clash of wills generating 'more heat than light'.

20.10.2 Persuasion and negotiation

Special circumstances demand skill in persuasion and, where necessary and allowed by the law bearing upon the circumstances in question, negotiation skills. Chapter 3 points out that influence is the common core. The practitioner must fulfil all of the criteria to create a positive impact upon the individual. Without achieving this, the practitioner has no hope of progressing to persuasion and *in extremis* negotiation—both being applied extensions of the influencing process.

In the case of port interviews, the compulsory nature of the questioning—spelled out within the Notice of Examination—risks generating within the detained person:

- negative perceptions of an invasive procedure;
- negative expectations of the approach that the interviewer will adopt;
- resistance in the form of minimal collaboration and minimal disclosure.

These can be overcome if the interviewer engages consistently in reciprocity and manifests throughout mindful RESPONSE behaviours.

Persuasion

We comment in Chapter 3 that persuasion is the intellectual face of influencing. It is about inviting the individual to:

- reflect upon what he or she has said or the way he or she is behaving;
- recognize the implications of what has been said or the behaviour;
- consider changing what has been said or to behave differently.

Investigative interviewing in special circumstances, whatever these circumstances might be, puts to the test the interviewer's ability to engage in ethical persuasion. This is characterized by:

- having a clear idea of:
  — your argument(s);
  — the evidence to back up your argument(s);
  — the benefit(s) to the individual should he or she take an appropriate action;
- moral commitment to:
  — tell the truth;
  — respect the individual as a person;
  — respect the individual's freedom to dissent and to choose;

- keeping calm;
- engaging in Quadrant 4 behaviours:
  — engaging continuously in RESPONSE behaviours;
  — being appropriately assertive;
- listening intently to what is said and listening actively to how it is said;
- engaging in SOFTENS behaviours;
- ensuring the individual fully understands by:
  — being explicit at all times;
  — presenting your position in a straightforward, matter-of-fact manner;
- coping with rejection of your argument—using positive rather than negative language, eg instead of saying, *You're wrong about that*, say:

  I accept that ^^^^however let's look more at what's at issue ^^ ^^ or
  *I accept that ^^^^ however I want you to know (consider) ^^^^*

- if necessary, re-stating your position (the argument, the evidence, the benefits);
- having re-stated your position, if the individual is still not convinced, accepting that:
  — he or she probably never will be convinced;
  — further presentation of your position will evoke a negative response and erode the relationship that you have established with the individual.

Negotiation

Actual and potential conflicts of interest are to be expected when interviewing in any special circumstance situation. In some situations, the interviewer has the power to negotiate—to concede in order to reconcile interests sufficiently so that the individual agrees to:

- to co-operate;
- do something even if he or she disagrees with it.

Where negotiation is an option, it boils down to what latitude of manoeuvre is open to the interviewer. In other situations negotiation is not an option.

As we point out in Chapter 3, negotiation must be ethical, ie *principled*: the interviewer has to see things from the individual's perspective. This is the basis for progressing from acknowledgement to adjustment of respective positions—concessions—to arrival at a mutually satisfactory agreement: a 'win'-'win' as opposed to a 'win'-'lose' outcome. Ethical, skilled negotiation is characterized by many persuasion behaviours and a few others.

- Preparing thoroughly.
- Always identity your BATNA (best alternative to a negotiated agreement)—the outcome acceptable to you in the event of not reaching agreement.
- Moral commitment to:
  — tell the truth;
  — respect the individual as a person;
  — respect the individual's freedom to dissent and to choose.
- Being explicit at all times.
- Keeping calm.
- Not being rattled by time pressure.
- Engaging in Quadrant 4 behaviours:
  — engaging continuously in RESPONSE behaviours;
  — being appropriately assertive.

- Listening intently and actively.
- Engaging in SOFTENS behaviours.
- Systematically questioning and probing (see Chapter 9) to:
  — understand barriers to resolution—particularly the individual's inhibitions, fears, aspirations, and his or her perceptions of constraints, available choices, and latitude to act in a given way;
  — gauge the individual's motives, priorities, needs, interests, issues;
  — clarify generalizations;
  — test assumptions.
- Identifying:
  — the key issues;
  — areas of common ground.
- Probing for areas of movement—offering brief, tentative proposals.
- Resisting—or keeping to a minimum—the making of instant counter-proposals to those made by the individual.
- Rarely saying *No*.
- Regularly summarizing areas of agreement.
- Taking a break if the individual consistently rejects your proposal:
  — summarize your proposal;
  — state you will stop the interview for [duration] to allow the individual to reflect.
- Distinguishing between 'needs'—important matters, issues, or points that you cannot compromise upon—and 'interests'—where you can concede ground.
- Knowing when to compromise (agree to concede what is demanded) where necessary—but minor ones at first.
- Remembering the power of reciprocity: if you give something, the other person feels obliged to give something in return.
- Allowing the individual to save face—if necessary by making small concessions.
- Reinforce agreement psychologically and the relationship subliminally by smiling sincerely or making an appreciative gesture.

Assisting offenders

The circumstances of conversing with an assisting offender are particularly complicated. Negotiation is likely to be part of the early phase of the process when moving the individual to a position of agreeing to assist. However, as the relationship develops across time, negotiation has to disappear, particularly in the later stages, when strict adherence to PACE is required. The decision point is likely to occur when the individual makes admissions concerning his or her own criminality. These will form part of a case against the individual. Negotiation is at an end.

Informants

Given the circumstances, and with the goal of acquiring intelligence product from an individual who in providing this exposes himself or herself to risk and retribution, persuasion will inevitably evolve into negotiation.

A handler is at risk of engaging in Quadrant 1 behaviours:

- maximizing the problem faced by the informant (debt, prison);
- demanding information on another criminal;
- emphasizing the handler's ability to grant or withhold assistance.

To adopt these behaviours takes influence beyond negotiation to coercion, presenting a forced choice, emphasizing domination, and minimizing or eliminating any show of concern. The use of excessive control will lead to feelings of resentment from the informant.

There are both short- and long-term consequences of mismanaging the balance of control and concern. In the short term, it is likely that the informant will seek to give as little information as possible—a natural reaction to coercion; while the long-term result is likely to be an uneasy, poor-quality relationship between informant and handler that neither values.

Manifesting Quadrant 4 behaviours, the practitioner must identify with the difficulty of the informant's situation and explain that there is a possible solution that could:

- reduce the individual's problem, eg debt, impending prison;
- maintain confidentiality;
- place a serious criminal behind bars.

Given this is ethical negotiation, the informant will make his or her own choice. The particular benefit of a relationship in which the handler does not coerce is that over time this builds trust—a vital influencing factor.

Port examinations

Practitioners must not rely on the power of the situation to produce interaction. This is particularly true in port examinations—the most coercive of special circumstances. The skills that will be on demand are those of persuasion, eg offering arguments for co-operating, such as the issue of refusal to admit entry, long delay waiting for the return flight, disruption of plans. Negotiation is not 'on the cards'.

Relatively quickly the individual perceives the practitioner as someone—a human being like the individual—satisfying a faceless authority and yet supporting the detainee in a situation which is giving both parties a problem to solve. This approach can be used even where the examination results in an arrest: the arrest is brought about by the inability to satisfy the requirements of the legislation: a mutual problem that both share and which is not the fault of interviewer or the individual.

20.10.3 Explanation

As in conventional investigative interviews, those conducted in special circumstances require the practitioner to engage in continuous explanation. Such explanation demonstrates professionalism, empathy, and an 'across' relationship that will develop into a constructive working relationship very quickly after first meeting.

20.10.4 Questioning

All that we have described in Chapter 9 concerning right question and right manner of questioning applies when conducting investigative interviews in special circumstances.

Dangers in using risky questions

Experienced practitioners are liable to fall into the bad habit of:

- posing an excessive number of risky—confirmatory 'yes'/'no'—questions;
- asking counter-productive leading and option questions;
- not pausing and failing to create pauses.

This bad habit stems from the perception that time is at a premium or that the individual, as a reluctant participant, will only give short answers. Confirmatory, leading, and option questions and not pausing certainly speed up the questioning process, but at the risk of generating short answers. This plays into the hands of the individual who wishes to engage in minimal disclosure. As we indicate in Chapter 9, it is essential to pose the right (productive) question, make the silence—pauses—work for you, and keep the pace down.

Choice of opening questions

Opening questions and topics must be carefully chosen. The preference in these circumstances will be to use open questions with oblique references or vagueness as 'hooks' to stimulate a response:

*Jim ^^ ^^ I was wondering ^^ what you knew about drug dealing on the seafront ^^ ^^*

This type of question would be challenged in a PACE interview, because of its vagueness, but is a better option in special circumstances.

A request for disclosure can also be included as part of the negotiation allowed in these circumstances, with an appropriate explanation.

*Jim you have agreed to give me information ^^ ^^ about the locations of drug dealing in [location]. ^^ ^^ It's really important that you give me as much detail as possible ^^ ^^ because I can then check this detail. ^^ ^^ The more of it that is correct ^^ ^^ then the more I can rely on what you tell me. ^^ ^^*

Dangers in using trailer questions

Trailer questions are very effective at triggering disclosure in conventional suspect investigative interviews where an explanation is required from the interviewee. The interviewer spells out a few nuggets of information/evidence in support of the allegation or disputed facts, pausing between each nugget, and rounding off with a productive question, eg an open question or a statement, such as, *We need to talk about this.*

Using trailer questions is risky in special circumstance interviewing, particularly in the early stages of interviewing. The interviewer has no control over how the individual will use the nuggets of information/evidence, and whether it will be combined with other information for a criminal purpose.

The necessity to probe

The second author of this book has all too often seen product from intelligence interviews that lacks detail for no other reason than the handlers have not wanted to probe the initial disclosure, because it presented the opportunity of direct action against a known criminal. Had this 'tempting' information been probed then, its provenance would have been found wanting, eg:

- reports of large amounts of stolen property in premises too small to accommodate them (implausible);
- revolvers with a magazine (impossible);
- high-value consignments of drugs in the possession of low-level addicts (illogical).

The message is clear. It makes no sense to leave disclosed information unprobed. Handlers must probe what the informant says.

20.10.5 Dealing with disruptive behaviour

The demands of special circumstances interviewing include the requirement to deal with disruptive behaviour that can affect the conduct of the interview, its course, and what the individual discloses.

- Assisting offenders can attempt to re-negotiate the conditions of their disclosure, as reality dawns about their predicament.
- Informants can become difficult when pressed for detail, or the amount of probing relating to their knowledge of a particular crime.
- The coercive nature of the port examination can give rise to resistance over the process itself, or dissatisfaction over the prospect of disrupted travel plans.

These behaviours must be managed in order for the interviewers to maintain control and achieve the investigative aim. The DEAL cycle can be used in any of the special circumstances and avoids unprofessional arguments. The specifics of the special circumstances present some powerful options if the third cycle of likely consequences is reached. These range from (at a low level) the port examination taking longer, to (at a high level), the arrest of the informant, to (at the highest level) withdrawal of assisting offender agreement or arrest.

The use of the DEAL cycle allows the interviewer to escalate their management.

20.11 Evaluation

The lack of recording during some special circumstance interviews,[13] absence of immediate evidential product, and the nature of the interviewing process are likely to be offered as reasons for a rushed evaluation of the interview, or no evaluation at all. We argue that where there are special circumstances, it is essential to evaluate the interview and the dynamic evaluation process put forward in Chapter 12 is well suited to this task. Planning documents, notes made during the interview, and reflective commentary by the interviewer after the interview all assist evaluation.

Given the special circumstances, evaluation must include assessment of credibility: *This is what the individual says. How confident are we that this is correct?* To answer this question requires reflection on:

- how the information was imparted, eg free recall or minimal disclosure after probing;
- the interviewee's behaviour;
- the circumstances of the disclosure;
- the interviewer's conduct;
- the structure of the interview;
- questioning and the effect upon the product, ie the individual's disclosures.

Assisting offender interview evaluations should include assessment of how the subject may perform as a witness. This assessment should be included in briefings of any relevant prosecutor.

Post-interview evaluation is crucial to the management of long-term informants. It assists the identification of patterns of disclosure over time, the assessment of risk, the formulation of tactics, and decisions concerning suitable handler attributes, eg experienced; assertive; male or female.

---

[13] Although there is no reason why recordings cannot be made.

20.12   **Chapter summary**

Investigative interviewing in special circumstances is challenging. It creates investigative opportunities but also poses risks. This chapter has demonstrated that the elements of GEMAC—the framework of the conversation management approach to investigative interviewing—can be successfully applied when faced with the demand to interview in special circumstances. Three diverse contexts—assisting offenders, handling informants, and port examinations—illustrate common requirements: to prepare and plan; to exert positive impact; to foster and sustain a positive working relationship; to establish rapport by explanation at the outset and across the entire encounter; to monitor the individual continuously; to manifest only Quadrant 4 behaviours; and to question appropriately. If these elements of GEMAC are observed the amount and quality of information disclosed will be significant. What is more, the practitioner will be well placed to engage in ethical persuasion and, where this is permitted, ethical negotiation. Post-interview evaluation, that should occur after every encounter, will reveal that conversation management flexibly applied in even the most challenging circumstances maximizes spontaneous disclosure and achievement of the investigative aim and objectives.

Reference Section

1. ASSESS +

1. Purpose

To collate (collect systematically) features of an individual's account and behaviour observed within a live (face-to-face; telephone) or recorded interview—when questioned within a particular context about the material time frame—enabling:

- assessment of the validity of the account and the individual's reliability;
- briefing of third parties without requiring them to view the recording;
- comparison with previous and subsequent assessments;
- planning for subsequent investigative and other actions.

2. Layout of ASSESS + form

The ASSESS + form (Box 1) has six sections covering different areas of observation, with a check box for the occurrence of material in the interview. These enable the recording of 'warning bells' in the form of anomalies, behaviour obstructing the conduct and progress of the interview, content potentially indicative of deception, and transient BASELINES behaviour change indicative of arousal occurring at a 'hot spot' when disclosing spontaneously or in response to questions.

3. Explanation of ASSESS + sections

3.1 Account problems

This section is used to note anomalies—oddities—observed in the individual's disclosures— initial and subsequent accounts and responses to questions—concerning the material time frame, ie circumstances with a potential bearing leading up to, during, and following the commission of the offence or other significant event.

Missing detail

The disclosure lacks detail on this matter.

Gaps

Between two points in the narrative it lacks one or more steps.

Jumps

These occur in two forms.

- A significant gap in time, eg *I saw him at the bar around eleven last night. This morning around ten or so I heard that he'd been found dead.*
- A sudden shift in location, eg *We were fighting like cats and dogs in the kitchen. I made it up to her in the bedroom.*

FOCUS		EXPLANATION	INDICATOR
A	**Account problems**	Anomalies in the person's disclosures concerning **everything that happened within the Material Time Frame and material facts.** *Note* The person's disclosures comprise: • his or her account(s) • his or her responses to requests for expansion and explanation of detail.	**Identifiable problems with detail** Missing detail. Gaps (= missing steps). Jumps (= big gap in time; sudden shift in location). Absence of reasonably expected detail (= 'non-barking dog'). 'Thin' story (= lacks detail throughout: 'agenda'-like account of 'what happened'). Non-specific (= vague or ambiguous). 'Sidesteps' (= passive verb use; 'not *really*...') Inconsistency (= doesn't 'fit' with prior detail). Contradiction (= different versions). Too 'pat' [**Note:** two versions compared] (= same wording, same order, little/no narrative reversal, too many descriptors). Narrative 'contrast' (= variation in detail). Other (specify).
S	**Sense problems**	The person's representation/explanation of events does not make sense when considered objectively.	**Detail which questions validity** Improbable (= difficult to believe). Impossible (= counter to reality: can't occur/be done). Nonsensical. Counter to reasonable behaviour. Other (specify).
S	**Struggling to give detail**	The person struggles, or is unable, to respond to the request for detail: even when reminded/encouraged to take time and to think before speaking.	**When probed the person** Struggles to go beyond the original story. Repeats minimal or non-specific detail. Admits inability to give further detail. Other (specify).
E	**Evasion**	The person avoids disclosing detail.	**When probed the person** Tries to change the topic. Answers the question with a question. Gives measured/evasive responses. 'Blanks' an echo probe (= repeats minimal or non-specific detail). 'Sidesteps' (= passive verb use; 'not *really*...') Other (specify).
S	**Sabotaging behaviour**	The person obstructs the process of: • being briefed/informed • being assisted • being called upon to give reasonable detail.	**When briefed/probed the person** Argues. Becomes angry. Becomes abusive. Threatens. Refuses to be helped. Refuses to co-operate. Other (specify).
S	**Significant expressive behaviour**	The person's vocal behaviour changes indicating: • physiological and psychological arousal • difficulties thinking—or thinking twice—before and while talking.	**When probed the person's speech has** Marked dysfluencies (not occurring before). Marked pauses before/when answering. Changes in voice pitch. Changes from self-control to gabbling. Other (specify).
+	**Context factors**		

Box 1. ASSESS +

Absence of reasonably expected detail: 'non-barking dog'

The individual gives no detail about an event or an issue that people in general could be reasonably expected to mention. The expected detail often concerns thoughts, emotions, and reactions, eg an individual describing in a very 'matter of fact' manner how he found his house burgled, eg *I drove up the path and saw the front door was opened. I got out, went in, and in the lounge I found all the hi-fi had gone and the plasma TV.* The individual could have been expected to disclose thoughts, emotions, and reactions concerning the open door, eg *I drove up the path and saw the front door was opened.* **I thought 'Someone's burgled us'.** *I got out.* **I was panicking 'cos I'd just spent a fortune on the entertainment system before we left. I rushed into the lounge.** *I found all the hi-fi had gone and the plasma TV.* **I thought 'I must check upstairs.'**

'Thin' story

The narrative lacks detail throughout. Like an 'agenda', it comprises a limited number of steps, with no detail given about any of the steps, or what happened between one step and the next.

Non-specific

What the individual says is vague or ambiguous.

'Sidesteps'

This occurs in two forms.

- Use of the passive that avoids naming the doer or doers of an action, eg *I was forced to agree; a plan was being put together.*
- Using 'not really' to avoid giving detail, eg *I couldn't really describe him.*

Inconsistency

Something said later does not 'fit' with something said earlier by the individual, or elsewhere by the individual or another person.

Contradiction

The individual gives more than one version.

Too 'pat'

The sequencing of detail is highly unusual.

- Events are described in chronological order with little or no narrative reversal. (Narrative reversal occurs when the order of telling is not the order in which events happened, eg *I called my Mum after I put the kids down.* It is very natural. It is highly unusual to tell a complete narrative without narrative reversal occurring.)
- Too many descriptive words precede the person, location, or item described, eg *it was a small, torn, white, plastic Tesco's bag.* Usually people put no more than two descriptive words in front of what is being described, eg *a small Tesco's bag.* Often people use just one, eg *a Tesco's bag.* They typically tack on descriptive words, eg *a Tesco's bag…small…white. It was torn.*

In such circumstances the individual should be asked to describe matters again. If this time there is still little or no narrative reversal, if there are still too many words preceding the item, and the individual uses the same or similar words and phrases when re-stating matters, this is indicative of a potentially 'pat' account.

Narrative contrast

This occurs in two forms.

- Greater level of detail concerning circumstances preceding and following the event relative to the level of detail about the event.
- Greater level of detail concerning the event relative to circumstances preceding and following the event.

Other anomalies

There is space in the section for the observer (assessor) to note other anomalies detected.

The significance of anomalies

The presence of anomaly does not necessarily indicate that the individual is lying. Every anomaly constitutes a 'warning bell': the more 'warning bells' the greater the requirement to probe the account and, wherever this is possible and appropriate, to test the validity of what the individual is asserting.

It follows that the more 'warning bells' the greater the question mark over the individual's reliability, especially if:

- there are sense problems concerning the representation or explanation he or she gives;
- the individual's behaviour gives cause for concern, ie he or she struggles to give detail, is evasive, engages in sabotaging behaviour, and manifests significant expressive behaviour.

3.2 Sense problems

As investigators and investigative interviewers, we have to make common sense assessments about the representation or explanation of events that an individual gives to us. We have to come to some conclusion whether it is:

- improbable—what is being said is difficult to believe;
- impossible—the representation or explanation is counter to objective notions of physical reality, ie what is being described could not occur or be done;
- nonsensical—the representation or explanation is patently absurd or preposterous;
- counter to reasonable behaviour—what the individual describes is counter to logic, may have happened, but it is counter to common sense.

There is space in the section for the observer (assessor) to note other sense problems.

3.3 Struggling to give detail

The individual's inability to deliver detail comes in a number of forms.

- Struggling to go beyond the original story—all the more significant if the initial account was 'thin' and when reminded of the ground rules for disclosing detail and requested to go over it again it emerged again as 'thin' and remains so when being probed.

- Repeating minimal or non-specific detail.
- Admitting inability to give further detail.

There is space in the section for the observer (assessor) to note other forms of struggling to give detail.

3.4 Evasion

If the account already has an anomalous lack of detail ('thin' account; significant missing detail; significant gaps; significant jumps; 'non-barking dogs'; 'sidestepping'), other behaviours potentially indicative of evasion become all the more significant.

- **Tries to change the topic. Interviewee:** *Rather than asking me about* [Topic A] *you should be asking me about* [Topic B]; **Interviewee:** *I tell you what I can say and that is* [discloses on a completely different issue].
- **Answers a question with a question.**
  — To block a line of questioning, eg **Interviewer:** *Could you tell me why you kept the Rolex having found it on the floor in Tesco's?* **Interviewee:** *Why would a man of my standing steal a watch?*
  — To force the interviewer to narrow the focus of questioning, eg **Interviewer:** *So what did he look like?* **Interviewee:** *What do you mean?* **Interviewer:** *A description.* **Interviewee:** *What of?* **Interviewer:** *What he was wearing.*
- **Gives measured/evasive responses ('reeling out bus tickets').** For example, **Interviewer:** *Could you describe the bag?* **Interviewee:** *It was black.* **Interviewer:** *And…* **Interviewee:** *Leather.* **Interviewer:** *Anything else?* **Interviewee:** *Medium-sized.* And so on…
- **'Blanks' an echo probe.** For example, **Interviewee:** *He got up and hit me.* **Interviewer:** *Hit you?* **Interviewee:** *Yeah.* (Interviewee remains silent, gazing at Interviewer, indicating that he or she has relinquished the talking turn.)
- **'Sidesteps'.** Using the passive form of the verb; saying 'not really' when asked to describe someone or something.

There is space in the section for the observer (assessor) to note other forms of struggling to give detail, eg referring the interviewer to someone else to answer—**Interviewee:** *Look I'm not your man for that kind of detail. You need to speak to* [name of person]?

3.5 Sabotaging behaviour

The individual obstructs the conduct of the interview despite:

- being briefed and informed fully about the *Route Map*—issues to be covered—and about the ground rules in the *Explanation* phase;
- being assisted to disclose detail, eg being given plenty of time to think; being advised to close his or her eyes, to create an image in his or her mind's eye, to 'go back' (context reinstate); in a face-to-face interview, asked to use illustrators to describe something non-verbally, to enact key actions, to draw a diagram or sketch, or to point out a position on a key location representation that is provided for this purpose;
- being reminded of the ground rules for 'as much detail as possible' and that 'there cannot be too much detail'.

Sabotaging behaviour comes in many forms.

- Arguing.
- Becoming angry.

- Becoming abusive.
- Threatening.
- Refusing to be helped.
- Refusing to co-operate.

There is space in the section for the observer (assessor) to note other forms of sabotaging behaviour.

3.6 Significant expressive behaviour

People manifest changes in their vocal (verbal and non-verbal) behaviour when they are psychologically aroused, physically aroused, or when they are having difficulties thinking—or thinking twice—before or while talking. Changes which occur when the individual is being probed are potentially significant. These changes in vocal behaviour occur in a number of forms. It is possible for more than one change to occur.

- Marked dysfluencies, eg the individual's speech becomes less fluent; he or she starts to stammer and stutter; he or she repeatedly 'stop and start'.
- Marked pauses—very long silences—occur before talking or when answering a question.
- Change in voice pitch, eg it rises indicating anxiety, stress, or tension.
- Change from normal, controlled speech to gabbling.

These behaviours are also included in the BASELINES tool for monitoring transient changes in behaviour.

There is space in the section for the observer (assessor) to note other forms of struggling to give detail.

3.7 Context factors

It is essential to assess any observed account and sense problems, difficulty in giving detail, evasion, sabotaging, and significant expressive behaviour in the context of what is known about the individual. This information is typically discovered in the Planning and Preparation stage, and added to across the course of interviews and other encounters with the individual.

You should enter in the Context section material that you judge as having a potential bearing upon the content of the individual's account and his or her behaviour in the interview, eg:

- Mental vulnerability.
- Previous character, eg propensity to make false allegations, propensity to give untruthful accounts when arrested and interviewed.
- Potential for the individual, or others, to benefit or to gain from what is being disclosed.

2. BASELINES

1. Purpose

To identify systematically transient changes in an individual's pattern of non-verbal and verbal behaviour indicative of psychological and physiological arousal occurring at the mention of particular subject matter—'hot spots'—that require:

- timely probing—including image-compatible questioning—of the behaviourally highlighted subject matter;
- planning for subsequent investigative and other actions concerning the subject matter.

2. BASELINES: potentially significant transient changes in behaviour

A very wide range of behaviours is liable to transient change when an individual is aroused. Commonly, but not always, transient change will occur in more than one behaviour. Box 2 presents BASELINES a checklist of:

- the more readily observable of these behaviours that you should focus your attention upon in order to identify a potentially useful baseline;
- observable changes that occur in these behaviours and typical causation for these changes.

2.1 Blink rate

Blinking is a reflex action, enabling tears to bathe the exposed eye. Our rate of blinking when we are not under pressure is relatively uniform, but is liable to vary according to ambient physical conditions. When we are aroused by particular subject matter our blink rate increases. It is extremely simple to monitor an individual's blink rate because we characteristically focus our gaze on the region of their eyes.

An unobtrusive way of registering blink rate is to tap your little finger against an available surface, eg the side of your leg if you are standing when talking to the individual. This technique has an additional bonus. Mentally counting whilst listening or talking to the individual can be very distracting. Tapping overcomes this. Your finger registers the tempo of blinking rather than the absolute number of blinks occurring.

2.2 Blood vessels

Large blood vessels extending from our necks to beneath our ears carry blood between our body and our brain. When aroused blood flow increases and these blood vessels enlarge. It is easily observed if an individual's neck is thick, relatively fleshy, or thin.

If you are sitting in a ten-to-two orientation to the interviewee the individual has to rotate his or her head slightly. In so doing he or she stretches the blood vessel over the muscle and cartilage of the neck enabling you to view the vessel much more effectively than if you were sitting face-to-face.

FOCUS OF ATTENTION		CHANGE AND TYPICAL CAUSATION
B	**Blink rate**	Increases [= eg intense emotion; frustration; anger; hostility].
	Blood vessels [neck]	Swelling [= eg intense emotion; frustration; anger; hostility].
	Blushing	[= eg intense emotion; frustration; anger; hostility].
	Body shift	Orientation in sitting position to an angle away from direct view [= terminating the topic] *Common parallel behaviour* Gaze aversion; pushing chair backwards; refusing to say anything else.
	Breathing	Increased rate; shallow; difficulty in breathing [= eg intense emotion; frustration; anger; hostility].
	Brow	Creasing ('omega') [= eg perplexity; disapproval; difficulty in remembering detail]
A	**Adaptors** [self-grooming; 'lint' picking; manipulating an item]	Increase in most people; decrease in some people [= eg intense emotion; frustration; anger; hostility].
S	**Shaking**	Body; limbs; hands [= eg intense emotion; frustration; anger; hostility].
	Sighing	Emission of deep, audible breath [= eg fatigue; impatience; growing frustration, annoyance or emotion].
	Sniffing	*Common parallel behaviour* 'Glistening' in nostril/lip area.
	Swallowing	Movement of throat/gullet [= dryness of mouth throat due to intense arousal].
	Sweating	Brow; armpits; hands [= eg intense emotion; frustration; anger; hostility].
E	**Eyes** • **Gaze**	• Upwards; sideways [= 'buying' thinking time—accessing material from memory]. • Downwards [= eg strong emotion; 'inner dialogue']. • Fixed—glaring or glowering [= eg dislike; frustration; anger; hostility]. • Aversion [= eg embarrassment; shame; guilt]. • Covering eyes [= eg embarrassment; shame; guilt]. *Common parallel behaviour* Failure to respond [= rejecting the 'talking turn'].
	• **Pupils**	Constriction [= eg intense emotion; frustration; anger; hostility].
	• **Tearfulness**	'Glistening'; actual tears [= eg distress].
	• **Eyebrows**	'Flashes' [= eg surprise; alarm; disapproval].
L	**Laughter**	Inappropriate relative to topic [= eg anxiety, embarrassment, shame, guilt]. *Common parallel behaviour* Smiling.
	Limbs	Leakage, ie movement of legs, feet, arms, hands [= eg intense emotion; frustration; anger; hostility].
	Lips	Biting, licking, tightening, trembling [= eg anxiety, embarrassment, shame, anger, guilt]
I	**Illustrators** [demonstrative/ emphatic hand/finger movements]	Decrease in most people; increase in some people [= eg intense emotion; frustration; anger; hostility].
N	**Nods** [= non-vocal 'guggles']	Increase or decrease [= eg intense emotion; frustration; anger; hostility].
E	**Expressiveness** • **Words** • **Speech pattern** • **'Tone of voice'**	Increase or decrease [= eg intense emotion; frustration; anger; hostility]. Dysfluency, ie difficulty saying words [= eg intense emotion; frustration; anger]. **RSVP** [= **R**hythm; **S**peed; **V**olume; **P**itch] changes [= eg intense emotion; embarrassment; shame; guilt; frustration; anger; hostility].
S	**Silence** [= protracted pause]	• Before/during 'talking turn' [= eg difficulty marshalling thoughts; intense emotion]. • Failure to respond, ie rejecting the 'talking turn' [= eg intense emotion; hostility].
	Smiling	Inappropriate relative to topic [= eg anxiety, embarrassment, shame, guilt].
	Sneering	Derisive smiling; may occur prior to/when speaking as an extremely fast upward movement of the side of the upper lip, before a change to a 'normal' smile [= eg disdain, insincerity, deception].
	Space	Pushing chair backwards—disengaging by increasing distance [= eg intense emotion; frustration; anger; hostility]. *Common parallel behaviour* Gaze aversion; body shift; refusing to say anything else.

Box 2 BASELINES: potentially significant transient changes in basic behaviour

2.3 Blushing

This reflex is impossible to suppress or disguise and is thus very easy to detect.

2.4 Body shift

When people are seated and finish what they have to say on a topic, and wish to terminate further talk on this topic, they tend to make a body shift. They move their bottom in the seat, sometimes also placing one or more hands on the arms of the chair or their upper thighs, and orientate their body at a more oblique angle to the other person. Often they also avert their gaze—looking away, upwards, or downwards—and may verbalize that they do not want to speak more on the matter, or state that conversation is at an end.

2.5 Breathing rate

Breathing, or respiration, rate increases when aroused. In extreme cases the person may start to hyperventilate, breathing at an abnormally rapid rate. Alternatively breathing may become shallow or laboured.

A useful way of monitoring breathing rate is to observe the rise and fall of the individual's shoulders and tummy.

2.6 Brow

When people are perplexed, disapprove of something, or have difficulty in remembering detail they furrow their brow. This creates a pattern of creasing called an 'omega' after the Greek letter: Ω.

2.7 Adaptors

Adaptors are self-grooming movements, eg rubbing one's chin, nose, brow, or neck; tugging one's earlobe; running fingers through hair; picking at fingernails or skin; 'lint'-picking (removing actual or symbolic fluff from clothing); and manipulation of items, eg fiddling with or moving a pencil or paper. For most people the rate of adaptors increases when they are aroused, but for other people it decreases.

2.8 Shaking

Shaking—rapid, marked trembling or movement of limbs or the entire body—is a common indicator of intense emotion.

2.9 Sighing

This stems from increasing weariness, impatience, frustration, or emotion.

2.10 Sniffing

A person who was not sniffing at the time of original baseline assessment, ie did not show signs of having a 'runny' nose associated with having a cold, may start sniffing when aroused. This is a reflex-like behaviour triggered by the excitation of nerves and sebaceous glands at the end of the nose where this joins the upper lip. A common parallel observable behaviour is glistening in this area, sometimes called a 'dew drop'.

2.11 Swallowing

The 'fight or flight' stress response includes the cessation of digestion. Salivation is the first stage of the digestive process. Extreme arousal causes the salivary glands to stop excreting saliva. The individual's mouth goes dry and swallowing occurs as a reflex response which is readily observable.

Always have water available in the interview room. This is not only humane, it is also a means of detecting arousal. When the interviewee reaches to drink this is a potential change in BASELINES: dryness of the mouth.

2.12 Sweating

The 'fight or flight' response triggers the secretion of sweat. This is observable when sweating occurs in the area of the forehead, under the arms evidenced by visible areas of dampness of clothing, and by the appearance of a 'dew drop' at the end of the nose. This propensity to sweat when aroused is a good reason for shaking an interviewee's hands on meeting and when departing.

2.13 Eye gaze

Upwards and sideways movement

Typically when people have the talking turn they 'buy' 'thinking time' to consider quickly what they're going to say by breaking eye contact and gazing upwards or to the side, then restoring mutual gaze and speaking.

Downwards movement

Typically when the subject matter is emotion-laden people gaze downwards, often also to the side when doing so. Sometimes the individual engages in what is called an 'inner dialogue' while looking slightly down, into the middle distance, remaining silent perhaps for some considerable time. The individual might look up, gazing away into the distance momentarily, before looking down again, or may continue gazing away into the distance.

In effect the individual is talking to himself or herself, ie retrieving information from memory store and considering this and current material in working memory, eg balancing up whether to say anything at all, or something else, on this topic.

Fixed gaze

Strong emotion may trigger an individual to look at you with a fixed gaze, ie to glare or to glower, triggered by negative perceptions of the topic, you, or both.

Gaze aversion

A common, selective interpretation of gaze aversion—sustained looking away—is that the individual is lying. This neglects the fact that people often look away when they experience feelings of embarrassment, shame, or guilt. It is also important to note cultural differences. In some cultures, eg Japanese, it is normal, polite behaviour to gaze away for a substantial period of time when occupying the talking turn.

Covering eyes

Covering eyes is a common behaviour when engaged in thought or affected by emotion or circumstances. The individual may use one hand, often coupled with looking down or to the side, and cupping the brow and cheek with the fingers. Alternatively, he or she might cup the brow with both hands and look down. Covering eyes often occurs during 'inner dialogue'.

2.14 Pupils

When people become extremely aroused their *irises*—the circular openings of their pupils— are liable to contract to a very small aperture.

It is important to bear in mind when making an initial baseline assessment that particular drugs affect pupil size:

- alcohol or opiates, eg heroin, dilate (open) irises;
- ecstasy and cannabis contract (constrict) irises.

2.15 Tearfulness

Tears that are welling or actually flowing are easily detected.

2.16 Eyebrows

The raising of an eyebrow is called a 'flash'. Like all facial movement 'flashing' of one or both eyebrows is easy to detect if you are alert to it.

2.17 Laughter

When any individual laughs inappropriately, ie when an issue is being covered that on common sense grounds is not a laughing matter, this issue merits probing.

2.18 Limbs

Unconscious movement of a limb is called 'leakage', a term devised by Freud. An indicator of arousal, it occurs in many forms, eg:

- legs, eg knee twitching/jigging (knee rising up and down quickly, either sustained or in bursts);
- feet, eg tapping (sole, heel);
- hands, eg clasping/clenching on knees or chair arms; rubbing against thigh;
- fingers, eg tapping.

Most 'leakage' is detected with your peripheral vision, particularly lower limb movement. Wherever possible, as part of your interview preparation arrange seating positions to enable you to have full view of the interviewee.

2.19 Lips

Biting, licking, trembling, and tightening of lips are all indicative of arousal.

2.20 Illustrators

Illustrators are emphatic and demonstrative hand and finger movements, eg pointing, tracing in space a route taken, direction, shape, or trajectory; emphasizing non-verbally something being said verbally. For most people the rate of illustrators decreases when they are aroused, but for other people it increases.

2.21 Nods

Nodding, ie non-verbal 'guggling', may increase or decrease relative to initial baseline when the individual is aroused.

2.22 Expressiveness

Words

When aroused an individual may increase or decrease the number of words that he or she uses, ie changing to either verbosity or terseness (sparing use).

Speech pattern

Our pattern of speech comprises a range of behaviours that provide clues to our thoughts and feelings. 'Ah' errors, eg *um, er, ah*, are normal behaviour. They buy thinking time when we are talking, often accompanied by gazing upwards to the right or left. You are listening for something else: potentially significant changes in the individual's fluency. If he or she was speaking fluently prior to interview or thus far in the interview but is now experiencing difficulty in finding or saying words—getting them out—this is noteworthy.

Very commonly occurring when aroused

- False starts (sentence switching), eg *I had to...well, I know that I...It was getting through to...*
- Poorly organized thoughts, eg *After he'd gone, I was relieved, well I didn't think she'd come back, I was upset...*
- Repetition, eg *I usually...usually walk back alone...*

Often occurring when aroused

- Stuttering, ie difficulty in voicing the beginning of a word, eg *I really...c..c..c..can't say...*
- Stammering, ie difficulty in controlling the timing of speech in the centre of words, eg *He was just stop..p..ping me...*

Less common when aroused

- Hanging utterance, eg *I would have said it...anyway I didn't say anything in the end.*
- Slips of the tongue, eg *I decided to meet...make my way home.*

'Tone of voice'

Changes in non-verbal, vocal features of speech—rhythm, speed, volume, and pitch conveniently remembered by the mnemonic RSVP (Box 3)—occur when the individual is

FEATURE	DESCRIPTION	DETECTION
Rhythm	Irregular tempo or beat in delivery.	More difficult
Speed	Slowed speech; speeded up speech—particularly *cluttering* = abnormally fast rate, often with syllables running into each other.	Easy
Volume	Raised, lowered, mumbling.	Easy
Pitch	Higher or lower in tone compared to previous utterance.	Most difficult

Box 3 RSVP 'tone of voice' changes

aroused psychologically or physiologically. These are the changes that you should be alert to when actively listening—listening with a 'third' ear.

Pitch is an extremely good indicator of arousal (emotional state) and attitude. Females tend to perform better in detecting variation in pitch. This is probably due to a combination of physiological difference, psychology, and experience. In conversation, females characteristically spend much more time than males listening and looking, sustaining the other person in the talking turn. Typically they listen more intently to what is said and how it is said, giving them the potential to pick up emotional clues. The good news is that irrespective of your gender it is possible to develop skill in detecting pitch change through practice in concentrated listening.

2.23 Silence

A protracted pause, ie manifest silence, occurring before an individual talks or when an individual rejects the 'talking turn' is significant.

2.24 Smiling

When any individual smiles inappropriately, ie when an issue is being covered that on common sense grounds is not a laughing matter, this issue merits probing.

2.25 Sneering

Sneering expresses derision or disdain. One form of sneering—a fleeting upwards movement of the edge and side of the upper lip—occurs very quickly before emerging as an apparently 'normal' smile. This pattern is often exhibited when any individual is not being entirely sincere or entirely truthful.

2.26 Space

Pushing back one's chair to increase distance between the interviewee and you, perhaps combining this with a change in body position or a refusal to say anything else, is a powerful signal that he or she is disengaging from the conversation.

3. Learning BASELINES

Don't try to learn BASELINES indicators by rote. The best way to develop awareness and skill gradually is by consciously observing closely people conversing with each other:

- in everyday life;
- TV interviews;
- quiz shows;
- plays;
- films.

An excellent means to developing intent listening skills—to detect changes in expressiveness—is the radio.

3. Enactment

1. Purpose

To obtain non-verbal disclosure of offence-related detail by observing the interviewee represent his or her experience by moving—or positioning—his or her body/limbs, yours or those of a third party.

2. Be prepared

2.1 Know the facts

Have the means to validate the enactment. Prior to the interview:

- wherever possible, visit key locations;
- obtain visual material, eg images, plans, photographs, video-recordings;
- study the material closely;
- optimally practise your remembrance of the images.

2.2 Have the necessary 'props'

Prepare and have with you the necessary 'prop', eg a ruler or a pencil to represent a knife.

2.3 Refusal to stand in order to enact

Paragraph 12.6 of Code C to PACE says that *People being questioned or making statements shall not be required to stand*. This is notionally ambiguous. The more immediate meaning is that obliging a person to stand, ie as a tactic to wear a suspect down, is unacceptable. Getting a suspect to stand in this inappropriate manner is quite distinct from asking the suspect to stand in order to enact—act out—something. However, a legal adviser might intervene to prevent the suspect getting up from his or her seat to enact. If this occurs it does not render enactment impossible. Be flexible: ask the suspect to verbally direct you, the second investigator, or the two of you, to turn and to move away from each other until the requisite angle or distance is reached.

3. Briefing the interviewee

Key element	Example
Explain use of enactment	*If we act out what happened—do what we did or someone else did—it can help us to describe something that might be difficult to do using words.* ^^ ^^
Demonstrate	*I'll show you what I mean by acting out what happened.* [Select a relevant example, eg how you closed the door and walked to your seat.]

Key element	Example
Check comprehension	*Can I check back with you that you understand what I mean about acting out what happened?* ^^ ^^
What is wanted	• *I'd like you to act out [what happened when [X] did [Y]].* ^^ ^^ [Note 1] • *(Where applicable) Using this* [point to 'prop' on the table] *as if it were* [state]. ^^ ^^ [Note 2]
Explain the 'roles' to be played	*I want you to act yourself* ^^ ^^ *and to imagine I am* [state], ^^ ^^ *and to imagine that my colleague is* [state].
Explain the 'prop'	*I'd like you to imagine that this* [ruler] *on the table is the knife.* ^^ ^^
Handling the 'prop'	*Can I ask you to pick it up and hold it in the way you saw it held at the time?* [Note 3]
Retrieve image	*I'd like you to get an image in your mind's eye of what happened just before* [X] *happened.* ^^ ^^
Restate what is wanted	*OK. I'd like you to act out [what happened when* [X] *did* [Y]]. ^^ ^^

Notes

1. Adjust these instructions to the task you require enacted.
2. Don't pick up the 'prop'. This would suggest how it was held. An alternative is to place it in the flat of your hand, ie your hand is the same as the surface of the table.
3. Because the interviewee picks up and holds the 'prop' you will not be criticized for shaping this aspect of the interviewee's experience, ie you didn't hand it to him or her.

4. Capturing the detail

KEY ELEMENT	REMARKS
Observe enactment closely	• Don't probe. [Note 1]
Create mental image	
Don't assist interviewee	• Don't mimic his/her movements. • Don't describe aloud ('verbally label') the observed movements. [Note 2] • Don't repeat what interviewee is saying. [Note 3]
'Repair' if detail is missed	Get a re-run of the missed detail, eg *I didn't quite get that.* ^^ ^^ *Can you show me that again?* ^^ ^^ [Note 4]
AT ANY TIME Mentally note/make a verbatim note of critical detail	• Parallel commentary, eg *I was extremely frightened...not taking in everything...; I'm really pushed to give any more...* • Correction (= another version), eg *No...on second thoughts...* [makes different movement].

KEY ELEMENT	REMARKS
Assess the enactment	• Assess match/mismatch with what you know (= external validation). • Assess the quality of demonstrated detail. [Note 5] • Don't probe. [Note 6] • Don't progress immediately to a drawing. [Note 7]
Reward	• Thank for the enactment, eg *That was a great help. Thanks.* ^^ ^^ • Move on to another topic.

Notes

1. Probing:
   - risks disrupting imagery;
   - prompting improvement—especially by the vulnerable, ie inducing confabulation, and by the would-be liar.
2. Labelling what you observe will rebound.
   - The interviewee will adopt your words, leading to subsequent legal argument concerning your role in shaping the interviewee's disclosures.
   - It helps the would-be liar to remember and tell a better story.
3. It helps the would-be liar to remember and tell a better story.
4. Repetition:
   - is risky: it helps the interviewee (particularly the would-be liar) to rehearse.
   - is useful: if the enactment:
     — involved a lot of detail; or
     — was extremely markedly imprecise/involved gross movements.
5. Markedly imprecise, gross or sweeping movement are a potential anomaly: a possible indicator of the interviewee not having experienced what he or she is describing. Note the anomaly for subsequent probing.
6. Probing at this stage will:
   - produce a rehearsal effect;
   - alert the interviewee that you have concerns.
7. A drawing at this stagte would be:
   - counter-productive—the enactment will have primed a fuller drawing;
   - a worthless test of validity: the enactment detail is still in the interviewee's working memory.

5.   Validating and probing the enactment

An interval reduces the rehearsal risk and enables effective validation.

Key element	Remarks
State requirement	Examples. • *I just need to make sure that we've got everything covered about what happened.* ^^ ^^ • *I'd like you to act out [what happened when [X] did [Y]].* ^^ ^^

Key element	Remarks
Observe enactment closely	Identify: • Replicated enactment (= potentially valid information; interviewee is potentially reliable source of information). • Enactment containing differences (= potentially invalid information; interviewee is potentially unreliable source of information).
Respond appropriately to a match	• Where necessary, probe for expansion or explanation. • Move on to another topic. • Towards end of the Probing phase obtain an enhanced drawing. [Note 1]
Respond appropriately to a mismatch or continued poor quality	• Don't mention the existence of a problem. • Don't probe now. [Note 2] • Move on to another topic. • Probe later for further enactment, expansion and explanation: after this moving on to another topic. • Towards end of the Probing phase obtain a drawing. [Note 1]
AT ANY TIME Mentally note/make a verbatim note of critical detail	• Parallel commentary particularly replication of earlier commentary. • Correction (= another version), eg *No…on second thoughts*…[makes different movement].

Notes

1. An interval reduces the rehearsal risk and enables further validation.
2. Probing at this stage will:
   • produce a rehearsal effect;
   • alert the interviewee that you have concerns.

4. Enhanced Drawing

1. Purpose

To obtain non-verbal disclosure of offence-related detail by a process of augmented drawing, ie:

- the interviewee creating a drawn representation of his or her experience with a potential to trigger further use of illustrator representation, enactment, or verbal disclosure;
- you creating a parallel representation (copy) of the interviewee's representation that you can annotate and label;
- using different colours to provide an 'audit trail' of disclosure: distinguishing initial spontaneously drawn material from material drawn in response to probing at different times.

Note. The parallel representation (copy) that you make is disclosable material.

2. Be prepared

2.1 Know the facts

Have the means to validate the drawing. Prior to the interview:

- wherever possible, visit key locations;
- obtain visual material, eg images, plans, photographs, video-recordings;
- study the material closely;
- optimally practise your remembrance of the images.

2.2 Have the necessary material

Drawing materials:

- white A4 size paper—sufficient for the interviewee and you;
- two black pens;
- two blue pens;
- two red pens.

3. Briefing the interviewee

For ease of explanation the instructions concern the drawing of a bar in which an attack took place.

Key element	Example
What is wanted	• Link to prior illustrator representation/enactment, eg *You remember a while back ^^ ^^ I asked you to show me what you remembered about the bar just before the attack took place. ^^ ^^* • *In a moment I'd like you to draw on this* [show interviewee his/her paper] *^^ ^^ what you remember of the bar ^^ ^^ just before the attack. ^^ ^^*
Put at ease	*Don't worry. ^^ ^^ It's not an art exam. ^^ ^^ We don't want a work of art! ^^ ^^*
Use the whole area of the paper	*When you are drawing what you remember of the bar ^^ ^^ I'd like you to use as much of the paper as possible. ^^ ^^* [Note 1]
Give interviewee his/her paper and BLACK PEN	[Note 2]
'Looking down' viewpoint	*Imagine that you are on the ceiling of the bar ^^ ^^ looking down from above ^^ ^^ down at everything below you. ^^ ^^ I'd like you to draw me a picture of what you can see ^^ ^^ looking down from above. ^^ ^^*
Check comprehension of 'looking down' and demonstrate if necessary	• *Can I check back with you that you understand what I want you to do? ^^ ^^* • (If not understood) *I'll show you what I mean by looking down and drawing what you can see. ^^ ^^* [Note 3]
Show on the paper and in the air	• *I'd like you to put in as much detail as possible in your drawing. ^^ ^^ There can't be too much detail. ^^ ^^* • *Use your fingers or hands ^^ to show me in the air if you find it difficult to draw something. ^^ ^^*
Check comprehension of 'draw the detail on the paper and in the air'	*Can I check back with you that you understand what I've said about detail ^^ and using your fingers and hands? ^^ ^^*
Share thoughts	*Now something very important. ^^ ^^* • *When you are drawing, ^^ I'd like you to talk me through what you are thinking. ^^ ^^* • *Tell me what you are drawing ^^ ^^ or want to draw. ^^ ^^* • *Say anything that comes into your head. ^^ ^^*
Check comprehension of sharing thoughts	*Can I check back with you that you understand what I've said about telling me what you are thinking ^^ and what you are drawing? ^^ ^^*
Parallel drawing	*When you are drawing on your paper ^^ ^^ I'll be copying what you are drawing on my piece of paper* [show interviewee your paper]. *^^ ^^*
Stopping to help and to keep up	*I will be stopping you from time to time ^^ to give you some help on drawing ^^ ^^ and also so that I can keep up with you. ^^ ^^*
Just ask	*If you want help, ^^ ^^ to have me explain something, ^^ ^^ just ask. ^^ ^^*

Key element	Example
Retrieve image	*So, imagine that you are on the ceiling of the bar ^^ ^^ looking down from above ^^ down at everything below you. ^^ ^^* *Some people find that closing their eyes helps. ^^ ^^* • *It helps them to get a better picture in their mind's eye. ^^ ^^* • *It helps them to remember what to draw. ^^ ^^ [Note 4]*
Restate what is wanted	*I'd like you to draw me a picture of what you can see ^^ ^^ looking down from above. ^^ ^^*

Notes

1. Pick up the paper you intend to give to the interviewee. As you give this instruction move your finger around the four edges of the sheet of paper, with you finger a short way in from the edge.
2. Black pen because this is the SE3R industry standard for capturing initial spontaneous disclosure.
3. Select a relevant example. The room in which you are sitting is probably the best for demonstration and comprehension. Create the initial stages of a drawing: the idea is to explain the technique, not for you to produce a detailed drawing.
4. If the interviewee is uncomfortable with closing his or her eyes, don't press the issue.

4. Capturing the detail

Key element	Remarks
Work together to capture detail	Implement a 'working together' cycle. • Observe the interviewee as he or she draws some material. • Come in politely to stop the interviewee, eg *As I said a moment ago ^^ ^^ I need to come in to copy what you've drawn on my paper. While I do that keep thinking hard about what you could see.* • When you have drawn the material, use a minimal prompt to get the interviewee drawing again, eg *OK got that ^^ ^^ Off you go again. ^^ ^^*
'Repair' if detail is missed	Get a re-statement, eg *I didn't quite get that. Can you talk me through what you were drawing there* [point]? *^^ ^^*
Identification and labelling	• If the interviewee does not state what a particular piece of drawn detail represents, ask him or her to tell you. [Note 1] • (Where applicable) Request annotation, eg *Can I just come in? You say that's a fruit machine. Could I ask you to write 'fruit machine' to show what it is? ^^ ^^* [Note 2]
Representing difficult detail	*So that's* [state]. *An easy way to show that kind of detail is* [explain and draw illustrative representation on a separate A4 sheet]. [Note 3]
AT ANY TIME make a note of critical detail	• Parallel commentary, eg *I'm not too sure about this bit…* • Correction (= another version), eg *No…on second thoughts…* [amends drawing].

Notes

1. You are asking for a label. This is sensible. It is not the same as probing. Probing to request additional detail during the initial drawing stage is too risky:
   - you are prompting the interviewee;
   - there could be more than one reason for absence of detail;
   - you may induce the interviewee—especially a vulnerable interviewee—to include detail that is not the case.

2. If the interviewee is illiterate or developmentally disadvantaged, regulate the flow of disclosure to enable you to label your drawing. The interviewee does not annotate.

3. Typically interviewees implementing the looking down perspective will not know how to represent people.
   - **A person viewed from above.** Use the SE3R industry standard symbol, a circle (representing the top of the head). Illustrate this on a separate blank piece of paper.
   - **A person laid on the floor or a surface.** Use a 'matchstick man' representation, giving the instruction about head and foot ends, eg *You say Alan was on the floor. A 'matchstick man' is an easy way to draw this.* ^^ ^^ *When you draw Alan put the matchstick man's head where Alan's head was pointing.* ^^ ^^ *Put his feet where Alan's were pointing.* Illustrate these instructions on a separate piece of paper.
   - **Direction in which a person was facing.** Instruct the interviewee to use an arrow head → attaching this to the circle representing the upright person or the circle representing the 'matchstick man's' head.
   - **Route/direction in which a person is moving.** Instruct the interviewee to use a dotted line with an arrow head to show the route and direction of movement →

   Very important. You must retain all sheets on which you demonstrated ways of representing detail as these are disclosable.

5. Probing after the interviewee has finished drawing

Unlike other non-verbal techniques—illustrator representation and enactment—it is sensible to proceed to probing immediately the interviewee has indicated that he or she has finished.

Key element	Remarks
Take back the interviewee's paper and pen	
Assess the drawing	• Assess match/mismatch with: — information known to you prior to this interview; — illustrator representation/enactment. • Identify areas for expansion (addition of detail) and explanation. [Note 1] • Don't alert interviewee to any concerns that you have.
Give interviewee his/her paper and BLUE PEN	[Note 2]
Probe appropriately	[Note 3]
AT ANY TIME Mentally note/ make a verbatim note of critical detail	• Parallel commentary, eg *I'm really pushed to give any more …* • Correction (= another version), eg *No … on second thoughts … [amends drawing].*

Notes

1. Common areas of probing include:
   - *directions*—indicated by an arrow, 'beak' on head;
   - *changes in position*;
   - *entry point/exit point/route taken*—indicated by a dotted line with an arrow head →
2. Blue pen because this is the SE3R 'industry standard' for capturing detail generated through probing.
3. Probing for extra detail implies extra tasks, eg:
   - the interviewee giving an illustrator representation prior to drawing the extra detail;
   - you giving advice and assistance on how to represent particular detail;
   - numbering sequentially changes in position.

6.   Signature and dating of the drawing

Key element	Remarks
Take back interviewee's paper and BLUE pen	
Enter interviewee's identifying detail and date using interviewee's BLUE pen	[Note 1]
Give interviewee paper and this BLUE pen	
Ask interviewee to sign	[Note 2]
Take back interviewee's paper and BLUE pen	
Sign your drawing using your BLUE pen	

Notes

1. If queried by the defence, forensic analysis of the inks will prove that the interviewee who signed did the drawing.
2. Unless the interviewee's vulnerability requires signing to be done by an accompanying third party, eg carer, intermediary, appropriate adult, reader (under para. 3.20 of PACE) Code C.

7.   Probing after signature of the drawing

If you decide later that further detail is required:

- both use red pens: the SE3R industry standard colour for representing detail obtained in final probing;
- conduct final probing in the same way as normal probing: see section 5;
- obtain a further signature and dating in the normal manner: see section 6.

5. The Griffiths Question Map (GQM)

1. Purpose

To improve interview effectiveness by recording (1) topic coverage, and (2) the sequencing and chronology of question usage, across the timespan of an interview enabling:

- comprehensive evaluation of subject coverage;
- detailed evaluation of questioning style and effectiveness;
- systematic identification of further interview areas;
- agreed areas for personal skills development.

2. Layout of the GQM©

The basic GQM (see Figure 1 and Appendix A) is designed to fit on a single sheet of A4 paper in landscape format, and has two distinct areas. The upper, shaded question mapping area, relates to questioning analysis. It is based on a hierarchy of questions., divided into productive and non-productive categories. The lower unshaded section is used for topic tracking.

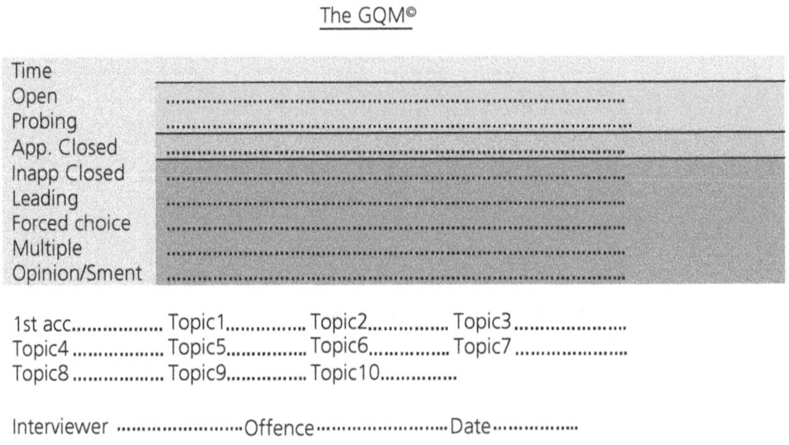

The GQM©

| Time |
| Open |
| Probing |
| App. Closed |
| Inapp Closed |
| Leading |
| Forced choice |
| Multiple |
| Opinion/Sment |

1st acc............... Topic1............... Topic2............... Topic3.....................
Topic4 .... Topic5............... Topic6............... Topic7 ....
Topic8 .... Topic9............... Topic10...............

Interviewer ....Offence........................Date................

Figure 1 The Griffiths Question Map (GQM)

The GQM can also be completed using Excel or dedicated software that introduces additional features. In automated versions, a question counter is attached to the bottom axis of the question analysis section.

Demographic information is also captured in the bottom section of the GQM, enabling accurate record keeping and thematic review across a number of areas (e.g. training course, offence type).

The different areas of the GQM can be used independently for targeted analysis of either questioning or subject choice, but ideally will be used together for capturing both the questioning strategy and subject coverage across a complete interview. The mapping of a complete interview would require multiple sheets.

3.   Be prepared

Completion of the GQM requires a minimum of one pen, a pencil and straight-edged ruler, and access to a recording of the interview. It is also possible to complete a GQM live, but this does require a high degree of proficiency and high level of concentration, as making accurate assessments of question type is paramount.

4.   Explanation of the GQM

4.1   Question mapping area

The question mapping area of the GQM is designed to plot each question used by an interviewer during an interview chronologically—resulting in a map of question usage across the whole interview or section selected for analysis. The completed map forms a unique visual representation of the interviewer's questioning style. Figure 2 shows an example of a sequence of seven questions plotted onto a GQM.

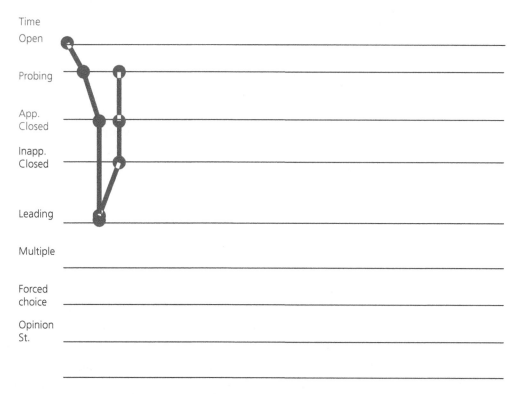

Figure 2 Example of a sequence of questions plotted onto GQM: open (o), probing (p), appropriate closed (ac), leading (l), inappropriate closed (ic), appropriate closed (ac), and probing (p).

Creating the question map takes place either listening to a recorded interview or live.[1] The mapper applies requisite knowledge of question types, to identify each question type as it used by the interviewer, and then places a dot on the relevant line, moving across the GQM from left to right as the interview proceeds. The dots are joined in order to show

---

[1] Completing question mapping live is not recommended until an assessor is fully conversant with the procedure and question definitions.

the chronology, and the question map will quickly start to take shape, as in Figure 2. This sequence is then followed throughout the interview.

Other considerations

- The GQM is designed as a focused assessment tool to note the questions used by the main interviewer in an investigative interview with a victim, witness, or suspect.
- The introduction and closure to any interview, need not be plotted.
- Summaries are not plotted and can be denoted by an 'S' on the map, along with their duration. Plotting recommences with questioning.
- Third party conversation, e.g. secondary interviewer, legal adviser, or appropriate adult, is also denoted in a similar manner using the symbol '3'.

Question types

There is an extensive body of published literature covering the subject of question types classification, and this subject is also covered in Chapter 8. From all of the literature it is accepted that questions can be broadly divided into two categories. These are *appropriate or productive* questions—associated, when used effectively, with gathering information and testing the validity of accounts provided; and *inappropriate or unproductive* questions—associated with, at worst, an oppressive style, and, at best, with an ineffective style of interview. The use of inappropriate questions produces either unreliable or insufficient information.

Within these two broad categories of appropriate and inappropriate, the GQM uses eight types of question, whose pragmatic classifications are derived from the published literature. Each of these question types is allocated a line on the map (see Figure 2). The question types used in the GQM are set out as a hierarchy, with the more productive question types situated at the top, and the least productive at the bottom. The individual classifications, within their categories are as follows.

Appropriate/productive

Open ended—Open questions are those that seek a wide response and give the interviewee a greater freedom to respond. They can be categorized as utilizing the active phrases such as 'Tell me...', 'Describe...', or 'Explain...' At a more skilled level they will include invitational statements, e.g. *'I'd like you to* tell me more about the trip to the pub...' Where an interviewee is co-operative such questions achieve the dual aim of allowing the interviewee to talk and limiting the amount of effort the interviewer has to put into composing further questions, allowing more cognitive capacity for listening, another key interview skill.

Probing or specific—these can be defined as questions commencing who, what, why, where, when, and how. Although 5WH questions seek more focused answers than open questions, they are still seeking information and are not completely closed questions in the way that some literature would suggest. Such questions are a vital part of an interview which is taking place in a legal setting, as they will assist in defining whether the actions of an individual are criminal or not. The vagueness of everyday speech is not sufficient for this setting and so obtaining precise information is critical. The critical factor is defining the active word within the question which defines the type of question. For example, 'Describe exactly *what* you did to the shop manager' is a probing question, as it reinforces the need for specific detail.

Appropriate closed 'yes'/'no'—this type of question is a clear example of how the context of a question is an integral part of defining its type, and is referred to in Chapter 8 as 'Risky' (Figure 8.1). Closed 'yes'/'no' questions are an essential part of a forensic interview but should be used with care. Here, then, is an illustration of two things: first how the same form of words used at different times of an interview could be either appropriate or inappropriate; and second, how there will be some subjectivity in any assessment. For example, the answer to the question 'Did you mean to break the window?' or 'Did you intend to push the shop manager through the window?' is important when determining the issue of intent in a criminal investigation. However, such questions should only be asked as clarification once an account as been obtained. Closed 'yes'/'no' questions are most appropriately used at the end of a line of questioning with regard to an issue or where a suspect is refusing to answer questions.

Inappropriate/unproductive

Inappropriate closed 'yes'/'no'—these may have the same word construction as an appropriate closed question, but will be inappropriate due to their timing and placing within the interview, e.g. early in an account. Some questions within this category can also be classified as leading. For example, 'Is that when you punched the shop manager?' is both leading and closed. It only fails to be a leading question if the interviewee has already stated he/she did punch the individual concerned.

Leading—defined as leading the interviewee to a particular answer. 'You know this was a serious assault don't you?'

Forced choice—giving the interviewee a number of choices. This type of question is also leading, but gives options instead of one preferred answer. 'Did you kick or punch the victim?'

Multiple—asking the interview a number of questions all at once. This is unproductive because in the event that the interviewee answers, it is not clear which question he/she is answering. It also indicates poor interview skill and can be especially dangerous for vulnerable interviewees. An example would be, 'Tell me what you did during the day, when you got home and just before going to bed?'

Opinion statement—not really a question at all but is included in the unproductive question section, as this type of behaviour is known to appear within poor interviews. This is defined as where an interviewer expresses an opinion or explicitly tells the interviewee what has happened in an effort to force agreement, e.g. 'I think you did assault this girl because I have interviewed her and she is telling the truth'. This is totally different to the invitational statement followed by a pause, e.g. 'the presence of your fingerprint suggests you have been inside that house...' In a suspect interview, they indicate a presumption of guilt by the interviewer.

4.2 Topic choice and duration

The topic coverage area of the GQM enhances evaluation of the interviewer's performance by cross-referencing the questioning strategy with detailed analysis of the topics covered.

- Each subject covered should be allocated a recognizable title, e.g. *conversation with shop attendant*, and a note made of the start and finish times, e.g. 21m–23m.
- Corresponding entries should also be made in the 'Time' section of the GQM above the question mapping area.
- Evaluation sessions can use this data to analyse whether the correct amount of examination was applied to relevant areas of the interviewee's account.

Computer versions of the GQM can display this information in chart form—providing visual results alongside the question map. See Figure 3.

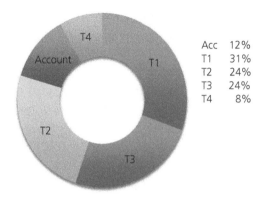

Figure 3 Chart showing relative time allocation of account and four topics within an investigative interview

5. Examples of completed GQM

The GQM produces individual maps for every interview, but certain typologies have emerged over time. Four examples are presented below:

1. The unskilled interview.
2. The skilled interview.
3. The oppressive interview.
4. The witness interview.

These four examples represent both positive and negative traits of questioning and topic coverage. Further discussion can be found in recent publications by the second author.[2]

5.1. The unskilled interview

This interview is characterized by a disorganised approach (as shown in Figure 4). The interviewer uses both appropriate and inappropriate question types, but with no structured movement from open to probing to explore relevant areas. The interview has two general areas of questioning but the interview also topic hops, i.e. asking several questions on one subject before switching to another subject and then returning to the first subject. Overall, this results in incomplete coverage of important subjects or repeated questioning on one area at different parts of the interview. The interview features regular use of inappropriate questions, most typically closed 'yes'/'no' questions at the wrong time, multiple questions, and leading questions generally. The interview fails to obtain a clear account from the suspect in this case, making evaluation of the evidence difficult.

---

[2] Griffiths, A. and Milne, R. (2006) 'Will it all end in tiers' in T. Williamson (ed.), *Investigative Interviewing: Rights, Research and Regulation*. Cullompton: Devon; Griffiths, A., Milne, R., and Cherryman, J.A. (2011) 'A Question of Control: The Formulation of Suspect and Witness Interview Question Strategies by Advanced Interviewers'. *International Journal of Police Science & Management*, 13(3), 255–67.

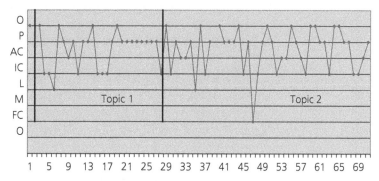

O =open, P=probing, AC= appropriate closed, IC = inappropriate closed,
L = leading, M = multiple, FC = forced choice, O = opinion/statement

Figure 4 GQM example of 'unskilled' interview strategy

5.2. The skilled interview

The skilled interview (shown in Figure 5) is characterized by a deliberate questioning strategy and the use of appropriate questions throughout. The interview is well organized, with relevant topics covered in detail through appropriate time allocation to each subject. The interviewer in this case is able to vary questioning strategy in different topics (see T1 v T3). The questioning strategy also features questioning funnels where topics are introduced with an open question, probed with more focused questions, and then closed with a 'yes'/'no' question.

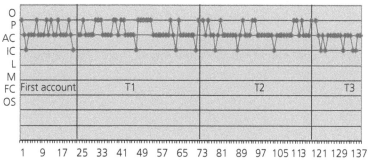

O =open, P=probing, AC= app. closed, IC = inapt. closed, L = leading,
M = multiple, FC = forced choice, O=opinion

Figure 5 GQM example of a skilled interview strategy

5.3. The oppressive interview

This interview is characterized by the predominant use of inappropriate questions and a guilt bias on behalf of the interviewer (see Figure 6). The oppressive interview features some elements also seen in the unskilled interview, but includes more of the forced choice, leading, and multiple question types. The interviewer in this case also hops between topics, but consistently returns to topics associated with the perceived guilt of the suspect. There is no discernible topic structure, or examination of the suspect's account. The oppressive interview strategy is also marked by premature and unsupported accusations of guilt made by the interviewer to the suspect. This particular interview was, following challenge by the defence, excluded from the evidence in a child abuse case and resulted in acquittal of the defendant.

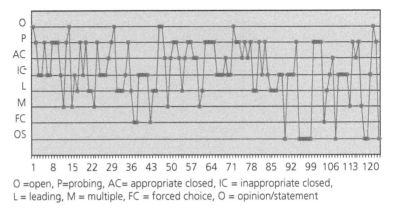

O =open, P=probing, AC= appropriate closed, IC = inappropriate closed,
L = leading, M = multiple, FC = forced choice, O = opinion/statement

Figure 6 GQM example of an oppressive interview strategy

5.4. The witness interview

This interview (see Figure 7) represents a fairly typical approach by police officers to the task of interviewing a witness. Even though the witness is compliant and willing to talk, the interviewer in this case has resorted to a directive approach after the first phase of the interview, using numerous probing questions instead of inviting recall from the witness. The account obtained is chronological through asking the witness to go from the beginning to end of the account. This favours the completion of a statement for criminal justice proceedings, over a witness-compatible approach of allowing the witness to relate the event as it comes to mind. The interviewer in this case has used appropriate question types but employed inappropriate sequences of questions that have constrained the interviewee and directed the flow of the interviewee for the convenience of the interviewer. There is not enough use of open questions.

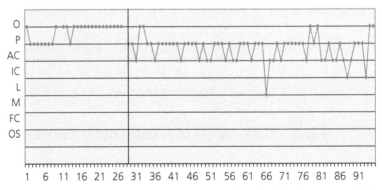

O =open, P=probing, AC= app closed, IC = inapp. closed, L = leading, M = multiple,
FC = forced choice, O = opinion

Figure 7 GQM example of witness interview strategy

6. Illustrator Representation

1. Purpose

To obtain non-verbal disclosure of offence-related detail by observing the interviewee's physical illustration of experience using his or her fingers or hands.

2. Be prepared

Have the means to validate the illustration. Prior to the interview:

- wherever possible, visit key locations;
- obtain visual material, eg images, plans, photographs, video-recordings;
- study the material closely;
- optimally practise your remembrance of the images.

3. Briefing the interviewee

Key element	Remarks
Explain use of illustrators	*Using* [a finger] [fingers] [a hand] [hands] *we can describe something that might be difficult to do using words.* ^^ ^^
Demonstrate	*I'll show you what I mean by using my* [finger] [fingers] [hand] [hands] *to describe something.* ^^ ^^ [Select a relevant example. Close your eyes. Produce an illustrator representation.]
Check comprehension	*Can I check back with you that you understand what I mean about using* [a finger] [fingers] [a hand] [hands] *in this way?* ^^ ^^
What is wanted	*I'd like you to describe to me* [X] *in that way* ^^ ^^ *Using your* [finger] [fingers] [hand] [hands] *as much as possible* ^^ ^^ *to show me what you are describing.* ^^ ^^

Retrieve image	• *I'd like you to get an image in your mind's eye of* [X]. ^^ ^^
	 • *Did you see how I closed my eyes when I was using my* [finger] [fingers] [hand] [hands]? ^^ ^^
	 • *Some people find that closing their eyes helps.* ^^ ^^
	   — *It helps them to get a better picture in their mind's eye.* ^^ ^^
	   — *It helps them to describe and show the detail.* ^^ ^^

Restate what is wanted	*OK. I'd like you to describe to me* [X]. ^^ ^^ *Using your* [finger] [fingers] [hand] [hands] *as much as possible to show me what you are describing.* ^^ ^^

4.   Capturing the detail

Key element	Remarks
Observe finger/hand movements closely	• Reassure the interviewee who says that he/she is not comfortable closing his/her eyes. [Note 1] • Don't probe. [Note 2]
Create mental image	
Don't assist interviewee	• Don't mimic his/her movements. • Don't describe aloud ('verbally label') the observed movements. [Note 3] • Don't repeat what interviewee is saying. [Note 4]
'Repair' if detail is missed	Get a re-run of the missed detail, eg *I didn't quite get that. ^^ ^^ Can you show me that again? ^^ ^^* [Note 5]
AT ANY TIME mentally note/make a verbatim note of critical detail	• Parallel commentary, eg *I was extremely frightened...not taking in everything...; I'm really pushed to give any more...* • Correction (= another version), eg *No...on second thoughts...*[makes different movement].
Assess the illustrator representation	• (Where applicable) Estimate the dimension described. [Notes 6–8] • Assess match/mismatch with what you know (= external validation). • Assess the quality of demonstrated detail. [Note 9] • Don't probe. [Note 10] • Don't progress immediately to a drawing. [Note 11]
Reward	• Thank for the illustration, eg *That was a great help. Thanks.* • Move on to another topic.

Notes

1. If the interviewee is really uncomfortable instruct to keep his or her eyes open.
2. Probing:
   • risks disrupting imagery;
   • prompting improvement—especially by the vulnerable, ie inducing confabulation, and by the would-be liar, ie making up detail.
3. Labelling aloud what you observe will rebound.
   • The interviewee will adopt your words, leading to subsequent legal argument concerning your role in shaping the interviewee's disclosures.
   • Repetition helps the would-be liar to remember and tell a better story.
4. Repetition helps the would-be liar to remember and tell a better story.
5. Repetition:
   • **is risky: it helps the interviewee (particularly the would-be liar) to rehearse;**
   • **is useful: if the illustrator representation:**
     — **involved a lot of detail; or**
     — **was extremely or markedly imprecise/involved gross movements.**

6. Use available material to assist you in estimating length, eg the edges of an A4 pad.
7. Aid to conversion: 10 cms = about 4 ins; 12 ins = about 30 cms.
8. Develop the skill of estimating length.
9. Markedly imprecise, gross or sweeping movements are a potential anomaly: a possible indicator of the interviewee not having experienced what he or she is describing. Note the anomaly for subsequent probing.
10. Probing at this stage will:
    - produce a rehearsal effect;
    - alert the interviewee that you have concerns.
11. A drawing at this stage would be:
    - counter-productive—the illustrator will have primed a fuller drawing;
    - a worthless test of validity: the illustrator detail is still in the interviewee's working memory.

5. Validating and probing the illustrator

An interval between initial illustration and subsequent validation and probing reduces the rehearsal risk and enables effective validation.

Key element	Remarks
State requirement	Examples. • *I just need to make sure that we've got everything covered about that* [X]. ^^ ^^ • *As before* ^^ *using your* [finger] [fingers] [hand] [hands] ^^ ^^ *I'd like to you describe everything that you can about* [X]. ^^ ^^
Observe finger/hand movements closely	Identify: • Replicated representation (= potentially valid information; interviewee is potentially reliable source of information}. • Representation containing differences (= potentially invalid information; interviewee is potentially unreliable source of information}.
Respond appropriately to a match	• Where necessary, probe for expansion or explanation. • Where applicable, consider obtaining enactment. • Move on to another topic. • Towards end of the Probing phase obtain an enhanced drawing. [Note 1]
Respond appropriately to a mismatch or continued poor quality	• Don't mention the existence of a problem. • Don't probe now. [Note 2] • Move on to another topic. • Probe later for further illustration, expansion and explanation: after this moving on to another topic. • Towards end of the Probing phase obtain a drawing. [Note 1]

Key element	Remarks
AT ANY TIME Mentally note/make a verbatim note of critical detail	• Parallel commentary particularly replication of earlier commentary. • Correction (= another version), e.g. *No...on second thoughts*...[makes different movement].

Notes

1. An interval reduces the rehearsal risk and enables further validation.
2. Probing at this stage will:

7. SE3R

1. Purpose

To represent comprehensively using SE3R formatted sheets detail contained in a document, real-time verbal account, or recording.[3]

2. Image the action as occurring now

We use the **past tense** to describe what has happened, eg *They went into the house*. When you are imaging you are observing past events as though they were happening now: before your eyes. To retain this sense of action 'in the present' you convert the past tense into the **present tense**: *They go into the house*.

3. Adopt an observer stance

When describing events, episodes, and continuous states people use the **first person** (*I* and *me; we* and *us*) to communicate their role as 'key player' in the account.

When imaging the account you are adopting an observer stance: so you switch the individual's first person into the third person, eg:

- Edward Smith's account says *At this point I got out of my car*. This becomes *At this point ES gets out of his car*.
- Mary Cooper's account says about herself and Luke: *We spent a couple of hours in Wantage*. This becomes *MC and L spend a couple of hours in Wantage*.
- Jack Twomy's account describes what Liam Donoghue did for him and Ciaran Leeson: *Liam took us to Funky Joe's*. This becomes *LD takes JT and CL to Funky Joe's*.

4. Abbreviate wherever possible

Abbreviations speed up the extraction process and create extra working space on the SE3R.

4.1 Use common abbreviations

In the early stages of learning SE3R use common abbreviations. For example: time of day—o'c (o'clock), *am* and *pm*; days—*Mon, Tue*, etc; months—*Jan, Feb*, etc; *DOB* (date of birth); locations—*Bham* (Birmingham), *Bton* (Brighton), *Soton* (Southampton), etc; directions—*N* (North), *SW* (South-West), etc; measurements—*in* (inch), *ft* (foot) *yd* (yard), *cm* (centimetre), *m* (metre), etc; *approx* (approximately); *dept* (department).

---

[3] For comprehensive coverage of SE3R, including how to apply the method to multiple sources of information and its applications, see Shepherd, E. (2008) *SE3R: A Resource Book*. Fourth edition. East Hendred: Forensic Solutions.

4.2 Use abbreviations distinctive to your work

For example, in the police/law context: *pb* (pocket book); *aka* (also known as); *HA* (home address); *aslt* (assault); *veh* (vehicle).

4.3 Use your own abbreviations

The only requirement is to be consistent when you use the abbreviation. Experiment with use of initial letters and also consider using the journalists' 'shorthand' technique: dropping out some (or all) of the vowels (a, e, i, o, u, y) and any non-essential consonants from words. For example: *w* (with); *fm* (from); *abt* (about); *twd* (toward(s)); *rd* (round); *st* (something); *sb* (somebody); *clw* (common-law wife); *fd* (friend); *htl* (hotel); *bdrm* (bedroom); *spk(s)* (speak(s)); *rtn* (return); *posn* (position); *WTTE* (words to this/that effect).

4.4 Use symbols

For example:

+ and	@ at	→ to (wards); forwards; in order to
∴ therefore	∵ because	↓ down(wards); ↑ up(wards)

Some symbols have very wide meanings. For example, ° means 'degree(s)' but is also the shorthand way of indicating order or sequence, e.g. 1° = first, 2° = second, 3° = third, 4° = fourth, and so on.

5. Commentary

Commentary gives the account giver's perspective on something.

- **Feelings** (attitude, disposition, emotion): *It is difficult for me to say this.*
- **An excuse or a justification:** *but I had no choice; I had no reason to be worried; because he had always been a heavy sleeper.*
- **Qualifying** (using a word or a phrase—a **qualifier**—to make something less absolute): *aboutsix; somewhere in the region of...; could not reallydescribe them.*

5.1 Disclosure concerning feelings, excuses, or justifications

Capture this detail verbatim and place it by the material to which it refers, eg *It is difficult to describe* becomes '*difficult to describe*' located beside the item that the individual has difficulty describing.

5.2 Significant qualifiers

Never change the substance of the qualifying word or phrase.

- If the text says *about*, write *about*, eg *about 2 pm*. If you fail to record the qualifier you make the disclosure more precise than the person actually said.
- Do not rephrase *a couple of...* as *two*.
- Do not aggregate, eg *three or so people* should not be converted into *some people*.
- Where applicable place quotation marks around the key word or words to highlight this detail for potential probing.

6. Annotate as you go along

Use the SE3R as a notebook. If you have an immediate thought about something, make an annotation adjacent to the detail or issue. Enclose your annotations in square brackets, ie [ ]. This usage comes from text processing contexts (eg publishing, academia): square brackets indicate that the words enclosed within them are not part of the original or source material.

There are many types of annotation.

- **Observations.** For example, **[Change in language use]** indicates the words used contrast with language use in the rest of the source.
- **Actions to be taken.** For example, **[Check]** indicates the requirement for confirmation or validation, **[Probe]** the need to expansion or explanation.
- **Questions to be asked.** For example, **[Who?]**; **[In what order?]**; **[Why?]**; or a question mark **[?]**.
- **Missing detail.** A question mark **?**—with or without square brackets—or **[Detail]**—highlights missing detail.
- **Other forms of oddity.** For example, **[GAP]** = missing step; **[VA]** = vague.

Common sense argues that you should never write any form of disparaging annotation on an SE3R. This is particularly important if your SE3R is, or is likely to be, subject to legal disclosure.

7. Corrections

If you make a mistake do not obliterate the error.

- Draw an X—crossed diagonal lines—through the error.
- Do not use correction fluid, eg Tipp-Ex or its equivalent.

8. Knowledge bins (KBs)

KBs are located at the bottom of the SE3R sheet. They are used to collate—assemble systematically—background detail on key topics: what my police colleague Mark D'Souza in Greater Manchester Police calls 'discussable topics', ie matters you may subsequently decide to probe.

- **Identities.** For example, an individual, a pair, or a group.
- **Locations.** For example, a building, physical area, or space (such as a shopping mall).
- **Objects.** For example a vehicle, computer, mobile telephone, or weapon.
- **Relationships.** For example, an association or connection.
- **Institutions.** For example, a company, a central or local government agency.
- **Routines and rituals.** A procedure or sequence of actions regularly followed, eg cashing up the till at the end of the day; securing the premises.
- **Plans and intentions.** Intended actions not embarked upon at the time the document was generated.
- **Issues.** Topics that are the subject of concern, apprehension, dissent and the like.
- **Explanations, excuses and justifications.** Offered by the individual, eg to account for the offence.

8.1   **Opening a KB**

When you identify a topic open a KB.

- **Give the KB a title.** Rather like an index card on a topic.
- **Use different sized lettering.** The detail becomes striking, easier to locate, and memorable, eg Elizabeth GREY.
- **Underline the title, or a key word.** The detail becomes more striking and memorable, and even easier to locate,, eg <u>Elizabeth GREY</u>.
- **Abbreviate the title.** Put the abbreviation in square brackets—eg <u>Elizabeth GREY</u> [EG]; <u>Thomas Cook Office</u> [TCO]—and use it throughout your SE3R.
- **Use a brief description to identify an otherwise unknown, unidentified, or ambiguous identity.** Open up a KB for any unknown, unidentified, or ambiguous identity and include in the title some brief descriptive detail to give this individual a discernible identity. For example, <u>Someone talking at bar</u>.
- **Use numbers to differentiate two or more similar identities.** The text may mention two or more individuals but not by name, eg four men in a bar would give rise to four KBs, <u>Male 1</u> [M1], <u>Male 2</u> [M2], <u>Male 3</u> [M3], and <u>Male 4</u> [M4]; two paramedics, <u>Paramedic 1</u> [PM1] and <u>Paramedic 2</u> [PM2]; three references to *someone*, eg **Someone holding knife [so1], Someone urging on [so2], Someone calling police [so3].**
- **Location of a KB.**
  — Typically people's accounts open with scene setting detail: identities, locations, biographical information, and so on. If you fill up KBs on your first SE3R sheet (= page 1), simply open up KBs on the second sheet (= page 2), and so on.
  — You do not have to fill up all KBs on an SE3R sheet before opening a KB or KBs on a subsequent sheet.
  — If you have a need to put something in a KB and there is one available at the bottom of the sheet, use it. If there is no available KB, go to the next sheet—or sheets—to locate a blank KB.
- **Additional KBs for a topic.** Open as many KBs on the topic as you require. You can keep track of two or more KBs for a topic by assigning them a sequential letter, <u>Elizabeth Grey</u> [EG] A, <u>Elizabeth Grey</u> [EG] B, and so on.

8.2   **Entering detail in a KB**

Enter initial detail, and any subsequent detail, in that topic's KB.

- **Sensible capture of detail.** Background knowledge detail is usually very significant, particularly in terms of evidence.
  — Capture the detail as fully but as succinctly as possible.
  — You can save space and time by maximizing the use of abbreviations.
  — Certain detail consider recording verbatim, using quotation marks. For example, *He is always drunk and repeatedly assaults his wife and children* would be entered as *'always drunk'* and *'repeatedly aslts wife + children'*.
- **Use bullets or numbering.** Bullets (eg •, –, ○, ⊙, □) and numbering make it easier to work with the contents of KBs.
  — They separate material, helping you to read and register detail.
  — Distinctive detail is more memorable, assisting memory consolidation.
  — In an interview, when you look down at your SE3R the KB detail is readily located, distinct from the rest of the detail, and immediately quotable.

- **Draw diagrams.** Always draw a diagram of what you are imaging. Incorporate into your diagram subsequent descriptive detail as this emerges across the account.

Collating detail in this manner is extremely valuable, eg it enables you to work out relative positioning, whether someone or something was or was not visible, or could or could not be reached, from where, and by whom.

A diagram can reveal what is frequently obscured by the words of the narrative. When turned into a concrete image the detail does not 'add up', eg it is inconsistent or contradictory, or presents an impossible set of circumstances. Do not be concerned that the diagram that you create may not correspond to reality. All you are doing is translating the descriptive words in the account into a mental image, and 'going public' on this image, ie creating a diagram of what you have in your 'mind's eye'.

Here are some simple guidelines for creating a diagram.

— **Draw the object from above.** Always draw the image as if you were looking down from above (an aerial view), eg the room; the house; approach routes to a location (roads, paths, etc); an intersection of roads, with relative positioning of vehicles; one or more individuals; a car, showing who was sitting where, location of bags, content of the boot, etc. You may have to image, and therefore draw diagrams, from a side, front, or rear view, eg a shopping bag, with its contents shown diagrammatically and listed beside the diagram; a jacket, perhaps with particular features, such as pockets; a handbag with a motif or a type of fastening. Sometimes you may need to draw a diagram to represent a view from a particular perspective, eg looking at something from an oblique angle.

— **Drawing people.** Draw a 'ginger bread man' shape. This allows you to record detail on the figure viewed from the front or rear, eg features; clothing. Depending upon the circumstances you may just need to draw part of the body, eg the individual's head; a particular limb.

— **Drawing a group.** When the text gives relative positioning of individuals in a group, represent each individual separately. If there is no such detail, simply draw a circle and place within this the identities of those in the group.

— **Standardized symbols.**

There are only two standardized symbols: any form of vehicle (eg a car, taxi, bus, truck, railway carriage, or even an aircraft) and a person seen from above (Figure 8).

— **Annotate.** Annotate your diagrams with verbal descriptions as appropriate, eg for a knife *serrated edge*.

Similarly enter dimensions, eg *about 8"*.

If you have an immediate thought about something, annotate the detail to which it applies, eg **[Probe]** or **[?]**

Figure 8 Symbols for a vehicle and a person (Note the wedge represents the direction in which the vehicle or person is facing)

8.3 Examples of KBs

Figure 9 shows examples of KBs that draw together detail within the statement given by Elizabeth Grey, the mother of a very young child who has been admitted to hospital with serious injuries. Note:

- **KB titles.** Underlined, second names in capitals, abbreviation in square brackets.
- **Use of 'white space', clear layout, underlining and bullets.** Making the detail easier to read and memorable.
- **Use of abbreviations.** This is an illustrative SE3R for a 'beginner'. Typically, there would be much greater use of abbreviation.
- **Quotation marks around verbatim detail of potential significance that merits probing.** For example:
  — *'always a heavy sleeper'*—*'always'* begs further expansion;
  — cannot *'really describe'*—the use of the word *really* suggests she could have given detail if pressed for this;
  — *'at all hours'*—what does she mean by this turn of phrase;
  — *'stormy'*—this needs expansion.

Figures 10 to 13 show the use of KBs to record detail as diagrams.
Note the following features.

- In Figure 10 the relative distances and the comment [**Check details**].
- In Figure 11 the wedge ('nose') indicating the direction in which TB was facing.
- In Figure 12 the chevron shape to represent it is a centre fold wallet.
- In Figure 13 the representation of relative position of JK, JK's bag, and the woman in the back of the taxi.

Elizabeth GREY [EG]	Simon TOWNSEND [ST]	Ross [R]	Chelsea [C]	Matthew [M]
• HA: 11 Newbury Grove Eaton ⊆ council flat. • Res. since Apr 95. • clnt of ST. • Worked as prostitute. • Works PT ∂ Tesco, Green Lane.	• EG's lodger. • Moved into EG's: Jun 98 • Father of M. • Uses flat for drug dealing. • Takes drugs. • "Drinks a lot."	• s/o EG. • Aged 4. • Conceived when EG working as prostitute.	• d/o EG. • Aged 2. • Conceived when EG working as prostitute.	• s/o EG + ST. • Died 25 Oct: — ∂ Readcliffe Inf. — aged 8 mths. • "always a heavy sleeper."

Mobile phone	Tesco's, Green Lane	Butts Centre	ST's "routine" w children	Relationship between EG + ST
• Owner: NK • Used to set up drug deals at EG's HA (23 Oct).	• EG's work loc.	• On way → EG's HA	• Takes children out "at all hours". • Causes EG + ST to argue "a lot". • ST persists w "routine"	• "Stormy". • EG wanted to end rel. "planning to throw Simon out as soon as I could afford to".

EG + ST Routine	Man 1 [M1]	Man 2 [M2]	Young Woman [W]	EG + ST's bedroom [bdrm]
• EG + ST argue. • ST hits EG "always".	• Name NK to EG. • EG cannot "really describe".	• Name NK to EG. • EG cannot "really describe".	• Name NK by EG. • EG cannot "really describe".	• Used by M(?) + W — morning 23 Oct. • At front of hse.

Figure 9 Examples of KBs

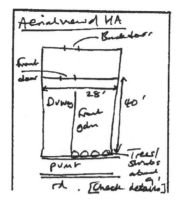

Figure 10 Example of KB

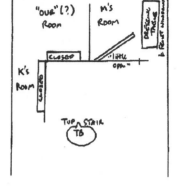

Figure 11 Example of KB

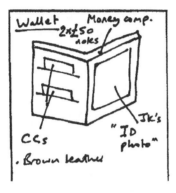

Figure 12 Example of KB

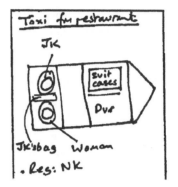

Figure 13 Example of KB

9. Event Line

This is used to represent detail on events, episodes, and continuous states.

- **Events.** These include actions, reactions, responses, utterances and dialogue, as well as the person's thoughts (reasoning). They are like action video-clips. The full description of an event includes time and place detail as well as occurrence detail. SE3R reveals how people often do not give full descriptions.
- **Episodes and continuous states.** These occupy a period, or span, of time longer than a single event. They are like longer video-clips, played at high speed. The person may subsequently describe events or smaller episodes within an episode or continuous state.

The initial **Survey** stage will have alerted you to potentially key events, episodes, and continuous states. The **Extract** stage enables you to identify methodically the full range of event and continuous state detail, significant and otherwise.

Starting with the first 'bite sized' chunk, which you were also processing for KB detail:

- identify each event, episode, and continuous state as it appears in the narrative;
- map the event, episode, or continuous state chronologically onto the Event Line.

9.1 What constitutes an event?

Very often sentences describe the occurrence of more than one event. For example, when Elizabeth Grey says: *I got up about six and fed Matthew* she is describing two events.

1. About six she gets up.
2. She feeds Matthew.

The use of the word *and* 'glues' the two events together. The solution is always to image what is being described. Elizabeth Grey's actions—getting up and feeding Matthew—cannot physically occur at the same time. Here the word *and* acts like a 'full stop'.

Look for clues to sequencing. When Elizabeth Grey goes on to say: *I then fed the other two after I put Matthew down*. The key word is *after*. This sends the following instruction to you: image the following action as occurring before the action you have just imaged.

With practice you will become very adept at recognizing events in written text, and distinguishing these from episodes and continuous states. This will have two spin-offs.

- When working with any document, imaging during the Survey stage will become 'second nature'. You will take in your stride instances of *narrative reversal* and *delayed mention* (when something is added much later in the text).

- When conversing with, or interviewing, people you will find yourself listening more intently and imaging the detail of what they are saying.

9.2 Event stems

When you identify an event draw a vertical (North-South) line—a **stem**—through the event line. It connects two notional areas of 'white space' above and below in which you record different types of detail (Figure 14).

Try to keep the detail within the box. Avoid writing too many words across the box: use the depth of the box. There is no rigid rule about the depth of the box.

- When learning SE3R it helps to put only four or five events, episodes, and continuous states on each SE3R sheet. As you get the measure of the technique you may wish to adjust this number.

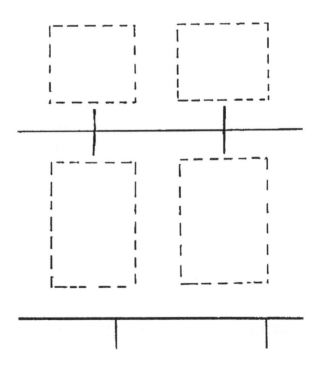

Figure 14 The notional areas of 'white space' available for recording event detail

- Do not put the first event stem (or where applicable episode/continuous state) on a page hard over against the left-hand end of the Event Line. Place this a short way in—about a fifth or a quarter of the way in—from the left-hand edge. This will give you flexibility, should subsequent disclosure require you to insert a prior event, episode, or continuous state.
- Leave an appropriately large gap between one event and another. Again this gives you the flexibility to cope with the requirement to insert later an event or episode/continuous state.
- Do not 'pre-draw' event stems on an Event Line. Pre-drawing stems wastes valuable time. The detail you are required to represent may not be a run of events, eg it might be a sequence comprising an episode, an event, another episode, a continuous state, and an event.

9.3   'Time and place' detail

Enter 'time and place' detail in the 'white space' area above the stem.

- **'Time' detail.** This includes: day, date, and time. Remember to enter any 'uncertainty' qualifier (eg *about*) or commentary (eg *'can't be sure but it was either…'*) by the detail in question.
- **'Place' detail.** This refers to location ranging from the most general to the specific.

The industry standard is a descending order of 'time' and 'place' detail (see Figure 15).

- Day.
- Date.
- Time.
- Location.
- More specific location, eg room.

People provide surprisingly little 'time and place' detail in their narratives. They do not give this detail for every 'step'. As you move from one event to another you do not need to replicate the day and date for events occurring on the same day (date). Where a change of day (date) is manifestly obvious you may decide to show this.

   You do not have to repeat the location above the stems representing actions taking place in the same location. Only ever put in the location detail above the stem when it is explicitly stated.

9.4   Duration detail

Duration refers to the passage of time between one event and another. For example, when Edward Smith says *I arrived about 8 o'clock. After about twenty minutes I left with Annabel*

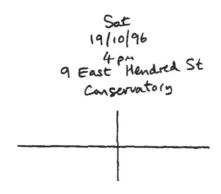

Figure 15 Representation of 'time and place' detail

Moon. In SE3R this is: *at about 8 o'clock ES arrives*; a time interval of about twenty minutes; *ES leaves with AM*.

You indicate duration by placing a bracket in an area of 'white space' extending to the right towards the next event. The extreme right end of the bracket (as you look at it) is where you place the stem of the next event. Write above the bracket the duration (Figure 16).

A bracket representing duration is called a 'coat hanger': at each end of the 'coat hanger' hangs an event!

An individual may describe a run of events and then specify duration, eg *All this happened over a period of about five minutes*. Simply draw a bracket extending from the top of the first event stem, over all the intervening events, and to the top of the last event stem.

9.5 Occurrence detail

Enter detail on **occurrences**—involving people, things, and objects—in the 'white space' area below the stem.

The amount of detail

An SE3R is **not** a statement in another form. The aim is to represent the image **not** to reproduce all the wording of the written text. Typically the image is simple, and hence the words beneath the stem are correspondingly few. Only use enough words to capture the image created in your mind's eye.

There will be occasions when, in your judgement, the essential wording of the text needs to be retained. A person may describe an occurrence, but the words used also express the person's interpretation of that occurrence. For example, the person's account says *The car crashed into the tanker* can be represented as *Car crashes → tkr*. It would be inappropriate—indeed incorrect—to substitute *Car + tkr collide*.

This example illustrates significant wording: key words and phrases. Think ahead to how the actual wording might be used at some future point. Nothing is as effective as referring to your SE3R in interview and reminding an individual of what was actually said. If you decide to capture the wording of the text verbatim, put this in quotation marks: these will highlight this detail as a potential issue for probing.

Representing actions

Actions are the commonest form of occurrence. Often they are physical events, with one or more people 'doing' something. Some are 'internal' events, eg the person describes an emotional response, or thinking something, or making a decision.

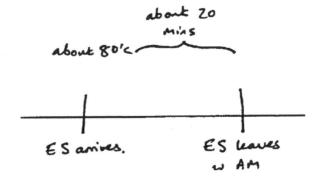

Figure 16 Representation of duration detail

532

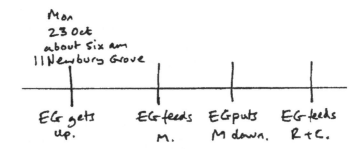

Figure 17 Representation of physical actions

Physical actions

Figure 17 illustrates the representation of physical ('doing') actions.

'X was done by A' (passive voice) descriptions

People describe occurrences mainly using the active voice, ie *A did X*. Action can be described another way, using the passive voice: *X was done by A*. For example, *The man hit Adam Kendon* (active); *Adam Kendon was hit by the man* (passive).

- Often people use the passive because they either do not know, or cannot remember, or think it unnecessary to state, the identity of who actually did the action, eg *I was told to go to reception; he was treated in Abingdon A & E*. They sidestep giving the detail.
- Would-be deceivers deliberately 'sidestep' to avoid disclosing critical detail concerning the doer of the action.

As soon as you detect a passive construction turn it immediately into its active equivalent. This reveals the missing detail.

- For example, in her account a female suspect—Christine Rogers—uses the passive construction twice when describing her involvement in the stabbing of Kelly Unwin: *The knife was handed to me. I was forced to stab her.*
- Turning the passive into the active reveals that she has avoided identifying the other person, or persons, involved in these two events.
  - **The individual who handed her the knife.** We can infer that it is only one individual because only one hand is required to hand over a knife.
  - **The individual, or individuals, who forced her to stab the victim.** We have to consider the possibility of more than one individual because forcing can be done by one or more. The past tense in the text, here *forced*, obscures whether one person or more than one person forced her. SE3R's requirement to use the present tense—*force(s)*—reveals the necessity to probe.
- Undisclosed detail revealed by the passive-active conversion generates Event Line and KB entries, as well as appropriate annotations.
  - Using a question mark ? to indicate the missing detail in the representation underneath the event stem.
  - Opening a KB for each unidentified individual.
  - Giving the KB a title—usually this captures the act done by the unknown individual.
  - Giving the title an abbreviation, eg **[NK]**—numbering these if there is more than one individual.
  - Putting the abbreviation by the ? in the occurrence detail.
  - Annotating, eg **[Who?]** to highlight the forthcoming need to probe.

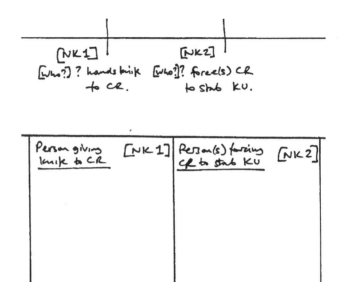

Figure 18 Turning the passive into the active to reveal undisclosed detail

Figure 18 shows these steps in respect of the disclosures by Christine Rogers.

Simultaneous occurrences

In SE3R simultaneous occurrences are represented by bulleted items under a single event stem. For example, Adam Kendon says *As I was turning round to face him the man hit me. I fell to the ground, grabbing hold of him as I did so*. The representation of these two events each comprising simultaneous occurrences is shown in Figure 19.

Unknown point of occurrence

Sometimes the text does not indicate at what point in the sequence of events a particular action occurred. Apply logic and put the event at the point that you reason it is most likely to have happened. Highlight this inference by drawing a circle on the top of the stem. This representation is called a **lollipop.**

For example, Annabel Moon says *I got in about 6 pm. Around 9.30 my mother called in reply to a message I had left on her answer phone*. You infer—but cannot be sure—that Annabel Moon made the call, leaving the message, after she got home. Figure 20 shows this sequence, with the inference represented by a lollipop. The eye-catching nature of a lollipop reminds you the timing of this event is not stated in the original and needs validating, if this is possible.

Uncertain order of occurrence

Sometimes an individual cannot say for sure which event came first, or in what order a number of events occurred. Put the events in the order stated in the text and create a lasso—in effect an extended lollipop—across the events. For example, Annabel Moon says *I went into the Post Office, the Bank, and John Lewis. But I cannot say in what order*. Figure 21 represents her unsure account.

Repetition of an occurrence

A lasso is used also to repetition. For example:

- Don Morris—a drug-taker—says *I called my supplier once or twice across the week* (Figure 22).
- Tom Horton says *Jack King came up to me a couple of times* (Figure 23).
- Martin Brown says *I visited Millie's two or three times* (Figure 24).

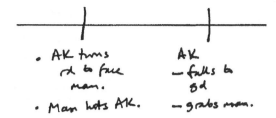

Figure 19 Representing simultaneous occurrences

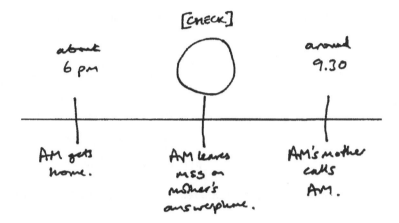

Figure 20 Representing an inferred point of occurrence (lollipop) (Note the annotation indicating the need to check the actual point of occurrence)

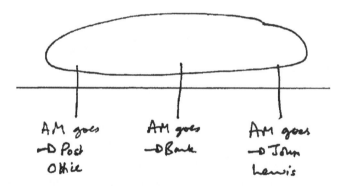

Figure 21 Representing an uncertain order of events (extended lollipop)

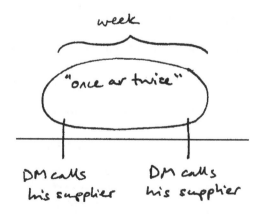

Figure 22 Representing repetition of an occurrence (extended lollipop)

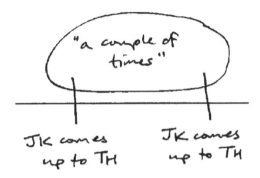

Figure 23 Representing repetition of an occurrence (extended lollipop)

Figure 24 Representing repetition of an occurrence (extended lollipop)

'Internal' actions

Represent the act of thinking as an 'internal' (mental) action, ie the person talking to himself or herself. Use quotation marks to capture the content of this inner speech. The same applies when representing 'internal' actions of assuming, reasoning or working out something.

Figure 25 illustrates the representation of Edward Smith's 'internal' action of thinking: *I thought that I really shouldn't be here. I decided to go.*

Caution! The word 'think' is sometimes used to express doubt or to communicate uncertainty, eg Mark Smith says *I think Anne and Richard went to Asda.* SE3R captures this internal process of doubt by using round brackets, eg *(MS thinks) Anne + Richard go to Asda.* 'Guess', 'suppose', and 'presume' are dealt with in the same way.

Often the individual will make a commentary when expressing doubt, eg *I'm not sure about what happened next* (commentary)...*I think that Anne and Richard went to Asda.* Capture the commentary verbatim—in quotation marks—putting it beside the detail to which it refers.

Representing interactions

Interactions are represented in exactly the same way as actions.

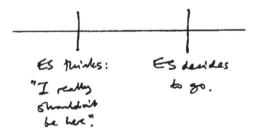

Figure 25 Representation of the 'internal' actions of thinking and deciding

Reactions and responses

There is only one distinction to be made here.

- If the reaction or response is a thought, represent like any other thought, ie capturing the content of the thought as 'internal' action—inner speech within quotation marks.
- Any other form of reaction or response, ie physical, emotional, or the act of deciding something, represent as a straightforward action.

Single utterances

When people report what was said they use either **direct** or **indirect speech.**

Direct speech

The person repeats, or quotes, the actual words used by the original speaker without making any changes. The reported words are placed within quotation marks. This provides the basis for creating a mental video clip, in which you see the individual and hear (as it were) the words being spoken.

Direct speech is transposed without change into an SE3R. Figure 26 illustrates this, showing an utterance reported in direct speech by Elizabeth Grey: *I shouted down to Simon. I said 'You bastard. For God's sake call an ambulance'.*

Indirect speech

The person reports what the original speaker has said indirectly. The words uttered are switched from the present into the past.

- **Direct speech:** *Tamsin said 'I am not interested'.*
- **Indirect speech:** *Tamsin said that she was not interested.*

Convert every instance of indirect speech into the direct speech equivalent. In her statement Elizabeth Grey says, *I told him to get out; She said she could not as she had other arrangements.* Figures 27 and 28 illustrate the conversions.

Dialogue

When people report dialogue they rarely report more than a two utterance exchange: *A said '......' B said '......'* Such dialogue pairs are called a 'two hander'.

SE3R makes the exchange in a dialogue pair more coherent—and therefore very impactful and memorable—by placing the participants' contributions under the same event stem, and bulleting each utterance In her account Elizabeth Grey:

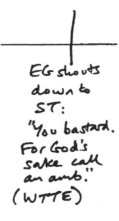

Figure 26 Representing direct speech

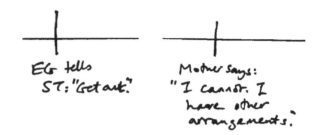

Figures 27 and 28 Examples of direct speech equivalents of indirect speech in Elizabeth Grey's statement

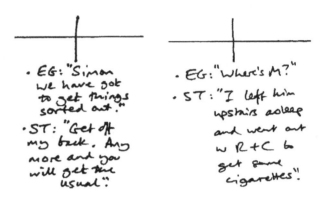

Figures 29 and 30 Examples of a dialogue pair under a single stem (Note the simple use of the colon and the omission of the word 'says')

- reports an exchange in direct speech: *I said 'Simon we have got to get things sorted out'. He said 'Get off my back. Any more and you will get the usual'*;
- reports an exchange in indirect speech: *I asked him where Matthew was. He said that he had left Matthew upstairs asleep and went out with Ross and Chelsea to get some cigarettes.*

Figures 29 and 30 illustrate this representation of dialogue

If the reported dialogue comprises two pairings in succession, then put the first pair under one stem, and the second pair under the following stem. If the reported dialogue runs into three utterances (*A said, B said, A said*), you can:

- either put the 'trio' of utterances under a single stem;
- or create a stem with a 'two hander', followed by a stem with the third utterance underneath.

Episodes and continuous states

As pointed out earlier, an episode or continuous state occupies a period, or span, of time longer than a single event.

When learning SE3R some people get confused about the difference between duration detail—a period of time between two events—and an episode or continuous state lasting for a specified period of time. To resolve this problem ask yourself a straightforward question: Is the description of a *completed* occurrence then followed by a span of time?

- **If the answer is 'yes'.** Represent the detail as an event, followed by a bracket indicating the stated passage of time.
- **If the answer is 'no'.** Represent the detail as an episode or continuous state that lasted for the indicated period of time.

For example, Edward Smith says *I bought a cup of coffee. I then bought another after about ten minutes.* This breaks down into three elements.

- *ES buys a cup of coffee* (= completed occurrence = event).
- A passage of time of about ten minutes.
- *ES buys another coffee* (= completed occurrence = event).

In contrast if Edward Smith had said *I talked to a girl for about ten minutes. Then I bought another coffee.* This breaks down into:

- A continuous state of affairs lasting for a stated duration *ES talks to a girl for about ten minutes*;
- *ES buys another coffee* (= event following the continuous state of affairs).

Some people worry whether the phrase went to is a continuous state or an occurrence. For example, Edward Smith says: *I went to Bristol. When I got there I went to the Halifax and then I went to Thomas Cook's in the High Street.*

- The first use of *went to* is an episode—an extended (unstated) period of time, travelling in a mode of transport (unstated).
- The other instances of *went to* are events: acts of entering.

A useful tip here. All vehicle journeys are continuous states.

Representing a single episode/continuous state

An episode or continuous state is represented by a continuous line located in an area of 'white space' above that assigned for recording day, date, time, or place. Enter above and/ or below this line the detail concerning the episode or continuous state.

The text may indicate the duration of an episode or continuous state, eg Elizabeth Grey says *He had been unwell throughout the night* It may only indicate when an episode or continuous state starts. Whether duration is stated or not, do not worry about how long the line for an episode or continuous state should be. You can always extend the line at a later stage.

As an initial representation draw a line of equivalent length to that of a duration 'coat hanger' between two events (Figure 31). Sometimes you may have to draw a slightly longer line to accommodate one or more events that occurred during the time span (Figure 32).

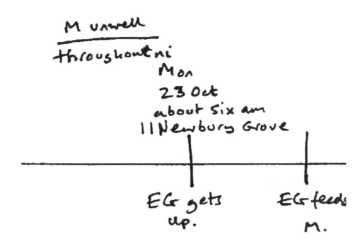

Figure 31 Example of single continuous state

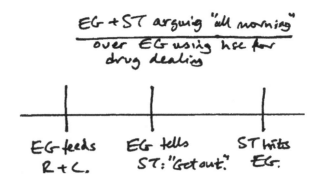

Figure 32 Example of single continuous state

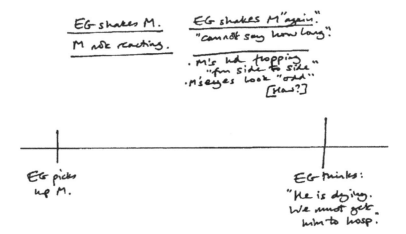

Figure 33 Representation of simultaneous and successive continuous states

If the duration is stated include this in the detail written above or below the straight line. You do not have to draw duration brackets ('coat hangers') above episodes or continuous states.

Representing simultaneous and successive episodes/continuous states

Figure 33 illustrates how simultaneous and successive episodes/continuous states are represented.

Representing events occurring during an episode/continuous state

The detail of event occurring during an episode is positioned below the episode or continuous state line and represented in the manner appropriate to the type of occurrence. If there are no events beneath an episode or continuous state, annotate your SE3R to remind you to probe for detail.

9.6   Identifying and highlighting material facts and material time frames
Material facts

Material facts (MFs) are details that you consider to have a direct bearing upon the case in hand and may be actually or potentially evidentially significant. You may want to highlight a MF, eg by lassoing it—drawing a circle around it. Use a pencil since this allows revision of your judgement and erasure of this annotation.

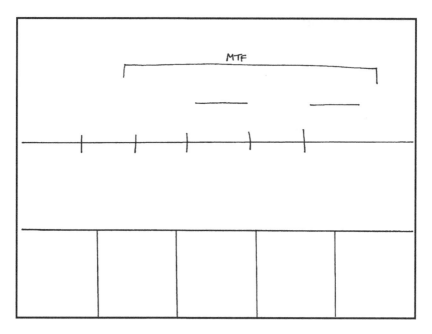

Figure 34 Highlighting an MTF (Event Line and KB detail omitted)

Material time frames (MTFs)

A material time frame (MTF) comprises the circumstances with a potential bearing on a case—leading up to, during, and following the commission of an offence. It may include a number of events—occurrences, episodes, or continuous states—or it may be just one episode or continuous state. There may be more than one MTF.

Decisions also have to be made concerning the **parameters** of the MTF, ie the **start point** and the **end point.**

You can highlight an MTF by drawing a continuous line above all the detail in the *Event Line*, extending this from the first to the last event, episode or continuous state in the MTF. An MTF, and therefore the MTF line, may extend over more than one SE3R sheet.

Annotate the line **MTF.** Where there is more than one MTF, number or letter the MTFs in sequence, eg **MTF1, MTF2, MTF3,** and so on.

Figure 34 illustrates the annotation of a MTF extending over four events and two episodes or continuous states.

10.   Annotating your SE3R

As explained earlier, annotation always goes in square brackets. Think of it as you talking to yourself, or a scratch note-pad within the brackets.

10.1   Anomalies

Examples of anomaly annotation:

> **[Missing], [THIN], [THIN ACCOUNT], [GAP], [JUMP], [NBD]** = 'non-barking dog', **[VA]** = vague, **[INCON]** = inconsistent, **[CONTRA]** = contradiction.

10.2 **Actions**

Examples of annotation for actions:

[CHECK], [PROBE] or [Q], [CHECK RECORDS].

10.3 **Think pad**

Get used to using your SE3R as a think/scratch pad and annotating it with your thoughts, eg:

[WHY?]

Index

Note: References to paragraph numbers relate to the main text. References to page numbers relate to the reference section